BECOMING A TEACHER OF READING
A Developmental Approach

Susan Davis Lenski
Illinois State University

Susan L. Nierstheimer
Purdue University

PEARSON

Merrill
Prentice Hall

Upper Saddle River, New Jersey
Columbus, Ohio

Library of Congress Cataloging-in-Publication Data

Lenski, Susan Davis.
    Becoming a teacher of reading: a developmental approach / Susan Davis Lenski, Susan
 L. Nierstheimer.
      p. cm.
    Includes bibliographical references and index.
    ISBN 0-13-060857-2
     1. Reading teachers—Training of—Handbooks, manuals, etc. 2. Reading (Elementary)
 3. Reading (Middle school) I. Nierstheimer, Susan L. II. Title.

LB2844.1.R4 L46 2004
428.4'071—dc21

2002038695

Vice President and Publisher: Jeffery W. Johnston
Editor: Linda Ashe Montgomery
Development Editor: Hope Madden
Production Editor: Mary M. Irvin
Design Coordinator: Diane C. Lorenzo
Text Design and Production Coordination: Amy Gehl, Carlisle Publishers Services
Cover Designer: Thomas Borah
Cover Photo: Getty Images
Production Manager: Pamela D. Bennett
Director of Marketing: Ann Castel Davis
Marketing Manager: Darcy Betts Prybella
Marketing Services Manager: Tyra Poole

Photo Credits: Bonnie Stiles, pp. 2, 4, 7, 36, 43, 65, 72, 74, 80, 86, 108, 123, 127, 142, 151, 156, 164, 176, 178, 187, 197, 201; Susan Davis Lenski, pp. 38, 117, 262, 321, 330, 334, 338, 345, 362, 367, 384, 401, 406, 411, 426, 432, 449, 456; Scott Cunningham /Merrill, p. 40; Susan Hodges, p. 49; Todd Yarrington/Merrill, p. 210; Susan L. Nierstheimer, pp. 212, 240; Tracy Strebel, pp. 214, 216, 229, 243, 251, 272, 287, 296, 304, 313, 454; Anthony Magnacca/Merrill, p. 332; Linda Wedwick, p. 394.

This book was set in Garamond by Carlisle Communications, Ltd., and was printed and bound by Courier Kendallville, Inc. The cover was printed by Phoenix Color Corp.

Pearson Education Ltd.
Pearson Education Singapore Pte. Ltd.
Pearson Education Canada, Ltd.
Pearson Education—Japan

Pearson Education Australia Pty. Limited
Pearson Education North Asia Ltd.
Pearson Educación de Mexico, S.A. de C. V.
Pearson Education Malaysia Pte. Ltd.

10 9 8 7 6 5 4 3 2 1
ISBN 0-13-060857-2

About the Authors

Susan Davis Lenski is a professor at Illinois State University, in the Department of Curriculum and Instruction, where she teaches undergraduate and graduate courses in reading, writing, language arts, and literacy theory. Dr. Lenski brings 20 years of experience as a public school teacher to her work as a professor, writer, and researcher. As a result of her practical experience and her grounding in theory, Dr. Lenski is a popular speaker for professional development programs and has consulted in the United States, Canada, and Guatemala.

Dr. Lenski has been recognized for her work by a variety of organizations. For her work in schools as a teacher, she received the Nila Banton Smith Award and led her school to receive an Exemplary Reading Program Award, both from the International Reading Association. In Illinois, Dr. Lenski was inducted into the Illinois Reading Hall of Fame, and at Illinois State University, Dr. Lenski was named Outstanding Researcher.

Dr. Lenski has coauthored six books, including *Improving Reading: Strategies and Resources,* and has published more than 50 articles in state and national journals. Her research interests include intertextuality during reading and writing, incorporating strategies into classroom practice, middle level reading, and preparing culturally responsive teachers.

Susan L. Nierstheimer is an assistant professor at Purdue University in West Lafeyette, Indiana. She teaches literacy courses to both undergraduate and graduate students and also conducts professional development workshops for classroom teachers.

A former kindergarten and first-grade teacher, Dr. Nierstheimer received her Ph.D. from Purdue University in 1996. While working on her doctorate, she received three outstanding teaching awards. Along with a team of literacy instructors, Dr. Nierstheimer also received Purdue's university-wide award, *Helping Students Learn: Innovations in Teaching,* for designing the innovation titled "The Impact of Authentic Assessment on Teaching and Learning."

Dr. Nierstheimer has done extensive work in professional development schools. As a member of the faculty at Illinois State University, she directed a 4-year, pilot PDS project with one cohort of students at Glenn Elementary School, Normal, Illinois, from the undergraduates' freshman year until their year-long, senior internship. The Glenn PDS project received the *Those Who Excel* award from the Illinois State Board of Education in 1999, which salutes those who have made outstanding contributions to education in Illinois.

Dr. Nierstheimer's research interests include preparing exemplary literacy teachers, helping young readers who find learning to read difficult, and forming partnerships with classroom teachers to improve literacy instruction. She has published numerous articles and has presented her research at local, state, and national levels.

Preface

Learning to become a teacher of reading is a complex, lifelong process. Teachers are always in the state of *becoming* as they learn from children, other teachers, scholars in the field of literacy, and themselves.

This text will guide you as you take your first steps on one of the most important journeys of your life: discovering how to help children learn to read and read to learn. To help you on your way, we present the information and experiences in this book in ways that provide meaningful access, guidance, and support. While a primary goal of this text is accessibility, the work is also rigorous and theory-driven, and is replete with classroom examples.

This book is grounded in a social constructivist perspective. We believe that people—whether primary grade students or university students—learn best when they can construct their own understandings in social contexts. For that reason, many of the activities within the book will encourage you to interact with your peers as you work toward becoming a teacher of reading. We present a social constructivist stance as a foundation for your own evolving theory of literacy teaching and learning. While we recognize that you will need to know other theoretical perspectives and offer alternative viewpoints throughout the book, we purposely chose to write from the viewpoint that we find most tenable; one that we hope you will adopt as you begin your literacy-teaching journey.

SOCIAL CONSTRUCTIVISM IN PRACTICE

Throughout the text, we try to practice what we believe, aligning information and learning experiences with a social constructivist stance. Thus we have worked to create a book that not only teaches constructivist theory, but uses it.

Beginning With the Learner

Taking into account our experiences and knowledge concerning how university students learn, we devote a complete, early section of this text to what you know most about: yourself. We ask you to explore who you are as a developing teacher, your previous beliefs and experiences as a literacy learner, what you know about children, and how you can learn to become a professional educator. Self-reflection is a thread throughout the book that we weave as we encourage you to develop and continue to examine an evolving theory of literacy learning. Embedded in this notion of an evolving theory of literacy is an emphasis on the importance of inquiry in teaching, the ongoing nature of learning, and an understanding that teachers *must* embrace ambiguity.

Integrated Text = Integrated Teaching

We believe that if we want prospective teachers to understand the importance of teaching literacy in an integrated fashion that it is only natural and meaningful that the material in the text is presented in an integrated way. Therefore, vital teaching and learning issues such as diversity and assessment that occur throughout a teacher's literacy block of time are integrated throughout this book rather than being separated into their own chapters.

A Workshop Approach

This text is designed to allow you to experience features of the reading/writing workshop with peers and with children in school or informal settings, providing opportunities for you to try out what you are learning in a learn-by-doing approach.

Interactive Technology

A Companion Website that accompanies this text extends the workshop approach through experiences that engage you in reacting to and reflecting upon what you're learning. In addition, there are mini-lessons and suggested assignments available on the Website that expand the text and address a range of topics such as setting up the literacy classroom, matching texts to children, and constructing lessons.

ORGANIZATION

We have organized this text in a developmental fashion under the following headings: *Early Readers* (grades K–2), *Interpretive Readers* (grades 3–5), and *Critical Readers* (grades 6–8). We recognize that developmental stages overlap, but we believe this organizational structure will provide helpful connections illustrating how literacy learning and teaching might occur on a developmental continuum. Topics are often reexamined as appropriate for each new developmental stage, as good teaching revisits ideas in different contexts.

To be an effective reading teacher, you need knowledge about the reading process, the skills necessary to apply your knowledge to classroom instruction (performances), and the dispositions to meet the needs of all students (as noted in the INTASC principles). Our book, therefore, devotes several chapters to each of these domains of teaching. We begin the book by appealing to preservice teachers' natural dispositions toward teaching. In Part 1 we also encourage you to review what you already know about teaching and learning, and present literacy theories that will be explored in and connected to later chapters.

Parts 2, 3, and 4, which cover the developmental stages of readers in depth, each begin with a chapter that helps you expand your knowledge about teaching and learning. Following this initial chapter are chapters that encourage you to *apply* your knowledge to instruction. These chapters develop your ability to teach reading. The book concludes with Part 5, which once again addresses teaching dispositions and helps you articulate your new understandings.

PEDAGOGICAL FEATURES

These features guide students through extended learning through observation, reflection, and application, enriching your understanding of the text.

- **You Try It** provides opportunities for readers to apply what they are learning in the text.
- **See for Yourself** offers interactive learning activities that connect ideas from the text to teachers and students in actual and virtual classrooms. Each activity gives you the chance to discuss your findings on our Companion Website's message board at *www.prenhall.com/lenski*.
- **For Your Portfolio** suggests portfolio entries that align with the INTASC principles as well as the IRA/NCTE standards and chronicle your learning in the course. Compile your entries online at our Companion Website at *www.prenhall.com/lenski*.
- **Advice for New Teachers** appears in a question/answer format and answers questions that preservice teachers might have about material presented in the text. These questions are answered by young teachers who have just begun their literacy teaching careers and have recently grappled with those same issues. We hope you will make connections through their experiences to the ones you are about to encounter.
- **Connections: What's Next?** helps readers see the overlap and progress in each reader's development. The developmental framework is charted at the end of each chapter as a part of this segment. This chart will help you keep the information you are learning organized in terms of what is involved in teaching students in each developmental stage while illustrating that the lines between stages are blurred
- **To Learn More** lists websites that expand on material presented in the text. Visit our Companion Website at *www.prenhall.com/lenski* to link to these important sites.
- **Margin notes** in each chapter contain definitions and questions that will cause you to reflect on new understandings or question your beliefs about pedagogy. These notes will contribute to your developing knowledge and evolving theory of literacy learning and can be used as an online journal. Visit each chapter's online journal on our Companion Website at *www.prenhall.com/lenski* to answer these margin questions.

RECURRING THEMES

- **Teaching diverse learners**—Classroom teachers need to feel prepared to teach and reach children of all cultures, races, ethnic groups, language abilities, and developmental levels. We believe that one way to instill this feeling of responsibility and efficacy in you as a future literacy teacher is by arming you with specific teaching strategies and knowledge through relevant and accessible learning opportunities. Each section of this text includes helpful strategies for working with all children in your future classrooms, including children who struggle, gifted children, English Language Learners, and children from diverse backgrounds.
- **Assessment as the centerpiece of instruction**—It is our belief that assessment lies at the heart of good instruction; therefore, assessment is highlighted in each part and woven throughout the text so that you understand its key role in teaching and learning.
- **Teaching comprehension strategies**—The purpose of reading is the construction of meaning. Rather than trying to "cover" comprehension strategies

in one chapter, we emphasize this often overlooked instructional component in each of the parts that deal with Early, Interpretive, and Critical Readers.

- **Working with words**—Throughout this text there are references to teaching phonics and resources for helping you understand teaching phonics and word analysis in an integrated and contextualized way to children of different ages.
- **Your evolving philosophy of learning**—As you prepare to be a teacher it is important that you examine your beliefs about children, teaching, and learning. Effective teachers continue to examine their beliefs throughout their careers as they continue to *learn more* about children, teaching, and learning; their new knowledge and experiences in the classroom challenge their previously held beliefs. The beliefs that teachers hold become the foundation of their philosophies of learning and guide how they teach and respond to their students. Throughout this text, you will be developing an evolving philosophy of literacy learning that will, no doubt, change over the term as you learn more about teaching and literacy. By the time you complete the course, you will have a clearly stated, articulate philosophy of literacy learning that will support your future practices in the classroom.

FOR YOUR PORTFOLIO

This book highlights experiences that lead to the creation of a standards-based teaching portfolio. The INTASC principles (Interstate New Teacher Assessment and Support Consortium) are used as one framework for your portfolio because the principles can be viewed as performance-based criteria against which developing teachers can be assessed.

You will also find ideas to develop portfolio entries based on the *Standards for the English Language Arts,* developed jointly by the International Reading Association and the National Council of Teachers of English. These national standards should guide your instruction as literacy teachers.

Students using this text are encouraged to use these standards-based suggestions as a foundation for the creation of a teaching portfolio. This portfolio will document your learning as well as reflect growth over time. At the end of the text are recommendations for ways to turn your learning portfolios into job search portfolios.

ACKNOWLEDGMENTS

This book would never have been written without the help and support of family, friends, colleagues, and many very special teachers. First, we would like to thank our families for giving us the time, space, and encouragement each step of the way—even when we were discouraged. We thank Fran Lenski for reminding Sue to keep writing, even when she'd rather have been reading mysteries, bicycling, or kayaking. We also extend heartfelt gratitude to Norm Niersheimer for his encouragement and support while Susan was absent and occupied with the computer for so long. Susan's children, Laura and Eric, cheered her on to the finish line!

We especially thank our parents, our first teachers, who taught us that reading is an essential part of life and surrounded us with books and love. These literacy role models are Sue Lenski's parents, David and Mildred Jepson, and Susan Niersheimer's parents, all career-long teachers themselves: John Hodges (deceased), Grace Hodges Dillman, and Dr. Beryl Dillman.

In addition, we are grateful to the many, many classroom teachers, administrators, colleagues, and professors who influenced our thinking. Among those we owe a special debt of gratitude are Jerry L. Johns, professor emeritus at Northern Illinois University, for introducing Sue Lenski to the world of higher education and writing for publication; Midge Rehmer, Briargate School, Cary, Illinois, for showing Sue how to be a dedicated elementary school teacher; and Flo Newbrough, Cary Junior High, Cary, Illinois, for teaching Sue how to incorporate the writing process in the classroom. We also thank John Godbold, our former department chair at Illinois State University, for encouraging the two of us to work together, and current department chair Rex Morrow for urging us to work with Merrill/Prentice Hall Publishing.

Carol Hopkins, Deborah Dillon, Maribeth Schmitt, and Susan Gunderson have been consistently wonderful mentors, as well as models of exemplary scholars/teachers for Susan Niersheimer at Purdue University. Vivian Hubbard provided support by continuing to be Susan's confidant, advocate, and lifelong friend. Sue Lenski invited Susan to collaborate on this book and showed her what perseverance is all about. These women have Susan's enduring gratitude.

Many of our colleagues helped us with different parts of this book, and we appreciate all that they did. First, we thank the featured teachers who shared their insights about the challenges of being a beginning teacher: Derek Schulze, Wilson School in East Peoria, Illinois; Janette Vandeveer, Murdock Elementary School in Lafayette, Indiana; and Linda Wedwick, Metcalf School in Normal, Illinois. We also thank Bonnie Stiles and Tracy Strebel, Armstrong School, East Peoria, Illinois, for their valuable input on the first 10 chapters, for their help in preparing some of the pedagogical features, for taking photographs, and researching websites. Thanks also to Kristen D'Alfonso, Central Middle School, East Peoria, Illinois, who contributed feedback concerning the section about middle level readers. For their work developing book lists, we appreciate Sarah Johnson, Glendale School, East Peoria, Illinois; Stacie France and Erexenia Lanier, Parkside Junior High, Normal, Illinois. We are extremely grateful to Jessica Wutz and Sofia Moore, graduate assistants at Illinois State University, for reading drafts of our manuscript and for developing questions for the instructor's manual. Susan Gunderson at Purdue provided expertise in the creation of materials for the book and Companion Website.

We would like to thank the reviewers of our manuscript for their comments and insights: Helen Abadiano, Central Connecticut State University; Debra Augsburger, Northern Illinois University; Laurie Ayre, King's College; Sandra Bodine, University of North Dakota; Carole L. Bond, University of Memphis; Diane Bottomley, Ball State University; Patricia P. Fritchie, Troy State University, Dothan; Sandra R. Hurley, University of Texas at El Paso; Leanna Manna, Villa Maria College; Michael Moore, Georgia Southern University; Ray Ostrander, Andrews University; Barbara Perry-Sheldon, North Carolina Wesleyan College; Ann Russell, Southwestern Oklahoma State University; Barbara Smith Chalou, University of Maine at Presque Isle; and William Earl Smith, Ohio University.

Finally, we are grateful to the professionals at Merrill/Prentice Hall for their help and encouragement. We continue to be impressed with Jeff Johnston and his team at Merrill/Prentice Hall for their outstanding list of publications. We are very proud to be on that list now. We thank Linda Montgomery for believing in our work and us—even when we weren't sure of ourselves. We are especially indebted to Hope Madden, our outstanding development editor, who guided us through the process of writing and preparing the book for publication. Mary Irvin, our production editor, Amy Gehl, who supervised the production of this book, Lorretta Palagi, who carefully copyedited our book, and Carlisle Publishers Services who did the proofreading also deserve our thanks.

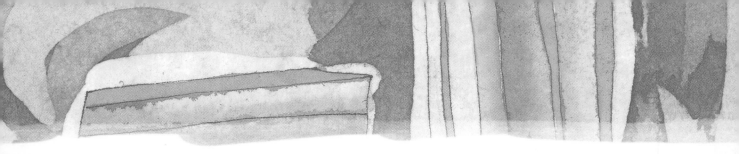

Discover the Companion Website Accompanying This Book

THE PRENTICE HALL COMPANION WEBSITE: A VIRTUAL LEARNING ENVIRONMENT

Technology is a constantly growing and changing aspect of our field that is creating a need for content and resources. To address this emerging need, Prentice Hall has developed an online learning environment for students and professors alike—Companion Websites—to support our textbooks.

In creating a Companion Website, our goal is to build on and enhance what the textbook already offers. For this reason, the content for each user-friendly website is organized by chapter and provides the professor and student with a variety of meaningful resources.

For the Professor—

Every Companion Website integrates **Syllabus Manager**™, an online syllabus creation and management utility.

- **Syllabus Manager**™ provides you, the instructor, with an easy, step-by-step process to create and revise syllabi, with direct links into Companion Website and other online content without having to learn HTML.
- Students may logon to your syllabus during any study session. All they need to know is the web address for the Companion Website and the password you've assigned to your syllabus.
- After you have created a syllabus using **Syllabus Manager**™, students may enter the syllabus for their course section from any point in the Companion Website.
- Clicking on a date, the student is shown the list of activities for the assignment. The activities for each assignment are linked directly to actual content, saving time for students.
- Adding assignments consists of clicking on the desired due date, then filling in the details of the assignment—name of the assignment, instructions, and whether it is a one-time or repeating assignment.
- In addition, links to other activities can be created easily. If the activity is online, a URL can be entered in the space provided, and it will be linked automatically in the final syllabus.

- Your completed syllabus is hosted on our servers, allowing convenient updates from any computer on the Internet. Changes you make to your syllabus are immediately available to your students at their next logon.

For the Student—

Common Companion Website features for students include:

- **Chapter Objectives**—Outline key concepts from the text.
- **Interactive Self-quizzes**—Complete with hints and automatic grading that provide immediate feedback for students.

  After students submit their answers for the interactive self-quizzes, the Companion Website **Results Reporter** computes a percentage grade, provides a graphic representation of how many questions were answered correctly and incorrectly, and gives a question-by-question analysis of the quiz. Students are given the option to send their quiz to up to four e-mail addresses (professor, teaching assistant, study partner, etc.).

- **Online Portfolio**—Provides opportunities to pull together reflections about chapters' For Your Portfolio prompts.
- **Web Destinations**—Links to www sites that relate to chapter content including all sites highlighted in each chapter's To Learn More section.
- **Message Board**—Virtual bulletin board to discuss each chapter's See For Yourself activity with a national audience.

  To take advantage of the many available resources, please visit the *Becoming a Teacher of Reading: A Developmental Approach* Companion Website at

  www.prenhall.com/lenski

Contents

PART IV TEACHING CRITICAL READERS   330

Note: Every effort has been made to provide accurate and current Internet information in this book. However, the Internet and information posted on it are constantly changing, so it is inevitable that some of the Internet addresses in this textbook will change.

PART
I

TEACHING BEGINS WITH YOU

You have embarked on an exciting journey—you have chosen to be a teacher! In just a few short years you will be standing in front of your own classroom of students who will be depending on you to help them learn in all areas, including reading. Although everything you do in the classroom is important, nothing is more significant than helping children in their literacy development. Distinguished author Frank Smith (1984) once said that the single most important thing a child will ever accomplish is learning to read. Soon, you will be a teacher who has the extraordinary responsibility of helping your students learn to read.

In this text, beginning with this chapter, you will be asked to reflect on many new concepts related to reading. Because you already know that *how* you look at issues influences how you interpret them, we would like to propose a "lens metaphor" to describe the teaching of reading. As a developing teacher of reading you will be looking at myriad issues related to literacy learning and teaching. At the start of this challenge we ask you to look first in the mirror—at yourself and your own experiences as a literacy learner and a student in schools. Then, we will guide you to a window where you will look at diversity in the world around you and the diversity that exists in today's classrooms. After learning about meeting the needs of diverse students, we will take a closer look at how people learn. You will use a magnifying glass to enlarge some of the concepts that you may have encountered in other college classes concerning researchers' hypotheses about what occurs during the learning process. After thinking about overarching learning theories, we will sharpen your focus further with reading glasses—the kind people use to make print appear much larger. With your reading glasses on, you will look at learning as it particularly applies to reading. How do children learn to read? How will you help them learn?

Finally, you will adopt a telescopic stance—one that allows you to step back and view everything at a distance so you can see the whole picture. At first this telescope will be low powered and able to focus only on parts that may be difficult to place in a framework. However, as you acquire more knowledge, assimilate new discoveries, and acquire multiple perspectives, you will be able to use what you have seen and experienced to sharpen your views of literacy learning and teaching processes. You will be able to see the patterns, order, and ways that all of this new information fits together. You will then be equipped to develop your own evolving philosophy of literacy learning. Your philosophy of literacy learning will begin to take shape in this course, but it will continue to evolve as long as you teach; new experiences and new knowledge will continually change your vision of how children learn and how you should teach. All the while, you will always be looking back in the mirror to reflect on yourself as a teacher; it all begins with and comes back to you!

chapter 1

Developing a Theory of Literacy Learning

Essential Learning Questions

- How do your own early experiences with reading affect your current beliefs about literacy learning?
- How can identifying your personal culture help you to better understand and value the various cultures represented in your classroom and also guide your instruction?
- What are the basic differences between behaviorist and social constructivist learning theories?
- How does the developmental level of your students influence which literacy learning theories you will employ most frequently in your classroom instruction?
- Why is it important for you to develop your own evolving theory of literacy learning? Why is it considered "evolving?"

Why do you want to become a teacher? Sometimes when students are asked this question they reply, "Because I love children!" This is a well-intended response and a commendable, even necessary, characteristic of a teacher. Many people choose to teach because they love children. Other prospective teachers say they want to teach because they love learning. That's another component of teaching: When you teach, you recognize the need for lifelong learning. Some people come to the teaching profession because of a special teacher. For example, did you have a teacher who inspired you in some creative way? Perhaps you are looking to become a teacher to open those doors for others. Many teachers choose their profession in order to help others learn. Helping others and making a difference in the world are still more reasons many have chosen to teach. Why have you chosen the teaching profession? In this chapter you will begin by exploring your own experiences as a learner and how they affect your view of literacy.

YOUR EXPERIENCES AS A LITERACY LEARNER

What you believe about literacy learning and teaching is often a product of your own experiences as a literacy learner. In this chapter, you will have an opportunity to reflect on an early literacy memory from your life and think about your literacy experiences as a student in school. Each of these activities and experiences is designed to help focus your attention on how beliefs and past experiences influence practices in the classroom.

Examining Your Beliefs

In this book we will encourage you to construct an evolving philosophy of literacy learning. A good starting place is to examine what you believe now about literacy learning. Indeed, the beliefs you now hold about literacy teaching and learning may shape your future teaching decisions and practices as you work with students. That is why it is so important to consider what you do believe about literacy learning, starting with your early memories.

Because we know that our own life experiences can influence our thinking as teachers, the following activity is designed to help you delve into a significant early memory about literacy. As you participate in the You Try It exercise, reflect on how your early literacy experiences influence what you think and believe today.

YOU TRY IT

Literacy Memoirs

Literacy memoirs are recountings of significant incidents from your life that involve literacy and reveal something about you. They often provide insight into families, personalities, and your own version of the truth (Routman, 2000). As you construct your stories, you may wish to gather data, by retrieving school memorabilia, talking with parents or siblings, or examining favorite storybooks.

Write about a significant early memory that you have about literacy learning or literacy in general. Select a story that you would be willing to share with your peers as part of a published book to use in the classroom with children. After you have written about your memory, type a simple version of your story for publishing as a children's book. In other words, first you will write a "long version" of your memoirs, then you will create a "shortened version" to be illustrated, typed, and then pasted into a blank book to share with your peers and perhaps children. For example, your children's book might be titled *My Grandmother Read to Me,* or *My Favorite Books,* or *Reading Groups I Have Known,* or *Learning to be a Writer,* and so on. An example of this project is provided here, starting with an excerpt of a longer literacy memoir written by an undergraduate student.

My Favorite Book

When I was three years old, up until I was about four, my favorite book was *The Monster at the End of This Book* (Stone, 1971). It was a Sesame Street book with Grover as the main character. Every night at eight o'clock, I got ready for bed. I brushed my teeth and put on my favorite furry pajamas with the feet at the bottom. Next, I walked over to my bookshelves and picked out the monster book.

"Dad, Dad, I'm ready!" I shouted.

"Are your PJs on, teeth brushed, and do you have a book ready?" he would yell from the family room.

"Yes. Hurry!" I said in my loudest voice.

When I heard him coming up the stairs, I would run and get into my bed. He always knew what book I was going to choose.

Next is a sample text for a children's book that could be created from the memoir written above. Imagine how you might illustrate this book.

My Favorite Book

When I was a little girl my very favorite book was *The Monster at the End of This Book!*
Every night at eight o'clock I went upstairs and got ready for bed.
I brushed my teeth.
I put on my pink pajamas with the feet at the bottom.
Then I picked up my favorite book, walked to the stairs, and yelled to my dad.
"DAD, I'M READY!"
I jumped into my bed.
My dad sat down on my bed and began to read.

Daddy used his Grover voice and each time he turned the page of the book, he said, "DO NOT TURN THE PAGE!"

Once my dad got so tired of the Grover book that he bought me six new books to read at bedtime.

But, I would have nothing to do with the new books.

I always wanted Grover!

School Reflections

As you wrote your literacy memoirs, then shared them with your peers, perhaps feelings emerged that helped you reflect on your experiences as a literacy learner and user. Some of you may have had joyous memories to recount. Others of you may have uncovered negative feelings. For instance, did anyone remember having to read aloud in school and feeling embarrassed when you made a "mistake" while reading?

Thinking about other literacy memories will be helpful to you as a developing literacy teacher. We now direct your attention to our changing world and your responsibilities to meet the needs of *all* children in your future classrooms.

◼ YOU TRY IT

Your Reflections on Learning to Read

Reflecting on your experiences as you learned to read, either at home or at school, is another way to help you understand what you believe now about literacy teaching and learning and why you believe it. Use the following questions as discussion prompts in small groups:

- Do you remember learning to read?
- Do you remember who taught you?

Eager to Learn to Read!

- What kinds of books did you read in school?
- If you had reading groups in your classrooms, what were they like for you?
- What did you like most about reading in school?
- What did you like least?
- Describe your favorite teacher of reading. Why was this teacher your favorite?
- Did you think you were a good reader when you were young?
- Do you think you're a good reader now?
- Do you like to read?
- Describe the role of literacy in your daily life now.

Did your discussions cause you to think about how your experiences in school as a reader influence what you think about literacy teaching and learning today? What did you discover about yourself?

YOUR EXPERIENCES WITH DIFFERENT CULTURES

As a literacy educator, you need to know that today's classrooms are increasingly diverse in terms of linguistic, cultural, racial, ethnic, and socioeconomic composition. Estimates by the U.S. Census Bureau (1998) indicate that people of color made up 28% of the nation's population in 2000, and the Census Bureau predicts that number will rise to 38% by 2020. The first two decades of the 21st century will also see an increase in the number of students in schools, so demographers predict that by 2020, students of color will make up 46% of the school-age population (Banks & Banks, 2001).

Currently, the teaching workforce looks much different from the general population and even more different from the student population. During the last decade of the 20th century, 90% of the teachers in the United States were White (National Center for Educational Statistics, 1993). In the early 2000s, the percentage of White teachers continues to hold at or above 90%.

Visit the online journal in Chapter 1 on our Companion Website at *www.prenhall.com/lenski* to answer these questions. Save your answers to your hard drive or to a disk to compile an online journal.

Cultural diversity is rapidly increasing in the United States. What do you predict will be your foremost challenge in teaching students whose cultures are different from your own?

In addition to the differences among students and the teaching workforce, the extent of the diversity of the student population is changing. In the last decade of the 20th century, approximately 20% of the children in the United States were children of immigrants (Dugger, 1998), and that percentage is increasing because a million people emigrate each year to the United States (Martin & Midgley, 1999). Therefore, finding teachers of certain races to teach students of that same race is not feasible (Gay, 2000). Instead, all teachers need to learn how to teach students from diverse cultural backgrounds.

The rapid changes in the cultural makeup of the nation's population will be occurring as you enter the teaching workforce. Therefore, you will need to think deeply about your own culture, the cultures of your students, and how you can apply what you believe about learning theories to your future classroom—regardless of your race or ethnic group.

Identifying Your Personal Culture

Who are you? What's important to you? The answers to these questions help define your culture. You might think that you have no identifiable culture, but that's not so. Culture is not only race or ethnic background; culture is a way of thinking that is "shared by a group of people who recognize the knowledge, attitudes, and values of one another, and who also agree on which cultural elements are better than others" (Cushnew, McClelland, & Safford, 1992, p. 19).

Groups of people with shared values band together to form implicit or explicit rules. These rules help define who is part of a group and who is not. Your culture, and the culture of others, can be identified by these rules and by material artifacts, social and behavioral patterns, and mental products.

Cultural groups.   One of the easiest ways to understand cultural groups is to think back to the social groups that were formed in your high school years. Young men may have formed a group if they played on the football team, were reasonably attractive, and had some degree of freedom to spend time together. Those who did not have free time because they had to work at part-time jobs or did not play football may have been excluded from that particular social group. In college you may also see students forming groups: sororities, fraternities, commuting students, students with children, and second-career students to name a few. These groups come about as a result of shared values.

When you graduate from the university you'll leave your current social groups and redefine your culture. Of course, all of you will share some commonalities. You'll all be college graduates and teachers. Other than that, the differences among you may be great. Take some time to examine who you are and the cultural values that you have.

YOU TRY IT

Identifying Your Personal Culture

Identify your personal culture by completing the following chart and writing a description of your culture. To find out about your own culture, you'll have to follow two steps: (1) Fill out a personal description chart and (2) Write a cultural description.

1. Personal Description Chart
   Using the blank chart supplied here, list pertinent information about yourself and add a few words and phrases containing background details. A sample chart follows.

Personal Description Chart (Sample)

Category	Background
Name	My name is Claire. That's short for Clarissa, my great grandmother's name.
Age	I'm 20 years old. It was difficult for me to leave the teen years because I'm a bit anxious about growing up.
Sex	I'm a female. I've found being a woman frustrating at times, especially in class. Teachers don't give me the respect they do the men in the class.
Race(s)	I'm a mixed race of Native American and White. Most people think that I'm European American because I look White.
Ethnicities	My ethnicities are Native American and German. My grandmother is a full-blooded Native American, and my grandfather is German. They met in the oil fields of Oklahoma.

Socioeconomic class	I come from a family that is middle class. My mother went to college and got a degree in social work, and my dad is a carpenter. He finished two years at a junior college.
Marital status	I'm single. I was engaged once for a couple of months, but I realized that I was too young to get married. I have no children.
Religion	My parents are Baptist and I still attend the Baptist church, but I am thinking of changing religions. I'm not sure what religion I prefer.

Your Personal Description Chart

Category	Background
Name	
Age	
Sex	
Race(s)	
Ethnicities	
Socioeconomic class	
Marital status	
Religion	

2. Personal Culture

   Write a brief description of your cultural identity in the form of a personal advertisement. Here is an example from the sample profile as a model.

   Single, Native American female, age 20, from a hard-working Baptist family who values friends, family, education, and religion. Likes to spend time shopping with friends, singing in a choir, and roller-blading. Finds pleasure in reading a good book, watching old movies, and talking on the phone. Wants to be a teacher in an urban school and hopes to marry and have several children.

Developing Positive Attitudes

After you have explored your cultural identity, think about how you would feel if the instructor in this course told you that your culture was inferior, deficient, or wrong. We asked you to explore your cultural identity so that you could recognize how personal and important culture is and that each person's cultural identity is equally precious.

Avoiding stereotypes.   Now that you understand the importance of personal cultures, think about your attitudes toward people who have cultures different from your own. It's easy to stereotype people with differences. In fact, some teachers base their expectations on race; for example, some teachers think that all Asian students will be strong academic achievers (Gay, 2000; Wong, 1980). This type of judgment can hinder a teacher's ability to make good instructional and interpersonal decisions. Teachers need to realize that all students have many forces influencing their cultures, and that students of one race might be socialized into the cultural patterns of a different group. Teachers should not look at a student, decide that student's cultural background, and then make blind judgments.

Even if your students belong to the same race or ethnic group as you, each student will have a somewhat different culture. If you teach at a school where most of the students live in the same neighborhood, the students in your class may be fairly similar. However, many of you will teach in schools where students are bussed to the school from different neighborhoods. In a class of 25 students you could have a wide range of cultural backgrounds, from highly educated to marginally literate, from wealthy to welfare, from living in large homes to homeless.

Understanding the Cultural Role of Language

Language is one of the elements that defines a person's cultural identity because language is the basis for thinking and communication (Vygotsky, 1978). No matter what language or dialect a person speaks, that language shapes his or her thinking and views of reality. As you learn to become a teacher, and especially a teacher of reading, it's important that you also think about the role of language in your life.

Dialects.   What language(s) do you speak? Are you a native speaker of English, or is English a second or third language for you? Do you know which dialect of English you speak? You might know that there are numerous English dialects in the United States (Wolfram, Adger, & Christian, 1999). A dialect is a certain variety of a language, with specific rules and vocabularies. For example, a cold carbonated drink might be called *tonic, soda, sodie, soda pop, sodie pop,* or *cola,* depending on your dialect. You might say *wash* or *warsh* for laundry. If you've ever traveled to Boston, New York, or New Orleans, you might find that understanding the native residents is a challenge. Dialects generally follow regional boundaries in the United States as you can see in Figure 1.1.

Standard English.   No one dialect is any better than any other; all ways of speaking should be valued. One of the dialects of English is Standard English, which is the dialect that is used in business, commerce, education, and the media in the United States. Your job as a teacher will be to speak and write Standard English and to teach your students how to speak and write it—not because Standard English is "right" or "correct" but because it is the language of power in our American culture (Delpit, 1995). People who speak other dialects of English are typically expected to also be conversant in Standard English. Even though you'll be teaching Standard English, you need to keep in mind that Standard English is merely one way of communicating. As a teacher, you should honor your students' dialects as you teach Standard English.

Standard English is the language in which most texts in America are written and that most people in positions of power speak. Why do you think it is important to teach your students Standard English?

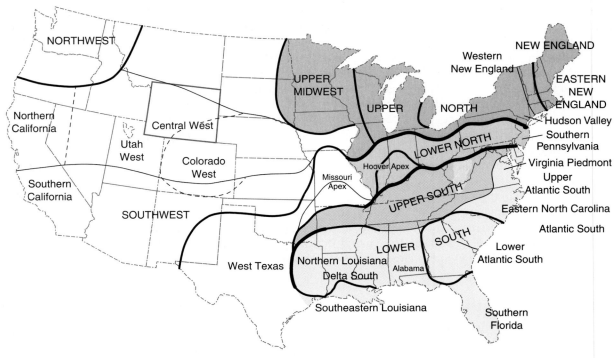

FIGURE 1.1   Dialect Map of the United States
From Carver, C. (1987). *American regional dialects: A word geography.* Ann Arbor: University of Michigan Press, p. 9.

Connecting Cultural Understanding to Teaching Reading

How should you cope with diversity in your classroom? Teachers used to believe that being "color blind" was the best way to react to students of different cultural backgrounds. Being color blind meant that you didn't pay special attention to the race or cultural background of your students. However, experts on multicultural education believe that being color blind to your students takes away from your ability to teach effectively (Banks & Banks, 2001). Lisa Delpit, a respected African American educator, writes: "If one does not see color, one does not really see children" (1992, p. 245). Acting color blind does not take into account individual student differences. Instead of being color blind, we encourage you to be "culturally fair" (Hodgkinson, 2000/2001).

Cultural fairness.   Cultural fairness means acknowledging, accepting, and acting on the cultural differences of your students. It means identifying the learning strengths and needs of your students and tailoring your instruction to those areas of strengths and needs. It means expecting your students to learn and providing learning environments and situations whereby your students can succeed. Cultural fairness means that you learn about your students and learn from your students, and that your instruction is not too difficult nor too easy (Moll, 2001).

Learning about students.   How do teachers learn about their students? One way teachers learn about students is through interest inventories and personal interviews (Johns & Lenski, 2001). Identifying students' interests can help shape your instruction. Moll (2001) also suggests that you learn about your students' families and identify their "funds of knowledge." Funds of knowledge are those areas of life in which the families of your students are extremely competent and knowledgeable. For instance, perhaps you find out that a student's family emigrated to the United States from Somalia and has extensive knowledge about weaving. You could develop teaching lessons that apply to the art of weaving and also invite the student's family members to share their knowledge with the class.

Assessing students.   You also should assess students' reading, keeping in mind what you know about students' cultures and their home language or dialect. As you assess students' reading, remember that learning hinges on background knowledge, so find out as much as you can about what your students already know and provide them with texts that have familiar subject matter. As students read, take into account that their pronunciation of words may be different from yours. Don't penalize them when you assess oral reading based on dialect or language differences. (For example, some children pronounce the word *ask* as *ax*.) Finally, as you assess students' reading, remember that you need to teach students what they need to know, not what they already know, and what they can learn, not what they are unable to learn.

Classroom Assessment

YOUR KNOWLEDGE OF THE LEARNING PROCESS

When you become a teacher, you'll be making lightning-quick decisions throughout your day. You'll be making decisions about what to teach, how to teach, and how to respond to students. Each of these decisions will be based on your beliefs about teaching, your instincts as a teacher, and the theories that you have generated about teaching and learning. As you think more about taking on the role of teacher, you'll realize how complex learning actually is. Because of the complexity of learning, teachers use their experiences, beliefs, observations, and knowledge to develop their own personal learning theories, which in turn shape the decisions they make in the classroom.

You know quite a bit about learning theories in general from your background and from other college courses. You can use this knowledge as you begin to make instructional decisions. When developing your personal learning theories, ask yourself the question, "How do people really learn?" Answering this question is not simple; in fact, you'll never have a final answer. For decades, researchers and theorists have been investigating learning processes. You can use the knowledge they have gleaned to help form learning theories that you can apply to your future teaching situations.

Behaviorist Theories

Learning theories are relatively new in human history. One of the first learning theories was developed by Thorndike in the early 20th century (Bell-Gredler, 1986); perhaps you read or learned about him in psychology class. Thorndike conducted experiments with chicks, dogs, fish, cats, and monkeys and drew conclusions about both animal and human behavior. In his experiments, Thorndike placed animals in cages that had a latched door and food just outside the door. He observed the animals as they attempted to open the door and get the food, and he measured the time it took for the animals to escape. From these experiments, Thorndike (1913) developed the theory of *connectionism,* which stated that responses are associated with stimuli during repeated learning attempts.

Classical conditioning.   While Thorndike was conducting experiments in the United States, another psychologist in Russia was thinking along the same lines. Pavlov also conducted experiments with animals to determine how they behaved. You're probably familiar with Pavlov's famous salivating dogs. Pavlov sounded a tuning fork immediately before giving meat powder to a dog. After repeating the experiment several times, the dog salivated at the sound of the tuning fork without the meat. Pavlov concluded that responses automatically occur after certain stimuli. His theory is known as *classical conditioning.*

Behaviorist principles assume that students learn by responding to a stimulus in a predictable way. Can you think of instances where your learning did not occur in a predictable way?

Behaviorism and education.   You may be wondering at this point about the relevancy of the theories of Thorndike and Pavlov to literacy learning. The work of Thorndike and Pavlov forms the basis for behaviorism, a theory made popular by Skinner (1953). *Behaviorism* is an umbrella term that covers a wide range of beliefs about learning. Behaviorism was extremely popular in the early and middle parts of the 20th century, and many teaching practices in schools today are still rooted in behaviorist theories.

Reading was taught primarily through a series of skills: drill, practice, and repetition. The curriculum was divided into discrete bits of knowledge and organized into a hierarchy of skills. Student learning was assessed through multiple-choice tests. From the era in which behaviorism held sway we have a long list of educational terms that are still used today: behavioral management, measurable behavioral objectives, behavioral modification, positive reinforcement, guided practice, mastery, and many more. You can perhaps relate to teaching and learning based on behaviorist principles.

Social Constructivism

The *social constructivist* theory is a combination of three theories that were developed in the last half of the 20th century: cognitive, constructivist, and sociocultural theories (Shepard, 2000). The seeds for these three learning theories were planted while behaviorist practices were at their height in schools.

Cognitive theories.   Beginning in the 1960s, theorists began to hypothesize that learners do not passively receive knowledge but that they actively participate in and process learning in unique ways. Behaviorists believed that the mind passively reacts to new information. Cognitive theorists, however, suggested that the mind actively tries to make sense of new information by applying it to existing knowledge. These new thoughts led to what has been called the *cognitive revolution* (Garner, 1985). One of the theories developed during the cognitive revolution was schema theory.

Schema theory supports the idea that there are cognitive structures, rather like file folders, stored in our memories that hold information. How many different "file folders" can you think of that contain categorized information that you know about the concept "dogs"?

Schema theory.   *Schema theory* was developed by Rumelhart (1980) who stated that knowledge is organized in the mind in structures called *schemata*. Schemata are the background knowledge that learners appropriate to make sense of new learning. You can think about the role of schemata by comparing the mind to a computer. When you turn on your computer, you boot up a specific application, such as a word processing program. This application allows you to access any number of files. Let's say that you open a file that contains a paper you've been writing for a history class. As you open the file, you find you have notes, references, and the first two pages of a paper. You use this partially completed work to continue writing your paper. Opening the computer files is analogous to accessing schemata during learning.

Schema theory is a key component of cognitive theory. Cognitive theory suggests that the mind actively accesses knowledge and applies that knowledge to make sense of new information. Think how different this theory is from behaviorist theory. Learners actively use their minds to construct meaning, which leads us to the second theory embedded in social constructivism: constructivist theories.

Constructivist theories.

Constructivism is a meta-theory that has been developing for the past several decades (Spivey, 1997). Constructivists contend that learners do not merely respond to stimulus as stated by behaviorists, but that knowledge is actively acquired, socially constructed, and created or re-created (Phillips, 1995). Constructivists believe that learners actively use their minds to construct their own individual meaning. This meaning is constructed using their background knowledge; and because every learner's background knowledge is different, every person's construction of meaning is unique. Learners also construct meaning in concert with other people. Knowledge, therefore, is socially constructed.

 Constructivist theory puts forward the idea that meanings from texts are constructed in social situations. In what ways do you think students can learn from each other?

Let's think about what this means to you. Think about a movie that you saw recently, one that was more complex than an action film. As you were watching the movie, you were constructing your perception of the movie in your mind. You may have been recalling other similar films, thinking about the main character's motivations, predicting what would happen next in the plot, and wondering how the movie would end. After the movie, you may have asked a friend a question about the movie to ascertain your friend's perceptions, which most likely were different from yours. The thinking process that you experienced is an active construction of meaning. You didn't just watch the movie and accept the visual and auditory input; your mind worked to make sense of the movie as you were watching. You didn't just accept your construction of meaning, you talked with others about their perceptions as well. Even while watching movies, you construct meaning in social ways, which illustrates constructivism.

Influence of Piaget.

Some of the beliefs of constructivism stem from Dewey's belief in experience as the foundation of learning (Dewey, 1938). More recently, however, constructivist perspectives have been developed from the theories of Piaget and Vytgotsky. Piaget's work has been extremely influential in several areas of education, but his writings during the 1970s have served as the foundation for constructivism (Fosnot, 1996). According to Piaget (1977), learners assimilate new information within existing knowledge structures, accommodate the knowledge structures to new situations, and move between assimilation and accommodation as necessary. These cognitive activities are quite different from behaviorist thinking. Piaget suggested that learners' minds are actively engaged in mental activities as they are exposed to new information.

Influence of Vygotsky.

Vygotsky added a new dimension to Piagetian constructivism. Vygotsky (1978) suggested that learners not only use their minds actively to develop new knowledge, but that they also use language and personal interactions to develop learning, as in the previous example of discussing a movie. Vygotsky's theories suggested that learning begins on the social level through language and then is internalized. The language events that most effectively facilitate

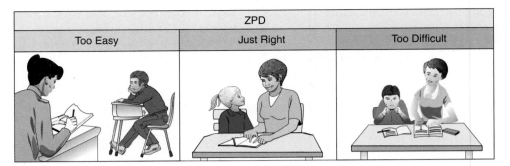

FIGURE 1.2 How ZPD Applies to Learning

learning are social, but they also involve learners and "more knowledgeable others" in these social interactions. As people learn, they have a sphere of actual and potential learning. A person's potential expresses what he or she is capable of learning: "The distance between the actual developmental level as determined through problem solving and the level of potential development as determined through problem solving under adult guidance or in collaboration with more capable peers" (Vygotsky, 1978, p. 84). This area of most effective learning is called the *zone of proximal development* (ZPD). Figure 1.2 illustrates how the ZPD applies to a child's learning.

Zone of proximal development.   The ZPD is a useful concept for you to understand. As you think about ZPD, think about how you learned different skills, such as learning to read. First, some of you may have learned to read outside of school, but most of you probably learned to read in school. Think about the social aspects of your experience. As a young child, you very likely had a parent or relative who read to you and with you. Then when you went to school, your teachers modeled reading by reading aloud, taught you letters and sounds, and organized literacy experiences for you. During these literacy experiences, you had opportunities to read with the teacher, with classmates, and alone. Much of your learning was social.

Early in this process, you could read, but you couldn't read everything. When you were in first grade, you couldn't read a biology textbook, even with help. That difficulty of learning would have been way outside your ZPD. In the same respect, when you were in high school, a first-grade story would have been too easy for you and also not appropriate. As you learned to read, you had to have materials that were in the range of your expertise. You could read more difficult materials with help, but only if those materials were within your ZPD.

Sociocultural theories.   Cognitive theory and constructivism suggest that learning is an active process, occurring in the mind but influenced by social interactions. Learning is also influenced by social and cultural relationships.

Individuals can learn alone but that learning is based on social mediation (Salomon & Perkins, 1998). Think about yourself learning something new. For example, let's say that your friend, Jeni, has a new computer game that you would like to try. Jeni tells you about the game, and you watch her play it while she discusses the aspects of the game. She then encourages you to learn it while she's at work. You boot up the computer and attempt the new game. Are you learning alone? In many respects you are; however, you also bring hours of socially mediated learning to the situation. While you try the new game, you're probably remembering past attempts at learning new computer games, strategies you've learned from others who you've played games with, and even conversations with Jeni about the new game. You are recalling socially mediated learning even while you're learning alone. Learning can be mediated socially in one-on-one instruction, in small groups, or in large groups.

Socially mediated learning. Learning is also socially mediated because much of your prior learning has been conducted in social situations or groups. Therefore, learning is socially mediated even when it occurs individually. Here's another example: Think of one of your college classes where the teacher taught by way of lecture. You were expected to listen to the teacher, take notes, read the textbook, and study for a test. Think about the times you turned to another student and asked for clarification and the times you formed study groups in preparation for a test. In those situations, you combined individual learning with learning in social situations.

As a classroom teacher, you will need to keep in mind that your students are social learners. Students learn best when they have the opportunity to collaborate with others and learn from their peers as well as from you. In a classroom where the teacher applies sociocultural theories, the teacher will also acknowledge the wealth of background knowledge each student brings to the class. The teacher will understand that students work alone and in groups and that all learning is valued.

Socially mediated learning is a term that describes learning that occurs and is enhanced in social settings. Name some of your learning experiences that were socially mediated.

Eclectic Approaches to Learning

Describing learning theories this way may seem black and white to you: Either you believe in behaviorist theories of learning or you believe in social constructivism. However, it's not that simple. Many teachers find themselves in the middle ground and take an eclectic approach, moving from one theory to another, drawing from both behaviorism and social constructivism.

An eclectic approach may mean different things to different people. Generally, though, teachers who consider themselves to be eclectic are atheoretical; that is, they don't believe in just one theory. Eclectic teachers' thinking and instructional practices may span from a strong belief in a transmission model to a strong belief in constructivist theories. Some teachers consider themselves eclectic because they are moving from beliefs in behaviorism to believing in a form of constructivism. Although it is preferable that teachers have consistent theories to guide their practices, it's often the case that teachers fall somewhere in the middle on a theoretical continuum.

You have been thinking about how students learn and how one's theory of learning is played out in the classroom. In the next section, you will focus your view specifically on literacy learning and how those theories relate to how children are taught to read.

YOUR KNOWLEDGE OF THEORIES OF LITERACY LEARNING

Many theories of literacy learning were proposed during the last half of the 20th century, and researchers continue to study the mysteries of exactly what happens when a person learns to read. You may be thinking, "Why do I care about theories? Just show me what to do!" It is important to learn about theories because even if you think you don't care about or need them, what you do in your future classrooms will be directly influenced by what you believe about how children learn to read—and that is your theory of literacy learning.

We have chosen to examine four major theories of literacy learning: the bottom-up theory, the psycholinguistic theory, the transactional theory, and critical literacy. We introduce these theories in this chapter, but we will explain them more thoroughly and make connections to them as they are woven throughout this book. As you study each theory, you should think carefully about their classroom implications and teachers you've known who have exemplified the theories in their teaching practices.

Bottom-Up Theory of Reading

 In bottom-up theory skills are taught *first* rather than *during* natural engagement with whole texts. What are your memories of trying to learn something new in small increments *before* you understood the big picture?

The *bottom-up theory* of reading stems from behaviorism and was popular in schools during the second half of the 20th century. Bottom-up means that when reading, readers first notice letters, then words, then sentences, and finally the meaning of the entire text, almost like climbing steps from the bottom up. This theory was made popular by LaBerge and Samuels (1974) who, at the time, believed that reading was an information processing activity and that decoding (figuring out) words and comprehending them (understanding meanings) were separate mental processes. Another name for the bottom-up theory of reading is the *skills approach*.

Like a . . . Teaching using the bottom-up approach is like learning to play the piano using notes and scales rather than music. For example, imagine learning to play the piano as a young adult. You contact a music teacher and ask for lessons. The teacher gives you a sheet of music that has the notes of the scale. During lessons you learn which note on the printed scale corresponds to the key on the piano. At successive lessons you learn more notes and more keys, but you don't play any songs. You continue learning the notes and the keys until you know them well. After you have mastered the notes, you begin to play simple songs.

Classroom application.   Not every teacher who teaches letters and sounds is using the bottom-up approach. Most kindergarten and first-grade teachers teach letters and sounds; the difference is in the way teachers approach them. If a teacher reads a story aloud to the class and discusses the words that begin with the letter *s,* that teacher is not using a bottom-up approach because she began with whole text. A teacher using a bottom-up approach has students complete a worksheet in which they identify pictures and circle the pictures that begin with the letter *s*. An emphasis on letters and sounds versus whole texts is the determining factor of the bottom-up approach.

Figure 1.3 provides an example of a four-square model that can help you understand the various literacy learning theories that we are describing here. A four-square model is useful in teaching students new concepts through analogy, definition, and an antithesis.

Psycholinguistic Theory of Reading

Psycholinguists, who combine knowledge from psychology and linguistics (how language works), reason that reading is primarily an active, meaning-making endeavor and that in order to make sense of the print on a page, the reader must begin with

Theory	Like . . .
Bottom-up theory Also called skills approach	Playing the piano by learning notes and keys before songs ![piano]
Definition	**What It's *Not***
Teaching reading using the progression of letters, sounds, words, and sentences before meaning	Teaching reading using books or stories as a context for learning about letters and sounds

FIGURE 1.3   The Bottom-Up Theory

the whole of the text, not the parts. *Psycholinguistic theory* is sometimes referred to as a *top-down model* in contrast to the theory you just learned (the bottom-up model). Kenneth Goodman (1965), a noted researcher in the theory of psycholinguistics, observed that readers access cueing systems, informational sources that allow them to make sense of print. Further, Goodman asserted that all readers make mistakes, which he called "miscues," and that those very miscues can provide evidence to teachers of what is happening in a reader's mind.

 The psycholinguistic approach contends that reading is primarily a meaning-making enterprise that requires readers to engage with whole texts *first*, before learning about the parts. Why would this be called a *top-down model* of reading?

Like a . . . The psycholinguistic theory of reading is like learning to play baseball. Pretend you're from a different planet and you have no idea what the game of baseball is all about. To help you understand, a coach takes you to a ballpark in order for you to experience what happens during a baseball game. You are able to see the players warming up before the game. Watching the batters face the pitchers while the umpire calls balls and strikes shows you that a batter gets only so many tries before he has to sit down. Or, you witness a batter hit the ball and start running down a base path toward an opposing team member who is standing there. A player far out in the field catches the ball and throws it to the waiting player who catches the ball in his mitt and touches the running player with it. The batter/runner then has to sit down; you are not quite sure but you have a hunch that it has something to do with the runner not reaching the base before the throw got there.

It might take a whole nine innings of careful observation before you understand the basic concepts of the game, but, gradually, you get the idea. Contrast the notion of seeing a whole game first versus learning all of the rules, regulations, and minutia of baseball without ever having seen a game before.

Classroom application.   You can often observe excellent teachers in the early grades who believe in the psycholinguistic theory of reading. In their classrooms, they read aloud daily to children, using expressive voices and pointing out brightly drawn illustrations in books. They ask children to predict what might happen next in the story and read on to see if those predictions come true. They purposefully demonstrate, in shared reading experiences using enlarged texts (Big Books), that books have letters, and words, and sentences. These teachers explain that when you look at the pictures, you can find information to help you figure out the words. They know that young children enjoy looking at whole books and reading some of the words before they even know all the names of the letters of the alphabet or all the sounds the letters make, especially after the teacher has read those books aloud to the children. Figure 1.4 describes the psycholinguistic theory using the four-square model.

Theory	**Like . . .**
Psycholinguistics	Watching a whole baseball game before learning all of the rules 
Definition	**What It's *Not***
Readers act on written language with the primary purpose of making sense.	Learning all the rules of phonics before being given a chance to read whole books

FIGURE 1.4   Psycholinguistic Theory of Reading

Transactional Theory of Reading

The transactional theory of reading, developed in the early 1970s by Louise Rosenblatt (1978), states that reading is a transaction between the reader, the text, and the social context. By *transaction,* Rosenblatt meant that when readers read, they bring their prior knowledge to the reading event and then that knowledge *combines* with the information from the text. The meaning that results from the combination of readers' prior knowledge and the text is influenced by the social and cultural background of each reader. Therefore, meaning from reading transactions is a combination of a reader's knowledge, the text, and the social context.

> **Like a . . .** The transactional theory of reading is like buying a car. When you buy a car, you bring your likes and dislikes, your transportation needs, and your money to a car dealer (or the Internet). The dealer offers cars that have certain characteristics—style, color, mileage, repair histories. When you decide to buy a car, you enter into a transaction. Influencing the transaction are the social mores of your age group. For example, young adults buy certain types and colors of cars, and that social information also is part of the transaction. When you buy a car, therefore, you bring your own preferences and needs to a situation where the dealer brings her cars, and your final decision is influenced by social knowledge.

Classroom application. Teachers who espouse the transactional theory of reading provide readers with many experiences with texts—through shared reading, guided reading, interactive reading and writing, reading workshops, literature circles, and so on. Before asking students to read, they conduct an activity so that students can access their prior knowledge in preparation for reading. During reading, teachers encourage students to use the information from the text along with their own knowledge to make meaning. After reading, teachers encourage discussion of multiple meanings of texts and discourage the notion that only one correct meaning exists for any text. Teachers who believe in transactional theory teach students about the visual cueing systems, or phonics, but instruction about letters and sounds is embedded within the context of whole texts. Figure 1.5 illustrates the transactional theory of reading.

Critical Literacy

Critical literacy is the most recent literacy learning theory put forward and it is continuing to be developed and refined in the early 21st century. Critical literacy is "an active, challenging approach to literacy that encourages students to be aware of the way that texts are constructed and how such constructions position readers" (Fehring & Green, 2001, back cover), which means that during reading, readers don't just construct meaning from print, they go beyond making meaning to analyzing text and forming judgments.

> **Like a . . .** A critical literacy approach is like reflecting on a discussion with a friend. If you are taking a critical stance, you're not being *critical* in the sense that you are *criticizing;* instead, you're looking at all the ins and outs, what's said and what's not said. For example, put yourself in the place of one of the two young adults engaged in this conversation:
>
> *Nicole:*   I'm going home this weekend to celebrate my 21st birthday. Would you come home with me?
>
> *Mark:*   I really have to study this weekend.

Transactional theory posits that readers construct meaning from text based on prior knowledge and experiences within the context of the reading. When you choose a book to read for pleasure, how does your background knowledge affect your understanding of the story?

Theory	Like . . .
Transactional theory	Buying a car
Definition	**What It's *Not***
Acknowledging the contributions of the reader, the text, and the social context in reading events	Teaching sounds and letters in isolation Demanding one right meaning of text

FIGURE 1.5   Transactional Theory of Reading

Another component of critical literacy is the evaluation of the political agenda of the author. As you read your daily newspaper, ask yourself, "What are the political viewpoints of this author?"

Nicole:	You usually don't study on weekends. But if you have to, you can study in the car.
Mark:	Well, I was planning on spending the weekend in the library. I have a paper due on Monday.
Nicole:	You can go to the library earlier this week. Don't you like my family? Is that why you don't want to go?
Mark:	Of course I like your family. I just have to study.

If you think about taking a critical stance, you'd reflect on the meanings *surrounding the words* of this conversation. You'd look at what Nicole and Mark *did* and *did not* say in the conversation and also *how* they expressed themselves. You'd make inferences about what each person meant. For example, perhaps Nicole was thinking, "I wonder if Mark is planning on breaking up with me," and perhaps Mark was thinking, "I might be placed on academic probation if I don't get good grades this semester." Taking a critical stance means looking at what authors include in texts and what that says about the author and about society.

Classroom application.   Students of all levels can practice critical literacy although the abstract thinking involved is best suited for readers in middle grades. Teachers who teach from a critical stance ask students to look for biases in text and to problemetize texts. This means that during reading, students identify what the text says

Theory	Like . . .
Critical literacy	Reflecting on a conversation 
Definition	**What It's *Not***
Examining texts and their relationships to society	Looking at surface meanings

FIGURE 1.6   Critical Literacy Theory

about society by what's stated and what's unstated. For example, when reading *The Three Little Javelinas* (Lowell, 1992), a version of *The Three Little Pigs* set in the Arizona desert, the teacher asks students how this story is different from other versions of *The Three Little Pigs* and what this story says about desert societies. The teacher does not just discuss the features of the text that make this story a fairy tale, she asks students to think more deeply and examine how the text illustrates cultures within society. Figure 1.6 illustrates critical literacy theory.

Combining Literacy Theories

When you're a teacher, you won't follow just one literacy theory; you'll probably use features of psycholinguistic, transactional, and critical theories. Furthermore, the proportion of time you spend teaching lessons derived from each theory will be different if you teach Early Readers (approximately grades K–2), Interpretive Readers (approximately grades 3–5), or Critical Readers (approximately grades 6–8).

Typically, as a teacher of Early Readers, you will spend more of your class's reading time teaching students how to use and orchestrate the cueing systems, based on the psycholinguistic theory of reading. You will also teach students to construct their own meaning from text (transactional theory) and, at times, will have your young students take a critical stance (critical theory).

As children progress in their reading abilities, they become more fluent and have to spend less time figuring out individual, unknown words. Use of the cueing systems becomes more flexible and automatic. Therefore, if you teach Interpretive Readers, you can spend more instructional time allowing children to respond to literature

FIGURE 1.7   A Developmental Approach to the Implementation of Literacy Learning Theories

through discussions, writing, drama, art, and other creative ways. Thus, if you teach grades 3–5, you will be relying more heavily on the transactional theory of reading. Of course, there will still be readers in your classroom who need support in accessing the cueing systems (the psycholinguistic theory) and others who are ready to launch into taking a critical look at the material they read (critical theory).

Most children in grades 6–8 are able readers who fairly seamlessly orchestrate the cueing systems and are experienced in responding to what they read through numerous ways of representing their reactions to text (transactional theory). It is during these grades that you, as a teacher, can take full advantage of these students' abilities to stand back from what they have read and look at it with analytical lenses to discern the multiple interpretations and political agendas that can be identified in printed material. In this way, you will be relying on the critical theory of reading.

In general, if you are a teacher who subscribes to social constructivism, the theory-use proportion that you would use as a teacher of Early Readers, Interpretive Readers, and Critical Readers would look something like the proportions drawn in Figure 1.7.

◢◢◢ YOU TRY IT ◢◢◢

Distinguishing Between Literacy Theories

Below is a list of student literacy practices that commonly occur in classrooms. Add other instructional practices that you remember from your schooling experiences. Write each phrase from the list on an index card. Then sort the cards into the four literacy learning theories that we have been discussing: bottom-up theory, psycholinguistic theory, transactional theory, and critical theory. Compare your sorting with other class members.

Instructional Practices

- Filling out worksheets,
- Writing in journals,
- Listening to a book read aloud,
- Trying to understand the author's message,
- Discussing a story,

- Participating in literature circles (book discussion groups),
- Learning the sounds of letters in isolation,
- Choral reading,
- Acting out a story,
- Discussing social implications of a story or book,
- Writing an editorial letter to a newspaper,
- Creating a painting that evolved from a story you read,
- Memorizing rules of phonics,
- Analyzing a political cartoon,
- Listening to books on tape while following along with text,
- Writing poetry about feelings evoked from a book,
- Using flashcards to learn new words,
- Critiquing a presidential speech,
- Developing a TV ad that sells a book to your classmates,
- Making up a puppet show version of *The Three Bears,*
- Interviewing a classmate about a novel,
- Evaluating websites for accuracy and political slant,
- Reading early reading texts and retelling the stories,
- Writing out definitions of vocabulary words,
- Constructing a diorama that depicts a scene from a story,
- Chanting the short and long sounds of the vowels,
- Learning to ask, "Does what I just read make sense?", and
- Crafting "Please Recycle!" flyers.

YOUR PHILOSOPHY OF LITERACY LEARNING

In the previous sections of this chapter, you addressed two essential questions: (1) How do people learn? (2) As a teacher, how can I support students in the learning process? You studied comprehensive, umbrella theories of learning, specifically behaviorism and social constructivism. These theories reflect our understandings of how people learn, so we can, in turn, use those theories to guide instruction in classrooms. Think about social constructivism as the umbrella that arches over three of the theories of literacy learning we discussed earlier: the psycholinguistic theory, the transactional theory, and critical literacy. The umbrella of social constructivism and the accompanying, related theories of literacy learning will be the frame for your evolving *philosophy of literacy learning;* this will guide how you teach students to read.

Assessment Matters

Classroom Assessment

Assessment plays a central role in every instructional judgment. Each child in an elementary classroom who is learning to read, and reading to learn, has different strengths and needs as well as different ways of approaching literacy tasks. The effective literacy teacher knows how to assess each child and make instructional decisions for that child based on the findings from those assessments. The assessment component is one that you will want to keep in mind as you gather knowledge for your evolving philosophy of literacy learning.

Sometimes, teachers and students think that assessment means giving tests and that the primary purpose of assessment is to give grades. Even though tests and grade giving are often associated with assessment, we believe that the primary purpose of assessment is to gather data to inform teaching. Just as the researcher gathers data, analyzes it for emerging patterns, and draws conclusions and implications from the findings, the literacy teacher needs to be adept and diligent at collecting and analyzing data. This is what we mean when we say that assessment informs instruction; knowing your students will guide you in what you need to teach.

How assessment can connect to social constructivism.   You have learned that social constructivists view learning as a process of actively constructing knowledge with other people in social settings. Students, then, construct their own understandings using their background knowledge as they interact with other people (peers and teachers) in classrooms. Perspectives that place assessment in an inquiry model would align with social constructivist theory (Fosnot, 1996). An inquiry model would acknowledge that each child's knowledge is unique because of differing prior knowledge, focus on process as well as product, and advocate the ongoing nature of assessment. Serafini (2000/2001) writes, "The teacher uses various qualitative and quantitative assessment techniques to inquire about particular learners and their learning processes. It is a process of inquiry, and a process of interpretation, used to promote reflection concerning students' understandings, attitudes, and literate abilities" (p. 387). Further, when teachers embrace an inquiry approach to assessment, students are invited into the cycle of inquiry, becoming partners-in-inquiry as they engage in self-evaluation and take active roles in understanding how they are being assessed and what those assessments mean (Thomas & Oldfather, 1995).

Authentic Assessment

Assessment based on an inquiry paradigm is sometimes referred to as *authentic assessment*. Authentic assessments are situated in classroom-based interactions while students are participating in ordinary learning activities. Figure 1.8 illustrates examples of the broad array of literacy assessment measures available to teachers. Some of the assessments shown in Figure 1.8 are an outgrowth of normal literacy activities (authentic assessments); others are situated in formal settings that are separate from day-to-day classroom interactions, such as when students are given standardized tests.

A few examples follow of some of the authentic assessment tools we will explore in this textbook. Note that one sentence in each of these examples begins "You can use this information to. . . ." We include this repeated sentence as a reminder that each assessment measure emphasized is designed to tell you about your students, then help you decide what and how to teach as well as to track students' progress over time. In addition, we are stressing the reflective stance that teachers must take when evaluating assessment data. They must continually ask, "What does this information that I have collected mean for co-learners: me as a teacher and my students?"

Classroom Assessment

Informal surveys.   Informal surveys help you find out about such things as children's interests, reading habits, hobbies, the kinds of books they like to read, and how they feel about themselves as readers. You can use this information to choose texts and other materials that interest and, thus, motivate children to learn. Further, knowing how children feel about themselves as readers will help you know how to support children's feelings of efficacy as literacy learners.

Classroom Assessment

Read and retell.   Using read and retell procedures allows you to assess children's comprehension after they have read a text. Rather than giving a formal test, you ask

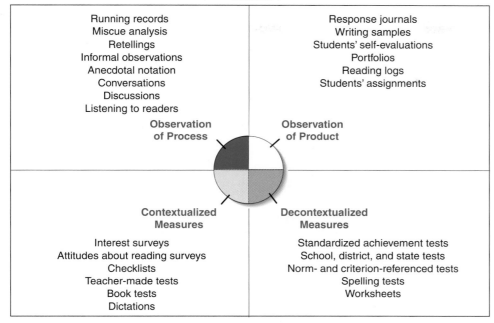

FIGURE 1.8 Assessment Options for Literacy Teachers

Adapted from Anthony, R. J., Johnston, T. D., Michelson, N. I., & Preece, A. (1991). *Evaluating literacy: A perspective for change.* Portsmouth, NH: Heinemann, p. 31.

the child to *tell you* about the text, prompting the child if necessary about such elements as the main characters, main ideas, and the setting. Sometimes you may opt to use a checklist or make notes that indicate children's levels of understanding of what they have just read. You can use this information to help you decide about the texts students are reading. Are the texts too difficult? Challenging enough? Interesting enough? You can also use this information to decide if there are strategies that your students need that could help their reading become more proficient and their understanding more complete.

Observations/anecdotal notation. As you teach, you will develop a systematic procedure for observing students as they engage in literacy activities. Observation of the reading and writing processes, for example, highlights students' strengths and needs as literacy learners. Anecdotal notes are brief, dated notes that teachers take as they observe students. Let's say your system is to observe and make notations about three students per day. You might write a note like this about your student, second-grader James:

> 10/23—James is anxious to read chapter books, but the ones that he's choosing, like the Boxcar Children series, are too difficult. *Reminder to self:* Try to direct James toward the Cam Jansen series to see if those catch his interest and are more appropriate for him, providing success.

Classroom Assessment

Classroom Assessment

Other assessment options.   Besides the exemplars we've already touched on, you will find explanations of many other forms of assessment in this textbook, including these:

- Checklists,
- Classroom discussions,
- Children's creative responses to literacy events,
- Interviews and informal conversations with students,
- Samples of students' work,
- Questionnaires,
- Journals,
- Records of books children have read, and
- Student self-evaluations.

You can use the information gleaned from each of these assessments to find out what your students know now and to decide with them what they need to know next.

Why So Much Emphasis on Assessment?

When you are a teacher, after each literacy assessment, you will reflect on your students as you analyze the data you have collected. Often you will find yourself asking these questions as you think about how you could help your students become more skillful and confident literacy users: What kinds of books should I provide? What topics are my students interested in that would engage them? Which strategies do I need to teach and encourage? What kinds of minilessons should I provide? What kinds of writing opportunities do I need to create? How can I best support my students' literacy development? How can I help my students take more ownership of their own learning? Because assessment is so central to effective literacy teaching, we will focus your attention on assessment each time it's presented. Look for assessment options in each chapter when you see the term "Classroom Assessment" in the margin. This term will be used as a reminder to keep assessment as a primary component of your philosophy and actions as a teacher.

Standards

In this textbook you will learn about various kinds of standards that will influence your developing philosophy of literacy learning. Standards are benchmarks of achievement that have been established by local, state, and national organizations to address a range of learning communities. We will consider two main categories of standards that exist: those that have been created for teachers and those developed for students in schools.

Standards for teachers.   There are standards for experienced teachers and another type that have been created for new teachers. The teacher education field is paying attention to standards in this time of high demand for quality teachers. Among the common goals of teacher educators is the preparation of new teachers who will have a positive impact on student achievement, be more attuned to students' needs, and be able to teach all children (Wise & Leibbrand, 2000). Darling-Hammond (2000) notes that although debates continue about best practices for training teachers, the quality and extent of teacher education matters now more than ever. To this end, a multistate cohort was created—the Interstate New Teacher Assessment and Support

Consortium (INTASC)—which is an assemblage of state agencies, higher education institutions, and educational groups dedicated to high-quality teacher preparation, licensure, and ongoing professional development of new teachers (Council of Chief State School Officers, 1992). INTASC principles are found throughout the For Your Portfolio sections in this textbook as a basis for understanding what is expected of you as a new teacher. The INTASC principles assess what you know (knowledge), what you can do (performances), and your intangible qualities as a teacher-to-be (dispositions).

Standards for students. For our purposes, standards for students in schools can likewise be separated into two groups: state content standards and nationally created standards. State and national content standards exist for each subject matter such as science, social studies, math, and language arts. As a literacy teacher, you will be responsible for meeting the standards of the state where you are employed under the realm of "language arts standards."

The literacy standards for students in school that we're going to concentrate on in this text are *Standards for the English Language Arts* (1996). These standards were developed by the International Reading Association (IRA) and the National Council of Teachers of English (NCTE), two large and respected professional literacy organizations. They will be referred to as the IRA/NCTE standards and will also be referenced in your portfolio entries as you think about how you will meet the literacy needs of your future students. As you complete both types of portfolio entries— those for new teachers (INTASC) and those for students (IRA/NCTE)—you will be challenged to think about the different aspects of literacy and literacy instruction and how standards have an impact on your developing philosophy of literacy learning.

Articulating Your Beliefs

It is important for each us as teachers to articulate what we believe about literacy teaching and learning and why. By putting what we believe into words, we begin to understand how those beliefs underpin our philosophy of literacy learning and how that philosophy directs what we do in the classroom. Regie Routman (2000) says, "Our beliefs about teaching and learning directly affect how and why we teach the way we do, even when we do not or cannot verbalize these beliefs. Therefore, it is important to articulate our beliefs and match them with practice: *If this is what I believe, how does that influence what I do in the classroom?*" (p. 17). Further, understanding your views about how children learn and the literacy research that supports your views will determine not only your teaching practices, but also your teaching effectiveness (Taberski, 2000).

You must be able to express your philosophy of literacy learning so you can understand how your views impact your teaching practices and effectiveness. However, this is a difficult enterprise and one that requires you to search for answers, not only within yourself, but also through your readings of relevant research, observation of expert teachers, and interactions with peers and students. Your philosophy will evolve from your own experiences as a learner, the knowledge you gain through study and from learning to be a responsive teacher, your understanding of the role of assessment, and what is expected of you as a new teacher as defined by standards for your students and for you.

Your philosophy of reading is essential because it defines both your beliefs and your practices. How will you begin to develop a philosophy of literacy learning?

CONNECTIONS: WHAT'S NEXT?

The rest of this text, including the provided experiences and activities, is intended to help you learn more about literacy learning and teaching so that you can become an effective literacy teacher. Social constructivism is the overarching theory of learning that will help you begin to understand the literacy knowledge base and how to translate that knowledge into practice. You are invited to become an active, engaged learner who draws on what you already know to construct new knowledge about literacy through social interactions.

This text, with its references to research, demonstrations, activities, and opportunities for reflection, is presented within your zone of proximal development (Vygotsky, 1978). Your instructor and more knowledgeable others such as noted literacy researchers and exemplary teachers will guide you through problem-solving experiences with the text, in collaboration with your peers. We believe this is how we all learn best. Through active engagement, you will study theories of literacy learning that will inform and support your *evolving philosophy of literacy learning*. These complex literacy learning theories will be presented in appropriate contexts so that you can make connections with them and use them to construct new understandings.

In the following chapters you will be journeying through the processes of understanding how to help students learn to read (and read to learn) from the early grades through the middle levels of school. Figure 1.9 presents the framework that we will use as a means of organizing this information for you as you progress through the next three parts: Teaching Early Readers, Teaching Interpretive Readers, and Teaching Critical Readers. We have loosely assigned grade levels to each of the sections to help you visualize how each developmental group might learn. The grade levels we've suggested are not firm in terms of the children you will teach in the future, because each child's development proceeds at a different rate. The grade levels simply provide a *general* frame of reference.

The developmental approach that we have adopted is divided into teaching methods appropriate for whole-group, small-group, and independent settings (see Figure 1.9). In addition, we will focus your attention on literacy learning theories, characteristics of students in those grades, and orchestrating instruction. You will learn about the centrality of assessment, how to plan, and how to become an effective teacher of reading, beginning with young children.

FIGURE 1.9   A Developmental Approach to the Teaching of Reading

	Early Readers	**Interpretive Readers**	**Critical Readers**
Theories underscored as readers develop:	Social Constructivism — Psycholinguistic / Critical / Transactional	Social Constructivism — Psycholinguistic / Critical / Transactional	Social Constructivism — Psycholinguistic / Critical / Transactional

FIGURE 1.9 *Continued*

	Early Readers	**Interpretive Readers**	**Critical Readers**
Whole-group instruction through:	• Read-alouds • Shared texts • Comprehension strategies • Working with words	• Read-alouds • Using basals • Literature-based models • Word-building strategies • Comprehension strategies	• Read-alouds • Common texts (e.g., basals, anthologies, trade books) • Comprehension strategies • Vocabulary instruction and word analysis • Researching • Critical reading • Reading content area texts • Studying and note-taking
Assessment ideas for whole group:	• Observations • Kidwatching • Anecdotal notation	• Portfolios • Open-ended questions • Rubrics	• Written retellings • Research projects • Interest inventories • Content-area histories • Cloze procedure
Small-group instruction through:	• Guided reading • Teaching for strategies • Working with words	• Basal readers • Literature anthologies • Fluency practice • Guided silent reading • Literature circles • Inquiry groups	• Book clubs • Trade books
Assessment ideas for small groups:	• Running Records • Retellings • Discussions with children	• Names test • Fluency checklist • Peer assessment • Inquiry rubric	• Student information card • Bio poem • "I Used to… But Now I…" poem • Observational checklist • Student self-assessment • Norm-referenced tests
Independent learning through:	• Independent reading • Reading/writing workshop • Making books • Reading the room	• Independent reading • Reading/writing workshop • Responding through writing • Reading logs	• Sustained silent reading and writing
Sociocultural contexts:	• Literacy partnerships with parents • Parents in the classroom • Home–school communication	• Reading/writing connection for life • Oral histories • Home literacy activities • Parent programs	• Parents as coaches • Funds of knowledge • Parent–student book clubs

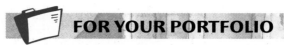

FOR YOUR PORTFOLIO

ENTRY 1.1   *My Dispositions as a Teacher*

INTASC Principle 9 states: *The teacher is a reflective practitioner who continually evaluates the effects of his/her choices and actions on others . . . and who actively seeks out opportunities to grow professionally.*

As you participate in experiences that prepare you to be a teacher, you will have many opportunities to reflect on what you are learning and who you are becoming. This supports you in developing into a *reflective practitioner,* as described in INTASC Principle 9. Here is a self-assessment for you to complete for your portfolio that asks you to reflect on what you know and believe about yourself as you begin this literacy course. The column on the left contains dispositions that effective teachers possess. Be honest as you evaluate yourself according to each of these attributes, using the spaces in the middle and right columns. An example of "love of learning" is provided for you.

My Dispositions as a Teacher

Disposition	How I demonstrate this disposition:	How I could develop this disposition more:
Love of learning	I read extra materials suggested by instructors.	I could subscribe to professional journals, such as *The Reading Teacher.*
Caring about children		
Hard working and resilient		
Organized		
Pursuing excellence		
Positive attitude		
Flexibility		
Unrelenting hope to make a difference		

ENTRY 1.2   *My Evolving Philosophy of Literacy Learning*

This portfolio entry is a starting place for the development of your evolving philosophy of literacy learning. You have already begun to think about what it is you believe and why; here are some questions and incomplete statements that will stimulate further thinking about what you believe. This exercise is designed to help you lay the groundwork in articulating your philosophy of literacy learning. At this point, your answers may be more like predictions or hunches—that is to be expected. Please date and keep this entry in your portfolio even after you make changes; it will be beneficial as you trace your new understandings and your development as a literacy teacher. You may find that you will hold fast to some of your beliefs and change others over time; that is why we refer to our philosophies as *evolving*.

Write your answers to these three questions:

- How do children learn to read?
- What should I teach when helping children learn to read?
- How should I teach children to read?

Finish these statements, relating them to literacy learning:

- All children can. . .
- All children need. . .
- Children learn. . .
- Everyone in the classroom. . .
- Learning should be. . .
- Children need opportunities to. . .
- Teachers need to. . .
- Teachers can. . .
- Teachers have a responsibility to. . .

ENTRY 1.3   *Helping English Language Learners*

IRA/NCTE Standard 10 states: *Students whose first language is not English make use of their first language to develop competency in the English language arts and to develop understanding of content across the curriculum*

In terms of your explorations of your own culture and language, as well as your reflection on theories of learning, write a paragraph in your portfolio that describes how using what you know helps you learn something you don't know. Then, using this as a reference point, write a second paragraph that addresses how you could help English Language Learners use their first language to make inroads into learning English. How would you help such students? Think about the power of social interactions, presenting materials in students' ZPDs, and the role of assessment in determining students' needs.

TO LEARN MORE

Helpful Websites

Visit our Companion Website at *http://www.prenhall.com/lenski* to link to the following sites:

Interstate New Teacher Assessment and Support Consortium

Read about INTASC, a consortium of state education agencies, higher education institutions, and national educational organizations dedicated to the reform of education and licensing of new teachers.
http://www.ccsso.org/intasc.html

IRA/NCTE Standards

Read about securing a copy of the International Reading Association and National Council of Teachers of English *Standards for the English Language Arts*.
http://www.reading.org/advocacy/elastandards/index.html

Constructivism in the Classroom

Learn more about what constructivism is, how it differs from traditional ideas about teaching and learning, and what constructivism has to do with the classroom.
http://www.thirteen.org/edonline/concept2class/month2/index.html

Integrating Constructivism Into the Classroom

Find ideas for integrating constructivist principles into the practices of teaching and learning.
http://www.stemnet.nf.ca/~elmurphy/emurphy/cle.html

Theory to Instruction

Provides a database for teachers interested in theory-based instruction.
http://tip.psychology.org/

Culturally Diverse and Tolerant Classrooms

Provides activities for teachers to help create culturally relevant classrooms.
http://curry.edschool.virginia.edu/go/capetown/

TEACHING EARLY READERS

From the title of this book you can tell that we have adopted a developmental perspective to the teaching of reading. That is, in this text you will learn about helping children develop from very early, emergent literacy learners to more proficiency as Interpretive and then Critical Readers. We believe that this developmental viewpoint will allow you to picture children as they grow as readers and also give you a chance to picture yourself as a teacher facilitating that growth.

In the chapters of Part II, you will learn about characteristics of Early Readers and instructional approaches for young literacy learners in whole-group, small-group, and independent settings. The approaches you will explore include reading and writing aloud, shared reading and writing, guided reading, independent reading and writing, and working with words.

Assessment ideas that will guide your teaching will be provided throughout. Assessment helps you understand what children already know, which allows you to focus on your students' strengths when planning instruction. You will also learn to teach for strategies that help Early Readers figure out unknown words and comprehend texts more readily. In addition, you will be provided with opportunities to try out what you are learning.

You will be introduced to a "new" second-grade teacher, Derek Schulze, who will share his perceptions about literacy teaching and learning by way of advice to you, who will soon be new teachers yourselves. We hope that you will feel a connection with Derek who has grappled with the same issues that you will soon face as literacy teachers.

Finally, in Part II you will investigate setting up a classroom for Early Readers that fosters their literacy development by providing emotional security, encouraged risk-taking, and the most engaging literacy learning opportunities that you can create. All of these elements—developmental characteristics, instructional approaches, assessment ideas, and applied activities for you—will be steeped in your need to understand each child's unique strengths and cultural backgrounds within their families and communities. It is a huge but exciting responsibility that you have committed to, and a career choice that is almost unparalleled in its significance. But we're guessing that you probably already know this. Let's begin!

Meet Derek Schulze

2nd Grade Teacher

Derek is in his second year of teaching second grade in a K–2 building located in an urban setting. He teaches reading using a basal series, supplemented with trade books. Derek has additional staff support for struggling readers and for those who need enrichment. He has developed listening, writing, reading, drawing, and computer centers that his students use during Literacy Workshop time. In the chapters about Early Readers, Derek will share his beliefs and practices of literacy learning in a column titled *Advice for New Teachers.*

Using Basals

Derek discovered in his first year of teaching that the stories in the basal adopted by his school district were not presented in order of difficulty. In fact, he found that the third story of the basal for his second graders was the most difficult to read and understand. To address this teaching challenge, Derek took his basal series home and assigned levels to the stories himself, using the categories of easy, medium, and hard. Then, he studied each category and ranked them further (e.g., very easy, somewhat easy, easy) and came up with nine levels within one basal for second graders. In this way, he reports that he "hops around the book all year," but is able to match his students with stories they are able to read.

Motivating Students

"I've learned that when I'm excited about a topic, it reaches over to the students. I didn't realize that at first. But if I enjoy something, my enjoyment is contagious." Derek believes that if you have passion about what you're teaching, then the students will be motivated to learn.

What I Wish I'd Known . . .

"I wish I'd known more about teaching reading. I admitted that when I interviewed for this job. But, soon after I was hired, I took a six-week course in literacy teaching from the district and that really helped. Also, I've learned from other teachers by not being afraid to ask.

"Another thing I wish I'd known is that you don't need to spend all your evenings and weekends grading papers. I did that the first year and it didn't really help me or the kids. I now use my energy actually teaching and thinking about what my students need."

chapter 2

Developing Your Knowledge About Early Readers

Essential Questions

- What are the classroom implications of children's physical, cognitive, and social development?
- How does emergent theory impact instruction in an early elementary classroom?
- Why is a print-rich environment critical for the literacy development of Early Readers?
- How does your knowledge of the cueing systems help you understand the reading process?
- Why does integrated, ongoing assessment need to be at the heart of your teaching?
- What factors are involved in motivating Early Readers?

Helping young children learn to read is an exciting and challenging responsibility. To be a purposeful and responsive teacher, you need to draw on all of the resources you have available throughout your career: your own experiences with children, information from your college courses, the expertise of your fellow teachers in the grade levels you teach, and your continued professional development as a literacy teacher. You should rely on the core body of knowledge that experts in the field of literacy have created for guidance. In this chapter we consider the core knowledge base associated with literacy teaching and learning as it applies to Early Readers.

If you are a teacher of young children, the first day of school will always be an exhilarating one. As the children arrive, you will notice that each one is excited, active, and unique! And while every child has unique strengths, needs, and experiences, as a beginning teacher you should think about general characteristics that young children have in common in terms of their physical, cognitive, and social development. These characteristics have important implications for you as you plan developmentally appropriate learning activities for Early Readers. *Developmentally appropriate* refers to activities that fit the children's physical, cognitive, and social characteristics. While reading the next section, think about how understanding young children's developmental distinctiveness will affect the life of your classroom and your instructional decision making.

Considering children's developmental characteristics and learning theories, you should then think about how young children acquire language and how oral language influences learning to read. Also consider how children learn about print, understanding that children become aware of print gradually, mirroring language acquisition. When children become aware of print, they progressively begin to understand that letters join together to form words, words form sentences, and print contains meaning. Children simultaneously start to understand that individual letters in our alphabet have names, and that letters have associated sounds when read aloud. Your new knowledge about how children process print will help you begin to understand how reading "happens." Developmental literacy learning processes are examined in this chapter to help you understand Early Readers and provide the foundation for your students' instruction.

 Visit the online journal in Chapter 2 on our Companion Website at *www.prenhall.com/lenski* to answer these questions. Save your answers to your hard drive or to a disk to compile an online journal.

Although children may have similar developmental characteristics, they are each different in many ways. How are some of the young children you know similar to and different from each other?

UNDERSTANDING EARLY READERS

We define *Early Readers* as children in kindergarten, first, or second grade. As you prepare to teach children in these grade/age groups (roughly 5 to 8 years old), it is helpful to understand their developmental characteristics in terms of physical, cognitive, and social features and how these impact literacy learning in school.

Physical Characteristics

You will notice a great diversity in heights and weights among your students. This period of time is one of fairly rapid growth—approximately 2.5 inches in height and 5 to 7 pounds of weight per year (Santrock, 1998). Children in K–2 classrooms are very active. They cannot and should not sit for long periods of time, nor are they able to attend to one task for an extended duration. It is not unusual for them to fidget while sitting, even if they are paying attention to what is occurring. Neither is it unusual for a kindergartner or first grader to fall out of a chair sideways for no apparent reason. Some children find it helpful to stand at their desks while working. They may complain that their hands "get tired" from writing and they often squeeze their pencils hard, with variable grasps. Early Readers can only focus on a sitting activity for 15 to 20 minutes. This physical restlessness and easy tiring does not mean that something is "wrong" with your students. They are not "hyperactive" and do not have "behavior problems." What it does mean is that, as a teacher of young children, you should create engaging, attention-keeping activities and change those activities often. You should vary children's school days, making sure to include many opportunities for physical exercise and movement.

Children's need to talk.   Young children are often noisy and their movements from one place to another require making noise because they have a lot to say and need opportunities to talk. In fact, young children often talk out loud to themselves as they are working on a task. Vygotsky (1962) called this self-talk *private speech,* a kind of speech that serves as verbal memory to guide the child, like a coach, in the successful completion of a task. You might, for example, hear a young child who is working on an art project say to himself, "Now I'm going to cut out this teddy bear and glue it on the page. Then I'm going to color all around it." The child is using private speech to rehearse, plan, and finish his project; his own language initiates and directs his actions.

Classroom application.   Physical developmental characteristics and the use of language as a mental tool have many implications for classroom learning. Language plays such an important role in helping children think, learn, and remember that as teachers you should not only be allowing talk in your classroom, you should encourage it (Bodrova & Leong, 1996). To require a silent, "no talking" classroom is to stifle the very means of learning for young children.

Likewise, because children naturally need to move around, you will want to provide opportunities for your students to spend time out of their chairs. Therefore, when you teach Early Readers, your classroom will be full of talk—a gently noisy place where children move about and exciting learning opportunities occur every day. More talk occurs during reading time because Early Readers do not read silently; they read words out loud, even when they are reading alone.

Jason prefers to stand while he reads.

Cognitive Development

In thinking about Early Readers' cognitive development, we proceed from a social constructivist viewpoint and draw on the work of Piaget and Vygotsky. Piaget (1977) believed that learners accommodate new information by fitting it into their existing schemata or patterns of behavior; he stressed that children actively construct their own cognitive worlds. Similarly, Vygotsky (1962, 1978) thought that children are active learners who use language in social contexts with more knowledgeable others to construct new understandings. Vygotsky also believed that learning and development are inextricably linked, one inseparable from the other, and supported by proper guidance.

Social constructivist viewpoints espouse children's ability to actively construct new understandings. How will this theory influence your teaching of young children?

Classroom application. In grades K–2, children's cognitive growth proceeds quickly when supported by a teacher who provides growth-enhancing events. The cognitive characteristics and related implications for literacy teaching shown in Figure 2.1, as suggested by Wood (1997), illustrate developmentally appropriate activities for young children.

Social Development

You have learned that children in the early grades like and need to talk and are quite social. They have begun to form friendships and may have one best friend.

- Young children learn best through repetitive activities, so you should supply opportunities for them to hear and interact with stories, poems, and songs over and over again.
- Early Readers learn best through lively investigation of manipulatives. It is a good idea to provide magnetic letters for them to build words, sentence strips that they can cut apart into words, and a wide variety of writing materials such as paint, markers, and colored pencils.
- Young children learn best when they can try out their early literacy learning in social settings. So you should furnish a dramatic play center that allows them to learn more about language through play and to practice their new reading and writing skills with classmates.
- Children learn best when they can practice new skills, so it is important to have a classroom library with daily time for independent reading. In the Library Corner, children are allowed to interact with books at their own developmental level, whether that is merely looking at the pictures, pretend reading, or conventional reading of texts.
- Children learn best when they receive supported risk taking, allowing for many "mistakes." Therefore, you will want to encourage your students to make predictions, take risks, and try new things while praising their attempts and approximations.

FIGURE 2.1 Developmentally Appropriate Activities for Early Readers

Companion Website

Approximations are attempts on the part of the child that are *almost* right. How does encouraging approximations help build a child's confidence as a reader?

Kindergarteners and first and second graders are sensitive youngsters who need approval, like to help, and find failure very difficult. Tears and even temper tantrums are not unusual.

Classroom application.   Allowing students of this age to work in pairs is a good idea because they are able to handle and can benefit from one-on-one interactions. Other social interactions such as dramatic play and "acting out" stories work very well with children in the primary years.

As their teacher, you will discover that you need to build on young children's successes and find ways to encourage risk taking so that children will feel psychologically safe. Other ways of making your classroom a positive place are to establish and maintain clear and consistent rules and routines. This will be important during your class's literacy block of time when some children may be reading independently, some children may be participating in centers, and some may be working with you in guided reading groups. Because of their social developmental characteristics, Early Readers need the security of knowing your expectations in the purposeful environment that you create.

Learning Centers

The physical, cognitive, and social characteristics of young children in the classroom can be demonstrated while thinking about how children interact with each other in centers during literacy time. *Centers* (sometimes called *stations*) are learning spaces that the teacher sets up to encourage active participation. Perhaps you remember playing in the House Learning Center in kindergarten, or doing experiments in the

Advice for New Teachers

Social Interaction

Dear Derek,

How do you allow students to interact socially in your classroom?

Dear New Teacher,

During our Literacy Workshop time I have centers set up that allow students to interact with and help one another. I also organize partner reading early in the school year. Partner reading has worked well for my students as a way to practice reading and to problem solve difficulty in texts with the help of a classmate.

Science Place, or reading in the Library Corner. Centers like these encourage use of language, independent and cooperative participation, and opportunities to learn about the world through play and experimentation.

Classroom Assessment

Observing students using centers.   A good place to observe children ages 5 to 8 exhibiting their physical, cognitive, and social developmental characteristics is while they are working in centers. Say that it is first-grader José's turn at the Writing Center. His teacher knows that physically he cannot attend to one project too long, so she sets the timer for 10 minutes for José's work on his writing project. He likes to write standing up at the table and his teacher knows that he needs that active stance in order to be most productive. He guides his own proceedings by talking in a soft voice to himself as he plans what he will write next. José needs the cognitive support of repeating what he knows best. Since he has learned the words *I, me, and, like,* and *Jason,* he uses those words often in the story he's writing, sometimes several times in the same sentence (Figure 2.2).

The teacher also knows that José needs to experiment with spelling without fear of being wrong, so although his writing will have many misspellings, the words will be approximations of correct spellings (such as *biks* for *bikes*). Socially, José is at an age when he works well with a partner, especially Jason. At the Writing Center, José reads his composition to Jason. Jason suggests that he add a picture to what he has written. José smiles, pleased at the attention his friend has given to his hard work. When the timer rings, José puts away his writing supplies and files his writing project into his portfolio to show his teacher later during a literacy conference.

Me and Jason ur Frns.
I like Jason.
Me and Jason like biks.
Me and Jason run and run and run.

FIGURE 2.2   José's Writing

Readiness Versus Development

Beyond considering developmental characteristics of Early Readers, it is important for you to think about how early literacy learning has been conceptualized in American schools in the past, how it is being regarded today, and how these perspectives will have an impact on your actions in the classroom. For many years, researchers and teachers alike believed that children had to possess certain skills, characteristics, and abilities before they were "ready" to learn to read: these beliefs underpinned readiness theory (e.g., Gates & Bond, 1936; Gray & Rogers, 1956). Those who believed in readiness theory supported the ideas that reading is a separate subject unto itself and that a period of preparation must come *before* formal reading instruction. For example, some teachers believed that children should be able to cut on a line with scissors, skip across a gymnasium with ease, or be able to write their names before reading instruction could begin. Until children could do those things, they reasoned, they were not "ready" to read.

Readiness theory supported the belief that reading could be broken down into a series of isolated skills that could then be arranged into a skill hierarchy that the teacher should follow in a fixed, prescribed order. Some reading textbooks, called *basals,* still publish scope and sequence charts that are constructed to guide teachers in presenting skills in a sequential manner. In addition, readiness theory advocates suggested that teachers should teach reading primarily through direct, systematic instruction. This means that teachers should proceed from a behaviorist learning perspective and take charge of the process of learning to read in a teacher-centered way.

Emergent Theory

 Teacher-centered classrooms are those that reflect behaviorist theory and in which the teacher controls all learning situations. How is a student-centered classroom different?

Even though remnants from readiness theory remain today, most teachers of early learners embrace an *emergent literacy theory,* which is a developmental perspective on how children learn to read (e.g., Clay, 1966; Teale & Sulzby, 1986). Clay (1991) explains that with a little knowledge about print, children can begin to learn to read, discovering new ways to work on printed text as they develop more knowledge about print. A developmental perspective encompasses the biological, cognitive, and socioemotional processes that are interwoven as a child grows and changes (Santrock, 1998). These processes of growth do not proceed in absolute, easily mapped out sequences; each child's growth and developmental pattern is unique, hence each child's development as a reader is unique.

Emergent literacy became a way of describing the reading behaviors of young children, and it aligns with the social constructivist perspective that we have identified in this book as the learning theory we find most reasonable. Emergent literacy theory is the belief that children are active learners who change and develop over time and are continually constructing new knowledge. Literacy learning is not viewed as the acquisition of a series of reading skills, but rather as a dynamic, ongoing process that begins long before children begin formalized school (Teale & Sulzby, 1986). Although there is no set of universally agreed-on developmental stages, many emergent theorists have drawn on the language developmental viewpoints of Piaget (1954, 1972), Vygotsky (1978), and Holdaway (1979). Oral language development is seen as fundamentally important as well as the connection between reading and writing. In addition, young readers and writers are believed to engage in the same types of literacy processes, though at a less sophisticated level, as those used by older children and adults (Harste, Woodward, & Burke, 1984; Vygotsky, 1978).

How Literacy Emerges

Immersion in print-rich environments, active experimentation, and supported risk taking are features of the emergent theory of literacy learning, as well as the following characteristics:

- Reading, writing, and oral language are all integral parts of literacy learning.
- Literacy learning begins *very early* in life; some say at birth.
- Literacy learning happens best through active and meaningful engagement with written language.
- Children's literacy learning is characterized by a progression through a series of developmental stages.
- Literacy education should be developmentally appropriate for children.

Further, Teale (1995) notes that emergent literacy "views reading and writing development from the child's point of view . . . [examining] changes over time in how the child thinks about literacy and in the strategies the child uses in attempts to comprehend or produce written language" (p. 71).

Classroom application. If you are a teacher of Early Readers who believes in emergent theory, you will use those beliefs to inform your practices in the classroom. Some of those practices include giving children plenty of time to interact with texts, daily story time and shared book experiences, and opportunities for individual and collaborative reading. You should also allow children in your classroom to engage with other more accomplished readers (Neuman & Bredekamp, 2000). In addition, you will want to provide daily literacy activities that are embedded in your routines such as morning message, notes to and among the children, learning center activities, and children's play time (Labbo & Teale, 1997).

Teaching isolated readiness skills, using volumes of readiness worksheets, and expecting perfect spelling when children attempt to write are not practices that align with emergent literacy theory. Instead you should concentrate on activities that help children as they are learning to construct meaning from print.

EARLY LEARNING ABOUT LANGUAGE AND PRINT

We know that language development begins very early in life, as early as birth (Chomsky, 1994). Consider the following scenarios. Have you ever watched an infant in a crib crying? When you approached the crib you may have noticed that the baby's cries began to subside as she saw your face and you began to interact with her. She was probably telling you something like "Pick me up" or "I'm hungry" or "I need to be changed." While she didn't have control of oral language yet, she was learning to "mean." She had already learned that if she cried in certain ways, someone would come.

If you were to come back in a few months, this same infant will have begun to expand her ability to "mean" as she tries out sounds that mean something to her and her caregivers. She may now say, "Ba, ba," which is her new language attempt at asking for a bottle. She feels powerful when she utters, "Ba, ba," because she knows what it means, her parents know what it means, and her new "word" gets her what she wants—a bottle! She is on her way to becoming a user of language. Soon her language will become more sophisticated as she strings two or three words together such as "Me go" or "Want red ball." At the same time she is learning to use language, she is talking to learn. You might hear her say, "This hot?" when she gets close to the stove. Her mother replies, "Yes. The stove is very hot!" The baby is discovering that she can get information by talking and that talking helps her learn things about the world. And, although you may have not considered it before, this storing of important information about language will help her learn to read.

Oral Language and Print Awareness

Oral language is the support structure for constructing meaning from text. And, just like learning to talk and use language is a natural process, so is learning to read. Children's language acquisition and print awareness go through approximate developmental stages as outlined in Figure 2.3.

Language and print emerges for children through their lived experiences before they ever get to school. And while each child's experiences are different, children go through some general stages of understanding on their way to becoming readers of print. We examine next children's beginning awareness of books and print and the role of environmental print in children's understanding of literacy.

Awareness of Books and Print

Babies as young as 4 to 6 months can benefit from looking at books with a parent or caregiver. Phillips (1997) declares, "an infant's brain thrives on words: feed her as

Characteristics	Approximate Age
Crying, cooing, babbling; becoming aware of environment and familiar people	0–6 months
First words associated with well-known objects and people	8–14 months
First sentences; speaks more often	18–24 months
More complex sentences; may repeat phrases from books; may pretend read	2.5–3 years
Imaginative language; may ask many questions; shows reading favorites	3.5–4 years
Talk becoming more conventional; begins to recognize words in environment; recites or sings the alphabet; asks for preferred books	4–5 years

FIGURE 2.3 Language Acquisition and Print Awareness

many as you can as often as you can" (p. 107). You may remember the bumper sticker "Have you read to your child today?" During early experiences with books and language, children begin to understand the integrity of the printed word, that reading is important, and that it is good to be able to read. When parents continue to read to their children, those children gain valuable knowledge about how books work, such as "words are talk written down." They learn about print stability (that the words in a story stay the same each time it is read) and they learn concepts about print that are fundamental understandings needed for reading.

Under the umbrella of concepts about print are the following: Words in English are written from left to right and top to bottom on the page; letters make up words and there are spaces between words; words have beginnings, middles, and ends; and the little marks on the page called punctuation help separate phrases and sentences and add emphasis.

Children learn what "book talk" sounds like by hearing phrases like "Once upon a time" again and again. In addition, children develop a sense of story by listening to books being read aloud. Knowledge of stories helps children interpret pictures and make predictions, thus playing an important part in helping them learn to read. Some young children have extensive knowledge about books and print; others need help from their teacher who will support their understanding about print through read-alouds and shared, guided, and independent reading.

Reading with grandpa.

Advice for New Teachers

Helping Inexperienced Readers

Dear Derek,

How can I help children who have had few experiences with books and print?

Dear New Teacher,

I am an avid believer in reading aloud to my second graders. I start every literacy time with a read-aloud—every day; I never miss it. My students look forward to it and so do I! Many times during read-aloud, we discuss new words or what's happening in the story. I believe that reading aloud to children helps all children, especially those who are less experienced with books.

Environmental Print

In our society, children are surrounded with print wherever they go. Besides in books and other printed materials at home, they see words on TV, in stores, covering grocery store items, and on trucks, buildings, and billboards. This print is called *environmental* because it's all around us. Most every child in America can tell you that the golden arches signify McDonald's or that the giant *K* means K-Mart. Environmental print supports emerging readers' knowledge of print by helping them associate meanings with words.

Environmental print plays an important role in helping children learn to read, but not all children have equal access to environmental print. In a study of two low-income and two middle-income neighborhoods, Neuman (2001) found that resources such as signs, labels, logos, and books were much more available to children in middle-income neighborhoods. Children in lower economic settings had to rely more on public institutions such as libraries for access to print; even then, the resources were less adequate. These findings have negative implications for the literacy development of children in lower income settings. If the children in your classrooms have not had fair entry into the world of print, it will be up to you as their teacher to provide it.

■ YOU TRY IT

Environmental Print Book

Go through magazines, newspapers, and advertisements, cutting out pictures of signs, labels, store logos, etc., that you think might be familiar to young children. Make a small book of the environmental print you have collected by gluing the collection onto construction paper that has been stapled together like a book. Glue one selection to each page. Sit down with a kindergartner or prereader and have the child "read" the book to you. Record the child's responses, just as he says them. For example, if you collected a KFC logo, he may call out, "Chicken!" That would be an accurate reading of KFC, don't you think? Bring to class your environmental print book and the responses you collected from your child. Share your findings with a partner. Ask yourself, "What did I learn about emergent literacy learners by engaging in this activity?" Perhaps you recognized that at very young ages, children try to make sense of those symbols we call print. They try to understand and repeatedly ask, "What does that say?"

The Purpose of Reading: Making Meaning

The ultimate goal of the complex process of reading is the construction of meaning. Clay (1991) asserted that reading is "a message-gaining, problem-solving activity that increases in power and flexibility the more it is practiced" (p. 6). Rosenblatt (1978) believes that while a text has inherent potential meaning, a reader brings the totality of his experiences to the text and constructs a personal understanding, or meaning, based on those experiences. Smith (1997) concurs: "It is not in print—nor even in speech—that the meaning of language lies. If there is to be any comprehension it must come from the meaning that a listener or reader *brings* to the language being attended to" (p. 58).

In addition to the personal response that readers bring to a text, Goodman (1967) notes that reading is a psycholinguistic guessing game, an interaction between thought and language that results from skill in selecting the fewest, most productive cues necessary to produce guesses that are right the first time. Weaver (1998) agrees when she states that "when a reader reads to construct meaning from text (rather than merely to identify words), various processes are going on simultaneously" (p. 25). The processes that occur simultaneously in meaning making comprise the recursive reading sequence. Each time a person reads, she goes through the continual recursive process of *sampling, predicting, confirming or disconfirming,* and *monitoring or self-correcting.* This sequence is illustrated in Figure 2.4.

 Environmental print is print that occurs all around us on signs, buildings, and in the media. How does environmental print help young children as emergent literacy learners?

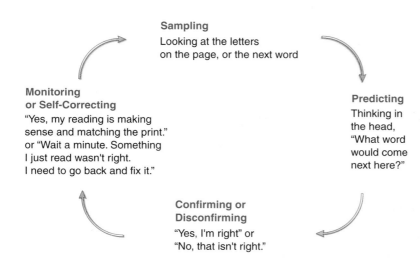

Sampling
Looking at the letters on the page, or the next word

Predicting
Thinking in the head, "What word would come next here?"

Confirming or Disconfirming
"Yes, I'm right" or "No, that isn't right."

Monitoring or Self-Correcting
"Yes, my reading is making sense and matching the print." or "Wait a minute. Something I just read wasn't right. I need to go back and fix it."

FIGURE 2.4   The Recursive Reading Sequence

In the midst of the recursive reading sequence, readers rely on information from their own background knowledge about how our language works; information on the page such as letters, words, punctuation, and illustrations; and the context of the reading experience itself.

The Reading/Writing Connection

The reading and writing processes are inextricably linked. When students learn to read, they construct meaning from printed language; when they write they compose messages using print from which others can construct meaning. Key to children's emerging literacy understandings is the notion that both reading and writing involve thinking and action as well as the flexible orchestration of many different sources of information and knowledge.

Most young children will notice and discover what they need to know about how print works in home and school settings. However, some children who seem to struggle as young readers may more readily enter the world of reading through opportunities to write and intentionally communicate using print. Gunderson (2002) notes:

> For young children who have become discouraged in their attempts to read, what better way to encourage them to become active participators in their own learning about the details of print than to try reading the very words they have just attempted to write (Chomsky, 1971)? In terms of social constructivism, the active construction of a meaningful message scaffolds the passive child's attention to letter formation, directional principals, spaces between words, conventions of print, and hearing and recording the sounds in words. Out of the act of writing, some early readers begin to link what they know in writing to what they know in reading; they discover the reciprocal nature of reading and writing. (pp. 1–2)

Early experiences with language and print through talk, books, the environment, and writing opportunities begin to shape and direct young children toward attempts at reading. When children begin to unlock meaning in print, they do so by tapping into sources of information that are called the cueing systems.

EARLY READERS ACCESSING THE CUEING SYSTEMS

When you look at any text and attempt to read that text, you draw from or search through sources of information that help you read the words. These sources of information have been referred to as *cueing systems*—systems that you, as an experienced reader, access with such speed, ease, and flexibility that you don't even recognize what you are doing. However, when you observe Early Readers you will notice how they use the cueing systems—meaning (semantic), structure (syntactic), and visual (graphophonic)— when trying to solve the words on the page. Figure 2.5 represents the three systems, which overlap in the middle where meaning is made. After examining the cueing systems, we will look at what young readers do as they attempt to orchestrate these sources of information.

Meaning Cueing System

The meaning cueing system is sometimes called the *semantic* cueing system, because it has to do with extracting meaning from the text, and *semantics* refers to the study of the meaning of language. Just as we noted earlier in this section, the primary purpose of reading is the construction of meaning; therefore, as a teacher of Early Readers, one

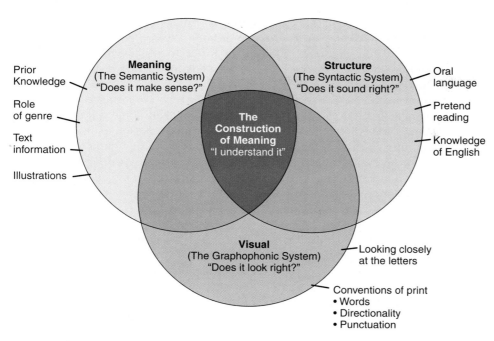

Prior Knowledge

Role of genre

Text information

Illustrations

Meaning
(The Semantic System)
"Does it make sense?"

Structure
(The Syntactic System)
"Does it sound right?"

Oral language

Pretend reading

Knowledge of English

The Construction of Meaning
"I understand it"

Visual
(The Graphophonic System)
"Does it look right?"

Looking closely at the letters

Conventions of print
• Words
• Directionality
• Punctuation

FIGURE 2.5　The Cueing Systems

of your primary goals is to help your students to continually ask themselves, "Does this make sense?" Some factors that help readers decide whether something makes sense are their prior knowledge, the genre of the text, the text itself, and the illustrations.

Role of prior knowledge.　　Readers' prior knowledge that they bring to a text is a composite of all experiences in their lives, all beliefs and biases, and all their knowledge about reading and that particular kind of text.

Imagine that a friend says to you, "You have to read this book! It is the best romantic novel I have ever read! You will love it!" You may already be thinking of your reaction. Perhaps you don't even like romantic novels, or perhaps your experiences with them have not been pleasant; you find them cloying and full of clichés. However, you take the novel gracefully from your friend so that you don't hurt her feelings. Your initial resistance to this book is a problem at first, but then something happens. You find out that the story takes place in a time in history about which you have a lot of knowledge. This connection starts to lure you into the story, and you begin to enjoy the book, especially the parts that deal with the historical knowledge you have. You are able to picture what is happening and why, make predictions about what will happen next, and are even able to read difficult words such as names of cities and castles. Because of your prior knowledge you are able to construct meaning.

Some children's prior knowledge does not match the kinds of texts that we as teachers present to them. Such a situation makes reading more difficult because they cannot link their prior experiences to what is happening in the story. That's why it is so important for you to tap into students' prior knowledge and prior experiences to find books that help them make essential *meaning* connections. Matching books to children's prior knowledge will ease your students' ability to monitor their reading comprehension as they continually ask themselves, "Does this make sense?"

Role of genre.   The genre of a text also supports readers' construction of meaning. *Genre* refers to the classification of a text according to its content and writing style. Following are just a few examples of differing genres: poetry, historical fiction, nonfiction, biographies, mysteries, and fairy tales. Remember our discussion earlier about romantic novels? They are a genre of literature. When you understand a particular genre, you are able to make more sense of the text. For instance, do you like to read mysteries? If you do you know the following: Usually some sort of crime has been committed, you will be introduced to various characters who could be the perpetrator, and you will discern many clues in the book that are written to both help you solve the crime and to confuse you. The more mysteries you read, the better you become at figuring out the perpetrator of the crime. Knowing and understanding how this genre works helps you unravel the "whodunit" and make predictions about the outcome as you access the meaning cueing system.

Text information.   The text itself is another venue for accessing the meaning cueing system. As you read, you gather more and more information in your head, at the story, paragraph, sentence, and word levels. Information in the text itself enables you to monitor your understanding and ask, "Does this make sense?" Think about an instance when you were reading a textbook for biology class that dealt with the topic of cell division. You found you understood the author's writing just fine until suddenly you stopped in your reading because something in subsequent paragraphs didn't tie in with your understanding from the beginning of the chapter. This act of "stopping" meant you were searching for information in the text itself, which is part of accessing the meaning cueing system—an attempt to make sense of the reading and monitor your understanding of cell division.

You can observe Early Readers stopping themselves and self-monitoring when trying a new word. Suppose a child comes upon the word *chalkboard,* as in Figure 2.6. She might say the word *chimney* because both words start with *ch.* However, she might pause at this point and say, "Wait. That didn't make sense because you don't

FIGURE 2.6   Using Meaning to Figure Out a Word

write on a chimney." If the child does this, she is trying to make sure that her reading makes sense, which is what we always want students to do.

Illustrations.   A final component of the meaning cueing system that we consider here is the book's illustrations. You should provide your young students with texts that contain abundant, rich illustrations. You will also teach your students that illustrations provide readers with valuable clues for figuring out words. To extend the example above about *chimney* instead of *chalkboard,* a teacher could say to the child, "Look at the picture. Read up to the hard word and then look at the picture. It will give you a clue about the word [chalkboard]." Helping Early Readers attend to the pictures and teaching them how to access information from the illustrations will help them connect meaning to their reading.

▚▚▚ YOU TRY IT ▚▚▚ ▐ ▌▐ ▌ ▚ ▚

Noticing How You Use the Meaning Cueing System

The following passage has blanks in the text. Read it and see if you can guess what the missing words are by using the meaning cueing system.

Once upon a _____ there was a princess who dreamed of someday living in a _____. Even at night when she slept, she _____ about the lovely palace and how happy she would be.

Did you guess that the missing words were *time, castle,* and *dreamed*? If you did you were accessing the meaning cueing system. From your prior knowledge you knew that the genre of fairy tales calls for *time* to appear after the words *Once upon a.* You probably guessed *castle* from looking at the illustration or from your genre knowledge. And you deduced that the last word would be *dreamed* because of the meaning of the text up to the point of the missing word (if the word *slept* gave you the clue) or because *dreamed* was used in the sentence before.

Structure Cueing System

The structure cueing system is sometimes called the *syntactic* cueing system, because *syntax* refers to the study of how sentences in a particular language are formed as well as the rules of grammar of that language. As a teacher of Early Readers, you will be supporting their understanding of how sentences are put together in English and the rules of grammar in formal writing, such as in textbooks, children's books, and other classroom reading materials. Some teachers like to use the phrase *book talk* when they ask their students "Does it sound right?"

Role of oral language.   Much of Early Readers' knowledge of English comes from their experiences out of school as users and hearers of language. At times, all of us speak in ways that are not conventional English—in other words, in ways that are not "book talk." For example, around your friends you might say things like "I ain't gonna do that!" Everyone understands what you mean and knows you might have even used the word *ain't* on purpose, for emphasis. However, in formal usage, chances are the written sentence would read "I'm not going to do that." Helping readers think about the structure cueing system means helping them ask themselves, "Does it sound right?" In other words, can I say it that way in conventional, Standard English? Would the words on the page read "I ain't" or "I'm not"? The structure cueing system is supported by children's natural language, their knowledge of English, and correct grammatical patterns and language structures that we would expect to see in books.

Pretend reading.   When children begin reading they use their natural language to guess what the words are. Perhaps you have observed a very young child "pretend reading" a familiar book—one that the child has had read to him. You will notice that some of the text that the child "reads" is exactly as printed and is being recited as the child remembers it. On other pages, the child makes up the words to match the illustrations. So, instead of saying "Goldilocks was so exhausted from all her adventures that she fell fast asleep," you might hear the child say, "Goldilocks was really tired from her great big day so she got up on the bed and went to sleep." Does that make sense? Yes. Does it sound right? Yes. In other words, the child's natural language is supporting the creation of a new text (one not on the page), but it still has meaning and it sounds like Standard English sounds.

Children use their knowledge of spoken language to guide their attempts at reading by thinking what would "sound right" in a particular situation. Because oral language supports early readers' attempts at reading, you will need to give children plenty of opportunities to talk in order to expand their understanding of spoken language and to have opportunities to speak with those who have a more extensive command of English oral language. In addition, teachers should provide Early Readers with texts that contain language that is close to children's oral language; their early books should sound much like they talk. Reciprocally, children's oral language will support their reading, and their reading will support their oral language.

Knowledge of the English language.   Children's knowledge of English as well as the grammatical structures that are appropriate for English varies from child to child and depends on many factors related to the child's experiences. Again, their knowledge of language structures is often evident in their talk. For children to be able to decide if a word "sounds right" or to answer the question "Can we say it that way?" depends on their prior experiences as users and hearers of the English language.

Later we will discuss ways to enrich children's oral language, especially for English Language Learners, but for now, remember these two things: First, the more you talk to young children, modeling conventional English usage, and the more you encourage them to talk, the more you will help them develop their knowledge of the structure (syntactic) cueing system. Second, the more you read to children and invite them to interact with the reading, the more familiar children will become with "book talk." They will be able to answer the question "Does it sound right?"

YOU TRY IT

Noticing How You Use the Structure Cueing System

Like the preceding You Try It feature, the following short passage has missing words. This time, however, think about your knowledge of how English words are put together in a certain order. Although you might not be 100% correct in guessing the missing words, you will be able to put in a word that would be an acceptable part of speech in the sentence.

> Once there was a student headed off to college who had a _____ sports car. He and his _____ were arguing about whether he should take it to _____ or not. _____ student wanted to take it but his father said, "Absolutely not!"

The missing words are *red, dad, school,* and *The.* How did you do? Would an illustration have been helpful? A colorful illustration would have helped you guess *red* but you knew from your understanding of English that the noun *car* would have had an adjective in front of it (in addition to *sports*). Knowing that, you may have guessed *hot* or *fancy* or *new.* All of those guesses would have been correct English usage. The next word may have been difficult to predict, but you knew that a noun was called for. You may have thought *mom* or *girlfriend* or you may have read ahead and seen *father* in the next sentence and used *father. School* was probably difficult to guess unless you've had this argument with your parents, but you knew, again, that the word needed to be a noun. Perhaps you supposed the word was *college* or *campus;* those would have worked, too. The final blank was easy. Everyone predicted *"the"* because so many sentences start with *"the"* in our language. Did you notice that as you were thinking about the *structure* of our language, you were also trying to make the passage make sense? At the same time, you were attending to the letters in the words (the visual cueing system). Perhaps you were able to see how one cueing system supports another as you extract meaning from text.

Visual Cueing System

The visual cueing system is also labeled the *graphophonic* cueing system, with *graphophonic* referring to our written alphabet as well as the conventions of print to which readers must attend. First, when you think visual cueing system, think "the letters on the page." When children are attending to the visual cueing system, they are using their knowledge of letter/sound relationships to make an attempt that "looks right" or matches the printed word on the page. It is what parents and teachers mean when they say, "Sound it out." What they are saying to the child is this: "Look at the letters, think about the sound that each letter makes, and blend the sounds together." You will learn from this book that as a teacher there are many more effective prompts for Early Readers than "sound it out" when you want them to pay attention to graphophonic cues.

Looking closely at letters.   Here is an example of a child attending to the visual cueing system. This sentence is printed on the page: "Red Riding Hood came upon a *wolf* in the forest." Instead she reads, "Red Riding Hood came upon a *fox* in the forest." Then she says, "Ooops. That can't be *fox,* it starts with a *w.* It must be w-w-wolf." The child in this example is focusing on visual cues.

Likewise, here's an example of how adults use visual cues. Have you ever been on an interstate highway trying to see the big green signs way down the road? Say you're looking for the turnoff to Chicago. You squint at the green sign up ahead and can see that the word on the sign starts with *C.* However, as you drive a little closer you notice that the word is too long to be *Chicago.* As you get even closer you can see that the word has a chunk of short letters in the center. Soon, you are able to read the sign. It says *Cincinnati.* You used visual cues to keep you from turning off in the wrong direction.

"Sound it out."   Obviously, visual cues are extremely important because graphic symbols represent the message in the text. All of us who read must attend to the letters; however, you will notice that Early Readers who struggle with learning to read typically are overly dependent on trying to "sound out" new words. Also, their parents and teachers often keep prompting them to "sound it out." Such children become so intent on saying the sounds of each letter to solve a new word, that in the intervening time spent on the unknown word they lose the meaning of the portion of the text they are reading. We will help you discover ways to help children who rely too heavily on the visual cueing system.

YOU TRY IT

Noticing How You Use the Visual Cueing System

This time, instead of missing words, letters are left out of words. Notice how you are able to figure out the words, even with some of the letters omitted.

Wh_n I h_v_ a pr_bl_m w_th my comp_t_r I alw_ys ask my r_ _mmat_. Sh_'s a comp_t_r sc_ _ nce m_j_r _nd knows how to f_gure out ev_ryth_ng. Plus, sh_ doesn't g_t m_d!

Were you able to read "When I have a problem with my computer, I always ask my roommate. She's a computer science major and knows how to figure out everything. Plus, she doesn't get mad!" If so, you were able to access the visual cueing system—looking at the letters that were printed to help you figure out the words with missing letters. Did you notice that it was the *vowels* that were missing? You relied on the consonants' sounds to help you figure out the words. If the consonants had been missing, your task would have been nearly impossible. Try it. What does that tell you about the importance of consonants in children's early reading and writing behaviors? Did you also observe yourself looking at the illustration (meaning cueing system) and thinking about the *kind* of word that would fit next in the passage (structure cueing system)? Even if you did the activity quickly with virtually no difficulty, you were orchestrating all three cueing systems simultaneously, which is what good readers do.

Companion Website

"Sound it out" is a phrase that many parents and teachers repeatedly say to readers. How could this prompt actually be detrimental to Early Readers?

Orchestrating the Cueing Systems

Readers need to access all three cueing systems—meaning, structure, and visual—when they read. When readers access all cueing systems, we say they are *orchestrating* the cueing systems. In other words, just like a symphony director signals different instruments when they are needed to play the musical piece, a reader uses different sources of information to read the words on the page. You do the same when you read.

Understanding the cueing systems as a teacher.   In this section you have been introduced to the reading process—what we believe occurs when people read. The more you observe emergent literacy learners deal with print, the more comfortable you will become with identifying how they utilize the cueing systems and ways that you, as their teacher, can support their new understandings. Your goal as a teacher of reading is to help children flexibly access all three cueing systems simultaneously, all the while monitoring their own reading. When young readers are able to do this, we say they are being *strategic*. Later in this book you will learn how to help children develop "inner control" to become strategic readers and you will learn how to foster independence—the primary goal of reading instruction (Lyons, Pinnell, & De-Ford, 1993). Meanwhile, it is important now to know that not all children develop their knowledge and use of the cueing systems in the same ways—and that is just one of the ways children in your classroom differ.

SEE FOR YOURSELF

Listen to an Early Reader Using the Cueing Systems

Visit the message board for Chapter 2 on our Companion Website at *www.prenhall.com/lenski* to discuss your findings.

On the Companion Website (*http://www.prenhall.com/lenski*) you will find an audio clip of an Early Reader reading a text. Listen to this segment several times, trying to match this child's reading behaviors with the cueing systems (sources of information) he is attempting to use. After you have listened to this child, write down your responses to the following questions:

- At one point in the reading, the child was clearly searching the meaning cueing system. How did you know that he was accessing this system? What did he do and say that told you he was thinking about meaning?
- At many points in the audio clip, the child went first to the visual cueing system to try to figure out an unknown word. Describe one of these instances. Was it a successful strategy for him? Why or why not?

Closely observing young students' reading behaviors will help you understand the reading process. What did you learn about the reading process and orchestrating the cueing systems from listening to the child read on the website? As teachers, we hope that the child goes first to the meaning cueing system because reading must make sense. We also hope that he asks himself, "If I were talking, would I say it that way?" (structure cueing system). Finally, we hope the young reader is continually sampling the letters to determine if the words he reads match what is printed on the page (visual cueing system). This all happens as he engages in the recursive reading sequence shown in Figure 2.4.

Assessing Students' Use of the Cueing Systems

We have already sent the message that assessment is at the heart of your teaching. Integrated assessment informs your instructional decisions and practices. When you get to know your Early Readers you should consider their place on the literacy development continuum (Tinajero & Ada, 1993). You also need to try to understand and value the diversity of experiences and backgrounds of the students in your classroom and accommodate those differences. Assessment can be accomplished through ongoing observation, conferencing with students, checklists, and self-assessment. Two ways that you can assess students' use of the cueing systems are through miscue analysis or Running Records.

Classroom Assessment

Miscue analysis and running records.   Literacy researcher Ken Goodman (1965) coined the term *miscue* to reframe educators' perspectives about students' reading "errors." Instead of thinking of students' departure from the text while reading as "errors," Goodman believes that when a reader miscues, she is still trying to make sense of the text. Further, miscues, when analyzed, can provide a window into the processing behaviors and language development of the reader. Miscue analysis involves tape recording the child's writing for later, in-depth examination. Weaver (1994) points out the following principles regarding miscue analysis:

- The construction of meaning from text is the central concern.
- Use of reading strategies is more important than reading speed, fluency, or accuracy.
- The focus needs to be on readers' strengths as well as needs.

Miscue analysis also involves a reading interview to learn about the child's perceptions and attitudes about reading and also a retelling of the reading selection to assess comprehension. Miscue analysis is an extremely effective and comprehensive way to analyze a student's reading behaviors, background knowledge, attitudes about reading, and use of strategies.

When learning about examining children's miscues, we will focus on Running Records, developed by Marie Clay (1985) as part of Reading Recovery®, an early-intervention program for struggling first-grade readers. Clay (2000) notes that Running Records not only reveal students' reading processing, they also assess text difficulty, capture a child's progress, and guide your teaching. Your knowledge of the cueing systems will help you understand which systems the child is or is not using when he miscues or comes to a difficult word.

As you've learned, good readers orchestrate the cueing systems in skillful ways that keep meaning making as the primary goal of reading. Good readers are continually cross-checking and self-monitoring their own reading. Running Records can tell you if your students are able to do that.

Teachers take Running Records while listening to a child read out loud in order to analyze the records later. One advantage of Running Records for classroom teachers is that only a blank piece of paper is needed for making standardized notations while listening to a student read orally.

The accompanying See for Yourself feature shows you a sample of a Running Record and is followed by a narrative describing what the Running Record means.

SEE FOR YOURSELF

A Running Record

Visit the message board for Chapter 2 on our Companion Website at *www.prenhall.com/lenski* to discuss your findings.

Connect to the Companion Website (*http://www.prenhall.com/lenski*). You will find the notation symbols used in a Running Record, the procedures for taking a Running Record, a sample record, and an explanation of what is revealed about the reader from the sample record. Take notes for discussion in class regarding what you can learn about readers by using Running Records.

Technology topic: Wireless devices for assessing reading.   Technological advancements are making it easier for teachers to assess students' reading "on the run" while listening to children read. Easy-to-use, compact, handheld systems (roughly the size of Palm Pilots) have been developed that can assess students' miscues, fluency, sight word knowledge, and even comprehension. As these systems become more refined and available, you may discover that they are useful tools for analyzing students' reading behaviors, measuring progress over time, and reporting to parents. (See the To Learn More section at the end of the chapter for a website reference.)

ACKNOWLEDGING DIFFERENCES AMONG EARLY READERS

Young children will come into your classroom on the first day of school with varying experiences with print. Some will have spent hours with parents and other caregivers looking at books and listening to books being read aloud. They will understand important beginning concepts about print: that speech can be written down, that words tell a story, that a story stays the same each time it is read, and that there is a one-to-one match between speech and print. Some children will have already begun to read, as early as kindergarten, and will be making steps forward into the exciting world of books.

Other children in your classroom will have had few experiences with books. This is not to say that they are from "bad" homes or have parents who don't care; there are many reasons why some children have had limited opportunities to interact with texts. Allington (1998) makes an important distinction between experience versus ability as these constructs apply to children. He notes that children who have had few experiences with books and print are often identified as lacking ability.

Instead of unquestioningly accepting labels placed on children, you will work from what students already know and immerse low-experience children in print, stories, read-alouds, and environmental print, providing the literacy-rich atmosphere they need. Regardless of children's literacy experiential backgrounds, you will be responsible for providing *all* children in your classroom with opportunities to help them develop as literacy learners.

In addition to students' varying experiences with print, the children in your classroom are likely to encompass all aspects of diversity including ethnicity, race, linguistic, social and economic differences, and differences related to ability and exceptionality. Part of the challenge and excitement of your first few days of the school year that continues throughout each year is the responsibility to get to know your students and to celebrate the wide range of diversity you will encounter.

Diversity Issue: Cultural Differences

In Chapter 1 you learned about your cultural heritage. Sometimes, culture has been linked only to race or ethnicity; however, culture encompasses much more, such as family customs, language patterns, religious traditions, shared attitudes, values, and goals of a society or subgroup, and countless unspoken rules of behavior that particular groups practice and understand. All of these differences reflect elements of cultural heritage.

Just as you explored your distinct cultural orientation, your students will come to you with unique cultural heritages that you must be prepared to value, especially if their heritages are different than yours. In her book, *The Dreamkeepers: Successful*

Teachers of African American Children, Gloria Ladson-Billings (1993) calls on teachers to teach in culturally relevant ways that are situated in students' prior knowledge and interests. She defines culturally relevant as "a pedagogy that empowers students intellectually, socially, emotionally, and politically by using cultural referents to impart knowledge, skills, and attitudes" (pp. 17–18). Cultural referents are not used to teach to the dominant culture, but are important features of the curriculum in their own right.

It is important for you to use cultural referents from your students' lives that they understand and to which they can relate. We are not suggesting that all children of any culture are alike, nor are we generalizing how all students should be taught. But researchers have suggested ways that you can infuse culturally relevant experiences into your classroom (e.g., Delpit, 1996; Diller, 1999; Ladson-Billings, 1993).

Let's say you are a second-grade teacher engaged in a yearlong theme in your classroom that revolves around the theme "harmony." You have been reading books to your young learners about how plants depend on rain and sunshine, how animals depend on plants for food, how people depend on one another and on plants and animals, and how these principles of dependency can result in harmony. If, for example, you are teaching African American children, you can find ways to make this theme culturally relevant. How might you do that? You could capitalize on many African American children's connections to extended family. By allowing children to communicate how grandmas and grandpas, aunts and uncles, and cousins provide emotional support for the family and share child-rearing responsibilities, you would not only be valuing your students' experiences, you would provide a natural connection to the concepts of interdependency and harmony that you are attempting to teach.

Diller (1999) states that by overcoming the "cultural discontinuity" that she once experienced with her first-grade students she was able to help her children learn and make connections in school. Among her strategies were to immerse her students in African American children's literature and to teach in culturally relevant ways. She writes, "When I touched the rhythm of their lives, they began to respect me and respond" (p. 823).

One extremely effective way to connect to students' cultural heritage is through children's literature. Hefflin and Barksdale-Ladd (2001) write that through literature, "children construct messages about their cultures and roles in society [offering] them personal stories, a view of their cultural surroundings, and insight on themselves" (p. 810). Figure 2.7 contains a list of recommended African American children's literature.

Culturally relevant teaching involves bringing in examples and experiences from your students' cultural heritage. How will you discover the cultural referents that are relevant to your students in the community in which you teach?

Diversity Issue: English Language Learners

"We think school is about equity and excellence, and that the charge to a modern diverse school is to develop a curriculum that is bilingual, multicultural, and option-filled" (Lapp, Fisher, Flood, & Cabello, 2001, p. 1). We entirely agree with this statement. So what does that mean for English Language Learners who will be in your future classrooms? The International Reading Association published a position statement subtitled *Honoring Children's Rights to Excellent Reading Instruction* (2000) that offers 10 basic rights that children have and can expect in their reading education. One of those rights states that literacy instruction should be provided in the child's native language whenever possible. We concur with this assertion and believe, as the position statement claims, that since the number of non-English-speaking students is increasing rapidly in American schools, sufficient attention and resources should be provided to help these children learn to read and write in English by using their first language as a foundation.

Degross, M. (1999). *Granddaddy's street songs.* New York: Hyperion.

Greenfield, E. (1977). *Africa dream.* New York: HarperTrophy.

Greenfield, E. (1988). *Grandpa's face.* New York: Philomel.

Grimes, N. (2001). *Danita Brown leaves town.* New York: HarperCollins.

Haley, G. E. (1970). *A story a story.* New York: Aladdin.

Johnson, A. (1989). *Tell me a story, Mama.* New York: Orchard.

McKissack, P. C. (1988). *Mirandy and Brother Wind.* New York: The Trumpet Club.

San Souci, R. D. (1989). *The talking eggs.* New York: Dial.

Steptoe, J. (1987). *Mufaro's beautiful daughters.* New York: Lothrop, Lee, & Shepard.

Thomas, J. C. (1996). *Brown honey in broomwheat tea: Poems.* New York: HarperTrophy.

Williams, S. A. (1992). *Working cotton.* New York: The Trumpet Club.

FIGURE 2.7 List of African American Children's Literature

Think about trying to learn a second language if you couldn't use your first. Perhaps you've had an opportunity to travel to a country where a language other than English was spoken. How did you communicate? Our guess is that you did a lot of pointing, maybe using a few words you had learned in that language along with English phrases. Perhaps you searched desperately for someone who could translate for you or you engaged in a sort of charades, acting out what you wanted. Now imagine yourself as a young child in school trying to learn to read in English if Spanish is your first language. Wouldn't you need support in Spanish in order to learn literacy concepts in English?

Researchers have noted that linguistic skills transfer relatively easily from the first language to the second (e.g., Baker, 1993; Hornberger, 1990). However, that means that if your first-grade students speak Spanish, and you're trying to teach reading in English, you will need to supply plenty of books in Spanish as well as English, post English/Spanish signs around your classroom, and access a speaker of Spanish who can provide the scaffolding the children need until the extra support can be gradually withdrawn. You also will have to guard against non-English-speaking students being classified as in need of special services simply because they do not speak the language.

As we delve more deeply into instructing young readers, you will learn multiple strategies for helping English Language Learners. For now, know that you will take advantage of their first language, allowing for exploration of oral language and opportunities to talk and learn in their first language as they move to their second. After all, you should be celebrating the fact that your students are becoming bilingual and are not limited to one language as perhaps you may be. In the meanwhile, you will concentrate on providing motivating and success-oriented experiences for *all* students in your classroom.

Diversity Issue: Children's Prior Experiences With Texts

Children who have had few experiences with books and print often score poorly on prekindergarten screening tests given to many students before they enter school; therefore, these children may be categorized as *not ready for school, developmentally delayed, immature,* or *slow* (McGill-Franzen, 1992). Unfortunately these unfairly assigned labels often "stick" to children and follow them throughout their school careers. Clay (1998) suggests an important alternative to trying to assess what children *don't* know. She suggests:

> What they [teachers] need to do is find points of contact in children's prior learning, the things that children *can* do, and spend a little time helping children firm up their grasp of what they already know. . . . Learner-centered instruction is about . . . starting where the learner already is and helping that learner move to a new degree of control over novel tasks. (p. 3)

MOTIVATING EARLY READERS

Motivating Early Readers is typically not the challenge for primary-grade teachers that it can be for those who teach older children. For the most part, that is because young children have not yet experienced school failure; they are convinced they will succeed and will learn to read. In fact, some become disappointed when they don't learn how to read on the first day! Most Early Readers are highly motivated and come to school anxious to learn to become readers just as their parents or older siblings are. However, you still need to build on that enthusiasm for learning by purposefully constructing engaging literacy activities for your young students, and providing ample opportunities for children to experience success.

In this section, we look at motivating Early Readers through principles of engagement. We examine keying into children's interests and thus stimulating their attention; a child (or adult) is more likely to pay attention or care about reading if the topic is one of interest. Then we consider giving children choices and encouraging success in reading by creating learning communities and setting up the conditions for active learning (e.g., Askew & Fountas, 1998; Cambourne, 1995, 1999). Finally, we challenge you to continually assess children's motivation to read.

Engagement

A component of motivation that must be addressed with Early Readers is engagement. *Engagement* can be defined as emotional involvement with the literacy events or opportunities being presented in the classroom. If children are not "engaged" with the learning activities you provide, learning is not likely to take place. Cambourne (1995) believes that engagement includes paying attention, a perceived purpose on the part of the learner, and active participation.

These principles of engagement can be applied to adult learners as well as children. Think about yourself and remember a time when you were really interested in what was happening in a college course. Perhaps you were participating in a workshop experience, preparing teaching materials for your future classroom. You paid attention because you wanted to create materials that were attractive and useful. You understood that there was a purpose for doing the activity; you knew that you would use the instructional materials with children. You actively participated as you cut, stapled, pasted, and printed the resources. You were an engaged learner. Furthermore, you were successful and left the class anxious to return the next day. That is exactly the feeling you want *your* students to have when they leave your classroom each afternoon.

Active engagement in the classroom.   Active engagement will occur in the classroom when Early Readers are working at the point of difficulty (their zone of proximal development) in terms of their physical, cognitive, and social development with just the right amount of challenge. If tasks are too difficult, children will become discouraged and stop trying; when they are too easy, children become bored and disengaged. Active engagement also requires students to take the lead in solving their own learning challenges and to make links to prior knowledge (Askew & Fountas, 1998).

"Young children . . . are experimenters who are trying out many pieces of the literacy puzzle" (Askew & Fountas, 1998, p. 128). When children come to a problem, let's say a word they do not know in a text, they need to feel that they have options to solve the word by themselves; you will learn how to equip them with strategies so that they can do so. You should provide individual help for those who need extra assistance. You will want to help Early Readers make connections between the new information your students are learning and what they already know. In this way, active learners will learn more about reading each time they read (Johnston & Winograd, 1985; Paris, Lipson, & Wixson 1994).

Children's Interests

As a literacy teacher, you should always be attempting to boost your students' interest in reading. Effective literacy teachers want children to enjoy reading, perhaps even "love to read." One of your best strategies for engendering interest in reading is finding materials that interest children; they have to be excited about what you offer them to read before you can expect them to like reading. Sometimes, students are presented with texts that the teacher (or the school curriculum director) finds interesting that they don't find interesting at all. Not only are children sometimes expected to read dull texts, but they are often given a plethora of reading follow-up activities, including multiple workbook pages that pertain to a reading selection that was uninteresting to them in the first place.

A colleague reported that when visiting a second-grade classroom, he approached a young reader whom he knew to be a gifted reader. As the child dutifully

Lem and Ashley enjoy a Big Book together.

was completing her workbook pages, following the requisite story read from the basal, he knelt down and whispered, "So, how do you like reading?" "I hate reading!" she replied. Puzzled by this response, he said, "But your teacher says that you're such a good reader." The child's eyes lit up, "Oh, you mean *reading!* I love to read!" He determined that the child's first remark about "hating reading" was related to what she thought her visitor was asking about: reading in school, something she clearly disliked. Conversely, she loved to read for her own purposes and the books that she cared about.

You can help children discover and keep the joy of reading by finding out what kinds of texts your students like to read. For example, at the beginning of the school year (and throughout the year), you should sit down with each child to ask questions about their interests. You can ask questions such as what they like to do after school, their favorite sports, TV shows, movies, or books. You will discover if they have hobbies, have special friends, or have taken vacations. All of these questions will yield valuable information about your students' interests. Some of your students will enjoy fairy tales, others scary stories like the Goose Bumps series. Some Early Readers will take pleasure in factual, nonfiction reading like books about dinosaurs, whereas others may prefer popular magazines that have stories about their favorite sports' heroes.

The Role of Choice

Just as you consider children's interests, you must realize that it logically follows that you would give them choices about what they want to read and the literacy tasks they take on. "Responsive teachers do not relinquish power; they *share* power and responsibility, providing a continually evolving balance between choice and structure" (Oldfather, 1993, p. 12). Although we have been discussing what *you* can and must do to set up the conditions for learning, you will want to share some of the decision making in your classroom with your students by offering them choices. Choice is a strong motivator (Figure 2.8); it allows children to feel empowered and responsible for their own learning by pursuing tasks that are of interest to them (Turner & Paris, 1995).

Just as you enjoy and learn more easily when you are given choices, children, even those as young as kindergarteners, should be able to select from a wide variety of developmentally appropriate literacy tasks that have been provided to meet their literacy learning needs. Again, it is you, the teacher, who will set up these appropriate choices; it certainly isn't an "anything goes" classroom environment.

For example, during the time you are working with individual small reading groups, the rest of the children may be involved in centers or working independently at their tables. Suppose you have a writing center set up in your classroom that has two

---

As a student yourself, you can relate to how important "choice" is to you. In each of the following examples, which choice do you appreciate more? Discuss your answers with your peers.

- Being told what your class project will be, or being given choices as to topic, methods, and presentation mode?
- Having one essay question to answer for a test, or having a choice of selecting one out of three?
- Being assigned to work with two other students for a class assignment, or having a choice of with whom you will work?
- Having your English instructor hand you a novel to read and respond to, or choosing the novel you will read?

FIGURE 2.8   The Role of Choice

computers, paper of different sorts, and various writing tools such as markers, pens, and pencils. The children at that center might choose to work on a rough draft of a story they are writing, put the finishing touches on the illustration of a poem the class wrote together, or discuss with a partner possible topics for their next piece. Choices such as these that are authentic and purposeful underscore for children the real purposes of reading and writing and help them feel in charge of their own learning.

Creating Success-Oriented Learning Communities

As the teacher, you should acquire reading materials for Early Readers that they are interested in, find exciting, and choose to read. And, as long as you are a teacher, creating a respectful, responsive classroom conducive to optimal learning will be your challenge (Oldfather, 1993). What does that mean?

Have you ever been in a classroom at the college level where you knew, almost from the first day, that you had little chance for success? You looked around and observed other students who were obviously going to experience no difficulty. They knew this and so did you. How did that feel? Perhaps you talked to your family or friends after you realized what was happening. "Most of my classes are going OK, but I have this one that is going to kill me!" Maybe someone tried to convince you that all you needed to do was buckle down and work really hard and you would succeed, but you knew differently. What were your options? Did you work diligently, being grateful to emerge at the end of the semester with a C? Did you drop the course and substitute another course? Did you end up failing the course? Whatever happened, do you remember that course, instructor, and subject matter with fondness and nostalgia?

Your classroom: A good place to be. If you have experienced failure or discouragement in school, you learned something. You learned how painful it is to feel that you couldn't succeed. You learned that as a teacher you never want your students to feel that way. You know that you want your students to come into your classroom believing that it is an emotionally safe place to be where all members are capable of achieving success and all are invited to the table (Cambourne, 2000). Further, you want your students to know that their voices will be heard, their experiences and contributions honored, and their very presence celebrated. Remember, unlike adults, children have few options. They cannot drop your course, or ask for a different teacher, or register for photography instead of reading. Therefore, you must make your classroom a place where failure is not an option and reading is seen as an enjoyable and "extremely worthwhile enterprise that will further the purposes of [each child's] life" (Cambourne, 2000, p. 513). Your students will experience success in your classroom early and often as you build on what comes naturally to young children: learning.

Consider this quote from a veteran educator in an urban setting concerning young children's motivation to learn:

> I've taught all kinds of kids, rich ones, poor ones, white ones, black ones. Some of the smartest youngsters I've worked with have been right here in this community, but a lot of the time they don't believe in themselves. School saps the life right out of them. You want to see intelligence walking around on two legs? Just go into a kindergarten class. They come to school with fresh faces, full of wonder. But by third grade you can see how badly school has beaten them down. You can really see it in the boys. (Ladson-Billings, 1993, p. 89)

If you teach Early Readers who have the natural enthusiasm for learning and belief that they will be successful as naïve entrants into the world of school, it will be up to you keep that inborn hunger for knowledge going. Conversely, if you teach older children who have experienced failure and begun to doubt their ability to learn, it will be up to you to rekindle the flame of hope in children's feelings of efficacy as students who not only can, but *will* succeed in your classroom. Let's look at how you find out where your students are on that continuum.

Classroom Assessment

Motivation to Read

Cambourne (1995) reports that learners are more likely to become engaged in literacy activities *if* the following conditions are in place: They believe they are capable of learning or doing the task, the activity has value to them (a purpose), they're free from anxiety and know they can safely take risks, and they respect and trust their teacher. It is important for you to set up these learning conditions, however, it is also important that you understand your students' motivation to read.

One method to assess your students' attitude toward reading is taken from the Elementary Reading Attitude Survey created by McKenna and Kear (1990). A few examples of the questions follow:

- How do you feel when you read a book in school during free time?
- How do you feel about reading for fun at home?
- How do you feel when the teacher asks you questions about what you read?
- How do you feel when you read out loud in class?

In this survey, you want to determine if students value reading, how they perceive reading tasks at school, and how they feel about reading for their own purposes. Another possible assessment for evaluating children's attitudes about themselves as readers can be practiced through one of your portfolio entries at the end of this chapter.

Reading interviews and other assessment measures can tell teachers how students feel about reading and about themselves as readers. Careful observation can also render vital information about engagement, children's interests, their choices, and whether or not they feel successful in your classroom. Remember your ultimate goal is not just helping children learn to read, but developing students who *choose* to read and starting them on the path to becoming lifelong readers.

CONNECTIONS: WHAT'S NEXT?

In this chapter you studied developmental characteristics of Early Readers including physical, cognitive, and social characteristics that influence their learning and your teaching. You considered theories of early literacy learning and how children gradually become aware of print and enter the world of words. Then, you looked closely at the reading process itself—what happens when people read—when you learned about the cueing systems. As a teacher of Early Readers, you should always analyze how your children orchestrate the cueing systems and the differences between and among your students. Differences in early reading processing, of course, are just one of the areas of diversity you will encounter. We also asked you to think about cultural and linguistic differences in your future classrooms. Finally, you considered the enormous, all-encompassing responsibility of motivating *all* of the learners that you teach.

In the next chapter, you will take this initial knowledge about early learners and apply it to literacy instructional practices. You will learn how to choose materials for Early Readers and incorporate reading and writing every day in an exemplary literacy learning environment. You will see how theory and the reading process come alive in your classroom!

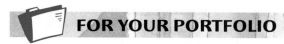 **FOR YOUR PORTFOLIO**

ENTRY 2.1:   *A Reading Interview*

INTASC Principle 8 states: *The teacher understands and uses formal and informal assessment strategies to evaluate and ensure the continuous intellectual, social and physical development of the learner.*

IRA/NCTE Standards for the English Language Arts 12 states: *Students use spoken, written, and visual language to accomplish their own purposes.*

The following assessment questions are adapted from the Burke Interview (1980) and are designed to tell you how each child feels about reading and especially herself as a reader. Select an Early Reader, perhaps a first or second grader, and ask her these questions, recording her answers to each question:

1. What do you think reading is?
2. When you are reading and come to a word you don't know, what do you do?
3. Who do you know who is a really good reader?
4. Why do you think he/she is a good reader?
5. Do you think you are a good reader? Why? Why not?
6. What would you like to do better as a reader?

Now, carefully analyze your child's responses. What did you learn about her as reader? For example, did the child say she was a good reader? If not, do you suppose that affects whether she likes to read? When you asked Question 2, did the child have strategies to try other than "ask the teacher?" If not, do you predict that she doesn't feel empowered as a reader to solve her own reading challenges? In your portfolio, write down the questions you asked, the child's responses (using a made-up name for the child), and what you learned from this exercise.

ENTRY 2.2:   *Embracing Diversity in My Classroom—Writing a Student Vignette and Teaching Plan*

INTASC Principle 3 states: *The teacher understands how students differ in their approaches to learning and creates instructional opportunities that are adapted to diverse learners.*

IRA/NCTE Standards for the English Language Arts 9 states: *Students develop an understanding of and respect for diversity in language use, patterns, and dialects across cultures, ethnic groups, geographic regions, and social roles.*

In this chapter, we considered cultural and linguistic differences among early learners. For this portfolio entry write a short, imaginary story about one of your future students. Think about meeting the needs of this diverse learner as you do the following:

1. Choose an area of diversity that is of interest to you. For example, you could consider cultural or linguistic differences. Or, you might consider giftedness, struggling literacy learners, or children with special needs.
2. "Invent" a diverse learner that could be in your future classroom and give the child a name.

3. As a part of the vignette, create made-up background information, including the following:
   - The child's family composition, including siblings,
   - The child's physical development,
   - The child's social and emotional adjustment in the classroom,
   - The child's school history, and
   - A summary of the child's strengths and needs as a learner.
4. After you have written your vignette describing your child and his/her personal and academic background, seek current research from the library or online that describes instructional strategies and resources that may help diverse learners in the classroom.
5. Use the information from your additional reading to write *specific* assessment options, such as a Motivation to Read Profile, instructional strategies, and resources that you could employ with *your* child. These strategies and resources could be ones that you discover in your research as well as your own perspectives as a developing teacher.

TO LEARN MORE

Helpful Websites

Visit our Companion Website at *http://www.prenhall.com/lenski* to link to the following sites:

Emergent Literacy Theory

Provides a detailed explanation of emergent literacy theory and a related project.
http://www.ets.uidaho.edu/cdhd/emerlit/intro.htm

Early Literacy Continuum Chart

Describes reading behaviors of Early Readers.
http://www.mcps.k12.md.us/curriculum/english/earlylit_cont.htm

The Cueing Systems

Explores semantic, syntactic, and graphophonic cueing systems.
http://www.mat-su.k12.ak.us/INS/curric/langarts/reading/cuesys.html

Assessment Ideas for Early Readers

Find teaching tips, tricks, references, and case studies.
http://teams.lacoe.edu/reading/welcome.html

Assessment Technology

The Wireless Generation presents handheld systems for assessing students' reading.
http://www.wgen.net

chapter **3**

Instructing Early Readers
in Whole Groups

Essential Questions

- Why is reading aloud so important for Early Readers?
- What is writing aloud and how does it help Early Readers?
- What are some of the benefits of using shared reading in your primary classroom?
- How can kidwatching assist ongoing assessment of students and focus your instruction within your students' zone of proximal development?
- Why do Early Readers need instruction in comprehension?
- How can you create a learning environment that will further your literacy goals and student learning?

Many preservice teachers worry most about what they will do when they get in front of a classroom. We're guessing that may be true for you, too, and that you might be thinking, "OK. We've talked about whether I'll be an effective teacher, various learning theories, about young children and how they learn to read but what will I do when I'm responsible for helping Early Readers? I'm really anxious about that!" This is a valid concern. So this and the next three chapters are devoted to how to instruct young children in reading.

In Chapter 1 we explored your *dispositions to teach*. We asked if you are the type of person who would make an excellent teacher. In Chapter 2 we built your *knowledge* base about Early Readers and the reading process. In Chapters 3, through 6, we address *performance;* that is, how will you help young children learn to read? In these chapters we discuss *instruction,* starting with instructing Early Readers in whole groups.

When you are teaching young children you are likely to begin with whole-group instruction—keeping the whole class together as you teach. Effective teachers of reading work with the whole group in order to start creating a community of learners right from the very first day, to establish classroom management routines, and to get a sense of the group as a whole. It is during this whole-group instructional time that you will begin to build informal judgments about such things as which children work together well and which do not, the kinds of literacy experiences your students have had, and hunches about where they are in terms of literacy understanding and development. On that very first day, you will begin your literacy instruction by reading to the children.

INCORPORATING READING AND WRITING ALOUD

What is the most important thing you can do for your Early Readers? *Read to them every day!* In fact, we believe that this is so essential we're asking you to take the pledge shown in Figure 3.1.

Why a pledge and why read every day? Because we agree with researchers who say that reading aloud is the single most crucial factor in young children's success in learning to read (e.g., Anderson, Hiebert, Scott, & Wilkinson, 1985). Distinguished educator and read-aloud advocate Jim Trelease (1995) noted that the following are among the benefits of reading aloud: It allows children to associate reading with pleasure, builds their background knowledge, and provides an adult literacy role model for them. Further, Trelease noted that reading aloud exposes the listener to new information, rich vocabulary, good sentences, and story grammar. Reading aloud also lets children hear beautifully written language composed by some of our best authors who exemplify the finest outcomes of the writing process. All of these benefits are especially important for children who may not have had many experiences being read to at home.

The Read-Aloud Pledge

I promise,
That when I teach young children,
I will read aloud to them
Every day,
Every day,
EVERY DAY!

FIGURE 3.1   Read-Aloud Pledge

You should read aloud every day.

How Do I Conduct a Read-Aloud?

You may be thinking anyone can read aloud to children, so what is there to know? You are partially right in that it is easy to do: Just pick up a book and read. However, since you want your literacy teaching to be purposeful and effective, there are some considerations for you to remember. Figure 3.2 outlines an effective read-aloud procedure for you to think about.

Visit the online journal in Chapter 3 on our Companion Website at *www.prenhall.com/lenski* to answer these questions. Save your answers to your hard drive or to a disk to compile an online journal.

Reading aloud to children provides many literacy learning benefits. How does reading aloud to children help them learn to read themselves?

Before Reading

- Know the book yourself. Read it thoroughly to test its appropriateness for a read-aloud and for your students.
- Gather the children and "set the stage" for the read-aloud. Some teachers sit in a rocking chair while they bring together children on the reading rug. Some teachers play soft music or turn on a reading lamp. Let your students know it's a special time of their day.
- Show children the cover of the book, reading the title as well as the names of the author and illustrator. Allow students to make predictions about what the book might be about. Accept all suggestions, asking, "What clues helped you make that prediction?" or saying, "That's a good guess."
- Ask children to connect their own experiences and prior knowledge to the content of the book as reflected in the cover illustration.
- Introduce the main characters or the topic of the book, the setting, and the genre (e.g., fairy tale, true story, mystery) to build interest.

During the Reading

- Read with expression! If there are characters, try doing different voices for each one. Also, read at a good pace, not too slowly, not too fast. Make the book reading a delightful, dramatic, interactive experience.
- Occasionally stop in the reading to ask questions that check for understanding and to see if children can predict what will happen next.
- Invite children to respond to and comment on the story as you read.
- Rephrase parts of the story that you discover are too complicated for your students to understand.
- If you're reading a longer picture book that seems to lose children's attention, paraphrase the story and move to the conclusion. Or stop reading, and choose another book.

After Reading

- Invite children to respond to the reading and tell you how they felt about the book.
- Lead a discussion, reminding the children about the plot, characters, events, and resolution of the book. Consider asking children to recall the sequence of the book (beginning, middle, and end).
- If you choose a nonfiction book, have children review and summarize what they learned from the reading. Encourage students to draw conclusions from the information learned.
- In your discussion, help children make connections to their own lives and their prior knowledge. Explicitly demonstrate those connections for the children if they are unable to do so.
- Consider a follow-up activity like an art or writing activity related to the book. However, for the most part don't overdo it on extension activities, and *never* test children on a read-aloud.

FIGURE 3.2 Conducting an Effective Read-Aloud Experience

What Kinds of Books Should I Choose for a Read-Aloud?

When you plan for a read-aloud, you will want to carefully choose the book you will be reading. Because you are working with early learners, the book is most likely to be a picture book. Is the picture book one that you find interesting and engaging? Do you think your children will enjoy listening to the story? If you're working with very young children, such as kindergarteners, very long picture books with complex story lines are usually not a good choice. Young children respond better to shorter, fast-paced stories. Your choices for kindergarteners and first graders may include the charts of poems, rhymes, and songs you use during shared reading (discussed later in this chapter).

For second graders, you might choose a chapter book that doesn't have illustrations, deciding to read a chapter a day, for example. Second graders love hearing ongoing stories like the Ramona books by Beverly Cleary. Keep in mind, children have listening comprehension levels far above their reading comprehension levels. An example of this notion is that even young children can describe a complex plot from a television show, but they would not be able to read the script.

In addition to thinking about the text, choose picture books that have large, wonderful illustrations that support the action of the story. You want to be sure that all of the children can see the pictures when they are sitting in front of you. Otherwise, you will spend much of your read-aloud time hearing cries of "I can't see!" Some illustrations are perfect for independent reading because of their small features and intricate details, like Stephen Kellog's illustrations in *The Day Jimmy's Boa Ate the Wash* by T. H. Noble. But for the purpose of a read-aloud, Kellog's pictures in a book like *Is Your Mama a Llama?* by Deborah Guarino are more appropriate for young children. Selected fiction books for read-alouds can be found in Figure 3.3.

Aardema, V. (1990). *Why mosquitoes buzz in people's ears: A West African tale.* New York: Dial.

Crews, D. (1992). *Freight train.* New York: Greenwillow.

De Paola, T. (1975). *Strega Nona.* New York: Simon & Schuster.

Dorros, A. (1991). *Abuela.* New York: Dutton.

Gonzalez, L. M. (1999). *The bossy gallito: A traditional Cuban folk tale.* New York: Scholastic.

Hill, E. (1990). *Where's Spot?* New York: Putnam.

Hoban, R. (1993). *Bread and jam for Frances.* New York: HarperCollins.

Keats, E. J. (1963). *The snowy day.* New York: Viking.

Kimmel, E. A. (1990). *Anansi and the moss-covered rock.* New York: Holiday House.

Lester, J. (1999). *John Henry.* New York: Dial.

Martin, B., Jr. (1990). *Brown bear, brown bear, what do you see?* New York: Holt.

Rathmann, P. (1997). *Officer Buckle and Gloria.* New York: Putnam.

Say, A. (1993). *Grandfather's journey.* Boston: Houghton Mifflin.

Schwartz, A. (1988). *Annebelle Swift, kindergartner.* New York: The Trumpet Club.

Viorst, J. (1995). *Alexander and the terrible, horrible, no good, very bad day.* Nashville, TN: JTG.

Williams, V. B. (1983). *A chair for my mother.* New York: Greenwillow.

Zemach, M. (1986). *It could always be worse: A Yiddish folktale.* New York: Farrar, Straus & Giroux.

FIGURE 3.3   Suggested Read-Aloud Books

Your repertoire of read-aloud books should include a wide variety of genres, and plenty of nonfiction texts (Hiebert & Raphael, 1998). By reading nonfiction to your children, you are helping them learn to extract information from texts and become familiar with the language patterns used in factual books. You can use the read-aloud time to build your students' background knowledge about topics you are studying in your classroom and to demonstrate strategies such as reviewing, summarizing, and listing the most important facts in a book.

 Many criteria are used to select books for reading aloud to young children. Which do you believe are most important?

Noticing Children's Awareness of the Cueing Systems

If you and your students enjoyed the read-aloud, it was an effective use of your instructional time—because the primary purpose of a read-aloud is enjoyment of reading. However, you can also use each read-aloud to think about how your students are comprehending written language as listeners, the connections they are able to make with the text, and the support they are receiving as readers themselves. This awareness of students' attention to the cueing systems is a type of informal assessment.

Classroom Assessment

When you are reading aloud, you are primarily supporting children's understanding of the meaning cueing systems and the structure cueing systems as suggested by the psycholinguistic theory of reading. (Because they are usually not looking at the letters, they are not paying attention to the visual cueing system.) Here are two ways you support the meaning cueing system: First, as children listen, they construct meaning from the words you are reading to them. Discussion and talk about the book clarify understandings. Second, when you show them the illustrations and talk about information a reader can get from the pictures, your Early Readers are learning that pictures contain clues about what is happening in the story and can be a source of information for figuring out the words. You can assess children's meaning-making abilities and listening comprehension through asking questions and listening to children's discussions, thus eavesdropping on their thinking processes and understanding.

You support children's knowledge of the structure cueing system during read-alouds simply by letting them hear profuse amounts of written language, specifically book language. Children who are unaccustomed to hearing book language and those who do not speak fluent English particularly need these experiences to support their knowledge of how English works; this will help them a great deal as readers. They will begin to be able to predict what word or kind of word would come next. For example, not all children who come to school will be able to predict that *time* usually follows "Once upon a . . ."; nor will some children be able to predict the *kind* of word that should come next.

You can better understand the structure cueing system by reading this sentence: "Yesterday, I went for a ride in a red _____." Even though you don't have any letter clues, as a proficient user of English, you know that the word will be a noun. So, the missing word might be *car, wagon,* or other such nouns that connote a vehicle. Read-alouds from every genre allow children to make accurate predictions about the kind of word that would come next in their early reading attempts, sharpen their abilities to access the structure cueing system, and help them become more effective readers of English.

What Is Writing Aloud and Why Do Teachers Use It?

Writing aloud, sometimes referred to as shared writing (e.g., Fountas & Pinnell, 1996), is a process by which the teacher acts as a scribe while children dictate the words or story to the teacher. We use the term *writing aloud* to help you remember that the teacher talks out loud about the writing process while writing in front of the children from their dictation. You will use a chalkboard, large chart paper, or an overhead projector when you write aloud.

Writing aloud capitalizes on children's interests, knowledge, experiences, and use of oral language. When you engage children in a write-aloud experience you demonstrate how written language works by recording their ideas. All children can participate and feel successful during this supportive literacy experience. Children can concentrate on composing—what they want to say—while you do what's hard for young children: the transcribing. You are also creating texts for the children to read later when you chart their stories and post them in the classroom.

Writing aloud involves talking about your thinking as you write in front of students. How does writing aloud serve to model composing strategies to children?

Another benefit of writing aloud is that while you write, you think "out loud," verbalizing how words work and drawing attention to letters, words, sounds, and conventions of print. Routman (1991) notes, "As children observe the teacher in the act of writing, the teacher makes explicit what he is doing—the thinking, the format, layout, spacing, handwriting, spelling, punctuation, discussion of vocabulary" (p. 51). We will show you how this works using three examples of writing aloud that are explored next: the morning message the language experience approach, and interactive writing.

The morning message.

The morning message is a good way to start your day when you are teaching Early Readers. The morning message serves as a transition bridge between home and school because you can use the time to take advantage of children's excitement about sharing news from home as well as to plan for the day ahead. It's a good idea to work collaboratively on the composition of this message as a way to guide students in recording the day's plan. A morning message should be a part of your daily routine, but should not take more than about 10 minutes to complete.

Figure 3.4 shows a sample morning message from a first-grade classroom. Read the message and then take a look at Figure 3.5, in which we discuss what the teacher might do and say during the composition of this text.

One of the beneficial outcomes of the morning message is that it helps students make the transition between home and school. What are some literacy learning benefits?

This teacher could use the morning message shown in Figure 3.4 as a way to remind students about what to expect during their school day such as continuing their author study of Patricia Polacco, making pencil and marker drawings that attempt to replicate Polacco's illustrative techniques, and looking forward to the physical education teacher's visit.

While the morning message does not require much time, it is a powerful instructional approach that holds children's attention because it is about *them*. Meanwhile, you are using this routine to teach about a wide range of literacy concepts needed by your Early Readers as well as setting up expectations for the goals of your school day.

Good morning, it is Monday!

   We have lots of news today. It's Shamika's birthday! She is seven years old. Jason and Carmelo had company on Saturday and Sunday. They had a terrific time! Tina lost her first tooth!

   Today we will listen to more Patricia Polacco books. Then we will work on the books we are making with pictures that look like Ms. Polacco's.

   Don't forget, the gym teacher comes today!

FIGURE 3.4   *A Morning Message*

- Start the message the same way every day (such as "Good Morning," and the date).
- Ask children to contribute news. "Does anyone have any special news that we should put into the message this morning?"
- Call on children who wish to share news. Then begin thinking aloud as you transcribe the information, verbalizing your writing/thinking process, and asking questions.
- "Oh, it's Shamika's birthday. We must put that in our message. Let's write, 'It's Shamika's birthday.'

  "Does anyone remember how the word *It's* begins? That's right, Tommy, it begins with an *i*.

  "Oh, good, Carlos, you remembered that it has to be a capital *I* because it is the first word of the sentence. Now, I'll put down the *t*. I need to add a special punctuation mark next to make the word *It's*.

  "Does anyone know the name of that mark and how it looks? Tina knows. Yes, Tina, it's an apostrophe. Let's all make one with our imaginary pens in the air. It's sort of like a comma, isn't it? Only it's up higher.

  "Now I've added the *s* and the word is finished. Let's read it together: *It's*.

  "Now I'm going to leave a space and then ask Shamika to spell her name out loud for us while I write it. I like how she reminded us we needed a capital *s*.

  "Names begin with capital letters, don't they? And, yes, we need to use that apostrophe again for *Shamika's*."

- Continue on with this type of thinking aloud, verbalizing reminders about spacing, moving to the next line on the board or chart paper. Point out spellings and special vocabulary, like *terrific*.

FIGURE 3.5 Sample Conversation While Writing Aloud the Morning Message

The language experience approach (LEA). The language experience approach (LEA) also capitalizes on children's interests and experiences and allows children to concentrate on composing while the teacher transcribes their accounts (Hall, 1981; Nessel & Jones, 1981). It differs from the morning message in that there is no set agenda and the teacher writes down exactly what children say.

The following steps outline the procedure for you to refer to when conducting an LEA. Often teachers use LEA with the whole class after they have had a shared experience such as a field trip, a special visitor to the classroom, or a new class pet.

Preparing for LEA:

1. Lead a discussion about what the writing will be about, such as an exciting shared experience. Ideas will come forth that can be included in the story.
2. Consider jotting down some notes (as sort of a rough draft) as the children volunteer their thoughts.
3. Have large chart paper on an easel with markers ready.

Transcribing Children's Words:

1. Call on someone who is willing to dictate the first sentence.
2. Write down exactly what the child says, repeating the words as you write. You can point out spellings, spacing, changing lines for the return sweep, etc.
3. Continue taking dictation until your students are satisfied that the story is finished.

Mrs. Spencer takes dictation from students after a trip to the fire station.

Reading the Story:

1. Read the story aloud to the class, pointing to the words with a pointer as you read.
2. Then children and you read and reread the story several times together, with children participating as "the teacher" using the pointer.

Follow-Up:

1. After you are through writing and reading, devote some time to word work. For example, you can ask children to come up to the chart, point to certain letters, find specific letters, use their fingers to measure spacing between words, sentences, etc. These activities are similar to those used in shared reading, which is discussed next.
2. Post the class story somewhere in the classroom where it can be read and reread later.

Figure 3.6 provides an example of story constructed by second graders after the arrival of a new pet. LEA texts, like the sample in Figure 3.6, can be placed on a wall in your classroom and become a text for shared reading.

Interactive writing.   Interactive writing shares characteristics with the language experience approach in that the teacher and the students construct a text together using the language of the children. It can be conducted in whole- or small-group settings. Interactive writing is an experience in which children and teachers negotiate what will be written, taking turns writing. Interactive writing differs from LEA, however, in that the teacher "shares the pen" (McCarrier, Pinnell, & Fountas, 1999) with students, allowing individual children to come to the easel and write down words, letters, or punctuation when they are able.

Rhonda the Hamster

We got a new hamster for our class, 2-H. We named her Rhonda. She has fuzzy brown fur and very long teeth. She likes to run on her wheel and drink from her water bottle that has a little straw on the bottom of it. She likes to sleep a lot. But, sometimes when we are reading quietly, she starts moving all her bedding stuff and furniture all around. It makes everyone put down their books and run to see what Rhonda is doing. We are taking turns taking care of her.

FIGURE 3.6   LEA Story

Another difference is that in interactive writing, rather than writing down children's dictation verbatim as in LEA, the teacher negotiates sentence construction with students and makes revisions, on the run, as he transcribes the sentences. In this way, the texts are often more readable for the students, with words that are repetitive, predictable, and easy to remember.

Here's an example. Let's say the teacher is sitting next to the easel with large chart paper and is transcribing his first-grade students' language contributions. The class is writing a story that is a variation on *The Three Little Pigs*. They have decided to title their story *The Three Little Mice*. Their story is about mice who are trying to find safe houses that will protect them from a mean cat. A segment of the conversation might go like this:

Mr. Samuel: Now, who wants to add the next sentence?

Louisa: Let's say: "Then, the second little mouse decided to look for a nice box to make his little house in so he would be safe from the mean cat."

Mr. Samuel: Excellent idea, Louisa! This is going to be such a good story! What if we write, "Then the second little mouse looked for a box." And, when we get to the word *mouse* will you come up and write it for us?

Can you see how the teacher changed the sentence to an easier, shorter format? That is because Mr. Samuel wants the students to be able to read and reread the story on subsequent days. Further, did you notice how he invited Louisa to write the word *mouse?* That is what we mean by "sharing the pen." At the same time, the teacher thinks aloud as he writes, modeling hearing sounds in words, spelling, spacing, and story construction. Interactive writing is an excellent tool for sharing writing with children, creating texts for children to read, and emphasizing the reading/writing connection through shared texts.

USING SHARED TEXTS

One of the best ways to start whole-group literacy instruction in the early grades is by using shared texts, often referred to as shared reading (e.g., Holdaway, 1979; Pappas & Brown, 1987; Teale & Sulzby, 1986). Shared reading is a process by which the whole group (your classroom) participates together in reading materials, such as oversized books, teacher- or student-made printed charts, poetry or song charts, or multiple copies of texts. Shared reading happens when a teacher gathers children together and invites them to read a text along with her to promote literacy learning and the joy of reading. During reading, the teacher or one of the students points to each word so that the whole group can follow along with the print while they say the words. When students read along with the teacher, less able readers are supported by more able readers, and they all are supported by the teacher and each other. Shared reading is a nonthreatening approach to reading that invites everyone to chime in as best they can in a choral reading, much like choir members support one another in singing. As a teacher, you can use shared reading daily with your young readers to involve them in reading for enjoyment and allow them to experience the accomplishment of expressive, fluent reading with the whole group.

Perhaps you remember participating in shared reading experiences in school or reading to a child while he followed along with you. Recall your literacy memoir from Chapter 1. Did you remember sitting in a parent's lap while your mom or dad pointed to words and you spoke the words along with them? If you did, those experiences were significant preparatory events to your learning to read. Shared reading offers children who have not had many opportunities for "lap time reading" the chance to follow along with words, engage in the story, and learn about how print works.

Other reasons for engaging students in shared reading include the sense of community it creates, the sense of story students develop, and the knowledge children gain about written language such as syntax (how our language is put together) and semantics (what the text/reading means) (Fountas & Pinnell, 1996; Routman, 2000). Through readings and repeated readings, children can learn concepts about print such as left-to-right eye sweep, following from top to bottom, and going from front to back in a book. In addition, they can learn more abstract concepts such as these: Speech can be written down, words can tell a story, a story stays the same each time it's read, and there is a one-to-one correspondence between speech and print.

Shared reading helps reinforce concepts about print. What concepts about print do children need to understand?

How Vygotsky's Theories Support Shared Reading

Remember our discussion of Vygotsky's theories of learning and his notion of zone of proximal development (ZPD)? Vygotsky's theories validate the use of shared reading in the classroom. For example, the ZPD—a range in which students can do something with the help of an adult that they cannot do alone—supports the practice of a teacher (the more knowledgeable other) engaging students in a shared reading experience. The teacher selects appropriate books and provides help in reading a text that students most likely could not read by themselves. This assisted performance allows children to achieve with help what they can almost do alone, in an area of learning that is *proximal* or close to emerging at any time. When this happens, children are given the gift of behaving like readers. The actions of a supportive, responsive teacher helping students, right at the cutting edge of their learning, are referred to as *scaffolding* (Wood, Bruner, & Ross, 1976).

Shared reading scaffolds children's early reading instruction. Scaffolding has been described by Rogoff (1990) as "guided participation." Through guided participation the child is supported by the teacher in problem solving *without* solving the problem for the child. The teacher supplies just the right amount of support, like scaffolding does on a building, until the child is able to solve the problem herself (like removing the scaffolding when a building can stand alone).

A good example of scaffolding is to think about a time when you helped a child, niece, nephew, or younger sibling learn how to ride a two-wheel bike (Figure 3.7). Remember how, at first, you held onto the bike and the child while running alongside? Then, you held onto the bike, more loosely, while still running with the new rider. Finally, you were able to let go and watch the delighted child ride off, elated

Scaffolding refers to providing just the right amount of support to a learner, then gradually withdrawing it. Can you think of an instance where someone scaffolded your learning of something new?

FIGURE 3.7   Scaffolding Learning

by the freedom and feeling of accomplishment. Through these actions you were providing just the right amount of support until you could remove your scaffold, and the child could handle the task alone.

In addition to the scaffolding that students receive from the teacher during a shared reading interaction, they are also receiving help from their classmates. Vygotsky noted that students learn most readily when they are learning with others in social settings; he believed that children's minds develop in the context of their social interactions embedded in a cultural backdrop (Vygotsky, 1962). Within the cultural backdrop of a school, you will create social settings that enable young children to move forward in their literacy development by conducting shared reading experiences.

Procedures for Conducting Shared Reading

Although you may not have an immediate opportunity to conduct a shared reading, read through the following list to identify some components important to a shared reading interaction.

1. Select the text.
2. Introduce the text to the class. Allow children to make predictions about the story.

3. Read the text to the children, pointing to each word, and inviting all children who can to join in on the reading.
4. Reread the text, still pointing to the words—more children will participate on the second reading.
5. Stop occasionally during the second reading to discuss features of the text, repeated phrases, surprises, illustrations, etc.
6. Discuss the text. Talk about favorite pages, illustrations, what children noticed.
7. Consider a follow-up activity that focuses on word study or a minilesson about conventions of print such as noticing that each sentence started with a capital letter.
8. If you have multiple, small copies of the text, show children where they can be found in the classroom library. Or, chart the words to the text on large chart paper so that it can be displayed in the classroom. It will become one of the known texts that children can use for independent reading and writing activities.

Selecting materials for shared reading.   In setting up a shared reading experience, you will need to select materials for your students to read with you. The texts should be enlarged, like Big Books, so that all children can see and follow along with you. Some teachers make their own Big Books or use large charts of poems, songs, or student-created texts. The texts that the class creates during morning message and through the language experience approach can be valuable resources for shared reading. A list of children's books for shared reading can be found in Figure 3.8. Here are some considerations to think about when selecting shared reading materials:

• Is the text one that children and you will enjoy? For example, does it have repetitive language, rhyming words, colorful illustrations, and some high-frequency words that the children know or can memorize?
• Is the text at the right level? At the beginning of the year the text should be *easy,* preferably printed in bold upper- and lowercase letters.
• Either by using a Big Book, chart, or multiple copies, can all children see the words as they follow along?
• Is the text an old favorite or one that you suspect will be a new favorite?

YOU TRY IT

Conducting a Shared Reading Experience

Now that you are familiar with what shared reading is and why teachers use it and have information about procedures and selecting materials, here is a chance for you to apply, practice, and make sense of what you have learned. On the Companion Website (*http://www.prenhall.com/lenski*) is a shared reading lesson for you to use with a group of children or a group of your peers. Teach the lesson, take notes on the outcomes, and discuss your reflections with your classmates.

The lesson is organized into the following components: before reading, during reading, and after reading. You can use this plan or create your own, using the format already provided. The lesson plan suggested on the Companion Website would be appropriate for an early shared reading experience with your new class of first graders in September and is based on the book *Five Little Monkeys* written and illustrated by Eileen Christelow (1989). This enlarged text has one sentence per page, following this pattern from the familiar rhyme: "Five little monkeys jumping on the bed. One fell off and bumped his head." For some first graders this lesson would seem easy, for others it would provide challenge. However, that is one of the major benefits of shared reading experiences: *All* children can participate and feel successful while enjoying a joint reading experience and the pleasure of the language.

Reflecting on your shared reading lesson.   Each time you teach a lesson or engage in an instructional interaction in this text such as the preceding You Try It feature, you should reflect on your actions and your success. Reflection is a way to assess your own teaching. Reflect on the following questions about yourself and your students (or your peers):

Classroom Assessment

- How did you generate enthusiasm for the lesson and interest in the book?
- Do you think your group enjoyed the shared reading? How could you tell?
- Having children make predictions is one way to enhance their comprehension. When you asked about the cover and subsequent pages, what did you think this would reveal about their understanding of the book?
- What was disclosed about prior knowledge of the content of the book and actions on the pages?
- Another way to build comprehension is to have conversations about the story. When you discussed what was happening during and after reading, how did your questions and their answers serve to add to the understanding of the story?

Becker, J. (1980). *Seven little rabbits.* New York: Scholastic.

Bennett, J., & dePaola, T. (1985). *Teeny tiny.* New York: The Trumpet Club.

Christelow, E. (1989). *Five little monkeys jumping on the bed.* New York: The Trumpet Club.

Delacre, L. (1989). *Time for school, Nathan!* New York: Scholastic.

Guarino, D. (1989). *Is your mama a llama?* New York: Scholastic.

Hutchins, P. (1986). *The doorbell rang.* New York: Scholastic.

Kovalski, M. (1987). *The wheels on the bus.* New York: The Trumpet Club.

Martin, B., Jr., & Archambault, J. (1989). *Chicka chicka boom boom.* New York: Scholastic.

Martin, B., Jr. (1992). *Polar bear, polar bear, what do you hear?* New York: Scholastic.

Numeroff, L. J. (1985). *If you give a mouse a cookie.* New York: HarperCollins.

O'Keefe, S. H. (1989). *One hungry monster.* New York: Scholastic.

Peek, M. (1985). *Mary wore her red dress.* New York: The Trumpet Club.

Shook, B. (1995). *My picture.* San Diego: Dominie Press.

Weiss, N. (1989). *Where does the brown bear go?* New York: The Trumpet Club.

Wescott, N. B. (1987). *Peanut butter and jelly.* New York: Dutton Children's Books.

Wood, A. (1984). *The napping house.* San Diego: Harcourt Brace.

FIGURE 3.8   Recommended Children's Books for Shared Reading With Early Readers (Available in Big Book Format)

Students and teacher publish wonderful class books that everyone can read.

Reflection entails critically thinking back on your teaching to problem solve difficulties and celebrate victories. How can reflection make your teaching more effective?

Classroom Assessment

- Word work is integrated into each literacy event with Early Readers. How did noticing repetitive phrasing, identifying familiar words, or adding to the Word Wall help your students?
- What might you change about your lesson next time? Why?

Kidwatching

Imagine yourself participating in shared reading with your students. You're reading a Big Book while your students sit on a rug in front of you. While you're reading along with students and pointing to the words on the page, you're also assessing your students' engagement with the activity. Your eyes are moving across the group of students, observing the extent to which the entire class is paying attention, honing in on students who are engrossed in the story, and noticing students who are wiggling around and not engaged. As you observe, you ask yourself questions about your instruction and about student learning. This type of observational assessment is called *kidwatching* (Goodman, 1978) and is often referred to as part of the category of informal, authentic assessment. Kidwatching is closely observing children, noticing what your students do, remembering it, and beginning to look for patterns of student learning.

The more you teach, the more automatic your kidwatching will become. Your observations, memory, and judgments about students are important aspects of assessment. However, you shouldn't rely solely on your memory about your observations. Memory is tricky. If you've ever compared your memory with someone else's you'll find that people remember things differently. Now think of the hundreds of student actions you'll observe in your class in one day. For that reason, it's a good idea to develop systematic assessment routines that can help you remember and record your anecdotes about student behaviors and actions.

Anecdotal Records

One assessment routine that you can use after any lesson involves anecdotal records. Anecdotal records are short notes that you take as you observe specific behaviors of students in your classroom. The behaviors you write on anecdotal records should be *factual*. For example, think about conducting a shared reading experience with your students. You notice that Samuel is sitting in the back of the class and is looking at the rug rather than at the Big Book. An anecdotal note about Samuel could read "Looking at rug, not at book." An example of a nonfactual note would be "Samuel is not paying attention." Remember as you take anecdotal records to write down only facts about your students' behaviors.

Before beginning to make any anecdotal records, you need to decide how you will manage the paperwork required for this kind of note-taking. You should develop a system that allows you to write brief notes about student behavior throughout the day (not just after shared reading) and be able to categorize them with other notes you have collected about individual students. There is no one right way to do this kind of record keeping. You will need to try a few ideas and see which one works for you. Some teachers prefer to take notes with a small computer right after a lesson. Others jot down notes on Post-It notes, index cards, or mailing labels attached to a clipboard. You can then transfer your notes to flip folders, binders, or sheets of paper as illustrated in Figure 3.9 (Hill, Ruptic, & Norwick, 1998).

After you have decided how you will take anecdotal records, identify two or three students to observe during every shared reading activity. Rotate which students

date
Students to observe today
Jacob Melissa Emily

date
<u>Jacob</u>
-Is reading with more confidence; reported: "I'm getting better at reading." -Wants to choose own books; says "I can choose my own books."

date
<u>Melissa</u>
says she: -Wants to read all of "The Kids of the Polk Street School" books -Still needs a bookmark to keep her place

date
<u>Emily</u>
Asked to work with a partner. Said, "I need someone to help me with the words." -Is choosing books that are too difficult: running records reveal only 80% accuracy

FIGURE 3.9   Systematic Anecdotal Notation

you will observe so that you take notes on each student every few weeks. You might decide to take additional anecdotal records during an activity, especially if you notice a particular student's behavior that you want or need to record. If you approach each lesson ready to take notes about *just a few students'* behavior, anecdotal note-taking becomes more manageable.

Analyzing anecdotal records.   Anecdotal records can help you plan instruction, and they can also help you identify patterns of student learning and make inferences; they are valuable resources when you are communicating with parents (Rhodes & Nathenson-Mejia, 1992). After you have taken notes on students in four or five situations, begin analyzing the anecdotal records. Let's say that you have taken anecdotal records during several weeks of shared reading. As you read the anecdotal records, you find that a great number of students are not engaged in the activity. At this point, you should probably think about the books you are choosing. They may be too hard for students to understand or uninteresting. Anecdotal records can help you think about your instruction through your notes on student behavior.

Anecdotal records can also help you identify patterns of student learning and make inferences. For example, imagine that you have four notes about Samuel, and in each note you have recorded that Samuel has chosen to sit in the back of the group and is not looking at the book. You have recognized a pattern of behavior. Now you should use the data on Samuel to make inferences about his learning. You could make the inference that Samuel isn't interested in reading. You might also wonder whether Samuel can see the words on the page or whether Samuel can hear you read. You can test the inferences you make by moving Samuel to a different spot in the group of students and by asking him whether he likes to participate in shared reading. You might also try involving him by letting him help hold the book or point to the words in the text. Whatever you decide to try, anecdotal records help you make informed decisions.

Diversity Issue: Accommodating All Children During Shared Reading

All students can benefit from participating in shared reading, and you may not need to make many modifications for student differences. However, your assessment of students' engagement may reveal that some students need special attention. As a responsive teacher, you should continually consider the needs of all children in your classroom.

Think of your assessment of Samuel through anecdotal records. You found that Samuel did not participate in shared reading activities. The inferences you made about him, taken with other assessments, might lead you to investigate his ability to see the book and hear you. Young students frequently have ear infections that interfere with their hearing. Because young students may not realize that their hearing isn't as acute as it should be, they don't let you know that they can't hear you. Therefore, if you notice students aren't engaged in shared reading, you should consider requesting hearing and vision screening. While you are waiting for screening reports, be sure the students in question sit near you.

Imagine that your anecdotal records reveal that Chai-Yu, whose parents have emigrated from China, isn't following you during shared reading. Additional observational assessments indicate that Chai-Yu is unusually quiet in class, never speaking or volunteering information. Although she knows a little English, you sense that she is fearful of speaking aloud in case her pronunciation is incorrect. You also notice that Chai-Yu doesn't play with the other children on the playground and that she never speaks to other children.

There could be a number of reasons why this child doesn't participate in classroom activities. You already suspect her lack of fluency in English. Calling Chai-Yu's parents may provide some information. On the other hand, you must be extremely sensitive to her parents' desire for their daughter to do well in your classroom. Therefore, you must not imply that Chai-Yu is doing poorly in school (Hurley & Tinajero, 2001). Rather, communicate your desire to help her feel comfortable enough to participate. If Chai-Yu speaks Chinese at home, find books written in her first language. Ask her parents to read Chinese children's books with her at home. Then, send home with Chai-Yu copies of the shared texts you create in English at school for her to read and practice. If one or both parents speak English, enlist their help in reading the shared texts with Chai-Yu. If school support personnel are available who are fluent in Chinese as well as English, inquire about receiving help for your student who is working toward bilingualism.

 ELL students in your classroom are learning to read a language that is different than the one they speak at home. How will you accommodate such children's linguistic needs?

DESIGNING INTERACTIVE COMPREHENSION ACTIVITIES

When we were young teachers, we expected that children would come to us understanding book language, with background knowledge about how stories were constructed and the ability to connect our reading materials to their lives and their prior experiences. *We* had come to school with these skills in place when we were children, so it seemed to us that all children would. We found out we were wrong. Many children in our classrooms needed our help and today's student will need yours. Maria (1989) contends that some students will begin school with "limited experiences with regard to reading comprehension which are more common for middle class children" (p. 296) and it is up to *teachers* and *schools* to assist children in removing barriers to comprehension (Goodman & Buck, 1997). By determining the common ground in what all children know and what they need to know, you can help your students understand a range of texts. This will be especially true for English Language Learners and children from culturally diverse backgrounds. Because we've already established that the purpose of reading is the construction of meaning, like the many exciting responsibilities we've reminded you of thus far, teaching children strategies for comprehending will be your job as well.

You need to show your future students how the words on the page must make sense and the strategies that help readers gain personal meaning from text. Through immersing your students in wonderful children's literature you will demonstrate that usually in stories something happens to someone in a setting that is described. Events occur and, more often than not, problems are solved. Similarly, using nonfiction texts, you will show students that those texts have information that readers can use to learn about the world. Fiction and nonfiction books in read-alouds and shared, guided, and independent reading are used to teach children how to better understand.

Routman (2000) examined her own ways of "knowing when she understands." Among her self-reflections are that she can retell the text orally to someone else, summarize what she's read, connect the text to something else she has read or experienced, be aware of the characteristics of the genre and how that helps her comprehension, and recognize when there are gaps in her understanding (p. 137). We imagine that you could create a similar list to analyze your own understanding of text. This process is called *metacognition*—thinking about your own thinking. When you teach children strategies that enhance their comprehension, you will be teaching them how to be metacognitively aware—to know when they understand and when they do not (Baumann, 1991; Baumann & Schmitt, 1986; Rosenshine, Meister, & Chapman, 1996).

Irvin (1991) notes that the reader, the text, and the purpose are the three primary influences on comprehension. We consider these three factors next as we

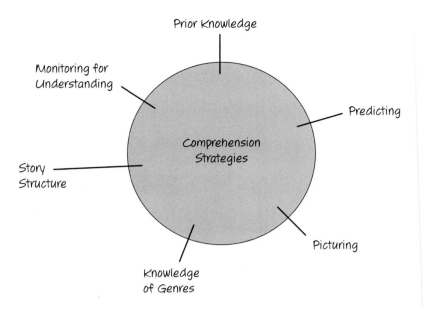

FIGURE 3.10   Comprehension Strategies

Metacognition refers to an awareness of one's own thinking. How can you foster metacognition in your students as you teach comprehension strategies?

supply you with selected activities to help children develop comprehension strategies in whole-group settings through accessing prior knowledge, predicting, picturing, knowledge of genres and story structure, and monitoring for understanding (Figure 3.10). When you teach young children, you need to think about the readers in your classroom, the kinds of books you provide, and the rationale you establish for the literacy events you present.

Prior Knowledge

What are your students' prior life experiences and prior knowledge? How can you help students make connections between prior knowledge and what they are reading in school? These important questions will guide your beginning literacy teaching decisions and your teaching of comprehension strategies. Schema theory can be helpful to you as you think about children's prior knowledge—knowledge that stems from children's experiences in life, with texts, and with language.

Schema theory.   *Schema theory* (Rumelhart, 1980), touched on in Chapter 1, advances the thought that when we learn something new, we can understand the new concept only as we integrate it with previously existing knowledge. *Schemata* are cognitive structures similar to file folders into which we organize information in our minds.

Think about young children and the schemata they possess as they make sense of their worlds. When a child is very young, for example, he may call all small to medium mammals "doggies," because that is how he has organized his knowledge about such animals. In the child's cognitive file folder labeled "doggies" are images of furry critters that walk around on four feet. Then, one day the young child sees a sheep in a field, points and says, "Doggie." "No," says his mother, "that's not a doggie, that's a sheep." Puzzled the child repeats, "Sheep?" "Yes," reiterates his mother, "sheep."

If you watch the little boy you can almost picture the process his mind is going through as he scrambles to create a new folder, a new schema labeled "Sheep" to accommodate this new information about animals that have tufts of gray/white fleece, eat grass in fields, follow each other around, and are not doggies. This example illustrates how learners integrate new information into existing knowledge. Pearson and Spiro (1982) call this process using an anchor point (dogs) as a bridge to help the learner develop concepts that he needs (sheep).

Schemata, as you can see, never stop changing; as we continue to learn, we refine our existing schemata. You can help young students develop as readers by expanding their life and language experiences and, hence, expanding their schemata. Among the ways you can do this is by taking field trips to museums, zoos, farms, and parks, and through technology support such as videos, CD-ROMs, and the Internet. These kinds of events provide platforms for enriching language experiences as you talk together in lively class discussions, write and then read LEA stories about your encounters, and make connections with texts, both fiction and nonfiction, about similar events. If you teach in an urban setting, for example, and are able to take a trip to a farm, think about how much new knowledge your students could gain about farm animals and how that new knowledge could stretch and enlarge their existing schemata. Then, imagine the stimulating discussions you could have, stories your class could dictate to you about their new knowledge, the research you could do on the Internet in communities of learners that support the social nature of learning (Fresch, 1999), and the books about the farm that you could read and discuss with your young students. All of these enrichment activities would further extend students' comprehension of new texts and uses of language.

Predicting

Prior experiences link closely with children's ability to predict what will happen next in a book. The more compelling literacy experiences your students have, the more they know about language and how books work; therefore, it becomes easier for them to predict book language and events. Proficient readers make good guesses, or predictions, as they are reading. The ability to make accurate predictions speeds up reading processing and enhances readers' comprehension as they confirm or reject their predictions. Consider your own reading: Have you ever been reading along in a novel when suddenly an event occurs that doesn't make sense? You figure that either you missed something or the writer went off on an unexpected tangent. At this point, you make a decision to keep on reading, hoping you'll figure out the unanticipated happening, or to reread the parts of the chapter where your confusion began.

One way you can help young children understand how to make good guesses and sharpen their predicting skills is by using a Directed Reading–Thinking Activity (DR-TA) (Stauffer, 1969) during a read-aloud. In a DR-TA, the teacher solicits predictions from students as she guides them in deciding if their hunches are accurate or need to be revised as she stops at predetermined points in the book to check children's predictions. This type of "thinking aloud" models for children what capable readers do in their own heads as they read text and monitor their own understanding. Figure 3.11 explains the procedure for conducting a DR-TA.

Picturing

Picturing or visualizing is another comprehension strategy that you can teach children. Sometimes teachers call this "getting a movie running in your head." Helping children to run that movie and picture what is happening in a story heightens

---

Before Reading
- Read the title of the book or passage to the students and show them the accompanying illustration.
- Ask children to make predictions concerning the content of the reading and their reasons for saying so:

    What do you think this book is going to be about?
    Do you see any clues on the cover that tell you that?

During the Reading
- Read a small portion of the text to the students.
- Stop and ask students whether their predictions are accurate or whether they would like to change their guesses:

    What are you thinking now?
    Do you want to change your predictions/guesses?
    What happened in the story that caused you to change your minds?

- Keep on with this pattern, allowing children to confirm or disconfirm their predictions.
- Call attention to the illustrations, key phrases, or vocabulary to help students make further guesses about what will happen next.

After Reading
- Discuss the process you just engaged in and why the students' predictions were or were not accurate and what might have led them to make changes along the way.
- Help students understand the prediction–confirmation sequence that proficient readers engage in as a comprehension strategy.

FIGURE 3.11   Directed Reading–Thinking Activity

comprehension. Perhaps you use this strategy as you read, being so sure of what certain characters in a book might look and act like that if an actual movie is made from the book, you are disappointed by the casting decisions. Davey (1983) suggests using a Think-Aloud procedure to help children picture how characters might behave and what is taking place in the story and, hence, make connections to students' experiences.

Let's say you are reading *The Cricket in Times Square* by George Seldon (1960) to your second graders, a book about a cricket who lands in the Times Square subway station via a picnic basket from his native Connecticut. During this read-aloud you could stop and model visualizing for your students:

- "As I'm reading this story, I'm picturing this tiny cricket alone and frightened in a new, noisy, and crowded place."
- "In my mind I can see him looking around and wondering what to do next."

As you read further to the part where Mario (the boy in the story) finds the cricket, you could stop reading again to say:

- "Now, I'm just picturing this scene of a small boy, picking up the cricket to show to his mother. Can you picture it in your mind, too?"

After you have demonstrated picturing scenes from the book in your mind, ask students to try to do the same. Explain how picturing helps you understand the words and the story better. Each time that you stop during read-alouds, ask children what they are picturing and ask them if they are running a movie in their heads.

Setting: Time   Place
Characters:
Problem:
Action: 1. 2. 3.
Outcome or Ending:

FIGURE 3.12   Story Map

Knowledge of Genres and Story Structure

As you read many different kinds of books with children, knowledge of various genres will help them understand what to expect in, for instance, a fairy tale or a poem or a mystery. Imagine that you are reading a mystery; you expect to receive clues from the author that help you solve the puzzle. If you are reading a biography, you expect to appreciate a famous person's life and to understand that person at a deeper level. You may have noticed we use the concept of "knowing what to expect" as we discuss genre knowledge; that is because again we are linking this comprehension strategy to prior knowledge and prediction. As you can see, the lines between various comprehension approaches are blurred and they often overlap. Knowing what to expect helps Early Readers comprehend texts from a variety of genres.

 Prediction plays a key role in comprehension. How are genre knowledge and prediction related?

Story maps.   Because narrative texts tend to dominate in the primary grades, one activity that may enhance comprehension of stories involves teaching your students story structure. Story structure lessons are not ends in themselves; rather, teaching about plot elements such as characters, setting, problem, action, and outcomes can be just one way to help children unlock meaning in stories. One activity that can highlight story structure for young readers is constructing a story map (Beck & McKeown, 1981). To complete a story map, the teacher guides the class in a discussion of the structure of a particular story and facilitates students' filling in the components of the map. An example of a story map appropriate for primary children is shown in Figure 3.12.

Web maps.   Web maps can also help children discern story elements or record important information from nonfiction texts (Bromley, 1996). Two examples of webs appropriate for kindergarten or first grade can be seen in Figure 3.13—one contains information children learned from a nonfiction text, *This Bird Can't Fly* (Canizares & Moreton, 1998), which compares nonflying birds to birds that fly, and one from a story (*The Gingerbread Man*). Both of these types of webs aid children's

Kindertgarten Web Map: *This Bird Can't Fly*
by S. Canizares & D. Moreton

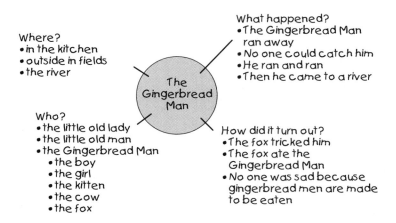

First-Grade Web Map: *The Gingerbread Man*

FIGURE 3.13   Web Maps

comprehension by providing graphic representations of important ideas from books that you and your students create together as you rethink and talk about texts.

Helping Children Monitor Understanding

You know that the primary purpose of reading is the construction of meaning. If a reader is calling out words and not understanding, she is not reading. Further, one of your primary goals as a teacher is to foster independence. Therefore, you will teach children to assess their own comprehension just as you do when you read. You recognize when what you're reading doesn't make sense. You want your students to recognize that, too, and monitor their understanding.

Monitoring is defined as "attending to the situation [reading] and noticing when things aren't quite right. . . . Monitoring strategies involve checking one's attempts to coordinate the variety of cues found in texts" (Schwartz, 1997, pp. 42–43). Some children seem to be instinctively strategic as they monitor their comprehension of text, but most developing readers will need guidance and supportive instruction. For beginning readers, reading is a complex task that requires the coordination of the cueing systems, accessing meaning, structure, and visual cues from the text, while attempting to monitor and self-correct.

Clay (1991) explains that as a teacher you will know when a child is monitoring by observing that when he miscues (makes a mistake in the reading), he rereads all or part of the sentence, or makes several attempts at a word including self-correction,

Advice for New Teachers

Monitoring Reading

Dear Derek,

How do you help children learn to monitor their own reading?

Dear New Teacher,

I use the following prompts, consistently. It would be good if you could memorize these phrases. These reminders help students pay attention when things aren't right as they read:

- I saw that you stopped in your reading. What did you notice?
- Why did you stop?
- I liked the way you went back and reread that sentence. What did you find out when you did that?
- I liked the way you worked out that word to make it make sense.
- Did it make sense this time? Were you right?
- How do you know when something doesn't make sense?

shows signs of dissonance, or asks for help. These are all positive signs that the child is trying his best to make sure the reading makes sense. Schwartz (1997, p. 47) suggests that you post the following sign in your classroom:

Readers Know That:

1. Good readers think about meaning.
2. All readers make mistakes.
3. Good readers notice and fix some mistakes.

When students know that all readers make mistakes and that strategies are available to help them understand text, they can learn to monitor their reading as you encourage them to talk to you about the range of strategies they are using to help themselves.

Asking children to think about their thinking and verbalize their cognitive processing are important steps in helping them self-monitor. Good readers self-correct often and read for meaning; self-monitoring and self-correction go hand in hand. Your goal as a teacher is to help all students self-monitor. You want all children in your classroom to say to themselves, "Reading is supposed to make sense. When it doesn't make sense anymore, I need to stop and find out why."

ORGANIZING THE CLASSROOM FOR EARLY READERS

When you teach Early Readers, how will you organize your classroom? Your first considerations are your students' needs and the literacy learning goals for those particular children at that grade level. You will be in charge of your daily schedule during Literacy Workshop time: selecting materials, setting up the physical arrangement of your classroom, developing supportive literacy centers, and providing for technology opportunities.

As a teacher you will create the *learning* environment. How is this different from creating the *physical* environment in the classroom?

Before we discuss each of these matters, let's review the fact that the most important and influential element of your classroom setting is the *learning* environment that you create, not the *physical* environment. As we have already emphasized, your classroom should be a good place to be; somewhere you and your students enjoy spending time—a place of psychological safety, acceptance, and laughter. In addition to creating a pleasant environment where the joy of literacy is celebrated, Cambourne (1995) notes that certain conditions must be in place to ensure optimal literacy learning. Among them are immersing children in print, demonstrating literacy concepts and skills for them, valuing their attempts, and creating motivating learning experiences that engender engagement. Once you understand and are able to create the kind of classroom environment and conditions for learning that your students need, you can begin to think about your daily schedule, how to arrange the physical space, setting up learning centers, and selecting materials.

SEE FOR YOURSELF

Cambourne's Conditions for Learning

Visit the message board for Chapter 3 on our Companion Website at *www.prenhall.com/lenski* to discuss your findings.

On the Companion Website (*http://www.prenhall.com/lenski*) you will find noted literacy researcher Brian Cambourne's (1995) conditions for literacy learning. Take notes on what he believes has to be in place to ensure optimal learning. Pay special attention to the role of "engagement." Bring your notes to class to discuss with your peers how each of these components plays out in elementary classrooms and also relates to learning at the college level.

Your Daily Literacy Schedule

In the primary grades roughly half of your school day will be devoted to literacy learning activities. How you decide to use this time may be influenced by outside factors such as when your students go to gym or art or other special classes. If you are able, however, try to work with administrators to schedule an uninterrupted block of time for reading instruction in whole-group, small-group, and independent settings. Figure 3.14 illustrates a workable schedule for your Early Readers during Literacy Workshop time.

Arranging the Physical Space

As you prepare to teach young children, you will also prepare the spaces in your classroom to facilitate learning and help you and your students feel organized and able to move through your days with purpose and order. Let's first consider a key element: arranging the floor plan in your classroom.

The floor plan.   Most of the classrooms where you'll work will not be as large as you'd like. However, if you are creative and sketch out your ideas before you start moving furniture, you will be able to make the most of the learning spaces you have.

Times and Activities	Instructional Setting
8:30–8:45 Free-Choice Reading	Independent
8:45–9:15 Opening Events Morning message; calendar; planning for the day	Whole group
Read-aloud Shared reading Interactive writing	Whole group
9:15–10:15 Reading Workshop Guiding reading and conferences	Small group
Independent reading and literacy centers	Small group and independent work
10:15–10:30 Working with Words	Whole and small group
10:30–11:10 Writing Workshop	Small group and independent work
11:10–11:30 Read-Aloud	Whole group

FIGURE 3.14   Sample K–2 Literacy Workshop Daily Schedule

Advice for New Teachers

Classroom Arrangement

Dear Derek,

How did you decide how to arrange your classroom?

Dear New Teacher,

I quickly realized that the way my classroom was arranged when I entered it wouldn't work for me or my students. So, I set up centers, a permanent classroom library area, a table for guided reading groups, and clusters of students' desks so that they can work collaboratively. I do change the seating arrangement fairly regularly, though. Students need to learn to work with many types of children, and some students simply *can't* work together.

It may seem strange to suggest this, but the way you arrange your classroom speaks to your philosophy of literacy learning. For example, if you embrace social constructivism, will you situate children's desks in straight, separated rows with your desk planted in the front of the room? Probably not. Instead, you will place your students' desks in clusters so that they are able to interact with one another and talk about the learning opportunities they encounter as they construct new understandings with the help of others (Vygotsky, 1978). You may also decide to position your own desk on the side or back of the room, supporting your belief that the teacher is the orchestrator versus the dispenser of all knowledge in the classroom. Lapp, Flood, and Goss (2000) state, "Desks don't move—students do in effective classroom environments" (p. 31) to explain their advocacy for active engagement in a busy, productive learning setting.

Bulletin boards.   Bulletin boards play an important role in your classroom space as you use them for student learning, student work, and organizational functions. When you plan for bulletin boards, be sure to leave some empty for your students to take charge of themselves. Giving students ownership of bulletin boards can help foster the kind of collaborative environment you want and signals your belief in the social construction of knowledge as well as shared power in the classroom.

One of the bulletin boards that you may want to establish in your classroom is the Message Board (Short, Harste, & Burke, 1996). A Message Board is an interactive space for children to write notes to each other or to the teacher and have them answered on the board. (See Figure 3.15 for an example of a Message Board.) The purposes of a Message Board can be varied and tailored to your particular students. For example, students can post important news that they want to share or ask the teacher questions about upcoming events in the classroom, or the teacher can put up reminders to the class.

FIGURE 3.15   Message Board

Besides student- and teacher-made bulletin boards, you should leave wall space open for the many charted stories and poems that you and your children will write together. Charted texts like these should be displayed at all times and changed as new ones are created. An appropriate activity for your young learners is to "read the room"; that is, they are invited to walk around the perimeter of the room, reading all of the displayed charted texts that they have helped to create. Wall space will also be used for the calendar, weather chart, rules for the class, and the "helper" poster. No doubt, you will change your classroom arrangement as new needs arise and as you learn about your students and how to organize their learning opportunities.

◼ YOU TRY IT

Arranging Your Classroom

Your task, for this You Try It feature, is to draw a diagram of an early elementary classroom floor plan that you believe would allow you to be an effective teacher of Early Readers. Your drawing will resemble those that interior designers create showing furniture placement for homeowners. Think about how your classroom arrangement reflects your philosophy of learning. Bring your diagram to class for sharing with your peers.

Some factors to consider:

- Furniture placement,
- Traffic flow,
- Comfort,
- Use of wall space,
- Organization of materials,
- Storage,
- Areas for centers,
- Reading spaces,
- Decorative accents that affect the environment, and
- Your desk placement.

Learning Centers

Learning centers are areas of your classroom that contain materials and activities that you have assembled in order to teach or extend the skills or concepts your children need to learn. You may be familiar with learning centers from your own elementary education years. Perhaps your primary classrooms had a writing center where you could compose stories, a math center where there were activities like Cuisenaire rods to manipulate, or a science center that invited you to perform simple science experiments. You may recognize that learning centers require active participation in small social settings (four to six students), supporting the social constructivist stance that we are encouraging (Morrow, 1997). Centers should have activities that range in difficulty from easy to challenging so that all children can succeed regardless of their development. Heterogeneous grouping is one of the advantages of center time—children of varying abilities and developmental stages work together. While students are involved in centers, you are able to work with students who are more homogeneous, in terms of their literacy learning strengths and needs, as the rest of the students are actively engaged.

When you develop a center, remember to ask yourself these questions:

- What is the purpose of this center?
- What kinds of activities will students engage in at this center?
- How can I ensure that each child who participates will experience success?
- How will children independently manage the activities at the center?
- What materials are needed?
- How will the materials be stored?
- If children create products at the centers, what will happen to those products? For example, will they go into a portfolio? Will the items be displayed on a bulletin board? Will I look at what the children create?
- Will there be record keeping at the centers and/or some type of assessment? If so, what will that be?
- How will I introduce the center, demonstrate its use, and monitor students' progress at the center?

Keep these questions in mind as we consider just three literacy centers for classrooms of Early Readers: the ABC Center, a technology center, and the Library Corner.

The ABC Center.   The ABC Center is appropriate for kindergarteners and early first graders to help children explore and talk about letters of the alphabet, including the letter names, sounds, and associated pictures or words. In this center, you could place both upper- and lowercase magnetic letters for children to manipulate. A posted class list with each of your students' names carefully printed is effective for children to use as they spell their classmate's names with the magnetic letters. Another good idea for the ABC Center is to place words that children are learning on posters in the center. For example, the words *I, a, am, the, like, see,* and *you* placed in the center could be compelling models for your students to copy using the magnetic letters or pencils and paper

You should include many alphabet books that help children to associate letters with pictures that begin with the letters/sounds they are learning. Some alphabet books have accompanying cassette tapes that your students can listen to with headphones. Other alphabet books are written all about one letter (e.g., The *B* book, with pictures of bumblebees, balls, baskets, books, etc.). Single-letter books allow children who are at the very beginning stages of literacy the opportunity to "read" books about letters and experience success.

In addition, writing materials should be available at the center so that children can practice writing the letters. The writing materials might include various kinds and colors of paper (lined and unlined), pencils, markers, and crayons. Think about providing small chalkboards and chalk, dry erase boards, easels with water colors, or even small sand trays for your students who are just starting to experiment with printing or tracing the letters. Can you see how the ABC Center could be constructed so that all children can participate and succeed no matter where they are on the literacy developmental continuum?

Technology topic: The technology center.   You will, no doubt, be afforded one or more computers in your classroom for use with your Early Readers. You will have to decide how you will use technology and how it fits into your philosophy of literacy teaching and learning. Our position is that technology is a valuable tool for enhancing literacy learning but it is just a tool; it does not replace either the roles of the teacher or books in the classroom.

Of course, technology must be integrated into your teaching as the definition of literacy continues to expand and change along with technological advances. Leu (2001) asserts that the central question we must ask is "How do we teach children to *continuously become literate?'* That is, "How do we help children learn to learn the new literacies that will continuously emerge?" (p. 568). Helping your students learn the new literacies can be encouraged at the technology center in your classroom.

For Early Readers, learning the keyboard is one of the skills that you will want to support. Software programs such as *Type to Learn Jr.* are designed for K–2 children to learn keyboarding competence as well as practice with the alphabet, high-frequency words, and sentences. As you already know, working at a computer station in a word processing program is motivating for children, especially for those who find transcribing difficult. When we discussed writing aloud, you learned that composing is much easier for young children than transcribing. Computers make the challenge of transcribing much easier once children possess keyboarding proficiency.

Teachers use the Internet to set up e-mail buddies for their students, engage in website projects, and conduct author studies. Let's say you are making your way through as many Eric Carle books as you can find; your students' favorite is *The Very Hungry Caterpillar* (1969) and they want to know more about the author. If you go to *http://www.eric-carle.com*, you and your students will find information about Eric Carle, lists of his books with each book cover pictured, and a museum of his picture book art. You can even sign up for free mailings. Many children's authors have such websites and they provide a wealth of engaging information to extend your literature studies. Creative teachers, like you, design activities that use technology to facilitate the learning of their students (Valmont, 2000). For example, Figure 3.16 lists websites that support Early Readers' learning of the alphabet as researched and suggested by Duffelmeyer (2002).

Be cautious and choosy if you are given the responsibility of selecting literacy learning software programs for your students and make sure you are able to preview the materials before you purchase. Remember that programs that offer only drill and practice are no more helpful than copious amounts of paper-and-pencil worksheets. Effective software programs are open ended, flexible, and allow for choice (Jongsma, 2001).

Connect to the Companion Website at *http://www.prenhall.com/lenski* to link to the following sites:

ABC Order
Helps children work on the order of the alphabet through color, objects, and sound.
http://www.learningplanet.com/act/abcorder.htm

Animated ABC's
See both upper- and lowercase letters as well as accompanying, associative pictures.
http://www.enfagrow.com/language008.html

These are the Letters of the Alphabet
Pictures and sentences with words beginning with certain letters appear, almost like an alphabet book.
http://pacificnet.net/~cmoore/alphabet/index.htm

Alphabet Soup
Letters float in bowls of soup at this fun learning site.
http://kayleigh.tierranet.com/abc.htm

Morris Farm Alphabet
First graders visit a farm, then build a website about their experiences.
http://www.lincoln.midcoast.com/~wps/jackson/alphabet.htm

FIGURE 3.16   ABC Websites

The Library Corner.   The Library Corner is a center that will always be in place in your classroom. Of course, it will change and evolve throughout the year, but wonderful children's books will always be available to your students in a welcoming, warm environment. Some of the elements of a cozy Library Corner from which you can choose include plenty of books in many different genres, including fiction and nonfiction; magazines, newspapers, encyclopedias, and dictionaries; posters; books made by the children; shelves and baskets for the books; a reading rug, pillows, stuffed animals, beanbag chairs, cushions, a comfortable chair or sofa; a lamp; and puppets or a felt board for acting out stories. The inviting atmosphere of the Library Corner addresses the affective domain of learning in that you are creating pleasing, comforting associations with books and literacy for the students in your classroom.

Of course, these are just three centers for you to think about. You will, no doubt, construct others in your classroom of Early Readers such as listening centers, writing centers, and centers that revolve around topics you are studying.

Selecting Materials

In other sections of this book, we make specific recommendations about text choices for your interactions with children while reading aloud, and during shared, guided, and independent reading. However, here we will make some generalizations about the texts you select for Early Readers. In their article entitled "What Makes a Good Book?" Giorgis et al. (2000) observe the following: Good books are those that withstand the test of time; relate to common experiences; explore family relationships; extend readers' knowledge; inspire readers to follow their dreams; and invite readers back again and again. You should collect trade books for children that meet those criteria. Trade books are books that are not textbooks and are separate whole texts unto themselves; they include fiction books like *Corduroy* by Don Freeman and nonfiction books like *The Amazing Life of Benjamin Franklin* by James Giblin. As we noted for the classroom library, you should select from a wide variety of fiction and nonfiction and choose from such genres as folk and fairy tales, poetry, mysteries, fact-based books, and biographies.

Early Readers need plenty of predictable books, meaning books that allow them to predict what will happen next. Predicting not only helps in their comprehension, but underpins their ability to predict what word would come next as they read beginning texts. Let's say you're using the predictable book *If You Give a Mouse a Cookie* (Numeroff, 1985) as a read-aloud. Once children get the idea that the mouse is gradually taking more and more advantage of the boy in the story, they will enjoy making predictions each time you stop and say, "Now, what do you think that clever mouse will want next?"

Your children will also benefit from repetitive texts—those that have a pattern with repeated words. Repetitive books allow children to repeat the words along with you during shared reading, memorizing the phrases with you and when they pick up the book on their own. *I Went Walking* (Williams, 1990), an engaging repetitive text, repeats the phrase "I went walking. What did you see?" throughout the story that young children love to chime in on as they quickly recognize the pattern. However, in addition to thinking about variety in content and genre, you must consider the range of difficulty in the texts you provide.

 Predictable texts allow for easy prediction about what might happen next. Repetitive texts repeat phrases throughout. How do these two types of texts support Early Readers?

A text gradient.   In terms of difficulty levels, your goal is to create a text gradient, which means that you should collect trade books that could be placed on a scale of complexity that extends from very easy to challenging for the readers in your classroom. "Creating a text gradient means classifying books along a continuum based on the combination of variables that support and confirm readers' strategic actions and offer the problem-solving opportunities that build the reading process" (Fountas & Pinnell, 1996, p. 113). When Early Readers are given texts at just the right level of difficulty—not too hard nor too easy—they are able to move forward in terms of their literacy development (Clay, 1991). Remember this: There are books that every child can read and feel empowered by; you will be gifting your students when you find those books and put them in their hands (Neuman & Celano, 2001).

Difficulty level depends on the child; it is not inherent to the book. On the other hand, certain criteria can help you decide the complexity of a book. Figure 3.17 lists some criteria to consider.

Please remember that you are leveling *books* not *children*. The leveled book baskets can be available in the Library Corner for independent reading as well as available for use with children during guided instruction.

Leveled texts are important for teaching young children because they allow you to match children with books they are able to read. Explain why leveled texts are just one type of reading material that you should provide to students.

Nonleveled children's fiction and nonfiction.

In addition to the leveled texts in your classroom for guided and independent reading, you should collect many copies of books that are notable children's literature as well as books that are factual and support the units you are studying in social studies and science. All of these books can be available for children during independent reading and Library Corner time and can serve as resources for their writing projects. Some of your fiction collection will be picture books, others chapter books for your more advanced readers. Chapter books are just like they sound: books that are longer in length and divided into chapters (e.g., *Charlie and the Chocolate Factory* by Roald Dahl, 1964). By second grade, children are extremely anxious to read chapter books, so be sure to gather chapter books that vary in difficulty from undemanding to more challenging.

You can also create materials for your Early Readers by charting poems, stories, and informational texts during shared reading and write-aloud activities. In addition, you should make books with and for the emergent readers in your classroom. Among the kinds of emergent texts that can be created by you and your students are alphabet books.

Making ABC books for children.

If you teach emergent readers (typically kindergarteners or early first graders), you can make simple books from plain or colored heavy paper that you staple together at the spine. If you intend to use the books for more than one year, laminate the pages for durability and consider using a spiral plastic binding. You might enlist the help of parent volunteers to assist with the book-making process.

- Look at the cover.
- Consider the length of the book.
- Examine the size of the print.
- Take into account the number of words per page.
- Look at the illustrations to decide how much they support the text.
- Notice the predictability of the language and the story.
- Count the number of high-frequency words.
- Skim the book for repetition of words or rhyming words.
- Judge the complexity of the story.
- Think about the interest level and familiarity of the topic to your students.

FIGURE 3.17 Determining Whether a Book Is "Easy" or "Hard"

ABC books are often the first type that you construct with students who need this support. Print the letters of the alphabet (upper- and lowercase) separately on each of the 26 pages of the book. Cut out or let the child cut out pictures that start with the letter on the page. You can buy inexpensive phonics workbooks with black-line alphabet pictures that are legal to copy. You can also cut pictures from magazines for your ABC books as shown in Figure 3.18.

Make sure the child associates the right sound with the picture. For example, if you're trying to illustrate "G is for gorilla," make sure the child is not saying "G is for monkey." Allow the child to glue the pictures next to the letters. As the child participates in this construction process, talk about the letter you are working on and have the child try to think of other words that start with the same letter. When finished, the children will have their own alphabet books that they can read and use as a reference to reinforce the names of the letters, the formation of the letters, and the associated sounds. This ABC book becomes an effective and supportive learning tool for emergent readers.

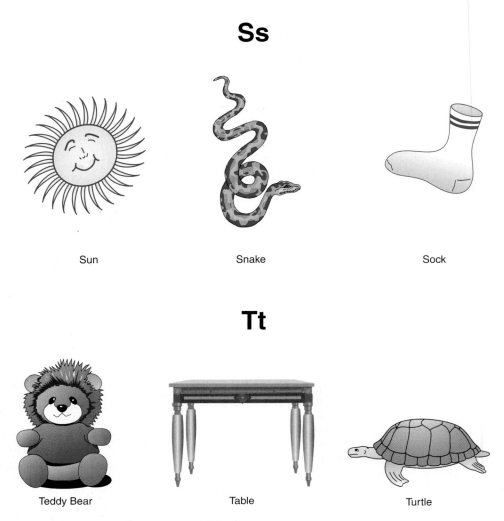

Ss

Sun   Snake   Sock

Tt

Teddy Bear   Table   Turtle

FIGURE 3.18   Samples From an ABC Book

CONNECTIONS: WHAT'S NEXT?

Teaching in whole-group settings is how you should begin your school year when you teach Early Readers. You should incorporate opportunities for many read-alouds and shared reading experiences, carefully selecting texts for each group of students that you teach. You should also make sure you are operating within the students' zone of proximal development by assessing the success of your literacy interactions. As you read aloud and use shared texts, you need to explicitly teach comprehension strategies such as building prior knowledge, predicting, picturing, learning about genres and story structure, and coaching children to self-monitor their comprehension as they read. Organizing your classroom in a purposeful and intentional way will further the literacy goals you and your students set for their learning.

In the next chapter you will learn approaches for teaching Early Readers in small groups. A large portion of your literacy time will be spent working with small groups as you instruct Early Readers in the strategies necessary to become effective, fluent readers. Figure 3.19 reminds you of where we have been: teaching Early Readers in whole groups, and where are going: teaching Early Readers in small-group settings.

Figure 3.19 reviews the developmental approach to reading that we are taking in this book. Notice that the darker shaded areas represent what you've learned in the chapter you've just read. The lighter shading indicates what you'll learn in the next chapter.

FIGURE 3.19   A Developmental Approach to the Teaching of Reading

	Early Readers	**Interpretive Readers**	**Critical Readers**
Theories underscored as readers develop:	Social Constructivism Psycholinguistic Critical Transactional	Social Constructivism Psycholinguistic Critical Transactional	Social Constructivism Psycholinguistic Critical Transactional
Whole-group instruction through:	• Read-alouds • Shared texts • Comprehension strategies • Working with words	• Read-alouds • Basals • Literature-based models • Word-building strategies • Comprehension strategies	• Read-alouds • Common texts (e.g., basals, anthologies, trade books) • Comprehension strategies • Vocabulary instruction and word analysis • Researching • Critical reading • Reading content-area texts • Studying and note-taking

continued

FIGURE 3.19   *Continued*

	Early Readers	Interpretive Readers	Critical Readers
Assessment ideas for whole group:	• Observations • Kidwatching • Anecdotal notation	• Portfolios • Open-ended questions • Rubrics	• Written retellings • Research projects • Interest inventories • Content-area histories • Cloze procedure
Small-group instruction through:	• Guided reading • Teaching for strategies • Fluency practice • Working with words	• Basal readers • Literature anthologies • Trade books • Guided silent reading • Literature circles • Inquiry groups	• Book clubs
Assessment ideas for small groups:	• Running Records • Retellings • Discussions with children	• Names test • Fluency checklist • Peer assessment • Inquiry rubric	• Student information card • Bio poem • "I Used to… But Now I…" poem • Observational checklist • Student self-assessment • Norm-referenced tests
Independent learning through:	• Independent reading • Reading/writing workshop • Making books • Reading the room	• Independent reading • Reading/writing workshop • Responding through writing • Reading logs	• Sustained silent reading and writing
Sociocultural contexts:	• Literacy partnerships with parents • Parents in the classroom • Home–school communication	• Reading/writing connection for life • Oral histories • Home literacy activities • Parent programs	• Parents as coaches • Funds of knowledge • Parent–student book clubs

FOR YOUR PORTFOLIO

ENTRY 3.1   *Creating the Learning Environment for Shared Reading*

INTASC Principle 5 states: *The teacher uses an understanding of individual and group motivation and behavior to create a learning environment that encourages positive social interaction, active engagement in learning, and self-motivation.*

For this portfolio entry, describe how you will, as a teacher of Early Readers, demonstrate the understandings outlined in INTASC Principle 5 when you create and conduct shared reading experiences. Base your response on your readings, discussions in class, and enacting and reflecting on a shared reading lesson. Discuss how the learning environment you create will influence the effectiveness of the lesson.

ENTRY 3.2   *The Morning Message*

IRA/NCTE Standard 6 states: *Students apply knowledge of language structure, language conventions (e.g., spelling and punctuation), media techniques, figurative language, and genre to create, critique, and discuss print and nonprint texts.*

When working with Early Readers one of the ways you will emphasize language and print conventions is through the creation of shared texts during writing aloud. A daily opportunity to write aloud is during the construction of the morning message.

For this entry, first explain what a morning message is and what purposes it serves in the classroom. Then, write a "simulated" morning message for a classroom of Early Readers. After you have created the message, describe *specific* features of language that you would point out to students as you co-construct the text with them. You might want to refer to Figures 3.4 and 3.5 for assistance with this portfolio entry.

◼◼◼ TO LEARN MORE ◢◣◼ ▮▮▮ ▮▮▮ ◼

Helpful Websites

Visit our Companion Website at *http://www.prenhall.com/lenski* to link to the following sites:

Companion Website

Reading Aloud

> Find out more about this important practice.
> *http://www.mcps.k12.md.us/curriculum/english/read_aloud.html*

More Reading Aloud

> Explores more read-aloud strategies.
> *http://www.education-world.com/a_curr/curr081.shtml*

Learning Centers

> Lists different types of centers for the elementary classroom.
> *http://vpsd6.vrml.k12.la.us:8000/~monah/Centers.htm*

Classroom Centers

> Provides printable centers that you can use in your classroom.
> *http://www.teachingheart.net/LC.htm*

Shared Reading

> Explores shared reading.
> *http://www.mcps.k12.md.us/curriculum/english/shared_reading.html*

Big Books

> Features Big Books published by Dominie Press.
> *http://www.dominie.com*

chapter **4**

Instructing Early Readers in Small Groups

Essential Learning Questions

- How can you effectively use a basal series to teach reading?
- In what ways will you use quality children's literature in your primary classroom?
- What are the benefits of using leveled texts in your literacy instructional program?
- How can you successfully match children with books?
- What is guided reading and how can you use it for primary reading instruction?
- What are some ways to help your young readers become *strategic* readers?
- What are some effective strategies to help students build fluency?

The theme of this section on teaching Early Readers in small groups could actually serve as a premise for this entire textbook: Children need and deserve to be provided with books that they are able to read. This statement may seem very obvious to you, one that all teachers should understand as a matter of course. In some classrooms, however, children are presented with texts that are too difficult for them. This results in discouraged and frustrated readers, and readers who are not making progress.

Children cannot get better at reading by trying to read books that are too difficult for them. Therefore, when you are a teacher, selecting appropriate materials becomes one of your most important tasks. The International Reading Association's position statement (2000) maintains the following: "Children have a right to access a wide variety of books and other reading materials in classroom, school, and community libraries" (p. 6). How can you ensure this right and choose the kinds of texts that are appropriate for Early Readers?

In Chapter 3, we thought about and analyzed teaching strategies for instructing young children in whole-group settings. In this chapter, we examine ways you can effectively teach Early Readers in small groups. Here you learn about selecting materials for instruction, managing guided reading and other techniques for grouping children, teaching comprehension strategies, and helping children build fluency.

SELECTING MATERIALS

What factors will influence your selection of materials for Early Readers? For some of you, your school district will have already made many decisions for you. Others of you could be at the opposite end of the continuum and find yourselves responsible for assembling all of the materials that you think are appropriate. We hope that no matter where you are on that scale, your first questions will be "How can I support my young readers' strengths and needs?" and "How can I select materials that my students find interesting?" With these questions underpinning our discussion, let's talk about selecting materials such as basal readers, children's literature, and leveled books for small-group instruction in primary classrooms.

Basal Readers

Many of you may remember using a basal (pronounced /*bay´ sull*/) reader in elementary school and progressing though the series from one level to the next as well as writing out answers to exercises in the accompanying workbooks. Basals are collections of materials produced for each grade level in elementary and middle schools that include children's copies of anthology-like texts, various supplementary materials such as workbooks, teachers' manuals, and sometimes trade books, Big Books, and manipulatives. Basal readers have been the primary instructional tool for teaching reading to elementary school children for the past 50 years (Winograd, Wixson, & Lipson, 1989). (Basal reading programs for older students are discussed later in this text.)

The fundamental learning assumption that undergirds most basal programs is that children can best be taught to read by progressing through a series of predetermined, sequenced learning steps using story selections from the basal and followed up by exercises in the supplementary workbooks. The assessment measures used to place children in certain levels of the basal series are often pencil-and-paper tasks such as reading a short passage, then answering questions about the story. Sometimes, children are placed in a certain level simply because they happen to be in that grade. Our position in this textbook is that Early Readers progress more readily with teacher guidance during guided reading using leveled trade books. However, if you do not have access to leveled texts in your future classroom, we want you to understand effective ways to use basals.

Using basal readers effectively.

Basal readers can be used effectively in the classroom when you are purposeful and selective in your use of basal materials as just one component of the collection of instructional materials you have available. Other instructional materials include wonderful children's literature, trade books, charted children's dictation, poetry, and songs you use to help young children read.

An advantage of basal readers as a resource for you is the wide variety of stories and reading selections from which to choose. As a beginning teacher of reading, you should understand how to use basal materials because of their widespread use and influence in schools; they are, in fact, still the major resource for beginning reading instruction in primary classrooms (e.g., Baumann & Heubach, 1996; Hoffman et al., 1998).

One way Fawson and Reutzel (2000) suggest for using basals effectively is to consider the stories in primary-grade basal readers on a range of difficulty, not necessarily in the order in which they appear in the series as determined by the publishers. Figure 4.1 is a sample of a list developed by a group of specially trained teachers who ranked stories from five basal publishers in order of difficulty, A–E. (The full chart can be found on the Companion Website at *http://www.prenhall.com/lenski*) If you use a basal, and don't have individual, multiple copies of trade books that have been leveled for you, such a chart could help you decide how to match children to basal stories as the children's reading proficiencies develop. In doing so, you will be offering children selections that provide just the right amount of challenge and support.

Besides finding stories to meet each child's unique strengths and needs from the basal series your school has chosen, you are also charged with making decisions about how to use the supplementary materials such as workbooks, tests, and the teacher's manual. You do not have to assign each story in the basal text, or all worksheets, or complete every activity suggested in the teacher's manual. You are the decision maker in the classroom and you should use good judgment with these resources, considering the guidance given to be recommendations rather than requirements (Winograd, 1989).

Publisher	Basal Title	Story Title	Author	Level
Scholastic	Beginning Literacy	In the City	S. Pasternac	**A**
Silver Burdett Ginn	Readables	Together	G. E. Lyon	**B**
Harcourt Brace	Picture Perfect	What I See	H. Keller	**C**
Scott Foresman	My Favorite Foodles	Hello, Mouse!	L. Hayward	**D**
Houghton Mifflin	Hello	The Foot Book	Dr. Seuss	**E**

From Fawson, P. C., & Reutzel, D. R. (2000). But I only have a basal: Implementing guided reading in the early grades. The Reading Teacher, 54, 84–97. Copyright by the International Reading Association. All rights reserved.

FIGURE 4.1   A Sample of Leveled Basal Stories for K–2 Students

Basal readers are most effective when used in an intentional and considered way as only one resource in a comprehensive reading program. Remember these guidelines when using a basal series with Early Readers:

- Ensure that your students are able to read and understand the selections you have chosen.
- Consider children's interests, strengths, and needs as readers when you decide which selections to use and which to leave out.
- Because you are the teacher, you do not need the teacher's manual to tell you what to do or provide questions and answers from each story or give you preset lessons that you must follow in a predetermined sequence.
- Not all children need to be taught the skills listed in sequence in the texts. If children already know those skills, or need other, more important skills, you must make those instructional decisions.
- Some workbook pages or worksheets may be thoughtfully prepared and provide excellent practice for your students' developing reading and writing abilities. Others may simply be busywork. It is up to you decide which of the worksheets to use and which to leave unused.
- Some prereading suggestions as well as some of the follow-up activities in the teacher's manual are engaging, creative, and worthy of your students' time. Others may be redundant, unnecessary, or simply take too much of your valuable literacy instructional time. Remember, what children need most during reading instruction is *time to read*.
- Supplement your students' reading materials with plenty of trade books and genuine, full-length children's literature.
- Use authentic assessment techniques such as teacher observations, read and retells, Running Records, and reading discussions with children. Do not depend on the assessments supplied by the series' authors to give you a total picture of children's reading abilities and needs.

Basal series have been compared to cookbooks in which recipes for teaching and assessing reading reside. Excellent teachers decide which recipes to use, which to modify completely, and which to leave out.

Concerns about basal readers.   Those whose special field of study is the teaching of best practices in reading instruction have questioned the overuse of basal readers in many classrooms. For example, some teachers have overrelied on the teacher's

Advice for New Teachers

Basal Decisions

Dear Derek,

You told us that you leveled the stories within the basal series in your second-grade classroom. What other important decisions do you make about the use of the basal series?

Dear New Teacher,

The school district chose the basal series for our schools and I use it as one tool for my developing second-grade readers. Here are some deliberate decisions I make:

- **Story selection:** I don't try to "get through" every story. Some of the stories interest my students and some don't. Some are too difficult. I select stories based on my students' needs and interests and supplement the basal with leveled texts and other trade books.

- **Teacher's manual:** The teacher's manual sometimes offers wonderful teaching ideas and suggestions. Again, it's just another instructional tool for me. I don't need to follow all of the steps recommended in the manual. For example, we don't spend a lot of time looking at the vocabulary words from the story ahead of the reading. Students find that boring and it takes away from the time they have for reading. We use more interesting vocabulary strategies, or we study vocabulary after reading when there is a context for the children to begin to understand the new words.

- **Workbooks:** I carefully select pages from the accompanying workbooks that I feel cause students to think and use multiple reading and writing strategies. I tell parents in my first-of-the-year meeting with them not to expect that all worksheets will be completed. Instead, I tell them that what they will see coming home is many pieces of authentic, original pieces of writing that will show their children's development over time as readers and writers.

manual as the primary guide for instruction in the literacy classroom. The lessons, skills, and application opportunities have been prewritten for the teacher. This practice puts the basal textbook authors at the center of instructional decisions rather than the teacher and the needs of his students.

In addition, assessment in basal programs often occurs after reading rather than before. Instead of using assessment measures to find out about children's strengths, needs, and interests, then planning instruction around those findings, basal programs often approach assessment as something teachers should do after reading, to "test" children on their learning. Thus, rather than assessment informing instruction, assessment is reduced to test giving and taking.

Another criticism that has occurred concerning basals is that when children read from a basal, they are reading from a collection of excerpted stories. The selections are typically lifted out of longer books and are incomplete and less compelling than the originals. Further, an anthology-like basal textbook denies children the excitement of holding and reading from a complete "real book" as they engage in reading.

Children's Literature

No discussion of reading in the primary grades would be complete without the inclusion of wonderful children's literature. Children working in small groups should have opportunities to select books from your classroom and school libraries that are beautifully illustrated and written by our most treasured authors. These books may first be presented to students at read-alouds and during shared reading, then they are set on shelves for your small groups of Early Readers to enjoy. When you read aloud to your students each day, these books develop into children's hit parade of books that they want to hold in their own hands so they can study the pictures and try to read the words themselves.

Your library should also include books that represent cultures of our pluralistic society. Norton (2001) writes: "Positive multicultural literature has been used effectively to help readers identify cultural heritages, understand sociological change, respect the values of minority groups, raise aspirations, and expand imagination and creativity" (p. 2).

You also want to remember the "old favorites." We are surprised by the number of children we talk to in schools today who have never met *The Three Little Pigs, The Gingerbread Man,* or *The Three Bears.* One way to combine a study of the old favorites with multicultural study is to look at familiar tales that appear in many cultures of the world. For example, although many Americans are familiar with the French adaptation of *Cinderella,* the Cinderella tale is found in countless versions such as Native American (*The Rough-Faced Girl,* Martin & Shannon, 1992), Chinese (*Yeh-Shen,* Louie, 1982), and Egyptian (*The Egyptian Cinderella,* Chimo, 1989).

Literature circles.   Even young children can begin to enjoy the language and art of children's books through the use of literature circles. Literature circles are composed of heterogeneous, small groups of children who read the same book for purposes of enjoyment, discussion, and response. Perhaps some of you have belonged to Book Clubs where you all read the same book, then get together once a month to discuss the book. What fun it is to listen to one another's interpretation of the same text. This is how literature circles can operate in primary classrooms as long as the teacher is there to provide the structure and guidance children need. A full discussion of literature circles is provided later in this text.

Listening to books on tape.   Sometimes accessing the more difficult language of "real" literature can be problematic for Early Readers. One way to scaffold their ability to do so is through providing books that have accompanying tape recordings. Not only are children able to read silently along with the taped reader, but they hear fluent, expressive reading that conveys the full meaning of the story. Sometimes books on tape are even complemented by music, adding another layer of interpretive support. As a teacher, you can gather children around a table to listen to a tape-recorded version of a book. Or, children can use headphones, which allows for "quiet listening" while other students are engaged in additional literacy activities.

Partner reading.   Another approach for encouraging students' access to the language of children's literature is through partner reading. In this approach, students sit side by side, either looking at the same book or two copies of the same book, and take turns reading to each other. Sometimes, teachers pair more capable readers with those who need some help so that more understanding takes place within the partnership. Opitz and Rasinski (1998) describe the benefits of partner reading: "[Partner]

Visit the online journal in Chapter 4 on our Companion Website at *www.prenhall.com/lenski* to answer these questions. Save your answers to your hard drive or to a disk to compile an online journal.

Multicultural literature should be a part of your classroom all year long. Why is this important?

reading is one of the most powerful ways to provide students with support" (p. 52). They report that students' comprehension and level of enjoyment can be accelerated through partner reading. Ultimately, the goal of learning to read is the enjoyment and satisfaction of reading.

Leveled Texts

You may have noticed in Figure 4.1 that the stories from the basal series were listed in order of level of difficulty. (Sometimes teachers use a letter-leveling system [A, B, C, etc.] as is done in Figure 4.1; others use numbers [1, 2, 3, etc.]; still others use a color-coding system.) Leveled texts can be placed in baskets or book boxes with colored stickers that allow you to keep them organized by level. For example, yellow stickers might denote emergent level; green, early readers; red, transitional; and blue, fluent reader level.

As a reminder, when we refer to *leveled texts* we are referring to books or stories that are arranged on a continuum from easy to more challenging, enabling teachers to match children to books (Fountas & Pinnell, 1999). For the purpose of guided instruction, as in guided reading, we recommend the use of leveled texts.

Benchmark books are individual books representative of each of the levels used in primary classrooms. How could a teacher use a collection of benchmark books?

Benchmark books. Some teachers establish benchmark books for their students. Benchmark books are individual, leveled texts that represent each of the levels. Teachers use these "benchmarks" to keep track of where individual students are on a reading development continuum. "Benchmark books are typically trade books that will be used exclusively for assessment purposes and represent a variety of grade level reading materials" (Fawson & Reutzel, 2000, p. 85).

Leveled texts will certainly not be the only reading resources you use with your children, but they will be the primary texts when you are providing guided instruction in small groups.

Why use leveled texts? When children are presented with books to read that are too difficult for them, they struggle through the reading, ending up losing the meaning of the passage as they get stuck on individual words. Reading becomes a laborious, painful affair for the child and the teacher. The process of reading—accessing the three cueing systems while self-monitoring and continually asking "Does this make sense?"—simply becomes too hard if the text is too difficult. As a teacher, you need to supply the children in your classroom with texts that they are able to read comfortably with relative ease, just as you do when you select a book.

Let's say you are going on a vacation to Florida and you are shopping for a book to take along. Do you choose a book on astrophysics in the 21st century? Or, do you select a novel that catches your interest because you like the genre, the author, and know it will be fairly easy to read and enjoy comfortably? Allington (2001a) says that "[if] we've made any mistake [in teaching], it's underestimating the importance of easy reading. I don't know why hard reading has gotten to be such an honor in schools, but performance levels and interest in reading are not shown to improve because of hard reading" (pp C1–C2).

How will I match children with books? Like all instructional decisions, this question is answered by assessment—by figuring out what the child can do without your help. Therefore, you should first get to know the child and make some informed hunches about where you think the child is in terms of literacy development. Taking this hunch as a starting place, you can select a handful of books that the child might be able to read.

For example, perhaps you are a first-grade teacher and you have been observing David during the beginning weeks of school. You have noticed that during shared reading he chimes in along with the other children in choral-reading fashion and has been able to come up to the charted stories and find some frequently occurring words like *the, can,* and *my*. However, you have also noticed that other words have caused him difficulty: *should, said,* and *they*.

In addition, when you clap out sounds of words to help develop segmentation of syllables, David has trouble with this activity. Therefore, when you sit down with David to assess his oral reading you select three books that are in the "easy" range but that might provide some challenge so that you can see what he can do. The three books that you choose are *Can You See Me?* (Lee, 1999), an emergent, level 1 book; *Water* (Canizares & Chanko, 1998), a level 2 book; and *Uncle Buncle's House* (Crowley, 1986), a level 3 book.

Because you feel that David might be able to read the book *Water,* you start with that one. You introduce the book to him, reading the title and pointing out the repetition of the word *water* throughout the book. The text proceeds in a predictable fashion: *A river is water. This is too. Rain is water. This is too,* etc. David begins reading with purpose and enthusiasm. However, you soon realize that this text is too hard. He struggles with the word *water* each time, even though you told him the word ahead of time in the book introduction and it appears throughout the text. He begins to exhibit signs of frustration. So, instead of even considering using the book *Uncle Buncle,* you pick up the book *Can You See Me?* This text has high support for the reader by cueing the change in each sentence with a change in the illustrations. The text progresses as follows:

> *Can you see my hair?, Can you see my eyes?,* etc. until the last sentence reads: *Can you see me?*

David rapidly catches on to the pattern in this repetitive text and proudly marches through it, reading with expression and commenting on the illustrations. The only problem he encounters happens on the last page when he reads, "Can you see my. . . " expecting the pattern to recur. However, he looks up at you and says, "No that word's not *my* is it?" You are pleased because he's monitoring his own reading by noticing that *me* is not the word *my*. Further, you have discovered through listening to David read *Can You See Me?* that level 1 books are where you need to begin reading instruction with him.

Through informal reading sessions like the one just described you can determine where to begin reading instruction with each student in your classroom and the level of books that your individual students need—books that they feel empowered by and are able to read.

A word of caution is needed, however. Just because you may determine that a book is "too easy" or "too hard" for a particular child, you may later find that you were wrong. So, use leveling criteria with the knowledge that they are not always accurate for every child.

Calculating the difficulty of a text.

A key component involved in matching children to books is calculating the difficulty level of a book *for a particular child*. Remember, what is difficult for one child may be easy for another. Therefore, difficulty level is always relative and it is not inherent in the text; *it depends on the reader*.

Here's how you calculate the accuracy of a child's reading and then transform that number into an understanding of the difficulty of that text for that particular child. First, take the total number of words in the text minus the number of errors. Then divide that number by the total number of words in the text, which will result in the percent accuracy of the reading.

(Total words − Number of errors) ÷ Number of words in text = Percent accuracy

Difficulty level of a text for a child:
  0–89% = Frustration level (but may be fine for shared reading or read-alouds)
  90–94% = Instructional level (this is the difficulty level of the books that the child should be reading for guided reading)
  95–100% = Easy level (this is the difficulty level of texts that the child should be reading *most of the time* for independent reading)

FIGURE 4.2   Reading Difficulty Level of Texts

Let's think about first-grader David again. If you had completed a Running Record on his reading of the book *Water*, you would have noticed that he miscued six times. That means that out of 37 words in the whole text, he missed 6. You could already tell by listening to him read that the book was too difficult for him but the formula shown in Figure 4.2 can be applied to show you more clearly how reading accuracy determines difficulty level. Using the formula for the accuracy of David's reading of the book *Water*, (37 − 6 = 31; 31/37 = 84%) accuracy, you can see that this book was at the Frustration Level for him. You knew that to be true as you saw his frustration and you made the decision to provide him with an easier book.

One caveat is appropriate here. Sometimes the accuracy calculation is not indicative of whether the child should be reading a particular book. You have to use your own judgment as a responsive teacher. Further, when helping children choose appropriately challenging books, teachers must always be gentle (have another book ready to suggest), tactful (never embarrass a child in front of classmates), and flexible (pay attention to a child's interest in a specific topic, therefore, *needing* to read a book even if it is too difficult).

Paying attention to the difficulty level of particular texts for particular students is one of your primary tools for matching children to books. When children have a guide, someone who can mediate the reading event for them, they can be presented with texts at the Instructional Level, that is, the level at which they are able to read with 90% to 94% accuracy. These types of texts are the ones you will provide students when you are conducting guided reading.

MANAGING GUIDED READING

There are different models of guided reading, but most involve a teacher working with a group of three to six children who are processing texts in similar ways and are able to read books at the same level of difficulty. When children engage in guided reading, each child reads the whole text to herself with the goal of reading increasingly challenging books over time. Guided reading is the bridge between shared reading and independent reading. In guided reading, children receive the instruction, support, and coaching they need to become independent, strategic readers (see Figure 4.3).

Derek conducts a guided reading group.

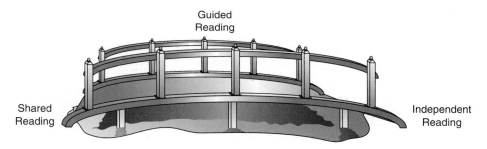

FIGURE 4.3   Guided Reading as a Bridge

Guided reading is the focal point of reading instruction for your Early Readers. Although guided reading is essential, it is just one part of your comprehensive, balanced literacy program, which should include reading aloud and shared and independent reading; in other words reading to, with, and by children (Mooney, 1990).

Guided reading is a bridge between shared reading and independent reading. Explain this metaphor.

Formats for Guided Reading

Different formats can be used during a guided reading session for Early Readers that involve more or less teacher support, depending on the needs of your readers. Figure 4.4 outlines a suggested guided reading lesson for young children. Note in the figure the role of the teacher and what the student group does during guided reading time. Note that students do not engage in round-robin reading. That is, they do not go around the circle, one reading a paragraph while the others listen. We believe that guided reading provides much more effective practice than round-robin reading by allowing students to read a whole text or passage by themselves.

Component	Teacher	Students
Brief book introduction	• Reads title • Takes students on a brief "picture walk" • Draws attention to a few new words • Asks students to make predictions about book	• Participate in book introduction • Comment about connections to own lives • Look at pictures • Make predictions
First reading	• Monitors reading • Listens to individual readers • Offers help if needed	• Read silently or in quiet voices
Second reading (optional)	• Praises use of strategies • Asks individual children how they problem solved during reading	• Read through the book again • May participate in a choral reading of parts of the text
Responding to the book	• Invites conversation about the book • Asks if predictions came true • Makes informal assessment of comprehension of text	• Talk about the book • Discuss predictions • Make connections to own lives • Do a brief retelling
Focus lesson	• Decides on a particular strategy or concept to use as a focus lesson	• Participate in focus lesson • Practice strategy
Follow-up (optional)	• May invite students to extend reading through writing, art, or drama	• Take part in extension activities, if offered

FIGURE 4.4   Format for Guided Reading Lesson

As readers become able to read more difficult books, guided reading meetings begin to resemble book discussion groups, with less teacher support and more autonomy on the part of students. In guided reading the scaffolding analogy is again useful; as your students become more capable readers, they won't need your guidance as much and you will gradually remove your support (Pearson & Gallagher, 1983).

When working with Early Readers you will need to group children together to provide them the guidance they require; while some children are working with you, others in the class will be engaged in literacy center activities or independent reading. The children you group together should be processing text similarly and have similar reading strengths and needs, based on careful observations you have made. You should offer children texts that are at the cutting edge of their learning, that provide just the right amount of problem-solving opportunities without being too difficult.

Choosing Books for Guided Reading

Once you have assessed your Early Readers and decided who might work together well in small groups based on their strengths and needs, you then need to decide which texts to present to each group. Remember, children *need and deserve* to be provided with books that they are able to read. At the same time, books need to provide some challenge so that children learn to become problem solvers and strategic readers. Fountas and Pinnell (1996) state that "[g]uided reading takes advantage of social support and allows the teacher to operate efficiently, to work with the tension between ease and challenge that is necessary to support readers' moving forward in their learning" (p. 6).

You should create a text gradient within your classroom so that books can be readily matched to readers. That is, if you start collecting books now for your classroom library that range from very easy to challenging, you can more easily match readers to books and teach focus lessons within each session targeted to a particular group of readers.

Brown (2000) suggests using texts to scaffold children's literacy learning by supporting them in their changing zones of proximal development and providing a link between what they already know and what they do not yet know about the reading process. She believes that rather than championing one kind of text for beginning readers "it [is] compelling to treat text as scaffolding, it [means] using particular types of texts at particular points in students' reading development" (p. 296). Figure 4.5, developed by Brown, illustrates Early Readers' developing understandings about reading. By studying the information presented in the figure, you can draw inferences about the kinds of books children need at different times in their reading development.

Teachers help students choose books in their ZPD. What does this phrase mean: "right at the cutting edge of children's learning?"

Focus Lessons for Guided Reading

During a guided reading session, many teachers find it helpful to include a focus lesson that directs children's attention to a particular strategy, phonics skill, or comprehension aid. Figure 4.6 contains a list of ideas for focus lessons for your Early Readers during small-group, guided reading instruction.

During each guided reading session you should enact focus lessons that help your students notice new features of print and develop new strategies for reading. Assessment will be ongoing as children change and grow in their reading abilities; therefore, your groups will be dynamic and continually changing as children's needs change. In addition to choosing books and preparing focus lessons for guided reading, we also need to consider assessment and the dynamic grouping aspects of guided reading.

Assessing Students for Guided Reading

As you've learned, authentic assessment is the centerpiece of instruction; it allows teachers to see what children understand at the time of assessment, and guides teachers in deciding what children need to know next. Consequently, you need to set up a systematic plan for learning about the readers in your classroom. Children's strengths and needs continually change and invariably they surprise us. Out of the many assessment options available to you, three assessment measures are discussed here that yield valuable information about the reading progress and literacy learning processes of your students: Running Records, retellings, and discussions with children.

Classroom Assessment

Running Records.   As you've learned, Running Records are a notation system for recording students' reading behaviors and students' patterns of responding while reading. Although learning to take Running Records can be a daunting undertaking,

Running Records are notations you make while a child reads aloud. What can you learn from a Running Record?

Phase 1: Learning About Print
- Understands that print is used to construct meaning
- Developing knowledge of print conventions (e.g., concept of word)
- Developing knowledge of letter names and sounds
- Developing basic levels of phonological awareness (e.g., detecting rhymes, syllable awareness)
- Uses prior knowledge to construct meaning
- Developing basic comprehension strategies (e.g., predicting, inferencing)
- Developing knowledge about and appreciation for different types of text
- Increasing motivation to become literate
- Increasing motivation to read for pleasure and information
- Relies heavily on memory, pictures, context, and selected letter cues to read text

Phase 2: Breaking the Code
- Understands the alphabetic principle (i.e., letters map to sounds in words)
- Developing more advanced levels of phonological awareness (e.g., blending, segmentation)
- Developing knowledge of simple spelling patterns (e.g., blends, digraphs, phonograms)
- Developing sight word vocabulary (e.g., *said, come, was*)
- Developing knowledge of decoding strategies (e.g., blending, chunking)
- Uses prior knowledge to construct meaning
- Continuing development of basic comprehension strategies (e.g., predicting, inferencing)
- Establishing coordination of decoding and comprehension strategies
- Increasing motivation to become literate
- Increasing motivation to read for pleasure and information
- Relies heavily on knowledge of letter–sound correspondences to read text
- May read aloud in a halting manner
- May produce nonsense words when reading aloud

Phase 3: Going for Fluency
- Developing more advanced levels of phonological awareness (e.g., segmentation, deletion)
- Developing knowledge of more complex spelling patterns (e.g., phonograms, prefixes, suffixes)
- Increasing automaticity in word identification
- Increasing fluency and expression when reading aloud
- Using a chunking strategy to identify unfamiliar polysyllabic words
- Using prior knowledge to construct meaning
- Continuing development of comprehension strategies (e.g., predicting, inferencing)
- Developing more sophisticated comprehension strategies (e.g., reading to learn, monitoring understanding, summarizing)
- Increasing coordination of decoding and comprehension strategies
- Increasing motivation to read for pleasure and information

From p. 297 in Brown, K. J. (1999/2000, Dec.–Jan.). What kind of text: For whom and when? Textual scaffolding for beginning readers. The Reading Teacher, 53 (4), 292–307.

FIGURE 4.5 Developmental Reading Phases and Their Characteristics

you can teach yourself a sort of Running Records "shorthand" by engaging in the You Try It exercise that follows. Even if you create your own personal notational system for analyzing Early Readers' behaviors, such a system can help you understand your students better and help you make informed decisions as their reading teacher.

- Concepts about print, such as directionality, left-to-right sweep, noticing how print is placed on the page
- Strategies for figuring out unknown words, such as the "skip it and come back" strategy
- Phonics lessons, such as learning about word families and patterns of spelling in words
- Comprehension aids, such as a Think Aloud, in which the teacher models how she thinks about what is happening in the story as she reads
- Noticing and practicing high-frequency words
- Vocabulary work on words whose meanings are unfamiliar to children

FIGURE 4.6 Guided Reading Focus Lessons for Early Readers

YOU TRY IT

Learning More About Running Records

On the Companion Website you will find samples of Running Records based on the instructions in Clay's *Running Records for Classroom Teachers* (2000). Study the samples with a partner, discussing what you can learn about a child's reading behaviors by analyzing Running Records. Then, answer the questions concerning what you learned about the reading process from this exercise, and how using Running Records in your classroom could affect your teaching decisions.

Retellings. Retellings are just what they sound like—recountings of stories or books told by children so the teacher can evaluate comprehension. You say to the child, "Tell me about the story (or book) you just read." Teachers can judge whether the child understands the main point of the story, the sequence of events, details, vocabulary from the text, and genre knowledge. Retellings uncover whether the child retains the basic structure of a story if it is a narrative text and the main ideas and supporting details of expository (nonfiction) texts. Retellings can also convey whether the text proved too easy or too difficult for the reader. Figure 4.7 contains information that you might find helpful when asking children to do a retelling.

YOU TRY IT

Retelling Practice

For this exercise, each student should bring a children's book to class. Then, class members should pair up and take turns being teacher and student. One partner (the student) should read a passage of the children's book that the other partner (the teacher) brought. After reading the passage, the "teacher" should conduct a retelling, using the prompts listed in Figure 4.7 and making notes as if listening to an Early Reader. Then, partners switch roles. Discuss what you learned about retelling from this experiment, and what you could learn about Early Readers.

Discussions with children. In addition to using Running Records and retellings to inform you about your students and what they understand about reading, setting up periodic, individual conferences with children to learn about their reading development

When asking a child to do a retelling, the session should be brief, relaxed, and not like taking a test. Your evaluation of the child's comprehension should cover what the child has read so far in a text. The following prompts can begin a retelling:

- Tell me about the book.
- What happened in the story?
- Tell me about your favorite parts.
- Who were the people (or animals) in the story?
- Where did the story happen?
- What else do you remember?

When evaluating a student's comprehension by using a retelling procedure, consider the following elements. Was the child able to do the following?

- Tell the main idea of the text.
- Recall characters, events, or setting.
- Describe details from the book.
- Provide the sequence of the story.
- Use some of the wording or phrases from the text.
- Relate personally to the book, speaking about it with authority.
- Retell the story with little prompting. Or, did the child need a lot of reminders to "tell me more?"

FIGURE 4.7   Information for a Retelling

Teachers confer with children during one-on-one reading discussions. Why is finding out how children feel about themselves as readers important?

is also valuable. At these one-on-one conferences, you can engage children in discussion and discover what interests children have, the kinds of books they like to read, why they choose the books they do, which books they find difficult, and which they find easy.

You can also help your young readers set reading goals for themselves during individual conference discussions. For example, if Joey only likes nonfiction books about dinosaurs, perhaps you can suggest fictional stories with dinosaurs in them. Or, maybe you can key into his interest in science and help him discover other interesting science books that broaden his horizons beyond dinosaurs.

Another example of goal setting could involve helping a child choose books that are at an appropriate reading level so that she is not continually frustrated. You may have to teach her how to tell when a book looks like it will be "just right" such as "You'll know a book is just right when you look at the cover, know most of the words, understand most of the ideas, like the topic, or you have some prior knowledge of the subject."

Dynamic Grouping for Guided Reading

Teachers make decisions about how to group children for guided reading. What kinds of information do teachers collect to make grouping decisions?

Guided reading groups are flexible and dynamic; they change based on the needs of the students. You, the teacher, should keep records of children's progress and needs and reconfigure your groups based on this information. "Any particular grouping is a hypothesis that is continually being tested" (Fountas & Pinnell, 1996, p. 99). Some teachers find it helpful to keep charts that record each child's placement in various groups to ensure that children are changing groups often and have the opportunity to work with a wide range of children in the classroom. Throughout the course of a school day, each child should be a part of many groups.

Mina and Mrs. Conway have a reading discussion.

Dynamic grouping is different than traditional ability grouping. How do they differ and why can any grouping be called a "hypothesis"?

Dynamic grouping is not the same as ability grouping. There are no "high," "middle," and "low" groups. Rather, every child is in a group that provides support, success, and appropriate challenge. Children who are grouped together for guided reading may have very different ability levels. Some of you may have varied memories of reading groups. Maybe you were placed in a "low reading" group and believe that had an impact on how you felt about yourself as a learner and a reader. Researchers have noted that children in lower groups receive different instruction and fewer chances to actually read (e.g., Allington, 1983a; Allington & McGill-Franzen, 1989).

Children may feel they have been labeled as "dumb" because of the reading group to which they were assigned. Here's a quote about reading groups from one of the author's own child:

> I didn't like them [reading groups]. . . . They were judgmental and made me feel like crap! The higher groups had some flashy, wonderful name that they got to pick. The low group got some name that the teacher picked out . . . some junk name . . . like in second grade we had planet names. The low group was 'Pluto.' How cheap and corny! The high group was 'Mercury.' Once we were the 'All Stars.' The high group was the 'Rad Racers!' (Nierstheimer, 2000, p. 35)

So that you do not replicate the damaging practices of ability grouping and labeling of children, you should instead use flexible, dynamic, needs-based grouping. Figure 4.8 compares and contrasts traditional reading groups with dynamic guided reading groups.

	Traditional Groups	Guided Reading Groups
Rationale for groups	Based on children's abilities; often long-standing	Based on children's strengths in processing texts; change regularly
Assessment	End-of-story questions; workbook pages; unit tests	Daily, ongoing teacher observations and record keeping
Texts	Basal stories; publisher-selected grade-level anthologies	Teacher-selected texts based on children's needs; multiple copies of individual books so children can read wide variety of choices
Teaching	Vocabulary pretaught; lesson follows sequence in teacher's manual; round-robin reading by children; focus on isolated skills and practice of skills on worksheets	Focus on reading for meaning and strategic problem solving in text; skills taught are related to children's reading behaviors while reading; each child reads whole text to herself

FIGURE 4.8   Grouping for Instruction

Advice for New Teachers

Grouping Decisions

Dear Derek,

How do you make decisions for grouping children together during reading?

Dear New Teacher,

I believe that children need to work in many different groups during the school week. For example, I have students working as partners, others who are grouped together for guided reading, and others who read together because they are interested in a certain topic. I keep a record of who has worked with whom and try to see that students have opportunities with many others and aren't labeled in any way.

   As I group children together for reading our basal stories, I keep in mind their strengths and needs as readers. These groups change often, however, since children grow and change in their reading development.

Diversity Issue: Teaching All Children

After reading about guided reading, matching children to books, and grouping students for instruction, you may be wondering if you will be able to teach all students. You might feel overwhelmed as you think about all of the students who may have special needs in your future classroom. Fortunately, Au (2001) has identified principles that experts in reading have agreed work for all children. As you think about teaching all children, you will want to consider these fundamental principles for your reading program.

1. **Link all language processes as often as possible.** As you develop reading lessons, plan your instruction so that your students engage in purposeful reading, writing, speaking, and listening.
2. **Help students develop ownership and purposes for reading.** Students need to read real books of their own choosing for their own reasons. Make time for choice in your reading program.
3. **Reject the behaviorist model of teaching.** The behaviorist model of teaching focuses on reading accuracy, drilling on isolated skills, and expecting single best answers. Learn to be supportive of students' miscues as they construct meaning from texts.
4. **Have high expectations for all children.** Work to develop students' sense of self-efficacy by holding reasonable yet high expectations for each student.
5. **Provide students with a variety of reading materials.** Encourage your students to read many different kinds of texts including magazines, websites, newspapers, and books. Variety fosters motivation and will result in more proficient, strategic readers.

HELPING EARLY READERS BECOME STRATEGIC READERS

When you learned about the cueing systems—meaning, structure, and visual—you learned that when young children orchestrate the cueing systems to construct meaning from texts, they often try going first to the visual cueing system, which sometimes proves unsuccessful for them. Attempting to "sound out" individual letters can result in interrupted reading and lost meaning. When children try to orally produce the sounds of each letter but do not rely on other strategies when they come to a difficult word, they get stuck; they are not being strategic readers.

Some literacy authors distinguish skills from strategies by noting that a skill becomes a strategy when the learner can use the skill independently by truly understanding how and when to use the skill. Routman (2000) notes that "strategies are the thinking, problem-solving mental processes that the learner deliberating initiates, incorporates, and applies to construct meaning" (p. 130). Knowing how and when to apply strategies is often referred to as *flexible strategy use*. Some reading strategies are ways of using the cueing systems to solve problems.

When children are intent on sounding out individual letters, they could instead ask themselves, "What word would make sense here and start with this letter?" or "What clue can I get from the illustration to figure out this word?" These strategy moves can help solve problem words. Good readers orchestrate the cueing systems in skillful ways yet keep meaning making as the primary goal of reading. Clay (1991) says that once children have acquired a repertoire of strategies for working out problems in text, they can teach themselves more each time they read.

Other reading strategies involve actions that allow young readers to apply skills such as accessing prior knowledge, making predictions about the text by thinking "What would I expect to come next?," and learning to track print by understanding the one-to-one match between speech and print. Your goal as a teacher of Early Readers is to help them become strategic readers who know how and when to apply certain strategies (Goodman, Watson, & Burke, 1996).

Strategies for Early Readers

In this section, we consider strategies that Early Readers need in order to be successful. The strategies that we address are print concepts, tracking print and one-to-one matching, and the "skip it and come back" strategy.

Print concepts.   As a teacher of Early Readers, you need to teach concepts about print in whole- and small-group settings. These are some of the understandings that fit under the umbrella of concepts about print:

- Words go from left to right and from top to bottom on the page (directionality).
- Books go from front to back.
- There are letters, and letters make up words.
- The print contains a message.
- There are spaces between words.
- There are marks on the page called punctuation that help separate phrases, sentences, and add emphasis.

Some Early Readers have extensive knowledge of the conventions of print. Others will need your help to understand conventions of print through shared reading experiences as in Chapter 3. You can provide such children with books that have few words per page that are printed in bold, clear print using both upper- and lowercase print. Figure 4.9 illustrates what these texts look like.

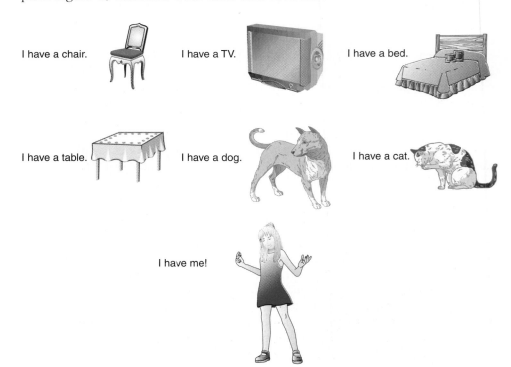

I have a chair.   I have a TV.   I have a bed.

I have a table.   I have a dog.   I have a cat.

I have me!

FIGURE 4.9   A Simple Text

Simple books allow children to apply the strategies you have been demonstrating such as front-to-back progression in a book, where the reader begins on a page, left-to-right sequence, and return sweep from line to line. As adults we take this knowledge for granted, and some of your students may already understand these principles; however, some will not and you will need to teach them.

Tracking print and one-to-one matching.   You should have already taught the concept of "words" and "spaces" and have used a pointer to demonstrate tracking print in shared reading experiences, but some children may need to learn how to track print independently. Children need to understand that there is a one-to-one match between what they say while focusing on a word that is printed on the page.

Encouraging children to point to each word, using their right-hand index finger (using their left hands causes them to cover up the text while trying to read), helps develop one-to-one matching skills (e.g., Shanker & Ekwall, 1998). In addition, while pointing, the child's action of placing a finger under the word extends a connection to the eyes and brain and directs his attention right to the word he is trying to read (Clay, 1991). Pointing also serves to help children keep their places while reading; therefore, some older readers may still need to point. You should not discourage pointing in older readers *unless* you believe that the act of pointing is keeping the reader from achieving fluent reading. Even then, you should proceed very carefully before discouraging pointing because some readers need this support.

The young child should point *under* the word to avoid covering it up, and the pointing should be precise and crisp (Clay, 1991). Unless the child is reading with relative fluency, you should insist that she point to the words while reading. Sometimes a child needs to be reminded to keep monitoring for one-to-one match. For example, she might get to the end of her reading and still have words left in the sentence. At that point, you can say, "You had some words left over, didn't you?" or "Try that again and make it match." Consistent reminders such as these quickly remind

Pointing while reading is important for most Early Readers. How does pointing to the words help children with their reading?

Christopher helps himself read by pointing.

Early Readers to use their strategy of tracking with print and matching their voice to the words. Some of the strategies that need to be demonstrated and encouraged for Early Readers are the following:

- Using pictures to help unlock meaning,
- Making predictions,
- Paying attention to the letters,
- Locating known and unknown words in texts,
- Supporting self-monitoring and self-correcting,
- Building on prior knowledge of above concepts,
- Beginning to see patterns of letters that occur in words, and
- Using cueing systems and reading strategies for solving unknown words.

Demonstrating the "Skip it and come back" strategy.   We are singling out this strategy for you to demonstrate to Early Readers because it is often very useful to them. The "skip it and come back" strategy is one in which the reader skips the difficult word (or says "mmmm" or "blank" for the skipped word), reads to the end of the sentence, then comes back to retry the difficult word. The meaning derived from the rest of the sentence gives the reader the cues necessary to figure out the unknown word. Proficient readers use this strategy almost unconsciously when encountering unfamiliar words.

Here's how to demonstrate this strategy:

1. Tell students that when good readers come to a word they don't know, they sometimes skip the word, read to the end of the sentence, and come back to the difficult word to figure it out.
2. Show them how this works. Use a sentence like this, written on the board with an illustration: *The boy laughed at his funny dog.*
3. Read the sentence to the children, stopping at the word *laughed*. Remind students that if you don't know a word you can skip it, read on, and come back.
4. Read the sentence this way: *The boy mmmm at his funny dog.*
5. Remind Early Readers that they always need to come back to the skipped word. Have students predict what the word could be. Ask them how they knew what to guess.
6. Show them how they used meaning (by reading the rest of the sentence and looking at the picture), how they used the structure of the sentence (it had to sound right, i.e., it had to be a verb), and how they looked at the first letter *l* to predict *laughed* instead of *giggled, chuckled,* or *snickered.*

By demonstrating and encouraging the strategy of "skip it and come back," you are actually teaching Early Readers how to become more proficient in orchestrating the cueing systems and, most importantly, how to keep meaning making as their primary goal in reading. Further, you are arming them with a much more compelling strategy than sound-it-out when they come to new, unknown words.

Teacher Prompts to Promote Strategic Readers

We have been referring to verbal reminders that teachers can give young readers to help them become more strategic in their reading of text and problem solving of difficult words. These reminders are often referred to as *prompts*. For you to be effective in supporting your young students, the language of your reading prompts needs to be specific and consistent because that's how children will remember what to do as you act as their reading coach.

Do you remember learning to play softball? When you picked up the bat, perhaps a parent/coach repeated these phrases to you, "That's right. Hold the bat over your shoulder but not on your shoulder. Stand sideways toward the pitcher, not directly facing him. Get ready for the ball to come to you." Chances are, you needed to hear these same specific and consistent words many times before you remembered what to do. Often the words of the coach are translated into private speech by the child (Bodrova & Leong, 1996; Vygotsky, 1978). In our example, after hearing the coach's words again and again you may have approached home plate with the bat in hand mumbling to yourself, "Not *on* my shoulder. Sideways. Get ready." Finally, you didn't have to verbalize the instructions any longer. You just remembered what to do; the learning had become internalized using language as a mental tool for you to become independent.

One of all teachers' primary goals is to help their students become independent. As a teacher of reading, the prompts that you provide students will lead to internalized learning and independence (Watson, 1999). Vygotsky and Luria (1930/1993) say internalization happens when external behaviors "grow into the mind"; your job is to let your consistent prompting "grow" into your students' minds until they can independently manage reading tasks and problem solving without you.

When children get stuck during reading, teachers prompt them to move forward. What are some of the phrases that teachers use?

Figure 4.10 lists teachers' prompts that you can use when you remind Early Readers to use strategies to help them in their reading. You will notice responses at the bottom of this figure that are appropriate for you to make when your students have been successful in applying a strategy.

As you've learned, the prompts in Figure 4.10 help readers think about strategies that they can apply while reading that will help them become independent. The clear and consistent language that you use will become private speech that the child uses to direct his own strategy usage.

YOU TRY IT

Strategy Chart

For this activity, make a strategy chart for Early Readers to use as a reminder of what to do when encountering an unknown word. Create a small poster, listing the strategies that children can try when problem solving new words. Try to add illustrations that might help prompt young learners. (Notice how "ask someone" is last on the list since you want to encourage independence.)

Word-Solving Strategies

- Look at the picture to help you.
- Get your mouth ready to say it.
- Think of what would start with that letter and make sense.
- Start the sentence again.
- Skip that word, read on, and come back to it. Now, what do you think it is?
- Where have you seen that word before?
- Put in a word that makes sense and go on.
- Ask someone.

Teachers teach Early Readers strategies for figuring out unknown words. What are those strategies besides "sound it out?"

We've noted that children need to flexibly orchestrate many strategies to be proficient readers. Just as a carpenter cannot work with only a hammer in his toolbox, a child cannot read successfully with only one strategy, such as "sound it out." In fact, poor readers tend to rely on primarily the visual cueing system and often ignore

Strategies	Teacher Prompts
Using pictures	Look at the pictures to help yourself.
Pointing for one-to-one matching	Read with your finger. Did that match? Try that again to make it match.
Solving unknown words	Get your mouth ready to say it. Start the sentence again. Skip that word and read on. Now, what do you think it is? Where have you seen that word before? Put in a word that makes sense and go on.
Accessing the meaning cueing system	Does that make sense? What would make sense here?
Accessing the structure cueing system	Does that sound right? Can we say it that way? Does it fit?
Accessing the visual cueing system	Look at how the word begins. What would make sense and starts like this? Run your finger under the word and say it as you look at the letters.
Using word analogies	Think about a word you know that looks almost like this word. Do you know other words that have the same chunks of letters in them?
Promoting self-monitoring and self-correction	Is that right? Check it. Try that again. Why did you stop? What did you notice? You found the hard part. Where was it? I saw you look at the picture and reread. What did you notice?
Encouraging strategy use	What can you do to help yourself? Try it. I like the way you worked that out. I saw that you tried _____ (fill in the strategy the child used) when you came to a hard word. That's what good readers do. You figured that out all by yourself. Good for you!

FIGURE 4.10   Strategies and Teacher Prompts

their errors and read on. As a teacher, you can arm all children with reading strategies that will help them become independent readers. You can help children acquire many tools in their reading toolboxes that will allow them to become independent, strategic readers. The poem shown in Figure 4.11 captures the essence of our discussion of independent reading strategies.

Independent Strategies

Jill Marie

When I get stuck on a word in a book,

There are lots of things to do.

I can do them all, please, by myself;

I don't need help from you.

I can look at the pictures to get a hint,

Or think what the story's about.

I can "get my mouth ready" to say the first letter,

A kind of "sounding it out."

I can chop the word into smaller parts,

Like *on* and *ing* and *ly,*

Or find smaller words in compound words,

Like *raincoat* and *bumblebee.*

I can think of a word that makes sense in the place,

Guess or say "blank" and read on

Until the sentence has reached its end,

Then go back and try these questions on:

"Does it make sense?"

"Can we say it that way?"

"Does it look right to me?"

Chances are the right word will pop out like the sun

In my own mind, can't you see?

If I've thought of and tried out most of these things

And I *still* do not know what to do,

Then I may turn around and ask for some help to get me through.

From Marie, Jill. (1993, May). Literary Poem: Independent Strategies. The Reading Teacher. 46(8), 710.

FIGURE 4.11   Poem Describing Independent Reading Strategies

HELPING STUDENTS BUILD FLUENCY

You have probably listened to young children read in a word-by-word fashion, stopping at each word as they point and decode the symbols on the page, even using a "reading voice" that they have come to associate with oral reading. This is a perfectly natural stage in reading development that most learners go through. However, if children remain at the stage of slow, nonfluent reading they can experience impaired comprehension, frustration, and an avoidance of reading altogether. Rasinski (2000) calls this type of reading "inefficient reading" and argues that teachers "need to take the notion of slow, inefficient, disfluent reading seriously. Even with adequate comprehension, slow and labored reading will turn any school or recreational reading assignment into a marathon of frustration for nearly any student" (p. 150). We agree with this statement and believe that as a literacy teacher you have a responsibility to help nurture your students' developing reading fluency.

Reading fluency is defined as easy, smooth expression and the freedom from word-by-word identification problems that might hinder comprehension (Harris & Hodges, 1995). "Fluent reading means solving problems 'on the run,' something all readers must do if they are to gain understanding" (Fountas & Pinnell, 1996, p. 151). Fluency also includes reading "using appropriate pitch, stress, and juncture; to project the natural intonation and phrasing of the spoken word upon the written text" (Richards, 2000, p. 535)—in other words, reading like talk sounds.

The difficulty of the text will influence the fluency of one's reading. For example, have you ever tried to read a conceptually dense passage aloud from one of your textbooks, like statistics? If so, your reading pace might have been halting and word by word at times. What we are discussing here, however, is helping Early Readers develop relative oral reading fluency when they are presented with texts that are at their instructional level in terms of difficulty—the "just right" books. Most children who lack fluency in their oral reading are probably reading from books that are too difficult for them—books that are at their frustration level.

As a teacher you need to model fluent reading for your Early Readers in whole-group settings through daily read-alouds and shared reading. Beyond that, in small groups, you can take simple texts like *Lunch at the Zoo* by Blaxland (1996) and demonstrate for children how to read in phrases or "chunks," adding expression and emphasis to certain words. For example, in this book, the zoo animals are each clamoring for food as the zookeeper arrives with their lunches. You can show the sentences to the children and demonstrate fluent reading.

Let's say you choose the page: "This is *my* lunch," said the elephant. "Yum! Yum!" Read the sentence first without intonation or phrasing. Next go back and model how the reading should sound. It will be in three chunks: (1) This is my lunch. (2) Said the elephant. (3) Yum. Yum. Then go back and read the page again adding voice emphasis on *my* and the *yums*. So the reading will sound like this (*italics* are used for emphasis, and dashes for short pauses): "This is *my* lunch,"—said the elephant.—"*Yum! Yum!*" You can also write the sentence on a long strip of paper and cut apart the words, helping children to put word clusters together in "talking chunks." Figure 4.12 contains

Level	Description of Oral Reading
1	Word-by-word reading primarily
2	Reads in two- or three-word phrases primarily, with some word-by-word reading
3	Reads primarily in phrases, little intonation, ignores some punctuation
4	Reads in phrases, generally smooth, but a little choppy at times
5	Reads fluently with expression

Published by Allyn and Bacon, Boston, MA. Copyright © 1999 by Pearson Education. Classrooms that work: They can all read and write, *2/e Allington. Adapted by permission of the publisher.*

FIGURE 4.12   A Simple Fluency Rating Scale

a chart developed by Cunningham and Allington (1994) that you might find helpful in thinking about as well as assessing children's oral reading fluency.

SEE FOR YOURSELF

Listening to Early Readers

Visit the message board for Chapter 4 on our Companion Website at *www.prenhall.com/lenski* to discuss your findings.

On the Companion Website *(http://www.prenhall.com/lenski),* you will find audio selections of three Early Readers reading texts at their instructional level; they are able to accurately read at least 94% of the words. As you listen to each child read, rate each child's oral reading according to the rubric given in Figure 4.12. Listening to children read is a simple, informal yet effective way to assess fluency, rate, and phrasing. Determine if any of the readers you heard need extra support in developing oral reading fluency.

In the See for Yourself feature, as you listened to the readers on the website, you may have decided that one or more of the readers needed assistance with fluency. If so, you probably wondered how a teacher might help such children. Some teachers believe that readers who lack fluency simply need more instruction at the word–sound level in isolation of real book reading (Allington, 1983b). Unfortunately, this often results in those students falling further behind because they are not given additional opportunities to practice fluent oral reading like "good readers do"; instead they get bogged down practicing word lists and memorizing words out of context. As an alternative to these unsuccessful teaching practices, we will explore specific approaches that have been found helpful in supporting students' developing reading fluency. The approaches that we will consider are repeated readings, paired reading, choral reading, ditto reading (Gupta, 2000), and dramatic expression.

> Fluency means reading with appropriate speed, phrasing, and intonation. How does fluency contribute to comprehension as well as motivation to read?

The Importance of Repeated Readings

We want to underscore the compelling influence of repeated readings. Consider sports in which you have participated like basketball. Haven't you practiced, and practiced, and practiced the same skills over and over again—like dribbling and shooting—in order to improve? This principle holds true for reading as well: Readers get better by reading. Young readers should be encouraged to read the same texts again and again. They will acquire confidence in their reading and collect "old favorites"—books they return to for pleasure reading when they are given choices during independent reading time.

When discussing the value of repeated readings, Routman (2000) asserts that "[w]ithin the comfortable territory of a well-known text, developing readers can practice multiple strategies and experience the success of reading with growing fluency and comprehension" (p. 130). When you enter a first-grade classroom and see a group of young readers clustered around an old favorite like Sue Williams' *I Went Walking* (1989) and you hear them enthusiastically reading together, "I went walking. What did you see? I saw a brown horse looking at me" you know that their teacher understands and values the importance of repeated readings.

Paired Reading

Paired reading is just what it sounds like: partners paired up to read together, taking turns reading from the same text. The values of this experience are based on students' learning from one another in social settings (building on your philosophy of social constructivism) in which they have opportunities to practice oral reading in front of a peer and receive support from that listener who can help the reader critique and improve her own oral reading proficiency.

As a teacher you can cultivate a positive learning environment for paired reading experiences by modeling for the students how these sessions should take place. Koskinen and Blum (1984) suggest that the teacher select a student to help her demonstrate paired reading in front of the whole class. This demonstration consists of showing children how pairs should sit side by side, sharing either the same book or having identical copies of the same text. One reader reads aloud first, while the other listens. The "listener" then offers encouraging suggestions about such fluency features such as the reader's use of expression, voices for the characters, and observation of punctuation. Then, roles are reversed as the listener becomes the reader, receiving encouraging comments from her partner. This procedure should be repeated several times, reading the same passage until both partners are satisfied that they are reading with intonation and proper phrasing. Partners may even choose to read the passages together repeatedly as a means of helping one another succeed in the reading.

When the teacher demonstrates this process with one of the students, she pretends to experience difficulty in the reading and shows her partner how to help her in a positive, supportive way by giving gentle feedback. All students can be asked to discuss the kinds of comments that would be helpful from a peer and those that would not be. For example, say you are practicing lines from a play that you have to read aloud in English class and you ask your roommate to listen to your lines. You want your roommate to help you get better at your reading by providing kind, constructive criticism—not be hurtful, abrupt, or judgmental when you are trying your best. This is how children feel, too. Once all students understand the way in which feedback should be given and received, they can proceed to practice paired reading on their own. Paired reading can be a powerful tool for improving students' oral reading fluency.

Choral Reading

Choral reading is another means of supporting the development of fluency. Choral reading involves pairs, small groups, or even the whole class participating in reading the same text together. As you already learned, choral reading is often practiced in settings such as shared reading experiences.

The power of choral reading lies in the support readers receive from one another. When children read aloud together from the same text they receive the same kind of support that you have received when singing in a choir (hence the "choral" connection). Perhaps you have sung as part of a musical ensemble and were given a new piece of music that caused you to be unsure of your part and the notes that you were supposed to hit. Sometimes a difficult passage of the music caused you to worry. However, if you stood in a cluster of strong voices, we presume it was comforting to let those voices hit the notes first in the difficult section while you followed just a fraction of a second later. Didn't you feel the reassurance of those other voices when you came to difficulty?

The same experience happens to Early Readers who are learning to read with accuracy and fluency. The support of other, sometimes stronger, readers helps them build confidence as they roll through the sentences using expression and appropriate pacing. In this way, choral reading builds a sense of teamwork and can even be used as part of a performance for other classrooms or parents (Opitz & Rasinski, 1998). Figure 4.13 suggests titles that contain pieces that work well for choral reading.

Ditto Reading

Children need many opportunities to hear proficient readers read fluently. Sometimes, due to questionable grouping practices, inefficient readers only listen to other inefficient readers (e.g., Zutell & Rasinski, 1991). Therefore, one of the purposes of ditto reading is to let all readers move from nonfluent reading to enhanced fluency by becoming explicitly conscious of how to do that. Ditto reading is an approach designed to help struggling readers in one-to-one tutoring situations (Gupta, 2000), but it is also supportive for Early Readers in small-group settings such as during guided reading.

This approach for helping promote oral reading fluency is one in which the teacher models for the children what nonfluent reading sounds like. By hearing another's voice reading in such a way, children are able to recognize and analyze nonfluent reading, and learn how to progress beyond that stage into more fluent reading. Here is how the procedure works:

1. The teacher initiates a focus lesson on fluency during guided reading or other small-group time. He explains that he is going to read from a book from the classroom library and that the students will evaluate his reading. The teacher emphasizes that this exercise is not for belittling or making fun of anyone's reading, but for helping all readers become more proficient.
2. The teacher reads a short passage of text in an expressionless, flat, monotone way. The children may giggle at this style of reading, which is good; enjoyment will capture their attention and make this focus lesson on fluency memorable for them.
3. Next, the teacher asks the children if that kind of reading sounds good—and why or why not.

Bryan, A. (1997). *Ashley Bryan's ABC of African American poetry.* New York: Atheneum.

de Regniers, B. S., Moore, E., White, M. M., & Carr, J. (compilers). (1988). *Sing a song of popcorn: Every child's book of poems.* New York: Scholastic.

Foster, J. (1988). *Another first poetry book.* Oxford, England: Oxford Press.

Goldstein, B. S. (compiler). (1989). *Bear in mind: A book of bear poems.* New York: The Trumpet Club.

Hopkins, L. B. (compiler). (1990). *Good books, good times.* New York: The Trumpet Club.

Leventhal, D. (1994). *What is your language?* New York: Dutton.

Martin, B., Jr., & Archambault, J. (1990). *Barn dance.* New York: The Trumpet Club.

Prelutsky, J. (1984). *The new kid on the block.* New York: Greenwillow.

Silverstein, S. (1974). *Where the sidewalk ends.* New York: Harper & Row.

Silverstein, S. (1981). *A light in the attic.* New York: Harper & Row.

FIGURE 4.13   Poems and Books for Choral Reading

4. The teacher then asks what needs to be done to make the oral reading sound "better" or "right."
5. One of the children could be called on to make the reading sound right. Or, the teacher can reread the passage, using expression, dramatic intonation, and appropriate pacing.
6. Next, the teacher and the children engage in discussing the first reading versus the subsequent reading(s).
7. Finally, all practice reading the passage together several times, putting voices together in a fluent manner.

By using the ditto reading approach, children are directed to attend to fluency skills they need to employ. This is important because you cannot expect children to instinctively understand what you want them to know and do. When you are explicit in your teaching expectations, and intentional in how you demonstrate those expectations, students are asked to become metacognitively aware—to think about their own cognitive processing. By becoming aware, children can change their reading behaviors through the conscious application of new strategies to achieve more fluent oral reading.

Dramatic Expression

Using dramatic expression as an extension of reading increases the joy of experiencing literature. It is also an effective way of promoting oral reading fluency. Readers Theatre involves children writing their own scripts for presentation in front of the class. The writing of their own lines and the dimension of performance provide authentic purposes for students to become familiar with each phrase of the dialogue and to deliver those words with vocal expression.

Drama can be extended further in the classroom through encouraging finger plays, staging poetry, using puppets, and acting out children's books. Galda and West (1995) note that drama can serve "as an immensely rewarding oral language experience as children plan, recall, argue, and create voices other than their own" (p. 184). These oral language experiences developed through the use of drama enhance expressive and fluent reading.

Many books are available that provide a "script-like" format. One such book is *I Am the Dog, I Am the Cat* by Hall (1994). In this beautifully illustrated book, the differences between dogs and cats are explored through alternately placed dog/cat pages where each is engaged in an activity or behavior that the other would totally disdain. This would be a perfect book for two small groups, or two individual readers to dramatize. Remember, the children can read from the book while they're "acting"; they do not have to memorize the text.

Another children's book we recommend using for dramatization is *Thomas' Snowsuit* by Munsch (1988). This story involves a little boy, Thomas, who refuses to put on his snowsuit no matter how hard his mother, his teacher, and the principal try to make him. Second graders love the irreverence of author Munsch's storytelling and revel in the disobedience of Thomas. It helps if you bring in props for your young actors like a winter coat, an old dress, and a sports jacket. When these pieces of clothing end up on different characters than they started out on, children are delighted. Students are guaranteed to deliver their spoken lines on cue, with expression. We believe you will enjoy adding dramatic expression to the repertoire of teaching strategies that you employ to encourage and support Early Readers' oral reading fluency in your classroom.

YOU TRY IT

Building Fluency

In this section you learned about various strategies for helping students build fluency: repeated readings, paired reading, choral reading, ditto reading, and dramatic expression. For this You Try It, select one of these teaching strategies and create a lesson plan for Early Readers using this format:

Objective:	To build fluency
Rationale:	[Write *why* fluency is important for readers.]
Materials:	[List the materials you will need.]
Demonstration:	[Explain how you will demonstrate the strategy for building fluency to your students.]
Practice:	[Tell how you will group for, facilitate, and monitor practice opportunities.]
Assessment:	[Describe how you will assess the students' understanding of the strategy they have practiced as well its effectiveness in building fluency.]

CONNECTIONS: WHAT'S NEXT?

This chapter explored effective ways for teaching Early Readers in small groups. You learned about selecting materials for instruction, managing and grouping for guided reading, helping young students become strategic readers, and assisting children in building fluency. Figure 4.14 reminds you of where we have been and where we are going.

You have learned about teaching *to* children in whole groups (e.g., reading aloud, shared reading), and *with* children in small groups (e.g., guided reading, partner reading) (Mooney, 1990). Now you will explore reading *by* children in independent settings as well as fostering positive relationships with students' first teachers—their families.

FIGURE 4.14   A Developmental Approach to the Teaching of Reading

	Early Readers	**Interpretive Readers**	**Critical Readers**
Theories underscored as readers develop:	Social Constructivism: Psycholinguistic, Critical, Transactional	Social Constructivism: Psycholinguistic, Critical, Transactional	Social Constructivism: Psycholinguistic, Critical, Transactional

continued

FIGURE 4.14 *Continued*

	Early Readers	Interpretive Readers	Critical Readers
Whole-group instruction through:	• Read-alouds • Shared texts • Comprehension strategies • Working with words	• Read-alouds • Basals • Literature-based models • Word-building strategies • Comprehension strategies	• Read-alouds • Common texts (e.g., basals, anthologies, trade books) • Comprehension strategies • Vocabulary instruction and word analysis • Researching • Critical reading • Reading content-area texts • Studying and notetaking
Assessment ideas for whole group:	• Observations • Kidwatching • Anecdotal notation	• Portfolios • Open-ended questions • Rubrics	• Written retellings • Research projects • Interest inventories • Content-area histories • Cloze procedure
Small-group instruction through:	• Guided reading • Teaching for strategies • Fluency practice • Working with words	• Basal readers • Literature anthologies • Trade books • Guided silent reading • Literature circles • Inquiry groups	• Book clubs
Assessment ideas for small groups:	• Running Records • Retellings • Discussions with children	• Names test • Fluency checklist • Peer assessment • Inquiry rubric	• Student information Card • Bio poem • "I Used to … But Now I…" poem • Observational checklist • Student self-assessment • Norm-referenced tests
Independent learning through:	• Independent reading • Reading/writing workshop • Making books • Reading the room	• Independent reading • Reading/writing workshop • Responding through writing • Reading logs	• Sustained silent reading and writing
Sociocultural contexts:	• Conferring with parents • Newsletters • Parents in the classroom • Reading parties • Reading at home	• Reading/writing connection for life • Oral histories • Home literacy activities • Parent programs	• Parents as coaches • Funds of knowledge • Parent–student book clubs

 **FOR YOUR PORTFOLIO**

ENTRY 4.1   *Guided Reading*

INTASC Principle 4 states: *The teacher understands and uses a variety of instructional strategies to encourage students' development of critical thinking, problem-solving, and performance skills.*

When you engage children in a guided reading lesson, you have used a particular approach to encourage students' independent word-solving and reading development. For this portfolio entry, write a paragraph describing the essential components of guided reading, the kinds of assessments used, how students are grouped for guided reading, and ideas for focus lessons. Then explain whether or not you will use guided reading in your future classroom and why small-group instruction is important.

ENTRY 4.2   *Evaluating Websites*

IRA/NCTE Standard 8 maintains: *Students use a variety of technological and informational resources (e.g., libraries, databases, computer networks, video) to gather and synthesize information and to create and communicate knowledge.*

One of the challenges you will face as you select materials for small groups of children is to evaluate sites on the Internet, looking for those that are appropriate, well conceived, visually appealing, and helpful to Early Readers. For this portfolio entry, locate a website that you believe could support young learners' reading development, as well as their technological competence.

Write a brief description of the site and why you chose it. Then, assume you have students in a primary grade who will work as partners at a computer station, using the website you have located. Answer the following questions, developed by Duffelmeyer (2002), as you think about the activity on the Internet you have chosen:

1. How will you introduce the activity?
2. What kinds of guidance will students need in order to engage in the activity?
3. What length of time do you believe students will need to complete the activity?
4. Will all students be successful with the site? Do you anticipate any points of confusion?
5. Are extension activities available to use as follow-ups to your computer activity?
6. How will you evaluate the success of this learning opportunity?

TO LEARN MORE

Helpful Websites

Visit our Companion Website at *http://www.prenhall.com/lenski* to link to the following sites:

Leveled and Benchmark Books

Provides helpful information on leveled texts and benchmark books for guided reading.
http://www.readinga-z.com/newfiles/leveledreaders.html

Early Minilessons

Provides a variety of minilessons posted by teachers to use during guided reading.
http://www.teachers.net/lessons/posts/1115.html

Carol Hurst's Children's Literature Site

Provides reviews of great books for children and ideas about how to use the books in the classroom.
http://www.carolhurst.com/

Literature Lessons

Lists a variety of lessons to use with children's literature at a range of reading levels.
http://www.teachers.net/cgi-bin/lessons/sort.cgi?searchterm= Literature

chapter 5

Instructing Early Readers Working Independently and With Families

Essential Learning Questions

- How will you help Early Readers select materials for independent reading?
- How can you prepare students for independent work during reading and writing workshops?
- How can you build home/school relationships that are beneficial for children, their families, and the school?
- How can you encourage parent participation in your literacy classroom?
- What are some guidelines for conducting a parent–teacher conference?

Six-year-old Maria pronounced, "I can do this by myself!" while beaming at her teacher, who watched the Early Reader pick up a book, sit down on the rug, and begin to read. Maria was moving toward becoming an independent reader. As you work with young learners, each action you take will be guided by your desire to help your students make choices, read strategically, and become confident, independent users of literacy. We agree that "the teacher's role is to provide the path to independence" (Bodrova & Leong, 1996, p. 3). Some have even suggested that our jobs as teachers require that we make ourselves obsolete—so that our students don't need us anymore. Although that imagery is a bit of a stretch for teachers of young children, you should employ teaching approaches and instructional strategies that will help your students move toward independence.

In Chapters 3 and 4 we asked you to think about teaching young children in whole and small groups by engaging in shared literacy activities where you, the teacher, would supply varying degrees of support for your students. This support can be represented by Figure 5.1, which illustrates the continuum of teachers' support ranging from high levels (as in reading aloud to children) to intermediate levels of support (as in guided reading) to no support at all (as in independent reading).

Of course, you cannot expect children to suddenly become independent readers. As in all of your teaching, you have to provide your students with demonstrations, practice, guidance, and time so that eventually your support can be withdrawn and students can manage independently. In earlier chapters, we learned about the decisions you must make as you select materials for young children. Here we learn that a good way to start fostering independence in your Early Readers is by helping *them* select their own reading materials.

HELPING STUDENTS SELECT MATERIALS

Each day, part of your literacy block of time should be devoted to independent reading. This time will be important for all Early Readers as they independently practice their developing understandings of print and construct meaning from text. You should encourage children to read books from a wide range of genres and difficulty levels. For example, you should facilitate your students' access to wonderful children's literature, nonfiction books about topics that interest them, newspapers, encyclopedias, and computer-generated text.

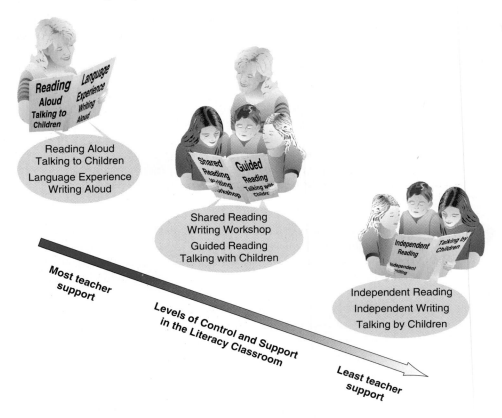

FIGURE 5.1 Teachers' Level of Support

As we have already discussed, however, it is essential that children spend most of their time reading books *that they are able to read*. When children engage in frequent, sustained independent reading experiences with books they are able to manage, they can build their confidence as readers, increase their fluency, and enhance their enjoyment of reading (Fountas & Pinnell, 1996; Holdaway, 1979).

Many of your students will automatically choose books that are in their range of proficiency in terms of difficulty. Others will need you to show them how to choose books. Remember, for a book to be considered an independent-level book for a particular child, the child should be able to read it with 95% to 100% accuracy. Remember, too, that a book that is difficult for one child will be easy for another.

Facilitating Book Choice

Some of you may harbor unfortunate memories of well-meaning teachers or librarians who felt it necessary to direct you to the books *they* wanted you to read. At some time in your schooling, you may have even dreaded library visits because you had no control over your choices. As a teacher, you do not want to replicate those experiences for your students. However, because you do want your Early Readers to have plenty of practice reading books that they are able to read and to experience the motivation that only success can bring, you will need to demonstrate to your students how to choose books.

Think-alouds.   Demonstrations of book choice can take the form of think-alouds (Roehler & Duffy, 1991) in which you purposely select a stack of children's books and model your reasoning by thinking aloud with your students about why or why not each selection might be appropriate, interesting, and beneficial for independent reading. Tharp and Gallimore (1988) note that modeling like this is "the process of offering behavior for imitation" (p. 47). Thus, by holding up books and modeling your thinking aloud, you will be showing children how they can imitate those thinking processes themselves. In addition, you will be generating responses from the children that will give you clues about how much they understand about the book choice responsibility. This will, in turn, help you know how to gradually withdraw your support of their choices of texts to read during independent reading.

For instance, you will notice children beginning to choose books on their own that match their interests, are at appropriate reading levels, and are from a wide range of genres. You will know then that you are no longer needed as a book-choice assistant.

The "By Myself" strategy.   One approach that teachers sometimes use for helping children choose books for independent reading is to create a chart with their students to help them make reading choices by themselves, for themselves. As you can see from the example in Figure 5.2, the "By Myself" Strategy can be constructed with children as you think together with them about choosing books to read all by themselves. The three categories that you post on a chalkboard, easel, or chart are: EASY, CHALLENGING, and HARD.

The "By Myself" Strategy chart could be printed on a large poster in your classroom and used as you and your students discuss books that are "easy," "challenging," and "hard" for *individual students*. (That is why the phrase "for me" is written after each category title.) You should make it clear to your students that it is all right to choose "easy" books for independent reading; after all, that is what you do when you choose books for your own pleasure-reading time. You don't want to spend

Visit the online journal in Chapter 5 on our Companion Website at *www.prenhall.com/lenski* to answer these questions. Save your answers to your hard drive or to a disk to compile an online teaching journal.

Thinking aloud about book choices is a helpful demonstration strategy. How does a think-aloud assist children in choosing books?

Too Easy Books For Me
- Someone has read this book to me.
- I know most of the words in this book.
- I can read this book easily and make it sound just like my teacher reads.
- I can read this book all by myself!

Challenging Books For Me
- I haven't read this book before.
- There are a couple words on each page that I don't know yet, but I think I can figure them out.
- Sometimes when I'm reading this book I sound like my teacher, and sometimes I sound a little bumpy.

Hard Books For Me
- There are lots of words on each page that I haven't seen before.
- I really don't understand what the book is about.
- My reading sounds very bumpy.
- I would need help to be able to read this book.

FIGURE 5.2 The "By Myself" Strategy for Choosing Books

your leisure, independent reading opportunities trying to decode difficult words and passages. However, you do want your developing readers to move forward, so encourage them to choose "challenging" books, too. Keep in mind that the goal here is to empower children to make choices for *themselves* and to help them understand and take responsibility for their own reading decisions.

Book introductions.   Marie Clay (1991) says that every child needs and deserves an introduction to a text before the child is given the text to read independently. Consider how you have learned to introduce yourself to a book. For example, when you pick up a novel at a bookstore, you begin making predictions about its content as soon as you hold it in your hands. If you're familiar with the author, you may have an idea of the genre or the likely quality of the writing. When you read the title and look at the front cover, you probably make more predictions about what the book is going to be about. Next, you might read the brief introduction or synopsis on the back cover of the book. The introduction added to the information you already gathered about the author and title usually helps you make up your mind about whether you will purchase the book.

During this selection process, which may last only a few minutes, the "movie" of this book has started to run in your head. You have become engaged (or not engaged) in the story and have already made several predictions about where this author might take you. Similarly, when you introduce books to children, one of your goals will be to engage students and help prepare them to make predictions. The more information they can gather from the book introduction, the more likely it is that they will understand the text and be able to make appropriate predictions at the word, sentence, and story level.

The type of book introduction you provide for your students will depend on several variables: their reading developmental level, their knowledge about the topic or content of the book, their experience with the words in the book, and their familiarity with the genre. As a teacher, you should consistently provide book introductions during read-alouds, shared reading, and guided reading.

To help children choose books for independent reading, you will need to remind them of how you provide book introductions for them during parts of your literacy day. But, your goal for independent reading time is for children to learn to introduce books to themselves. You will again rely on modeling the processes involved in the way you introduce books to yourself and allow children to practice the procedure with you and with one another.

A good strategy is to let children introduce a book to a partner, then have the children switch roles using a different book. Similar to the criteria delineated in the By Myself strategy, these are some of the features you want children to notice when they introduce books to themselves and decide whether or not to choose the book for independent reading:

- The cover,
- The author,
- The pictures,
- The amount and size of the print,
- The thickness (length) of the book,
- Their familiarity with the book or topic, and
- The difficulty of the words. (Teach children the "three-finger rule": If there are three or more words on a page they don't know, it's too hard. For emergent readers, it would be the "one- or two-finger rule.")

What kinds of information about texts do students glean from book introductions?

Some Early Readers consistently choose books that are too difficult for them to read. How can you help such children make better choices?

■■■ **YOU TRY IT** ■■■ ■ ■■ ■ ■ ■ ■ ■■

Book Introduction

For this You Try It, each of you should bring to class a children's book that you have read. After you have paired up with a classmate, pretend you are a teacher who is introducing the book to an Early Reader. Read the title and author's or illustrator's name, ask your partner to make predictions about the text, then tell a little bit about the book in order to engender interest and start building comprehension. You can try reading a passage from the book or ask your partner to do so. Discuss why book introductions are essential and how they promote students' motivation to read.

Making Books With Children

You may have trouble locating enough books that are easy enough for students at the emergent and beginning stages of reading. An alternative to using books that are too difficult for your Early Readers is to make books with and for them. Teacher/student-made books build on children's store of known words and prior life experiences. Since you understand that creating books containing some words that children already know is based on Vygotsky's notion of ZPD, as a teacher you should construct texts that are exactly in students' "zone," that is, where children can succeed in reading with minimum help (Vygotsky, 1978).

A powerful learning experience is to have children participate *with you* in the book making process. In this way, the books become personally important to the children. Further, the meaning is clear because the children themselves participated in the creation process and they are actively involved in the construction of knowledge. Making books is a social constructivist activity; you engage in an educational dialogue with the child during the process of making the book, negotiating decisions and constructing meaning together in a social setting (Bodrova & Leong, 1996; Newman, Griffin, & Cole, 1989).

Procedures for book construction.   Before beginning a book, engage the child in a real conversation concerning what the child already knows, like family, food, pets, interests. These distinctive experiences can be the foundation of the kind of book you create. For example, if you find out that the child has a cat, choosing cat stickers for a sticker book would be a good choice.

Here are some steps to follow when making a book with an Early Reader:

- Use blank books of about six to seven pages. Staple down the left side of the spine.
- Talk with the child about life experiences before beginning.
- Decide on a theme that connects to the child's experiences.
- Remember that your goal is to create an easy, readable book so compose only one sentence per page that will fit on one line (i.e., no return sweep).
- Start each sentence with an anchor word—one that the child knows—such as *I* or *A*.
- Place the text in the same place on each page, preferably at the bottom of the page below the illustration.
- Use good-sized upper- and lowercase print unless the child only recognizes certain words, like a name, in all capital letters.

Making books with children is an effective way to increase your collection of easy books for students. Why is book making such a compelling learning experience for Early Readers?

- Overemphasize spaces between words.
- Make sure the illustrations are simple and very clearly associated with the text.
- Let the child participate as much as possible in the book making process (e.g., placing stickers, gluing magazine cutouts, or illustrating the pages), but do the transcribing yourself for readability purposes.
- Invite the child to read the book to you when finished, then celebrate the child's success.

Figure 5.3 contains brief descriptions of books, some of which are suggested by Susan Gunderson and Tammy Younts of Purdue University based on their experiences with children in the Reading Recovery® program. These books can be made with Early Readers and then placed in their own personal book baskets of favorite, independent reading texts.

If you are interested in some additional creative ideas for making books with children we suggest the idea-filled title, *Making Books: Over 30 Practical Book-Making Projects for Children* (Johnson, 2000).

- **A sticker book**
  Let's say you find stickers of colored leaves. You and the child then set about the task of making a book with the following pattern:

  Many Colored Leaves!

  I see a red
  leaf.

  I see a yellow
  leaf.

  I see a green
  leaf.

  This particular sticker book supports the emergent reader by following the same pattern of text on each page, cueing the color word by the color of the leaf on the sticker. It also provides success for the child in both planning the layout and assembling the book and being able to read it.

FIGURE 5.3   Teacher/Student-Made Book Ideas

- **An "environmental print" book:** *I Go To . . .*
  For an emergent reader, use cutouts of restaurant logos from newspaper or magazine ads or logos taken from printouts at websites.

  Let the child help you construct this book by first letting him choose from a variety of restaurant logos that you have collected.

  The key here is *the child has to recognize the logo and be able to name it.*

  Paste a logo to each page where the phrase "I go to _____" is written. (The logo goes in the blank.)

  Negotiate the simple text for the final page of the book with the child based on the child's experiences and oral language. This provides a successful reading experience for emergent readers. For example, the book might end "No more food!" or "I am full!"

- **A book specifically based on the child's store of known words**
  For a particular emergent reader use the child's known words such as *LAURA, EMILY, I, MOM, DOG;* /m/ as in *my* are the words this child, Laura, can recognize.

  Then make a pattern book, such as:
  I see LAURA.
  I see EMILY.
  I see MOM.
  I see my DOG.

  Note that many of the words contain capital letters because this is how the child knows, recognizes, and writes these words. Use the form the child knows in the text of the book. The purpose is to create a book the child can read independently with success. Understanding of conventional use of capital and lowercase letters will come later.

- **No Problem book:** Begin by drawing a face on the cover of the book, discussing facial features such as eyes, nose, ears, hair, etc.

  Then, on each consecutive page leave off one feature of the face. (For example, on the first page leave off the nose. The text would read "No nose." Then, on the next page quickly draw the face with no eyes. The text would read "No eyes.")

  Let the child help you decide what facial feature to leave off. Continue in this pattern until at the end the whole face is complete again and write underneath it: "No problem." For example:

  No Problem

  No eyes.
  No nose.
  No ears.
  No mouth.
  No hair.
  No problem!

FIGURE 5.3 *Continued*

- **Book from an LEA:** Use a class dictation from a shared experience, as in the Language Experience Approach, to create a predictable book that students in a kindergarten or first-grade class could read with little or no assistance.

Example of an LEA text:

Our Trip to the Zoo
I saw a monkey. (Trisha)
I liked the tigers and the lions. (Matthew)
I saw a kangaroo and her baby. (Melissa)
There were lots of ducks in the pond. (Samantha)
The polar bears were in the water. (Jason)
We got to eat ice cream. (Jennifer)

Example of an easy-to-read book from the LEA text that could be illustrated:

Our Trip to the Zoo
"I saw a monkey," said Trisha.
"I saw the tigers and the lions," said Matthew.
"I saw a kangaroo and her baby," said Melissa.
"I saw ducks," said Samantha.
"I saw polar bears," said Jason.
"We ate ice cream," said Jennifer.

FIGURE 5.3 *Continued*

YOU TRY IT

Make a Book for Early Readers

Using the ideas for making books in this chapter, make a book for Early Readers that is bright and inviting and durable enough to last, laminating it if possible. Remember to print in clear, large print using both upper- and lowercase letters. Illustrate the pages with pictures cut from magazines, or stickers, or your own colorful drawings. If you choose to construct a book using a child's known words, invent your "own child" and the words that she knows to form the basis of the text you construct. Share your emergent texts with your classmates, explaining how you would use this book with a child.

Madison and Tyler are reading the room.

Reading the Room

Another effective way to provide materials for young students is by filling the walls of your classroom with poems, charts, Big Books, and stories that have been read by the children during shared reading. After sharing these texts together in whole- and small-group settings, they can be used by individual children during independent reading as they "read the room." When you have demonstrated how this is done, as well as set guidelines for behavior, you can encourage children to independently travel around the circumference of the classroom reading from the printed material posted there, providing pointers for children who need and enjoy that support.

A teaching idea tied into the "reading the room" approach is to attach zippered plastic sandwich bags next to each posted poem that contain sentence strips from the poem, cut into words (see Figure 5.4 for suggestions on how to do this). The child's task is to reconstruct the poem as if she were putting pieces of a puzzle together. When the child has the whole poem reconstructed, she can read it to herself or to the teacher or to a peer. In this particular exercise, the child is engaged in "making the words make sense," paying attention to conventions of print (such as capital letters and punctuation), and experiencing success as she effectively reconstructs and reads a familiar text.

Children enjoy reconstructing posted poems as they "read the room." What are the literacy learning benefits of reconstructing texts?

Texts for Independent Reading

Since you are encouraging your students to read, read, read, you will need to develop a classroom library that supplies them with texts. You will have to be creatively tenacious in your pursuit of reading materials, including contacting your administrators for

Here's how to use this teaching idea:

1. During shared reading, introduce a new poem like this familiar one to the whole class, written on chart paper:

Apple Tree

Way up high in an apple tree,
Two little apples looking down at me.
I shook that tree as hard as I could.
Down came the apples, Mmmm they were good!

2. Leave this poem posted for several days for rereading and add motions to your class's enthusiastic chanting.
3. When you're sure everyone is familiar with the poem, write another copy of it on thick paper.
4. Using four different brightly colored markers, put a colored dot under each word on both poems—the one for the wall and the one for cutting up. (For example, put purple dots under each word in line 1; orange dots under each word in line 2; green dots, line 3; and pink dots, line 4.)
5. Cut apart the poem on thick paper, word by word.
6. Put all the cut-apart words in a zippered plastic sandwich bag.
7. Post the full poem on a bulletin board.
8. Use a pushpin to attach the plastic bag of words next to the posted poem.
9. Show children how to reconstruct the poem on the floor, like a puzzle. Have a child help with the demonstration.
10. Call attention to how the colored dots, as well as the poem on the wall, can help them make matches.
11. When the poem-puzzle is complete, let the child use a pointer to read the whole poem to the class.
12. Rejoice in the success of the experience!
13. Demonstrate how to place the words back in the plastic bag and attach it to the bulletin board.
14. Tell children that when they read the room, one of their learning tasks will be to reconstruct poems that will cover the walls as the year progresses.

FIGURE 5.4   Cut-Apart Poem and Reconstruction

financial support, engaging your school librarian, asking parents for donations of books, shopping at used book outlets, ordering from trade book companies, or even writing grants that might fund your classroom library. In doing so, consider genres, tailoring book selections for individual children, and your familiarity with your books.

Genres.   In addition to covering the walls of your classroom with an array of genres such as labels, songs, poems, class-composed stories, pocket charts, and Word Walls, you will need to create a collection of books from a wide range of genres that represent many cultures and traditions from which your students can choose.

Early Readers need alphabet books, counting books, children's literature, class-published books, reference materials such as dictionaries and encyclopedias, and those that accompany the topics you are studying. Often these topic-related books will be nonfiction. Richgels (2002) writes, "Informational texts can be valuable sources of content knowledge and provide emergent readers and writers with opportunities to explore the workings of written language" (p. 586).

Collecting Books

Dear Derek,

As a new teacher how did you collect enough books for your classroom? How were you able to afford it?

Dear New Teachers,

I started collecting some books when I was an undergraduate. But, I really got excited about building a classroom library when I was hired for my first job. I became a book scavenger! I went to garage sales and contacted teachers who were retiring and might be giving their books away. Books don't have to be new to be part of your library. It's surprising how much kids enjoy reading old encyclopedias and textbooks.

Also, I was able to get in on a grant to our school. My colleagues and I shared money that provided us with about 300 books per classroom. I would urge new teachers to search out grant money, like those offered by the major bookstore chains, to help with the cost of assembling a classroom library.

Nonfiction books are sometimes underused in the primary grades, but may, in fact, be the kinds of books that appeal to and motivate your students the most. Yopp and Yopp (2000) argue that young children are interested in and are able to read informational texts; they agree with those who say that we are shortchanging our young students if we do not provide them with abundant nonfiction texts from which to choose (e.g., Moss, Leone, & Dippillo, 1997).

Diversity issue: Tailoring book selections for individual children. One goal that should be foremost in your mind as you create your classroom library will be meeting the reading needs of your students. When you spend time in any primary classroom, you will notice the range of differences among children in just one class. Let's say you are in a second grade; some of the readers will be reading at an emergent stage, while others will be ready for chapter books. We have discussed leveled texts (little books) for beginning readers, but you will also need to think about books for those who are ready for more difficult texts.

Transitional chapter books are available that are tailored to meet students' developing needs for more complex text, more characters, and multifaceted plot lines as they graduate from easier-to-read books. Sometimes these transitional chapter books are published in a series and can be quite exciting for your first and second graders as they make their way through the series. Examples of these series are Kids of the Polk Street School and New Kids of the Polk Street School by Patricia Reilly Giff, Junie B. Jones by Barbara Park, and Henry and Mudge by Cynthia Rylant. A sample of transitional chapter books can be found in Figure 5.5.

Brandenberg, F. (1984). *Leo and Emily and the dragon.* New York: Yearling.

Clifford, E. (1978). *Help! I'm a prisoner in the library.* New York: Houghton Mifflin.

Dahl, R. (1998). *Fantastic Mr. Fox.* New York: Puffin.

Delton, J. (1988). *Pee Wee Scouts Camp Ghost-Away.* New York: Yearling.

Delton, J. (1990). *Hello Huckleberry Heights.* New York: Yearling.

Giff, P. R. (1984). *The beast in Ms. Rooney's room.* New York: Yearling.

Peterson, J. (1986). *The Littles.* New York: Scholastic.

Rylant, C. (2000). *The case of the climbing cat (High-rise private eyes).* New York: Greenwillow.

Smith, R. K. (1978). *Chocolate fever.* New York: Yearling.

FIGURE 5.5   Transitional Chapter Books

To facilitate children's book selections during independent reading, you may want to think about assembling individual book baskets for your students. (You can use small inexpensive plastic containers or even shoeboxes for your book baskets.) Book baskets should contain books that individual students and you have selected together that are at that "just right" reading level. For instance, Latasha may be making her way through the Junie B. Jones series. So, her basket would have one or two of those books as well as perhaps a biography that has captivated her and a book of riddles that second graders find hilarious. Simultaneously, Latasha's friend Cindy, who is at a different developmental reading level, has a book basket with a few leveled texts, an easy-to-read chapter book like *Frog and Toad Are Friends* by Arnold Lobel (1970), and a children's dictionary that she enjoys reading to learn new words.

Book baskets can also be created to house books of the same genres, same series, same illustrator, or same levels of reading difficulty. This is another purposeful way to organize your classroom library and help your students with their decision making during independent reading.

Be thoroughly familiar with your books.   As you can see, it is essential that you be familiar with the books you gather so that you can organize them into categories and levels. In addition, you must know the books that you have in your classroom collection so that you can guide and support children in their book choices. Finally, your knowledge of books must correspond to your knowledge of your students and their strengths and needs as developing readers so that you can suggest just the right book for them at just the right time.

ENCOURAGING INDEPENDENT READING AND WRITING

We say that the goal of literacy teaching is to create independent readers and writers who choose to engage in reading and writing. Yet our actions do not always support what we say. Do you remember having a favorite book, like a novel, in your school desk that you would sneak out and read when you were supposed to be doing other schoolwork? Perhaps you were clever at placing the novel inside your textbook, then holding the textbook at just the right angle in front of you on the desktop so you could be reading what *you* wanted to read instead of the assignment. You probably ended up getting caught and reprimanded for reading the wrong text. You may have thought to yourself, "Why did I get in trouble for *reading?*"

While we understand that all teachers have assigned readings that are part of their curriculum, independent reading time, in which students select what they read, needs to be a part of every school day. Concerning changes in schooling that would result in better readers, Allington (2001a) notes: "If I were required to select a single aspect of the instructional environment to change, my first choice would be creating a schedule that supported dramatically increased quantities of reading during the school day" (p. 24). When you teach, time must be set aside for independent reading of texts that children want to read. Some of this reading takes place during guided reading, some during center time, but it should also take place as dedicated silent reading time.

You also may have school memories of writing assignments that failed to interest you because you had no choice about what to write. Lack of choice in writing often turns students into nonwriters and fosters negative feelings toward writing in general. "I hate writing" sometimes means "I hate to write about what my teacher wants me to write about." Therefore, when you teach young children, you need to offer time during which they are encouraged to compose texts of their own choosing, about topics that interest and engage them.

In this section we explore fostering independent reading and writing through promoting silent reading during Reading Workshop and promoting self-selected writing during Writing Workshop. We begin with events that typically occur during Reading Workshop. Reading Workshop in this text is defined as that chunk of the Literacy Workshop framework in which the teacher and students are engaged in small-group and independent work—specifically guided reading, reading conferences, independent reading, and literacy centers.

Promoting Silent Reading

As a part of Reading Workshop, children need time every day to read silently by themselves. Because we are talking about young children, this time is often whisper reading time. Emergent readers may use this time to sit and look at books, quietly talking through the books using the pictures as a source of their narratives or remembering phrases from listening to the book read aloud. Early Readers may select books from their baskets of old favorites and read some of the pages while improvising on other pages when the text becomes too difficult. Or perhaps your students enjoy magazines that you've ordered for your classroom. More fluent young readers may curl up on a beanbag chair with a transitional chapter book like *Henry and Mudge and the Tall Treehouse* by Cynthia Rylant (2001), enjoying the adventures of the would-be detective Henry and his trusty sidekick dog. Whatever the difficulty levels or genre choice, the important thing is that students are reading, by themselves, every day.

SSR, DEAR, WEB, RAP.   Teachers use different labels to signify independent reading. SSR (Sustained Silent Reading), DEAR (Drop Everything and Read), WEB (Wonderfully Exciting Books), and RAP (Read Any Place) are some of the titles used in elementary classrooms to mean special times of the day during which everyone reads, often even the teacher. During these periods of independent reading, the focus is on enjoyment, engagement, and practice—all of which result in more proficient readers who choose to read. In order for independent reading to be a success in your classroom, you need to create an inviting environment, provide materials that allow for choice, and provide time for response and assessment.

Creating an inviting environment for independent reading.   Children need to feel comfortable and at ease during independent reading time, just like you do. Suppose you just purchased a novel that your friend recommended as a "must read!" A few of

A cozy loft provides a great place for independent reading.

you may sit at a desk as you begin to read the novel that you're so anxious to get into, but we're guessing that many of you will lounge in a comfortable chair, or lie on a couch, or nestle onto a pile of blankets on the floor as you embark on the journey with your new book. Similarly, children need inviting spaces that foster getting lost in a book. You might provide reading rugs, an old couch, a reading loft, big pillows, or cozy reading corners for your students. Soft, incandescent lighting from lamps rather than the harsh glare of overhead fluorescent lighting is also a way to suggest that it's time to relax with a favorite book or story.

Providing for choice.   We've already discussed the importance of providing your young readers with a wide variety of materials ranging from storybooks to magazines to newspapers to encyclopedias. Among the reasons for such collections of texts is that it affords children with *choice* in selecting what they will read during independent reading. As you know from your own experiences, choice is an important component affecting motivation (e.g., Guthrie & Wigfield, 1997; Turner & Paris, 1995). When children are given choices about what they will read, they feel empowered and enthused. Gill (2000) notes that when a child is given a choice of texts he will often strive for successful reading by choosing books that are familiar and that he can read fluently. Over time, the child will gain the confidence to select unfamiliar, more challenging texts—no longer relying on the scaffolding provided by familiar texts.

Assessing Independent Reading

As teachers, sometimes our best intentions fall short. This can happen during independent reading time when students may read for 5 minutes and declare they're finished, or complain that they have nothing to read, or simply refuse to use the time reading. These are pitfalls that can be avoided by planning ahead and watching for signs that your students are losing interest in independent reading.

Although we suggest you spend at least part of your independent reading time reading books yourself to model good reading-for-pleasure behavior for your students, you will need to spend some of the time assessing independent reading. You should know what your students are reading and if they are engaged with the texts they have chosen. You should also conduct brief conferences on a systematic basis. Sometimes, this assessment will take the form of walking around the classroom, stopping to notice your students' choices and level of engagement, and making anecdotal notes to yourself to use in student–teacher conferences. These conferences, which are a daily part of your Literacy Workshop time, are platforms for succinct conversations about what children are reading and allow you to use your observational notes and the child's responses to make judgments about what they are accomplishing during independent reading.

Paired discussions. First-year teacher Lee-Daniels (2000) noticed DEAR burnout among her second graders who were disengaging during voluntary reading time. To salvage what she knew was a vital component of their school day, she paired students who had similar interests and had copies of the same book. The partners each independently read 10 pages at a time, then discussed those pages with the other. As a teacher, you can casually listen in on children reading together and their subsequent talk to assess whether independent reading is going well or not. Children's discussions also provide a social setting for sharing thoughts and ideas gained during silent reading and support your social constructivist learning framework.

Response logs. Some teachers find reading response logs helpful but because your primary purpose is *reading* during this time of the day, you will want to require only short entries such as the title of the book, number of pages read, and brief remarks about the texts in a reading log notebook that children have with them during the Literacy Workshop time. See Figure 5.6 for a sample of a student's reading response log.

Classroom Assessment

Paired discussions can help Early Readers stay engaged during independent reading time. How can you use this as an assessment opportunity?

Classroom Assessment

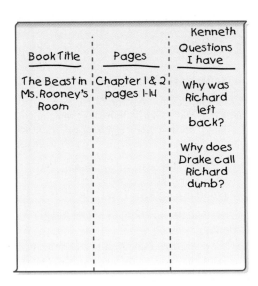

FIGURE 5.6 Student's Reading Response Log

Promoting Self-Selected Writing

Although the primary focus of this textbook is teaching reading, we do want you to consider teaching writing as well and how you can create the conditions that foster students who *choose* to write. Many effective teachers find that using a Writing Workshop approach helps their young writers develop writing abilities and skills. Calkins (1994) suggests that Writing Workshop should occur as a predictable, daily event as students engage in the writing processes of thinking about what to write, creating drafts, conferring with others, revising and editing, and finally publishing. You will have to explicitly teach children about the writing process. Figure 5.7 lists some guiding principles.

During Writing Workshop children work at an individual pace and are not all at the same stage in their writing at the same time. One child may have just finished a piece and be brainstorming topics to write about for a new piece. Another student may be signed up for a conference with her teacher to discuss editing and revision. Still another might be working with a parent volunteer who is helping him transcribe his writing onto the computer and then bind the pages for publication.

 The writing process emphasizes the steps that writers take to produce a piece of writing. How is this approach different than looking at writing solely as a product?

Guiding writers.   The workshop approach helps children learn to be writers, find their voice, and experience the satisfaction of seeing their written work published (Atwell, 1987; Calkins, 1994; Graves, 1983). The teacher guides the writing process by conferring with individual students and by providing minilessons to whole- or small-group gatherings on topics that she notices the children are struggling with, based on her observations. Here are some examples of minilessons during Writing Workshop for young writers: leaving spaces between words, using capital letters at the beginning of sentences, where to look for help when you come to a word you don't know how to spell, or putting a punctuation mark at the end of sentences.

Early writers, like kindergarteners, will often use drawings as their communication medium when you ask them to write. This is a perfectly normal stage and way

Stage of the Process	Questions
Choosing a topic	What am I going to write about?
Audience	Who is my audience and what do I want them to know?
Knowledge	What do I know about this topic? Do I need to find out more?
Composing	How can I get a draft down on paper?
Revision	How can I add, change, delete, reorder, or remove parts of my writing? (*Note:* Children think that revision is the same as editing, so they have to be taught the difference.)
Editing	I need to proofread, as well as use conventional English and correct spelling as a courtesy to the audience who will read my work. Did I do this?
Publishing	Do I want to publish this piece of writing or just keep it in my writing folder?

FIGURE 5.7   Principles of the Writing Process

for them to write. When you accept a child's drawing, she will gladly interpret it for you, telling you "what it says." Gradually, you can request that students add a letter or even words to their pictures that describe what is happening. Sometimes these letters or letter-like figures that children add contain great meaning. The example in Figure 5.8 shows a kindergartener's drawing and accompanying text as translated to her teacher. As you can see, she has conveyed quite a bit of important information by using developmental spelling and an illustration.

As children mature, teachers should focus on craft lessons as a means of helping them develop into sophisticated writers who will learn more about writing each time they write. Just as we learn to read better by reading, we learn to write better by writing. Fletcher and Portalupi (1998) note that "writing teachers need to have a deep and profound knowledge of writing and this knowledge should include a sense of how writers grow as they move through the grades and move toward proficiency" (p. 2). Some of the craft lessons Fletcher and Portalupi suggest for developing writers in grades K–2 include learning about the beginning, middle, and end of stories; using details to create "mind pictures" for the reader; using illustrations to convey information; and using details to describe the setting.

Conferring with writers.   Meeting with individual students during Writing Workshop is imperative. Calkins (1994) asserts that these conferences are the heart of teaching writing. She reminds us that we need to always keep this fundamental principle in mind as teachers: It is the *writer* we are trying to help, *not the writing.* During one-on-one conferences, you can ask the child questions about the writing process like these:

- How did you decide to write about this topic?
- Which parts of the writing are going well? Which parts are difficult?
- Tell me about what you have down so far.
- What are you going to add to or change in your writing next?

Classroom Assessment

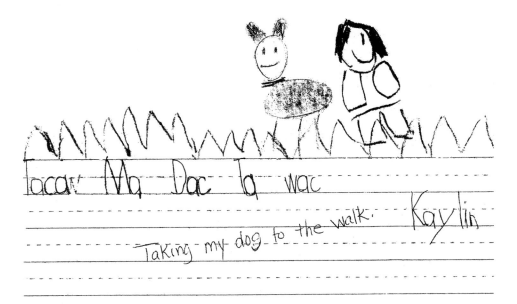

FIGURE 5.8   Kindergartner's Drawing With Accompanying Text

Conferring with writers can help develop their competency.
What are topics of discussion that could guide young writers?

- How are the illustrations helping you tell the story?
- Do you have any questions about your writing?
- When you are finished with this piece, what are going to do with it?

You can also use your conference time to share what you've observed about the writer during workshop. For example, you might use a checklist that assesses the student's level of involvement and development during Writing Workshop. In addition, you can ask the child to self-assess his progress during Writing Workshop, keeping in mind that the goal is fostering *independent* writing.

FACILITATING READING AND WRITING WORKSHOPS

In this chapter you have been studying ways to help children choose books for independent reading and to encourage reading and writing on their own during Reading/Writing Workshops. This information may have caused you to wonder, "If I don't keep the class together as a whole group or working in small groups, and the kids are doing independent tasks, how will I manage this? Will my classroom be chaotic and disorganized? How will I keep track of who's doing what?" These are important questions for you to think about because independent work time can become unmanageable if you don't have a plan and you don't establish practiced routines with your students.

Practiced Routines

We believe that setting up Reading/Writing Workshops in which children have the freedom to read and write based on their own choices provides for children's optimal literacy development. As you have already guessed, independent work can turn into "aimless wondering around" if your students don't understand what's expected of them during workshop time. It will be up to you to teach your students how to operate independently and purposefully in the classroom. How will you do that?

Whole and small groups first.   As we've mentioned before, you should begin the school year teaching your students together as a whole group. Until early learners understand how to conduct themselves in a whole group, it is very difficult for them to understand how to work independently. For example, at the beginning of the year you will teach your young students how the daily schedule works. They should learn that when it's story time they're to come from their desks or tables to the Reading Rug to listen to a read-aloud. You will teach them that they need to keep their hands to themselves, take turns speaking, and listen while you read.

Similarly, students should learn with your guidance to participate in choral readings with their peers during shared reading and how to take turns coming up to the chart to write words during shared writing experiences. These "school behaviors" may be new to your students and they will have to be modeled and practiced many times before students understand your expectations. Once your Early Readers are able to conduct themselves in whole groups, you can move to small-group activities such as guided reading. This step, too, requires much perseverance and practice.

When children know how to function in whole- and small-group settings, you can then implement Reading and Writing Workshops in which a portion of their time will be independent work. Remember, when you manage your classroom, withdrawing teacher support in terms of controlling students' behavior parallels the withdrawal of your support as a teacher during the phases of literacy teaching and learning. (Refer again to Figure 5.1 earlier in this chapter.)

Teaching independence by setting guidelines.   Good teaching always involves modeling and then providing opportunities for practice; this is how you will proceed when you teach children how to work independently. You begin by modeling behavior in a whole-group setting.

   Let's say that you wish to teach children how to conduct themselves during independent reading. Because you want your students to take responsibility for their own behaviors as well as their own learning, a good idea is to have a class meeting to brainstorm with your Early Readers some of the guidelines or rules for Reading Workshop. (You'll do the same for Writing Workshop.) Write down all suggestions the students have about behavior during this time. Then, work toward achieving consensus concerning the most important guidelines and record them on a chart that will stay posted in the classroom throughout the year. Try to keep the rules as simple, straightforward, and positive as possible (avoid too many "don'ts"). Figure 5.9 contains the "Rules for Reading Workshop" constructed by a second-grade class along with their teacher.

Teaching independence by role playing.   After students have established the community rules for Reading or Writing Workshop, model these behaviors by role-playing them with individual children in front of the whole group. For example, think about showing children how to read quietly with a partner. Ask two students to come to the front of the class. Seat them side by side and have them demonstrate quiet reading and responding for their peers. Now have the students read and talk in loud voices. Discuss the impact of loud talking on the rest of the students who are engaged in quiet reading. Denton and Kriete (2000) note that after a role play, the teacher summarizes

---

Rules for Reading Workshop

* Respect and help each other.

* Always stay busy.

* Read books from your desk, the book baskets, the class library, or the centers.

* Remember to record your reading in your reading log.

* When you read with a partner, read quietly so others can concentrate.

* Follow the directions at the centers and put materials away.

* Ask a friend if you have a question when the teacher is working with guided reading groups.

* Do not disturb others.

* Read, read, read!

FIGURE 5.9   Sample Second-Grade Reading Workshop Rules

the input students have generated and encourages everyone to practice the ideas in daily classroom life.

Or, let's say you want to model what children can do when the teacher is busy with guided reading groups. Role-play this situation by pretending you are working diligently with a small group of readers. Have another child act as if she has a question she cannot figure out by herself. Elicit suggestions from the rest of the students about options the child can try other than disturbing the teacher and the reading group. Those suggestions might include the following: Try thinking of an answer yourself, ask a neighbor, or write the question down and ask the teacher later when she is free.

Independent workshop activities call for management guidelines and expectations. How will you set those guidelines in a primary classroom?

Classroom Assessment

Practice, practice, practice.   Once rules have been established by and for the class, an integral part of community building, it is imperative that you hold children accountable for following those guidelines. Otherwise your Reading/Writing Workshop time can turn into pandemonium where little is being accomplished. Children should begin practicing routines in small time increments, perhaps just 5 to 10 minutes at first then gradually increasing time devoted to the activity as the year progresses (Tierney & Readence, 2000).

Class meetings.   An important goal for your students is that they learn to assess themselves. After each of the first independent literacy sessions, you can hold class meetings to assess the effectiveness of workshop time. Using the chart that you and your students constructed, ask questions such as these: "Did everyone stay busy? Why or why not? Who was able to stay focused on their reading or writing the whole time? How were you able to do that? I noticed Jerome had a question but he didn't interrupt guided reading. How did you solve your problem, Jerome?" Questions like these support self-reflection and self-assessment and put the responsibility back on students to monitor and regulate their own behavior.

Similarly, when things don't go well, you and your students will have to determine strategies for remedying those challenges as well as setting up consequences. For instance, let's say that Matt keeps forgetting to record his reading in his reading log. Maybe the consequence will be that his reading log has to be checked by a peer each time after independent reading until Matt can remember to make his notations without reminders.

Class meetings can be forums for students to assess their own success as learners and citizens. Why do you believe that self-assessment is essential?

Independent reading and writing with early learners will take patience, perseverance, and practice in order for them to understand and carry out expectations. As your students learn the routines and how to handle materials, as well as themselves, you should continually praise them for jobs well done.

More Literacy Centers

In Chapter 3 you learned about creating learning stations such as an ABC Center, a technology center, and a Library Corner. Here we introduce some additional ideas for centers for you. Some teachers prefer to conduct Literacy Workshop time without the use of centers; they rely solely on sustained silent reading or children's independent work during workshop time. As a new teacher, however, we recommend that you provide centers for your students as a supplement to your literacy program. You can create centers for your students that provide active practice in using their developing literacy skills. Figure 5.10 contains some suggestions for centers that are motivating and supportive for Early Readers. Other literacy centers that may come and go in your classroom include such ideas as using the overhead projector, a Big Book corner, or a Drama Corner.

Advice for New Teachers

Keeping Your Balance

Dear Derek,

The more I learn about literacy teaching and learning, as well as managing the classroom, the more concerned I become about how I will be able to do it all!

Dear New Teachers,

I felt that way, too. The good news is that you don't have to do it all. I have found that you must prioritize and first do the things that are most important. And, frankly, sometimes things I've tried don't work for me. When this happens I change and try something else, rotating ideas until I find a schedule, or materials, or an approach that works best for me and my students. To keep from getting overly stressed, I have to know my limits and keep my kids' needs at the center of my teaching.

Writing—For this center, gather a wide variety of writing materials such as pens, markers, crayons, and a choice of papers for children's work. Also include reference resources such as word lists, dictionaries, and high-frequency word charts.

Word Study Center—This center should contain materials that encourage children to play with letters and words and learn more about how words work. Among the materials you should assemble are magnetic letters, letter cubes, word cards, small chalkboards, dry-erase boards, and alphabet books.

Listening—Place tape recorders with earphones in this center along with children's books that have accompanying tape-recorded versions. Children can follow along with the books and read silently as they listen to the books on tape.

Unit-Based Centers—As you study topics in science, social studies, and math, students will want to learn more about those topics through literacy activities. These centers will change as your units of study change with books, research materials, manipulatives, and learning games rotating in and out.

FIGURE 5.10   Literacy Centers for Early Readers

Each center that you create needs to be thoughtfully planned and managed so that students' experiences move them forward as literacy learners. Ford and Opitz (2002) write: "Instruction away from the teacher needs to be as powerful as instruction with the teacher. Like instruction with the teacher, it needs to be grounded in knowledge of the children—their reading and writing abilities and their degree of independence" (p. 717).

The listening center is always a good place to hear stories and follow along in the book.

Introducing and managing centers.   Centers that you create should allow children to work without your assistance; therefore, you need to set clear expectations for the children, demonstrate the use of each center, and allow children to practice the routines, with your guidance, before you can expect them to manage independently. Typically, teachers establish some type of rotational system so that after 20 to 30 minutes, children move to a different center. Storage places for all materials should be labeled and children should understand and know how to maintain them.

Teachers who successfully manage centers find that introducing them one at a time, not all at once, works best. In other words, at the beginning of the year you will not have all your centers ready for students to start the first day. Rather, you will introduce them gradually, not launching a new one until children fully understand and can effectively use a center already in place. Just as you learned about constructing class rules, modeling and role-playing appropriate behavior with and for the children during independent work time, you will do the same for your class's centers.

This may mean one center a week until all centers are open. Students must practice effective learning behaviors in each center as well as how to care for and store materials. Show your students how each container in a center is labeled (such as "Pencils," "Pens," "Markers") so that everything can be returned to its place and students leave each center ready for the next group. In addition, you will need to demonstrate and practice moving from one station to another, with as little confusion as possible, if you establish a rotational system.

Suppose you've decided to introduce the Writing Center. You will gather your students around the center and explicitly teach what the center is for as well as point out materials such as individual folders for children's work and the resources for accessing words students need to spell. Then, take the whole group back to the Reading Rug to construct a charted checklist to be posted in the Writing Center. This checklist will be a visual reminder for the children about housekeeping duties such as where to place materials when finished and about what to do when you need help. Repeat this procedure for each center you introduce.

Centers should be introduced to Early Readers one at a time. Why is this good practice?

You will find that occasionally students have difficulty remembering how to manage themselves during workshop time. Some children need only a gentle reminder to get them back on track. Others may need firmer consequences. Usually, having to sit out of centers for a day is enough of a consequence for most children to remind them of their responsibility to be good citizens during center time. You may even have to "reintroduce" centers, practicing routines, procedures, and transitions all over again. Some teachers are fortunate enough to have parents who come into the classroom to help during workshop time, making centers run much more smoothly.

ENCOURAGING READING AND WRITING WITH FAMILIES

Thinking about teaching children in independent settings causes us to think very deeply about the individual child. And, when you focus on the individual child, you must consider each child in the context of his home and family. Knowing this, you also know that the most important partners in the classroom are the parents or guardians of your students. In this book we use the term *parent(s)* to refer to any person or persons responsible for providing the majority of primary care for the child. That may include relatives of the child such as grandparents, foster parents and guardians, and sometimes even older siblings. Because these individuals are serving as parents, we will refer to them as such.

When considering your work with future students' parents, Spielman (2001) cautions that we teachers not consider ourselves as the dispensers of knowledge to parents. Instead we need to partner with parents, as equals, in the literacy education of their children. Spielman believes that following questions need to be asked in all literacy initiatives with parents:

- Do family literacy programs work on equalizing the inequities of our school systems?
- Do they begin with a healthy respect for parents' knowledge?
- Do teachers use parents' knowledge in developing curriculum?

You can begin fostering positive partnerships with parents by welcoming parents to your classroom. As a new teacher, it is sometimes daunting to have parents walk into the classroom when you are teaching. You may be worried if "instructional chaos" reigns at the particular time they choose to visit. While that may be a bit unnerving the first time or two it happens, keep in mind that parents will judge you over time, not on one occasion *if they feel welcome in your classroom.*

For those of you who are parents (as well as those who will be someday), nothing feels more unsettling than sensing that you're unwelcome in your own child's classroom. No one likes to feel unwanted, especially in those places where your child is being educated. Besides being children's first teachers, parents also know their children better than anyone else. When you use parents' knowledge of their children, their desire to help their children succeed, and their assistance in the classroom, you will have garnered a most valuable asset for the sake of your students and the success of your teaching/learning community.

Parents need to feel welcome in the school and in your classroom. How can you extend a feeling of welcome and joint partnership to your future students' parents?

Therefore, except on rare occasions (for instance, when you are testing), make every effort to let your students' parents know that you not only want them to visit, but that you are counting on their help as partners in the education of their children. You can advocate for parents to be partners in your classroom by encouraging parents' help with literacy development at home, benefiting from parents' involvement at school, and promoting regular, honest communication.

Literacy Partnerships With Families

Your classroom instruction and classroom life will be more successful if you work daily to remember students' sociocultural contexts and to integrate what you are teaching with students' lives outside of school. We know that the ways parents approach literacy in the home has a great deal of influence on the success of their children in schools (Jordan, Snow, & Porche, 2000).

You might think that all parents know how to support their children's literacy at home. However, many families of the students in school today do not know that they should help their children because they did not experience help from their parents in their formative years (Fields & Spangler, 2000). Reading to young children at home is taken for granted in many American homes. However, researchers have found that some immigrant groups are surprised at a teacher's request for them to read to their children to help in the literacy education of their children.

Diversity issue: Parents' expectations.   In American schools we expect young children to learn the alphabet. Many of the parents of our students, however, have not had the experience of learning the alphabet in schools and cannot understand why teachers place such importance on the letters of the alphabet (Ada & Zubizarreta, 2001). In interviews with Mexican immigrants, Valdés (1996) found that parents were surprised at teachers' request for their children to learn the alphabet because in their experience of reading instruction in Mexico, syllables rather than the letters of the alphabet were emphasized. The same differences hold true for other aspects of learning of young readers. You know how important it is for parents to read aloud to their children. However, in some homes reading aloud is not only unfamiliar (Teale, 1986), it is also resisted.

In a study of Chinese American parents, Ernst-Slavit, Han, and Wenger (2001) found that the practice of reading aloud is not common in typical Chinese households; some Chinese parents felt that teachers were shirking their responsibility by asking parents to read to children at home. Because of these parents' background experiences with schooling, they held distinctly different views of their roles as parents than teachers held for them. The Chinese parents believed that teachers were supposed to teach students to read and write, as they had experienced in their home country. They understood that parents were responsible for teaching their children how to behave in preparation for schooling. Furthermore, the parents that Ernst-Slavit et al. interviewed lived frugally and had few resources to buy books or even to travel to public libraries so their children could use the library's book collections.

Building bridges.   If a lack of understanding exists between you and parents of your students, you should attempt to build bridges that help you and families connect with one another. As we've discussed, families sometimes struggle "to reconcile the familiar sociocultural patterns of functioning in their homes and communities with the vastly different and often confusing environment of the public school" (Nistler & Maiers, 2000, p. 671).

Literacy initiatives.   You already know that you will recommend books, advocate reading to children every day, and encourage parents' involvement with children's schoolwork. You may want and need to go further. For example, Morningstar (1999) started using home response journals with her class's parents as a means of helping teachers and parents learn from each other about children's literacy development. Barillas (2000) instituted a program that enrolled her students' Mexican and Mexican American parents in a writing project. Students and their parents engaged in voluntary writing assignments (in their first language, Spanish, and then later in English) that culminated in published works by all, shared at an end-of-the-year celebration. Barillas reports the benefits of this program: "The first [benefit] has been to encourage reading, writing, and discussion about school assignments at home. Second, because parents' experiences and knowledge are valued and recognized in the classroom, bonds of respect and appreciation for their culture, language, and identity are affirmed through this celebration of literacy" (p. 308).

Literacy backpacks.   Another way in which you can keep in touch with students' lives is to use literacy backpacks, which can be purchased, created by the teacher, or co-created between the school and families. They consist of a collection of literacy materials around a theme that are placed in a backpack and travel back and forth between the school and home for parents to enjoy with their children.

Let's say you are studying the weather with your first graders. A literacy backpack might contain a nonfiction book about the weather, a read-aloud book like *Cloudy With a Chance of Meatballs* (Barrett, 1978), a laminated weather game, and a literacy log in which the student and the parents can write responses to the shared literacy experiences. Jongsma (2001) explains, "Each time the packs go home, families read what other families have written, then add to the journals with adventures of their own. Students enjoy reading what their classmates and their families have written in the traveling journal" (p. 58).

Involving Parents in the Literacy Classroom

Parents can be invaluable help to you and your students in the literacy classroom. They can listen to children read, monitor learning centers, organize your classroom library and leveled books, make books and other teaching/learning materials, and provide extra help for those children who need it. Further, as children engage in the writing process, parents can serve as transcribers for children who can dictate but not yet write. They can assist in helping children edit and revise their work. Parents can take children's written work and type it on a word processor, demonstrating for children conventional spelling, grammar, and punctuation. As the publishing process comes full circle, parents can help children bind their stories or books and make covers for their published work.

Similarly, Nistler and Maiers (2000) described a family literacy program in which family members came into the classroom to help with literacy activities during the day. They helped with morning message, read-alouds, the poem of the week and related word work, cooking activities that involved reading and following recipes, and assisted with learning centers. Nistler and Maiers report:

> We found that by working closely with families we can further understand parents' beliefs, attitudes, and perceptions of the roles they play in the literacy development of their children. In turn, parents are able to give voice, through their actions, to the commitment they feel for their children to succeed. (p. 680)

Parents as tutors.   A specific way to involve parents in helping the students in your classroom is to enlist them as literacy tutors. Veskauf (1999) suggests recruiting parents, then offering a short training session, teaching them supportive teaching approaches such as helping children to become independent word solvers when they come to difficult words. Veskauf initiated a tutoring model in which parents read to the child, modeling good fluent reading, then the child reads to the parents. She noted that by inviting parents into her classroom as tutors, students' reading confidence and competence improved and parents' feelings of connection to the school and their children's learning were enhanced.

SEE FOR YOURSELF

Discovery Packs

Visit the message board for Chapter 5 on our Companion Website at *www.prenhall.com/lenski* to discuss your findings.

Connect to the Companion Website *(http://www.prenhall.com/lenski).* There you will find a link to Discovery Packs. Look under Primary Literature and Arts Discovery Packs. See what you think about these for-purchase materials for your Early Readers. How could they be used for fostering home–school literacy connections? How might your school be able to purchase such materials? How might you be able to construct similar-type packets yourself?

http://www.demco.com/discoverypacks.htm

Communicating With Parents

The more you understand families and the more they understand your purposes and interactions with their children, the more effective the teaching and learning will be in your classroom. Communication will require your commitment to listening as well as speaking so that a true dialogue can occur that promotes and honors parents' voices. Because language differences might exist between you and your students' parents, you may need to enlist the help of translators for written and spoken communication.

Before the school year even begins, write a letter home introducing yourself to your students' families. (See a sample introductory letter in Figure 5.11.) You might even want to visit your students' homes as a way of presenting yourself, letting parents know what they can expect for their children in your classroom, asking for their help as partners in their children's education, and learning about your students' families. Other means of communication throughout the school year include a beginning meeting, parent–teacher conferences, newsletters, and calls and notes.

Your first parent meeting.   As you begin the school year, it is important for you to help your students' parents understand your reading program and the kinds of literacy experiences and activities you will be providing their children. You may want to discuss your beliefs about early literacy learning, your goals and expectations for the children, scheduling and time issues, meeting individual students' needs, and your beliefs about the role of parental involvement in children's literacy development.

The children's book *Leo the Late Bloomer* by Robert Kraus (1971) is an excellent read-aloud for your first parent meeting. In this engaging book Leo, a young tiger, has a father who is extremely anxious that Leo is a slow learner. The mother tiger keeps advising patience and says, "A watched bloomer doesn't bloom!" This book wonderfully illustrates the developmental and individually unique nature of learning and also addresses parents' worries about their children in a very gentle and entertaining way.

> August
>
> Dear Parents,
>
> I'm pleased to welcome you and your children to first grade! You and I will work together to help your children grow as readers and writers, and watch how they change and develop between now and springtime. This year will be an exciting one for all of us!
>
> When you stop by the classroom you will see plenty of literacy activities like daily read-alouds, reading Big Books together on the Reading Rug, and small-group reading instruction. You will also observe your children becoming more skillful writers as they participate in Writing Workshop and even create their own books.
>
> Watch for books and writing that your children bring home. You can be a big help to your young children if you read to and with your first grader and share the joy of their developing writing.
>
> I hope you can attend our first Parent Meeting. There you will learn more about your first grader's reading and writing programs and ask any questions you might have. I look forward to meeting each of you and invite you to visit our classroom any time you're able.
>
> Sincerely,
>
> Mrs. Bertolucci

FIGURE 5.11   Introductory Letter From Teacher to Parents

A colorful, easy-to-read handout that explains some of the information you present at the first meeting is helpful so parents have something to take home and refer to later. This handout should contain simple literacy activities that parents can do with their children as well as a list of excellent children's books that parents can use as a resource as they select books for their families.

Parent-teacher conferences.   You probably remember your own parents attending parent–teacher conferences and feeling nervous about what the teacher was going to say about you. Some of you may have attended such conferences as parents yourselves and been nervous about what the teacher was going to say about your child. Right now you may be wondering, "How could my presence as a teacher in a conference make anyone uncomfortable? I'm too worried about what parents will think of me!" This dance of insecurity is often played out between the teacher and the parent without either party being totally aware of the two-sidedness of the apprehension. Parents are especially vulnerable if they feel inferior in educational background, linguistic understanding, or cultural knowledge of how schools work in this country.

To work diligently to allay the apprehension of your parents, consider the following guidelines for parent–teacher conferences:

- Make every effort to be welcoming by creating a cordial and comfortable environment for your conversations.
- Communicate positive information about your students as often as possible.

- Let parents know that you and they are on the same team—working to help their child.
- If there is a concern to problem solve regarding a student's progress, let parents know about the concern you want to discuss ahead of the conference. Never "ambush" parents by denying them advance time to prepare questions in order to think together with you on behalf of their child.
- Don't talk down to parents but explain everything thoroughly to make sure they understand what you are saying. Avoid educational jargon and abbreviations such as "LD" or "ADD." If you do use an abbreviation (e.g., IEP), explain exactly what it means, using examples for clarification.
- Be very careful about what you say to parents about their children. For example, if a child is experiencing difficulty in learning to read, you would never say, "Your child is far behind the other readers in this class." You should, instead, discuss ways that you and the parents can partner to help the child learn to read.
- Above all, parent–teacher conferences should be two way—not just a time for you to report on a child's progress, but also a time for you to *listen*.

YOU TRY IT

Write a Letter for a Parent Conference

For this You Try It, you will use pieces from a collection of a child's writing portfolio to report to his parents. Your letter will indicate growth over time in this child's literacy development.

I can write my name.

I can write numbers.

Anthony 8/31

It is the boat.

Anthony 10/20

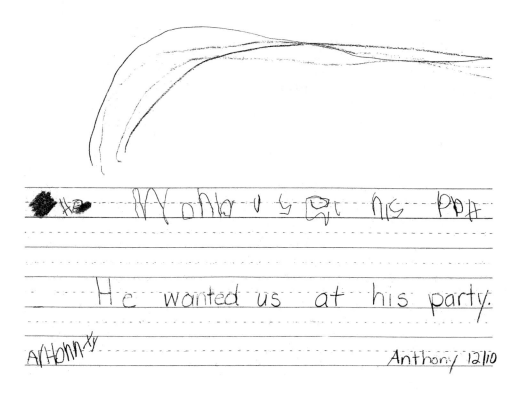

Monter is git his por

He wanted us at his party.

Anthony

First Grade, First Grade, What do you see?

I see paul looking at me.

Anthony 4/12

Anthony is one of your first graders. You and his parents are pleased with the progress he has made in your classroom. Study the four pieces of writing that you see, collected between August and April. Create a letter to Anthony's parents that describes his growth and development as a writer over time. This could be a letter you would share at Anthony's spring parent–teacher conference. In this positive and informative letter, be sure to highlight what this first grader *knows* about writing at each stage as supported by the samples you have assembled.

Regular newsletters.   Most primary-grade teachers believe that sending home newsletters on a regular basis is a useful way to communicate with parents. These can be done on a weekly, bimonthly, or monthly basis. Children can and should participate in the construction of your class newsletter; it is an excellent, authentic opportunity for writing. Newsletters can contain news from your classroom, highlight special projects that your students are accomplishing, and announce upcoming events. Figure 5.12 shows a section of a newsletter written by second-grader Trisha, explaining independent reading time in her class. Trisha had help from her teacher in the editing and revision process, but all of the ideas were hers. Not only do regular newsletters keep you in contact with parents, they celebrate the wonderful literacy events that are occurring in your classroom.

Calls and notes.   It doesn't take much time to pick up a phone or write a quick note to report something good that has happened to a student that day in your classroom. Parents sometimes get conditioned to receiving only bad news from teachers; it is delightful to receive "random reports of kindness" from their child's teacher. How very pleased would you be to return home after work, push the play button on the answering machine and hear this message?

> Hello, Ms. Simmons. This is Grace Perez. I just wanted you to know that Tina had a wonderful day at school. For the first time, she chose her own book, sat down on the Reading Rug, and read the whole book all by herself. I'm so proud of the progress she's making! I'll see you soon.

Short, unexpected messages like this one not only honor the accomplishments of your students, they strengthen your relationship with parents by letting them know how much you care about their children (e.g., Noddings, 1995). Each of you, as university students, can tell whether or not a teacher cares about you, and you

Open communication between home and school is critical to effective teaching and learning for your students. In what ways will you engender open, honest communication?

DEAR Parents,

Every day at 12:30 we DEAR. That means "Drop everything and read." We get to choose books out of our book baskets and e read for 20 minutes. The teacher reads, too. I am reading <u>Freckle Juice</u> by Judy Blume. Cindy is reading <u>Frog and Toad Are Friends</u> by Arnold Lobel. What books are you reading? If you want to, come to our class at 12:30 and DEAR!

by Trisha

FIGURE 5.12   Newsletter to Parents

know what a difference it makes in your learning. When you truly care about the children you teach, you will enhance their learning and earn their parents' respect and trust as someone who wants their children to succeed.

CONNECTIONS: WHAT'S NEXT?

Instructing Early Readers who are working independently has caused us to consider not only teaching situations but students' sociocultural contexts and lives outside of school. In terms of the classroom, you learned about helping students select reading materials for independent reading, providing time, structure, and settings for self-selected reading and writing, and facilitating reading and writing workshops. You also learned about additional literacy centers that you can use during workshop time and how to introduce and teach children to manage centers.

Then, you focused on students' families and how to develop respectful, genuine partnerships with parents where communication is honest and ongoing. You learned about the importance of parental involvement in students' literacy development and how parents can help in the literacy classroom. Perhaps most importantly, you were reminded that teachers must constantly be aware of students' sociocultural contexts as they develop curriculum and offer literacy instruction relevant to students' lives. These contexts are outlined in Figure 5.13, the framework for the developmental approach to the teaching of reading. Next, we will explore an important topic for all Early Readers: Working with words in whole-group, small-group, and independent settings.

FIGURE 5.13   A Developmental Approach to the Teaching of Reading

	Early Readers	Interpretive Readers	Critical Readers
Theories underscored as readers develop:	Social Constructivism: Psycholinguistic, Critical, Transactional	Social Constructivism: Psycholinguistic, Critical, Transactional	Social Constructivism: Psycholinguistic, Critical, Transactional
Whole-group instruction through:	• Read-alouds • Shared texts • Comprehension strategies • Working with words	• Read-alouds • Using basals • Literature-based models • Word-building strategies • Comprehension strategies	• Read-alouds • Using common text (e.g., basals, anthologies, trade books) • Comprehension strategies • Vocabulary instruction and word analysis • Researching • Critical reading • Reading content area texts • Studying & notetaking

continued

FIGURE 5.13 *Continued*

	Early Readers	**Interpretive Readers**	**Critical Readers**
Assessment ideas for whole group:	• Observations • Kidwatching • Anecdotal notation	• Portfolios • Open-ended questions • Rubrics	• Written retellings • Evaluating research projects • Interest inventories • Content-area histories • Cloze procedure
Small-group instruction through:	• Guided reading • Teaching for strategies • Fluency practice • Working with words	• Basal readers • Literature anthologies • Trade books • Guided silent reading • Literature circles • Inquiry groups	• Book clubs
Assessment ideas for small groups:	• Running Records • Retellings • Discussions with children	• Names test • Fluency checklist • Peer assessment • Inquiry rubric	• Student information card • Bio poem • "I Used to… But Now I…" poem • Observational checklist • Student self-assessment • Norm-referenced tests
Independent learning through:	• Independent reading • Reading/writing workshop • Making books • Reading the room	• Independent reading • Reading/writing workshop • Responding through writing • Reading logs	• Sustained silent Reading and writing
Sociocultural contexts:	• Conferring with parents • Newsletters • Parents in the classroom • Reading at home	• Reading/writing connection for life • Oral histories • Home literacy activities • Parent programs	• Parents as coaches • Funds of knowledge • Parent–student book clubs

 FOR YOUR PORTFOLIO

ENTRY 5.1   *The Reading/Writing Workshop*

INTASC Principle 4 states: *The teacher understands and uses a variety of instructional strategies to encourage students' development of critical thinking, problem-solving, and performance skills.*

For this entry in your portfolio, describe how students' independent work during Reading and Writing Workshop supports the intention of INTASC Principle 4.

ENTRY 5.2   *A Parent Brochure*

INTASC Principle 10 reads: *The teacher fosters relationships with school colleagues, parents, and agencies in the larger community to support students' learning and well-being.*

In this chapter you learned about the importance of working with parents as partners. For this entry, select an early grade level (K–2) and create a brochure that highlights and explains your literacy program for parents. Remember not to include too much information, but briefly explain your daily schedule and what you hope to accomplish with their Early Learners. Also, in your brochure emphasize some important ways in which parents can support their children's literacy development such as daily read-alouds, trips to the library, and talking and listening to their children.

ENTRY 5.3   *Texts for ELL Students*

IRA/NCTE Standard 10 says: *Students whose first language is not English make use of their first language to develop competency in the English language arts and to develop understanding of content across the curriculum.*

In this chapter you learned about providing materials for Early Readers to choose from during independent reading time. IRA/NCTE Standard 10 suggests the need to supply texts for English Language Learners (ELLs) in their first language(s).

For this portfolio entry, locate three children's literature books that are printed in both English and a second language. Create an annotated bibliography of these three texts. Provide complete citations, including ISBN numbers. Then write a short description of each book, why it would be an appropriate choice for Early Readers, and how you could use the book with ELL students.

▰▰▰ TO LEARN MORE ▰▰▰ ▰▰ ▰ ▰▰ ▰▰ ▰

Helpful Websites

Visit our Companion Website at *http://www.prenhall.com/lenski* to link to the following sites:

Conferring With Parents

Provides information on how to conduct conferences with parents.
*http://www.ccc.adventist.org/educ/mentor/
ccc_education_parent%20teacher%20conference%20lett.htm*

Personal Contacts With Parents

Provides information on the importance of becoming acquainted with the families of students.
http://www.ed.gov/pubs/ReachFam/perscon.html

Home-to-School Connection

Lists links to articles that deal with communicating and interacting with parents.
http://www.educationworld.com/preservice/learning/parents.shtml

The Reading Workshop

Lists components of a Reading Workshop and how to make them work for you in your classroom.
http://www.mcps.k12.md.us/curriculum/english/rdr_wkshop.htm#ind_reading

chapter **6**

Early Readers Working With Words

Essential Learning Questions

- Acknowledging that phonics has an essential place in the instruction of reading and writing for Early Readers, how will you learn to provide effective phonics instruction?
- What are some of the terms used for teachers of phonics that you need to understand?
- How is developmental spelling important to children's literacy development?
- What important information can samples of children's writing give you about their development as readers and writers?
- What is *phonemic awareness* and how can you foster phonemic awareness development in Early Readers?
- Why are Word Walls and activities like word sorts beneficial for Early Readers in helping them understand how words work?

Let's pretend you're taking a test and the task is for you to read the message shown in Figure 6.1. Unless you already know how to read Greek, you will soon become frustrated, maybe at first glance, and declare, "I can't do this!" The marks on the page simply hold no meaning for you. Now imagine that others around you are reading the message with relative ease. The test giver notices you are not working hard enough at decoding, so she nudges you and says, "Sound it out!" So you try again. Perhaps if there were an accompanying picture you could make guesses about what the words say, but there isn't, and you don't know what the symbols mean; you are left helpless.

These feelings of frustration and helplessness are what young children experience when we place print that they are unable to read in front of them. Remember our discussion of the cueing systems: semantic, syntactic, and visual? In this chapter we concentrate on the visual—the cues we get from paying attention to the letters on the page. Specifically, we are going to explore how we can help Early Readers unlock the meaning in words by accessing the visual cueing system to break the code. (By the way, the translation of the Greek message in Figure 6.1 is "Reading, Writing and Printing in Greek.")

We learned to read so long ago that it is hard for us to remember that at one point someone helped us figure out that letters had names, were associated with sound(s), and could be linked to make words; that words could be strung together to make sentences; and that we could read those sentences to make sense of print. Now, it's our turn to deconstruct those early understandings about how our alphabetic system of print works so that we can help our students understand it, too.

In this chapter, we discuss a range of word decoding approaches including teaching letters and sounds in context, the language of phonics instruction for teachers, phonemic awareness, and assessing students' knowledge of how words work. Good teachers dedicate time for word study as part of their daily Literacy Workshop schedule. Our position is that you can make extremely effective use of 15 minutes per day for exciting, engaging activities related to word study.

Kyle uses magnetic letters to learn new spelling words.

Διαβάζοντας, γράφοντας και τυπώνοντας ελληνικά

FIGURE 6.1   Sample of Greek Writing

Explicit time is needed for word study, but children should also be supported in learning about words throughout their school day. Let's say you have been studying words that "belong to the same family," like the *an* family. Your students can become word detectives who look for words that end with the letters *an* all day long and you can call attention to their discoveries. Pinnell and Fountas (1998) write, "As students have numerous opportunities to encounter words in a variety of contexts, they use many words, become flexible as word solvers, and, in the process, build the vocabularies they need for quick, automatic reading and writing" (p. 263).

UNDERSTANDING PHONICS

We begin with the word *phonics* because it is often misunderstood and used as a catch-all phrase referring to everything related to word work in the classroom. Some educators use the term *phonics* to mean a teaching *method*. We define *phonics*, rather, as the knowledge of the relationships between letters and sounds and the ability to combine or blend those sounds represented by letters into words. To be good readers, students need to understand how speech sounds are connected to print symbols, and they need to possess the ability to decode unfamiliar words. Children's literature can be a valuable tool in your word study program. Not only will your students be enjoying wonderful books, they will be learning about words and how sounds are represented in print. Figure 6.2 lists books you can use with young children to help teach letter/sound relationships.

Ahlberg, J., & Ahlberg, A. (1978). *Each peach pear plum.* New York: Scholastic.

Cameron, P. (1961). *I can't said the ant.* New York: Coward-McCann.

Carle, E. (1991). *My very first book of words.* New York: HarperFestival.

Gordon, J. R. (1993). *Six sleepy sheep.* Honesdale, PA: Boyds Mills Press.

Higgins, J., & Steig, W. (1980). *The bad speller.* New York: Windmill.

Macmillan, B. (1990). *One sun: A book of terse verse.* New York: Holiday House.

Martin, J. (1991). *Carrot parrot.* New York: Simon & Schuster.

Martin, J. (1991). *Mitten kitten.* New York: Simon & Schuster.

Olbigado, L. (1983). *Faint frogs feeling feverish and other terrifically tantalizing tongue twisters.* New York: Puffin.

Shaw, N. (1986). *Sheep in a jeep.* Boston: Houghton Mifflin. (There are other "sheep books" in this series by Shaw.)

Sherman, I. (1983). *Walking, talking words.* New York: Harcourt Brace.

Showers, P. (1981). *The listening walk.* New York: Harper & Row.

Zeifert, H. (1987). *Baby buggy, buggy baby.* Boston: Houghton Mifflin.

FIGURE 6.2   Children's Books That Help Teach Letter/Sound Relationships

Phonics Teaching Considerations

For some time, controversy has surrounded the topic of phonics teaching and its place in the elementary classroom. We concur with those whose position is that reading and writing are "meaning-centered processes [taught] through experiences with connected text" (Dahl & Scharer, 2000, p. 586). Further, we support the notion that phonics should be taught in contextualized, meaningful ways along with reading and writing rather than as a prerequisite to them. Cunningham (2000) writes:

> Everyone agrees that children must read and write; in fact, if you had to choose between teaching either phonics or reading and writing, you would always choose reading and writing. But you don't have to make a choice. You can engage the children's minds and hearts in reading good literature and finding their own voices as authors, *and* at the same time, teach them how our alphabetic language works. (p. viii)

Authentic literacy experiences.   Figure 6.3 of a student's writing for real purposes illustrates her developing understanding of the alphabetic principle: that each speech sound of a language should have its own distinctive graphic representation (Harris & Hodges, 1995). In this piece, Sharadyn is petitioning her teacher (Miss T.) for extra recess time and has found her voice as an author. Notice her attempts at applying the alphabetic principle and phonics generalizations as in the words *reesones* (representing the long *e* vowel sound) and *mone and grone* (representing the silent *e* generalization). Also, see how *pritt* shows the extra syllable in the word *prêt-ty*. Do you see that even her spelling mistakes show a sophisticated understanding of how our language works? Her teacher chose not to correct this paper, because Sharadyn's writing has an authentic function and presents a sound argument for her viewpoint.

In this text we echo the position of the International Reading Association (IRA) concerning the role of phonics in reading instruction (1997):

1. The teaching of phonics is an important aspect of beginning reading instruction.
2. Classroom teachers in the primary grades do value and do teach phonics as part of their reading programs.

Visit the online journal in Chapter 6 on our Companion Website at *www.prenhall.com/lenski* to answer these questions. Save your answers to your hard drive or to a disk to compile an online journal.

The International Reading Association is a professional organization for teachers of reading. How will joining professional organizations support your evolving theory of literacy learning?

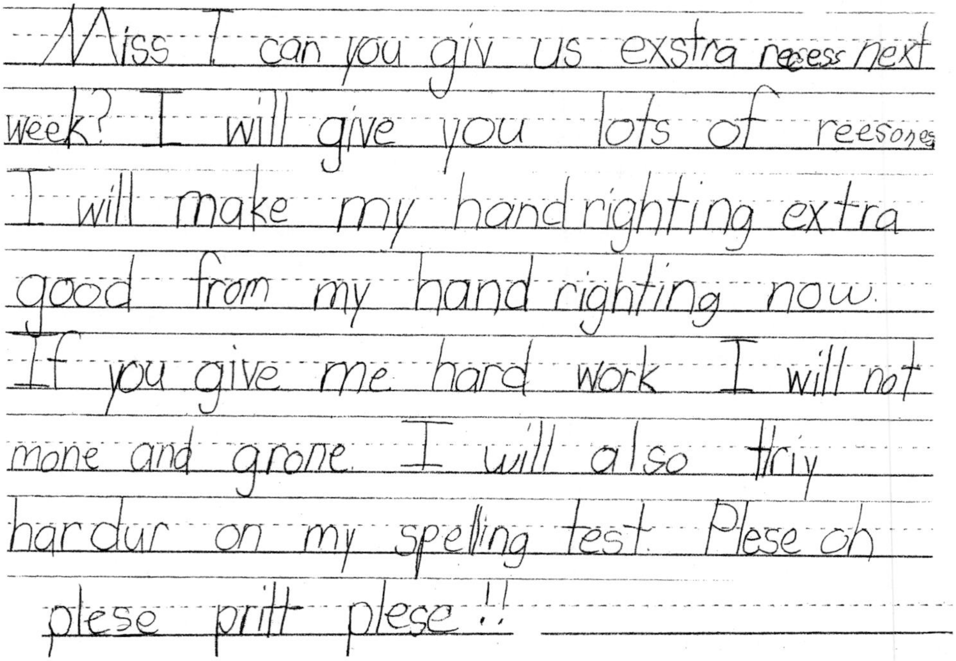

> Miss I can you giv us exstra recess next week? I will give you lots of reesones I will make my hand righting extra good from my hand righting now. If you give me hard work I will not mone and grone. I will also triy hardur on my spelling test. Plese oh plese pritt plese!!

FIGURE 6.3   Sharadyn's Recess Petition

3. Phonics instruction, to be effective in promoting independence in reading, must be embedded in the context of a total reading/language arts program.

Whole-to-part teaching.   We believe that as we provide children with experiences with whole texts through read-alouds and shared readings, we teach about sounds, letters, and words in the context of marvelous experiences with whole texts. Sometimes, this is referred to as a whole-to-part perspective. You begin with whole books and stories, then move to the smaller parts of analyzing the words within those texts. This practice is contrasted with a part-to-whole perspective, in which teachers begin with letters and then proceed to words, sentences, and whole texts. Part-to-whole teaching is also referred to as *synthetic phonics* and generally includes a heavy emphasis on learning the "rules" of phonics.

The role of early literacy learning and print-feature awareness is discussed in a 1998 position statement by the IRA and the National Association for the Education of Young Children. In this paper these groups state the following:

Early learners can:

- Enjoy being read to and themselves retell simple narrative stories or informational texts,
- Use descriptive language to explain and explore,
- Recognize letters and letter/sound matches,
- Show familiarity with rhyming and beginning sounds,
- Understand left-to-right and top-to-bottom orientation and familiar concepts of print,
- Match spoken words with written ones, and
- Begin to write letters of the alphabet and some high-frequency words.

What teachers do:

- Encourage children to talk about reading and writing experiences.
- Provide many opportunities for children to explore and identify sound/symbol relationships in meaningful contexts.
- Help children to segment spoken words into individual sounds and blend the sounds into whole words (for example, by slowly writing a word and saying its sound).
- Frequently read interesting and conceptually rich stories to children.
- Provide daily opportunities for children to write.
- Help children build a sight vocabulary.
- Create a literacy-rich environment for children to engage independently in reading and writing.

Because we believe that children learn about words more readily using the whole-to-part premise, we will discuss embedding phonics instruction in a balanced reading program, and we will show you how to do this in your classroom. We begin by discussing how to build on children's developing awareness of print.

Whole-to-part instruction involves starting with the whole of a text, like a book or poem, and then focusing on individual features of print. How is whole-to-part instruction like the top-down model of literacy learning described in Chapter 1?

Diversity issue: Helping ELL students with phonics.   Peregoy and Boyle (2001) note that although little research has been done on phonics instruction for English Language Learners, several principles provide effective practice for ELL and *all* students. These principles include teaching spelling patterns rather than rules (e.g., using word families); teaching phonics in meaningful contexts; allowing enough time to enhance phonics instruction through real reading and writing; and applying informal assessments to measure ELL students' progress and need for further instruction.

Young children who are learning English can be helped by using plenty of pictures for associating new language understanding, as long as the pictures you choose are part of those students' prior knowledge. In other words, it's not very helpful to use a picture of an ostrich to teach the short *o* sound if the child has no prior knowledge of "ostrich." Always make sure that the phonics learning experiences you provide connect to students' backgrounds.

Rodriguez (2001) suggests that for ELL students who have already started to read and write in another language you use *cognates,* or words that are very similar in spelling in English as they are in the students' native language. Students who speak languages that use the Roman alphabet have some of the same Greek and Latin roots as English. Students who speak Spanish, for example, will find some of the same word parts in both languages, which can make English easier to learn. These words become anchors for students as they are learning English. For Spanish-speaking learners, some of the words that are cognates follow:

English Word	Spanish Word
alphabet	alfabeto
hospital	hospital
hotel	hotel
class	clase
color	color
family	familia
flower	flor
memory	memoria
pilot	piloto
television	television

Effective teachers always employ the practice of using what students already know to teach the unknown. In the case of cognates, this may be a helpful tool for you to use with your ELL students. It would be natural to show your English-speaking students how cognates appear in other languages as part of your word study program.

SELECTED TERMS OF PHONICS INSTRUCTION FOR TEACHERS

As a teacher of Early Readers, you will teach concepts and use materials that require *you* to understand certain terminology about letters, sounds, and their relationships in the English language. This vocabulary will appear in reading teachers' textbooks, teachers' manuals that accompany basals, books that you purchase for your professional libraries, and workshops that you attend as a teacher. It is not our intent here to include every possible phonics term that you will come across. Rather, we have attempted to record those key words or phrases that you will most likely encounter first. We have already explored the terms *phonics* and we will add more terms to your knowledge bank of vocabulary related to phonics instruction.

This book emphasizes that when teaching new vocabulary to children, those new words need to be connected to something or contextualized. Therefore, here we contextualize the language of phonics instruction by providing teaching examples, showing how and why a word/concept is important to learn. These teaching examples or classroom applications include active practice that entail students *doing something,* thus emphasizing the importance of active learning.

Note that the specialized vocabulary used in the teaching of phonics is for you, *not for your students.* Teaching Early Readers words like *onsets* and *rimes* would probably confuse them. Instead, use terminology like *beginnings of words* and *ending chunks,* explaining to children what those phrases mean.

 The language of phonics instruction is important for you to learn as you use professional books and teachers' manuals. Why is it important for you to know these terms?

Consonants

Consonants are letters that are not vowels and generally have a firm sound because of restriction to the breath channel when spoken. Examples: *b, c, d, f, g.*

Classroom application: Teaching individual consonants.   Some kindergarten teachers like to have Letter Days, days on which they concentrate on certain letters, like the letter *b.* On B Day (or Week), invite kindergarteners to bring in objects or pictures of items that begin with the letter *b.* These items can then be placed in the "B Box." The children might bring in such objects as a *book, baby bottle, bell,* or pictures cut from magazines such as *Bear in the Big Blue House,* a *bumblebee,* a *boy.* Have children come up to the B Box and one at a time put their contribution into the box while saying with exaggeration *b-b-b-bear.* Then have the other children join in with the naming of the object. That day or week, encourage students to look for the letter *b* when they read and write. All activities associated with letter learning should be playful and use what children know and can do like work alphabet puzzles, sort letters in ice cube trays, play letter-based board games, use ink-stamp pads with letter stamps, and paint letters at the Art Center.

YOU TRY IT

Noticing the Importance of Consonants

Children hear consonants first as they make their first attempts at spelling because the consonants are what they hear most readily. You can see this as you look at children's early writing. Read the following excerpt from *A Bargain for Francis* by Russell Hoban (1992) that has most of the vowels missing.

Th_n th_t g_rl l_st s_m_ _f h_r m_n_y _nd sp_nt th_ r_st _n c_ndy. Sh_ n_v_r g_t th_ tea s_t.

Our guess is that you were able to read the text: "Then that girl lost some of her money and spent the rest on candy. She never got the tea set," even though you couldn't rely on vowels. Instead, you relied on the sounds you associate with the consonants. Another reason you were able to decipher the text is that consonants appear so much more frequently than vowels in the English language. Therefore, when young children begin to compose messages, they mostly put down the consonants. As an accomplished reader you used consonant sounds, the meaning cues to make sure the passage made sense, and structural cues to construct words that "fit" properly such as nouns, verbs, and conjunctions.

Another effective teaching practice for consonants and vowels alike is to have students make individual alphabet books that Early Readers can use as their own personal references to the letters. Some teachers have children make their own alphabet books using cut-out pictures from magazines or phonics workbooks. Others make class books where each child contributes a page to the book. For example, Jeff makes the *b is for boy* page, Lizzie makes the *c is for computer* page, Manuel makes the *d is for duck* page, and so on, until all 26 letters have pages constructed by members of the class.

Consonant Blends

Consonant blends consist of two or more letters blended together where each letter retains its original sound. Examples: *bl, fl, gr, str.* (Also, referred to as consonant clusters.)

Classroom application: Teaching about consonant blends.   Once students have learned the consonants, have them take out the following letter blocks: *s, e, l, l, p, w, m* and place them on their desks (see Figure 6.4). Ask them to make the word *sell* at their desks using their letter blocks. After allowing them time to do so, write

FIGURE 6.4   Making Words

and spell the word together on the chalkboard. Next, ask if they can add *p* to the word *sell* to make the word *spell*. Children should be allowed to help one another. Again, write *spell* on the board while chanting the letters together. Repeat the process, making the words *swell* and *smell*. Finally, talk about blends that sometimes begin words, like *sp, sw,* and *sm*. Students might separate those letters out and listen to the chunks of letters that "still say their names."

Vowels

Vowels are represented by the letters *a, e, i, o, u,* and sometimes *y* and *w*. Vowels can also be defined as speech sounds that are made by an unrestricted vocal passage way. (Saying each of the vowel sounds aloud illustrates how the mouth is either partially or fully open with little tongue or teeth involvement.)

Classroom application: Teaching about the vowel a.   This lesson concentrates on words that have the short vowel *a* in a consonant, vowel, consonant pattern—sometimes referred to in teaching circles as the CVC pattern, as shown in Figure 6.5. First construct a silly sentence with children on the Reading Rug: *Pam, a fat cat, sometimes sat on her mat reading a map.* (We recommend keeping the use of silly sentences like this one to a minimum, since no one talks that way. Sometimes, though, such sentences can help make a point for Early Readers.) Next, chart the sentence on an easel and read it together.

Then, solicit volunteers from the students to circle the words that have the CVC pattern with the *a* in the middle. After students have identified *Pam, fat, cat, sat, mat,* and *map,* use your sentence strip chart to invite children up to spell those same words using letter cards. Discuss the sound that the *a* makes when it is in the center of a short word (CVC) like *cat.* Talk about how that knowledge can help students when they encounter words with an *a* in the middle in their reading and writing. For example, write the words *rat, mad, tap,* and *fan.* See if the children can transfer their new understandings to these words.

Consonant Digraph

A consonant digraph is a kind of consonant cluster in which letters stand together to make one sound. Teaching digraphs should be reserved for children who already have good control of consonants and consonant blends. Examples of consonant digraphs that can be found at the beginning of words are *ch, wh, sh,* and *th* (e.g., *church, whale, shop,* and *that*). Examples of consonant digraphs that can be found at the ends of words are *ck, nk, ng, ch, sh, th,* and *tch* (e.g., *clock, pink, ring, beach, dish, tooth,* and *witch*).

$$\frac{c}{c} \frac{a}{v} \frac{t}{c}$$

FIGURE 6.5   The CVC Pattern (Consonant–Vowel–Consonant)

Classroom application: Teaching students to notice digraphs.   Here's something to try to get students to notice *ch* and *sh* at the beginning of words:

- Write the words *ship* and *cheese* on the board as in Figure 6. 6.
- Draw a picture of each next to the words.
- Talk about the letters *sh and ch* and the sounds they make at the beginning of words like *ship* and *cheese*.
- Hand out stacks of eight cards to each child that have the following words on them: *shop, shoe, shower, sheep* and *church, chain, chimp, check.*
  - Ask the children to sort their cards, putting *sh* cards in one stack and *ch* cards in another stack.
  - Partner up the children and let them check each other's stacks and try to read the cards.
  - Read the cards together exaggerating the *sh* and *ch* sounds.
  - Let the children make a small illustration on each card to remind them of the word and strengthen their association with it.
  - Have the children place their cards in their word storage boxes.

Word storage boxes contain individual collections of words printed on index cards that students know and can refer to often for sorting and word game activities (see Figure 6.7). Recipe card boxes work well for the purpose of storing words. Students can use their word boxes as personal dictionaries that help them remember how to spell words. These boxes foster special ownership of literacy learning for children and help them feel successful as they watch their word banks grow.

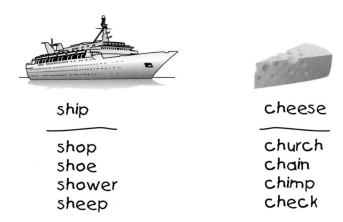

ship   cheese

shop   church
shoe   chain
shower   chimp
sheep   check

FIGURE 6.6   Learning About Consonant Digraphs

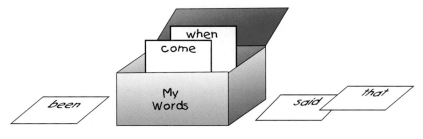

FIGURE 6.7   Word Storage Boxes

Onsets and Rimes

An *onset* is what linguists use to describe all letters *before* a vowel in a word. In the word *king,* the *k* is the onset. If the word were *bring,* the onset would be *br.* Onsets are related to rimes in that rimes are what follows the onset. In our examples above of *king* and *bring,* the rime is *ing.* Figure 6.8 contains some of the most common rimes in the English language that form the basis of frequently occurring spelling patterns as suggested by Wylie and Durrell (1970). Sometimes rimes are referred to as phonograms or letter chunks that form *word families.* When children are taught the spelling patterns of word families, they are empowered to read and spell many more words. Johnston (1999) writes, "This ability to hear, see, and use the rime as a reliable cue for reading new words and spelling words that sound alike offers students a powerful insight into how English spelling works" (p. 64).

Classroom application: A lesson using onsets and rimes.   Refer to the photo on p. 187 that portrays a young learner working with onsets and rimes. For this classroom application, the teacher selected various onsets (such as *cl, w, t, ch, p, tr, k, st, fl, br*). Post the onsets in the upper compartments of a pocket chart. Below the onsets, insert multiple copies of the rime *ick.* Allow the child to make as many real words as he can by combining the onsets and rimes. In this example, you see that some of the words he has made are *brick, slick, quick,* and *lick.* Can you see how this active practice with onsets and rimes helps him understand the underlying principle of learning new words by analogy? The child is learning "If I know the word *sick,* I can figure out *brick, slick,* and many other words that end in the letters *ick.*" The child should be able to transfer this knowledge to learning other new words through analogy.

Sight Words or Sight Vocabulary

Sight words are words that are so familiar to readers that they are recognized instantly and automatically. Teachers work hard with young readers to help them develop a bank of known words that they recognize on sight. Sometimes teachers use

ack (tack)	ay (day)	ip (sip)
ail (nail)	eat (meat)	it (sit)
ain (rain)	ell (tell)	ock (rock)
ake (lake)	est (nest)	oke (broke)
ale (sale)	ice (mice)	op (hop)
ame (game)	ick (kick)	ore (store)
an (pan)	ide (slide)	ot (not)
ank (tank)	ight (night)	uck (duck)
ap (clap)	ill (hill)	ug (bug)
ash (trash)	in (win)	ump (jump)
at (hat)	ine (mine)	unk (skunk)
ate (skate)	ing (king)	
aw (saw)	ink (sink)	

FIGURE 6.8   Common Rimes in English With Sample Onsets

Sean learns about word families using onsets and rimes.

Word Walls or even small word charts taped to children's desks to help them remember certain words. Often, important-to-know sight words can also be found on lists of high-frequency words.

Classroom application: Reinforcing sight words.   When Early Readers are reading a text that says, "I can run and play," they might stumble on or confuse the words *can* and *and*—these words look very similar to young eyes. On a dry-erase board, write down the two sight words that you want them to know as anchor words: *can* and *and*. Discuss how they look alike as well as how they look different. Teach *one* of the words that day intensively. For this example let's use the word *can*. Let the children take turns coming to the dry-erase board and writing the word while the others chant *c-a-n*. Clap the letters while saying, "*C-a-n* spells *can*." Whisper the letters. Shout the letters. Draw the letters in the air with imaginary pencils. Draw the letters on each other's backs with fingers for pencils. Trace the letters in sand. Make the letters with water on a chalkboard. Use as many ways as possible to reinforce the sight word *can,* so that the next time that small group of children comes to the word *can,* they absolutely, positively, no-doubt-about-it will know it.

High-Frequency Words

High-frequency words are those that appear most often in our written language. In fact, Fry, Fountoukidis, and Polk (1985) found that only 100 words account for almost half of the words we need for reading and writing (see Figure 6.9). Further, only 10 words: *the, of, and, a, to, in, is, you, that,* and *it* make up one-quarter of all the words we need as readers and writers. When looking at the 100 most frequently occurring words in our language in Figure 6.9, it's clear that many of these words are abstract. Typical high-frequency words such as *of, some, were,* and *very* are ones

the	is	see	how
and	as	very	come
a	up	are	look
to	so	this	get
he	one	will	again
of	out	like	two
in	were	go	we
was	him	no	too
his	there	would	about
it	when	just	saw
I	then	back	good
you	my	now	more
on	he	over	did
they	not	by	made
said	down	big	off
she	have	do	didn't
for	their	old	some
that	went	can	new
with	could	if	red
but	what	your	long
her	them	who	around
all	from	away	know
had	came	where	through
little	into	or	other
at	me	an	put

FIGURE 6.9   100 High-Frequency Words

that Early Readers struggle learning because they hold no concrete meaning for children. Many are abstract (What is a "some"?) and many do not follow the pattern of phonics rules children attempt to apply. (For example, *of* spelled phonetically would probably be *uv*.)

Classroom application: Attaching meaning to high-frequency words.   Cunningham (2000) suggests activities that help children associate meaning with some of our functional, high-frequency words that they typically have trouble remembering. One of the activities she proposes assists Early Readers in learning the words *of* and *for*, which students often confuse when they are reading. For this activity, we suggest building on children's known words, such as foods that they like (e.g., pizza, cake, and Pepsi). Hand out three index cards to students. Taking the food words, teacher and students write phrases and illustrate them together, so that each child will have three illustrated cards with one phrase on each card: a slice *of* pizza, a piece *of* cake, a can *of* Pepsi. When the phrases are written and the pictures of the pizza, cake, and Pepsi can are drawn, you personalize the meaning of the words by adding the child's name to learn the word *for.* As in, a slice *of* pizza *for* Adrian, a piece *of* cake *for Jamie,* a can *of* Pepsi *for* Michael. Children then keep these cards in their desks, word boxes, or folders as reminders of these two difficult words.

 When students have a large core of known words, those words become anchors that they can depend on as they encounter unknown words. How will you help students increase their bank of known words?

Companion Website

Developmental Spelling

Developmental spelling is also called *invented* spelling. However, we prefer the adjective *developmental* because it describes exactly what it is: a temporary stage in a child's development as a speller/writer.

Although not strictly a phonics term, developmental spelling is important to understand because it is a normal and *temporary* spelling stage. It provides vital evidence of what children understand about our language and its written representation, and it informs your teaching about what students are ready to learn next.

When they look at their kindergartener's or first grader's writing some parents are unduly concerned with spelling "errors." We can help dispel parents' fears by explaining how appropriate and wonderful such writing is. Point out that just as their children went through the developmental speaking stage of "baby talk," which has come and gone, their spelling behaviors will be temporary as well. Harris and Hodges (1995) note that "invented spellings are used both to study young writers' emerging awareness of conventional spelling patterns and as an instructional strategy in beginning writing as the child moves toward conventional spelling" (p. 123). Your goal as a teacher will be to help move your children forward in their understanding of spelling as they move from developmental to conventional, standard spelling.

Classroom application: Analyzing developmental spelling. Look at the child's developmental spelling in Figure 6.10. Even though you may be able to read this note easily, what may strike you first is what the child does not yet understand about writing and spelling. The child is attempting the message: "We got on the bus. When we got there, we planted a tree. After we planted the tree, we rode to school." As

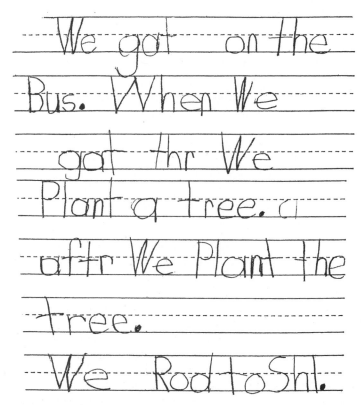

FIGURE 6.10 Kyle's Writing

teachers, however, we don't want to approach a child's writing with either a red pencil in our hands or our minds. Instead, we advocate asking yourself these three questions (Beaver, 1997):

1. What does this child understand now about writing and spelling?
2. What does the child almost know?
3. What does the child need to learn next?

Look again at the sample in Figure 6.10. Concerning Question 1, the child understands these concepts:

- Words have particular spellings.
- Letters represent sounds in words.
- Letters and words go from right to left, and top to bottom.
- Spaces are needed between words.
- Print contains a message that you want someone else to understand.
- Punctuation is needed to separate thoughts.
- Capital and lowercase letters are used.

Concerning Question 2, this is what the child almost understands:

- Some words need capital letters.
- Sometimes you need to use punctuation.
- Writers often use sequence writing such as a *first, then,* and *last* pattern.
- In reading material that Early Readers are familiar with, the last sentence is often different than the others: There needs to be an ending.

Concerning Question 3, this is what the child needs to learn next. Remember, *choose only one or two* of the most important concepts you think would move this child forward. In this example, you might choose only one or two of the following:

- Helping the child learn to add some descriptive words, like adjectives, could help develop his writing. What color bus? What kind or size of tree? He could also be encouraged to add an illustration to further enrich his message.
- The child uses the word *we* in almost every sentence, yet is consistently using a capital *W.* The focus could be on teaching the child to spell *we* without a capital when it doesn't need one.
- The child wants to write the word *planted.* Teaching him to reread his writing to check for whether the spelling *Plant* matches the sounds needed for *planted* could be the focus of your minilesson when you confer with him.
- The child is unsure about the principle of starting sentences with a capital letter. Praising him for the times he has used this convention and showing him which words do not need a capital could be the focus.

Figure 6.11 illustrates a primary benefit of encouraging developmental spelling—writing for real purposes. In this writing sample, second-grader Dominica transferred her job qualifications from her handwriting to the computer to make it look more professional. She remarked, "I'm trying to get a job. It has to look good." Her teachers, who have continuously supported Dominica as a writer, have opened the door for this child to use literacy for her own authentic purposes.

Our intent is to give you a core of key vocabulary terms that you will encounter when you teach Early Readers. The key terms presented here are just a beginning of the terminology that can be found in materials related to teaching phonics and teaching how words work. However, some states and districts require a test to gauge new teachers' phonics knowledge so you may have to prepare for such a test. A phonics-related term that you will need to understand thoroughly as a teacher of Early Learners is phonemic awareness.

1. windexing
2. dustening
3. vaeckumien
4. werching dishis
5. sckrebeingkishin fiors
6. skrebing sterarz
7. wotering plans
8. orgnizing cuberds
9. unloting dichwers
10. loting dichwerchers
11. If you hav a baby i well babysit and cklin up it's tyows and feed thaer mel to them
12. vacuom the fonitcher
13. mack beds
14. wi the kishin taboll
15. sutel the baby dun for a nap
16. organwz evretheing

FIGURE 6.11   Jobs I Can Do

PHONEMIC AWARENESS

Phonemic awareness is defined as the ability to recognize that words are made up of individual sounds, to hear those individual sound units, and to manipulate the sound units (Cunningham, 2000; McCormick, 1999; Wilson, Hall, Leu, & Kinzer, 2001). Yopp and Yopp (2000) are more specific when they say, "Phonemic awareness is an awareness that a speech stream consists of a sequence of sounds—specifically phonemes, the smallest units of sound that make a difference in communication. It is a phoneme that determines the difference between the words *dog and hog. . .* " (p. 130). Heilman (2002) notes that children need to understand that "words have small sounds that can be pulled apart and put back together; sounds in words have a specific order; sounds in words can be counted; sounds in words can be moved, removed or replaced to make new words; several sounds can be represented with many different letters" (p. 29). When young children are able to hear our spoken language and differentiate the sounds they hear as well as manipulate them, we say they have phonemic awareness.

 Phonemic awareness involves only speaking and listening, *not* the written forms of words. How does hearing individual sounds in words help children as both readers and writers?

Relationship of Phonemic Awareness to Reading and Writing

Phonemic awareness plays a part in both reading and writing. Children's level of phonemic awareness has been correlated to their degree of achievement as Early Readers (Hoffman, Cunningham, Cunningham, & Yopp, 1998; Yopp & Yopp, 2000). When children engage in developmental spelling they are revealing their level of phonemic awareness. Clay's assessment *An Observation Survey* (1993) includes a test called *Hearing and Recording Sounds in Words*. This test involves dictating sentences to children in order to evaluate whether they are able to listen to the phonemes in words and then record them on paper. For example, one of the sentences dictated to Early Readers and Writers is: "The bus is coming. It will stop here to let me get on." Figure 6.12 shows a sample of a child's writing of this dictation. The more sounds a child can hear and represent, the more likely she is to be able to read those sounds/words when she encounters them in print, reflecting again the reciprocal nature of reading and writing.

Regarding the connection of phonemic awareness to reading and writing, Clay (1991) notes that writing slows down the process of managing text and may help a child make more straightforward connections between letters and sounds. Sipe (2001) clarifies further:

> It is possible that, at least for some children, writing may be an easier "way into" literacy than reading. In reading, the message is not known, but in writing the writer already knows the message. In reading, the task involves going from letters and letter sequence to sounds, whereas in writing the process is reversed: going from sounds (which are already known and automatic) to letters. (p. 266)

Activities That Foster Phonemic Awareness

Explain the difference between the terms *phonics* and *phonemic awareness.*

Whereas some children come to the classroom with phonemic awareness securely in place, others will need support and instruction. Yopp and Yopp (2000) outline criteria that should shape instruction in phonemic awareness. They say that phonemic awareness instruction should be child appropriate, including playful and appealing activities; deliberate and purposeful; and only one part of a comprehensive literacy program. Further, they suggest a sequence for instructional activities found in Figure 6.13. Notice that the order of instruction parallels the conceptual understandings of children concerning phonemic awareness: word, syllable, onset and rime, and phonemes (Goswami & Bryant, 1990).

Activities that focus on rhymes.   Activities that focus on rhyme capitalize on children's natural love of language play. Even babies love to hear themselves play with sounds and learn to manipulate them. Babies, for example, play with sounds they can produce such as "ba, ba, ba, ba," and then change to "ma, ma, ma, ma." Their giggling as they engage in speech play may signify their understanding that they have created a marvelous string of sounds that they are able to control.

When young children are introduced to nursery rhymes and rhyming language in poetry and books, their caregivers are taking advantage of the joy of language. Try

the bs is c me it wl stop her t

let me Get Dn

FIGURE 6.12   Sample of Lily's Writing on the *Hearing and Recording Sounds in Words* Assessment

Instruction	Example
Activities that focus on rhyme	Let's think of something that rhymes with cow. (now)
Activities that focus on syllable units	Clap twice for Harry's name. Har(clap) – ry.(clap)
Activities that focus on onset and rime	Say just the first part of brown. (/br/)
Activities that focus on phonemes	Let's put these sounds together. /ch/-/ā/-/n/(chain)

From Yopp, H. K., & Yopp, R. H. (2000, October). Supporting phonemic awareness development in the classroom. The Reading Teacher, *54(2)*, 130–143.

FIGURE 6.13 A Sequence for Phonemic Awareness Instruction

this: Put in some sound effects to *Hickory Dickory Dock* by clicking your tongue twice at the end of lines, as well as chiming a clock, and adding a running down sound:

> Hickory dickory dock. (click, click)
> The mouse ran up the clock. (click, click)
> The clock struck one, (bong!)
> The mouse ran down. (bllliinnngggg)
> Hickory dickory dock. (click, click)

Through activities like this young children begin to notice that words that "end the same" rhyme.

Naturally, children who come to school having heard countless hours of nursery rhymes and early rhyming books may have an easier time understanding the concept of rhyme. Others who haven't had these experiences, especially English Language Learners, will need more exposure to rhymes, poetry, and songs as well as explicit instruction concerning words that rhyme. One reason that detecting rhyme is an early learning skill is that it doesn't require children to manipulate sounds. They only have to learn to *hear* the rhyme.

SEE FOR YOURSELF

Rhyming Activities

Visit the message board for Chapter 6 on our Companion Website at *www.prenhall.com/lenski* to discuss your findings.

Connect to the Companion Website *(http://www.prenhall.com/lenski)* and see a teacher leading her kindergarten students in learning about rhyming. Notice how she uses a nursery rhyme and a game-like activity. What features of these lessons help her students learn about rhymes? Why are the activities so engaging? Discuss your observations with your classmates.

A good starting place for all Early Readers is to use students' own names as teaching tools. Children's names are extremely important to them. Even more significant to children is that once they have learned to recognize their names in print, those printed symbols become tangible representations of themselves. With this in mind, it's easy to see why using students' names can be so powerful.

Inserting students' names into familiar rhymes works well to help teach rhymes. We don't recommend rhyming games using the child's name itself because that can become the fodder for playground teasing: slim Kim, scary Larry, etc. However, classes can cowrite a variation on a familiar verse. For example, Andrew's name was added to the following variation of *Mary Had a Little Lamb* here:

> Andrew had a little cat,
> Whose fur was white as snow,
> And everywhere that Andrew went,
> The cat was sure to go.

Phonemic awareness instruction proceeds from focus on rhymes, to syllables, to word families, to phonemes. Why would a teacher of Early Readers begin with rhyming words?

Other students' names as well as animal names could be substituted to make different poems that could be published and illustrated in a class book. Remember, the point here is to use children's names to personalize the verses (and thus engage the children) and to help them listen for and identify the words that rhyme (*snow* and *go*). At this point, you aren't as concerned about the spellings of rhyming words as you are about helping children to *hear* and *understand* the concept of rhyme. Also, remember that phonemic awareness relates to auditory (hearing) and speaking awareness, not the printed representation of words.

Activities that focus on syllable units.   Pinnell and Fountas (1998) define a syllable as "a minimal unit of sequential speech sounds composed of a vowel sound or a consonant vowel sound combination. A syllable always contains a vowel or vowel-like speech sound" (p. 64). Say the following words: *school, textbook, university,* and notice that in these words with one, two, and five syllables, each syllable has a vowel sound or a lone vowel, like the *u* in *u-ni-ver-si-ty.*

Children's names can help again when teaching syllables. Clapping the syllables of students' names is a good way to teach syllabic division. For example, try clapping *Vic-tor, E-liz-a-beth,* and *Jess-ie.* After clapping, students can try finger snapping and stomping to the syllables of their names. The accompanying See for Yourself feature highlights a teacher working on listening for syllables with her students.

SEE FOR YOURSELF

Learning About Syllables

Visit the message board for Chapter 6 on our Companion Website at *www.prenhall.com/lenski* to discuss your findings.

Connect to the Companion Website *(http://www.prenhall.com/lenski)*. Here you will see a short lesson as a teacher works with students on hearing syllables in words. What prompts and props does she use to augment her lesson and how do those work to keep students engaged? What would you change about this lesson?

Activities that focus on onsets and rimes.   We've mentioned that sometimes the endings of words after the vowel, rimes, can be used to create word families. Listening to and recognizing rhymes begins when children are in the emergent stage of literacy learning, but teaching about word families should not begin until children are at the stage when vowels begin appearing in their developmental spelling (Invernizzi, Abouzeid, & Gill, 1994; Johnston, 1999).

Working with word families builds on the notion that our brains are pattern makers that instinctively look for patterns. So, when teaching children that *black, tack,* and *sack* belong to the same family they can relate to the concept of having the same "last name" as well as learn to look for this letter pattern in future words such as *pack*. Recognizing the ending chunk *ack* helps children to gain access to words they've never seen before. If they can manipulate a new beginning letter/sound to the familiar ending chunk they will be able to decode the unfamiliar word. Teaching onset and rime patterns allows children to quickly increase their collection of known words and also supplies them with a strategy for figuring out new words. Children become empowered when they understand that "If I know *cap*, then I can figure out words like *lap, tap,* and *snap*." In addition, "the study of word families offers a friendly route to phonics instruction" (Johnston, 1999, p. 66).

 Our brains instinctively look for patterns. How does teaching children about word families capitalize on the inclination to notice patterns?

▰▰▰ **YOU TRY IT** ▰▰▰

Playing With Onsets and Rimes

Using either lowercase magnetic letters, letter blocks, or cut-out paper letters, decide on a word family to use for this activity. (See Figure 6.8, which lists common rimes in English with sample onsets.) Let's say you decide on the *ip* family. Take out the letters *i* and *p*. Now, begin adding initial consonants like *b, c, d, f, g, h, j, k, l, m,* etc. Next, decide which are real words in English: *hip, lip, nip, rip, sip, tip, zip*.

Now, think about the fact that it was engaging to be *doing* something while you were thinking and learning. That's extremely important for you as well as for 6-year-olds. Consider how you could use this activity with Early Readers. How could you help students see how learning one language pattern (the *ip* family) can help them understand many new words? How could you help those children who don't understand the point of the activity? How could you challenge those who need it? For example, what if you challenged students to add more than one letter to the beginning of *ip,* such as two letters, *bl, dr, sl, tr*? Or three letters such as *str*?

Activities that focus on phonemes.   As discussed earlier, phonemes are those small units of sound made up of a letter or cluster of letters that determine whether a word reads *book, look,* or *shook*. An effective method to help children focus on individual phonemes is one that Clay (1979) developed based on the work of Elkonin (1973), a Russian psychologist. This method involves using "sound boxes" that represent each phoneme in a word.

Let's say that you are working one-on-one with first-grader Madina as she composes a message. Madina says that she is going to write the sentence "We have a flag." She takes out her paper and writes *We,* she uses the Word Wall to copy *have,* writes *a,* then stops. The conversation, then, might proceed like this:

Madina: I don't know how to spell *flag*.

Teacher: Let's take out a practice piece of paper and use our sound boxes to figure it out. How many sounds can we hear in the word? Say it slowly with me and stretch it out: *f-l-a-g*. How many sounds did you hear? That's right, there are four sounds in the word.

If the child is unable to hear the four sounds go ahead and draw the four boxes anyway on the practice piece of paper, saying there are four sounds in the word. Figure 6.14 is a drawing of this method of hearing sounds in a word. Once you have drawn the four boxes, take out four pennies or four round place markers below each box. Next you could say:

> *Teacher:*   Madina, we are going to listen for the sounds in the word *flag* and use our pennies before we write the letters. I want you to push the pennies into the boxes as we stretch the sounds out together again. Get ready. Put your finger on the first penny.

Next you and Madina say the word slowly again: *f-l-a-g.* It's important to help children learn to "stretch" words out slowly as they speak them in order to help them hear each sound. As you say the word, show the child how to push a penny up into each box representing each phoneme (one penny each for the *f, l, a,* and *g*). This process can be repeated several times until you are sure the child understands the concept of listening for the sounds in the word. Then, let the child push the pennies into the boxes. Finally, you move away from using the pennies to helping the child put a letter in each of the boxes.

> *Teacher:*   Madina, we've been listening for the sounds. I want you to write letters in the boxes now. Stretch the word out again: *f-l-a-g.* What letter do you think goes in the first box?

You and Madina continue in this manner, letting her do the writing, until the word is complete and in the boxes, at which time you should praise her for her work. You may have to help her with the *a* in the middle of the word. If she gets too bogged down with getting the correct vowel, go ahead and tell her. Remember, each

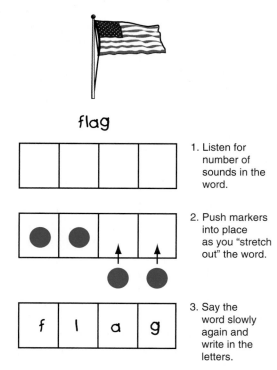

FIGURE 6.14   Sound Boxes for Hearing Sounds in Words

Madina listens for sounds in words using sound boxes.

of these teaching approaches should be pleasant for you and the child, not painful. When all of the letters are in the boxes, have Madina copy the word from the boxes onto her paper in the sentence she is creating. Figure 6.14 represents this use of sound boxes, and the accompanying See for Yourself feature shows a teacher using sound boxes to teach sound segmentation.

SEE FOR YOURSELF

Teaching Using Sound Boxes

Visit the message board for Chapter 6 on our Companion Website at *www.prenhall.com/lenski* to discuss your findings.

Connect to the Companion Website *(http://www.prenhall.com/lenski).* The teacher in this segment is using sound boxes (Elkonin boxes) to teach children how to segment sounds in words. Notice how children engage in this lesson using their eyes, ears, voice, and hands to learn about sound segments. Create a minilesson using sound boxes to "teach" to a peer. Why is this method such a powerful teaching/learning strategy?

Sound boxes focus children's attention on the individual sounds in words and their corresponding letters. Why would some words (e.g., *their* or *would*) be ineffective to use with sound boxes?

An important point to make here is that you would only use this method once or twice at the most in a short teaching session. Your intention is to help the child learn to listen for phonemes and how to represent them with letters. Overusing this method will stress the child and turn writing into a laborious, protracted process. Eventually, with repeated use of the sound box method, children learn to use the strategy by themselves until they no longer need that extra help.

You may have noticed in this example of working with Madina using sound boxes that the teacher must carefully use methods and make changes in her approach based on the child's responses. This reflects the teacher's on-the-run assessment of what the child understands and what she does not yet understand. In addition, you will need to conduct regular assessments that document children's developing literacy understandings over time.

TEACHING PHONICS

In the same way that young children begin to understand the function of print in books and notice print in their environments, they begin to become aware of certain letters and words. They start to pay attention to specific letters that are important to them. Noticing individual letters happens before children begin to associate sounds with letters. Many children know the letter "K" from K-Mart signs. They also begin to recognize the letters in their names. In fact, if a little girl's name is Katie she may claim that the letter on the big sign is "her letter." Children often are possessive of the first letter of their names and generally don't want to share that letter with other people, such as their classmates.

Although not a prerequisite to experiences in reading—children can and do read easy books before they know all the letters—at some point children need to know the letter names. That is, they need to attain grapheme awareness: the marks that we call letters. When teaching young students, you should help them notice that each letter has a different shape and name. Integrated, natural, and engaging activities will assist students in acquiring the visual discrimination and memory needed to learn the letter names.

One effective way to teach the alphabet to young children (besides singing the *ABC Song*) is through the reading of alphabet books during read-alouds, shared reading, and independent reading. A list of excellent alphabet books for Early Readers is presented in Figure 6.15.

Angel, M. (1996). *An animated alphabet.* New York: David R. Godine.

Base, G. (1986). *Animalia.* New York: Puffin.

Bond, M. (1991). *Paddington's ABC.* New York: Viking.

Erhlert, L. (1996). *Eating the alphabet.* New York: Harcourt Brace.

Garten, J. (1994). *The alphabet tale.* New York: Greenwillow.

Hobby, H. (2000). *Toot and Puddle: Puddle's ABC.* Boston: Little, Brown and Company.

Martin, B. (1989). *Chicka chicka boom boom.* New York: Simon & Schuster.

Potter, B. (1995). *Peter Rabbit's ABC and 123.* London: F. Warne.

Thornhill, J. (1988). *The wildlife A-B-C: A nature alphabet book.* New York: Simon & Schuster.

Van Allsberg, C. (1987). *The Z was zapped.* Boston: Houghton Mifflin.

Wildsmith, B. (1996). *Brian Wildsmith's ABC.* Austin, TX: Star Bright Books.

Wood, A. (2001). *Alphabet adventure.* New York: Blue Sky Press.

FIGURE 6.15   List of Alphabet Books

Important Word-Related Concepts for Children to Understand

At the same time children are learning individual letters, they begin to notice that letters can be strung together to form words. *A, and,* and *the* are frequently among the first words children recognize because they appear so often in print and are short in length. Other words that children find easy to recall might include *I, mom, dad, cat,* and *dog.*

Not all children understand what the concept *word* means, however. Here are some ways to teach the concept of *word:* Point to words while reading enlarged texts during shared reading; talk aloud while writing a text on the chalkboard or chart, saying, "Now, I am going to write another *word.*" Using enlarged texts of connected writing, cup your hands around different words (some teachers call this making fences around words), or purchase or make a "mask" that frames words so that children can focus on individual words.

From the teaching of the names of letters and the concept of *word,* teaching will progress to additional literacy terms that teachers use and assume young children understand. Simple teacher directions such as "Look at the beginning of the word" confuse some children. They may be thinking "Which word?" or "Where is the beginning?" Remember as a teacher of young children the need to explicitly teach the language of reading instruction. The language of reading instruction represents concepts that children have to understand if you want them to attend to the features of print that you are describing while you are teaching. Sometimes we, as teachers, may think that children do not have control of concepts about print such as left to right directionality or word boundaries, when they actually are baffled by the language we are using as we talk about print. Among the terms related to print that some children need to be taught are those represented in Figure 6.16.

In order for children to focus on certain features of print, they have to understand what you are asking them to notice. What are some of the language/concepts children need to understand in order to study words without becoming confused?

Active Practice

We cannot emphasize enough that when teaching phonics to Early Readers, all activities that involve noticing how letters and words work should be engaging and involve *active practice.* Returning to the recurring theme of motivation, it is essential

---

- Letter
- Words
- Sentence
- Beginning of the word, sentence, page, story
- Ending of the word, sentence, page, story
- Middle of the word, sentence, page, story
- Top
- Bottom
- Spaces between letters, between words
- Quotation marks (talking marks)
- Period

FIGURE 6.16 Language of Reading Instruction to Teach Children

that children be excited and curious about learning how our written language system works, the patterns they can expect, and how they can become empowered to participate in the writing and reading of our language.

Active practice is encouraged each time you let your students *do something*. The doing might be manipulating magnetic letters, working with letter blocks at their tables, sorting letters or words, holding up word cards in front of the class, maneuvering sentence strips at the chart in the Word Study Center, or cutting apart sentences and reconstructing them. They are not engaged in active practice when they are working in workbooks doing things such as drawing lines from a list of words to the sentence with blanks where each word belongs. These types of activities are finished quickly by those students who already understand the concepts involved; thus, they have learned nothing new; and signify nothing to those students who do not understand what they are being asked to do. Two teacher-friendly texts that we recommend for ideas on active word practice are by Cunningham and Hall: *Making Words: Multilevel, Hands-On, Developmentally Appropriate Spelling and Phonics Activities* (1994b) and *Making Big Words: Multilevel, Hands-On Spelling and Phonics Activities* (1994a).

Active practice during word study means that students are encouraged to *do something*. What are some word-learning activities that require children to be actively engaged?

Word Walls

An example of a word-learning tool that can provide active practice is a Word Wall (Cunningham, 1995). Word Walls are display areas on a bulletin board where key words can be placed for easy referencing by students who need help with spelling or decoding. To create a Word Wall, place newly learned words in alphabetical order, adding about five new words a week to the display (Gunning, 2000). It is helpful to use colored markers or colored backgrounds to help differentiate between words. Also, cutting around the configuration of each word can help children remember how certain words are shaped like the difficult-to-learn *w* words (see Figure 6.17).

Figure 6.18 shows two different kinds of Word Walls. The first is from a kindergarten classroom at the beginning of the year where the teacher has posted the students' names under their starting letter of the alphabet. The Word Wall with names helps Early Learners make initial connections to the alphabetic principle (something new) by linking it to the children's names (something they already know). The second wall is for high-frequency words and serves as a dictionary on the wall for students.

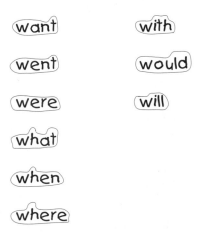

FIGURE 6.17   Word Configurations: The Difficult *w* Words

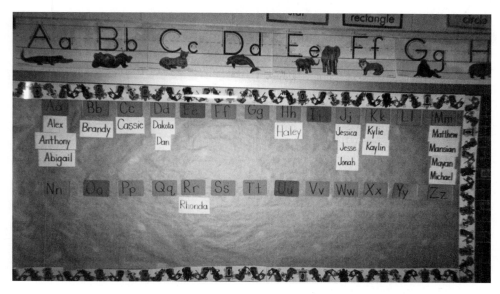

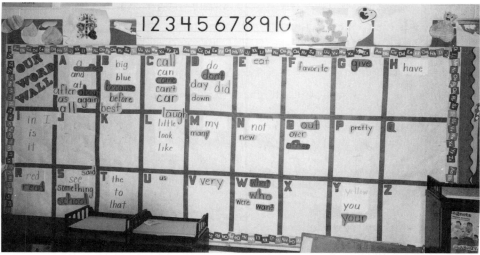

FIGURE 6.18 Two Kinds of Word Walls: Names (top) and High-Frequency Words (bottom)

Cunningham (2000) reminds us that if words stay on the wall and are not used on a daily basis through interactive exercises, then Word Walls become useless. She suggests that the teacher initiate game-like activities throughout the day that cause children to notice and use the Word Wall. For instance, let's say your students are waiting in line to go to the gym. Play a quick Word Wall game by saying, "One of our Word Wall words has three letters and means *large*. Who can guess what it is?"

Other more formal interactions with the Word Wall could occur during your Working with Words time slot. A popular Word Wall game is called "Be a Mind Reader" (Cunningham, 2000). In this game, the leader (you or one of your students) gives clues until children guess the word. Students number their scratch papers from one to five. Then, the leader gives clues. After each clue the rest of the students write down a guess next to the number. The idea is to have the leader say all of the clues while those who already have figured out the word remain quiet. When the clues are all read, then the leader can ask, "Who got the word after one clue? (two, etc.)"

1. It's a word on the wall.
2. The word has six letters.
3. It ends with an *e.*
4. It has two of the same letters in the center.
5. It means small. (*little*)

The main purpose of using Word Walls is that they provide your students with "an immediately accessible dictionary for the most troublesome words" (Cunningham, 2000, p. 76).

Word Sorts

Word sorts are a "word study routine in which students group words into categories. Word sorting involves comparing and contrasting within and across categories" (Bear, Invernizzi, Templeton, & Johnston, 2000, p. 372). Through sorting words children can form generalizations about words, connect patterns between words, and improve their visual memory for familiar words. Individual words are printed on index-size cards for sorting. The words used for word sorts should have some connection to students' lives, like their names, their siblings, their pets, as well as words from familiar books, words from signs in the room, and other words they know on sight.

Pinnell and Fountas (1998) offer these suggestions for word sorts:

- Words can be sorted by how they sound, like rhyming words or words that start with the same letter sound, or end with the same sound.
- Words can be sorted by how they look. Children can look for patterns in words like words with *ee,* words that have double consonants in the middle, or words that end with *ed* or by the number of letters in a word.
- Words can be sorted by connections between units of meaning like prefixes, suffixes, contractions, etc.

Word sorts allow children to divide word cards into designated categories. What kinds of phonics characteristics do children learn to notice by sorting words?

Other categories for sorting can be created by the teacher or the students. For example, things that grow, kinds of pets, people in my family, things that are green, words I need to learn better, words I already know. The possibilities are endless. Word sorting builds on the brain's inclination to look for patterns while affording children active practice during your Working with Words sessions.

ASSESSING STUDENTS' AWARENESS OF HOW WORDS WORK

In this text we have stressed the centrality of assessment as it serves to inform your teaching. When thinking about children's knowledge of how words work, it is essential to regularly assess what it is the child knows and can do. Here we will discuss various means of assessing your students' understanding of sounds/letter/words and their relationships.

Classroom Assessment

Observation Survey

One of the most useful tools for gathering information about Early Readers is Clay's *An Observation Survey of Early Literacy Achievement* (1993). In the introduction to this survey, Clay writes that through systematic assessment and observation we are able to reduce our uncertainties about our students and improve our literacy instruction. Clay's text offers valuable suggestions that allow us to monitor children's literacy development including:

- The reading of continuous text (Running Records),
- Letter knowledge,
- Reading vocabulary (known words when reading),
- Writing vocabulary (known words when writing),
- Concepts about print, and
- Hearing sounds in words (through dictation).

Phonemic Awareness Screening

The Consortium on Reading Excellence (1999) suggests a phonemic awareness screening procedure for kindergartners through second graders that measures whether children can detect rhymes, count syllables, match initial sounds, count phonemes, compare word lengths, and represent phonemes with letters. Their assessments involve conversations with the child about the concept you are measuring, then using pictures for the child to point to or draw a line between to indicate the correct pictures.

Based on this idea, you could create an easy assessment for your students. For example, if assessing the child's ability to detect rhymes, you could initiate a discussion about rhyming words like *rock, sock, lock,* and *clock.* Next you present the child with a page of pictures on which are some picture-words that rhyme and some that do not. Then, "read" each of the pictures to the child. Finally, ask the child to point to or draw lines between picture-words that rhyme as in Figure 6.19.

Using Rubrics

Writing rubrics can be used to assess students' writing progress over time. The rubric in Figure 6.20 was developed by literacy professionals as one means of evaluating a second grader's writing, linking the attributes to their state standards. When using this type of assessment, record the date, then score a child's piece of writing by assigning

Classroom Assessment

Classroom Assessment

FIGURE 6.19 A Teacher-Made Assessment for Detecting Rhymes

Second-Grade Writing Rubric
East Peoria/District #86

Indicators	0	1	2	3	4
CONTENT	Consists of one sentence	Of little interest No specific descriptions or examples (NARRATIVE) Does not express emotions or feelings	Mildly interesting Few specific descriptions or examples (NARRATIVE) Some emotions or feelings expressed	Fairly interesting Some specific descriptions or examples (NARRATIVE) Expresses feelings or emotions/not effectively	Captures reader's interest Several vivid descriptions or examples (NARRATIVE) Effectively expresses emotions/feelings
ORGANIZATION	Consists of one sentence	Topic is not clear No evident beginning middle, and end	Topic is evident but not clear Beginning, middle or end omitted	Stays on topic w/1 or 2 exceptions Beginning, middle, and end are evident but not clear	Stays on topic Has a clear beginning, middle, and end
FLUENCY	Consists of one sentence	Choppy/run-on sentences Sentences do not vary No transitions	More choppy/run-on sentences than natural expression Little variation in sentence length Some transitions	Some sentences flow naturally but not throughout the paper Some variation in sentence length Transitions throughout but may be stilted	Sentences flow naturally from one to another Sentences vary in length Transitions between sentences are natural
CONVENTIONS	Consists of one sentence	Little evidence of conventional spelling Little evidence of correct conventions * capital letters * ending marks	Conventional spelling evident (50%), but not used throughout Correct conventions evident, but not used throughout * capital letters * ending marks	Most words (75%) are spelled conventionally Conventions are generally correct with some errors * capital letters * ending marks	Spelling is conventional (90% of the words used) Convention use is consistent but not perfect * capital letter * ending marks * subject/verb agreement * paragraph form

Scoring
15–16 Exceeds standard
11–14 Meets standard
10 or less Does not meet standard

FIGURE 6.20 Writing Assessment Rubric

a number to each of the cells and adding up the total. In a few weeks, you assess the child's writing again, hopefully noticing growth. Each time you look to see whether the child is employing the targeted characteristics. In this way, a child's development as a writer could be tracked over time. In addition, this type of assessment allows you to know in which areas you need to support the child's learning through demonstration and practice opportunities.

In this section on assessing students' understanding of how words work, the measures described do not involve grade giving or error counting. Instead, they grow out of the perspective that the primary function of assessment is to tell you, the teacher, what you need to teach next. Through systematic observations, surveys, checklists, and documenting change over time you are provided with windows into the literacy-processing minds of your students that will allow you to make teaching decisions that will move your students forward.

CONNECTIONS: WHAT'S NEXT?

In this chapter we have been exploring the importance of word study for young learners and how best to employ word study in the context of your literacy program. We have emphasized the value of using children's literature and students' everyday reading opportunities as platforms for helping them make connections to features of print. We have also emphasized that working with words should be engaging, involve active practice, and be connected to reading and writing for real purposes. These are important elements in *all* effective literacy teaching.

Next, we move on from thinking about Early Readers and turn our attention toward children that we call Interpretive Readers. Just as you learned characteristics of young children, you will begin by finding out about intermediate-grade children: how their physical, social, and emotional characteristics affect their literacy learning. All the while, you will keep in mind that even though we have organized this textbook on a developmental continuum, the lines are blurred because all children are different and proceed at different developmental rates.

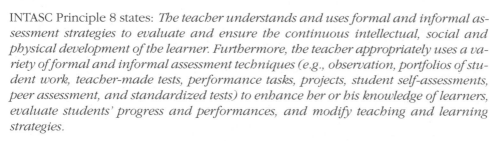

FOR YOUR PORTFOLIO

ENTRY 6.1   *Assessing Students' Awareness of Concepts of Print*

INTASC Principle 8 states: *The teacher understands and uses formal and informal assessment strategies to evaluate and ensure the continuous intellectual, social and physical development of the learner. Furthermore, the teacher appropriately uses a variety of formal and informal assessment techniques (e.g., observation, portfolios of student work, teacher-made tests, performance tasks, projects, student self-assessments, peer assessment, and standardized tests) to enhance her or his knowledge of learners, evaluate students' progress and performances, and modify teaching and learning strategies.*

Presented here is part of a checklist of concepts about print administered to kindergartner Shelly by her teacher. A checkmark has been placed by concepts Shelly understands and blank spaces remain next to concepts she does not yet know. The teacher handed an easy book to the child and asked the following questions:

Shelly, can you show me the front of the book?	✓
Where is the back of the book?	✓
Where do we begin reading the story?	✓
Look at this page in the book. Can you point to the words?	✓
Here's a page that has lots of words. (There are two lines of print.) Where do your eyes go when you get to the end of a line?	
Where is the first word on this page?	
Can you put your fingers around a word?	

Using the assessment here, and your understanding of the importance of knowing about children, answer these questions concerning this child.

1. What does she know about print now?
2. What does she need to know next? Describe which concepts about print you would teach Shelly that she does not yet understand. Also describe *how* you would teach these concepts.

ENTRY 6.2   *Defining Literacy Terms*

IRA/NCTE Standard for the English Language Arts 3 states: *Students can apply a wide range of strategies to comprehend, interpret, evaluate, and appreciate texts. They draw on their prior experience, their interactions with other readers and writers, their knowledge of word meaning and of other texts, their word identification strategies, and their understanding of textual features (e.g., sound–letter correspondence, sentence structure, context, graphics).*

For this entry, make a list of the literacy terms discussed in this chapter for helping children develop phonemic awareness and phonics understandings as part of their repertoire of word-solving strategies as described in IRA/NCTE Standard 3 (students' ability to identify words and understand textual features).

Here is a list of some of the terms we've been studying in this chapter:

- Phonics,
- Whole to part,
- Consonants,

- Consonant blends,
- Vowels,
- Consonant digraphs,
- Onsets and rimes,
- Sight words,
- High-frequency words,
- Developmental spelling,
- Phonemic awareness,
- Rhymes,
- Syllables,
- Phonemes,
- The language of reading instruction,
- Word Walls, and
- Word sorts.

For your portfolio entry, describe what the term means and how it is related to students' developing awareness about how words work. You may also want to include details about how you would teach the concepts to early learners.

An example of an entry is listed here:

Alphabet books —books that highlight individual letters of the alphabet and their corresponding sounds, through text and illustrations. Alphabet books help young learners make visual and conceptual associations between letters and sounds. Alphabet books that children make themselves can be especially effective in students' making personal connections with letter/sound relationships.

ENTRY 6.3 *Revisiting My Evolving Philosophy of Literacy Learning*

For this portfolio entry we ask that you revisit your evolving philosophy of literacy learning. Early in this course, you wrote about what it is you believe and why. This time we want you to look at what you wrote at the beginning of the term and determine changes you would make in articulating your philosophy of literacy learning based on the knowledge you have gained after engaging with this text and your co-learners. At this point, you have grown in your knowledge of literacy teaching and learning and your answers may be different from those you gave earlier.

Please date and keep this entry in your portfolio after you make changes; it will be beneficial as you trace your new understandings and your development as a literacy teacher. You may perceive that you will hold fast to some of your beliefs and change others over time; that is why we refer to our philosophies as *evolving*.

This time, as you write your answers to the following questions and sentence starters, back up your stated beliefs with information you have learned from this course and new knowledge you have constructed or co-constructed with your peers.

- How do children learn to read?
- What should I teach when helping children learn to read?
- How should I teach children to read?

Finish these statements, relating them to literacy learning:

- All children can. . .
- All children need. . .

- Children learn. . .
- Everyone in the classroom. . .
- Learning should be. . .
- Children need opportunities to. . .
- Teachers need to. . .
- Teachers can. . .
- Teachers have a responsibility to. . .

TO LEARN MORE

Helpful Websites

Visit our Companion Website at *http://www.prenhall.com/lenski* to link to the following sites:

Word Walls

Explains Word Walls and a variety of ways to use them in your classroom.
http://www.coe.ilstu.edu/portfolios/students/wjmirow/
word%2520walls%2520web%2520page.htm

Word Walls K–3

Describes Word Walls to use in kindergarten through third-grade classrooms.
http://www.k111.k12.il.us/lafayette/fourblocks/
word_wall_grade_level_lists.htm

Word Work in the Four-Block Model

Provides ideas and examples of working with words for different levels of readers.
http://www.wfu.edu/~cunningh/fourblocks/block4.html

Poems and Games, K–2

Lists K–2 poems and games that help with reading and writing.
http://www.bbc.co.uk/education/wordsandpictures/

Literacy Materials

Catalogs excellent letter and word learning materials for sale to K–2 teachers.
http://www.abcstuff.com

III

TEACHING INTERPRETIVE READERS

Interpretive Readers, that is, students who are in intermediate grades, will seem much more mature than Early Readers. They are more independent—physically, emotionally, and academically—than their younger counterparts. You can give Interpretive Readers assignments that they can complete alone or in groups; almost all of them will be able to read chapter books; and they are beginning to develop their own interests. Furthermore, many students in the intermediate grades are able to *interpret* texts, rather than just read them for simple understanding. That's because as children mature, they develop cognitive capabilities. As children reach the middle childhood years, they increase their ability to think logically (Piaget, 1952). This logical thinking ability allows students to use their knowledge to interpret texts, which is why we call them Interpretive Readers.

The intermediate grades are often a watershed for many students. Some Interpretive Readers will have been successful in the primary grades and will continue to be successful in school throughout the grades. Others will be so advanced by third grade that you, as their teacher, will have trouble keeping up with them and will find that your biggest challenge is to *challenge them*. Still other students who have been successful in the primary grades will begin to struggle with reading. This may be because by third grade, students are expected to read much more complex texts, fictional and informational, which will prove to be too difficult for some students. For those students who struggled in the primary grades, reading will all of a sudden "click"; these students will finally catch on and will begin to make rapid progress.

The gap of reading progress among students will begin to widen by third grade, and with that widening gap, you will need more than ever to meet the needs of individual students. To do this, you will have to understand the characteristics of this age group and how Interpretive Readers process print. In addition, you will need to address a wider variety of students with special needs, and you will need to think, maybe for the first time, about motivating students. Along with this knowledge about Interpretive Readers, you will need to develop a classroom environment conducive to learning, and teach strategies that help your students become proficient readers.

Meet Janette Vandeveer

Multigrade Intermediate Teacher

Janette has been teaching for 3 years in a multiage classroom with third-, fourth-, and fifth-grade students. Her literacy program is based on small-group instruction using literature, writing, working with words, and silent reading blocks. In this part, Janette will answer questions you might have in the feature titled *Advice for New Teachers.* Here she shares some wisdom that she's gained as a new teacher.

You Can't Do It All the First Year!

Janette reports that she has succeeded well at organizing and managing the word work segment as well as "SQUIRT" (Super Quiet Uninterrupted Independent Reading Time) during her class's literacy time. However, her goal is to bolster her reading program while the other students in her classroom are engaged in constructive, independent activities. She says, "Next year I want to consistently pull small reading groups together, collect all the materials I need for each group, and figure out what I need to do in order to have my other students doing beneficial activities, not seatwork-type busywork. Management is part of it, but I ask myself: Are they [the rest of the students] learning anything? However, I've learned that you can't do it all the first year. You have to be patient with yourself and add things in little by little as you become more knowledgeable, competent, and confident."

Who Needs Theory?

"When I graduated," says Janette, "I didn't even think about theory. I remember sitting in college thinking, 'Don't tell me that. Just tell me what to do!' Now, I want to know *why* am I doing this and how does it work? And, *is* it working?"

What I Wish I'd Known. . .

"Things I wish I had known my first year: Every child is different; not every class is the same. You can learn a lot from other teachers. I've been challenged in teaching reading and I've had to read stacks of books and attend conferences. You can find research articles and you can find out how other people have done it, but to actually go out and do it yourself, then you have to really reflect and figure out the way that *you* know and understand. Learning to teach is a never-ending process."

chapter **7**

Developing Your Knowledge About Interpretive Readers

Essential Learning Questions

- What characteristics of Interpretive Readers have implications for classroom instruction?
- How does the transactional theory of reading influence your understanding of the way Interpretive Readers process print?
- What are the "ingredients" of a reading event and what impact does each have on students' reading?
- Why is differentiated instruction crucial when teaching Interpretive Readers?

Interpretive Readers are distinctly different from Early Readers and Critical Readers. We are not suggesting that children move from one stage to another when they are promoted to a new grade, but that children in each age group have commonalties of which you should be aware. Interpretive Readers, in general, are learning the physical skills necessary to play games, developing a sense of themselves as unique individuals, learning how to work and play with their peers, becoming more independent, developing values, and increasing their abilities to read at a deeper level (Havighurst, 1952).

Children in the intermediate grades are learning how reading and schooling work. If children feel secure about their foundational skills of reading, they use reading to learn about the world and their lives. Children in the intermediate grades begin to form a realistic picture of their reading progress through a newly acquired ability to perceive themselves as others see them.

The intermediate grades are also a time when students are held more accountable for their reading progress—locally and nationally. Many state and national reading tests begin to be administered in the third or fourth grades. And although educators agree that all children learn at their own rate, once they reach third grade, students are often expected to match grade-level standards. The pressure of accountability often leads teachers to place a great deal of emphasis on testing and meeting standards even though Paris (2001) reminds us that elementary school readers need authentic purposes for learning that are embedded in integrated instruction. Because of the budding maturity and increased accountability placed on Interpretive Readers, it would be helpful for you to understand what makes Interpretive Readers unique compared to other age groups.

UNDERSTANDING INTERPRETIVE READERS

Physical Development

Children in middle childhood, ages 7 through 11, are in a period of stable growth, unlike when they were younger or in early adolescence. Children in intermediate grades grow more slowly, gaining only an average of 5 pounds and 2 inches per year (Berger & Thompson, 1991). Along with this slow, steady physical growth, many children become more adept at controlling their bodies. They are now able to hit a baseball, make free-throw shots in basketball, and run a mile. Many children become

Intermediate-grade students are often proficient at keyboarding.

slimmer, losing their "baby fat," and develop stronger muscles. During this time, children rapidly develop athletic skills and become more interested in team sports. As a teacher of Early Readers, you may have entire groups of children hanging on your arms during recess, but Interpretive Readers are more likely to be off playing games with their friends.

Fine-motor control.   During grades 3 through 5 most children develop more precise fine-motor control. Many young children have difficulty writing and drawing pictures, but by third grade, most children have developed the hand and finger coordination necessary to be able to write, draw, and use a keyboard. Typically, children at this age begin writing in cursive script rather than manuscript printing. Although some schools teach cursive writing in second grade, third grade is the time when children most often make rapid progress writing in cursive. The intermediate grades are also appropriate grades to teach keyboarding skills. Many children come to third grade with hours of experience playing computer games and even typing on the computer, but few will know how to correctly position their hands on the keyboard for rapid and accurate typing.

Early development of girls.   For many girls, middle childhood is the best time of their lives (Pipher, 1994). During this time, girls tend to develop in patterns similar to those of boys; they become involved in team sports, they develop friendships, and

Visit the online journal in Chapter 7 on our Companion Website at *www.prenhall.com/lenski* to answer these questions. Save your answers to your hard drive or to a disk to compile an online journal.

The changes students experience in puberty are described more fully in Chapter 11. How do you think your reading instruction should be adapted for students entering puberty?

they enjoy learning about life. Young girls are not constricted by society's notions of what girls should be or do. They are, in some sense, free of gender roles that are imposed on older females. However, during grades 3 through 6, many girls begin to enter puberty. With puberty, and the hormonal changes that occur, comes a new self-consciousness and an intense interest in boys. As a teacher, you may find that a fourth-grade girl who enthusiastically engaged in classroom activities in the fall is by spring more concerned with her looks, her weight, and her social status.

Classroom application.   Because Interpretive Readers are learning to play in teams with rules and are increasingly independent, they are much more willing to engage in more independent literacy activities such as literature discussion groups. Frank, Dixon, and Brandts (2001) organized a type of a book club with their intermediate-grade readers. The class was divided into four groups of students with varying reading abilities. Students were asked to choose a book to read, to read that book more than once, to write a letter to the group discussing the book, and to talk about the book during discussion time. These types of group activities work well with Interpretive Readers who relish their growing reading competence and find pleasure in taking control over their learning.

 You will learn more about grouping activities in subsequent chapters. How does active, engaged learning exemplify social constructivist theories?

Social and Emotional Development

When was the first time you went to a movie or the mall without your parents? For many children it's during middle childhood. During this time, children become much less dependent on adults; they begin to make their own decisions about what to

---

Advice for New Teachers

Active Learning

Dear Janette,

I know that intermediate-grade students have lots of energy and need to learn through activities. How can I teach my students what they need to know if they're moving around?

Dear New Teacher,

Developing active learning lessons will take a bit of creativity if you are to adapt your teaching plans so that your students can move about freely. I try to be sensitive to my students' needs, so I incorporate movement whenever I think it's appropriate. One day I was conducting a word building lesson, which is an interactive activity, when I noticed that the students were listless and distracted. It was good weather outside, so I took students outside and modified the lesson into a relay race. The students perked up right away, and I was pleased to see that they were even paying attention to the phonics skills I was teaching.

My advice to you is to look for opportunities such as the example just given to incorporate active learning. If you keep your mind open, you'll be able to develop lessons that include movement.

wear, what clothes to buy, and what books they want to read. Children at this time develop social cognition—the understanding that how people relate to each other influences personal bonds—and they begin to develop friendships. Friendships develop into clubs and groups. You might remember in your elementary school years forming private clubs with rules about who could or could not be a member, or joining groups such as Girl Scouts or Boy Scouts.

Children in middle childhood also begin to understand social roles. If you teach younger children, they may be shocked to see you at the grocery store, but children in intermediate grades understand that teachers can also be parents, spouses, and members of families (Watson, 1984). Children also begin to understand their own personalities. They learn that people can be different from each other, and that one of their friends might be hard working and motivated while another might be easy going. Along with this self-revelation, though, comes a barrier to positive self-esteem.

Self-esteem.   As children become more aware of their personalities, they often become more self-critical and sometimes their self-esteem begins to drop (Berger & Thompson, 1991). Younger children tend to have high self-esteem, but when children reach the intermediate grades, they tend to become aware of their shortcomings and failures. This is especially true in school. During the primary grades, most children believe they can learn to read, and they are motivated to continue trying— even in the face of failure. By the time children reach third grade, however, they become aware of their level of success compared to others in their class. They know who are the "good readers" and who are the "struggling readers." This new awareness tends to lower children's self-esteem, even for the good readers, because children in middle childhood begin to blame themselves for their failures. When young children have difficulty in school, they tend to blame it on outside forces—luck, the teacher, their peers—but intermediate-grade children blame themselves (Powers & Wagner, 1984). Self-blame can lead to lower self-esteem and also to a personality adaptation called *learned helplessness.*

Learned helplessness.   As children develop greater capacity for self-reflection and as they struggle to develop positive self-esteem, many children become reluctant to learn new skills. This reluctance to learn may turn into learned helplessness. Learned helplessness is hopelessness: Children believe that nothing they can do will help them improve their learning. Often children who are not motivated to learn are actually experiencing learned helplessness. Their past failures have taught them that they cannot succeed no matter what they do, so they see no reason to even try. As a teacher, you'll probably have children who don't believe they can read well or can learn to read. This will be especially true if parents or teachers have told the children that their lack of success is due to low ability. These children often develop a sense of inferiority that can lead to more school failure. If they succeed at a task, they attribute success to luck rather than to ability. They then enter a negative spiral: attribution of success to luck, attribution of failure to self, feelings of inferiority, low self-esteem, lack of motivation, learned helplessness. Girls and students from minority groups are especially susceptible to these feelings of learned helplessness (Berk, 1996).

Diversity Issue: Cultural mediators.   Children from families who represent minority groups face additional barriers to positive self-esteem. According to Vygotsky (1978), social relationships are one of the building blocks of mental and personal development. Social relationships become internalized as mental functions. Therefore, the relationships those students have in classrooms with their peers and with their teacher can become the basis for their view of themselves.

When children observe that their families and their language usage are not valued in school, they may develop a poor sense of self and even give up on schooling. Díaz and Flores (2001) suggest that teachers must bridge the gap between home knowledge and school learning by becoming a cultural mediator. You already spent some time considering your own cultural identity in Chapter 1; as a teacher, you'll also need to become familiar with the cultural backgrounds of all of your students. As you learn about your students' cultures and the values they hold, it will be important to your students' social development that you respect their cultural backgrounds and languages. One specific way to be a cultural mediator is to read books aloud to students that illustrate a variety of cultures. As you choose books, you can try to match students' cultural backgrounds to books, but you need to be cautious about assigning stereotypes. Students who come from Spanish-speaking homes may or may not relate to books set in rural Mexico, for example. If your students are from Mexico, however, you can read books from a variety of settings in Mexico and hope that your Mexican students relate to some aspect of the different books. You can find book lists on multicultural literature at the websites listed in Figure 7.1.

America's Stir-Fry Multicultural Books
Contains information about more than 150 multicultural and bilingual books and audio and videotapes. Includes a downloadable catalog and book reviews.

http://www.americas-stirfry.com

South Asian Children's Books and Software
Contains a brief introduction to a list of books as well as links to other websites that sell books or software. Some of these books are translations, but most were written in English.

http://www.umiacs.umd.edu/users/sawweb/sawnet/kidsbooks.html

Multicultural Literature in the Elementary Classroom
Contains a list of citations from the ERIC database that addresses the topic of selecting and utilizing multicultural children's literature as well as the significance of such materials in shaping the views of children toward cultures other than their own. Directions for securing full-text copies of these records are also given.

http://www.indiana.edu/~eric_rec/ieo/bibs/multicul.html

Books About Multicultural Topics
Contains bibliographies of books on different parts of the world.

http://www.monroe.lib.in.us/childrens/multicultural.html

Making Multicultural Connections Through Trade Books
Focuses on multicultural trade books for elementary-age children. These books were selected because they represent a specific culture and its traditions, history, folktales, or current peoples.

http://www.mcps.k12.md.us/curriculum/socialstd/MBD/Books_Begin.html

Multicultural Children's Literature: Authorship and Selection Criteria
Contains information from the ERIC database on authorship and selecting criteria for multicultural children's literature. Directions for securing full-text copies of these records are also given.

http://www.indiana.edu/~eric_rec/ieo/bibs/multicu2.html

FIGURE 7.1 List of Websites for Multicultural Books

YOU TRY IT

Student Interview

You will need to practice to learn how to become a cultural mediator for intermediate-grade students. One way to learn this important skill is to interview a child, learn about that child's culture, and begin to find books that match that culture in some way.

Identify a child in grades 3 through 5. You might have a cousin, niece, or nephew at this age, or you might have access to students in schools. If possible, find a child that has a different culture from your own.

Remember, culture is not limited to ethnic heritage. You might be of European American heritage from a suburban area. A child of European heritage from an urban or rural area would have a different culture. Ask the child's parent or guardian if you can talk with the child about his family and background for a school assignment. Show the parents the list of questions you will ask and get their approval before the interview begins. Emphasize that you are not a member of any governmental agency. (Some families are afraid of immigration officials, if not for themselves, for others.) Ask the child if you can talk with him and ask questions about his family. If the child agrees, develop a list of questions aimed at an understanding of culture, or use the list of questions that follows. After you have interviewed the child, compare your results with other members of your class. Then use your knowledge of literature to select books that could match the child's culture.

Interview Questions

- What languages do your parents and grandparents speak? Do you know what country your ancestors were from?
- Does your family attend church, synagogue, or mosque?
- What holidays are special to your family?
- What favorite foods does your family eat?
- What does your family do on weekends?
- Is there anything that makes your family different from other families?

Cognitive Development

Children in middle childhood develop significantly in the ways they learn. Young children tend to be very concrete and exacting; they don't understand subtleties, and they have difficulty making inferences and drawing conclusions during reading. As children mature and develop, however, they begin to think more deeply and are able to not only "read the lines" but "read between the lines." Most intermediate-grade children have experiences reading longer books and completing complex learning assignments. By the time children reach third grade, most of them are reading chapter books that have complex story plots, and many of them read informational books that have conceptually dense material. Because of the cognitive gains children make at this age, they can interpret more complex text.

Children in middle childhood develop a whole host of new skills during the intermediate grades. Students become more able to focus on tasks during this time, and they are less distractible, which is one of the reasons why they are able to work independently with much more ease. Intermediate-grade children can also remember more information than younger children and can play more complex games, such as chess. They are also expected to learn more content material, and students are expected to study and memorize information for tests. Another important cognitive difference between Interpretive Readers and Early Readers is that older children can begin to transform information by considering the different aspects of information, and they can synthesize multiple sources of information, such as in writing summaries and reports. Finally, the knowledge base of Interpretive Readers expands rapidly due to increased cognitive capabilities and many experiences reading a variety of books.

Piaget's stages.   During the intermediate grades, most students begin to think logically, rather than intuitively, and are able to classify objects into categories. These traits, and others, illustrate what Piaget (1952) termed the *concrete operational* stage of development. Piaget studied children throughout his long career as a psychologist and researcher. One of his theories was that children move through developmental stages of cognitive growth (Figure 7.2). Although subsequent research has cast doubt on the generalizability of Piaget's stages, we can use his work as a foundation to understand

Approximate Age	Stage	Characteristics	Major Acquisitions
Birth to 2 years	Sensorimotor	Uses senses and motor abilities to learn.	An object still exists when it is out of sight.
2–6 years	Preoperational	Uses symbolic thinking, including language. Thinking is egocentric (thinks only from own perspective).	Uses language as a means of expression. Imagination flourishes. Begins to understand multiple points of view.
7–11 years	Concrete operational	Understands and applies logical operations. Interprets experiences rationally.	Understands conservation, number, classification, and other concrete ideas.
12 years and older	Formal operational	Thinks about abstractions and is able to speculate.	Ethics, politics, utopia, and social and moral issues become important. Able to view ideas from multiple perspectives.

FIGURE 7.2   Piaget's Stages of Cognitive Development

how children learn throughout their lives (Berger & Thompson, 1991). As you read the stages, understand that children do not move from one stage to another at a specific time and at a certain age. Instead, children move from stage to stage (and back and forth between stages) depending on the task and their motivation.

Language development.   Language develops rapidly during middle childhood. According to Berk (1996), young children entering school typically have a vocabulary of approximately 10,000 words. By the time children finish elementary school, their vocabulary has expanded to more than 40,000 words, which represents an average gain of more than 20 new words each day. During this time, most children are able to read longer books, and, as a result, they are exposed to many new words. In addition, children at this age are able to internalize the rules for learning new words, such as learning how to use prefixes and suffixes to read and understand new words. Therefore, experiences with language and a new facility for figuring out new words foster rapid vocabulary growth.

Vocabulary also develops through the explicit teaching of new words (Blachowicz & Fisher, 2000). Children will learn many words through reading, but they also need instruction to help them learn academic vocabulary. When you teach Interpretive Readers, you should help them link new words to their background knowledge, develop conceptual understandings of new words, understand the relationships between words, and develop independence in vocabulary acquisition (Lenski, Wham, & Johns, 2003).

 Many strategies for the explicit teaching of vocabulary can be found throughout this text. What vocabulary strategies do you already know that would be appropriate for Interpretive Readers?

Diversity issue: Code-switching.   Many of you will have students for whom English is not their first language, that is, English Language Learners (ELL). ELL students typically make impressive language gains during intermediate grades, both in English and possibly in their home language. Think for a moment about children who are native speakers of English. Children in the primary grades develop language and grammar skills and this progress continues throughout the intermediate grades. For example, young children often use the nonstandard phrase "*Me and Aaron* would like to write a story together." It's not until children become more proficient with language that they use the standard form "Aaron and I." Language develops in all Interpretive Readers whether or not they speak English as a first or second language.

As ELL students are learning English, however, they may need to code-switch (Berzins & Lopez, 2001). Code-switching is the process of switching back and forth between languages during a single conversation or thought. An example of code-switching follows:

Teacher:	What did you do this weekend, Rosa?
Rosa:	I went *al cine* with my *hermanito*. (I went to the movie theater with my little brother.)
Teacher:	What movie did you see?
Rosa:	I saw *la pelicula Titanic*. (I saw the movie *Titanic*.)

As you can see, Rosa used her knowledge of both English and Spanish to talk with her teacher about what she did over the weekend. Rosa was able to compose parts of sentences in English, but she reverted to Spanish for more difficult words. Code-switching is part of the language development of ELL students and should be encouraged rather than discouraged (García, 2000).

Humor.   One of the delights in working with Interpretive Readers is that they finally understand jokes. Because many children at this age have progressed to the concrete operational stage and because they have increased vocabularies, students often en-

Barrett, J. (1970). *Animals should definitely not wear clothes.* New York: Macmillan.
Berger, M. (1991). *101 Wacky state jokes.* New York: Scholastic.
Coville, B. (1989). *My teacher is an alien.* New York: Pocket Books.
Gutman, D. (1996). *The kid who ran for president.* New York: Scholastic.
Hirsch, P. (1988). *101 Dinosaur jokes.* New York: Scholastic.
Macauley, D. (1987). *Why the chicken crossed the road.* Boston: Houghton Mifflin.
Monsell, M. (1988). *Underwear.* Morton Grove, IL: Albert Whitman.
Nancy, J. L. (2000). *Letters from a nut.* New York: Scholastic.

FIGURE 7.3   Humorous Books for Interpretive Readers

joy humor. Younger children often tell "Knock, Knock" jokes, but Interpretive Readers are able to read and tell jokes, and are even developing their own sense of humor. You can help children develop a sense of humor by reading humorous books to them or by encouraging them to read humorous books independently. A list of humorous books appropriate for intermediate-grade students is given in Figure 7.3.

OBSERVING INTERPRETIVE READERS PROCESS PRINT

Once students reach intermediate grades, they should be fairly adept at orchestrating the cueing systems. Interpretive Readers will be able to use their knowledge about language cues to make sense of print as they read. Most of them will know enough sight words that they can read fairly fluently, and many students will automatically use reading strategies, such as sampling, predicting, and confirming. Interpretive Readers will also begin to read silently with more comprehension. As students in intermediate grades become more skillful using cueing systems and simple strategies, they begin to have more cognitive space to think about texts more deeply. At this time, the demands of reading in school change. Students are given more difficult texts to read: longer chapter books, nonfiction materials, and textbooks, in addition to the more familiar genre of fiction. During the intermediate grades many students make rapid progress in reading and are able to read the challenging texts. Students who have difficulty learning to read, however, will need to review those skills and strategies that were taught in the primary grades and also learn the strategies that can help them become Interpretive Readers.

To understand how Interpretive Readers process print, you need to refresh your memory about how people learn. From a social constructivist viewpoint, learning is a social process in which learners construct individual meanings using their background knowledge as a lens to make sense of text. These constructions of meaning are not developed in a vacuum, but are framed within particular social contexts. As you consider the ways in which Interpretive Readers process print, use your knowledge of social constructivist learning theory to weave together the ideas presented in this section. Here you will learn a reading theory that is compatible with social constructivism, the *transactional theory* of reading. The transactional theory suggests that three components of any reading situation interact: the reader, the text, and the context.

 You were introduced to the transactional theory of reading in Chapter 1. How does the transactional theory fit into your own evolving theory of literacy?

Transactional Theory of Reading

In earlier chapters you learned the differences between social constructivism and behaviorism. Students are not blank slates for you to "write" knowledge on as believed by behaviorists; instead, when students engage in social interactions involving language, they think and learn. The notion that students construct their own knowledge is one of the premises of social constructivism. Using social constructivism as a theoretical framework, then, reading becomes a process of thinking: of thinking about reading cues and of thinking about meaning.

One theory that emphasizes the point that reading is thinking is the transactional theory of reading (Rosenblatt, 1978). The transactional theory suggests that reading is a transaction between the reader, the text, and the context. This theory was developed in opposition to behaviorist thinking, which viewed the reader and the text as separate entities, with meaning residing in words, not people, and being the same for all readers. Instead, Rosenblatt theorized that readers, texts, and contexts are linked during the reading process. Each of the components of reading contributes to the meaning that readers construct during reading events.

The idea that reading is a transaction may be new to you, or at least the terms may be new. Let's think about a situation that is more familiar to you: when you applied to college. When you decided to pursue a college degree, you probably sent away for an application, or you accessed one from the college's website. The application acts as the "representative" from the college in that it "asks" you for information about yourself. As you completed the application, you brought your own background and other pertinent information to the situation. You sent the college your application and a transaction occurred. The college reviewed and accepted your application. They communicated their acceptance to you, and you decided to attend the college. Because of the transaction, your future and that of the college would intertwine. You would change (because of the college) and so would the future of the college (because you would be there).

Something similar happens during reading. The reader enters a situation in which she decides to learn about a specific topic or wants to enter into the lives of others through the story. The reader has a purpose for reading, and that purpose guides the selection of reading material, which results in the reader choosing a text. The text is an author's views on a subject, or, in the case of fictional texts, an author's story. The author has written the text at an earlier time, so the text is the representative of the author. The reader enters the reading situation, bringing her purposes, background knowledge, and linguistic ability. The reading event is situated in a social context, such as reading for school. During reading a transaction occurs: The reader changes as a result of the reading, and the text changes. The text in the reader's mind is no longer the same text that was published by the author; it's now a construction of meaning within the reader. In other words, the words did not stay on the page containing universally agreed upon meaning. Rather, the meaning is unique to each reader because of each person's background experiences and prior knowledge. Figure 7.4 illustrates the relationship between the three main components of reading: the reader, the text, and the context.

A shared journey.   The transactional theory of reading describes reading as a shared journey between readers and authors. The transaction that occurs between readers, texts, and contexts is not only experienced by Interpretive Readers. Early Readers also bring their background knowledge, interests, and abilities to texts and contexts, but Early Reading focuses more closely on cueing systems, as described by psycholinguistic theory. The transactional theory, however, does apply to all readers—Early Readers, Interpretive Readers, Critical Readers, and Adult Readers. Each of these groups experiences reading as a function of the individual reader, the text, and the context.

Reader

Text

Context

FIGURE 7.4   Transactional Theory of Reading

Transactional Theory: The Reader

Readers come to reading situations with unique knowledge and abilities. When you teach reading to Interpretive Readers, consider the metaphor of "a party" to understand what each reader brings to any reading situation. Imagine yourself planning a party for several good friends. You invite your friends to the party, and they bring food or drink, individual personalities, different agendas, and a variety of expectations—based on past experiences. You don't know beforehand how successful the party will be for each of your friends; you bring people together, and they take away different experiences. Teaching reading is like that. You'll be bringing a group of students together to read, but they'll all be very different. What they bring to the reading situation will, in many respects, determine the outcomes of their reading experiences. Some of the ingredients that readers bring to reading events are background knowledge, interests, linguistic abilities, and abilities to apply reading strategies.

Background knowledge.   When you become a teacher, you'll be amazed at the differences among your students—not only their cultural differences and the wide range of reading abilities in your class, but the differences in their background knowledge. Readers bring their background knowledge to each reading situation and use it to construct meaning from a new text. Knowledge is organized in students' minds in schemata (Anderson & Pearson, 1984). During reading, schemata are accessed and new information is sorted into the schemata. Each of your students will have distinctly different experiences with and knowledge about the texts you use in the classroom and will bring different amounts and types of background knowledge to reading those texts.

Background knowledge, as you might remember, is a central notion in constructivism. In order for readers to make meaning while reading, they access the background knowledge available from schemata to make sense of the text. Let's say you ask a small group of students to read the book *So You Want to Be President* (St. George & Small, 2000). In your group of six students, you have one student who is new to the United States, one student whose parents are involved in politics, one student who loves to watch the history channel, and three students who have no specific knowledge about the presidents. As the students read the book, each brings a different knowledge base about presidents to the reading of the book.

Individual motivation and interests.   Background knowledge is only one component that your students will bring to each reading event. Each reader will also bring his own motivation and interests. Motivation in reading is a combination of a student's personal goals, values, and beliefs as they apply to a specific text (Guthrie & Wigfield, 2000). All of us have reading preferences and different motivations to read. For example, imagine that your friend gives you a copy of a new diet book. You've heard about this diet, know friends who have tried the diet, and have heard positive news reports from doctors about the diet. You are thinking about losing 10 pounds, and you were looking for a book to read over the weekend. How motivated would you be to read this book? On the other hand, let's say that you are satisfied with your current eating habits, have several books on your shelf that you've been waiting to read, and have no plans in the near future to diet. What's your motivation now? These examples illustrate how motivation to read varies among readers, especially when books are presented to them *by someone else.*

All of your students also bring different interests to reading situations. Some students will be interested in reading fictional texts and others will be more interested in reading informational texts. Students have preferences about the types of fiction they prefer. Some students prefer adventure stories, some prefer mysteries, others prefer real-life stories. It's hard to say what captures a particular student's interest, but it's important to find out what interests students because students tend to become more engaged in reading when they read topics or genres that interest them (McPhail, Pierson, Freeman, Goodman, & Ayappa, 2000). This will be especially important for reluctant readers—those who can read but choose not to read.

 You will find ideas for promoting motivation throughout this text. How do you motivate yourself to read?

YOU TRY IT

Interest Inventories

Each student has very different interests. Students bring their individual interests to reading situations as part of the transaction that occurs during reading. Often teachers ask their students to complete an interest inventory to determine students' interests.

Administer a copy of an interest inventory to a student in the intermediate grades. (Sample interest inventories can be found on the Companion Website: http://www. prenhall.com/lenski.) Bring your results to class and discuss the differences among the students you have interviewed. Use the following questions to guide your discussion.

- What trends in interests do you find?
- How are students' interests different from each other?
- How do students' interests change the transaction or reading?

Linguistic abilities.   Each student also has unique linguistic abilities. Young readers learn how to manage the cueing systems of language, and each student will have different areas of strengths and weaknesses. Some students will be able to make accurate predictions about words through the use of contextual clues (the meaning cueing system), whereas other students will rely more heavily on visual clues. Not all of your students will have the same ability to orchestrate the cueing systems. Furthermore, each of your students will have different personal vocabularies, or lexicons. Your students will have had different experiences with stories and language and will know the meanings of different words. So, not only do readers bring their own unique background knowledge to reading situations, they bring their own ability to read words and make meaning of the text.

Use of strategies.   A final ingredient readers bring to reading situations is their ability to control the processes of reading (Pressley, 2000). When students read, they should use a wide variety of strategies to make meaning from the print. You'll learn more about these strategies later in this section, but for now, know that when intermediate-grade students read, they use strategies before they read, while they read, and after they read. Before reading, a reader might preview the text, set purposes for reading, and choose appropriate reading strategies for the demands of the text. While reading, readers check their understanding, reread difficult sections, make inferences, and get the gist of the selection. After reading, readers summarize and synthesize what they read and respond in some way. Each reader applies these reading strategies in different ways (Blachowicz & Ogle, 2001).

You might be thinking at this time, "I don't think I use these strategies when I read." You do, but you may not realize it. Experienced readers use all of these strategies automatically and have incorporated them into their reading routines. For students in intermediate grades, however, using strategies is relatively new. Most students in the primary grades have had enough experiences with texts to be comfortable applying cueing systems so that when they reach the intermediate grades, students are able to develop their ability to apply strategies that help them control the processes of reading.

Transactional Theory: The Text

When intermediate-grade students read, they use a text. Any reading material is considered to be a text, and even though Early Readers also read texts, the texts of Interpretive Readers are much more demanding—the chapter books are longer, basal reader stories are more complex, and more content-area reading is expected (i.e., science books). Some students enter third or fourth grade feeling successful only to find that the texts expected at the intermediate grades are much more difficult. Read the excerpt from the first-grade text in Figure 7.5 and think about how this passage engages readers in the content. Texts for Interpretive Readers are typically less engaging and more densely packed with facts and new vocabulary terms.

Readability of text.   You may be wondering what makes texts difficult. Reading researchers have determined that many aspects of texts make reading more difficult. Among them are sentence length, number of unknown vocabulary words, and word length (Klare, 1984). How difficult a text may be is sometimes measured with a readability formula. These formulas use two or more of the components of texts, such as sentence length and the total number of syllables, to provide an approximate grade level. Readability formulas are frequently used to measure classroom materials, such as basal reader stories and content-area textbooks. You might hear a textbook sales representative say, "This social studies book was written at a fourth-grade level." When you hear these types of statements, you will know that the text was measured with one of the many readability formulas. As a teacher, however, you will find that these so-called "reading levels" may not be helpful for you in selecting materials for your students.

First-Grade Passage

Many plants grow from **seeds.**
Look at the plant flowers.
Flowers of plants make seeds.
Find the seeds in this flower.

A seed opens when it begins to grow.
A plant grows from the open seed.
A growing plant makes more seeds.
Look at the seeds in the picture.
What plants will grow from the seeds?

FIGURE 7.5   First-Grade Science Passage

Readability formulas are appealing in many ways, but they can also be mis-leading. For example, you already know that each reader brings different back-ground experiences to reading events; therefore, no one text could possibly be set at a reading level for students with wide variances of knowledge. Another reason why readability formulas are problematic is that most of them don't take into account concept density, or how many ideas are presented in short passages. For example, read the following selection (Plato, 1983), consider at which grade this passage should be taught, and predict the passage's readability.

> "Well then," said Parmeides, "If there is a one, of course the one will not be many. Consequently, it cannot have any parts or be a whole. For a part is a part of a whole, and a whole means that from which no part is missing; so whether you speak of it as 'a whole' or as 'having parts,' in either case the one would consist of parts and in that way be many and not one. But it is to be one and not many. Therefore, if the one is to be one, it will not be a whole nor have parts." (p. 24)

At what grade level would you suggest this passage be taught? Probably not at the intermediate grades. According to a popular readability formula, however, this text is written at a fourth-grade reading level. You can see why readability formulas don't give us an accurate rendering of the difficulty of text. Because readability formulas are frequently used in schools, you should be aware of their use.

Technology topic: Online readability programs.   Figuring out the readability of passages used to be a time-consuming venture. To determine the readability, you had to count syllables, words, and sentences and apply these numbers to a chart. Now, however, you can input passages on the computer, and the computer calcu-lates the readability. For example, some word processing programs calculate the number of words in a selected passage and others calculate actual readabilities. You can also find readability formulas online: The Fry and the SMOG formulas provide directions, tables, and graphs. Their websites are listed in the To Learn More section at the end of the chapter.

Text structure.   Texts are also organized into different structures. Narrative texts are organized into what Stein and Glenn (1979) call *story grammar.* Story grammar is a way to characterize the organization of narrative texts using terms that describe the plot such as *initiating event, internal response, attempt,* and *resolution.* Teachers use different terms to describe the organization of narrative text. Many elementary teachers use these terms: setting, characters, the problem, events, solving the problem, and ending.

Nonfiction texts are also organized into recognizable structures. Nonfiction structures are typically organized into the structures of main idea–detail, problem–solution, cause–effect, and comparison–contrast. Take this textbook, for example. Most of it is written in the main idea–detail structure, but some passages are organized with the problem–solution, cause–effect, and comparison–contrast text structures. Text structures are another component that affects the transaction that occurs during reading.

Transactional Theory: The Context

Reading does not occur in isolation, even when you are reading alone. Reading consists of a transaction between readers, texts, and also contexts. The context of reading is where reading occurs, but not just the physical space. Context includes the cultural and social backgrounds each of the readers brings to the reading situation. Context of reading, therefore, can be considered in two ways: patterns of socialization and learning environments.

 The context of reading is one of the applications of sociocultural theory. How else can you apply sociocultural theories to reading processes?

Patterns of socialization.   Each of us has been socialized into different attitudes about print, reading, and the content of the text. For example, Lori, a Native American student, told us about her experiences reading American history in school. Lori recalls that in fifth grade she resisted reading American history even though she was an excellent student with adequate background knowledge on the subject. Lori's socialization emphasized a strong identification with Native American issues, and she was aware of the distortions of American history as it was taught in school at that time. Lori simply could not read history without becoming upset. As a result, she refused to read fifth-grade history assignments.

Reading in a relaxed environment.

While this example may be extreme, print exists in social contexts, and all of us have been socialized in many ways about print. Perhaps when you think of picture books you get a warm feeling because your mother and father read you lots of books when you were young. Perhaps you become anxious when you read math books because you had trouble with math in high school. These examples further illustrate the social contexts that readers bring to reading.

Environments as context.   You can also think about the context of reading as a reading environment. Where do you like to read best? Some of us like to read lying down on a sofa; others like to read while sitting in a chair. Most likely few of you prefer reading while sitting in an uncomfortable school desk with 25 of your friends sitting in close proximity. Another question. Do you read with noise or without? The environment of reading is also a factor in the transaction of reading.

ACKNOWLEDGING DIFFERENCES AMONG INTERPRETIVE READERS

You've probably heard the popular slogan "All Children Can Learn," and you might wonder how you can teach a classroom of students who have a wide array of differences so that each one learns to read. That, of course, is one of the biggest challenges of teaching. It's one thing to teach a group of students, and quite another for each child to learn. Thomas and Bainbridge (2001) argue that as we consider a classroom of students, we need to remember that indeed all children can learn, but that they will not all learn at the same rate and the same way. Therefore, as a teacher of Interpretive Readers, you will have to pay close attention to the differences among your students so that each one can learn to the fullest degree possible.

In a typical classroom of intermediate-grade students, you will have between 25 and 30 students. If you teach a heterogeneous group (mixed-ability group), you may have students who can't read above a pre-primer level and students who can read high school textbooks. You may have students who know little English and students who were reading when they were 3 years old. You may have students who have been identified as being in need of special education, Title 1, bilingual classes, and gifted education. Each of these students needs a differentiated curriculum. As a classroom teacher, you are the primary educator of your students, and although some of your students may be taught in special classes, it will be your responsibility to see that all children *do* learn.

Interpretive Readers With Special Needs

You may find that you have more students with special needs in the intermediate grades than do primary-grade teachers. There are two reasons why this is so. First, teachers often wait to test students who are experiencing difficulty in school until second grade. Some students who struggle in kindergarten and first-grade seem to "catch up" by second grade, especially if they have not had many literacy experiences prior to schooling. The second reason why teachers wait to refer students for testing is because many kindergarten and first-grade classrooms already have intervention programs (e.g., Reading Recovery™, teacher aides, parent volunteers). If students still struggle with reading after participating in intervention programs in kindergarten and first grade, teachers look for other causes of reading problems. Therefore, teachers of Interpretive Readers will have more students who have been identified as having special needs in their classrooms.

As a teacher of reading, you'll have students with a variety of special needs in your classroom. What do you already know about instructing students with special needs?

Teaching in an Inclusive Classroom

Many students with special needs are now included in regular classrooms. *Inclusion* means that students with special needs are assigned to regular classrooms for the entire day rather than assigned to a special education classroom and mainstreamed into regular classes. Many included students are given support in the regular classroom. Support might include physical accommodations, assistive personnel, professional development, and technical services. Categories for special services include learning disabilities, mental retardation, hearing impairments, speech or language impairments, visual impairments, serious emotional disturbances, orthopedic impairments, autism, traumatic brain injury, attention deficit disorder, attention deficit–hyperactivity disorder, and other health impairments.

Inclusion has changed the way teachers view students with special needs. As a teacher, you can't relinquish the responsibility for your students with special needs; you are the primary educator of all of your students. It is your responsibility to orchestrate instruction so that students with special needs are truly part of the classroom. In an article titled "Including 'the included,'" Howard Miller (2001) writes, "In order for full inclusion to occur, children must become genuine members of the class. They should be fully engaged and accepted by their peers, not just treated politely and professionally by their teacher" (p. 820). Miller goes on to say that one of the most important things teachers can do for students with special needs is to acknowledge differences among students. He writes, "Instead of pretending everyone is the same, we need first to accept the worries, the fears, the concerns, and the prejudices—our own and those of our students—and then take action" (p. 821). In other words, you need to learn about your students with special needs, just as you learn about students of different cultures.

Teaching students with learning disabilities.   By far the largest number of students with special needs in the country are students with learning disabilities. Students with learning disabilities account for more than half of the population of students with special needs (U.S. Department of Education, 1998). Students with learning disabilities have a disorder in one or more cognitive process: memory, auditory perception, or visual perception. The learning difficulty does not have other causes, such as visual or hearing impairment, and students with learning disabilities do not score as well on achievement tests as they do on intelligence tests. Often students with learning disabilities will have difficulty learning how to read and write.

Students with learning difficulties who have difficulty learning to read will probably have a special education teacher instructing them for a segment of the school day. The special education teacher might assist the student with reading in your classroom or in small groups outside of the classroom. As a classroom teacher, you will also provide reading instruction for these students. To do this, you will need to collaborate with the special education teacher to discuss assessment options and the kind of instruction you should provide. You don't need a background in special education to know how to teach students with learning disabilities in reading. You can apply what you are learning about teaching reading to every student. In fact, Worthy, Broaddus, and Ivey (2001) write, "The only principle that is now accepted for instructing struggling learners is what applies to all learners: For students with reading and writing challenges, as well as for all students, instructional plans must be based on the students' strengths and challenges, interests and goals" (p. 258). Use what you know about good teaching of reading to develop plans for students with learning disabilities.

Advice for New Teachers

Teaching Students With Special Needs

Dear Janette,

I know that I'll have many students with special needs in my classes over the year, but I'm concerned that I don't have the training to work with students with so many different needs. How do I prepare for teaching students with Down syndrome, autism, and learning disabilities and still teach a classroom of other students?

Dear New Teacher,

I'm glad that you're interested in meeting the needs of all of the students in your classroom. As a classroom teacher, the students assigned to you will be your responsibility. However, you won't be left alone to teach students with special needs. You'll work in collaboration with special education teachers who are knowledgeable about the ways to best teach students with special needs. Collaboration takes time, so it will be important for you to leave time in each day—even if it's only a few minutes—to discuss instructional adaptations for the students in your classroom who have special needs.

Struggling Readers

Some students who have difficulty reading will not be labeled with a learning disability and will not be eligible for special education services. These students are often called *at-risk readers* or *struggling readers*. McCormick (1999) identified these general characteristics of struggling readers:

- Their problems result from differing sources.
- They are found in all IQ ranges.
- They are reluctant about making attempts at reading.
- They want to learn to read.
- They avoid reading because of lack of success.
- They don't believe they can learn to read.

Teaching Title I students.   Some of the struggling readers in your class will be eligible for Title I services. Title I is a federal program to provide assistance for students who have difficulty reading, who are not identified as in need of special education services, and who have a discrepancy between intelligence and achievement. Students may go to a Title I teacher for special reading classes, or the Title I teacher might teach the student in the regular classroom. Students in Title I are supposed to be getting *extra* support in reading, which means that Title I classes should not replace classroom teaching of reading. Instead, you should address the needs of Title I students in the same thoughtful manner that you address the reading needs of all of your students. Title I services should be *added to* an already comprehensive reading program.

Day 1

15 minutes	Strategy instruction (whole-group instruction)
30 minutes	Literature discussion groups using common text (heterogeneous small groups)
15 minutes	Self-selected reading (individual students)

Day 2

30 minutes	Self-selected reading (individual students)
	Strategy instruction to one or two small groups based on need
30 minutes	Activities based on common text (whole group)

FIGURE 7.6 Flexible Grouping Reading Schedule

Grouping for instruction.   Students who struggle with reading will need additional reading instruction. Some teachers think that if they group students who struggle with reading together for instruction, they are doing students a disservice. That thinking stems from our history with grouping students. In the mid-20th century, students were grouped by ability, or *tracked*. Although ability grouping was convenient for the teacher, students were often short-changed. Students in the lowest groups were given less authentic reading to pursue, more worksheets, and less time to discuss reading, and they fell further and further behind the other students (Allington, 1983a; Stanovich, 1986). Then in the 1980s, some educators thought that all children should be taught in one group with the same text (Nagel, 2001). Students who had difficulty learning, however, were unable to read with the group and did not progress in reading as much as expected.

 Teachers have recently begun experimenting with flexible reading groups in programs such as guided reading. How can flexible reading groups meet the needs of students with special needs?

You've learned about flexible grouping for students in the early grades, and you'll find that flexible reading groups work differently with students in grades 3 through 5. You might not use guided reading with Interpretive Readers, but you can flexibly group students so that you address individual needs by grouping students into literature discussion groups, whole-class instruction, and independent reading (Evans, 2001; Radencich & McKay, 1995). A sample schedule for grouping Interpretive Readers is shown in Figure 7.6.

Identifying Gifted Readers

Some of the students that you teach in the intermediate grades will be gifted readers. Many schools will have procedures for identifying gifted readers just as they have for identifying students who have learning problems. Typically, gifted readers are identified by intelligence tests, reading achievement tests, and teacher recommendations (VanTassel-Baska, 1998). Some students who are identified as gifted will surprise you because they will be underachievers. Others will be the shining stars in the classroom. Identifying gifted readers can be difficult, and teachers aren't always aware of the kinds of characteristics that make up gifted readers and writers. Characteristics of gifted readers and writers are listed in Figure 7.7 (Piirto, 1999; Van Tassel-Baska, 1998).

Gifted underachievers.   You might picture a gifted student as a boy who has his nose in a book reading *War and Peace*. Teachers often hold stereotypes of gifted students that prevent them from noticing brilliance. Several historical figures were not recognized for their talents during their schooling, including Albert Einstein, who

- Reads widely.
- Has a large vocabulary.
- Remembers what was read.
- Is curious.
- Has complex thoughts and ideas.
- Demonstrates logical thinking.
- Understands relationships and comprehends meaning.
- Produces original or unusual ideas.
- Exhibits idealism.
- Has a fine-tuned sense of humor.
- Displays an ear for language.
- Writes with an unusual use of figures of speech (e.g., alliteration, personification).
- Uses sophisticated syntax (e.g., hyphens, parentheses, appositives).
- Displays a willingness to play with words.

FIGURE 7.7   Characteristics of Gifted Readers and Writers

did not do well at school, and Thomas Edison, who was always at the bottom of his class. In your classroom, you might also have a budding Einstein. Who are the underachieving gifted students and how can you identify them?

Tannenbaum (1983) has described four types of students who could be gifted but do not exhibit high achievement. The first type of student has had general abilities overestimated. You may have attended school with someone who could read early and was considered to be gifted, but never really excelled in later years. When students have had expectations of them set too high, they may become discouraged under the pressure. A second type of underachieving gifted student does have the ability to excel but does not have the drive or the motivation. A third type of student lacks encouragement from home and school, and a fourth type becomes distracted with other issues and never achieves full potential. According to Whitmore (1980), there are also school-related causes for underachievement. Students who don't feel respected at school, who never have the opportunity to show leadership, and who are bored with the curriculum could also be gifted underachievers.

Gifted underachievers can be difficult to spot. Butler-Por (1987), however, suggests that teachers look for students who score high on intelligence tests but do mediocre classroom work as possibly being gifted underachievers. Another way to identify students who may be gifted is to look for students who persevere at high levels of performance on tasks of their own choosing compared to work in school or who show differences in excelling when reading books of their choosing versus required reading. An intermediate-grade student who has read all of Stephen King's books but who fails reading tests on your classroom novels could be a gifted underachiever.

Diversity issue: Gifted students from diverse backgrounds.   Students from diverse backgrounds have been underrepresented in gifted education programs because of the identification procedures of most gifted programs. Most gifted programs use intelligence tests as baseline information for entry into the programs. Intelligence tests, however, are not culture free (Ford & Harris, 1999). Many of the questions on intelligence tests are geared toward the middle class and are unfamiliar to students who have a different cultural background from the mainstream population. Students who have cultural backgrounds that are not consistent with tests used for identification

should be given different opportunities to enter gifted programs. Ford and Harris recommend that, as a teacher, you should be aware of gifted students from diverse backgrounds by giving nontraditional tests, such as a checklist based on cultural characteristics, or by asking for community members to nominate students for gifted programs.

An example of alternative identification of gifted students is described by Bernal (1974) who suggests that teachers of ELL students should look for the following characteristics, which are not measured by typical gifted identification procedures:

- Rapidly acquires English language skills.
- Exhibits leadership ability.
- Has older playmates and easily engages adults in conversation.
- Enjoys intelligent risk-taking behavior.
- Is able to keep busy and entertained.
- Accepts responsibilities at home normally reserved for older children.
- Is "streetwise."
- Is recognized by others as able to succeed in the mainstream culture.

Classroom application.   You might have heard some teachers say that gifted students will learn to their potential without a differentiated curriculum, or that they use gifted students to "tutor" struggling readers, or that what's good for gifted students is good for everyone. We would like you to reconsider these ideas. Equal education is not fair education—neither for students with learning problems nor for gifted students. Gifted readers need differentiated instruction to the same extent that students with learning problems do. You don't have to differentiate all assignments, but you should be aware of the kinds of reading instruction that works best for gifted students. The recommendations for gifted readers are the kinds of things that you may do for all students, but perhaps to a different extent. VanTassel-Baska (1998) recommends the following types of reading activities for gifted students:

- Use an inquiry-based study of children's literature such as junior great books programs.
- Encourage and provide time to pursue free reading based on student interest.
- Individualize your reading program to take into account your students' reading potentials.
- Form literacy groups of students with similar interests for discussions of books.
- Provide literature that is broad based in form and rich in language.
- Utilize children's literature that involves finding solutions to problems.
- Introduce students to new genres of books.
- Provide the opportunity for author study by having students read several books by the same author.
- Provide the opportunities for topic study.

Respecting Students' Differences

As you acknowledge the differences among the students in your classroom, you need to respect your students for their differences. Intermediate-grade students are quick to internalize labels that you give them. When you're in schools, you may hear teachers talk about their students saying, "Oh, she's in my low group," or "She's one of my at-risk students." These statements, called *deficit-based statements,* carry

"Labeling" students has been a part of education for decades. What are your experiences with labeling of students in schools?

subtly negative messages and influence the teacher's thinking and expectations (Fennimore, 2000). Perhaps you even have memories of teachers who used deficit-based statements about you or your classmates. If you have had these experiences, you'll know that giving labels can be discouraging for the learner and can even be a mark of disrespect. As you acknowledge differences among students and as students are classified in schools as *learning disabled, struggling reader, English Language Learner,* or *gifted,* it's important that you look beyond the label to the real students who are in need of your expert teaching.

SEE FOR YOURSELF

Learning About Students With Special Needs

Visit the message board for Chapter 7 on our Companion Website at *www.prenhall.com/lenski* to discuss your findings.

Read one of the books listed below about students with special needs or from diverse backgrounds. As you read, try to identify with the main character. Ask yourself questions such as those that follow and then record your insights in a journal. Also, think about ways you could incorporate these books into your classroom teaching.

- What is it like to have a learning disability?
- How do people treat you if you come from a different place or speak a different language?
- How do your peers treat you if you're different from them?

Books With Characters With Special Needs

Betancourt, J. (1993). *My name is Brain.* New York: Scholastic.
Boor, E. (1997). *Tangerine.* San Diego: Harcourt Brace.
Fleming, V. (1993). *Be good to Eddie Lee.* New York: Philomel.
Fraustino, L. R. (2001). *The hickory chair.* New York: Arthur A. Levine.
Gantos, J. (1998). *Joey Pigza swallowed the key.* New York: HarperCollins.
Garfield, J. B. (1994). *Follow my leader.* New York: Puffin.
Hamilton, V. (1999). *Bluish.* New York: Blue Sky Press.
Holt, K. W. (2000). *My Louisiana sky.* New York: Yearling.
Jones, R. (1996). *Acorn people.* New York: Bantam Doubleday Dell.
McElfresh, L. E. (1999). *Can you feel the thunder?* New York: Antheneum.
Philbrick, R. (1993). *Freak the mighty.* New York: Scholastic.
Polacco, P. (1998). *Thank you, Mr. Falker.* New York: Philomel.
Voight, S. (1986). *Izzy Willy Nilly.* New York: Simon & Schuster.
Wood, J. R. (1995). *The man who loved clowns.* New York: Hyperion.

CONNECTIONS: WHAT'S NEXT?

This chapter introduced you to Interpretive Readers, students who are beyond the beginning stages of reading and are typically in grades 3 through 5. We discussed how the development of children at this age impacts reading instruction and how you must be aware of developmental issues if you teach intermediate grades.

We also elaborated on a literacy theory that was introduced in Chapter 1: the transactional theory of reading. The tenets of the transactional theory should have a great deal of usefulness for you. In general, when you think about the reading process, you should remember that reading is a transaction between the reader, the text, and the context. This premise can help you as you develop your own theory of literacy. As you think about each aspect of the reading process, you'll begin to develop a richer notion of what happens when we read.

Finally, we presented more information on teaching students with special needs and those from diverse backgrounds. As a teacher, you'll need to carefully plan instruction for students with special needs, and you'll need to think of creative ways to teach students from cultures that are different from your own. The ideas that we presented in this chapter can be applied to Early Readers and Critical Readers, and because this issue is so crucial in teaching today, we will revisit it in later chapters.

In Chapter 8 we will address instructional issues pertinent to Interpretive Readers. We will begin by describing instruction that you will deliver to the entire group. You've already learned many teaching strategies in earlier chapters that you can adapt, and we'll suggest others that are especially appropriate for students in the intermediate grades.

FOR YOUR PORTFOLIO

ENTRY 7.1   *Developing Teaching Cases*

INTASC Principle 2 states: *The teacher understands how children learn and develop, and can provide learning opportunities that support their intellectual, social and personal development.*

Write a teaching case[*] (e.g., short story) about an intermediate-grade student. Your teaching case should have information that describes the student in question, details a critical incident, and provides an instructional plan. Use the teaching case as a way to describe your knowledge of the intellectual, social, and personal development of an intermediate-grade student.

ENTRY 7.2   *Students With IEPs*

IRA/NCTE Standard 11 states: *Students participate as knowledgeable, reflective, creative, and critical members of a variety of literacy communities.*

Students who have been identified as having special needs are given an individualized educational program, or IEP. Classroom teachers often collaborate with special education teachers to create IEPs and work with them to plan instruction and to monitor student progress. On the Companion Website (http://www.prenhall.com/lenski) you'll find links to sample IEPs. Collaborate with another student in your class to

---

[*]To read examples of teaching cases, link to Literacy Cases On-Line at http://literacy.okstate.edu.

develop instructional plans based on the recommendations of one of the IEPs. (You might leave some areas blank until after you've read the pertinent chapters in the text.)

ENTRY 7.3 *Multicultural Literature*

IRA/NCTE Standard 1 states: *Students read a wide range of print and nonprint texts to build an understanding of texts, of themselves, and of the cultures of the United States and the world: to acquire new information; to respond to the needs and demands of society and the workplace; and for personal fulfillment. Among these texts are fiction and nonfiction, classic and contemporary works.*

Providing intermediate-grade students with multicultural literature expands students' views of themselves and the world while connecting to the children in your classroom who come from a variety of cultural backgrounds. Access one or more of the websites listed in Figure 7.1, or find a website of your own that lists multicultural books. Choose several books from the list to read that represent cultures other than your own. Read the books and prepare a portfolio entry. For the entry, include the following:

- A full reference for the book,
- A brief annotation (summary) of the book,
- Instructional ideas for the book, and
- Activities that would extend the book that might include art, music, writing, and technology.

TO LEARN MORE

Helpful Websites

Visit our Companion Website at *http://www.prenhall.com/lenski* to link to the following sites:

Transactional Theory

> This website lays out Rosenblatt's transactional theory of reading and writing and how it may help us to read and write.
> *http://www.bsu.edu/classes/newbold/210/theory2.html*

Transactional Theory and Literacy Criticism

> This article talks about transactional theory and how it applies to literary criticism and the teaching of literature, and suggests a "reciprocal, mutually defining relationship" between the reader and the literary text.
> *http://www.ed.gov/databases/ERIC_Digests/ed284274.html*

Diversity in the Classroom

> This site links you to a variety of articles written about diversity in the classroom.
> *http://www.lessonplans.com*

Coretta Scott King Award

This award honors African American authors and illustrators for outstanding contributions to children's and young adult literature that promote understanding and appreciation of the culture and contribution of all people to the realization of the American dream.
http://www.ala.org/srrt/csking

Barahona Center for the Study of Books in Spanish for Children and Adolescents

Contains a searchable database of "more than 6,000 in-print books that deserve to be read by Spanish-speaking children and adolescents (or those who wish to learn Spanish)." Headings and descriptions are bilingual.
http://www.csusm.edu/csb/intro_eng.html

Readability

Contains two online readability formulas, the Fry and the SMOG.
http://school.discovery.com/schrockguide/fry/fry.html
http://www.cdc.gov/od/ads/smog.htm

chapter **8**

Instructing Interpretive Readers in Whole Groups

Essential Learning Questions

- Under what circumstances would you use a basal reader?
- What are the various ways of organizing a literature-based approach to reading instruction?
- What are the benefits of using portfolios in assessing literature-based instruction?
- Why are word-building activities still important for intermediate-grade students?
- Why is it important to *model* comprehension strategies?

Interpretive Readers exhibit many differences from Early Readers, one of which is their independence. If you teach students in intermediate grades, you'll need to conceptualize reading instruction in a different manner from what we discussed in the chapters on Early Readers. Many of the components of your reading program will remain the same: You'll still read to your students; you'll still assess students informally; you'll still try to motivate students to embrace literate lives; and you'll orchestrate whole-group, small-group, and independent literacy activities. Many of these activities, however, will look different.

One of the biggest differences between instructing Early Readers and Interpretive Readers is the difference between the types of whole-group and small-group activities that you plan. Much of the whole-group instruction for Early Readers focused on shared reading and writing. Interpretive Readers are able to read longer and more complex text than Early Readers so shared reading is not as effective a teaching strategy for them. Instead, you are likely to organize your whole-group instruction around a different type of reading approach: the use of a basal reader or literature-based program. When you use either a basal reading approach or a literature-based approach, you'll spend part of your time teaching to the entire class and part of the time instructing students in small groups. You'll use whole-group instruction to create a classroom community, like you did with shared reading, and to introduce texts or concepts that all students need to know. Because most intermediate-grade students begin to personalize their achievement and feel unsure about their abilities, you'll need to approach grouping with heightened awareness. As always, however, as you assess your students' literacy strengths and needs, you can organize instruction that meets their academic needs as well as their needs to be contributing members of your classroom community.

TEACHING WITH BASAL READERS

At one time using basal readers was the most common reading approach in the United States—up to 95% of our country's students were instructed using basal reading programs (Anderson, Hiebert, Scott, & Wilkinson, 1985). Basals are not quite as popular now, but they still are widely used as the foundation for a teacher's reading program. As a matter of fact, you probably used a basal reader during your elementary school experience.

What Is a Basal Reading Program?

A basal reading program is a collection of student texts, student workbooks, teachers' manuals, and supplementary materials organized grade by grade that are sometimes used throughout an entire school or district. Basal programs are created and based on the principle that reading instruction should be taught through a systematic, predetermined sequence of instructional skills and strategies using reading selections that are at or near the student's grade level, reading ability, and interest. Basal reading programs are comprehensive, but they are designed to be the core of a reading program—not the entire literacy curriculum.

A team of authors that includes literacy educators and publishing house editors designs basal readers. These teams decide on the philosophy of the book, the literature to be included, and the types of skills and strategies to be described in the teacher's manual. The author team also agrees on the types of supplementary materials that will be sold with the program. You can find the names of the author team members in the front pages of the teacher's manual.

Because each student text typically has its own name, basal reading programs are referred to by the name of their publisher. For example, if you ask a teacher what basal reading program she is using, she might say "Scott Foresman," or "Open Court" rather than the name of her grade-level book. Seven companies currently publish basal reading programs:

Harcourt Brace

D.C. Heath

Houghton Mifflin

McGraw-Macmillan

Open Court

Scott Foresman

Silver Burdett & Ginn

Student texts.   You're probably familiar with student texts for basal readers—they're reading books. Typically, basal readers for intermediate grades have one or two student texts for each grade level. A fourth-grade basal series might include a 4-1 book and a 4-2 book. The texts contain a selection of stories, informational articles, and poetry that are written for each grade level. The texts are not arranged in order of difficulty, with the easiest stories first in the book, but are most often arranged by theme. As a result, some of the more difficult stories in the text could be near the beginning, which might be problematic for some readers. The inclusion of stories having various levels of difficulty is an attempt to meet the needs of students at different reading levels.

Student workbooks.   Most basal reading programs provide student workbooks to accompany the student text. The workbooks are designed for students to independently practice the needed skills that are recommended in the teacher's manual. Some teachers use student workbooks as *seatwork,* or work that students do quietly at their desks.

Teacher's manuals.   If you're wondering how to teach a story in a basal reader, all you have to do is refer to the accompanying teacher's manual. The teacher's manual provides a wide variety of instructional suggestions for teaching a selection—more

Tim and Ron work quietly at their desks.

ideas than you could possibly try. Often the student text is reproduced in the teacher's manual with teaching ideas written in the margins. In the front pages of teacher's manuals you can also find sections that describe the underlying philosophy of the basal reader.

Supplementary materials.   Basal reading programs come with a wide variety of supplementary materials. The supplementary materials that might be included with a particular basal reading program are listed in Figure 8.1. Many of the materials that accompany basal reading programs could be useful to you as a teacher. Sometimes schools house supplementary materials in central locations like storage rooms. It is up to you to ask about this and to determine the school's policy on sharing the materials. You should judiciously select supplementary materials that will support your reading program.

Audiotapes	Picture cards	Tests
Big Books	Resource notebooks	Trade books
Black-line masters	Response journals	Videos
Leveled books	Rhyme posters	Word cards
Manipulatives		

FIGURE 8.1   Supplementary Materials for Basal Readers

Visit the online journal in Chapter 8 on our Companion Website at *www.prenhall.com/lenski* to answer these questions. Save your answers to your hard drive or to a disk to compile an online journal.

Basal reading programs are structured, organized approaches to teaching reading. How do basal readers fit with your beliefs about literacy learning?

Basal Reading Versus Literature Anthologies

Basal readers represent one of the dominant reading approaches used in schools today. Basal reading programs are based on a structured approach to reading. Some teachers, however, like the organization of a basal reader, but prefer authentic literature as texts. Therefore, most of the basal publishing companies also publish literature anthologies.

There are two major differences between basal readers and literature anthologies. First, traditional basal readers contain stories that are written by authors employed by the publishers and are written specifically for that reading book. Literature anthologies, on the other hand, typically contain excerpts from books or stories that are first published as children's literature (Hoffman et al., 1994).

The second difference is the type of instruction suggested in the teacher's manual. In basal readers, instruction typically follows the directed reading activity (DRA) format. The teacher's manual recommends ideas for preparing students to read, such as developing background knowledge, preteaching vocabulary, and encouraging motivation. The teacher's manual also provides comprehension questions to ask while students are reading. After reading, teachers are encouraged to ask additional comprehension questions, extend comprehension through writing, and teach specific skills. The reading skills that can be found in basal readers generally include finding the main idea, identifying facts and opinions, sequencing, and so on.

Literature anthologies have a different instructional emphasis. The teachers' manuals for literature anthologies typically present fewer skills and more strategies that students can use to comprehend literature. For example, literature anthologies often have students identify plot outlines, construct character analyses, and discuss themes.

Assessing Student Progress

The different basal reading programs approach assessment in different ways. Some programs provide skill tests at the end of stories or units that assess student progress on reading skills, such as finding main ideas or identifying prefixes in individual words. Other basal reading programs provide a range of informal reading assessment options such as Running Records and observational checklists. Because the different basal programs approach assessment in different ways, you should use a program's assessment philosophy as one of the criteria you use to evaluate a basal series' advantages and disadvantages.

Basal Reading Instruction

When you use a basal reader, you'll have a teacher's manual to use as a guide for your instruction. Many of the strategies found in the teacher's guide are described in this text, so you should be familiar with the instructional recommendations. Some of the strategies that you're learning now are not found in basal readers, but you can still use them. As a teacher, you will make decisions about which instructional strategies to teach; the teacher's manual is just a guide.

The use of a teacher's manual can present opportunities for teacher decision making. How will you make decisions about what to use from a teacher's manual?

Whole-group instruction.   Much of the instruction for basal readers is directed toward the entire group. For example, imagine that the basal reader has a story about a circus elephant. You might have the entire group of students brainstorm what they know about elephants in the circus. After students have discussed their knowledge

Assessment

Dear Janette,

I already feel as if I know how I want to assess the literacy progress of my students, and I'm concerned that I won't be able to use that knowledge if I use a basal reading program that has an assessment component. Should that keep me from using a basal reader?

Dear New Teacher,

Your decision about whether or not to use a basal reader should hinge on many factors—what you believe about assessment is one of those factors. However, if you want to use a basal reader, you can still conduct the types of assessment that you know and are comfortable using. For example, you can take Running Records of your students' reading even if that isn't part of the basal assessment recommendations. Also, you need to remember that you can adapt a basal reading program to fit your needs and the needs of your students.

of elephants, you might preteach the new vocabulary words in the selection. Again, this instruction is designed for the entire class of students. After these prereading strategies are presented, students should read the selection. If you have students for whom the reading is too difficult, you might pair them with more adept readers and have those partners read the story together. Otherwise, students should probably read silently. After students have read the story, you can discuss the story with the whole group and ask students to respond to the story through writing. The teacher's manual might suggest teaching a specific skill with the story (e.g., sequence of events), which you can choose to do or to omit. In any case, you'll probably teach the skill to the entire class.

Grouping with basal readers.   Should you ever group students when using a basal reader? Basal readers are designed so that most of the instruction is directed to the entire class, but some basal reading programs also include leveled books for guided reading groups. If you are using a basal reader but prefer teaching using guided reading groups, Fawson and Reutzel (2000) suggest leveling the stories in the texts and teaching them the same way you would when organizing your class using guided reading. This type of teaching frequently occurs in primary classrooms because there are so many "levels."

Diversity issue: When students can't read the basal.   You may have students in your classroom who can't read the basal reading selections for your grade level. These students may be English Language Learners, struggling readers, or students with special needs if you have an inclusive classroom. Scala (2001) states: "In inclusive class-rooms, students with disabilities learn with their peers and respond with the motivation that comes from being part of the intellectual and social mainstream" (p. 5). Students with special needs, or any struggling readers, benefit from being part of the class, but you'll still need to think about how to make reading experiences successful for them.

One way to address the needs of struggling readers is to provide extra reading groups for them. In these groups, you should summarize the story, preteach the vocabulary, and read sections of the story together. Some teachers feel that these students gain an advantage over the rest of the class when they provide them with supplementary reading groups. But if your goal is for all readers to be successful, giving students the kinds of experiences that maximize success is a good idea. And extra reading time can help your English Language Learners, struggling readers, and students with special needs be successful readers in a basal reading program.

Should You Use a Basal Reading Program?

You're probably wondering right now if a basal reading program is right for you. It's good to consider your views about basal readers, but when you become a teacher, you may not be able to choose which reading approach you want to use. Some states, districts, and schools have committees that make these decisions, and, as a teacher in that district, you'll be required to use the approach chosen by that committee. In some schools, however, you'll be able to make your own decision about whether to use a basal reading program or another approach. As you think about your views on basal readers, you should also think about your own theory of literacy learning as well as the advantages and disadvantages of using basal readers.

As a beginning teacher, you might prefer the security of a teacher's manual and a preselected group of stories to teach. The stories in basal readers typically have a good multicultural balance and often include attractive artwork. You may also want to use the supplementary materials associated with basal reading programs.

On the other hand, some students do not find the stories in basal readers interesting and may prefer to read trade books. Because student motivation in the intermediate grades is critical for student success, you might want to consider using a basal reading program as just one component of your reading program. The important principle to remember, however, is that the published material does not teach students to read; teachers do. How teachers use basal reading programs, or other reading approaches, will make the difference in student achievement (see Pressley, Allington, Wharton-McDonald, Block, & Morrow, 2001).

▰▰▰ YOU TRY IT ▰▰▰

Basal Reading Program Evaluation

At some point in your teaching career, you may be asked to serve on a reading textbook selection committee for your school or your district. Or, you may take a teaching job where a basal reader has already been selected for you, and you may be required to use it to teach reading. Teachers who are on textbook selection committees or who peruse a basal for their own purposes use criteria for evaluating the book.

Locate a teacher's manual for a basal reading program and use the following criteria to determine whether you would choose to use the basal or not.

Selection Criteria

1. Locate and read the information about the approach taken by this basal reading program. In what ways does the approach taken by this publisher fit your own literacy learning theory? How is it different?
2. List the kinds of stories that are included in the student text. Do you agree with the balance between classical children's literature and current stories? Are the cultures of your students well represented in the text?
3. Are suggestions given for ways to adapt your teaching for all of your students?
4. Does the reading difficulty of the stories seem appropriate for the majority of your students?
5. Are the student texts inviting and attractive?
6. Are the supplementary materials useful?
7. Does the teacher's manual connect reading to the other language arts (i.e., speaking, listening, writing, viewing)?
8. Are the assessments appropriate for good literacy instruction?
9. Is the teacher's manual easy to read and to use? Are the skills and strategies suggested in the teacher's manual ones that you would use?
10. Are students taught specific decoding and comprehension strategies? If so, how are they taught?

LITERATURE-BASED APPROACHES

When you were in elementary school, your teacher probably relied on a basal reader for much of your reading instruction. Now, however, literature-based approaches are much more popular. "Over the last decade we have seen the approaches to teaching reading and writing change dramatically. Instead of using published basal reading series and workbooks to teach reading, many teachers are now using children's literature" (Buss & Karnowski, 2000, p. 1). Using children's books as texts, instead of stories from a reading book, is the heart of a literature-based approach to reading.

Using children's literature as the basis for your reading program has appeal for many teachers and students (Norton, 1997). Some teachers find that they can be more enthusiastic when they use an authentic piece of literature as the basis for teaching rather than the excerpts found in basal readers and literature anthologies. Many students also find trade books to be more motivating than basal readers. Because motivation for both teachers and students is a critical component of the reading process, you should carefully consider using a literature-based approach for at least a part of your overall reading program.

If you decide to use trade books as part (or all) of your reading program, you have more control than with a basal over what and how you teach reading. You also have to spend more time thinking about what to teach, and you have more decisions to make. One of your first decisions will be which books to use as your main texts. Yopp and Yopp (2001) believe that teachers who use a literature-based approach to reading need to *know* children's literature. Of course, you can't know all of the books available for the grade level you teach, but you need to know which books would be appropriate to use as the focus of your instruction. After you have

Motivation for reading is part of the reading context that you learned about in Chapter 7. In what ways can using trade books for instruction motivate intermediate-grade students to read?

selected the books that you think would be appropriate to use, you need to read the books, identify themes to use in your instruction, decide on word analysis and comprehension strategies that apply to the book, and develop a list of student assignments and related projects. Although this may seem like a great deal of work, it's worth it to have lessons grounded in authentic texts that engage students in learning.

Organizational Approaches

If you decide to use a literature-based approach to teach reading, you have to decide how to organize your instruction. You can approach literature-based instruction in a number of ways; three types of approaches addressed in this chapter are genre studies, author studies, and thematic studies. If you decide to use one of these approaches, however, you don't have to stay with that one for the entire year. You can alternate between author studies, for example, and thematic units. Or, you might teach a few books of a particular genre, conduct an author study, and then go back to teaching a different genre.

Genre studies.   You've probably heard the word *genre* in some of your children's literature or English classes. "A genre is a kind or type of literature that has a common set of characteristics" (Lukens, 1999, p. 13). You're probably also familiar with writing genres, such as persuasive papers. The genres you can use to teach literature in intermediate grades include biographies, fables, fantasy, folktales, mysteries, poetry, and realistic fiction.

Once you decide on a genre to teach, you should read several books from that genre, choosing those that would be most appropriate for your students. Then you need to think about the characteristics that make the books in this genre similar. For example, intermediate-grade readers are beginning to be interested in the world outside their own family and community, so many students begin reading biographies at this age. Biographies can be either fiction or nonfiction; they usually are written in chronological order; the main characters are fully developed; the setting is authentic; the author uses stylistic elements such as dialogue, anecdotes, and flashbacks; and they have a central theme (Buss & Karnowski, 2000). A list of biographies can be found in Figure 8.2.

Once you have chosen the genre books that fit your students and curriculum and have identified the common elements, you should develop lessons that fit the genre and that help students become more strategic readers. For example, one of the characteristics of biographies is that their characters are more fully developed than those of many other literary genres. (Mysteries, for example, typically have characters who are flat and stereotypical, but they have more complex plots than do biographies.) When planning your instruction for biographies, therefore, you should link the strategies you teach to the text you are teaching.

A wide variety of reading and writing strategies are found throughout this book. What other reading and writing strategies apply to teaching biographies?

One strategy that works well if you're teaching biographies is the Plot Line of Life (Calkins, 1986). A Plot Line of Life is a time line listing key accomplishments of the character along with the date on which they occurred. Some students will be creative and draw illustrations to match the accomplishments on the time line. Because most biographies are written in chronological order, time lines are typically straightforward.

You might be wondering how a strategy like the Plot Line of Life promotes strategic reading. As you teach students to develop a time line from a biography, you can

Adler, D. (1992). *A picture book of Harriet Tubman.* New York: Holiday House.

Anderson, W. (1992). *Laura Ingalls Wilder: A biography.* New York: HarperCollins.

Black, S. (1989). *Sitting Bull and the battle of the Little Bighorn.* New York: Silver Burdett.

Cha, D. (1996). *Dia's story cloth: The Hmong people's journey to freedom.* New York: Lee & Low.

Conklin, T. (1994). *Steven Spielberg.* New York: Random House.

Davidson, M. (1981). *The Golda Meir story.* New York: Scribner's Sons.

Fritz, J. (1977). *Can't you make them behave, King George?* New York: Coward-McCann.

Green, C. (1992). *John Philip Sousa.* Chicago: Children's Press.

Lepscky, I. (1984). *Pablo Picasso.* New York: The Trumpet Club.

McKissack, P., & McKissack, F. (1998). *Young, black, and determined: A biography of Lorraine Hansberry.* New York: Holiday House.

Schroeder, A. (1996). *Satchmo's blues.* New York: Doubleday.

Stanley, F. (1991). *The last princess: The story of Princess Kaiulani of Hawaii.* New York: Aladdin Books.

Zhensun, Z., & Low, A. (1991). *A young painter: The life and paintings of Wang Yani—China's extraordinary young artist.* New York: Scholastic.

FIGURE 8.2 Biographies

also draw their attention to the organizational structure of the book (including chronological order) and you can help them identify important information, both of which are strategies that support comprehension.

Author studies. Students in the intermediate grades often choose to read multiple books by a single author. Another way to organize literature-based instruction, therefore, is by teaching books by the same author. If you decide to use several books by the same author, you need to first decide which author to study. You can make this decision by observing the books that students read in the classroom, by using one of the required books from the school curriculum as the basis, or by simply choosing your favorite author. A list of authors that would be appropriate for intermediate-grade readers can be found in Figure 8.3.

An author study is very different from a genre study. Books in a specific genre have common characteristics. This may not be true about different books written by the same author, so you should use the historical–biographical approach to literature when you conduct author studies. The historical–biographical approach "considers a work in the context of the author's life and times. People using this approach often look at how the author's life affects the work" (Davis & Jepson, 1991, p. 28).

To conduct an author study using the historical–biographical approach to literature, teach about the life and times of the author from resource books or from the Internet. (Many authors currently have their own websites.) Have students learn as much as they can about the author's life. Then have students develop a data chart of the information that they collected about the author. An example of a data chart about Eve Bunting can be found in Figure 8.4.

Lloyd Alexander	Ralph Fletcher	Gary Paulsen
Avi	Jean Fritz	Robert Newton Peck
Natalie Babbitt	E. L. Konigsburg	J. K. Rowling
Judy Blume	Gordon Korman	Cynthia Rylant
Matt Christopher	C. S. Lewis	Louis Sachar
Beverly Cleary	Jean Little	Jon Scieszka
Roald Dahl	Lois Lowry	Jerry Spinelli
Paula Danzinger	Barbara Park	Lawrence Yep
Paul Fleischman	Katherine Paterson	

FIGURE 8.3   Author Studies for Intermediate-Grade Readers

Source: Website *http://falcon.jmu.edu/~ramseyil/bunting.htm*	Source: Back of book	Source: Author index
Has written picture books, novels, and nonfiction.	Born in Northern Ireland.	Wrote more than 100 books.
Writes because she wants to share what she knows.	Came to U.S. in 1958. Lives in CA.	Lots of awards Caldecott—Smoky Night
Writes about all kinds of things—race, death, war, problems.	Also writes short stories.	Has 3 children.
Did not always want to write! Began when she was 40! Took a college class.	Likes to write about birds.	First book: The Two Giants

FIGURE 8.4   Data Chart for Eve Bunting

After students have learned about the author, have them read several books written by that author. You might teach one book to the entire group, but this would also be a perfect opportunity to divide students into small groups and assign different books to each group. Students in the groups can read the books independently or you can use literature circles. As students read, they should identify the elements of fiction that the author uses: plot, setting, characters, and theme. After students have read two or more books by the same author, ask them to compare and contrast the books they have read. Finally, have students write a summary of what they

Most students like to study about authors.

learned about the author along with samples from the author's books. As students compile information about the author's life and the author's books, they are making inferences and drawing conclusions—important strategies that build reading comprehension.

Thematic studies. One of the most popular methods of organizing literature-based instruction is through thematic studies. Thematic instruction centers on a topic or issue, such as holidays, celebrations, science or social studies concepts, award-winning books, or issues such as coming of age, problems, and family relationships. When teachers organize literature around themes, they also often provide instruction in other subjects that deal with the theme.

To organize your instruction by themes, you first have to decide what theme you want to teach. You might decide to develop a theme that fits your curricula—such as life cycles, communities, or relationships—or you might ask students to choose a theme. Then you need to develop a list of books that have elements that apply to the theme. Some teachers organize their literature-based instruction around the Caldecott and Newbery Medal award-winning books. The Newbery Medal is awarded yearly to the book with the best story line and the Caldecott Award is given to the picture book with the best illustrations. Other teachers prefer to teach books with contemporary issues, such as "problem novels" (Figure 8.5).

If you organize your instruction around themes, you might decide to begin the unit with a strategy in which students identify their feelings and beliefs about the theme, such as an Anticipation/Reaction Guide (Herber, 1978). An Anticipation/Reaction Guide

Literature circles are an instructional approach in which students read books in small groups. They are described in detail in Chapter 9. What other ways could you use to encourage students to read a variety of books by the same author for an author study?

Haddix, M. P. (2000). *Among the hidden.* New York: Simon & Schuster.
Hesse, K. (1997). *Out of the dust.* New York: Scholastic.
Koss, A. G. (2000). *The girls.* New York: Penguin.
Lowry, L. (1994). *The giver.* New York Bantam Doubleday Dell.
McDonald, J. (1997). *Swallowing stones.* New York: Random House.
Paterson, K. (1977). *Bridge to Terabithia.* New York: HarperTrophy.
Pearson, M. E. (2001). *Scribbler of dreams.* San Diego: Harcourt.
Spinelli, J. (1990). *Maniac Magee.* Boston: Little, Brown.

FIGURE 8.5   Problem Novels

Theme: Problems

Directions: Circle "Yes" if you agree with this statement and "No" if you disagree.

Before Reading			**After Reading**	
Yes	No	1. Everyone has problems.	Yes	No
Yes	No	2. All problems are equal in difficulty.	Yes	No
Yes	No	3. People respond differently to problems.	Yes	No

FIGURE 8.6   Anticipation/Reaction Guide

is composed of a series of statements that elicit students' opinions about a topic. Having students discuss their opinions before reading books from a thematic unit helps focus students' thoughts on the main theme. You can also discuss students' views after reading the books you've provided. An example of an Anticipation/Reaction Guide can be found in Figure 8.6.

Caveats.   You should begin thinking about the organizational approaches to teaching literature that you prefer. However, you may need to adapt your preference when you get a teaching position. Some districts and schools have lists of books that you will be required to teach at a particular grade level. You may be given lists of books that you cannot teach, because they are taught in a different class or grade level. If you find yourself in such a situation, you will need to be flexible about your choice of books. If you don't agree with certain reading selections, volunteer to join a committee to revise the list of core books.

◢◢◢ YOU TRY IT ◢◢◢

Collecting Materials for a Literature-Based Unit

Use your knowledge of trade books to develop a list of books that could be taught at one of the intermediate grades. Follow these directions to help you develop your lists:

1. Select a grade level that interests you.
2. Decide whether you want to develop a list by genre, author, or topic; then title your unit.

3. Ask teachers for their book suggestions.
4. Use the websites listed at the end of the chapter to find ideas for books.
5. Use the chat room at the Companion Website (http://www.prenhall.com/lenski) to ask your classmates about their favorite books.
6. Ask intermediate-grade students for lists of books they like.
7. Read as many books as you can.
8. Create a list of books that could be used for a literature unit.
9. Decide which strategies apply most directly to your literature unit.

Cooperative Grouping

When you use literature-based instruction, you'll teach many lessons to your entire class. Within this instruction, however, you can engage students in learning by using cooperative grouping strategies. Traditionally, schooling has been competitive and individualistic. Think back to your schooling experiences. How often did you try to get a better grade than your classmates compared to the times you tried to accomplish something with a small group? Most of you probably had more of a sense of competition in schools rather than cooperation. You might find the same sense of competition in college. However, promoters of cooperative grouping such as Johnson and Johnson (1990) believe that work outside of school is typically accomplished by cooperation rather than competition.

If you were to think about examples of working to achieve a goal or accomplish a task outside of the school environment, you'd probably come up with more examples of cooperation than competition. For example, consider the following scenario:

> Fatima, Corrine, and Tara decided to student teach in a large city away from their hometowns. They needed to rent an apartment close to the school because none of them had a car that was reliable for long commutes. Three months before they were to move to the city, the three women met to develop a plan of action. Fatima searched the Internet for places to rent; Corrine scanned newspapers; and Tara contacted friends in the area. They combined their knowledge and developed a list of apartments to see during their next trip to the city.

In this scenario, the three women did not compete to see who would be the first to find an apartment. They divided the tasks to accomplish a shared goal. Johnson and Johnson (1990) suggest that in the world outside of school, cooperation exists far more than competition. Teachers, therefore, should use cooperative grouping strategies as part of their classroom routines in order to foster the cooperative skills students need in life.

Think–Pair–Share.   Think–Pair–Share (Bromley & Modlo, 1997) is a cooperative learning strategy that you can use for any grade level and any subject whenever you ask students a question. In fact, this strategy can make the difference between dull instruction and engaged learning. When you use Think–Pair–Share, you ask students to think about their answers before raising their hands; you ask them to tell their answers to another student; then you have them share with the entire class. In a classroom discussion, Think–Pair–Share would look something like the following:

Teacher: We are going to begin a genre study this week on biographies. What can you tell me about biographies? Think about this for a moment. (Allow several seconds of silence.)

You learned how important accessing prior knowledge is to constructivist teaching. In what other ways can cooperative learning practices promote constructivist teaching?

> Before we discuss this genre, turn to your partner and discuss your knowledge about biographies. (Allow several minutes for paired discussion.) Now, what can you tell me about biographies?

This type of teaching allows students to retrieve information stored in their schemata before they engage in whole-class discussions. If you don't give students time to think, oftentimes students will raise their hands to respond without having much to offer to the discussion. Or, your students might not volunteer any of their own knowledge, and you'll spend your time "telling" your students what they already know.

Student Teams–Achievement Division.   A second cooperative grouping strategy is Student Teams–Achievement Division (STAD) (Slavin, 1988). You can use this strategy when you're introducing new information that you want everyone to learn. For example, say you're teaching about the author Gary Paulsen. You want the students to know certain facts about Gary Paulsen's life. After teaching a lesson, group students into four-member mixed-ability teams. Tell the students that it is the group's responsibility to make sure each member of the team learns all of the information. Provide teams with ideas for learning the information and give the group time for work. After a set time period, conduct a group discussion or have students write what they know about Gary Paulsen.

Jigsaw.   A third cooperative grouping strategy is called Jigsaw (Aronson, Stephens, Siles, Blaney, & Snapp, 1978). Jigsaw is similar to STAD, but with Jigsaw each group member is responsible for a portion of the material. You should use Jigsaw if you want students to learn about a topic, but it's not necessary for each student to learn all of the material. For example, say you're teaching about the Newbery Medal books. You give brief summaries of a variety of books to the class, divide the class into groups, and ask each student to share his or her information with the group. After students have shared what they know, you can discuss Newbery Medal winners with the entire class knowing that different students will contribute different ideas.

Assessing Literature-Based Instruction

When you assess literature-based instruction, you need to assess several different reading processes. You should assess your students' knowledge of the texts that they're reading, their comprehension of the material, their responses to reading, and their vocabulary knowledge, use of reading strategies, and motivation to read. Obviously, one test cannot measure all of these components of reading. The best way to assess literature-based instruction is through portfolios.

Classroom Assessment

Portfolio collections.   Portfolios are collections of work samples. Artists, architects, models, and investment bankers commonly use the term *portfolio* to describe a collection of work. Models, for example, develop a portfolio of photographs of themselves along with lists of places where they have worked. A model would not place every photograph of himself in a portfolio; he'd only gather pictures that represented different aspects of his talent. He could then use the portfolio to present to prospective employers who would evaluate the portfolio's contents. Although one or two photographs may be much better than the rest, the portfolio would be evaluated in its entirety rather than on one or two pieces.

You can see how the portfolio concept applies to the assessment of reading. One reading test cannot represent the total picture of a reader, but a collection of different kinds of tests and samples of a student's work can accurately portray how well a student can read and write.

Several different types of portfolios could be used to assess a student's reading progress. Among the most popular types of portfolios are showcase portfolios, which are collections selected by students of their best work, and documentation portfolios, which provide a record of student progress (Gredler, 1999).

Portfolio artifacts. The most important feature of portfolios is the selection of portfolio artifacts. Farr and Tone (1994) suggest that teachers select some of the portfolio entries and that you give students the opportunity to make additional decisions about what to include in their portfolios. The portfolio should include a variety of types of assignments (e.g., not all should be responses to literature). The list in Figure 8.7 provides some ideas for portfolio entries.

Evaluating portfolios. A collection of portfolio artifacts is merely a collection of materials until you make some evaluative decisions. Consider the example of a model's portfolio. A prospective employer would not look at just one photo but would make decisions about the entire portfolio. In the same way, as a teacher, you need to assess the entire portfolio to interpret the results and to make evaluative decisions.

Rhodes and Shanklin (1993) suggest developing a list of key questions to use when evaluating portfolios (Figure 8.8). The questions you develop should focus

Different types of assessments are presented throughout this book that can be collected in portfolios. How does portfolio assessment support social constructivist philosophies?

Classroom Assessment

Classroom Assessment

- Tests on novels
- Running Records or miscue analyses
- Audio or video recordings of student's readings
- Lists of books read
- Written responses to literature
- Retellings
- Story maps
- Pictures of posters or projects
- Inquiry project summaries
- Journals or self-reflections
- Vocabulary tests
- Reading surveys
- Observational checklists
- Anecdotal records
- Student self-assessment

FIGURE 8.7 What to Place in a Reading Portfolio

---

1. Is this portfolio representative of what I've seen in the classroom? If not, what other artifacts should be included?
2. What are the student's reading strengths?
3. What areas of instruction should I emphasize to build on these strengths?
4. What difficulties does this reader face?
5. What can I do to address the student's difficulties with reading?
6. What insights can I glean from the student's reflections and self-assessment?

FIGURE 8.8 Questions to Ask to Evaluate Reading Portfolios

around two areas: how well the student is reading and what instructional approaches you should take to scaffold the student's reading progress. The same list of questions can be applied to each portfolio so that your assessment of your class's portfolios is comparable.

SEE FOR YOURSELF

Evaluating a Reading Portfolio

Visit the message board for Chapter 8 on our Companion Website at *www.prenhall.com/lenski* to discuss your findings.

On the Companion Website *(http://www.prenhall.com/lenski)* you'll find reading portfolio artifacts representative of a fourth-grade student. Read the portfolio entries as if you were the child's teacher. As you read, apply the evaluative questions from Figure 8.8 to the portfolio and develop a summary of the student's work and an instructional plan.

Of course, simply reading a portfolio won't give you the same rich understanding of a student that you would have from teaching the student throughout the year. However, it will give you a sense of how to read multiple portfolio entries and make evaluative decisions.

TEACHING WORD-BUILDING STRATEGIES

Most of your intermediate-grade students will be proficient in using cueing systems to figure out unfamiliar words. They should know the sounds that represent all of the letters and letter combinations (including vowels), and they should be adept at figuring out word chunks that have regular spelling patterns. The word strategies that students learn in the primary grades are the foundation of knowledge they need about reading words, but learning about words should not end in second grade. Intermediate-grade students also need instruction in word-building strategies, not as an end in itself, but to support comprehension. As Strickland, Ganske, and Monroe (2002) state: "Skilled readers process print quickly and efficiently, so they can devote their full attention to meaning" (p. 90).

Much of the instruction in word building in the primary grades consists of applying phonics rules and using the cueing systems. In the intermediate grades, you can add to your students' existing knowledge by teaching them more complex word analysis strategies, such as understanding how words are put together with root words, prefixes, and suffixes. They also need more sophisticated instruction on using context clues in reading. Furthermore, Interpretive Readers begin reading more difficult text so they come across vocabulary words that are new to them. Therefore, you should begin spending time explicitly teaching students words that they will encounter in their reading. Much of this instruction will be directed to your entire class.

Root Words

Many of the words in the English language are made up of word parts: root words and affixes. Root words are the part of the word that "carries the main component of meaning and that cannot be further analyzed without loss of identity" (Harris & Hodges, 1995). Affixes are the prefixes and/or suffixes that are added to root words. For example, the word *rereading* consists of the prefix *re,* the root word *read,* and

afternoon	everyone	peanut
airplane	everything	playground
anyone	eyebrows	quicksand
backbone	firecracker	rainbow
barefoot	fireplace	raincoat
baseball	flashlight	rowboat
basketball	football	sandpaper
bathtub	goldfish	snowball
billboard	hallway	sunrise
bookcase	headlight	sunset
campfire	highway	sunshine
classroom	homesick	teenager
deadline	jellybean	thunderstorm
downhill	maybe	toothbrush
driveway	motorcycle	uphill
earthquake	outside	without

FIGURE 8.9   Compound Words

the suffix *ing*. Some root words are combined to form compound words, such as *playground*. (Figure 8.9 lists some common compound words.) Knowing about root words and compound words provides an additional tool that readers can use when they come to a word they don't know.

Word sorts.   One of the most effective ways to teach root words is to explain how some words are put together to your whole class. Emphasize the role of root words in many multiple-syllable words. You learned about word sorts for Early Readers in Chapter 6. This same interactive activity is effective for Interpretive Readers when used with more complex word analysis tasks. When using a word sort to teach root words, write root words, prefixes, and suffixes on small cards. Give a small group of students a set of cards and have them make words using the different word parts. Encourage students to name the types of word parts as they make words, such as root words, prefixes, and suffixes.

 Words sorts can be applied in many instructional situations. How else can you use word sorts for instruction?

Context Clues

Intermediate-grade students should have experience using context to figure out unknown words just by their use of the cueing systems. However, there are more ways to figure out words in context than just using the surrounding words. Authors sometimes provide the meaning of new words in the context of the sentence or paragraph, and astute readers can learn new words just by a careful reading of the context of a passage. Some ways in which authors provide meanings through context follow:

Definition or description: Words are directly defined.
Appositive phrase: The definition of the unknown word or the word itself is in a phrase set off by commas.

Linked synonyms: The unknown word is used in a series of known words.

Comparisons and contrasts: The word can be defined by its opposite in the sentence.

Examples: The word can be defined by examples in the sentence.

Classification: The word can be defined by its relationship to known words.

Experience: The word can be defined by applying previous experience to the unknown word.

Learning the Meanings of Words

What does it mean to "know" a word? Is it being able to recite one of the definitions for the word? If you've ever had a teacher assign you to write the definitions for vocabulary words, you know that merely writing definitions doesn't help you learn new words. Knowing a word means that the concept of the word is in your speaking, writing, reading, and/or listening vocabulary. That means that you can understand and use the word accurately in a variety of modalities. Having students copy words from dictionaries or glossaries won't promote that type of rich understanding of words.

Word learning is primarily accomplished through wide reading (Wittlesea, 1987). When students read, they encounter new words in an authentic context. As they process these new words, they use their knowledge of the story and the passage to build a conceptual frame around the word, which means that they situate words in multiple contexts. This process builds vocabulary in most readers.

Although reading is the primary way students develop richer vocabularies, teachers can support vocabulary development by creating word-rich classroom environments, by helping students become independent word learners, and by using vocabulary strategies that mirror effective word-learning behaviors (Blachowicz & Fisher, 2002).

Vocabulary Self-Collection.   If students are to become strategic readers, they will need to become aware of new words in their reading, independent of your instruction. One strategy that encourages students to independently look for new words is Vocabulary Self-Collection (VSS) (Haggard, 1986). To begin the VSS process, ask students to independently look for words in their reading that they would like to learn. Divide the class into small groups and have students share their words. After students have shared their individually selected words, have each group select one word to share with the class. Take one word from each group and list the words on the board, again using the motivational properties of choice. From that list, have students vote for one of the words to learn. Teach students the meaning of that word, and encourage students to write any of the words that intrigue them in their vocabulary notebooks. Encourage students to find definitions for their words from their reading, from others, and from resources such as dictionaries. Tell students that they should continually be learning new words and that using VSS and vocabulary notebooks can help build their vocabulary. An example of a students' vocabulary notebook entry can be found in Figure 8.10.

Knowledge Rating Scale.   Good readers monitor their knowledge of the words they encounter while reading. Knowledge of words is a gray area, not black or white. For example, perhaps you've heard the word *amiable,* and you have an idea about the meaning of the word—you might even have a visual image of an amiable person. However, you may not be really clear about what *amiable* means in the sentence "Her classmates considered her to be an amiable young woman."

"The Tunnel"

Vocabulary   8-19-93

Pg.78 –
        Contrition – 78a
        Chivalry – 78a
        Supplication – 79a
        Uncomprehending – 79a
        Gravely – 79b
        Beseeching – 81a
        Frond – 81b

1. Write original sentence
    underline word
2. Write word + definition
3. Write own sentence

FIGURE 8.10   Sample Student Vocabulary Notebook Entry

	Know it well.	Have seen or heard it.	No clue!
Soothingly			
Strolled			
Shebang			
Scorching			

FIGURE 8.11   Knowledge Rating Scale

The Knowledge Rating Scale (Blachowicz, 1986) helps readers monitor their knowledge of a word's meanings by using a survey format. Use a Knowledge Rating Scale when you want students to access their prior knowledge about a group of words and to determine how well they know the word. To use the strategy, select several words from a passage that you think students may or may not know. Develop a survey like the one shown in Figure 8.11 taken from the first chapter of *Bridge to Terabithia* (Paterson, 1977). List the words next to columns for students to rate their knowledge of the word as "know it well," "have seen or heard it," or "no clue!" Have students discuss their knowledge of the words in small groups so they can share their prior knowledge and discuss the words' meanings. Then discuss the words with the entire class. If there are words that none of the students know, tell them the meaning of the word as it is used in the text.

The Knowledge Rating Scale is a vocabulary strategy that makes use of students' knowledge through discussion. How is this strategy a good example of social constructivist teaching?

Vocabulary Word	Personal Associations
Strolling	Walking on beach Walking down the hall before school Running out of time in a basketball game - strolling and dribbling
Definition To walk leisurely Picture	Opposites Jogging Running because I'm late for class Hurrying

FIGURE 8.12   Four Square Vocabulary Strategy

You used the Four Square strategy in Chapter 1 to learn some terms about literacy theory. In what ways did Four Square help you learn new terms?

Four Square.   Because word knowledge encompasses more than just knowing a definition of a word, students need strategies to help them think about words in broader ways than mere definitions. In the Four Square strategy, students consider not only the word's definition, but also make personal associations with the words and list opposites of the word. You can even have students include a picture with the definition. Some teachers use Four Square with all of the new vocabulary words they introduce. An example of the Four Square strategy is shown in Figure 8.12.

TEACHING COMPREHENSION STRATEGIES

Taylor sat at her desk reading *Sideways Stories From Wayside School* (Sachar, 1978). She held the book in front of her propped on its spine, her feet were crossed neatly beneath her desk, and she had an expression of concentration on her face. The teacher watched as Taylor's eyes moved across the pages and as she turned pages at reasonable intervals. After the silent reading time was over, the teacher asked Taylor what she thought of Chapter 3. Taylor said nothing; her face was a blank.

Taylor was unable to verbalize anything from her reading. Although she read the words and perhaps even vocalized some of them, Taylor did not construct meaning from the print. She did not comprehend the text.

The goal of reading is comprehension; however, many students read books without constructing any meaning whatsoever. They move their eyes over the print without it making any sense. Good readers, however, actively construct meaning as they read, and they monitor those comprehension processes (Paris, Lipson, & Wixson, 1983).

Teaching students how to use their mental processes for comprehension has been the subject of research for two decades. Research has clearly indicated that teachers who help students relate what they're reading to their background knowledge, form mental images, question as they read, summarize, and respond personally to their reading can improve their comprehension (Pressley, 2002; Rosenblatt,

1978). Teachers, however, cannot just *tell* students to use their background knowledge. Just like young students who don't know what the term *word* means, most intermediate-grade students won't understand what you mean if you just tell them they need to comprehend the story. Effective teachers model the comprehension strategies that good readers use and provide students with opportunities for them to try these strategies independently (Pressley, 2002).

Strategies: What Are They?

In this book we use the term *strategy* or *strategies* often. A strategy is "a systematic plan, consciously adapted and monitored, to improve one's performance in learning" (Harris & Hodges, 1995, p. 244). In other words, a strategy is a blueprint or game plan that someone uses deliberately in order to accomplish something more effectively.

Here's an example of how you might use strategies in preparing for a test. Rather than trying to memorize the 300 pages that you are accountable for, you might reread your notes, noticing the places where you placed double underlines or big stars to emphasize important concepts. Another strategy you might employ is listening closely when your instructor gives hints about specific items that could be on the test. Or perhaps you and a partner get together to study and quiz each other, comparing your pooled knowledge and best guesses about what will be on the test. These are all examples of strategic study skills that you consciously employ.

In the realm of literacy learning, we hope that students use strategies, as they become more proficient readers. Fountas and Pinnell (1996) remind us, however, that just as you can't observe a strategy directly (it's in the mind of the learner), you can't teach strategies directly either. Rather, good teachers teach *for* strategies by demonstrating what good readers do and by allowing students to practice a strategy until they can use it automatically and independently.

You will learn about strategies that students use to construct meaning, while being aware of what they are doing. The awareness piece is critical to learning because then students are able to apply strategies when appropriate and decide for themselves whether they are working or not. Examples of student, literacy-learning strategies include these:

- Strategies for figuring out new words,
- Strategies for monitoring reading,
- Strategies for maintaining fluency,
- Comprehension strategies,
- Study strategies, and
- Research strategies.

Sometimes, we will refer to teaching strategies that are related to student strategies. Teaching strategies are those designs or actions that teachers use intentionally to accomplish hoped-for results with and for students.

Comprehension Strategies

Each reading situation is different, but typically good readers think about their topic before reading and predict what will be in the text. During reading, good readers visualize what they're reading, question, and confirm or revise predictions. After reading, good readers may reread confusing parts, summarize what they've read, and connect what they've read to other material (Blachowicz & Ogle, 2001). To teach

You will find a variety of comprehension strategies that are appropriate for intermediate-grade students throughout this book. How can you incorporate comprehension strategies in your teaching?

Courtney and Elizabeth apply comprehension strategies while reading independently.

these comprehension strategies, you should model them through think-alouds. For example, say you were teaching *Witness* by Karen Hesse (2001) to your fifth graders. Before reading, you should model what good readers do: Think about the topic and make predictions. You could say something like the following:

> I decided to read *Witness* (Hesse, 2001) because I read Hesse's book *Out of the Dust* (1997) and I enjoyed it very much. *Out of the Dust* was a novel about the Dust Bowl, and I wondered whether *Witness* would be a similar type of story. I read the dust jacket and found that *Witness* takes place in a Vermont town in 1924 when the Ku Klux Klan moves in. The story is about a young African American girl and a Jewish girl. I know that the KKK actively hated these two cultural groups, so I predict that the girls will encounter hatred from people who don't even know them. I don't know what will happen, but I predict that the girls will have a difficult time understanding why the KKK members hate them so much.

Prereading

Before teaching a reading selection—whether from a basal reader, a literature anthology, or a trade book—you should draw your students' attention to some of the features of the story by conducting activities that have students predict what will be in the story, connect ideas from the story to their background knowledge, and make students aware of the organizational pattern of the text (Readence, Moore, & Rickelman, 2000). Most Interpretive Readers will be familiar with plot outlines (or story grammar), which you learned about in previous chapters of this book. You can take advantage of students' knowledge of story to create interesting prereading lessons that forecast the plot and capture students' interest in reading.

Words or Terms:

Annie Rye	Georgia	Piney Woods	Elouise
Fishing	half-sisters	violence	helpful
Snakes	cross burning	scared	family

Setting	Characters	Goal or Problem
Action	**Resolution**	**Other Things**

FIGURE 8.13 Predict-O-Gram for *Down in the Piney Woods* (Smothers, 1992)

Predict-O-Gram. A Predict-O-Gram (Blachowicz, 1986) capitalizes on students' ability to predict what will happen in a story using the elements of fiction (Figure 8.13). Before students read a story, identify key words or terms that are used in the text. Give students a copy of a Predict-O-Gram and the list of terms. Have them "predict" which words apply to the different parts of the plot. After students have made their predictions, ask them to share their charts and compare their predictions. You could also have students keep their Predict-O-Grams with the story they're reading so that they can confirm their predictions.

Story impressions. Another prereading strategy that encourages students to make predictions is the story impressions strategy (McGinley & Denner, 1987). Story impressions combine prediction with writing. To use the strategy, create a list of key words or terms that illustrate the story. You should include words about each of the elements of fiction: characters, setting, plot, conflict, and theme. Give the list of words to students and ask them to develop a story using the words in the order in which they are written. After students have individually written stories, have several students share their writings.

An example of terms for a story impression for the story *Lions at Lunchtime* (Osborne, 1998) follow:

Jack	Frog Creek	Library	Africa	Warrior
Annie	Lion	Tree house	Hyena	Lunch

During Reading

During reading students need to apply the monitoring strategies they have learned so that they can construct meaning from their reading. Some Interpretive Readers do not apply strategies during comprehension and as a result read through texts without knowing what they have read. As a teacher, you will need to remind students that reading is a thinking activity, and that they should ask questions during reading, and if their comprehension fails, they should apply fix-up strategies.

Comprehension bookmark.   As students read, you should model comprehension strategies such as forming mental images, summarizing, and questioning. As you model these strategies, remind students that they should apply these strategies as they read. A bookmark (Figure 8.14) that prompts students with sentence starters often helps readers remember to comprehend as they read.

Monitoring logs.   All readers experience situations when their comprehension falters—even expert readers. Good readers, however, are aware of breakdowns of comprehension and apply fix-up strategies that help them understand what they're reading. As you model and teach comprehension strategies, many of your students will internalize the strategies and use them as they read. Other students, however,

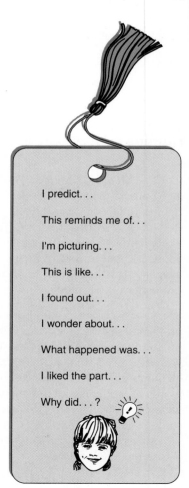

I predict. . .

This reminds me of. . .

I'm picturing. . .

This is like. . .

I found out. . .

I wonder about. . .

What happened was. . .

I liked the part. . .

Why did. . . ?

FIGURE 8.14 Comprehension Reading Strategies Bookmark

will have difficulty applying the strategies you teach. Your goal is to teach students to use these fix-up strategies as their comprehension breaks down.

One way to help students learn how to automatically apply fix-up strategies during reading is to draw their attention to times when their comprehension breaks down using a monitoring log like that shown in Figure 8.15. A monitoring log provides students with a place to record times when they had difficulty with text and to list the strategies they used to overcome their problem. Model the use of the monitoring log with your students using several different texts before you ask them to use the monitoring log on their own.

Good readers use fix-up strategies when their comprehension falters, such as the strategies found in this chapter and others in this book. What kinds of fix-up strategies do you use to increase your comprehension?

After Reading

After students read, they need the opportunity to reflect on the meaning they have constructed and to extend their thoughts. Strategies in which students use different modalities, such as art and drama, are especially effective.

Sketch to Stretch.   Some students are able to convey their thoughts more readily through art. For that reason, Short, Harste, and Burke (1996) developed the strategy Sketch to Stretch. When students engage in Sketch to Stretch, they work in groups to develop a drawing that represents the theme of the story or a central concept. After creating the drawings, students then share their sketches and discuss what they learned from the story. The sharing of sketches and discussion often lead students to think more deeply about the story and to extend their comprehension.

Story pyramid.   A story pyramid is a strategy that is often used in intermediate-grade classes to extend comprehension and to help students understand story elements. A

Page and paragraph	My problem was.	What I tried.	How it worked.
	Word I didn't know Confusing sentence Lost concentration Didn't know about Distracted Other	Reread Took a mini-break Used a highlighter Looked up a word Summarized Asked a friend Thought harder Other	Great Pretty well Not too good Not at all
P.4 ¶2	Word "parlor"	Used content	Worked!
P.7	Lost track of story	Reread from page 5.	OK
P.12 ¶8	Meaning of paragraph	Thought about it	I think I get it.
P.15	Distracted	Shut door of room	good

FIGURE 8.15   Monitoring Log for *Emily* (Bedard, 1992)

story pyramid is a type of poem: Each line is a certain number of words about a specific topic (Figure 8.16). To have students write story pyramids, first make sure students have a good understanding of the characters, plot, setting, and theme of the story. Then have them write a story pyramid using the following form:

Line 1: Name of main character
Line 2: Two words describing the main character
Line 3: Three words describing the setting
Line 4: Four words stating the problem
Line 5: Five words describing one event
Line 6: Six words describing a second event
Line 7: Seven words describing a third event
Line 8: Eight words describing a final event
Line 9: Nine words stating the solution to the problem

Readers Theatre.   Interpretive Readers can build comprehension of text by acting out stories through Readers Theatre, dramatic representations, and pantomime. Readers Theatre, as described by Martinez, Roser, and Strecker (1998/1999), is a dramatic production of a story that relies on a reader's reading rather than acting, props, and costumes. According to these authors, Readers Theatre can aid students' fluency, comprehension, and confidence. To have students participate in Readers Theatre, you first need to select a script or have students write a script for you. Then have students choose parts and practice these parts until they can read them fluently. Finally, stage the production by having students sit in chairs facing the audience and read their lines. Students can use scripts as they read.

Asking questions.   Questioning is another of the comprehension processes that active readers engage in subconsciously. As they read, good readers ask questions to guide their comprehension. Self-questioning shapes readers' thinking and promotes monitoring of comprehension. For example, as you're reading this section, you might be asking yourself some of the following questions:

- What kinds of questions do good readers ask?
- Do I ask questions as I read?
- How do I teach students to ask questions?

Phoebe
Guilty, scared
Now, small town
Mick's sudden unexpected death
The fight over a tattoo
Zoe thinks Mick can be here.
Phoebe speaks about Mick at the assembly.
Phoebe writes in cement Mick Harte was here.
Phoebe understands that Mick's accident was no one's fault.

FIGURE 8.16   Story Pyramid for *Mick Harte Was Here* (Park, 1996)

As with all of the reading strategies that you want students to internalize, you should model questioning as part of your teaching routine.

Teachers often conduct discussions after students have read a passage of text and ask questions during that time. Bloom (1956) identified a hierarchical classification (called a taxonomy system) of areas of thinking that apply to teacher-generated questions, as follows:

- Knowledge,
- Comprehension,
- Application,
- Analysis,
- Synthesis, and
- Evaluation.

The first two types of thinking on the list, knowledge and comprehension, involve students' ability to remember and understand information. Application, analysis, synthesis, and evaluation involve the ability to use higher level thinking abilities to apply and evaluate information. Although Bloom's terms are used by some reading teachers, the reading terms of *literal, interpretive, applied,* and *critical* are more common (Blachowicz & Ogle, 2001).

Question–answer relationship.   Bloom's taxonomy relates to the types of questions you ask students, but how should students think about answering these questions? Raphael (1982) suggests that there are four types of question–answer relationships (QAR): Right There, Think and Search, On My Own, and Author and Me. You can teach your students to use QAR to determine the types of textual material they need to answer questions. For example, to answer a Right There question, students should refer to the passage to find the answer. A Think and Search question necessitates students looking through the text to make inferences. When students answer an On My Own question, they need to use their prior knowledge to develop an opinion, and when given an Author and Me question, students should use their prior knowledge and text clues provided by the author.

Assessing Comprehension

Comprehension can be difficult to assess. Teachers typically assess comprehension informally by observing classroom discussions, by retellings, and formally by giving tests on the materials that students have read. Tests often consist of objective questions where there is one right answer, such as multiple-choice questions, true–false questions, and short answers. Developing fair objective questions is very difficult to do, and objective questions tend to promote a view of reading that suggests that there are "right answers" to all questions about texts. Because we are encouraging you to think about comprehension as an individual's construction of meaning, objective tests provide you with little useful information about a student's reading comprehension. An alternative to objective tests is to ask students to answer open-ended questions.

Open-ended questions.   Open-ended questions ask students to think about significant concepts in the story they have read and to relate them to their own knowledge. For example, open-ended questions about Lois Lowry's (1989) *Number the Stars* include the following:

- In what ways did Annamarie show courage?
- How did Annamarie take on adult responsibilities?

You'll learn more about conducting discussions later in this book. What further ideas do you have about questioning during discussions?

Classroom Assessment

Score 4	Demonstrates good knowledge of the key ideas from the story.	Demonstrates good understanding of main point of the story.	Makes fully supported connections to life, other books, or other subjects.
Score 3	Demonstrates adequate knowledge of the key ideas from the story.	Demonstrates adequate understanding of main point of the story.	Makes somewhat supported connections to life, other books, or other subjects.
Score 2	Demonstrates some knowledge of the key ideas from the story.	Demonstrates some understanding of main point of the story.	Makes few connections to life, other books, or other subjects.
Score 1	Demonstrates little or no knowledge of the key ideas from the story.	Demonstrates little or no understanding of main point of the story.	Makes no connections to life, other books, or other subjects.

FIGURE 8.17   Rubric to Score Open-Ended Responses

Classroom Assessment

You should use a variety of methods to assess reading comprehension that can then be placed in a student's portfolio. What types of assessments and artifacts other than the rubric could be included in a portfolio?

- In what ways are Annamarie's characteristics like or unlike you?
- The treatment of the Jewish people during the Holocaust was unjust. What other unjust situations occur today?

Rubrics.   You can assess students' reading comprehension by applying students' written or orally stated answers to a rubric. Rubrics are a holistic method of assessing student work that can be used in a variety of situations. If you use a rubric, you need to have some idea in your mind (or on paper) of what constitutes a paper that would fit in each of the scoring areas. For example, you need to have in mind what you believe your students could write that would constitute a "score 4 paper." Some teachers collect benchmark papers, or papers that they consider represent each level of excellence for an answer to a question. Figure 8.17 illustrates an example of a rubric to score open-ended responses.

YOU TRY IT

Using a Rubric to Assess Open-Ended Questions

You'll find several examples of student responses to open-ended questions from the story *Love That Dog* (Creech, 2001) on the Companion Website at http://www.prenhall. com/lenski. Read this short book and develop your own sample answer. Then use the rubric found in Figure 8.17 to score the students' responses. Compare your answers with those of your classmates or use the chat room to discuss answers with other classmates.

CONNECTIONS: WHAT'S NEXT?

In this chapter, we presented ideas for teaching Interpretive Readers as a whole group. We discussed different approaches to reading—basal reading programs, literature anthologies, and trade books—and encouraged you to make an informed decision about the type of reading approach you use. No matter what materials you use to teach reading, however, you need to prepare lessons that use instructional strategies so that students learn how to process text strategically. We presented a variety of strategies that you can use for Interpretive Readers, but we also suggest that you use strategies found in other chapters of this book as you prepare for teaching. You can contextualize the major ideas presented in this chapter by looking at the highlighted sections in Figure 8.18.

In Chapter 9, you'll find information about teaching Interpretive Readers in small groups. Intermediate-grade students learn in many ways, and one of these ways is through small-group instruction. When you group students, you have the opportunity to work with them in a more personal setting. Small-group instruction for Interpretive Readers, however, will be different from what you've learned about Early Readers. For Early Readers we recommend that you use guided reading for small-group instruction. Interpretive Readers usually respond better to grouping options such as literature circles. As always, though, you should take what you've learned throughout the book and apply it to your students and teaching situation, no matter what age your students are.

FIGURE 8.18 A Developmental Approach to the Teaching of Reading

	Early Readers	Interpretive Readers	Critical Readers
Theories underscored as readers develop:	Social Constructivism — Psycholinguistic — Critical — Transactional	Social Constructivism — Psycholinguistic — Critical — Transactional	Social Constructivism — Psycholinguistic — Critical — Transactional
Whole-group instruction through:	• Read-alouds • Shared texts • Comprehension strategies • Working with words	• Read-alouds • Using basals • Literature-based models • Word-building strategies • Comprehension strategies	• Read-alouds • Common texts (e.g., basals, anthologies, trade books) • Comprehension strategies • Vocabulary instruction and word analysis • Researching • Critical reading • Reading content area texts • Studying and note-taking

continued

FIGURE 8.18   *Continued*

	Early Readers	**Interpretive Readers**	**Critical Readers**
Assessment ideas for whole group:	• Observations • Kidwatching • Anecdotal notation	• Portfolios • Open-ended questions • Rubrics	• Written retellings • Research projects • Interest inventories • Content-area histories • Cloze procedure
Small-group instruction through:	• Guided reading • Teaching for strategies • Working with words	• Basal readers • Literature anthologies • Fluency practice • Guided silent reading • Literature circles • Inquiry groups	• Book clubs • Trade books
Assessment ideas for small groups:	• Running Records • Retellings • Discussions with children	• Names test • Fluency checklist • Peer assessment • Inquiry rubric	• Student information card • Bio poem • "I Used to… But Now I…" poem • Observational checklist • Student self-assessment • Norm-referenced tests
Independent learning through:	• Independent reading • Reading/writing workshop • Making books • Reading the room	• Independent reading • Reading/writing workshop • Responding through writing • Reading logs	• Sustained silent reading and writing
Sociocultural contexts:	• Literacy partnerships with parents • Parents in the classroom • Home–school communication	• Reading/writing connection for life • Oral histories • Home literacy activities • Parent programs	• Parents as coaches • Funds of knowledge • Parent–student book clubs

FOR YOUR PORTFOLIO

ENTRY 8.1   *Reading Strategies*

INTASC Principle 4 states: *The teacher understands and uses a variety of instructional strategies to encourage students' development of critical thinking, problem solving, and performance skills.*

In this chapter you learned about strategies for teaching reading to Interpretive Readers. Choose one of these strategies, describe it, and discuss how it could serve to meet one of the INTASC standards. This exercise is designed to give you practice in thinking about how you will meet each of the standards when you are a teacher.

ENTRY 8.2 *Author or Genre Study*

IRA/NCTE Standard 12 states: *Students use spoken, written, and visual language to accomplish their own purposes (e.g., for learning, enjoyment, persuasion, and the exchange of information).*

The teaching of authors and literary genre are ideal for individual study and class presentations. For example, you might assign your students to research their favorite authors and develop a website, a brochure, or a speech about the author.

In preparation for this assignment, develop your own presentation that you could use as a model for your students.

TO LEARN MORE

Helpful Websites

Visit our Companion Website at *http://www.prenhall.com/lenski* to link to the following sites:

American Library Association: Newbery Medal Award

Provides information about the Newbery Medal and lists of award winners. *www.ala.org/alsc/newberry.html*

American Library Association: Caldecott Medal Award

Provides information about the Caldecott Medal and lists of award winners. *www.ala.org/alsc/caldecott.html*

The Children's Literature Web Guide

Provides information about Internet resources related to books. *http://www.acs.ucalgary.ca/~dkbrown/index.html*

Authors

Contains lists and information about authors of children's books. *http://www2.scholastic.com/teachers/authorstudies/authorstudies.jhtml*

ISLMC Children's Literature & Language Arts Resources

The Internet School Library Media Center (ISLMC) provides information about authors, illustrators, genres, and book awards. *http://falcon.jmu.edu/ramseyil/childlit.htm*

Portfolios

Discusses how to use portfolios for elementary students. *http://www.ed.gov/databases/ERIC_Digests/ed334603.html*

Readers' Theatre

Provides scripts for Readers' Theatre performances and has many links to helpful sites. *http://www.aaronshep.com/rt*

Children's Literature Activities for the Classroom

Offers teachers the opportunity to retrieve literature by grade level. Lesson plans are provided, along with other links to be used when teaching with trade books. *http://members.aol.com/Mgoudie/ChildrensLit.html*

chapter

Instructing Interpretive Readers in Small Groups

Essential Learning Questions

- Why is small-group instruction important in your balanced literacy program?
- What types of grouping plans would you prefer in your intermediate classroom? Why?
- In what ways can small-group literacy instruction be assessed?
- How can literature circles be effective in meeting the needs of your students?
- In what ways are inquiry groups a vital part of a literacy program?

Because you can't provide the types of instruction your students need by relying solely on whole-group instruction, you also need to instruct Interpretive Readers in small groups. The type of grouping practices we recommended for Early Readers, such as guided reading, may not work well for intermediate-grade teachers. Students in intermediate grades need more independence than do Early Readers; they need more time to read silently; and their motivation to read may begin to wane. On the other hand, many Interpretive Readers have developed the ability to use the cueing systems to read unknown words and are fluent readers. Therefore, the types of reading strategies that you need to teach Interpretive Readers are usually different from those you teach Early Readers.

Many intermediate-grade students can decode words, but they may have difficulty comprehending text. At this age, students often have difficulty sustaining comprehension over the length of an entire book, they struggle with monitoring their understanding, and they have difficulty understanding text features (Szymusiak & Sibberson, 2001). Some students, however, will still struggle with the cueing systems, will have difficulty with phonics, will lack fluency in reading, and will have difficulty comprehending text. Other students will comprehend text easily and need to apply higher order thinking strategies rather than constantly reviewing comprehension and decoding strategies. Small-group instruction can provide the venue for meeting students' various needs.

SMALL-GROUP INSTRUCTION

Reading is a complex process that is a transaction between the reader, the text, and the context. Because of the vast differences among readers, different students will have different needs that can only be met through small-group instruction. Think about teaching a class of 28 fourth graders to read more proficiently. A portion of your reading program will probably consist of whole-group instruction using a basal reader, a literature anthology, and/or novels. Whole-group instruction is useful for providing explicit instruction in strategies that all students need to learn, for allowing students to share common texts, and for reviewing recently taught strategies (Radencich & McKay, 1995). Some intermediate-grade teachers spend most of their instructional time teaching to the entire group, but we believe this is a mistake. We concur with Strickland, Ganske, and Monroe, (2002) who write, "One of the misconceptions paralleling the advent of holistic approaches to literacy was the trend toward total whole-group instruction throughout the day" (p. 42).

Visit the online journal in Chapter 9 on our Companion Website at *www.prenhall.com/lenski* to answer these questions. Save your answers to your hard drive or to a disk to compile an online journal.

You learned about the purposes of teaching to the whole group in Chapter 8. What are the limitations of whole-group instruction that necessitate the use of small-group instruction?

Grouping for Struggling Readers

Some Interpretive Readers who have been struggling with reading in the first and second grades will continue to have difficulty reading in the intermediate grades (Juel, 1988). Students who struggle with reading will have difficulty with the complexity of the text that you use for whole-class instruction; they may not be able to read the text at all. Continued instruction with texts far above their reading ability frustrates students and does not help them learn to read better. To learn to read, students must use the cues available in the text coupled with their experiences to construct their own personal meanings. If you read the text to them, or if they hear the text from other readers, they might be able to construct meaning, but they are deprived from using their own minds to read the words on the page. It might surprise you that some students can't read a book that you might have read in fourth or fifth grade, such as Katherine Paterson's *Bridge to Terabithia* (1977). Asking struggling readers to read that text would be like asking you to try to learn reading from a medical dictionary.

Struggling readers need more time with reading instruction than do the rest of the students in your class. They need extra small-group reading time to read and reread text, to bolster their confidence, and to apply the strategies that you teach (Strickland et al., 2002). Before you say "That's not fair to the other students," think about this scenario. You are attending a golf class this semester, not because you want to learn how to golf, but because the class fits your schedule and you need a physical education credit. In your class are several students who were members of their high school's golf team and who play golf regularly. You, on the other hand, have never played golf and have poor eye–hand coordination. Now let's imagine that one of the requirements to pass the class is to hit a golf ball 100 yards. The seasoned golf players can accomplish this feat with one or two warm-up swings. How about you? Will you need more time practicing than the other class members?

The same principle holds true for struggling readers. Students who have difficulty reading in the intermediate grades need extra small-group instruction in reading so that they can read text that is commonly read at their age level. In addition, they need easier texts that allow them to practice their reading while experiencing success.

SEE FOR YOURSELF

Grouping Ideas for Struggling Readers

Visit the message board for Chapter 9 on our Companion Website at *www.prenhall.com/lenski* to discuss your findings.

Practicing teachers have a variety of methods at their disposal to provide struggling readers with additional reading time. Listen to the two intermediate-grade teachers on the Companion Website *(http://www.prenhall.com/lenski)* who have practical suggestions for grouping struggling readers. You might also ask intermediate-grade teachers in your area how they work small-group instruction for struggling readers into their schedules. As you listen to the teachers and those you interview, think through the following questions:

- How does this teacher's view of struggling readers compare with my own perspective?
- What complexities has the teacher discussed that I haven't considered?
- What can I learn from this teacher that will help me teach struggling readers to read?

Diversity issue: Grouping for English Language Learners.   English Language Learners (ELL) also need extra instruction in small groups. Many of the students who are learning to read in English need different kinds of instruction, such as additional vocabulary instruction, a greater use of visuals, and more practice pronouncing words. Small groups are the best places for these types of instructional activities so that ELLs have a safe place to practice and take risks as they learn a new language.

Grouping for gifted readers and writers.   You might be thinking, "Well, at least the proficient readers and writers won't need extra groups. They can learn on their own and even help other students." Research on gifted children, however, shows that gifted readers and writers also need the opportunity to work at their own levels. Ellen Winner (1996) writes that gifted students may lose their motivation to learn if not given challenging activities as children. Think about this. Let's say again that you're in that golf class, you love to play golf, and you're very good. If the class is targeted only for beginners, you may begin skipping class, and may not even do well in the course because you're so bored. If the instructor only has you help the neophytes with their golf swing, you may become angry and frustrated because you can't play at your own level. Gifted readers feel the same way in schools. If they only read material that is below their ability level, and if much of their day is spent "tutoring" other students, they may lose their love of learning. So, you also need to provide occasional small-group activities for gifted readers and writers.

You may also want to occasionally form groups of only gifted girls or gifted boys. After two decades of research on gifted girls, Reis (1998) has come to the conclusion that gifted girls need opportunities to work alone, without gifted boys. In mixed gender situations, gifted girls too often stay quiet and do not use their talents. In fact, Reis has found that gifted White girls are the most overlooked subgroup in schools, even more ignored than students of minority groups.

Flexible, needs-based groups.   Not all small groups need to be formed by ability. There will also be times when you need to create small groups of students with mixed abilities to help them make progress on a needed skill or strategy. Assessment will reveal the literacy strengths and weaknesses of each student, and, at times, you should group students who need special instruction together for a lesson. Explicit teaching and strategies are necessary for students to gain access to school literacies (Wilkinson, 1999). Szymusiak and Sibberson (2001) suggest that flexible, needs-based groups in the intermediate grades can be used to teach students how to select books, to learn about an author or a new genre, to develop comprehension strategies, to study words, to discuss books, and to develop higher level thinking.

 All readers need instruction at an appropriate instructional level. How does this principle apply to your theory of literacy learning?

Grouping Options

You will have many options for grouping intermediate-grade students—so many options that your biggest problem may be deciding which ones to use. Students in third through fifth grade are able to work independently, so your grouping options are varied. Your choice may depend on the grouping option that fits best with your own view of literacy, your teaching style, district or school mandates, and the materials that are available. Because most of you do not yet have teaching positions, you should consider which set of grouping options you think fits best. When you obtain your first teaching position, you may have to adjust your opinion based on state, district, or school mandates; the school population; and the materials.

Basal reading groups.   Many of you will teach using a basal reader or a literature anthology for much of your reading instruction. For some of your instruction, you'll have all of your students reading the same story so you can introduce strategies to the class as a whole. If you teach using a basal reader to the entire class, however, you should also divide your class into groups for instruction that fits their reading levels. Many of the teacher's manuals have suggestions for struggling readers, ELL students, and gifted students that you can use for instructional purposes.

Another way to use basal readers for small groups is to teach the basal as a set of leveled stories to use in guided reading groups (Fawson & Reutzel, 2000). As you learned in Chapter 8, the stories in third-grade basal readers could range from early second grade to late fourth grade in terms of difficulty. The differences in difficulty in the stories make basal anthologies appropriate for use for guided reading. One of the roadblocks teachers find in using guided reading is the number of books needed to successfully implement the program. Because many teachers have access to basal anthologies, Fawson and Reutzel suggest leveling the stories in the basal readers to use in guided reading.

A third way to use basals in small-group instruction is to implement "visiting basal reader selection groups," in which students use the basal reader to select the stories they want to read (Reutzel, 1999). Students browse through copies of the basal reader, reading the table of contents, looking at the illustrations, and scanning the stories. After browsing, they can ask the teacher questions about any of the selections. Then students vote on the stories they want to read. The teacher forms groups based on the students' interest in the basal stories.

Guided reading groups.   Guided reading is a successful method of instructing Early Readers in small groups. So, is guided reading also appropriate for intermediate-grade students? Pinnell and Fountas (2002) have suggested guided reading for students in grades 3 through 6 and have developed a list of leveled books to use for those purposes. Other experts in teaching reading, however, recommend that guided reading be adapted in a couple of significant ways for older students. In a book titled *Beyond Leveled Books,* Szymusiak and Sibberson (2001) write that relying on leveled books for students in intermediate grades is counterproductive. Motivation for reading becomes more complex for older children, and students' interest in topics becomes central to the text that they are given to read. Szymusiak and Sibberson write, "If we know that children are unique and the reading process is complex, why would we limit our ability to match children with books by relying on a leveled list created by a person or a company that doesn't know us or our children?" (p. 15).

A second difficulty with using lists of leveled texts is that students do not learn how to set their own purposes for reading. Their goal in reading becomes reaching the next level of text rather than establishing real purposes for authentic reading. In discussing guided reading for students in intermediate grades, Regie Routman, a well-respected educator, writes: "Some schools have witnessed a leveling craze that has extended through grades three through five. Some teachers have grown accustomed to selecting books based on leveling guidance, and feel that they cannot conduct guided reading groups without it. But leveling books in these grades is neither a good nor appropriate use of teacher time" (2000, p. 84). Instead, Routman suggests that intermediate-grade teachers use books for reading groups that are "developmentally appropriate, interesting, and relevant as well as accessible" (p. 84).

A third difficulty with guided reading for Interpretive Readers is the emphasis on oral reading. Although this emphasis is appropriate for Early Readers, older students need to spend time reading silently. Because of this need, Whitehead (1994) suggests guided *silent* reading. During guided reading, children read leveled texts aloud in groups so that the teacher can listen in and scaffold their use of the cueing systems. During guided silent reading, students are divided into groups by needs. Each group is given a different book to read. Students read the books silently away from their group. While reading, students are encouraged to use self-monitoring strategies such as bookmarking. (See Figure 9.1 for an example.) The teacher meets with each group two or three times per week to discuss a prearranged number of chapters in the book and to suggest comprehension strategies for difficult passages. Because the level of the books has been matched to the reading level of the students, all students should be able to read the books without much difficulty. The teacher's role, then, is to scaffold the students' use of self-regulating comprehension strategies.

Needs-based groups.   Another grouping option is flexible needs-based groups. As stated earlier in this chapter, students need different types of instruction based on their individual reading needs. Some groups of students, such as special education students, struggling readers, gifted readers, or English Language Learners, need to meet regularly—although not every day. You might meet with the students who have difficulty reading three or four times a week while you meet with gifted readers only once every two weeks. You will have to develop a systematic pattern for meeting

FIGURE 9.1 Strategy Bookmark

with students based on their needs and your teaching schedule. In addition, you should occasionally meet with students on an ad hoc basis, which means that if a group of students is having difficulty with a particular strategy, you should schedule a time for those students to meet with you to learn more about that strategy. These groups should have flexible membership and should only meet as many times as it takes to help students learn the particular strategy.

Classroom Assessment

Grouping through assessment.   Needs-based groups should be changed based on students' needs. Intermediate-grade educators Szymusiak and Sibberson (2001) write, "Every few weeks, we complete a master list of students and their needs for reading instruction and use it to form flexible small groups and plan whole-class lessons and individual instruction" (p. 63). Figure 9.2 illustrates how you can use assessment to develop reading profiles on students to form needs-based groups.

Literature circles.   Students in intermediate grades are vying for independence and are beginning to form unique interests. At times, some students may resist reading the books you have selected for them—even if you think the books will interest them. To address the needs of Interpretive Readers, Daniels (2002) developed a small-group instructional option called *literature circles*. Literature circles are much different from guided reading groups. They are based on student selection of materials to read; different groups generally read different books; they are typically mixed-ability groups; and students are responsible for leading their own discussions and monitoring their own learning.

Student	Observations
Francisco	Understands basic English Reads fluently Doesn't apply comprehension strategies Selects books about soccer English vocabulary weak
Tanya	Reads Junie B. Jones books Difficulty decoding multisyllable words Motivated reader Uses self-monitoring strategies
Vinnie	Reads mostly nonfiction books Comprehension strong No difficulty decoding Uses strategies during reading Needs to apply higher level thinking strategies

List of Groups

Group Members	Purpose
Francisco, Emily, Katy, Ted	Vocabulary building Fluency
Kenny, Tanya, Ann	Decoding: Three-syllable words with suffixes
Vinnie, Norma, Bethany	Connecting themes of stories to current news stories

FIGURE 9.2   Creating Needs-Based Groups

Book Clubs.   Book Clubs are another type of small-group instructional option, in many ways similar to literature circles, but the teacher typically selects the book students read in groups and often everyone reads the same book. Students are divided into mixed-ability groups, led by students, to discuss the book.

Inquiry groups.   A final type of grouping option is inquiry groups. In inquiry groups, students are grouped based on the interests they pursue through reading and writing. They research a topic and present that information to an audience. Students are typically divided into mixed-ability groups.

Mixed-ability and homogeneous groups.   You've probably noticed that some grouping options call for mixed-ability groups, whereas others are reliant on homogeneous groups. When you were in the intermediate grades, you were most likely divided into homogeneous groups, that is, groups of students who read at approximately the same level. More recently, however, the trend in schools has been to teach to the whole group, or to use cooperative mixed-ability groups. You might be wondering how to decide which type of small-group instruction is best. We would like to suggest that you use a combination approach because each type of grouping pattern has benefits for students learning to read. We believe that students should have some reading instruction with text at their own levels that supports homogeneous grouping. On the other hand, research on grouping practices indicates that when students spend too much time in homogeneous groups, their learning suffers (Weinstein, 1976). Therefore, we would like you to carefully consider the types of grouping options you prefer. Figure 9.3 reviews those options.

You will learn more about literature circles, Book Clubs, and inquiry groups later in this text. What personal experiences do you have with these types of grouping practices?

Grouping Plans

You might be wondering how to decide which small-group option will work best for your students. The good news is that teachers of intermediate grades have so many interesting and effective grouping plans from which to choose. The bad news is that developing a coherent reading program is more difficult using all of these choices.

We would like to suggest that you develop a small-group instructional plan based on the model of instruction you prefer for the bulk of your teaching. As you think about a combination of options, you'll want to consider these critical components of your overall program:

- Explicit teaching of word-building and comprehension strategies,
- Explicit teaching of elements of literature (i.e., plot, setting, characters),

Instructional Methods	Type of Group
Basal reading groups	Homogeneous
Guided silent reading	Homogeneous
Needs-based groups	Homogeneous or mixed ability
Literature circles	Mixed ability (can also be homogeneous)
Book Clubs	Mixed ability
Inquiry groups	Mixed ability

FIGURE 9.3   *Small-Group Options*

- Common texts for students to read and discuss,
- A strong literature component,
- Both teacher-selected and student-selected books
- Opportunities for students to read texts at their own reading levels, and
- Opportunities for students to apply reading strategies.

Using basal readers.   If you prefer teaching from a basal reader or if your school district mandates basal reading instruction, you might decide to develop a plan centered on instruction with basal readers (Figure 9.4). Basal reading selections are typically taught to the entire class, which is a mixed-ability type of instruction. If you use a basal reading approach, you'll also have students working in mixed-ability cooperative groups so that all students construct meaning from the stories. Because much of your instruction will already be in mixed-ability groups, you'll need to balance that with instruction tailored to the needs of your students. Students will need to read texts that are at their own level, so you'll need to develop small-group instruction, using the basal or other materials that provide students an opportunity to read at their own level. Teaching from a basal is very teacher directed, so you should supplement that instructional model with one in which students have more autonomy and independence, such as literature circles.

Using a literature-based approach.   If you're teaching primarily from literature to the entire class, you also need to supplement that teaching with strategy instruction in needs-based groups. You should also consider interrupting your teaching of novels with short stories from a literature anthology. No novel is popular with every student, and students can become disengaged from learning if they spend weeks reading a book they don't particularly like. Figure 9.5 provides a plan for using literature-based reading.

Whole-Class Instruction

Weeks 1–5	Weeks 6–8	Weeks 9–14	Weeks 15–18
Basal reader	None	Basal reader	Basal reader

Small-Group Instruction

Weeks 1–5	Weeks 6–8	Weeks 9–14	Weeks 15–18
Basal groups	Literature circles	Basal groups	Basal groups

FIGURE 9.4   Semester Grouping Plan Using Basal Readers

Whole-Class Instruction

Weeks 1–5	Weeks 6–8	Weeks 9–14	Weeks 15–18
Novel 1	Novel 2	Short stories	Novel 3

Small-Group Instruction

Weeks 1–5	Weeks 6–8	Weeks 9–14	Weeks 15–18
Needs-based groups	Inquiry groups	None	Needs-based groups

FIGURE 9.5   Semester Grouping Plan Using Literature-Based Reading

Using literature circles.   An entirely different sort of grouping plan should be considered if your primary means of instruction is through literature circles (or Book Clubs) (Figure 9.6). If you use literature circles as the basis for reading instruction, you'll need to make room in your reading program for the explicit instruction of strategies and for literary elements through the teaching of short stories from a literature anthology. As you'll learn later in this chapter, literature circles are based on reader response and do not provide an avenue for teaching strategies. You might also vary the types of literature circles your students use so that students can read texts at their own level as well as select their own texts to read in mixed-ability groups.

Using guided silent reading.   A final grouping option is based on guided silent reading. If your students need a great deal of time reading text at their own level, you might consider using guided silent reading as the basis for your program (Figure 9.7). If you're using this plan for small-group instruction, you'll need to supplement your teaching with the teaching of short stories from a literature anthology and novels so that students have opportunities to read in mixed-ability settings.

Assessing for Small Groups

Classroom Assessment

Throughout this text we've encouraged you to think about assessment as the centerpiece of reading instruction: You need to know what your students need to learn before you make instructional decisions. In Chapter 7 we discussed using portfolio assessment to make decisions about student progress. In this chapter, we present some additional assessment ideas so you can make decisions about creating small-group instruction.

Whole-Class Instruction

Weeks 1–5	Weeks 6–8	Weeks 9–14	Weeks 15–18
Short stories	Short stories	None	Short stories

Small-Group Instruction

Weeks 1–5	Weeks 6–8	Weeks 9–14	Weeks 15–18
Lit circles	Lit circles	Lit circles	Lit circles
Homogeneous	Mixed ability	Homogeneous	Mixed ability

FIGURE 9.6 Semester Grouping Plan Based on Literature Circles or Book Clubs

---

Whole-Class Instruction

Weeks 1–5	Weeks 6–8	Weeks 9–14	Weeks 15–18
Short stories	Short stories	Short stories	Novel

Small-Group Instruction

Weeks 1–5	Weeks 6–8	Weeks 9–14	Weeks 15–18
Guided silent reading	Guided silent reading	Guided silent reading	Inquiry groups

---

FIGURE 9.7 Semester Grouping Plan Based on Guided Silent Reading

Classroom Assessment

Assessing phonics knowledge.   Many of your intermediate-grade students will come to you already knowing basic information about the sound/symbol relationship in the English language. However, some students will need further instruction in phonics elements. Many intermediate-grade teachers who primarily teach students using a basal reader approach or a literature-based approach teach to the whole class and may not know which students need additional instruction in phonics. Not all students need this assessment; only those students who you find have unusual difficulty reading. These students may refuse to read the texts you assign, or they might have poor comprehension. If that is the case, you might give them the *Names Test* (Cunningham, 1990) to determine whether they need additional instruction in phonics. This test should be conducted one on one in a setting where there is privacy so no student is embarrassed (Figure 9.8).

Classroom Assessment

Assessing reading fluency.   Another hindrance to comprehension is a lack of reading fluency (Johns & Bergland, 2002). Intermediate-grade students may be able to decode words but read so haltingly that they are unable to construct meaning from the passage. If this is the case, they'll need to be given extra opportunities to read text at their own level and will need instruction in phrasing and intonation in reading. To assess reading fluency, you should have students read text to you privately

---

Directions

1. Write or type the 25 names on individual cards.
2. Prepare a scoring sheet with all of the names listed in order. Provide room to write the student's answers.
3. Have one student at a time read the names.
4. Record the student's answers by marking syllables with a check if correct and writing the student's pronunciation if they are incorrect.
5. To score, count words correct when all syllables are pronounced accurately regardless of which syllable the student accents.
6. Count the number of names pronounced correctly, and look for patterns of strengths and needs.

The Names Test

Jay Conway	Wendy Swain
Tim Cornell	Glen Spencer
Chuck Hoke	Fred Sherwood
Yolanda Clark	Flo Thornton
Kimberly Blake	Dee Skidmore
Roberta Slade	Grace Brewster
Homer Preston	Ned Westmoreland
Gus Quincy	Ron Smitherman
Cindy Sampson	Troy Whitlock
Chester Wright	Vance Middleton
Ginger Yale	Zane Anderson
Patrick Tweed	Bernard Pendergraph
Stanley Shaw	

From Cunningham, P. M. (1990). The Names Test: A quick assessment of decoding ability. *The Reading Teacher, 44,* 124–129.

FIGURE 9.8   Names Test

that is matched to their independent reading level and then you can apply the reading fluency rubric given in Figure 9.9 to determine whether students need additional instruction in reading fluency.

Managing Small-Group Instruction

Small groups are much easier to manage in intermediate-grade classrooms than in younger children's classrooms. Students in grades 3 through 6 are much more independent and can read or write at their desks while you meet in groups. You also might consider developing one or more centers in your classroom such as those suggested for Early Readers. Centers can be effective for Interpretive Readers because they allow students to move freely and they appeal to students' need for independence. McLaughlin and Allen (2002) suggest the following centers for intermediate-grade students:

Centers are more common in primary grades than in intermediate grades. What benefits do you think centers would have for intermediate-grade students?

- **Writing Center:** writing materials, writing prompts, pictures, stickers, and stamps
- **Vocabulary Center:** words for word sorts, Word Bingo, acrostics, riddles
- **Making Words Center:** letter tiles
- **Poetry Center:** copies of poetry books, writing materials
- **Drama Center:** copies of Readers Theatre scripts

	Not fluent 1	2	Fluent 3
Accuracy[*]	**Below 90%**	**90–94%**	**95–100%**
Fluidity	Hesitates frequently Little rhythm Extended pauses Repetitions Choppy reading	Occasional hesitations Some pauses Some repetitions Smooth reading Fairly smooth reading	Few hesitations Few pauses or repetitions

Phrasing	Word-by-word reading
	Ignores punctuation
	Inappropriate breaks
		Some inappropriate
		  breaks
		Mostly phrased
		  correctly
			Phrased in
			  meaningful
			  chunks of text

Expressiveness	Monotone, or little
	  expression
	Fails to mark end of
	  sentence with
	  intonation of voice
		Minimal expression
		Some correct
		  intonation
			Appropriate
			  stress, intonation,
			  and expression

[*]Make a check each time the student reads a word incorrectly. Find the percentage of incorrect to correct words. For example, if a student misses 14 words in a passage containing 122 words, the student has read 108 words correctly. Divide the number of words read correctly by the total number of words to obtain a percentage, in this case, 88.5%.

$$\frac{\text{Number of words} - \text{number of miscues}}{\text{Number of words}}$$

FIGURE 9.9 Reading Fluency Rubric

Using Centers

Dear Janette,

I know that I'll want to use centers if I teach primary grades, but I never thought of using centers for older students. Do intermediate-grade students still like to use centers?

Dear New Teacher,

I think centers are great for older elementary students. Students at this age are able to work independently with little difficulty, so management of centers is relatively easy. Further, intermediate-grade students like the freedom of movement and choice that centers provide. I also find that my students can be really creative when they use centers; I think this is because they are able to choose to work on things of interest to them. Try centers; I think they'll work for you, too.

LITERATURE CIRCLES

Literature circles are one of the ways to group Interpretive Readers. "Literature circles are small, peer-led discussion groups whose members have chosen to read the same story, poem, article, or book" (Daniels, 2002, p. 2). You may have experienced literature circles in your own schooling or you might have heard about them in other college classes. If you participated in literature circles or have heard about them, you might be familiar with any number of adaptations. Literature circles have been used for more than a decade, and many teachers have discovered different ways to implement them in classrooms.

According to Harvey Daniels, one of the originators of the concept, literature circles have 11 characteristics (Figure 9.10). If you're organizing instruction into small groups using literature circles, the students will be in temporary, task-oriented groups, similar to guided reading groups. The students are grouped by the books they want to read. Each group of students selects one book to read, reads the book, responds to the book, and discusses the book in their literature circles. Your role as the teacher is to facilitate all of these activities.

As you read about the characteristics of literature circles in Figure 9.10, you can see why they are so appropriate for Interpretive Readers. Students in the intermediate grades are becoming independent and want to make their own choices. Worthy, Broaddus, and Ivey (2001) write that intermediate-grade students are "more likely to make a personal investment in their reading when they have some choice about what to read and when they have their own purposes for reading" (p. 101). Using literature circles gives students these choices. Students at this age are also becoming

1. Students *choose* their own reading materials.
2. *Small temporary groups* are formed, based on book choice.
3. Different groups read *different books.*
4. Groups meet on a *regular, predictable schedule* to discuss their reading.
5. Kids use written or drawn *notes* to guide both their reading and discussion.
6. Discussion *topics come from the students.*
7. Group meetings aim to be *open, natural conversations about books,* so personal connections, digressions, and open-ended questions are welcome.
8. The teacher serves as a *facilitator,* not a group member or instructor.
9. Evaluation is by *teacher observation and student self-evaluation.*
10. A spirit of *playfulness and fun* pervades the room.
11. When books are finished, *readers share with their classmates,* and then *new groups form* around new reading choices.

From Daniels, H. (2002). Literature circles: Voice and choice in book clubs & reading groups *(2nd ed.). Stenhouse! Portland, ME (emphasis in original).*

FIGURE 9.10   Characteristics of Literature Circles

interested in their peers, so student-centered discussion is also appropriate. Furthermore, the theory behind literature circle fits nicely with the transactional reading theory. By implementing literature circles, you're handing off some of the control of your classroom to students. This shift in the balance of classroom power needs to be conducted carefully because some of your students (and possibly you) will need to learn new ways of acting in the classroom.

 Literature circles were developed using aspects of social constructivist learning theory. How do literature circles fit your theory of literacy learning?

Preparing Students for Literature Circles

You may be intrigued with the idea of literature circles and wonder how to begin them. The first thing to remember is to start slowly. You may not be able to run a "genuine" literature circle during your first few months of teaching because you'll need to prepare your students and yourself for a method of reading that is new and different.

Introducing literature circles.   One way to introduce literature circles is to teach response activities to the entire class. For example, you could begin by reading a book to students, such as *Jamaica Tag-Along* by Juanita Havill (1989). In this story, Jamaica, a young girl, tries to follow her older brother, Ossie. After being rebuffed by Ossie, Jamaica learns how important it is to be kind to younger children. After you read the story, have students respond to the story by writing a hypothetical journal entry from either Jamaica or Ossie. An example of a fifth-grade student's entry can be found in Figure 9.11. (Notice that this student went beyond the story and created something of a sequel.)

After the students have responded to the story, ask them to discuss the story by talking about their own personal experiences being either an older or a younger sibling. During the discussion, try to keep students talking by asking probing questions such as "Can you tell me more about that?" and "How did that make you feel?" Keep your own comments to a minimum. During literature group discussions, you want your students to initiate topics and manage the discussion.

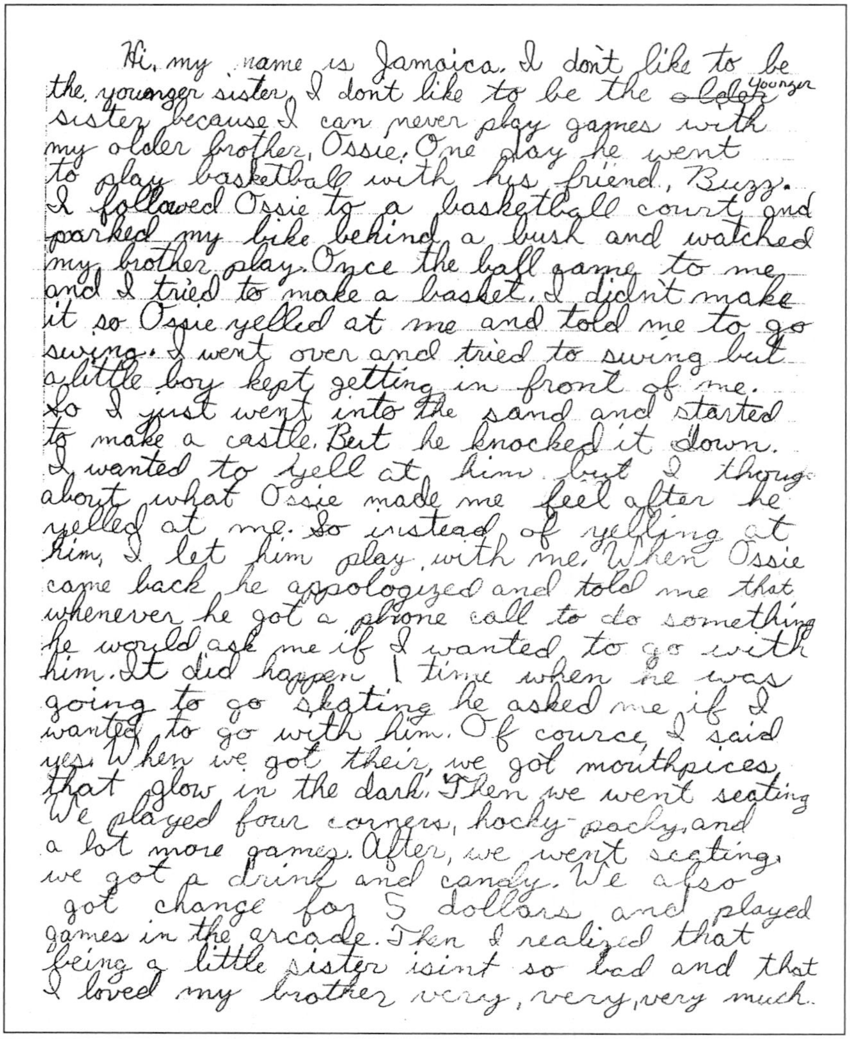

> Hi, my name is Jamaica. I don't like to be the younger sister, I don't like to be the ~~older~~ younger sister because I can never play games with my older brother, Ossie. One day he went to play basketball with his friend, Buzz. I followed Ossie to a basketball court and parked my bike behind a bush and watched my brother play. Once the ball came to me and I tried to make a basket. I didn't make it so Ossie yelled at me and told me to go swing. I went over and tried to swing but a little boy kept getting in front of me. So I just went into the sand and started to make a castle. But he knocked it down. I wanted to yell at him, but I thought about what Ossie made me feel after he yelled at me. So instead of yelling at him, I let him play with me. When Ossie came back he appologized and told me that whenever he got a phone call to do something he would ask me if I wanted to go with him. It did happen 1 time when he was going to go skating he asked me if I wanted to go with him. Of cource, I said yes. When we got their, we got mouthpices that glow in the dark. Then we went seating. We played four corners, hocky-pocky, and a lot more games. After, we went seating, we got a drink and candy. We also got change for 5 dollars and played games in the arcade. Then I realized that being a little sister isint so bad and that I loved my brother very, very, very much.

FIGURE 9.11   Fifth-grade Response to *Jamaica Tag-Along*

Helping students select books.   The first thing you have to do if you want to use literature circles is gather sets of books. Ideally, you'll have dozens of sets of books with two to six books of the same title in a set. Realistically, however, you may only have a few sets of novels. If that's the case, you'll have to assign the books to students; and, although that alternative isn't optimum, you might not have any other choice. Students do need a balance between teacher-selected and student-selected books, so if you assign a book for literature circles, be sure to provide students with other opportunities to choose books to read (Zimelman, Daniels, & Hyde, 1998).

If you have a number of sets of books to use for literature circles, Steineke (2002) suggests that you prepare a ballot listing the books you have available, such as that shown in Figure 9.12. Give a quick book talk describing each book, then pass copies of the book around so that students can gauge its difficulty and look at the cover. After that have students rank the books in the order in which they would like to read them.

Title	Author	Ranking
Nothing But the Truth: A Documentary Novel	Avi	3
Bud, Not Buddy	Chistopher Paul Curtis	1
Out of the Dust	Karen Hesse	4
Maniac McGee: A Novel	Jerry Spinelli	2

FIGURE 9.12   Book Selection Ballot

Ann is browsing through selections for literature circle ideas.

Forming literature circle groups.   Students in literature circles are grouped by the text they want to read. Students, therefore, are not grouped by ability, but by interest. The number of students in each group may be determined by the number of copies of the chosen books you have, but, if possible, the groups should be between two and six students, with many teachers preferring four students per group (Hill, Noe, & Johnson, 2002). If you have students rank their choice of books, you can make the final decisions about group membership based on additional information you have. Many students try to form groups around friendships rather than interest in books, and these types of groupings may be productive, but at times you may decide to form groups based on other factors. As you create literature circle groups, you should take into account students' book preferences, interests, and reading levels, as well as group dynamics such as which students work well together and which do not.

In order for literature circles to be effective, you need to have a knowledge of books that would be appropriate for your class. What books do you think would be good for intermediate-grade students?

Conducting Literature Circles

Once you have formed literature circle groups and students have copies of books, you're ready to schedule literature circles into your reading program. After scheduling, your role will be one of facilitator. You'll decide what students need to learn, conduct minilessons at the beginning of each session, observe group discussions, keep records, make notes, and help solve problems. And you'll probably need to continually remind yourself that your role in literature circles is to scaffold student learning, not to explicitly teach reading strategies.

Scheduling.   Literature circles generally take around 45 minutes in all: 5 minutes for a brief minilesson that helps students successfully participate in the day's activities; 30 minutes for reading, responding, or discussing the book; and 10 minutes for debriefing. Many teachers schedule literature circles every day, but some teachers do not have enough time in their schedules for a daily 45-minute literature circle. If that is the case, you might schedule literature circles three times a week. Many teachers use literature circles all year long, but other teachers prefer scheduling literature circles for 3 or 4 weeks every grading period. There are any numbers of ways to schedule literature circles, but teachers often need to practice creative scheduling so that they can fit different types of learning activities within a school year.

Minilessons.   The minilessons you conduct for literature circles should directly relate to the day's activities. If students are reading, you might offer some suggestions for responding to reading. For example, if students are discussing, you should suggest ways to conduct a successful discussion. Some teachers begin literature circles by assigning students roles to play during discussions (Daniels & Bizar, 1998), such as Discussion Director, Passage Master, Word Wizard, Summarizer, and Artful Artist. For a minilesson, then, you would model one or more of the roles. For example, if you were the Word Wizard using the book *Out of the Dust* (Hesse, 1997), you might say:

> When I was reading, I kept running across the word "kerosene," and I didn't really know what it meant. I figured out that it must be some type of flammable liquid, but I had never heard of it. I looked up the word in the dictionary, but the definition didn't tell me much more than I already knew. I love the sound of that word, and I kept saying it over and over: kerosene, kerosene, kerosene. My grandfather heard me, and he asked what I was doing. I told him I was a Word Wizard and that *kerosene* was a word I was learning. He told me how his grandparents had kerosene lamps when he was young, and then I really understood the word because I've seen kerosene lamps in movies.

Daniels (2002) suggests that you teach two types of skills during minilessons: social and thinking skills (Figure 9.13). Teachers often teach thinking skills during reading class, but rarely do they teach the types of social skills that are necessary during discussions, especially student-led discussions.

◢◣◥◤ YOU TRY IT ◢◣◥◤

Conducting Minilessons

When teachers start using literature circles, they often have difficulty deciding what to teach in minilessons. Using the list of possible minilessons from Figure 9.13, prepare a lesson that you could teach to an intermediate-grade class. If you have access to a group

Social Skills	**Thinking Skills**
Take turns	Make connections
Listen	Visualize
Make eye contact	Put yourself in the story
Share airtime	Reread to clarify
Include everybody	Check and confirm facts
Don't dominate	Make inferences
Don't interrupt	Draw conclusions
Value ideas	Evaluate the book, author, characters
Respect differences	Notice words and language
Disagree constructively	Look for patterns
Stay on task	
Support your view with the book	

From Daniels, H. (2002). Literature circles: Voice and choice in books clubs & reading groups (2nd ed.). Portland, ME: Stenhouse.

FIGURE 9.13   Literature Circle Minilessons

of students, teach the lesson to them. If not, teach to a small group of your classmates. As you prepare your minilesson, consider the following questions:

- Does this lesson facilitate reading or thinking processes?
- Will this lesson facilitate discussions about literature?
- Does this lesson fit my own theory of literacy learning?

Responding during reading.   The purpose of literature circles is not to teach students about story, but to have them "live the story." The explicit teaching of reading strategies is not taught in literature circles; those activities are reserved for other aspects of the reading program. Instead, literature circles are based on Rosenblatt's reader response theory. Reader response theory suggests that readers can approach texts aesthetically (with personal responses) and efferently (to gain information). Literature circles were developed to provide students with aesthetic reading experiences (Daniels, 2002).

The bulk of the time (30 minutes or so) spent in literature circles is for students to read, respond, and discuss books. Students can read independently, in pairs, or in small groups—depending on the book's difficulty and the students' needs. As students read, they should write their reactions in response logs, write ideas on sticky notes, or use role sheets that describe discussion roles. Students can write whatever they want, but they need to remember that these written notes will be used as the basis for literature circle discussions. Some teachers provide students with response ideas in minilessons such as those listed in Figure 9.14.

Discussions about literature.   Literature circle discussions should mirror the type of discussion friends have about books. Think about times when you spontaneously told a friend about a book you were reading. You may have discussed the characters, the plot, the author, or other topics. You may have liked the book, felt indifferent, or even hated the book. But you felt as if you had something to communicate, and you wanted to talk about that book with someone.

Characters

How do I feel about this character?
How do the characters change in the story?
If I were the character, what would I do?
How are the characters like or different from my family or friends?
How would you change a character if you could?

Plot

What happened in the story?
What was the problem and how was it resolved?
How did the plot surprise you?
In what ways was the plot interesting?
How could the plot have been different?

Author

Why do you think the author wrote this book?
How did the author create suspense or humor?
What does the author have to know to write this book?
How do you picture the author?
What would you ask the author if you could?

FIGURE 9.14   Response Questions

It's those types of emotions you want to evoke in your students—strong feelings about books. And, you will want your students to share their thoughts in an environment that feels safe to them. Therefore, you need to pay close attention to students as they discuss their books, watching for students who feel silenced by their peers.

To begin discussion groups, you may want to remind students about the social skills they learned in minilessons. Then have students move to places in the classroom so that their group is sitting together, away from others. If your classroom is small, you might ask the librarian if students can use the learning center to discuss their books. During the first discussions, you might suggest a few topics for students to begin, but encourage students to discuss their own topics as they surface. It might take several attempts at discussion before intermediate-grade students use all 30 minutes, so monitor the discussions, and when conversation lags, have students present their last ideas then close the literature circles for the day.

YOU TRY IT

Literature Discussions

The best way to understand literature discussions in literature circles is to participate in them yourself. Choose a book that you think would be appropriate for intermediate-grade students and ask three or four of your classmates to read it as well. After you have read several chapters, get together to discuss what you have read. Focus the discussion on the plot of the book and your response to your reading. After the discussion, write a memo to yourself about the event. Save the memo so that you can better plan literature discussion groups when you're a teacher. As you write your memo, consider the following questions:

- Did everyone participate in the discussion?
- How did I feel during the discussion?
- What did I learn from my classmates?
- How can I apply this experience to teaching?

Assessing Literature Circles

One of your roles as a teacher during literature circles will be to assess your students' reading progress. You can do this by using some of the assessment strategies that you've already learned in this text, such as kidwatching, taking anecdotal notes, peer conferences, and using checklists. You can also have students conduct peer assessment.

Peer assessment.   In a book on literature discussion groups for intermediate-grade students, Evans (2001) describes one of the reasons for having students conduct peer assessments. She writes, "I wanted to use assessment techniques that would be consistent with my beliefs about the instructional practice of literature discussion groups, techniques that would allow for multiple voices, diminish my role as sole evaluator, and increase the students' voice in the assessment process" (p. 88). Peer assessment fills the bill.

To have students assess themselves and one another, you first need to establish the criteria for assessment. One way to determine criteria is to keep track of the mini-lessons you present and list them as possibilities for an assessment tool. Because students will be using the assessment, ask them which of the items they think should be included on an assessment. Then work with your students to develop a simple rating system, such as "plus," "check," and "minus." After a group discussion, have each of the students fill out the assessment on their literature circle members. A sample peer assessment for Raffie, Serena, Mario, and Wanda, who were discussing Ruby Bridges's *Through My Eyes* (1999), can be found in Figure 9.15.

You've learned a variety of assessment techniques in this text. What other assessment tools would be appropriate to assess literature circles?

Classroom Assessment

Integrating Literature Circles Into a Reading Program

Literature circles were developed as a way to have students select their own reading, respond aesthetically, and develop their own topics for discussion. Literature circles are effective at accomplishing these goals, but they should not make up the entire reading program. The strength of literature circles is a foundation on reader response, but reader response theory doesn't include some of the other types of reading instruction, such as explicit teaching of reading strategies. In order for students to become strategic readers, you'll want to instruct students on certain reading strategies in a teacher-directed manner. For example, you'll probably teach intermediate-grade students how to decode words of several syllables. Some students will not learn this type of reading strategy without instruction. Therefore, you should balance teacher-directed instruction with student-directed activities, such as literature circles, in your reading program.

Some intermediate-grade teachers balance their reading programs by implementing literature circles 3 days a week, alternating literature circles with a more direct approach to teaching, such as teaching short stories from a literature anthology

Name	Rating	Reason
Me Raffie	+	I took turns and listened carefully. I spoke my mind!
Serena	✔	She kept interrupting when people talked.
Mario	+	He sort of directed talk by nodding to people. It was cool.
Wanda	+	She didn't talk much but she listened real good.

FIGURE 9.15   Literature Circle Peer Assessment Form

or basal reader. When instructing short stories, teachers emphasize story structure and literary elements, and probably teach to the entire group at the same time. Other teachers alternate weeks between teaching a common text and having students participate in literature circles.

▰▰▰ YOU TRY IT ▰▰▰

Developing a Reading Schedule

As you develop a schedule for your reading program, you will need to take into account grouping patterns, types of instruction, available materials, student needs, and your school schedule. Use the information below to develop a reading/writing schedule that includes literature circles, filling in the schedule provided.

Resources

    Class set of one literature anthology
    Class sets of 8 different novels
    Seven sets of 4–8 books each
    Classroom library with 200 books
    School library with adequate collection
    Small public library

Monday	Tuesday	Wednesday	Thursday	Friday
Opening (8:15–8:30)	Opening (8:15–8:30)	Opening (8:15–8:30)	Opening (8:15–8:30)	Opening (8:15–8:30)
Music (8:30–9:00)		Music (8:30–9:00)		
	Phys. Ed. (10:30–11:00)		Phys. Ed. (10:30–11:00)	
				Art (10:45–11:30)
Lunch (11:30-12:30)	**Lunch (11:30-12:30)**	**Lunch (11:30-12:30)**	**Lunch (11:30-12:30)**	**Lunch (11:30-12:30)**
Math 1:00–2:00	Math 1:00–2:00	Math 1:00–2:00	Math 1:00–2:00	Math 1:00–2:00
Thematic instruction based on Social Studies or Science (2:00–3:00)	Thematic instruction based on Social Studies or Science (2:00–3:00)	Thematic instruction based on Social Studies or Science (2:00–3:00)	Thematic instruction based on Social Studies or Science (2:00–3:00)	Thematic instruction based on Social Studies or Science (2:00–3:00)
Dismiss 3:30	Dismiss 3:30	Dismiss 3:30	Dismiss 3:30	Dismiss 3:30

FORMING INQUIRY GROUPS

"You have a twenty-page research paper due at the end of the semester." You've probably heard statements like this throughout your schooling experience and especially in college. Are you cringing? If so, you're not alone. Many college students hate to write research papers. You might be thinking that as a teacher you won't subject your students to research assignments. But, wait. Researching has an undeserved bad reputation in schools—one that we hope you'll change with your students.

Researchers and educators have found new ways for students to conduct research that fits the social constructivist theory that we have recommended. Researching may have many different names. In this section we're going to approach researching as an act of inquiry and encourage you to include inquiry groups as a small-group option in your balanced reading program.

What Is Inquiry?

"Inquiry is our curriculum and our way of life. It is asking questions, searching for answers, and finding multiple ways to find answers" (Rogavin, 2001, p. 9). When you think about inquiry, think about the natural questions you and your students have about life. For example, you might be wondering right now how you will find your first teaching job. That's a question you will need to research. To find answers, you might ask other students, contact a placement office, search the Internet, ask a professor or advisor, or read a book about finding a job. You will be "researching" this topic because you have an actual need and an authentic reason for your question and your search. The outcome of your research will not be a 20-page paper, but most likely it will be a group of actions based on your findings.

Inquiry in schools can be just as meaningful as the example about finding ways to obtain a teaching position. Your students will have their own inquiry needs that you can use as the "curriculum" for their learning. In most of the small-group options we've presented thus far, we've presupposed a curriculum of learning that is external. In other words, it has come from "outside" the students. The curriculum in other grouping options has been literature or a content topic, mostly determined by you, the teacher. In inquiry groups, teachers "lead from behind" as Gordon Wells (1986) has phrased it; you'll let students determine what they want to learn and how to learn it.

 Inquiry learning is a good example of social constructivist theory. How do you think inquiry in the classroom exemplifies social constructivism?

What is your role, you might ask. Years ago, John Dewey (1938) described the teacher's role as one in which she establishes a classroom learning environment and orchestrates experiences for students so that students can raise questions. Or, as Freire (1985) wrote, inquirers need to be problem posers, not merely problem solvers. These problems, or questions, are the basis of inquiry.

Finding Topics for Inquiry

Before you can form inquiry groups, you need to work with your whole class to help them develop topics, or questions, for inquiry. The example that we used earlier of you researching job opportunities is an obvious research topic for preservice teachers. Your students' inquiry topics might be a bit more subtle.

Short, Schroeder, Laird, Kauffman, Ferguson, and Crawford (1996) write that three sources of knowledge are necessary as inquirers develop questions: personal and social knowing, knowledge systems, and sign systems. Personal and social knowing are students' own experiences. As students think about topics of inquiry, they need to draw on their prior knowledge because thinking about what we know leads us to thinking about what we want to learn (Ogle, 1986). A second source is knowledge systems, or ways knowledge is organized into topics, such as mathematics, history, and science. The third type of knowledge is a knowledge of sign systems. Sign systems are alternative ways to represent knowledge including music, art, movement, dance, and drama (Siegel, 1984). You might be thinking, "Of course, there are many methods of expression. How does this relate to inquiry groups?" For years, inquiry in schools has meant writing research papers with footnotes and reference pages. This type of externally imposed inquiry has often resulted in students' hating the very word "research." Short and her colleagues (1996) remind us that "[o]utside of school, learners do not use only reading and writing to create and share meaning. They have multiple sign systems available" (p. 11). If you want students to become engaged in real inquiry, you need to think beyond the bounds of the traditional research paper to the sign systems available to all inquirers, and those that appeal most to students who are conducting inquiry.

Encouraging questioning attitudes.   If you were told to conduct an inquiry project about any topic you wanted, how would you feel? Many students find that type of open-ended assignment overwhelming. Therefore, to begin inquiry groups, you will need to lay some foundational groundwork by encouraging students to ask questions throughout the day. Frequently, teachers don't encourage students to ask questions because they are so busy "covering" the curriculum. However, if you want students to become inquirers, you'll need to encourage questioning throughout the school day, not just during inquiry groups.

In a book titled *The Research Workshop,* Rogavin (2001) suggests a number of ways you can promote inquiry in your classroom, including these:

- Tell students that their questions, comments, and observations are welcome.
- Compliment students when they ask questions or make observations using such comments as "That's a really good question."
- Keep a bulletin board of questions students have raised. Allow students to write their questions on an index card and post the questions they have raised outside of class as well as inside class.
- Don't allow students to make fun of the questions other students have asked.
- Tell students that all questions should be valued.
- Provide students with time to think of questions.
- Have students keep a writer's notebook with ideas they conceive and questions they raise.

Brainstorming ideas.   Even with an environment that encourages questions, some students may not have ideas for inquiry topics unless you help them brainstorm ideas. You need to remember that your students are novice inquirers and may need you to guide them in developing questions to ask. Allen (2001) writes: "Students might not know they have a passion for a topic unless we bring it to their attention" (p. 27). Intermediate-grade students have passion about many topics, but at times it will be your job as a teacher to help them connect with their interests.

One brainstorming technique that works well with Interpretive Readers is to develop a list of questions that students can answer in their journals or in small groups (Figure 9.16). The questions should probe different areas of the students' lives. Frequently, one or more areas of interest will emerge from the answers to these questions.

Forming groups.   Once students have begun thinking about topics of inquiry, you can divide them into groups to discuss areas of interest. The groups should not be divided by ability, but by interest. Because inquiry is such a personal activity, you should give students as much leeway as possible to divide into groups. Some students may want to work alone, and you should honor those requests as well. However, as

---

1. What books, magazines, or Internet sites have I read recently that have intrigued me?
2. What music or musical performers do I like?
3. What historical time periods or people are of interest to me?
4. What current affairs have I been interested in?
5. Which artists or types of art appeal to me?

FIGURE 9.16   Brainstorming Questions

Rivka brainstorms ideas for an inquiry project.

the teacher, you always have veto power in any group membership. For example, you might have a group of English Language Learners who are grouped together for much of the day, and you want them to work with other students to strengthen their language skills and social interactions. Or, perhaps you have a gifted student who worked alone during the previous inquiry project whom you would like to encourage to work with other students. In cases like those, you might need to intervene in the group selection.

K-W-L. Once students have formed inquiry groups with a general topic, you may want them to complete a K-W-L chart (Ogle, 1986). K-W-L stands for what students *Know,* what they *Want* to know, and what they have *Learned* (Figure 9.17). K-W-L charts can be used in a number of ways, including during the beginning of inquiry groups. As students gather into groups, have them list what they know about their topic first. This allows students to access their prior knowledge about the topic and to let their minds range over the different aspects of the topic. It's a good idea to give students two or more group sessions to list what they know. Once students begin listing what they know, they'll continue to think about the topic for several days, remembering more each day. After students have worked on their "Know" list, have them begin brainstorming what they want to know. It's this list that is crucial for students as they focus on areas of inquiry.

FIGURE 9.17 K-W-L Chart

Technology Topic: Finding Electronic Sources

Some intermediate-grade students will have many hours of experience surfing the Web and will want to use the Internet for their inquiry projects. Roe (2000) suggests that when students begin inquiry projects they use a variety of media as they search for information, such as encyclopedias on CD-ROM, audiotapes, videotapes, educational television, videodiscs, and digital videodiscs (DVDs). Many students are unaware of the many resources available electronically in addition to the Internet. As students conduct inquiry, therefore, make a variety of sources available to supplement Internet research.

Inquiry Projects

You have students conducting inquiry in groups, and they have learned vast amounts of interesting material. How do they synthesize their learning in such a way that they can learn more about their topic and remember what they have learned? You might have students write a collaborative research paper using the traditional research format. However, more interesting options exist.

Transmediation. Rief (1999) writes, "We must expand our notions of literacy to include all that we know and can do visually, physically, mathematically, and even sensually—through touch, taste, and sound. These ways of knowing can enrich our lives as learners" (p. 3). Remember the different sign systems (i.e., dance, drama) that are a crucial component of knowledge resources? *Transmediation* is when you recast knowledge from one sign system into another, such as creating a dance from a musical piece or drawing pictures related to a poem.

One interesting way to have students present inquiry projects is by asking them to create songs, poems, dance, or drama from their learning. You can have students practice this transformation by a strategy called Sketch to Stretch which was introduced in Chapter 8 (Short, Harste, & Burke, 1996). In this strategy, students draw a sketch of their interpretation of a passage. Students familiar with creating sketches from stories will have the foundation for transmediation, or reframing language into various sign systems. An example of a poem and picture that a student wrote after researching the Statue of Liberty is given in Figure 9.18.

Multigenre research papers.   Another alternative to traditional research papers is the multigenre research paper (Romano, 1995). A multigenre research paper is a paper that uses different genres in the paper, such as diary entries, bumper stickers, letters, essays, and stories. Allen (2001), a proponent of multigenre research papers, defines them like this: "The best way I can describe a multigenre paper is to say that each piece in the paper utilizes a different genre, reveals one facet of the topic, and makes its own point" (p. 3). Multigenre papers are not organized like traditional pa-

FIGURE 9.18 Student Poem

Advice column	Interview	Poem
Announcement	Journal entry	Poster
Bedtime story	Jump rope rhyme	Prescription
Biographical sketch	Legend	Realistic fiction
Bumper sticker	Letter	Report
Catalog description	List	Speech
Diary	Love note	TV commercial
Diet	Motto	Warranty
Epilogue	Mystery	Yearbook inscription
Fairy tale	Myth	Yellow pages ad
Fortune	Persuasive speech	
Horoscope	Picture book	

FIGURE 9.19   List of Genres

pers but are like a collage, an artistic expression of thought and meaning. If students are to write multigenre papers, they need to be familiar with a wide variety of literary genre, not just the typical ones. Allen suggests that students keep a resource notebook with three parts: one devoted to models of genre, the second filled with drafts of writing, and the third with research notes. Figure 9.19 contains a partial list of genre that could be used for multigenre papers.

Managing Inquiry Groups

Your role in managing inquiry groups will be as a teacher/facilitator. As you watch students researching, your role will be to provide resources when necessary, to make suggestions, and to keep students on task. Some teachers conduct their own research while students are working in inquiry groups so that you can model researching behaviors for students. Rief (1999) suggests writing one paper per semester or year, not as often as students do, so you can devote the bulk of your time to helping students. However, conducting research while students are working in inquiry groups will help you reflect on the research process, which, in turn, will help you be a better teacher. And, you might also find out about something of great interest to you.

Assessing Inquiry Projects

Inquiry projects cannot be graded with a simple "A" or "B." Because of their complexity, inquiry projects are better scored using a rubric so that you can evaluate the different components of the work. As you evaluate the projects, Jane Hansen (1998) suggests that you are actually finding the "value" in the work. Hansen's perspective sheds a refreshing light on assessment. Instead of looking for what's wrong in the project, therefore, you should consider looking for what's of value. As you assess inquiry projects, you should consider your instructional purposes and goals, and create a rubric that will help you determine whether the students' projects have met those goals. A sample rubric for assessing inquiry projects can be found in Figure 9.20.

Part of the Balance

Inquiry groups are part of your entire reading and writing program; they are not your entire program. In writing about inquiry groups, Romano (1995) states, "It seems clear to me that if we want students of any age to become one with literacy, we must afford

Classroom Assessment

A rubric for assessing inquiry projects can be found in Chapter 13. How would you develop a rubric to evaluate inquiry?

Name_____   Date_____

Score 3	Project demonstrates a sincere interest by the authors and compelling questions.	Authors used a wide variety of sources and answered questions thoroughly.	Presentation was interesting to and appropriate for the audience.
Score 2	Project demonstrates mild interest by the authors and interesting questions.	Authors used several sources and answered questions in part.	Presentation was mildly interesting and somewhat appropriate.
Score 1	Project demonstrates little interest by the authors and questions that were not interesting.	Authors did not use many sources and did not answer questions.	Presentation was not very interesting and did not reach the audience.

FIGURE 9.20   Rubric to Assess Inquiry Projects

them chances to achieve optimal psychological experience through reading and writing" (p. 193). We agree. However, as students work in inquiry groups, you might find that they are so enthusiastic that you don't want to go back to teaching literature or using your basal reader. We believe inquiry groups are a vital aspect of a literacy program, but we would also like you to remember that Interpretive Readers also need explicit teaching of reading strategies. Therefore, we would like to encourage you to embed inquiry groups into a complete reading program that incorporates whole-class instruction, small-group instruction, and independent work.

CONNECTIONS: WHAT'S NEXT?

In this chapter, we presented some ways to work with Interpretive Readers in small groups (Figure 9.21). We highlighted two types of grouping—literature circles and inquiry groups—that are especially appropriate for students in intermediate grades. Literature circles and inquiry groups, however, are not the only ways to form small groups. We suggest a variety of other grouping options in other parts of this text. As with all of the ideas presented in this part, you can adapt most of them to Early Readers and Critical Readers. You can also use what you've learned in the other parts to help Interpretive Readers. As you develop your repertoire of small-group options, you can decide which ones you think would work best for you in your particular teaching situation.

As you know, teaching students in whole groups or small groups isn't your entire reading program. You also need to provide intermediate-grade students with time to read independently, and you should encourage your students to read at home. These topics will be discussed in Chapter 10.

FIGURE 9.21 A Developmental Approach to the Teaching of Reading

	Early Readers	**Interpretive Readers**	**Critical Readers**
Theories underscored as readers develop:	Social Constructivism Psycholinguistic Critical Transactional	Social Constructivism Psycholinguistic Critical Transactional	Social Constructivism Psycholinguistic Critical Transactional
Whole-group instruction through:	• Read-alouds • Shared texts • Comprehension strategies • Working with words	• Read-alouds • Using basals • Literature-based models • Word-building strategies • Comprehension strategies	• Read-alouds • Common texts (e.g., basals, anthologies, trade books) • Comprehension strategies • Vocabulary instruction and word analysis • Researching • Critical reading • Reading content area texts • Studying and note-taking
Assessment ideas for whole group:	• Observations • Kidwatching • Anecdotal notation	• Portfolios • Open-ended questions • Rubrics	• Written retellings • Research projects • Interest inventories • Content-area histories • Cloze procedure
Small-group instruction through:	• Guided reading • Teaching for strategies • Working with words	• Basal readers • Literature anthologies • Fluency practice • Guided silent reading • Literature circles • Inquiry groups	• Book clubs • Trade books
Assessment ideas for small groups:	• Running Records • Retellings • Discussions with children	• Names test • Fluency checklist • Peer assessment • Inquiry rubric	• Student information card • Bio poem • "I Used to… But Now I…" poem • Observational checklist • Student self-assessment • Norm-referenced tests

continued

FIGURE 9.21   *Continued*

	Early Readers	**Interpretive Readers**	**Critical Readers**
Independent learning through:	• Independent reading • Reading/writing workshop • Making books • Reading the room	• Independent reading • Reading/writing workshop • Responding through writing • Reading logs	• Sustained silent reading and writing
Sociocultural contexts:	• Literacy partnerships with parents • Parents in the classroom • Home–school communication	• Reading/writing connection for life • Oral histories • Home literacy activities • Parent programs	• Parents as coaches • Funds of knowledge • Parent–student book clubs

 FOR YOUR PORTFOLIO

Companion Website

ENTRY 9.1   *Integrated Instruction*

INTASC Principle 1 states: *The teacher understands the central concepts, tools of inquiry, and structures of the discipline he or she teaches and can create learning experiences that make these aspects of subject matter meaningful for students.*

As an intermediate-grade teacher, you will most likely be teaching several subjects, not just reading. An important benefit to teaching all subjects is that you can integrate reading with the other subjects that you teach.

Small-group work, such as literature circles and inquiry groups, are perfect for integrating several subjects. Using either literature circles or inquiry groups as your instructional approach, develop an integrated unit plan that you could teach in the intermediate grades.

Entry 9.2   *Writing for Audiences*

IRA/NCATE Standard 7 states: *Students conduct research on issues and interests by generating ideas and questions, and by posing problems. They gather, evaluate, and synthesize data from a variety of sources (e.g., print and nonprint texts, artifacts, people) to communicate their discoveries in ways that suit their purpose and audience.*

Reading is just one of the language arts. In addition to reading, students need to learn how to speak, write, listen, and use media effectively. Small-group instruction is a good venue for working with students on the other language arts. As students work in an inquiry group, for example, you can help them develop presentations that suit their purpose and audience.

Develop a lesson plan for a type of inquiry group (such as a multigenre research paper), and expand the lesson so that students are not only researching, but are presenting their information by speaking, listening, writing, and media. Prepare a list of methods for presenting the outcome of the inquiry.

TO LEARN MORE

Helpful Websites

Visit our Companion Website at *http://www.prenhall.com/lenski* to link to the following sites:

Balanced Literacy Program

Discusses the components of a balanced literacy program. Also includes assessment techniques.
http://www-titleone.ncsd.k12.wy.us/WHATISBA.htm

Teacher Resources

Contains links to articles and resources about balanced literacy.
http://www.teachersplanet.com/subjects/ballit.shtml

Literature Circle Resources

The literature circle resource center is designed to support teachers as they plan and use literature circles in their elementary and middle school classrooms.
http://fac-staff.seattleu.edu/kschlnoe/litcircles/

Introducing Literature Circles

These sites offer everything you need to get literature circles started in your classroom. A large amount of resources are available to download.
http://home.att.net/~teaching/litlessons.htm
http://www.literaturecircles.com

Leveled Reading

Lists 440 titles sorted by reading level 1.0–8.9.
www.tamu-commerce.edu/coe/shed/espinoza/s/ellis-b-rdlevl.html

Researching

Offers ideas for conducting inquiry groups.
http://www.heinemann.com/research

Instructing Interpretive Readers Independently and With Families

Essential Learning Questions

- Why is independent reading an important component of your intermediate-grade literacy program?
- What are some of the factors that influence motivation and how can these increase your students' love of reading?
- How does reading workshop fit social constructivist learning theories?
- What are some effective ways to assess students during reading workshops?
- What are some effective ways to involve intermediate-grade parents in their children's literacy learning?

Interpretive Readers need time in school to read books of their own choosing. Part of your reading instruction should be targeted to the entire class; some of your instruction should be provided to small, flexible groups; and a significant amount of time should also be scheduled for some type of independent reading program.

Independent reading is the time when students apply the reading and writing strategies that you've taught them. It also gives them the chance to follow their own interests. Students in intermediate grades begin to become intensely interested in a variety of topics—many that you won't be teaching in your classroom. Independent reading time provides students with the opportunity to learn about topics that interest them rather than topics that you have selected for them. Independent reading also helps students feel a part of your classroom community. "When students feel the liberation that comes from having a say in what they read and write, they have a stake in creating and maintaining a classroom that stimulates and supports deep learning, freeing you as the teacher to concentrate on how you can best guide, inform and strengthen their abilities" (Booth, 2001, p. 8). With independent reading you are honoring students' potential as developing readers.

Independent reading can take a variety of forms. You might give students 20 minutes per day for sustained silent reading (SSR), or you might decide to implement reading and writing workshops. Whatever instructional decision you make, however, the success of your independent reading program will hinge on your students' motivation to read. Therefore, you may have to actively promote motivation to read in your intermediate-grade classroom.

If students are motivated to read, they will also read at home. Some students, however, do not have books available for them to read at home, and some parents are unaware of the role they should play as reading models for their children. Your role as a teacher, therefore, is to help students bridge the gap between school reading and home reading by encouraging students to read and write at home and by promoting parental involvement in students' literacy lives.

MOTIVATING INTERPRETIVE READERS

Motivating students to read becomes an important issue once students reach intermediate grades. When students are in the primary grades, they tend to love everything about school, including reading. But once they get a little older, some students decide that they don't like to read and don't want to read. In general, the internal motivation students have toward learning in schools decreases steadily from third grade through high school (Anderman & Maehr, 1994).

Why does motivation begin to wane in the intermediate grades? Barrett and Boggiano (1988) suggest that one of the reasons why students' motivation lessens as they grow older is because they become more perceptive about their ability to succeed in school. Young children often are unaware of their ability or their successes. They seem to be eternally optimistic about their learning. Older children, however, begin to compare themselves to their peers. They notice how well they are doing compared with other students, and they begin to internalize the feedback they have received from their teachers.

During the time that students begin internalizing and personalizing success or failure in school, instruction begins to change. In the intermediate grades, teachers spend more time teaching decontextualized subjects; that is, they tend to spend less time teaching integrated thematic units and more time teaching discrete subjects such as science and social studies. According to Cordova and Lepper (1996), when learning is moved outside of the contexts in which students can connect their learning to their everyday lives and interests, their motivation tends to decrease.

Not every student in intermediate grades will lose the motivation to read; many will love reading. As a teacher of Interpretive Readers, however, you need to address reading motivation in ways that teachers of Early Readers do not. You need to learn how to structure your lessons to maximize students' natural inclinations to read, and also to be sensitive to the motivational needs of your students. Intermediate-grade students are not all avid readers, but you can make a difference in the number of students who are motivated to read.

Visit the online journal in Chapter 10 on our Companion Website at *www.prenhall.com/lenski* to answer these questions. Save your answers to your hard drive or to a disk to compile an online journal.

Creating a classroom in which students are motivated to read is essential for intermediate-grade teachers. What motivational strategies worked for you (or your children) in school?

Motivation and Reading Success

Teachers often say, "If only my students were more motivated, they would be much better readers." Teachers instinctively know that motivated readers are better readers, but the relationship between motivation and success is complex (Guthrie, Wigfield, Metsala, & Cox, 1999). Motivation to read is a combination of energy, direction, and persistence and is an internal process that is influenced by personal beliefs, perceptions of the value of reading, and the students' goals (Guthrie & Wigfield, 2000; Ryan & Deci, 2000). But what forces shape students' beliefs, perceptions, and goals? It's different for each student.

Think about what you read and what motivates you to read. Let's say that you recently have developed an interest in strength training. You have never before taken much interest in the muscular–skeletal system; in fact, during biology classes dealing with the topic, you found it hard to stay awake. But with your new interest, you decide to go to the library and find books that explain how muscles work. You read four books in one weekend about muscle development in preparation for a meeting with a personal trainer at your health club. What motivated you to read these books? Probably your new interest.

The same scenario holds true for many intermediate-grade students. At this age, students begin to develop their own personal interests, many of them based on popular culture, or trends, but some based on other factors. Students are highly motivated to read and learn about these interests. A recent example is the Harry Potter books. Teachers who can't get their students to read textbooks, find the same students reading lengthy and complicated Harry Potter books and other books and games relating to Harry Potter. So really, it's not that students are unmotivated; they simply may be unmotivated to read your choices of books.

Motivation and attitudes toward reading.   Students who are not motivated to read may or may not have a poor attitude toward reading. McKenna, Kear, and Ellsworth (1995) suggest that motivation is different from attitude toward reading. Think about students who are not really motivated to read, even though they have a positive attitude. These students might like reading during school but rarely read themselves or vice versa. Some students, on the other hand, are motivated to read, but don't really enjoy reading; they have a negative attitude toward reading. Many students who have poor attitudes toward reading have experienced difficulty learning to read. When a task is difficult and students have experienced failure for a number of years, their natural tendency is to avoid it.

As a teacher, you should develop lessons that motivate all students to read, and you may also want to address negative attitudes toward reading.

Motivation to Read Profile.   Motivation is a key issue in the development of intermediate-grade students' reading ability. Although teachers can determine students' motivation to read to a certain extent by observation, motivation to read surveys can augment your personal knowledge about how students feel about reading. One survey dealing with motivation is the Motivation to Read Profile (MRP) (Gambrell, Palmer, Codling, & Mazzoni, 1996). The MRP has two forms: One is a multiple-choice survey and the other is an interview survey. The questions in Figure 10.1 were adapted from the MRP interview survey.

The MRP interview is a student self-report measure, which means that students describe their views about their own reading. One of the limitations of a self-report survey is that some students will write answers that they think *you* want to hear. Therefore, you should make use of self-report surveys in conjunction with other assessment measures.

Classroom Assessment

Advice for New Teachers

Motivating Students to Read

Dear Janette,

I hate to admit this, but I was never much of a reader when I was in school. I want my students to have a better experience. How can I motivate students to read when I don't read much myself?

Dear New Teacher,

When you were in elementary school, there weren't as many high-quality children's books as there are now, so many new teachers aren't the readers they could be. The best way to create enthusiasm in yourself about reading is to begin reading children's books. You might start by going to a public library or large bookstore and reading several picture books. Just enjoy the pictures and the message. If you can, read some of these books to a young child. Savor the child's interest and enthusiasm. Then begin reading longer books. Scan through several books until you can find a topic that interests you and an author whose style you enjoy. Read several books from that author and create book talks for those books. Continue reading books and you'll find that you'll become an enthusiastic reader in no time.

1. Did you read anything at home recently? If so, what did you read?
2. Do you have any books at school (in your desk/locker/book bag) today that you are reading? Tell me about them.
3. Tell me about your favorite author.
4. What do you think you have to learn to be a better reader?
5. Do you know about any books right now that you'd like to read? Tell me about them.
6. How did you find out about these books?
7. What are some things that get you really excited about reading books?
8. Who gets you really interested and excited about reading books?

Adapted from Gambrell, L. B., Palmer, B. M., Codling, R. M., & Mazzoni, S. A. (1996). Assessing reading motivation. The Reading Teacher, 49, *518–533.*

FIGURE 10.1   MRP Interview Questions

Motivation and "fun."   Some teachers think that to motivate students, they need to make reading "fun." But that's not so. Every person must tolerate a certain amount of boredom and drudgery in life. No matter who you are, some of your activities will be routine, even boring. For example, you have to brush your teeth and make your bed in everyday life. And there are always dirty dishes to wash. In reading, you might have to read things that you would not normally choose to read: directions for new computer software, job applications, or textbooks. There's a difference between motivation and fun. As a teacher, you'll certainly want students to enjoy reading, but if you fall into the trap of trying to always make reading fun, you'll do your students a disservice—and you'll place undue pressure on yourself.

Students respond positively to many factors that may not be "fun" in the most general sense of the word. Students who read a challenging book, or figure out a difficult unknown word, or organize information from text in a new way may be working and concentrating so hard that it's not fun. But they are motivated to complete the task, and they feel a sense of accomplishment when it's over. Reading and learning are motivational in many ways that are not necessarily fun.

SEE FOR YOURSELF

Motivation to Read

Visit the message board for Chapter 10 on our Companion Website at *www.prenhall.com/lenski* to discuss your findings.

Take the Motivation to Read Profile interview survey from Figure 10.1 to determine your own motivation to read. As you think about how motivated you are to read, know that whether or not you are a motivated reader, you need to motivate your students to read. Make reading a higher priority for yourself if you are not currently a motivated reader. Your students must perceive that you value reading yourself and view it as an important part of your life. After taking the MRP survey, find a student in the intermediate grades to interview. Draw conclusions about how motivated this student is to read and think about ways you can emphasize motivation when you become a teacher.

Extrinsic Motivation

As a teacher, you can appeal to two types of motivation: extrinsic and intrinsic motivation. "The term extrinsic motivation refers to the performance of an activity in order to attain some separable outcome and thus contrasts with intrinsic motivation, which refers to doing an activity for the inherent satisfaction of the activity itself" (Ryan & Deci, 2000, p. 71). In reading, extrinsic motivation is analogous to the desire to complete a task that is separate from the content of the text rather than to understand or enjoy what was read (Meece & Miller, 1999). Extrinsic motivation, therefore, is asking students to read to receive external recognition, rewards, or incentives—not for the pure enjoyment of reading.

Extrinsic motivation was one of the hallmarks of the behaviorist learning theory (Ryan & Deci, 2000). Much of behaviorism is based on the idea that behavior change is based on rewards and punishments, and although many contemporary teachers do not follow behaviorist tenets any longer, the vestiges of external motivational programs are often found in schools today in the form of incentive programs.

Incentive programs.   Many teachers seem to believe that students won't read unless they are encouraged to do so by a gimmick or an incentive program. Incentive programs are based on the idea that students should receive rewards for reading. The prizes could take the form of stickers, candy, coupons for pizza, or any other number of other rewards. Some teachers find that incentive programs increase the number of books that students read (Guthrie & Wigfield, 2000), but research also indicates that incentive programs can decrease students' natural inclinations to read by making them dependent on rewards and recognition (Barrett & Boggiano, 1988). Researchers Deci, Koestner, and Ryan (1999) found that threats, deadlines, and imposed goals also decreased students' intrinsic motivation. When students feel that they've lost control over their choices and pace of reading, they begin to lose their desire to read.

 Many teachers use incentive programs to motivate students to read. What incentive programs have you seen in schools?

Intrinsic Motivation

Intrinsic motivation, as contrasted with extrinsic motivation, means engaging in an activity for its own sake. Think about the kinds of things that motivate you—that you do without anyone telling you to do. Some of you may be intrinsically motivated to read; no matter what your schedule, you'll find time to read. Writers are intrinsically motivated to write. In the movie *Quill,* for example, when the Marquis de Sade's paper and pens were taken away, he wrote on his bed linens using his own blood. Athletes exercise without anyone forcing them to work out; musicians sing or play because they want to. In general, people are intrinsically motivated to engage in certain activities that they choose.

A number of factors encourage intrinsic motivation in schools. Students who are in classrooms where they feel secure and valued tend to be intrinsically motivated more often (Ryan, Stiller, & Lynch, 1994). When students are in situations where risk taking is discouraged, they begin to lose their internal motivation. So, as a teacher, one of your priorities should be to create an inviting environment so students feel free to take risks.

Another factor that encourages intrinsic motivation is the opportunity for self-determination. When students have the opportunity to read books of their own choosing and for their own purposes, they tend to be more interested, motivated, and confident than students who are not given the opportunity for self-determination (Ryan & Deci, 2000). You can use this knowledge when you teach to create an environment that encourages students to want to read.

Intrinsic appeals.   You might be wondering how to encourage students to become intrinsically motivated or whether it's even possible to motivate someone else. You'll be relieved to know that teachers can make a huge difference in the motivation of their students. Encouraging intrinsic motivation is subtle, however, and hard to pinpoint. Think of teachers in your past who motivated you. These teachers were not necessarily the easiest or the most fun, and the subject may not have been of interest to you. Yet, these teachers motivated you. How?

Rinne (1998) suggests that all subjects have latent intrinsic appeal, and that teachers can apply these appeals to any lesson at any grade. He suggests that when teachers appeal to novelty, surprise, anticipation, security, challenge, or application, they intrigue students' natural curiosity and interest. Teachers don't have to prepare elaborate lessons to motivate students. They can motivate through just a few words. However, Rinne cautions that not every student is intrinsically motivated by any single appeal but that a percentage of students will probably be motivated by each one.

Here's how teachers can facilitate students' intrinsic motivation through various appeals. First, teachers can appeal through novelty. Novelty is something new and different. For example, when introducing *The Scrambled States of America* (1998) by Laurie Keller, you could say, "Have you ever wondered what the United States would be like if the states decided to change places?" This novel idea will pique many students' interest and will motivate them to read the book. Notice how this approach is different from saying, "If you read this book, you will get five points for your team"—an extrinsic motivational approach. Examples of other intrinsic appeals can be found in Figure 10.2.

Book talks.   Book talks are another method of appealing to student's intrinsic desire to read (Fader, 1976). A book talk is a short (2-minute) "commercial" for a book. Typically, you give book talks on four or five books, which are then displayed and

Intrinsic appeals are embedded in good instruction. In what ways have you observed teachers using intrinsic appeals?

Intrinsic Appeal	Description	Examples
Novelty	Something new	We're going to read something different today. I'll bet you've never met anyone like the characters in this book.
Surprise	Something unexpected	You won't believe what happens… Just wait until you read this.
Anticipation	Prompts suspense	Be sure to look for… Let's see if…
Security	Reassurance, familiar	You already know… This is just like…
Challenge	A reachable goal	What do you think about…? Can you…?
Application	Using skill elsewhere	You'll be able to use this… After you learn this, you'll be able to…

Adapted from Rinne, C. (1998). Motivating students is a percentage game. Phi Delta Kappan, 79, 620–627.

FIGURE 10.2   Intrinsic Motivational Appeals

made available for students to read. The purpose of giving book talks is to expose students to many books and to motivate them to read. Book talks appeal to intrinsic motivation by focusing on the content of the books, rather than asking students to read and keeping track of the number of books they have read.

To give a book talk, you can present a short summary of the book, or you can relate the book to a personal experience, use props, tell the book in first person, prepare an interview with a character, read an engaging excerpt from the book, or any other creative way to stimulate students' interest in reading. Several examples of books talks appropriate for Interpretive Readers can be found in Figure 10.3.

Book talks are an excellent way to share books with students. How else can you let students know about books that they might want to read?

YOU TRY IT

Book Talks

Develop a list of novels and informational books that would be of interest to students in intermediate grades. Select six books and prepare books talks for each of them. Develop book talks using each of the five examples described in Figure 10.3 and create a new type of book talk. Present the book talks in class.

FACILITATING READING WORKSHOPS

Intermediate-grade students need time to read, and they need the opportunity to use their literacy skills to follow their own interests. Some teachers provide their students significant amounts of independent reading and writing time (such as sustained silent reading and writing); other teachers prefer to organize independent reading and writing around a workshop approach.

Reading and writing workshops were developed by Nancy Atwell (1987), Lucy Calkins (1994), and Donald Graves (1994) to provide students with opportunities to read and write for authentic purposes. In a reading and writing workshop, students select their own books to read and write for their own audiences. (Because this text concentrates on the teaching of reading, we limit the discussion of workshops to reading workshops.) As you implement a reading workshop in your classroom, however, you can expand it to include writing so that your workshop is truly an integrated reading and writing workshop.

Organizing Reading Workshops

You're probably wondering how reading workshops are organized. There is no one method of managing reading workshops, but here we present some ideas that have worked for us.

Scheduling reading workshops.   You need to set aside a regular chunk of time for students to participate in reading workshops. Depending on the other elements of your reading program, we suggest you set aside 30-minute sessions at least twice a week. You might say, "There's no way I can fit reading workshop into my crowded schedule." Fletcher and Portalupi (2001) suggest that you ask yourself what other lessons workshops can replace. Are you spending class time having students read textbooks? Perhaps you can use textbooks as a whole-class literacy lesson and replace that time with reading workshop. In any case, you have to be creative as you schedule all of the subjects that need to be taught in the intermediate grades in order to give students

Relate the book to a personal experience.

My dad and I lived alone in a small apartment for five years, and I was really used to it. Then Dad got married to a woman with four other kids! We couldn't fit into our apartment, so we all moved into my stepmother's house. I had to share with my stepsister: a room, a phone, a television, and a computer. Just when I thought the adjustments were over, we had a real family problem—my dad was in an accident and broke his leg. We all had to pitch in together to make things work.

My situation was like what happened to Annie Rye from Piney Woods, Georgia, in many ways. However, Annie Rye encountered even bigger problems than my family did. They were faced with violence and racism. You'll have to read the book *Down in the Piney Woods* by Ethel Foorman Smothers (1992) for more details.

Use props. (Bring old-fashioned doll as a prop.)

If dolls could tell their stories, what would they say? In the book *Hitty: Her First Hundred Years,* by Rosemary Wells and Susan Jeffers (1999), Hitty is a doll carved from a piece of mountain ash wood in Maine in 1829. In this book, Hitty tells a hundred years' worth of adventures including leaving Maine to sail on a whaling ship, becoming shipwrecked on a tropical island, getting lost in India, and being sent to a soldier in the Civil War. As Hitty tells her stories, you'll learn about the world of the 1800s and early 1900s and be fascinated by the doll's experiences. And you'll think, "What kinds of stories would dolls today tell?"

Tell the book in first person, using dialect if appropriate.

For this book talk I'm going to pretend I'm the character Jason Hawthorn, and I'll be talking the way he did in the book.

My name is Jason Hawthorn, and I live in Dawson City way north near the Arctic Circle. I need money, real bad. You see, me and my brothers were cheated by a no-good rascal out of our means of living, our sawmill. I aim to buy it back, and I've got a chance. I can win $20,000 in a canoe race to Nome and find gold there to boot. My sweetheart, Jamie Dunavant, will be my partner in the Great Race across Alaska. I expect to have some mighty exciting adventures. You can read all about them when I finish the race in my book called *Down the Yukon* by Will Hobbs (2001).

Prepare an interview with a character from the book.

Interviewer:	Mark, what made you decide to climb Mt. Everest?
Mark:	I like physical challenges, and I thought climbing the highest mountain in the world presented me with the biggest challenge I could find.
Interviewer:	How old were you when you attempted the climb?
Mark:	I was 16, the youngest person to try to climb at that altitude.
Interviewer:	How did you train? You don't live in a mountainous area?
Mark:	I ran up flights of stairs in the tallest building in my town. That wasn't the best way to train, for sure, but I ended up being fit enough for the trip.
Interviewer:	Did you reach the summit?
Mark:	I'll let you read the book *Within Reach: My Everest Story* by Mark Pfetzer and Jack Galvin (1998) to find the answer to that question.

Use quotations or excerpts from the book.

"Polar climates are intensely cold and dry with very strong winds. Cold air moves from the poles toward the Equator, helping to stop the Earth from getting too hot. Antarctica is the coldest and windiest place on Earth, with average winter temperatures of −76 degrees Fahrenheit and roaring, ferocious winds of up to 180 (mph) producing blizzards and snow drifts. An unprotected person could freeze solid in minutes." (Taylor, 1999, p. 4)

Read Barbara Taylor's *Pole to Pole* (1999) to find out more.

FIGURE 10.3 Book Talk Examples

Mr. Sandberg conferring with Aaron.

time to learn on their own. Independent reading activities, like reading workshops, should be one of the priorities in your schedule. Figure 10.4 provides a sample reading schedule that incorporates a reading workshop in a balanced reading program.

Facilitating book selection.   Teachers of Early Readers spend a great deal of effort trying to match the difficulty of books to a student's ability to read. This strategy is appropriate for students who are learning to read. For those intermediate-grade students who are reading independently, however, you'll need to facilitate book selection in other ways. At times, students should read books that are "just right" for their reading ability, but at other times, students may want to read books that are easy or difficult. Interpretive Readers tend to match the content of the book to their interests rather than matching books to their reading ability.

Intermediate-grade students are developing reading habits during independent reading that could last through their lives. Think about the independent reading that you do. You probably read books on a variety of subjects that encompass different reading levels. During reading workshop you should give students the same leeway in book selection as adult readers have. However, if you notice a student who is always reading a book that is too difficult or too easy, you should steer that student toward books that are more appropriate.

Reading workshop is based on the premise that students need to use reading for their own purposes. How does reading workshop fit social constructivist learning theories?

Monday	Tuesday	Wednesday	Thursday	Friday
SSR 15 minutes	Whole-class strategy lesson	SSR 15 minutes	Whole-class strategy lesson	SSR 15 minutes
Whole-class strategy lesson	Small-group skill lessons	Whole-class strategy lesson	Small-group skill lessons	Whole-class strategy lesson
Novel study or basal reader lesson	Reading workshop 30 minutes	Novel study or basal reader lesson	Reading workshop 30 minutes	Novel study or basal reader lesson

SSR = sustained silent reading.

FIGURE 10.4   Sample Reading Schedule

Series books.   Many intermediate-grade students "discover" series books by third grade and will want to read books from a specific series for reading workshop. Many of the series books have plots that interest students at this age, and you shouldn't discourage students from reading these books during reading workshop. You want students to read according to their own choices during this time, not books that you have selected. However, sometimes students stick with a book series because they are unfamiliar with other books to read. In that case, you should recommend other books, possibly even other series of books. A list of series books appropriate for intermediate grade students can be found in Figure 10.5.

Structuring reading workshops.   So what happens during reading workshops? Do students simply select books to read? Giving students time to read is certainly a major component of reading workshops, but you should consider other components of reading workshops. First, you should provide students with some sort of class meeting that deals with skills or procedures. These meetings should last only a few minutes and should focus on making the workshop run smoothly. For example, you might need to give students tips on how to select books appropriate for their needs, or you might focus on classroom rules during workshop. In any case, you need to set the stage for workshops so that they are successful.

After spending a few minutes giving directions or instructions in a class meeting, you should give students a significant amount of time to read silently. Some teachers allow students to read any place in the room or in a nearby hall, whereas others ask students to sit at their desks. As a new teacher, you should begin with procedures that make workshop successful for you and your students. You can adjust the rules as you go.

Because purposes for literacy are intensely personal, many students work alone during the time to read, but some students may also choose to read in small groups. For example, say you are teaching a class of 29 fourth graders. Perhaps 6 students are interested in reading the Harry Potter series, 5 students are interested in reading Nancy Drew books, and the remaining students have their own individual reading interests. During reading workshop time, the students who want to read Harry Potter or Nancy Drew books might meet to read together, to share books, or to discuss the books they have read.

Title	Author
A Series of Unfortunate Events	Lemony Snicket
Amelia Bedelia	Peggy Parish
American Girls	Pleasant Company
American Sisters	Laurie Lawlor
Animal Ark	Ben M. Baglio
Animal Emergency	Emily Costello
Arthur	Marc Brown
Bailey School Kids	Debbie Dadey
Beezy	Megan McDonald
Cam Jansen	David Adler
Chip Hilton Sports Series	Coach Clair Bee
Commander Toad	Jane Yolen
Dear America	Various authors
Dinotopia	Various authors
Dinoverse	Scott Ciencia
Frog and Toad	Arnold Lobel
Goosebumps	R. L. Stine
Hank the Cowboy	John R. Erickson
Hardy Boys	Franklin W. Dixon
Henry and Mudge	Cynthia Rylant
Junie B. Jones	Barbara Park
Little House	Laura Ingalls Wilder
Magic Tree House	Mary Pope Osborne
Nancy Drew	Carolyn Keene
Nate the Great	Marjorie Weinman Sharmat
Pee Wee Scouts	Judy Delton
Pinky and Rex	James Howe
Pippi Longstocking	Astrid Ericsson Lindgren
Sailor Moon	Various authors
Sweet Valley Jr. High	Jamie Suzanne
The Amazing Days of Abby Hayes	Anne Mazer
The Baby-Sitters Club	Ann M. Martin
The Boxcar Children	Various authors
The Royal Diaries	Various authors
The Saddle Club	Bonnie Bryant
Thoroughbred	Various authors

FIGURE 10.5 Series Books for Interpretive Readers

Responding Through Writing

As students participate in reading workshops, they should be given the opportunity to respond to their reading through writing. When students respond in writing, they express their thoughts and feelings about the book, the characters, the plot, or any other aspect of the story. Students do not go back to the text to find out more about

Dear Will Hobbs,

 I just read your book, *Wild Man Island*. Boy, was it ever exciting! I chose the book because my teacher said I would like it. He was right! I really liked it because it was set in Alaska. I want to go to Alaska and see a grizzly but my dad keeps saying next year. I was so scared when Andy was going into that cave but I knew he would be all right. I didn't know that he would make such a great discovery (you know what I mean).
 Thanks for writing such an awesome book.

From,
Ryan

FIGURE 10.6   Letter to Author

Reader response is an instructional application of the transactional theory of reading. How do other comprehension strategies apply to the transactional theory of reading?

what the author has written about the character, nor do they make inferences about characters. Instead of looking to the author for illumination, students look within themselves. Asking students to respond personally to their reading promotes reading comprehension and is an appropriate type of reading instruction to provide to the entire class.

Letters to authors.   One way to have students respond to a text is to have them write a letter to the author of the book—even if the author is no longer living. Students write to the author and express their personal feelings about the book, and tell the author how the book affected them (Figure 10.6). Students need not send the letters; writing a personal response is the aim of the lesson. According to Moutray, Pollard, and McGinley (2001) who analyzed 3,600 student-generated letters to authors, "when students are encouraged to think by engaging in reader response activities, teachers are promoting exploration for understanding and clarification of attitudes" (p. 34). The authors continue: "letter and journal writing provide expressive formats for students to explore texts, themselves, and life" (p. 34).

YOU TRY IT

Letter to Authors

As the authors of this text, we care very much what you are thinking and feeling as you read this book. We wrote this book so you could learn how to become a terrific teacher of reading, but we also care how this book makes you feel. To experience writing a letter to an author, please write to us. Tell us your thoughts, feelings, and the concerns you have as you read this textbook. Feel free to send your letters to us at the addresses listed in our biographies.

Two-column response chart.   When students read, they often come to parts of the text that they could comment on, but they don't have the chance. Frequently, the books that students read for school are the school's property, and students can't

Book *Molly's Route 66 Adventure*

Quotations from the book	My response
In the cave, a guide led us along underground passages lit by thousands of tiny lights.	Boy, would I like to see this cave. I've never been to a cave. I'll bet it's scary but WAY COOL!
We almost got hit by a tornado!	How amazing! We don't have tornadoes where I live. Did it sound like a train?
I held my breath every time a bucking bronco threw a rider.	I know what you mean. Rodeos are great fun but people do get hurt.
I got LOTS of kicks on Route 66.	It sounds like a fun vacation. I'm going to ask my parents to take me!

Quotations from American Girl. (2002). Molly's Route 66 Adventure. Middleton, WI: Pleasant Company.

FIGURE 10.7 Two-Column Response Chart

highlight, underline, or record their responses. A two-column response chart (Oll-mann, 1992) provides a place for students to record quotations or lines from the story and their response to the statements (Figure 10.7).

Tell students that they can respond to statements from the story using a two-column response chart. Develop and duplicate charts for each student. Model how to use the chart with an example from a book that you are using with your class. Give students several examples before asking them to use two-column response charts independently.

Response questions.   When students read without reflecting on the text, they often miss underlying issues of the story. When students have the chance to stop and reflect on their reading, they deepen their understanding, think of questions, and increase their comprehension (Berger, 1996). When given response journals, however, some middle-level students don't know what to write. To prompt the thinking of some students, you can give them a list of response questions to use as they read (Figure 10.8). If you have students use a list of response questions, model how they would use this list and encourage them to add their own ideas.

Technology topic: Making connections to media.   The media and popular culture both influence your students' thinking and views about life (Parsons, 2001). In some ways, viewing media is similar to reading. In both situations, the viewer (or reader) needs to attend to details, make inferences, and draw conclusions. Students, however, rarely think of using comprehension strategies when viewing media. Parsons (2001) suggests that you have students respond to media in the same way they respond to text—through writing.

Encourage students to think about media viewing by having them write in their journals how television programs, movies, or videos they have seen connect to the

1. Why do you think the author wrote this book?
2. How do you picture the author?
3. What would you ask the author if you could?
4. How would you describe the main characters?
5. Would you choose one of the characters to be your friend?
6. How are the characters like your friends or family?
7. How would you change the characters if you could?
8. Which parts of the plot interest you?
9. How does the story make you feel?
10. Which passages of the book are most effective?

FIGURE 10.8   Response Questions

Good readers automatically make connections from the books they read to other aspects of their lives, including media. What connections to media have you made while reading?

books they are reading. (You might need to remind some of your students about topics that are appropriate and inappropriate for discussions in school.) A list of response questions from which students can choose can be found in Figure 10.9.

Assessing Student Progress

Should you assess students during reading workshop? Some teachers prefer to use reading workshop as a time when students read independently and assess student progress in other areas of their reading program. But if you use reading workshops for a large part of your reading program, you should develop some assessment techniques that match the principles of reading workshops.

Classroom Assessment

Reading logs.   Hansen (2001) writes that the role of decisions in both reading and writing is crucial, so one of your assessment strategies could be to assess and scaffold students' decision-making abilities in reading workshop. Reading logs work well to give you a window on the students' decisions about reading. A reading log is simply a record of the books and pages students have read during each reading workshop. You might also provide a column for students to write notes to themselves (Figure 10.10). Each student should record information in their logs at the end of a workshop session. You can collect students' reading logs periodically to learn about student decision making.

The goal of assessment in reading workshop should be to inform your teaching, not to make evaluative decisions. There is a difference. For example, if you have students record the books they have read in a reading log, you learn valuable information. You learn the types of books students select, how difficult the books are, and how long it takes a student to read a book. It would be inappropriate to assign a grade to this information—you can grade students elsewhere. Instead, you might offer suggestions to students about books to read or how to read more quickly (or more slowly). Use the information you get from assessing reading workshop to provide you with instructional information that students need to become better readers.

Classroom Assessment

Conferencing.   A second method of assessing student reading during reading workshop is to hold individual conferences with students during the silent reading time. The goal of conferences is to discuss students' reading choices with them and to learn about students' progress while reading independently. To hold conferences, develop a schedule for each workshop session, conferencing with three or four students each

1. What programs, movies, or videos have you seen recently?
2. Why did you decide to view these programs?
3. What did you like or dislike about them?
4. How was this program like your own world?
5. What theme or message was portrayed from the program?
6. What images were most vivid?
7. What did you feel as you were watching?
8. How would you rate this program? Why?
9. How does this program connect to the book you are reading?

FIGURE 10.9 Connections to Media

Date	Book/Author	Pages Read	Notes
Jan. 12	Lions at Lunchtime Mary Pope Osborne	1-32	This is the fourth Magic Tree House book I've read.
Jan. 13	Lions at Lunchtime Mary Pope Osborne	33-70	I think I'll start a different series.
Jan. 15	Captain Underpants Dav Pilkey	4-93	Cassie said to read this. It's OK.
Jan. 18	Pony Pals Here's my Pony Jeanne Betancourt	1-27	I love this book. It's a new series for me. I'm going to get another one next week.

FIGURE 10.10 Reading Log

time. Keep conferences short—5 minutes should be adequate—and rotate class members so that you conference with each student every few weeks.

During conferences you should talk with students about the books they're reading, perhaps using their reading logs as a reference for discussion. Or, you could have a list of questions prepared similar to those shown in Figure 10.11. Ask the questions and jot down notes, but leave plenty of time for students to volunteer opinions about their reading.

1. What book are you reading now?

2. How did you choose this book?

3. How well do you like this book?

4. How difficult is this book for you?

5. What do you like about this book thus far?

6. Please read a paragraph to me from a page you've already read.

7. Could you retell that paragraph for me?

FIGURE 10.11   Conference Questions for Reading Workshop

ENCOURAGING READING AND WRITING WITH FAMILIES

When students reach the intermediate grades, your communication with parents may change. Often when students reach third or fourth grade, they are given more difficult texts to read and many students are evaluated with letter grades. Parents whose children have experienced success in school may now find that their children are experiencing difficulty. Many parents of students in intermediate grades consider themselves to be active participants in schools; the U.S. Department of Health and Human Services (1998) reports that the parents of 39% of students in grades 3 through 5 are highly involved with their children's learning. However, many parents who have had time to devote to their young children may now find themselves busy with new babies, more time-consuming jobs, or other commitments. Despite the large number of parents who still take an active role in the schooling of their children, the time many other parents are willing to devote to school activities may begin to wane.

Some parents of children in intermediate grades will be more available to assist in the literacy development of their children than others, so Epstein (1997) suggests that intermediate-grade teachers expect parents to vary in their levels of involvement. Think about parents in the ways that you think about the students in your class. Not every student reads the same number of books, writes the same number of stories, or learns in the same way. And you adjust your teaching accordingly. When you think about parental involvement, remember that parents are different too—just as different from each other as are the students in your classroom. Therefore, don't expect all parents to be equally involved with their child's literacy learning.

Parental involvement is, of course, a great boon to their child's learning. The values and skills that parents teach children are beneficial to overall development as

The Smith family reads at the dining room table.

well as to literacy learning (Purcell-Gates, 2000). Some parents, however, may not be used to participating in literacy events with their children. In fact, more parents than ever before have themselves had little or no schooling and have low levels of literacy (Meier, 2000). Therefore, the first step in encouraging reading and writing at home is to learn about the home cultures of your students. As you learn about your students' families, you can encourage your students to read and write more frequently at home; you can involve parents in their children's literacy learning, and you can include parents in school literacy activities.

Involving parents in their children's literacy learning is an important part of a teacher's job. What ideas do you have for working with parents?

Parental Involvement

Parents from all ethnic backgrounds are interested in helping their children succeed in school, and most parents have high expectations for their children (Ada & Zubizarreta, 2001; Moles, 1993). Parents from some cultures, however, have a different perception about parental involvement than you do. You've already learned that parents are important teachers and that a child's literacy experiences in early years lay the foundation for literacy development. You've also learned about the importance of practicing reading and writing at home as well as at school. These perspectives come from a way of looking at literacy—one that is prevalent among teachers in today's society.

Diversity issue: Different perspectives.   All parents teach their children many skills and abilities, some of which deal directly with school learning and some of which do not (Purcell-Gates, 2000). In some cultures, however, parents believe that their job is to teach their children life skills and that it's the school's job to academically educate their children (Rodríguez-Brown, 2001). For example, research indicates that in some families, especially those of newly arrived immigrants, parents believe that they should teach their children to be respectful to elders, to care for family members, and to develop a good character rather than work on literacy (Faltis, 2001). Moreover, some parents don't feel comfortable conversing in English and are intimidated by teachers and schools (Rodríguez-Brown, 2001).

Try to put yourself in the place of these parents. Think of yourself in a country where the customs and the language are different. Many of you know how to speak

Some parents may feel uncomfortable coming to school events and talking with you. How can you make these parents feel more at ease?

a foreign language, say, French. But even if you've taken 4 years of French in high school and 2 years of French in college, you would still make many linguistic blunders if you lived in Paris. Now imagine someone you care about, a child or a younger brother or sister, enrolling in school in Paris. You don't know much about the French school system, you are not truly fluent in the language spoken at school, and you deeply want the child in your care to succeed in her new home and school. Do you think you might feel insecure about your interactions with the child's teachers?

Diversity issue: Oral histories.   As you learn about differing parental expectations, you can take a proactive stance by inviting all parents to become involved with their child's literacy learning by encouraging parents to share oral histories with their children (Ada & Zubizarreta, 2001). To invite parental sharing, send home oral or written questions—in English and in the students' home language—that encourage parents to share their histories with their children. Don't insist that these conversations be in English, though. Any increased amount of language activity in the home, in any language, improves the language base of children. Another idea is to author a personal book yourself, or make a tape recording or videotape, of a story from your life. You can send this story home with children (include a tape player if necessary) as a model. Then encourage parents to tell their stories to their children.

SEE FOR YOURSELF

Oral Histories

Visit the message board for Chapter 10 on our Companion Website at *www.prenhall.com/lenski* to discuss your findings.

Listen to the oral histories presented on the Companion Website *(http://www. prenhall.com/lenski)*. Then develop a story from your own life. Write it as a personal story, tape record it, and post it on the Companion Website. You can include pictures if you wish. After you write your story, include questions or prompts that could facilitate parental storytelling.

Encouraging Students to Read and Write at Home

One of your goals as a teacher will be encouraging your students to love to read and to voluntarily read and write at home. Because reading and writing are skills that take extensive practice, and because there simply is not enough time during the school day for students, they also need to practice reading and writing at home. Sometimes we think of school-related reading and writing as the only valid type of literacy activities that students should do at home. That isn't true. You should encourage your students to read all sorts of materials at home and to write for many different purposes.

Classroom library.   You can encourage reading and writing at home by providing students with short reading books and writing materials that they can take home. It helps to have a classroom library of paperback books from which students can choose. When you get your first teaching job, you might be lucky and inherit a classroom with a large collection of books, but don't count on it. More likely you will

---

- Request books for holiday presents.
- Ask parent organizations for funding.
- Host a paperback book exchange among students.
- Periodically exchange sets of books with colleagues.
- Hold garage sales.
- Visit second-hand bookstores.
- Go to public libraries.
- Attend library book sales.
- Apply for grants.
- Attend publishers' warehouse sales.
- Join book clubs:

Scholastic Book Club, Inc.
P.O. Box 7503
Jefferson City, MO 65102-7503
(800)724-2424

Trumpet Book Club
P.O. Box 6003
Columbia, MO 65205-6003
(800)826-0110

Troll Book Clubs
100 Corporate Drive
Mahwah, NJ 07430
(800)929-8765

FIGURE 10.12   Obtaining Reading Materials

need to develop the library yourself. You can order inexpensive books through school book clubs. Typically when you order a set amount of books, you also receive bonus points that you can use to order free books and other classroom materials. When you're a teacher, you can also ask your students whether they want to purchase books from these book clubs. Many students love ordering books, and their orders help you develop a classroom library. Additional methods of developing a classroom library are listed in Figure 10.12.

Home literacy activities.   Another way to encourage reading and writing at home is to help students identify the types of reading and writing they do as a matter of course in their lives. You'll be surprised and so will your students when you consider all of the reading and writing that students do at home. Figure 10.13 details a partial list of home reading and writing activities. Post the list on a display, encourage students to become aware of their home reading and writing, and ask them to add items to the list when they think of more ways they read and write at home.

Involving Parents in Their Children's Literacy Learning

It's important to encourage your students to read and write at home, but you also want parents to become involved in their children's literacy learning. Parental modeling can work wonders. However, some parents aren't used to reading with their children and may find it stressful. Some parents may view reading with their children as an added responsibility and may even find it a totally foreign concept. For example, some parents come from countries where children's literature is scarce so they are unfamiliar with the concept of children's books (Janes & Kermani, 2001).

Reading at Home	Writing at Home
Recipes	Messages
Grocery coupons	Directions
Video game directions	Letters and notes
Newspapers	E-mail
Credits at the beginning or end of movies	Lists
Letters	
E-mail	
TV guide	
Music	
Shopping lists	
Menus	
Bus schedules	
Labels on food containers	

FIGURE 10.13   Reading and Writing at Home

Having students write their own newsletters gives them the opportunity to reflect on their week's activities and what they've learned. How does this activity illustrate social constructivist theories?

Newsletters.   There are many ways you can encourage parents to play an active role in their child's literacy development. First, you need to continue communicating with parents about their child's schooling. You learned about sending home newsletters to children in the primary grades, and this activity is also appropriate for intermediate-grade children. Figure 10.14 shows a copy of a newsletter written by Josh Ames for the parents of her fifth-grade students at Sunny Lake Elementary School. Some teachers send home weekly newsletters that they develop, but if you are teaching students in grades 3 through 5 you can also ask them to write the newsletter. Some teachers develop a framework for the newsletter and ask different students to type or print news articles about different activities in the columns. If you have many students that speak a language different from English, you should include sections in the children's home languages. However, you also need to have an older student or an adult translate those sections for you, so you're sure the students have accurately summarized the classroom activities. At the end of the week, you can read the newsletter and edit it a final time. Then have copies made and send the newsletter home, either on Friday afternoon or early in the next week.

Public libraries.   You can involve parents in their child's literacy learning in many other ways. For example, you might take a field trip to the pubic library and invite parents to attend. Call the library first to find out the paperwork necessary for applying for library cards. Send home a note carefully explaining the rules for obtaining library cards and informing parents about the documents they'll need. If parents are recent immigrants and don't have the required documents, explain to them that they can bring their children to the library to read books there. When parents arrive at the library, have a librarian provide a tour of the children's section and other sections of interest. Hand out library card applications and help parents complete the forms if necessary. Encourage your students and parents to visit the library regularly.

Sunny Lake Elementary

Mr. Ames' 5th Grade Reading Newsletter

Dear parents,

It has been a joy getting to know your children throughout the first few weeks of class. Our goal as a class is to generate strong friendships that develop and grow during the year. Thank-you for the support and time you have put in to starting the year off right.

The purpose of this newsletter is to give you a snapshot of the 5th grade literacy program. Reading is an integral part of all subjects areas, therefore I am informing you of what I believe is to be the best way to teach reading. In this newsletter you will find:

*My philosophy of reading
*Components of a balanced literacy program
*Effective reading strategies for your child
*A+ book list
*Reading websites for you and your child

A+ Book List

Check out these awesome books. They will get your child ready for our upcoming units.

Island of the Blue Dolphin, O'Dell Scott

A Year Down Yonder, Richard Peck

Hatchet, Gary Paulsen

Cells, Wonder World

Jackie Robinson Breaks the Color Line, Andrew Santella

More Perfect Union: The Story of our Constitution, Betsy & Giulio Maestro

---

My philosophy

"A child who does not read has no advantage over a child who cannot read."   - Anonymous

as had a tremendous affect on the way I view reading. I truly believe that when we read we are setting the groundwork for our future learning experiences. There are many things that happen in our mind when we read. At a young age we start to develop our own reading strategies. As we develop as readers our minds construct meaning when we read, the construction of meaning (comprehension) should be the number one goal for all readers. When we start to comprehend we then can enjoy what we read.

Furthermore, reading is developed through practice. Tiger Woods did not get where he is today without discipline and practice; the same can be said about reading. The more you read, the more you know. As your grow and develop as a reader you are preparing your mind for future learning experiences.

Literature Circles

One way that your child will be engaged in interactive reading with their classmates is through literature circles. Literature circles are small discussion groups of students that have chosen to read the same book. The groups will be meeting regularly throughout the week. The type of discussion that goes on will bring meaning to what they read. Different interpretations and perspectives will enhance your child's knowledge and learning experience. We will be reading the book *Dear Mr. Henshaw*, by Beverly Cleary as a read-aloud to introduce the students to lit circle and the components of the circles. A great website to check out is http://fac-staff.seattleu.edu/kschinoe/litcircles/index.html. This will allow you to explore more about literature circles.

Reading Websites

www.scholastic.com
This is a very interactive website that is useful for you and your child. There are tips for smart parenting, book lists, book characters and you can even order books online.

www.ala.org
The American Library Association offers a wide range of topics. By clicking on, "Kids, Parents and the Public," you will be able to access the Newberry Award list, Caldecott list, reading websites and more!

www.isbe.state.il.us
Parents, this website is for you. The Illinois State Board of Education offers statewide school report cards. Check out Sunny Lake Elementary's reading scores!

www.beverlycleary.com
This site will give your child an in-depth look at Beverly Cleary's characters, her life, and fun games. Check out the character report on Leigh from *Dear Mr. Henshaw*.

www.amazon.com
This is a great site to read reviews on books, even order them. I recommend this site because of prices.

www.magickeys.com/books/
This site is wonderful for the student reader. Your child can read stories off the internet, with illustrations. It also offers riddles, mazes, and pages they can print off.

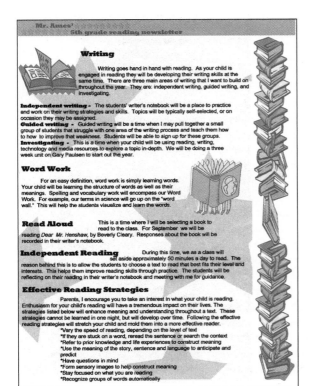

Writing

Writing goes hand in hand with reading. As your child is engaged in reading they will be developing their writing skills at the same time. There are three main areas of writing that I want to build on throughout the year. They are: independent writing, guided writing, and investigating.

Independent writing - The students' writer's notebook will be a place to practice and work on their writing strategies and skills. Topics will be typically self-selected, or on occasion they may be assigned.

Guided writing - Guided writing will be a time when I may pull together a small group of students that struggle with one area of the writing process and teach them how to how to improve that weakness. Students will be able to sign up for these groups.

Investigating - This is a time when your child will be using reading, writing, technology and media resources to explore a topic in-depth. We will be doing a three week unit on Gary Paulsen to start out the year.

Word Work

For an easy definition, word work is simply learning words. Your child will be learning the structure of words as well as their meanings. Spelling and vocabulary work will encompass our Word Work. For example, our terms in science will go up on the "word wall." This will help the students visualize and learn the words.

Read Aloud

This is a time where I will be selecting a book to read to the class. For September we will be reading *Dear Mr. Henshaw*, by Beverly Cleary. Responses about the book will be recorded in their writer's notebook.

Independent Reading

During this time, we as a class will set aside approximately 50 minutes a day to read. The reason behind this is to allow the students to choose a text to read that best fits their level and interests. This helps them improve reading skills through practice. The students will be reflecting on their reading in their writer's notebook and meeting with me for guidance.

Effective Reading Strategies

Parents, I encourage you to take an interest in what your child is reading. Enthusiasm for your child's reading will have a tremendous impact on their lives. The strategies listed below will enhance meaning and understanding throughout a text. These strategies cannot be learned in one night, but will develop over time. Following the effective reading strategies will stretch your child and mold them into a more effective reader.

*Vary the speed of reading, depending on the level of text
*If they are stuck on a word, reread the sentence or search the context
*Refer to prior knowledge and life experiences to construct meaning
*Use the meaning of the story, sentence and language to anticipate and predict
*Have questions in mind
*Form sensory images to help construct meaning
*Stay focused on what you are reading
*Recognize groups of words automatically

FIGURE 10.14   Sample Newsletter

From Josh Ames, Sunny Lake Elementary School.

Include Parents in School Literacy Activities

Your day will be filled with literacy activities, and many of these activities can include parents. Inviting parents to participate in school literacy activities motivates intermediate-grade students to excel. Parents love to see their children perform, so you might have informal poetry readings, Readers Theatre, or short plays where you can invite parents. Once again, however, some parents may not be comfortable coming to the traditional types of school activities, such as performances, parent–teacher conferences, and curriculum nights. These types of activities are steeped in typical white middle-class discourse practices and may be threatening to some parents (Edwards & Danridge, 2001). If the parents of your students have low attendance at typical school functions, think of ways in which you can provide a less threatening way for parents to become involved in school literacy activities.

Parent programs.   One successful program that teachers have used is to invite parents to school a half hour before school begins for "Muffins with Mom" or "Donuts with Dad." At these short meetings you can encourage parents to read with their children and show them the types of chapter books that are appropriate for students in grades 3 through 5. Another idea is to recruit a few willing parents to act as leaders and to contact parents and invite them to the school. Have a leader provide transportation for the new parent or have them meet the parent at the school door. Then offer both parents coffee and escort them to your classroom. Informally give the parents a classroom tour and show them their children's desks. Give the parents your school telephone number and the times you can be reached. Some schools have refrigerator magnets with these numbers. Encourage the parents to contact you and to visit again.

CONNECTIONS: WHAT'S NEXT?

You've learned in this chapter that Interpretive Readers may need you to encourage them to read so that they continue to love reading throughout the intermediate grades. You can promote motivation to read through a variety of intrinsic and extrinsic activities, but especially through activities that encourage students to choose their own books and read independently. Most Interpretive Readers will be fairly fluent readers by this point and will have enormous numbers of interesting books that they will be able to read. Your job as a teacher will be to direct students to books that interest them and to give them time to read during school.

Another important component of Interpretive Readers' literacy learning is reading and writing outside of school. Many families are supportive of their children's literacy development and will work with you to help their children learn. As you work with families, it's important to know that you need to learn about the parents (or guardians) of your students as well as provide parents with ideas to endorse reading and writing at home. You can see how this information fits with other things you've learned by looking at the framework in Figure 10.15.

This chapter concludes the part on Interpretive Readers. The next part, beginning with Chapter 11, describes the development of middle level students who we call Critical Readers. Critical Readers are students that are in middle school or junior high school. You can use what you've learned about Early Readers and Interpretive Readers with these older students, but you will also learn about the development and additional instructional strategies that are especially appropriate for Critical Readers in Part IV.

FIGURE 10.15 A Developmental Approach to the Teaching of Reading

	Early Readers	**Interpretive Readers**	**Critical Readers**
Theories underscored as readers develop:	Social Constructivism Psycholinguistic Critical Transactional	Social Constructivism Psycholinguistic Critical Transactional	Social Constructivism Psycholinguistic Critical Transactional
Whole-group instruction through:	• Read-alouds • Shared texts • Comprehension strategies • Working with words	• Read-alouds • Using basals • Literature-based models • Word-building strategies • Comprehension strategies	• Read-alouds • Common texts (e.g., basals, anthologies, trade books) • Comprehension strategies • Vocabulary instruction and word analysis • Researching • Critical reading • Reading content area texts • Studying and note-taking
Assessment ideas for whole group:	• Observations • Kidwatching • Anecdotal notation	• Portfolios • Open-ended questions • Rubrics	• Written retellings • Research projects • Interest inventories • Content-area histories • Cloze procedure
Small-group instruction through:	• Guided reading • Teaching for strategies • Working with words	• Basal readers • Literature anthologies • Fluency practice • Guided silent reading • Literature circles • Inquiry groups	• Book clubs • Trade books
Assessment ideas for small groups:	• Running Records • Retellings • Discussions with children	• Names test • Fluency checklist • Peer assessment • Inquiry rubric	• Student information card • Bio poem • "I Used to… But Now I…" poem • Observational checklist • Student self-assessment • Norm-referenced tests

continued

FIGURE 10.15   *Continued*

	Early Readers	Interpretive Readers	Critical Readers
Independent learning through:	• Independent reading • Reading/writing workshop • Making books • Reading the room	• Independent reading • Reading/writing workshop • Responding through writing • Reading logs	• Sustained silent reading and writing
Sociocultural contexts:	• Literacy partnerships with parents • Parents in the classroom • Home–school communication	• Reading/writing connection for life • Oral histories • Home literacy activities • Parent programs	• Parents as coaches • Funds of knowledge • Parent–student book clubs

FOR YOUR PORTFOLIO

Companion Website

ENTRY 10.1   *Communicating to Different Audiences*

IRA/NCTE Standard 4 states: *Students adjust their use of spoken, written, and visual language (e.g., conventions, style, vocabulary) to communicate effectively with a variety of audiences and for different purposes.*

You learned a variety of strategies and activities in the chapters in Part III that encourage students to tailor their language to their audience. Some examples are multigenre research papers, letters to authors, responses to literature, and so on.

Develop a chart that lists the different strategies that you're learning that include some aspect of communication, write a short definition for the strategy, explain its purposes, list its audience, and gauge the formality of its writing style. Be prepared to explain your chart to your peers. An example follows.

Strategy or Activity	Definition	Purposes	Audience	Style
Letter to author	To write a letter to an author of a book I've read	To learn more about the author and to ask questions about the writing of the book	The author	Letter format Moderately formal Educated vocabulary

ENTRY 10.2 *Topical Lists of Books*

IRA/NCTE Standard 2 states: *Students read a wide range of literature from many periods in many genres to build an understanding of the many dimensions (e.g., philosophical, ethical, aesthetic) of human experience.*

In order for students to read a wide range of literature, they need time to read through independent reading, reading workshops, and reading at home. In addition, they need a teacher who is familiar with many types of literature at their age level.

Use your knowledge of children's literature to develop topical lists of books appropriate for Interpretive Readers. For example, many students in intermediate grades are interested in individual and team sports. Develop lists of books about such sports as basketball, soccer, figure skating, and climbing. Use several different genres (i.e., biographies, adventure, informational) to develop your lists.

TO LEARN MORE

Helpful Websites

Companion Website

Visit our Companion Website at *http://www.prenhall.com/lenski* to link to the following sites:

Independent Reading

Gives an explanation of independent reading.
http://www.eduplace.com/rdg/res/literacy/in_read3.html

Authors and Illustrators

Gives information about authors and illustrators who are popular with children.
http://www/clau.org/authatof.htm

International Reading Association

This website for reading professionals contains links to several parent brochures and pamphlets.
http://www.reading.org

Parental Involvement

Provides several links to ideas that teachers can use to connect with parents regarding their children's education.
http://www.ameritech.com/education/technology/products.html

Teacher's Role

Includes a large section on parental involvement and the teacher's role with links to abstracts of articles.
http://www.indiana.edu/~eric_rec/leo/digests/d115.html

Hard to Reach Parents

Offers a transcript that deals with reaching the hard to reach parent. Large resource of ideas with several links.
http://www.nea.org/heatoday/9710/chat.html

When you think about teaching reading, you probably picture yourself teaching *young* children to read. The images that come to your mind might be of teaching the alphabet or of reading aloud to children sitting on a rug. You might think that only young children or older struggling readers need reading instruction in schools, but that's not so. All middle level readers still need reading instruction (Humphrey, 2002).

Many of the students who reach the middle level can read at a basic level. In fact, the National Assessment of Educational Progress (NAEP), a national test given to students in grades 4, 8, and 12, indicated that more than 60% of the eighth-grade students tested could read at a basic level (Donahue, Voelkl, Campbell, & Mazzeo, 1999). While the NAEP scores show that the majority of middle level students are able to read at a basic level, the scores also reveal that a good number of middle level readers still need instruction in reading. Basic reading isn't sufficient for the 21st century when citizens need to read complex texts—from tax documents to important health information (Rand Study Group, 2002). Although high levels of literacy are needed for all students, the NAEP scores indicate that only 4% of eighth-grade students can read at an advanced level. Indeed, the case for teaching reading in the middle level has never been stronger.

Because we believe that middle level students have been overlooked in teacher preparation programs, we've given middle level students the same attention in this text as we've given Early and Interpretive Readers. We use the term *Critical Readers* for students in the sixth through eighth grades because one of the goals for middle level literacy is the ability to read critically, not just to interpret text. Critical Readers, you will find, need a different type of instruction than do their younger counterparts. Although Critical Readers also need to read in whole groups, small groups, independently, and with their families, the percentage of time middle level teachers spend teaching in each of these areas differs from that of younger students. Moreover, Critical Readers spend a large part of their day reading informational text and content-area materials. Therefore, we've organized this part a bit differently. We begin by discussing the developmental aspects of middle level students as we did with the other groups, but because middle level teachers spend most of their time teaching to the entire group, we spend two chapters discussing whole-group instruction: One deals with fictional texts and the other with content-area instruction. Then because middle level teachers do not spend much time instructing in small groups, we discuss small-group instruction along with independent reading and reading with families.

Meet Linda Wedwick

Novice Middle School Teacher

Linda has been teaching seventh-grade language arts for 2 years. She teaches four classes, each in a 75-minute block. Her language arts classes are integrated with the seventh-grade social studies teacher, so she teaches a great deal of content-area reading and writing. Linda also makes time for reading and writing workshops, an approach that she thinks is important in middle level classes. Throughout this part, Linda answers questions you might pose about teaching at the middle level. In addition, here she shares with you her thoughts about teaching Critical Readers.

Middle Level Students Need Choices!

Linda believes that one of the most important pieces of advice she can give a new teacher is to give students choices. Linda tries to give her students choices wherever she can. In the part of her class that she integrates with the social studies teacher, Linda tries to give students choices about which historical novels they will read, the research that she assigns, and the group projects that she gives. Student choice is one of the reasons Linda has implemented reading and writing workshops. During workshops, students can choose (with her guidance) the books that they read and the types of writings that they compose. In addition, Linda tries to provide her students with frequent independent reading and writing times. She tries to give students extended time to read or write at least twice a week.

Theory Needs to Align With Practice

Before Linda began teaching, she got a master's degree, and she feels as if she received a solid foundation in the theories of literacy learning. Linda espouses constructivist theories, and she tries to model her teaching practices according to her beliefs. For example, during reading workshop, Linda asks students to respond to their reading in journals, which she reads. She asks students to respond personally to books as well as to understand the elements of fiction. Linda also expects students to discuss books beyond the literal level. She wants them to experience texts deeply, to compare books in meaningful ways, and to talk about books passionately.

Hot Tip: Know Young Adult Literature

Linda said that if she could give a new teacher one hot tip it would be to know young adult literature. Middle level students are extremely aware of their teacher's knowledge of books and love of reading, and they respond to their teacher's attitude toward reading. Linda loves to read and spends some time every week reading young adult literature. She keeps a list of the books that she reads and uses the list to give book talks and to recommend books to students. One of Linda's goals for all of her students is to love reading by the time they're finished with the first semester. She believes her knowledge of books helps her achieve this goal.

chapter

Developing Your Knowledge About Critical Readers

Essential Learning Questions

- In what ways do middle level students grow and change?
- What is *critical literacy* and how does it apply to middle level readers?
- What strategies do Critical Readers use while reading?
- How can middle level teachers differentiate instruction to meet the needs of *all* of their students?
- Why is motivation an important issue for middle level teachers?

The early teen years were not long ago for many of you, so you may have recent memories of what it's like to experience the transition between childhood and adulthood. As you read this chapter you may be able to relate to many of the experiences of this age group and some of the knowledge about what classroom instruction should look like. However, much of the information in this chapter will be new to you. Middle level instruction is rapidly changing as more teachers leave behind traditional instruction that is based on behaviorist models and as they begin to embrace social constructivism. In classrooms where teachers base their instruction on social constructivist principles, students use their literacy skills to learn from text and also to address issues of social justice (Bean, 2000). Teaching critical reading for social justice may not have been part of your schooling, but it is now part of many middle level classrooms.

The organization of schooling typically is different for early adolescents than it is for younger students. Young children are often schooled in self-contained classrooms, but when students reach the middle level, they frequently attend middle schools. Middle schools house students in grades 6 through 8, but they may also contain fifth-grade or ninth-grade students. In middle schools, early adolescents experience a different kind of schooling: a greater number of teachers, departmentalization, less access to teachers, more extracurricular activities, and larger numbers of students.

To understand how to teach students in middle level grades, or what we have termed *Critical Readers,* you will need to review what you know about the developmental changes of early adolescents, reader response and critical literacy theories, acknowledging differences among students, and issues of motivation.

 Visit the online journal in Chapter 11 on our Companion Website at *www.prenhall.com/lenski* to answer these questions. Save your answers to your hard drive or to a disk to compile an online journal.

Social justice is a concept that encourages equality and fairness for all people. In what ways should the advance of social justice be part of a literacy program?

UNDERSTANDING CRITICAL READERS

When students reach their early adolescent years, or ages 10–15, they begin a time of rapid growth and change. It is during these years when most young people enter puberty, sparking a series of changes unlike any other in their lives. As adolescents enter puberty, they begin experiencing physical, emotional, social, and intellectual changes. The changes that occur cause inconsistencies in students that take even seasoned teachers by surprise. A student may act mature, focused, and responsible one day only to act irresponsibly another day. A student who can grasp an abstract concept one day may have difficulty understanding simple ideas the next. And a student who wants to be treated as an adult may at times revert to childlike behavior. Early adolescents are in the transition time between childhood and adulthood, and that transition is rarely a smooth one. The onslaught of hormones associated with puberty causes inconsistent, even bizarre, behavior in many students.

The changes that students face during early adolescence dictate reading instruction that is responsive to their specific needs. To meet their needs, you first should access your current knowledge of the physical, emotional, social, and intellectual development that characterizes early adolescents, and learn how to teach Critical Readers during this time.

Physical and Emotional Development

The most noticeable change that early adolescents experience is their physical development. Between the ages of 10 and 14, most adolescents enter puberty, or the time when they move from childhood to adulthood. As students enter puberty, they experience growth spurts and gain height, weight, and muscular strength. Many youths grow between 2 and 4 inches and gain 10 pounds or more per year (Van Hoose & Strahan, 1988). Some youngsters grow so fast that they become awkward and gangly. As adolescents grow, they develop adult bodies, capable of reproduction. These physical changes cause many young teens to be overly aware of their bodies, even obsessed with their looks.

Many young teens use reading to make sense of the physical changes that are occurring to them. Novels with characters who are experiencing physical change and growth or who are obsessed with their looks provide young adolescents with characters with whom they can identify. Novels also present story lines with the conflicts and problems that teenagers experience, and, more importantly, they provide a variety of ways to resolve problems. Many teens use novels as sources of information as they search for ways of coping with new body images. Coming-of-age novels that address the developing bodies of young teens and some of the issues common to adolescents can be found in Figure 11.1.

Energy level.   As middle level students enter puberty and acquire adult physical characteristics, their bodies experience rapid hormonal changes. The flooding of hormones in the body causes adrenaline to be released in large quantities (Robinson, 1998). At these times, the students are bursting with energy and need to move. At other times, students are lethargic, also a function of hormonal changes. During these times, students become easily fatigued. Because early adolescents alternate be-

Bennett, C. (1998). *Life in the fat lane.* New York: Delacorte.

Blume, J. (1970). *Are you there God: It's me, Margaret.* New York: Dell/Yearling.

Blume, J. (1971). *Then again, maybe I won't.* New York: Bradbury.

Byars, B. (1993). *Pinballs.* New York: HarperCollins.

Creech, S. (1997). *Absolutely normal chaos.* New York: HarperCollins.

Haddix, M. P. (2001). *The girl with 500 middle names.* New York: Scholastic.

Howe, J. (2001). *Misfits.* New York: Atheneum.

Naylor, P. R. (2001). *The grooming of Alice.* New York: Aladdin.

Ryan, P. M. (2000). *Esperanza rising.* New York: Scholastic.

Van Praunen, W. (2001). *Flipped.* New York: Alfred A. Knopf.

FIGURE 11.1   Coming-of-Age Novels

tween boundless energy and draining fatigue, teachers need to create flexible lesson plans that encompass different activities.

Teachers shouldn't expect middle level students to sit quietly during a 40-minute class period. Early adolescents need variety, but they also need a teacher who is sensitive to their energy levels. For example, imagine yourself as a seventh-grade teacher. The students have just read *Stargirl* by Jerry Spinelli (2000), and you have prepared probing questions that you hope will lead to a rousing class discussion. You're excited about this class, anticipating an enjoyable class period listening to students take sides and argue their points. You meet the class at the door, and as you welcome each student to your reading class, you notice the students are dragging themselves into class, staring listlessly ahead. A few students are their typical enthusiastic selves, but as a whole, the class is unnaturally quiet. You try to raise the students' energy levels by your questioning, but your attempts fall flat. After several minutes of trying to engage students' interests, you recognize that the lesson you have prepared does not match the needs of your class. At this time, you can choose to become frustrated with the students, or you can change your plans and try your initial idea another time.

Related emotional changes.

The physical changes that early adolescents experience trigger all sorts of emotional changes, and hormonal fluctuations cause new emotions. Teens lack the experience to control these new feelings so they tend to be moody, easily offended, and sensitive to criticism. As the bodies of young teens steadily mature, their emotions range erratically from calm and tranquil to unsettled, angry, and belligerent. One thing you can be certain of when working with middle level students is that their emotions will be unpredictable. Robinson (1998) describes middle level students as a "walking set of opposites." Small events can trigger major bouts of insecurity, depression, and even suicide. Irvin (1998) states that middle level students entering puberty have erratic and inconsistent behavior that results from anxiety and fear. Feelings of inferiority swing to superiority in a matter of moments.

Developmentally appropriate instruction.

We often hear about designing developmentally appropriate instruction for Early Readers, but rarely do we read about ways to develop instruction that fits the needs of middle level readers. Armed with knowledge about the physical development of middle level readers, you can design instruction that is both fun to teach and appropriate for young adolescents. For example, some educators recommend a cross-age tutoring program to address literacy needs of struggling middle level learners (Jacobson et al., 2001). In this program, the researchers paired 21 seventh-grade students who needed assistance in reading with small groups of third-grade students. The middle-grade students were taught reading strategies that they, in turn, taught the younger students using grade-appropriate texts. This program was successful for the middle-grade students, and was also beneficial for the younger students.

Cross-grade tutoring illustrates ways in which teachers can design instruction that acknowledges the physical and emotional development of early adolescents. With this program, students moved to another location to tutor, which gave them the opportunity to physically move. More importantly, however, the teens were engaged in a meaningful activity (helping young children) and were in control of the situation. They were not passively listening to a teacher describe reading strategies; they were learning, talking, and teaching. These activities allowed for self-directed movement.

You might think that because reading is a cognitive activity that it's not possible to incorporate physical activity into reading classes. In one sense, that's correct. Reading

At times the energy level of middle level students will not match your lesson. What are some ways in which you can respond to such a situation?

Emily and Hannah learn through reading with Cassidy and Brianna.

does not expend the energy that playing basketball does. There are many ways, however, in which you can design instruction so that students can move around or at least have some control over their movements. Some additional activities that offer physical movement are Readers Theatre, literature circles, Book Clubs, and dramatization.

Social Development

Socialization is one of the developmental tasks of early adolescents. During the teen years, young people need to learn how to relate to peers of the same and opposite sex, achieve a gendered social role, create emotional independence from parents and other adults, and prepare for career options (Swanson, Spencer, & Petersen, 1998). As teens develop their own identity, they reconsider the values of their families and society in general, test choices, and try different roles. At this time, young people begin to develop their own style of dress and experiment with different looks. Early adolescents begin to identify with groups that have formed in and out of school and merge their individual identity with the characteristics of the group.

Experimentation with identity roles is important for adolescents. At this age students begin to see themselves as important people outside of their family unit and are trying out ideas that will eventually form the basis for their own identity. For the first time in their development, young teens are able to consider alternative perspectives and acknowledge a variety of points of view (Brown & Theobald, 1998). The ability of middle level students to take other views into account coupled with their desire for self-determination leads them to question societal, family, and school traditions and to develop their own social groups.

As students bond with social groups, peer pressure becomes more intense. The importance of peers has been publicized in the last decade; however, both sides of that story haven't been told. Researchers have made some startling discoveries about the influence of peers. Adolescents are certainly more influenced by their peers than are younger children. As teens mature and develop their own social roles, they begin to form an identity separate from their parents' identities. This leads to a certain amount of differentness, and even rebellion. However, families also influence young teens. Researchers Brown and Theobald (1998) distributed a survey to 1,000 middle and high school students and asked what they considered to be the best thing about school. The answers of 7th- and 8th-grade students indicated that peers and academics were equally important. By 9th grade, however, the importance of peers considerably surpassed that of academics, but by 11th grade peers and academics evened out once more. Irvin (1998) concluded that "peer groups usually reinforce rather than contradict the values of parents. . . . Young adolescents tend to form friendships similar to the relationships they have with their families" (p. 19).

Families and adults are important to teens, but Csikszentmihalyi and Schmidt (1998) report that young people spend very little time with their families, and even smaller amounts of time with their fathers. "Typical American adolescents spend only three minutes a day alone with their fathers, and half of that time is spent watching television" (p. 11). Because so little time is spent with other adults, the role of teachers becomes more important. Csikszentmihalyi and Schmidt continue: "The only adults many teenagers encounter on a sustained basis are teachers" (p. 12). Teachers, therefore, can play a key role in helping young teens develop positive social relationships.

Advice for New Teachers

Group Work

Dear Linda,

I understand that middle level students need to socialize, but I'm worried that if I let them talk with each other, they'll spend all of their time off task. Do you have any suggestions?

Dear New Teacher,

I had the same concern when I started teaching last year. One of my biggest worries was "controlling" the class. I'll admit that during the first few weeks of school I didn't allow the students to work in groups, but then I noticed that the students weren't volunteering much in class discussions. So I told them I was going to give them time to discuss in groups, but that I would expect them to stay on topic. That first time I divided them into groups, I walked around the room making sure that the conversations stayed close to the topic, and I was amazed at how rich their discussions were. I now trust my students to talk together, but I occasionally nudge them back to topic if they stray.

Reading workshops were discussed in Chapter 10 and are appropriate for students of all ages. In what ways can reading workshops promote the socialization of middle level students?

Using peer pressure.   Knowing about the social needs of early adolescents can help you become an effective middle level teacher. Young teens need much attention from the adults in their lives, but they also need time to develop relationships with their peers. You can use this knowledge as you develop a reading program for your middle level students. Williams (2001a), for example, implemented a reading workshop approach with her middle level readers. In developing her reading workshop, Williams had students read books independently at their own level, read with partners, share summaries of books with other students, and predict outcomes in groups. Connecting the social nature of young teens to a literacy activity promotes both socialization and literacy.

Another way you can use peer pressure to your advantage is to provide students with ample time to share books they have read. Middle level learners are more likely to read a book recommended by a peer than a book recommended by an adult. Therefore, as a middle school teacher, you might consider developing activities with your middle level students to share favorite books with each other.

Emphasizing popular culture.   Teenagers develop their own cultures, separate cultures from society at large. These cultures are distinguished by music, art, fashion, and media. You can use popular culture to invite middle level learners into the culture of literacy (Alvermann, Moon, & Hagood, 1999; Stevens, 2001). Of course, you have to be careful when you use popular culture in the classroom that you don't expose students to violence or sex. You can, however, use popular forms of media, such as rap, to engage middle level learners in literacy activities (Paul, 2000). Or you might consider using movie magazines as a basis for reading assignments (Wilson, 2001). Additional ways to use popular culture are to have students set their poetry to music, write an analysis of a music video or video game, write a review of a movie or television program, and develop website evaluation tools. Any way you can connect teen culture to literacy helps students understand that reading is not simply a school-based activity, but a skill that permeates their lives.

SEE FOR YOURSELF

Popular Culture Word Sort

Visit the message board for Chapter 11 on our Companion Website at *www.prenhall.com/lenski* to discuss your findings.

Although you may feel like it hasn't been very long since you were in the middle grades, fads change so quickly that you might be "out of touch." To learn about the newest fads of interest to middle level learners, interview one girl and one boy who are in grades 6, 7, or 8. Ask the following questions:

- What are your favorite television programs?
- Who is the most popular music group?
- What is your favorite movie?
- Who is your favorite movie star?
- Who are the athletes you like best?
- What are your favorite video or computer games?
- What social groups are in your school?
- What look is "cool" in your school?
- What slang expressions do your friends use?
- What do you do in the evenings and on weekends?

Consider tape-recording the interviews so that you can replay them at your leisure. As you remember the interviews, write down examples of popular culture on index cards, one to a card. You should have a number of cards filled out, at least 20. In groups of three or four, organize your index cards into categories. Category headings might include things like sports heroes, popular movies, and free-time activities. Use this information to develop reading activities that relate to your students' interests in popular culture.

Intellectual Development

Students in the middle grades also make striking intellectual changes during grades 6 through 8. The most prominent change is that students move from concrete to abstract thinking. George and Lawrence (1982) identified additional dimensions of cognitive development that early adolescents experience. They found that young adolescents move from:

- Concrete to abstract thinking;
- An egocentric to a sociocentric perspective;
- A limited to a broad perspective of time and space;
- A simplistic to a complex view of human motivation;
- A reliance on slogans toward the construction of a personal ideology; and
- Concrete thinking toward the development of a capacity for complex, higher order conceptualizing.

Abstract thinking.   Early adolescents begin to have the ability to think abstractly. At the beginning of the middle grades, most students still function at Piaget's concrete operational level of thinking. An example of concrete thinking as it applies to middle level reading is when students have the ability to understand *what* happens in a story but not *why* it happens. To illustrate, many students are able to understand literal information such as the *plot* of a novel. That would be thinking at the concrete stage. These students may not, however, be able to discern the *theme* of that same novel, which is an example of thinking more abstractly.

The change from concrete thinking to abstract thinking does not occur overnight, nor does it always occur for every student. Students who are able to understand a political cartoon, for example, may still not be able to identify bias in a text—both examples of abstract thinking. Abstract thinking will come more quickly for some students than others, but remember that cognitive development is not like physical development. Students who grow 3 inches will not lose that height the next day. With cognitive development, new ways of thinking occur sporadically, but they do tend to develop for most students during the middle level years.

 Piaget's stages of development were described in Chapter 7. How does knowing about stages of development influence your teaching?

Metacognitive development.   Another characteristic of the intellectual development of middle level learners is their new ability to think about what they know, or metacognition. Although younger readers can learn this skill, when students reach early adolescence, they have more capacity for introspective thinking. During the middle level years, students find metacognitive strategies easier to learn. When they take tests, young teens begin to question why their answers are correct or incorrect. As middle level learners become more aware of their own knowledge, they begin to question authority.

Sociocentricity.   A third aspect of the intellectual development of early adolescents is their egocentricity. During the middle years, students tend to view the world only from their own perspectives. They also begin to develop a sociocentric perspective, in which they become concerned with issues of social justice and question the meaning of life. Many young teens start questioning the relevance of schooling because they tend to want their learning to be meaningful to them as they are observing how the adult world works. As middle level students' intellectual development progresses, many students also become idealistic, expecting life to be fair and just.

Questioning the author.   You can design engaging literacy activities for students who are moving from concrete to abstract thinking, who are developing the ability to think metacognitively, and who are developing a sociocentric perspective. One strategy that meets the needs of each of these areas of intellectual development is Questioning the Author (Beck, McKeown, Hamilton, & Kucan, 1997). This strategy is used by students as they read nonfiction text. As they read, students need to think of the author as separate from the text—as a human being who has made writing choices that may or may not be appropriate for the reader. During reading, then, the students "talk to the author," asking questions that they need answered for rich comprehension. For example, students could ask the following questions:

- Why did you include this example in the text?
- What do you mean here?
- What background do you have in this area?
- Do you have any contact with readers my age?
- Why didn't you use more common vocabulary?

As students "question the author" during reading, they use their developing intellectual capacities. The Questioning the Author strategy is an abstract process; students are not looking for specific information from text, they are trying to develop questions that help them understand the text more deeply. This process also encompasses metacognition. Students need to monitor their comprehension as they read, so they can develop appropriate questions. Finally, as students read, they move away from themselves toward asking larger questions about the text, an example of sociocentric thinking.

SEE FOR YOURSELF

Questioning the Author

Visit the message board for Chapter 11 on our Companion Website at *www.prenhall.com/lenski* to discuss your findings.

The most effective way to teach students how to think critically is to model strategies aloud for them. Questioning the Author, for example, is a difficult strategy to describe. When you model the strategy, however, you reveal your mind's inner workings and provide examples for ways students can think.

To learn more about the Questioning the Author strategy, access the Companion Website *(http://www.prenhall.com/lenski)* and listen to undergraduate students using the Questioning the Author strategy as they respond to portions of the previous section.

OBSERVING CRITICAL READERS PROCESS PRINT

When students reach the middle level grades, the way they process text begins to shift. Successful readers in middle schools adopt four different roles as they read: code breaker, text participant, text user, and text analyst (Freebody & Luke, 1990). By the middle grades, most students will automatically use cueing systems to problem solve words, although some students will need instruction on breaking the code of language. Many middle-grade students will also successfully interpret text through the flexible use of reading strategies and will be text participants and text users. Texts become even more difficult in middle grades, so middle-grade students will also need continued instruction on regulating their reading processes. By middle school, students are ready to embrace the fourth and most challenging role in reading: to become a text analyst, or to learn to read critically.

Critical reading is a developing field; therefore, much of what is presented in this section might be new to you. In your own schooling, you may have learned how to distinguish facts from opinions and to identify propaganda techniques. These critical reading strategies were popular in the 1980s and are still part of school curricula today. Some of you may also have had training in identifying the structure of arguments and in identifying warrants and claims. Teaching argument as critical reading was promoted in the 1990s (Unrau, 1997). Vestiges of both of these aspects of critical reading theory can be found in schools and are useful to know and to teach. However, by the end of the 1990s, theorists redefined critical reading to conform to a larger educational movement called *critical pedagogy* (Siegel & Fernandez, 2000). At present, critical reading, then, is defined as "an active, challenging approach to literacy that encourages students to be aware of the way that texts are constructed and how such constructions position readers" (Fehring & Green, 2001, back cover). Critical reading is a way to read that analyzes and evaluates texts so that the readers view texts as a means of understanding cultures and societies. Cadiero-Kaplan (2002) describes critical literacy in slightly different terms that might resonate with some of you: "Students involved in a critical literacy curriculum read the world and the word, by using dialogue to engage texts and discourses inside and outside the classroom" (p. 377).

 Critical literacy suggests that readers view texts from a broader perspective. In what ways does critical literacy theory fit your own evolving literacy theory?

Not all middle school readers take a critical stance toward text. Critical reading, however, is considered an important goal for all students. The two largest professional literacy associations, the International Reading Association (IRA) and the National Council of Teachers of English (NCTE), have stated in the national *Standards for the English Language Arts* that students need to "question assumptions, explore perspectives, and critique underlying social and political values or stances" (IRA/NCTE, 1996, p. 71). So, as we discuss critical reading, remember that while critical reading is an important reading objective for middle-grade students, it is a goal that may not be reached for all students.

New Critics Approach

In order for you to understand critical reading, it will help you to think about the ways you learned how to approach text in high school and college. Because critical reading is so new to the educational field, you probably didn't have teachers who were trained in a critical approach to reading. Many of you had teachers who taught with a formalist approach called *New Criticism*. New Criticism was the preferred instructional model of teaching literature in the 1960s and 1970s. Although your teachers may have been trained after the height of New Criticism, many teachers today still follow that approach.

New Criticism is an approach in which students attempt to examine and analyze texts by trying to understand what the author was communicating through the text (Wimsatt & Brooks, 1964). Think back to literature classes. Did any of your teachers require you to try to figure out what the author was saying? When you proffered an interpretation, did the teacher ever tell you that it could not possibly be what the author intended? Did your teachers refer frequently to literary critics rather than asking you to decide on the meaning of a text? If so, your teachers were likely operating under the New Critics approach, and you probably were not encouraged to read critically. Critical reading requires that readers think for themselves while reading—not try to understand someone else's thinking.

New Criticism: Meaning resides in text.   Thinking back to what you know about learning theories, you might have predicted that New Criticism aligns with behaviorism more closely than it does with constructivism. If you're trying to understand what the author intended when you read, then you're assuming that the meaning of the text resides in the words on the page. This approach to reading, then, does not consider the reader's background knowledge, experiences, interests, and biases; meaning is the same for every reader regardless of personal experiences. If that's the case, then there is one interpretation for text, and one right answer for questions teachers ask. Teachers approaching reading from a New Criticism perspective believe that meaning resides in text, and many teachers still teach from that position.

Reader Response Theory

When students read critically, they need to form their own opinions and construct their own meanings. An alternate theory of reading consistent with the constructivist approach was developed in the late 1970s as a means to counter the New Criticism approach to text. As educators became more knowledgeable about ways people learn, they acknowledged the prior knowledge that readers bring to reading situations and admitted that readers cannot really discern an author's intended meaning. They also came to believe that reading is more than an analysis of a literary critic's interpretation of the formal structure of text. As educators became interested in constructivist ways of thinking, Rosenblatt (1978) proposed a theory of reading that emphasized an individual reader's experiences. She reasoned that readers approach text as a "lived through" experience and that readers don't merely try to analyze text but actually experience it. Those who believe in reader response theory understand that reading is a transaction between the reader, the text, and the context. In her research, Rosenblatt developed the transactional theory and furthered that theory by discussing an instructional approach: reader response.

The transactional theory of reading was discussed in Chapter 7. In what ways does reader response theory logically follow the transactional theory?

Some of you may have had teachers who espoused reader response theory. If so, you probably wrote journal entries or talked with your peers in response to your reading, and your experiences with reading were valued as much as the teacher's interpretation of the text. Your teacher did not ask you to try to figure out what the author intended, but wanted to know what *you* thought and how *you* felt about the text. More students today than in the past report that their teachers are asking these types of questions, but the numbers are still low (Donahue, Voelkl, Campbell, & Mazzeo, 1999).

As you think about reader response, you might be wondering how to determine whether readers *understand* the texts they are reading. Well, it depends on what you mean by the word *understand*. There are varying degrees of understanding. Reader

Journal writing supports and extends reading comprehension.

response theorists do not believe that any response to a text indicates complete understanding of text. Instead, responses show how the reader interprets the text—and there are times when readers' interpretations do not match what was written. As you learn ideas for instruction in later chapters, you'll come to understand how to encourage individual constructions of meaning that are balanced with logical interpretations of text.

Reader response: Meaning resides in readers.   Those who believe in reader response consider the meaning of text to be constructed by the reader. Meaning does not exist in the text, only in a reader's mind. The idea that meaning resides in people can be illustrated by the frequently debated question: If a tree falls in a forest with no one to hear it, does it make a sound? You could probably argue this question for days without ever coming to a conclusion. We have a similar kind of conundrum in reading. In writing about reader response, Galda and Guice (1997) state, "a text is merely inert words without a reader" (p. 311). Text is an author's written communication. Is there meaning without someone else reading the words? Those who believe reader response theory would say no. Meaning only exists within the minds of a reader, not in the text.

Adopting a stance toward text.   Rosenblatt (1994) had more to say about responding to text than that meaning resides in people rather than words. She suggested that readers read for different purposes, and as they read, they adopt a stance toward that text. For example, you have adopted a stance toward reading right now. You are very likely reading to learn new information. This type of reading differs

The concept of a reading stance implies that readers, texts, and contexts are important aspects of literacy theory. In what ways will knowledge about reading stance influence your teaching?

from reading for pure enjoyment, although we hope you're also enjoying this text. As you think about stance in reading, know that some texts signal readers to carry away meaning, and others are typically read from an experiential point of view. If you're reading for the primary purpose to find out something, you're reading from an *efferent* stance. For example, you probably read most of your college textbooks to carry away meaning, so you're adopting an efferent stance. If you were reading a young adult novel such as *Walk Two Moons* by Sharon Creech (1994), you'd be reading from an *aesthetic* viewpoint. You'd read primarily for the story and to "live" the story through the characters.

When students read, they adopt a stance somewhere along a continuum that ranges from efferent to aesthetic. Different reading situations and purposes, however, can influence the stance that you take when you read. For example, imagine yourself reading the classified advertisements in a newspaper. In one scenario, you've just accepted your first teaching position and you have decided to rent an apartment for a year. You read the classified advertisements in search of an apartment that meets your needs. As you read, you're looking only for apartments that meet your budget, are located within driving distance of your school, and that accept pets. As you scan the ads, you're asking questions, selecting ads to read more closely, and discarding ads that don't meet your requirements. You're reading from an efferent stance because you're reading to carry away meaning.

In a second scenario, imagine yourself visiting your college roommate in a town that you'd never visited before. You pick up a newspaper and scan the classified advertisements. As you read the ads for apartments, you're reading to form impressions, not using the text to accomplish something. As you read, you compare the costs of apartments to your own experience and you visualize the apartments described in the ads. In this case, you're reading more from an aesthetic stance than an efferent stance.

Although the same texts can be read from different stances, in general, fiction is read from a more aesthetic stance, and nonfiction is read from a more efferent stance. Figure 11.2 illustrates how some of your reading could be considered on the continuum of reading stances.

A Critical Approach to Reading

If students are to read critically, they first need to approach text from a reader response perspective, trying to construct their own meaning rather than relying on others to tell them what text means. They also will adopt a stance while reading, from an aesthetic to an efferent stance. Approaching text from a perspective of reader response is a prerequisite for reading critically. If students read without trying to determine the author's intention, they are free to read the text knowing that different readers will construct different meanings based on their prior experiences. However, simply constructing individual meaning is not reading critically.

Critical Readers do more than take an efferent or aesthetic stance toward text; they adopt a *critical* stance toward text. Readers with a critical stance recognize that texts are written versions of an author's view of reality and that they represent par-

---

Efferent	Aesthetic
Textbook → News magazine → Fashion magazine → School newspaper → Romance novel → Letter	

FIGURE 11.2   Reading Stance Continuum

ticular social and political values. Critical Readers also recognize that they use their own cultural and social views to frame their own interpretations. Furthermore, Critical Readers consider the social and political relationships involved in reading by identifying their own positions in relation to the text, by considering the author's position as a writer, and by acknowledging the connections that all readers make while reading. Critical reading is "part of a real attempt to read the social: to make sense of the texts and signs of our culture" (Gilbert, 2001, p. 81). Critical reading, therefore, is more than constructing meaning; it suggests that readers use their reading of texts to understand the social realities of the world and to actively contribute to changing their cultures and furthering social justice (Kempe, 2001).

 Critical Readers take into account social and political relationships implied by the text. In what ways is critical reading important for diverse classrooms?

Forming reasoned judgments.   The first step toward critical reading is for readers to form reasoned judgments. Critical Readers understand that any one text represents one view of the world, and that to come to a reasoned judgment about any issue, other views should be taken into account. This is especially true in today's information society because readers are flooded with information from print and electronic sources. Readers simply cannot believe everything in print or on the Net; they must have strategies to discern which information is valid and which is not. To form reasoned judgments, readers need to be able to look for assumptions, reasons, justifications, and implications in texts and to interpret texts fairly (Paul, 1993). You might be wondering how students actually move toward forming reasoned judgments during reading. A number of strategies are available to Critical Readers during reading, as listed in Figure 11.3 (Chapman, 1993; Unrau, 1997).

Adopting a critical stance.   Middle school readers who become Critical Readers need to begin the process of taking a critical stance by forming reasoned judgments as they read. In addition, they should blend their responses to text with their critical thinking ability to acknowledge the "power of the text on the reader as well as an understanding of *why* the text exercises that power" (Soter, 1999, p. 114). To further critical reading skills, middle school students can become researchers of language, explore the ways diverse cultures are represented in literature, and problematize

- Deciding what is important in text
- Connecting current texts to past texts
- Constructing tentative hypotheses while reading that are actively verified, modified, or abandoned
- Inferring what information is needed to fill gaps in understanding
- Evaluating and integrating information
- Identifying claims and arguments
- Comparing and assessing arguments and counterarguments
- Identifying beliefs that shape an argument or counterargument
- Evaluating the consequences of beliefs, decisions, and actions
- Monitoring, managing, and reflecting on thinking
- Acknowledging that thinking arises from and is associated with schemata
- Observing and becoming sensitive to social interactions that shape knowledge and beliefs

FIGURE 11.3   Critical Reading Strategies

Picture Books

Bloom, B. (1999). *Wolf!* New York: Orchard.

Browne, A. (1985). *Piggybook.* New York: Alfred A. Knopf.

Cronin, D. (2000). *Click, clack, moo: Cows that type.* New York: Simon & Schuster.

Feiffer, J. (2001). *I'm not Bobby!* Manhasset, NY: Hyperion.

Keller, L. (1998). *The scrambled states of America.* New York: Scholastic.

Lovell, P. (2001). *Stand tall, Molly Lou Melon.* New York: G. P. Putnam's Sons.

St. George, J., & Small, D. (2000). *So you want to be president.* New York: Philomel.

Thaler, M. (1989). *The teacher from the Black Lagoon.* New York: Scholastic.

Chapter Books

Haddix, M. P. (2000). *Among the hidden.* New York: Simon & Schuster.

Hinton, S. E. (1967). *The outsiders.* New York: Dell.

Koss, A. G. (2000). *The girls.* New York: Penguin Putnam.

Lowry, L. (1994). *The giver.* New York: Bantam Doubleday Dell.

Martin, A. M. (2001). *Belle Teal.* New York: Scholastic.

McDonald, J. (1997). *Swallowing stones.* New York: Random House.

Pearson, M. E. (2001). *Scribbler of dreams.* San Diego: Harcourt.

Spinelli, J. (1997). *Wringer.* New York: HarperCollins.

Woodson, J. (2001). *Hush.* New York: Scholastic.

FIGURE 11.4   Selected Books Appropriate for Problematizing Texts

texts as they read (Comber, 2001). Students become researchers of language by reading with a view toward the specific words authors choose to create an emotion or to set a tone. For example, Edgar Allan Poe is well known for choosing words that evoke emotions such as *dark, dreary, weak, weary.* Middle school readers need to recognize that all writers choose words, either consciously or unconsciously, to influence readers. Critical Readers also recognize that texts are not neutral—they influence and establish social identity and power relationships (Luke, O'Brien, & Comber, 2001). Critical Readers, therefore, recognize that texts can reproduce or challenge cultural relationships. Critical Readers also problematize texts. To problematize text, Critical Readers look for the ways in which reality is constructed in texts by asking and answering questions as they read. Books that would be appropriate for problematizing are listed in Figure 11.4.

▬▬▬ YOU TRY IT ▬▬▬

Problematizing Texts

Select a book from the list in Figure 11.4 to read. Some of the books are picture books and others are chapter books. While reading ask the questions that follow. Then form small groups and discuss the books you read and your critical reactions to them. Also discuss ways in which you could encourage middle-grade readers to become Critical Readers of text.

- Why do you think the author told that particular story? How does the author represent social and cultural relationships? For example, which groups have power and which do not?

- How are various cultural groups represented?
- How are conflicts resolved?
- What does the story tell you about the author?
- What's missing from this story?
- What does this story tell us about our culture?

ACKNOWLEDGING DIFFERENCES AMONG CRITICAL READERS

The differences among Critical Readers will be striking. The most obvious differences will be physical. Some students will look like young children and others will look as mature as your college friends. In fact, if you are a young middle level teacher you may be mistaken for a student! Other differences won't be apparent by sight but will be clear once you begin teaching. You'll find that the range of reading levels will increase to 8 or more years in a single class. You could have some students who can barely read second-grade material and others who will be able to read college textbooks. Students' abilities to think abstractly also vary, and their emotional stability fluctuates.

If you teach middle level students in a middle school (as opposed to a kindergarten through eighth-grade building), acknowledging differences among Critical Readers may be apparent, but it will also be more difficult to meet their individual needs. Unlike elementary schools where a teacher instructs a group of 25 to 30 students for most of the day, middle schools are typically departmentalized—you will not be the teacher of a class; you will teach a subject. Reading is taught as a separate subject in some middle schools, but more often students won't have a "reading" class. Reading may be taught in English class using literature or novels as texts, or it may be taught in content-area classes as reading-across-the-curriculum. In both cases, your job will be to acknowledge the differences among your students so that all of them become proficient readers.

If you teach middle school, therefore, you probably won't teach a "reading" class. However, you might teach English, language arts, math, science, social studies, art, or physical education. Or, you could teach two or three of these subjects. Many middle schools currently are organized into teams. If you teach in a team, you will work with three or four other teachers to teach a specified number of students. You will probably be responsible for teaching two subjects to 50 or 60 students.

If your school does not espouse teaming, you might teach up to six classes with 30 or more students in each class—that's a total of 180 students not counting any additional students you have in study hall or homeroom or for extracurricular activities. Acknowledging differences among students becomes a more formidable undertaking in middle school when you have a greater number of students with more differences among them, less class time, and adolescent hormones to consider. Meeting the needs of this wide variety of students is a challenge, but fortunately, with increased diversity has come a number of new ideas about ways to teach all children at the middle level.

Struggling Readers

You could have many struggling readers in a middle level class if you define a struggling reader as a student who cannot read material commonly used at that grade level. Imagine you have just been offered a job teaching seventh grade. From your experience and your college studies, you think that teaching *The Witch of Blackbird Pond* by Elizabeth George Speare (1958) would be a good choice. You know that this book has been successfully taught in seventh grade for decades, and it has current appeal as well. When you meet your students, however, you find that half of your group cannot read this novel. You find that you have a large number of struggling readers.

Why so many?   Why do so many students fail to meet basic reading standards by middle school? There are a number of reasons for this high number of students who struggle with reading, some of which you'll have control over and others that you won't. Many societal factors influence educational outcomes. For example, more children than ever live in poverty in the United States; at least one-half of the students in the nation live at or near the poverty level by the time they are 15 (Taylor, 1996). Children in poverty face challenges that can impede learning. They may be homeless or move frequently. They may not have physical necessities, such as food. They may have to care for younger children and have little time to read and study at home. These and other factors influence academic progress, but they are beyond your control for the most part.

Other reasons for the large number of struggling readers in middle school *are* under your control. Cambourne (2001) suggests that one reason why students fail to learn to read is that they haven't had reading and writing strategies demonstrated effectively. You can make a difference here. Much of the teaching at the middle level has been primarily teacher directed, using the New Criticism model of teaching that was described earlier in this chapter. Experts in the teaching of struggling middle school readers, such as Primeaux (2000), suggest that instruction should be framed from the social constructivist view of learning. When you approach teaching from a social constructivist perspective, you identify students' needs and interests, tailor instruction to their needs, teach skills in the context of authentic texts, and provide opportunities for choice. Understanding the social constructivist learning theory and being able to develop lessons using that approach will be your most effective way to address instruction for struggling readers in middle schools.

Support services.   Fewer support services are available for struggling readers in the middle level grades. Because Title I was created to boost the reading achievement of K–6 readers, few middle schools offer Title I services. Many middle school students, however, have been identified as having learning disabilities. In general, a greater number of boys and students from diverse backgrounds will be among the group (Lerner, 1993). Most of the students with learning disabilities will be "included" in your classroom rather than "pulled out" for special classes. Some of these students will have support services; however, many middle school students resist going to special classes for reading, and they may not even want special support in the classroom. When students reach middle school, their peer group status becomes more important to them than their academic interests, so many students oppose special assistance of all forms. Therefore, as the classroom teacher, you will have to differentiate instruction for struggling readers in your classroom.

Students with learning disabilities.   Students with learning difficulties will also be coping with the adjustments that come with early adolescence. Because of the changes that occur in young teens, many students with learning problems will have low self-esteem and may be passive about learning to read to the extent that they exhibit traits of learned helplessness where they feel hopeless about ever learning to read in school (Richek, Caldwell, Jennings, & Lerner, 2002). Many special education students begin to feel that they will never succeed in school, and statistics indicate that they are correct. Only 35 percent of students with learning disabilities graduate from high school (U.S. Department of Education, 1998).

Students with special needs have been discussed throughout the book. In what ways does meeting the needs of *all* students fit your evolving literacy theory?

Classroom application. To teach the struggling readers in your middle school classroom, you'll have to provide all students with the opportunity to read both at their independent reading level and grade level texts (Primeaux, 2000). Finding independent level materials for all students is a challenging responsibility. Students in eighth grade who are reading at a third-grade level won't read third-grade books such as *Encyclopedia Brown* stories. Instead, you will need to find materials that match the students' reading abilities yet are of interest to their age group. Lenski, Wham, and Johns (2003) suggest finding high-interest easy-to-read texts for struggling readers needing independent level reading. Many publishers currently offer special series of books to meet this need. Figure 11.5 includes a list of resources that offer high-interest, easy-to-read books for middle school students.

Students From Diverse Backgrounds

In many areas of the United States, middle level classes seem like a mini-United Nations; students from many diverse cultures, backgrounds, and languages make up a good portion of middle level classes today. In middle schools, you may have more diverse classrooms than teachers of younger students because some families don't emigrate until their children are older (Igoa, 1995). Having students in your class from more diverse backgrounds presents additional challenges. As a middle level teacher, you will need to have at least a basic understanding of the cultural groups represented in your classroom.

Identifying authentic literacy tasks. Middle level students need relevant schooling experiences even more than younger students do. As students reach early adolescence, many of them begin to reject learning that doesn't apply to their current needs and immediate gratification tendencies. As a middle level teacher, you will have a curriculum, and possibly state standards, to use as a basis for your instruction. However, you also can develop instructional lessons that meet the cultural needs of your students that might be outside your curriculum. For example, in his work with Latina/o students, Jiménez (2001) found that Spanish-speaking students needed to be literate in both Spanish and English in ways that were not then being taught in schools. Some of the students in his study who were struggling with reading in schools were actually language brokers in the home, translating language and print material for older adults. These students were also reading teachers of younger siblings. These literacy

---

Cobblestone
Easy-to-read science and social studies materials

EMC Paradigm
Adapted classics

Jamestown Publishers
Easy-to-read and adapted short stories

Steck-Vaughn
Easy-to-read science, literature, social studies, math, and health materials

Wieser Educational
Adapted classics

FIGURE 11.5 Sources for High-Interest Easy-to-Read Books

tasks, language brokering and teaching, were not taught in the middle school the students attended but were literacy skills that were relevant to their lives. Jiménez recommends that teachers use their knowledge of students' lives to amend literacy tasks not commonly found in school curricula to fit students' actual literacy needs.

English Language Learners.   Teaching English Language Learners (ELL) to read English is a delicate balancing act (Gersten & Jiménez, 1994). Giving students texts that are too difficult for them to read will not help them learn how to use reading strategies. On the other hand, research indicates that teachers have lower expectations of ELL students (Gersten & Jimenez, 1994) and that many teachers assume that students cannot comprehend text until they become fluent in English (García & Pearson, 1991). As a result, middle level teachers tend not to teach ELL students the kinds of sophisticated cognitive strategies that they need. Instead, middle level ELL students report using only low-level thinking strategies, such as concentrating and rereading (Padrón, 1998). Although these strategies are useful during reading, by middle level grades all students should be using strategies that take more cognitive ability, such as predicting, making inferences, and drawing conclusions. Teachers of middle school students should take into account the cognitive development of all students, whether they are native English speakers or English Language Learners, and teach all students reading strategies using appropriate texts.

 Strategies for teaching diverse learners can be found throughout the text. Which ideas will you incorporate into your teaching?

Gifted Critical Readers

"The United States is squandering one of its most precious resources—the gifts, talents, and high interests of many of its students" (U.S. Department of Education, 1993, p. 1). During the past decade, much attention has been paid to the needs of struggling readers and students from diverse backgrounds and less interest directed toward the needs of gifted students. Teachers often think that struggling readers need their help, but that gifted students will be able to learn on their own. That's not necessarily so. A governmental report summarizing research on gifted education states, "In a broad range of intellectual and artistic endeavors, America's most talented students often fail to reach their full potential" (U.S. Department of Education, 1993, p. 5). Unlike other industrialized nations, the United States has not emphasized developing challenging instruction for its gifted students.

Many middle level teachers ignore the needs of gifted readers. Baskin (1998) writes that the academic attention that gifted students receive in the elementary school frequently diminishes by middle school. Middle school teachers tend to "teach to the middle" according to Tomlinson (1992). "Teaching to the middle" means that instruction is tailored for students who are achieving near grade level, and that the needs of gifted readers and struggling readers are not being met. Researchers Westberg, Archambault, Dobyns, and Salvin (1993) conducted a study across the United States to determine how gifted students were taught in middle schools. They found that gifted students received less attention than other students, that they had fewer chances to respond to challenging questions, and that they were frequently used to teach students of lower abilities. The researchers also found that some teachers provided students with more time for independent reading, but that the gifted students did not automatically select books that would challenge their minds, so this practice alone was ineffective.

Classroom application.   One way to challenge gifted readers is to help them select books to read that will stimulate their intellect. The novels that you teach to your entire class may be of interest to gifted readers, but they may not be challenging. Having students read classics such as the works of Charles Dickens would be chal-

Anonymous. (1971). *Go ask Alice.* New York: Simon & Schuster.

Avi. (1991). *Nothing but the truth.* New York: Avon.

Cooper, S. (1973). *The dark is rising.* New York: Simon & Schuster.

Dickinson, P. (2001). *The ropemaker.* New York: Delacorte.

Myers, W. D. (1999). *Monster.* New York: HarperCollins.

Nir, Y. (2002). *The lost childhood.* New York: Scholastic.

Tolkien, J. R. R. (1966). *The Hobbit.* New York: Houghton Mifflin.

Wulffson, D. (2001). *Soldier X.* New York: Viking.

Yen Mah, A. (1999). *Chinese Cinderella: The true story of an unwanted daughter.* New York: Delacorte.

FIGURE 11.6   Recommended Books for Gifted Middle School Readers

lenging, but possibly not interesting. Instead, you should keep your eyes open for books like the following:

- Novels with complex story lines,
- Novels filled with rich language,
- Themes that deal with social issues, and
- Novels whose main characters are older adolescents or young adults.

Figure 11.6 contains a list of books that are appropriate for many gifted middle school readers.

MOTIVATING CRITICAL READERS

Motivation for school learning tends to decline for Critical Readers. As young teens enter the middle grades, they experience rapid physical changes and have an increased interest in finding their place in the world. As teens search for personal identity, they have a heightened need to be accepted by a peer group, and they avoid situations where their status is threatened. Coupled with young adolescents' internalization of school success or failure, school learning becomes less of a priority for many middle level students.

There has, however, been some encouraging evidence in the research on motivation for middle-grade readers. Although the National Assessment of Educational Progress found that approximately half of the eighth-grade students surveyed reported reading 10 or fewer pages each day for school (Donahue et al., 1999), additional evidence suggests that middle level students actually like to read. In a review of three large surveys, Krashen (2001) stated, "contrary to popular opinion, most teenagers read a lot" (p. 16). He concluded that between 72 and 85 percent of the teenagers surveyed read frequently outside of school and that 64 percent rated reading positively. The evidence, therefore, on motivation and middle school reading suggests that middle school students have the potential to see themselves as readers, but that school reading may not be important to them.

 Students from any grade level may or may not be motivated to read. What strategies have you already learned to motivate students to read?

Why Motivation Declines

Researchers have identified three possible reasons why motivation for school learning declines for middle level readers. First, the organization of school changes for most students from a self-contained classroom to a departmentalized setting. Oldfather and

Wigfield (1996) found that the relationship between students and teachers plays a key role in students' motivation. Younger students typically are in schools where they have a few teachers who know them well and who listen to their personal likes and dislikes. As students move into middle schools, however, they often have a greater number of teachers who have less of an opportunity to know each student on a personal basis. Furthermore, young teens begin to turn to peer relationships rather than to adults for personal affirmation, and are less inclined to care about pleasing teachers. Taken together, the relationships between students and teachers are different for adolescents than they are for younger children, and that difference affects students' motivation to read.

A second reason why motivation declines for Critical Readers is that the classroom environment is usually different in middle level grades. Eccles and Midgley (1989) found that elementary classrooms tend to be more collaborative places where students can pursue individual interests, and where students have more opportunity for self-expression and self-determination. As students enter middle level grades, they yearn for more personal autonomy and less outside control. Conversely, schooling in the middle grades allows students fewer choices and less control.

A third reason has to do with the students' sense of self. As students become older, they have had six or more years of feedback from teachers on their school success. Students who have heard for years that they are not "good readers" lose their desire to continue trying to learn to read and feel alienated from school. When students identify themselves as readers, learners, and knowers, they are typically motivated to act in accord with their identity as a learner. Students who have identified themselves (or have been identified) as "struggling readers" also act on that identity and, hence, shun reading. Often these students have attributed their lack of success to inability and feel powerless to improve their reading (Irvin, 1998).

Aliterate Readers

Many Critical Readers are aliterate, or *students who can read but choose not to read*. Aliterate readers are not all alike, however. Young adolescents, and indeed all of us, have situations in our lives that change our reading habits.

Each student's reading history is different, but there are some similarities among students. In a study of aliterate readers, Beers (1998) interviewed middle school students and developed five different reading identities, as described in Figure 11.7. While not every middle level reader will fit into a neat category, the five reading identities help us consider the range of reasons why students choose to read. Knowing about reading identities can also help us choose activities to motivate students. For example, Beers found that avid readers want to choose their own books, have teachers read parts of books, meet authors, and go to the library. Uncommitted or unmotivated readers, on the other hand, find trips to the library to choose books overwhelming. They prefer to choose books from a narrowed selection, perhaps from 30 or 40 popular titles or a dozen familiar authors. They like hearing teachers read entire books, not just parts of books because they will not necessarily read the books on their own. They also like to read illustrated books and want to read nonfiction as well as fiction, such as newspapers and magazines. Although these ideas may help you as a teacher of middle level readers, no one idea will work for all unmotivated readers. Instead, ask your students. Ask them why they like or dislike reading and in what kinds of activities they would like to engage. Giving young adolescents choice and a degree of control over their own learning goes a long way toward motivating aliterate readers.

Avid Reader	Dormant Reader	Uncommitted Reader	Unmotivated Reader	Unskilled Reader
Enjoys reading	Enjoys reading	Does not enjoy reading	Does not enjoy reading	Cannot read
Makes time to read	Does not make time to read	Does not make time to read	Does not make time to read	May/may not make time to read
Identifies self as reader	Identifies self as reader	Does not identify self as reader	Does not identify self as reader	Does not identify self as reader
Defines reading as "way of life"	Defines reading as "neat experience"	Defines reading as "knowing words"	Defines reading as "saying words"	Defines reading as "figuring out words"
Views purpose as entertaining	Views purpose as entertaining	Views purpose as functional	Views purpose as functional	Views purpose as functional
Has aesthetic transactions primarily	Has aesthetic transactions primarily	Has efferent transactions primarily	Has efferent transactions primarily	Has efferent transactions primarily
Has positive feelings about other readers	Has positive feelings about other readers	Has positive feelings about other readers	Has positive feelings about other readers	May/may not have negative feelings about readers

From Beers, K. (1998). Choosing not to read: Understanding why some middle schoolers just say no. In K. Beers & B. G. Samuels (Eds.), Into focus: Understanding and creating middle school readers *(pp. 37–63). Norwood, MA: Christopher-Gordon.*

FIGURE 11.7   Middle-Grade Reading Identities

YOU TRY IT

Reading Histories

Each of your students' reading histories will be different, and so will yours. Earlier in this text you remembered how you learned to read, now we would like you to think about your reading history. During your life you may have been an avid reader, then a dormant reader, and back to an avid reader. Or perhaps you were an unmotivated reader for several years. Or perhaps you have been an avid reader, but you have so much reading to do for school right now that you don't find time to read. Develop a reading history that profiles your motivational history. Use the reading identities described in Figure 11.7 to help you describe your stages.

Creating Motivational Contexts

As a middle-grade teacher, you'll have to work hard to develop a classroom environment that encourages students to read. You'll be facing a general decline in motivation for school learning and a greater number of aliterate students. On the other hand, you'll have more students who are able to read complex text, students who are able to think abstractly, and students who are eager to question, analyze, and critique. As you think about ways to create contexts for motivating middle-grade readers, you might use the acronym Edward Hootstein (1996) developed: RISE. RISE stands for *r*elevance, *i*nterest, *s*atisfied learners, and *e*xpectations for success.

Relevance.   Middle level students demand that school be relevant to their lives. As students develop sociocentric capacities, they try to understand how they fit into larger society, they question life's meaning, and they ask unanswerable questions. During this time in their lives, middle level learners have little patience for learning that doesn't answer their questions about how life works. They want school to make sense to them, to be relevant to their lives, and they are often unable to connect their personal world with the academic world without assistance.

Making school relevant is not a new phenomena. In the early 20th century, Dewey (1913) suggested that connections be made between learning and subject matter. Dewey's notions were the precursor of later theories, including social constructivism. Social constructivist teachers are aware that each student brings unique knowledge to every learning event, and that through the process of learning, students add new knowledge to existing knowledge states. If learning is to occur, students must access prior knowledge. Through this process, learning can be made relevant with teacher guidance, middle level learners, however, don't always make the links between their lives and their learning, and instead rely on teachers to make those links visible.

Let's consider how you as a middle level teacher could make learning relevant. Let's say that you are teaching *My Brother Sam Is Dead* (Collier & Collier, 1974), a story about brothers who fight on different sides in the Revolutionary War. Middle school students may not understand the relevance of this story because it is set in the 18th century. To make relevance visible, you could begin the story by asking students for examples of times when they and their siblings (or close friends) had diametrically opposing beliefs or opinions. (For example, one teen believes in strict gun laws while another believes in little or no government control over the possession of firearms.) You could lead a discussion about the reasons why young adolescents have differing views and apply that principle to the brothers, Tim and Sam, in the novel. Helping students see how their reading is relevant motivates them to read and to think about literature.

Interest.   Finding reading material that piques students' interests is an important aspect of motivating students to read. Students who read texts that are of interest to them spend more time reading and have higher achievement (McLoyd, 1979; McPhail, Pierson, Freeman, Goodman, & Ayappa, 2000). One of the great things about teaching middle level reading, however, is that reading is not topic oriented. Once you are aware of students' interests, you can tailor your curriculum to take into account those interests.

What captures students' interests? Because middle-grade students have more experiences with books than younger students, they have specific types of books they like and don't like (Purves & Beach, 1972). Among the researchers who have recorded text preferences for middle-grade students, Lowery-Moore (1998) found that mystery and horror books are favorites of middle school students, that girls like reading romance and series books, and that many boys prefer nonfiction. Furthermore, because middle level students are in the midst of becoming adults, many students are interested in learning about the general and gendered topics from the adult world.

When you teach middle level learners, however, you shouldn't only use texts that are of interest to the students at that time. One of the hallmarks of early adolescents is curiosity embedded in naiveté. Students may not know that a topic will interest them until you teach it. For example, young teens may not have read much about the Holocaust by sixth grade. If you introduce a number of books about the Holocaust, some students will become interested and begin reading books about that topic; others won't. Therefore, as a middle level teacher, you need to take students' interests into account, and also to act as a more knowledgeable other to introduce new concepts, authors, topics, and genres to students.

Satisfied learners.   Students in middle grades are less likely to respond favorably to the kinds of incentive programs that exist in elementary classrooms, nor do rewards play a key role in middle school learning. Instead, extrinsic rewards tend to have a detrimental effect on the reading motivation of all students, including young teens (Lepper, 1988). When you consider the developmental needs of early adolescents, the rewards schools can offer seem insignificant. For example, middle-grade students exhibit strong interest in peer relationships, with students of the same sex and with those of the opposite sex. Students whose main concern is being accepted by their peers are often indifferent to rewards that teachers can offer. Middle-grade teachers need to reflect on the needs of young teens as they develop motivational contexts that generate satisfied learners.

An important component of motivation is the ability to set and achieve personal goals (Ames, 1992). When students set personal goals, they take control over their own learning. Setting goals is different from extrinsic rewards. Students who set goals are internalizing and organizing their learning rather than allowing their teacher to tell them what to do and how to learn. Students who are setting learning goals are keeping track of their achievements, not for their teacher or for a reward, but for their own satisfaction. Encouraging students to set personal goals, therefore, can encourage satisfied learners.

Setting personal goals is a familiar task outside of school for middle level learners. Students who play sports often keep track of their accomplishments—their batting average, the time it takes to run a mile, their shooting percentage—so keeping track of personal reading goals will appeal to many students. One way for students to keep track of their goals is through the use of reading contracts. A reading contract is an agreement between you and individual students about the number and type of books they will read (Figure 11.8). Reading contracts may encourage some middle level readers to become satisfied learners.

Expectations for success.   You've heard the saying "Nothing succeeds like success." That saying is especially true for middle level students. Because of the numerous physical, emotional, and social changes young teens experience, their egos tend to be fragile. The fragility of their egos and their sensitivity to criticism make ongoing success especially important. Therefore, it will be important for you to help your students feel confident.

Confidence is the belief that you can succeed, and it is an important aspect of motivation (Ryan & Deci, 2000). Middle-grade students, especially those who have had difficulty with reading, may not be confident readers. Instilling confidence does not mean making it easy. When an activity is too easy, students do not feel personally satisfied when completing the task. On the other hand, if a task is too difficult, students tend to give up and lose their confidence altogether (Gambrell, 1996). The challenge for middle-grade teachers is to provide students with reading activities that are neither too difficult nor too easy.

```
┌─────────────────────────────────────────────────────────────┐
│                                                               │
│   Name  Jody Mallicoat                 Date  9-16-01          │
│   Class  Reading                       Period  1st            │
│                                                               │
│                                                               │
│   For the next quarter, I agree to read the following:        │
│                                                               │
│        Total number of books:  6                              │
│                                                               │
│        Total number of pages:  1800                           │
│                                                               │
│        Genre of books:    Mystery                             │
│                           Historical Fiction                  │
│                           Adventure                           │
│                                                               │
│                           _____                      │
│                                                               │
│                                                               │
│       Jody Mallicoat               9-16-01                    │
│     ─────────────────────        ─────────────               │
│     Student's signature            Date                       │
│                                                               │
│        Mrs. D'alfonso              9-16-01                    │
│     ─────────────────────        ─────────────               │
│     Teacher's signature            Date                       │
│                                                               │
└─────────────────────────────────────────────────────────────┘
```

Reprinted courtesy of Jody Mallicoat and Kristen D'Alfonso.

FIGURE 11.8   Reading Contract

Technology Topic: Web Literacy

Many middle level students are motivated to search the Internet even when they are not motivated to read print text. Reading on the web is different from reading books, and the strategies that are useful for web reading are different from the reading strategies that students need to construct meaning from books. Web literacy:

- Permits nonlinear strategies of thinking;
- Allows nonhierarchical strategies;
- Offers nonsequential strategies;
- Requires visual literacy skills to understand multimedia components;
- Is interactive, with the reader able to add, change, or move text; and
- Enables a blurring of the relationship between reader and writer (Sutherland-Smith, 2002).

Because some students are more adept at web literacy than print literacy, it may be helpful to incorporate Internet reading in your class to supplement the reading of text. Even though web literacy relies on different strategies than print reading, students who read on the web are furthering many of their overall literacy skills and should be encouraged to read from the Internet as well as from books.

CONNECTIONS: WHAT'S NEXT?

In this chapter you learned about middle level students—about the physical, emotional, social, and intellectual development patterns that make this group unique. Along with a review of the developmental patterns of young teens, we presented additional theories of reading. We discussed reader response, reading stance, and critical literacy. We chose these theories to discuss with Critical Readers because older students are more able to read in the sophisticated ways represented by reader response and critical literacy. However, you can apply all theories of reading to Critical Readers, just as you can apply the theories presented in this chapter to younger readers.

Because Critical Readers are different in many ways from Early and Interpretive Readers, we suggest that instruction in the middle grades looks different from instruction for younger students. You can apply all of the good strategies you've learned from the previous chapters to early adolescents, but you also need to take into account the students' ages and needs as you develop your reading program.

In the next three chapters, we present ideas for you that we think work especially well with middle-grade students. We have continued the same structure in these chapters that you've already encountered: ways to teach students in whole groups, small groups, independently, and at home. However, we've changed the amount of space devoted to each type of instruction. When you teach middle level students, you'll find that you spend more time teaching to the entire group. Therefore, we have divided whole-group teaching activities into two chapters: one dealing with teaching literature and one dealing with teaching reading across the curriculum. In these chapters, we discuss how to support students' ability to read and understand words as well as to deepen their comprehension of text. Even though most of your teaching will be to the entire group, you will also want to differentiate instruction using other grouping patterns. We present these ideas in one chapter where we have combined small-group instruction, independent reading, and reading at home with their families.

Teaching Critical Readers is a challenging but exciting job. We hope that our treatment of middle level students helps prepare you to teach students of all levels.

 **FOR YOUR PORTFOLIO**

ENTRY 11.1 *Comparing Student Needs*

INTASC Principle 2 states: *The teacher understands how children learn and develop, and can provide learning opportunities that support their intellectual, social, and personal development.*

Compare the needs of middle level learners to students in primary and intermediate grades using a comparison chart. Then write a curricular plan that takes the developmental needs of Critical Readers into account. Think in terms of the following categories:

- Physical,
- Emotional,
- Social, and
- Intellectual.

Comparison Chart

	Early Readers	Interpretive Readers	Critical Readers
Physical			
Emotional			
Social			
Intellectual			

ENTRY 11.2   *Topical Book Lists*

INTASC Principle 5 states: *The teacher uses an understanding of individual and group motivation and behavior to create a learning environment that encourages positive social interaction, active engagement in learning, and self-motivation.*

One of the ways to motivate middle level students to read is to be knowledgeable of the books that might interest them. Create a database of young adult books that could be used for students in grades 6 through 8. Think of six topics that might be of interest to students. Then, develop a list of different genres of books, videos, magazine articles, and other media that apply to the topic. Post one of your lists on the Companion Website (http://www.prenhall.com/lenski). A partial example follows:

CIVIL RIGHTS
BOOKS

King, C. S. (1983). *The words of Martin Luther King, Jr.* New York: Newsmaker.
Parks, R. (1996). *Dear Mrs. Parks*. New York: Lee & Low.
Parks, R., & Reed, G. (1994). *Quiet strength: The faith, the hope and the heart of a woman who changed a nation*. Grand Rapids, MI: Zondervon.
Thomas, J. C. (2001). *The blacker the berry*. New York: HarperCollins.

NONPRINT SOURCES

Public Broadcasting System. (1986). *Eyes on the prize* [videos]. New York: Author.

Martin Luther King, Jr., website. (n.d.). http://www.lelandstandford.edu/
groupu/King/KingBios/briefbio.htm.

"I Have A Dream" website. (n.d.). http://www.newsvanna.com/Gravity/
mlktribute.

TO LEARN MORE

Helpful Websites

Visit our Companion Website at *http://www.prenhall.com/lenski* to link to the
following sites:

Critical Literacy

This comprehensive site discusses critical literacy, its importance,
questions asked of texts, what critical literacy looks like in the classroom,
where to find more ideas to use with students, and much more.
http://www.discover.tased.edu.au/english/critlit.htm

International Reading Association

An international professional reading organization's website. Look for the
position statement on adolescent literacy.
http://www.reading.org

National Assessment of Educational Progress

Reports the most recent scores and gives long-term trend results.
http://nces.ed.gov/nationsreportcard/reading.asp

National Middle School Association

Visit this professional middle school organization's website.
http://www.nmsa.org

Reader Response Theory

This online article discusses the history of reader response and describes
the theory.
*http://www.press.jhu.edu/books/hopkins_guide_to_literary_theory/entries/
reader-response_theory and criticism.html*

SERI Gifted and Talented Resources

Links to resources, professional organizations, and publications for those
interested in the education of gifted students.
http://seriweb.com/gt.htm

chapter 12

Instructing Critical Readers Using a Common Text

Essential Learning Questions

- How would you use basal readers, literature anthologies, and trade books to teach middle level readers?
- How would you use prereading strategies in your teaching?
- What are appropriate word-building strategies for middle level readers?
- Why is reading comprehension such an important issue for middle level readers?
- How can you facilitate middle level students' critical reading?

Middle-grade teachers most often teach students using a common text, meaning that teachers instruct all of the students at the same time with the same text. If you think back to your middle level years, you probably remember an English or a language arts teacher teaching from a literature book or a novel. Picture whether the teacher used more than one text. Probably not; the teacher most likely used one text for all students in your class. We called that type of teaching *whole-group instruction* in earlier chapters; whole-group instruction is more frequently referred to as *using a common text* in middle level grades.

Teachers in middle level grades use a common text as a matter of course, probably because teaching large numbers of students in short periods of time makes grouping difficult. This type of teaching, however, has the potential to support several of your instructional goals including the following:

- Encouraging community building,
- Discussing ideas of interest to all students,
- Introducing skills and strategies that all students can use,
- Promoting whole-class discussions, and
- Demonstrating the democratic ideal where each class member gives voice to opinions.

These instructional goals are important in middle level classrooms and can often be achieved best by teaching to the whole group.

SELECTING COMMON TEXTS

You will have the same range of teaching materials from which to select in middle level grades as the teachers of Early and Interpretive Readers do: basal readers, literature anthologies, and trade books. Your selection process may, however, be different. If you teach in a middle school, you may be in a departmentalized setting—you might teach reading, English, or language arts to more than one class of students. You might teach in the traditional 45-minute period, or you might teach in a double period of 90 minutes, or some other configuration. Depending on how your curriculum is organized, you might be responsible for teaching writing, spelling, vocabulary, and grammar, as well as reading. Furthermore, reading at the middle level takes a different perspective. Students use reading as a tool for learning, and, therefore, you should

Visit the online journal in Chapter 12 on our Companion Website at *www.prenhall.com/lenski* to answer these questions. Save your answers to your hard drive or to a disk to compile an online journal.

The materials you select should be based on your beliefs about literacy. What do you believe about teaching reading to middle level students?

concentrate less on teaching reading processes and spend more time applying strategies to all texts. As you consider selecting materials, therefore, you need to consider your teaching responsibilities and the focus of the teaching of reading in your school.

Remember, it doesn't matter so much which type of text you select—there are reasons why you might choose each of the types of text. What is more important is *how you use these materials*. Regardless of the text you select, you should proceed from the same theoretical perspective, instructional principles, and selection of strategies. In other words, you can use basal reading programs, literature anthologies, and/or trade books while embracing social constructivism and providing engaging and purposeful instruction.

Basal Reading Series

Basal readers are far less common in middle level grades than in elementary grades. Reading is typically taught in English or language arts classes in middle school, and the skills and strategies that are taught generally emerge from reading literature rather than from the skills that are found in basal readers. Furthermore, students in middle school become extremely sensitive about texts that appear juvenile. Middle school students want to look grown up, and the books they carry to class need to match the students' desire for maturity.

Basal readers were discussed in detail in Chapter 8. Under what conditions would you teach using a basal at the middle level?

In some situations, however, basal readers are appropriate in middle schools. Some basal readers have texts aimed at kindergarten through eighth grade. If you teach in a K–8 building, your administrators may want your entire school to use the same basal reading series. Or, if you teach in an area that expects you to concentrate on reading skills and strategies rather than on literature, you might be given a basal reader to use as a main text. If you use a basal reader in the middle level, you will need to pick and choose which strategies to teach and which ideas to use from the teacher's manual, depending on the needs and interests of your students.

Literature Anthologies

Literature anthologies look similar to basal readers in some respects. They are typically hardbound books containing a series of stories. Important differences, however, do exist. Basal readers generally include excerpts of stories or books, whereas literature anthologies have short stories. Excerpts of stories are short selections from a longer book. For example, some literature anthologies print chapters from popular young adult novels. A short story, on the other hand, is a "brief fictional prose narrative designed to create a unified impression quickly and forcefully" (Harris & Hodges, 1995, p. 233). Short stories are crafted so that they contain more sophisticated elements of fiction, such as foreshadowing and symbolism, which are taught in middle schools.

Thematic units.   The content of literature anthologies is frequently divided into two types of thematic units: concept units and genre units. Concept units are organized along a concept or a theme such as "courage" or "coming of age." Each concept unit contains several short stories and one or more of the following types of texts: poems, essays, informational pieces, and graphic displays. Literature anthologies that are organized around concept units provide a theme that you can use to teach each type of text represented in them.

A second type of thematic unit is a genre unit. Some literature anthologies are divided into genres such as fictional stories, nonfictional texts, poems, and essays.

Within each unit, the genre might be divided into smaller units of study. For example, fictional stories might be organized around the conflicts typically found in fiction: character versus society, character versus nature, character versus another character, and character versus himself. Some middle school teachers prefer this type of organization of content. Middle school students often have little experience with literary genre, and an in-depth study of each genre can encourage students to read more diverse types of texts. Also, middle school students are expected to be able to read content-area texts in the other classes they take (i.e., science, social studies, math). Learning how to read different types of text can be useful in reading-across-the-curriculum efforts.

Teacher's manual.   The teacher's manual of a literature anthology is also unlike the manuals that accompany basal readers. Literature anthologies come with fewer ancillary materials, such as workbooks, black-line masters, and teaching suggestions. Typically, the teacher's manual provides some background information about the selection, information about the author, a summary of the story, a few teaching ideas, and comprehension questions. The teaching ideas will concentrate on having students understand how literature is written and how to read literature rather than on reading strategies. This distinction is important. If you teach from a literature anthology, you will need to supplement the ideas in the teacher's manuals with your knowledge of the skills and strategies that Critical Readers need to learn.

Trade Books

Whether you use a basal reading series or a literature anthology as a main text, you should supplement your instruction with trade books, which is an educational term for young adult (YA) literature. Most middle level students prefer reading YA literature to anthologies or basal readers. Trade books come in paperback or permabound books that students love to carry around. Not only are paperback books lighter, they mirror the reading of adults. Novels are also more interesting because they are directly written for middle school students. Some of the selections in basal readers and literature anthologies were written for young teens, but many of them were written for adults so those selections are not as intrinsically interesting to students as YA literature is.

Teaching YA literature, does, however, have some disadvantages. First, YA selections are longer than the shorter pieces in basal readers and literature anthologies, which means you will be teaching the same book for several weeks. If students are not interested in the book and refuse to participate in class, they will lose days' worth of instruction. Therefore, selecting interesting YA literature to use is of the utmost importance. A second disadvantage is that you will have to develop many of the instructional lessons yourself without the aid of a teacher's manual.

Selecting young adult literature.   If you decide to teach middle school students using YA literature, you should balance your selections between novels and informational selections, classics and new books, and differing cultural perspectives. Many middle school students enjoy reading novels. Novels are an "extended piece of fictional prose" (Harris & Hodges, 1995, p. 168). When you teach novels, therefore, you'll have the opportunity to teach the elements of fiction, such as character development, plot structure, and theme. Novels are also ideal for promoting discussions about topics of universal appeal. If you teach using YA literature, however, you should also select informational texts. Some students, especially boys, prefer informational

Using Trade Books

Advice for New Teachers

Dear Linda,

I want to teach using trade books, but I'm concerned about teaching all of the skills and strategies that I know my students need to learn. How do you know if you're teaching all of the right things?

Dear New Teacher,

I know exactly what you mean. I believe in teaching from literature, so I developed my entire reading program using trade books. I didn't have a basal reader or a literature anthology to use for my strategy instruction, so I accessed our state's reading and language arts standards from the state board's website and used the standards as the basis for my instruction. The standards in our state are comprehensive, so I was able to develop lessons for the novels that aligned with state standards and taught students the skills and strategies they need to know.

texts to novels (Brozo, 2002). Using informational texts can provide you with the opportunity to have students read to identify important information, to prioritize information, and to summarize.

As you think about selecting YA literature, you should also try to balance classics, or books that have been taught to middle school students for decades, with books that have popular appeal. Classics are books that are well written, contain universal truths, and have endured the test of time. An example of a classic that is taught in middle school is *White Fang* by Jack London (1964). Classics are beneficial for most middle school students because they are the source of a cultural body of knowledge in mainstream America. Because classics will not interest every student, you should also include currently popular books in your list of YA literature to teach. To select a currently popular book, you might use a current Newbery Medal winner or a book that you notice other students are reading.

A sample book list that contains a balanced approach to YA literature is given in Figure 12.1.

Resources.   If you teach YA literature, you will have to carefully read the book yourself and develop teaching lessons on your own; you won't have a teacher's manual to refer to. You will need to apply your knowledge of teaching the skills and strategies appropriate for Critical Readers to the novel you teach. Some teachers rely on old ways of teaching. They develop vocabulary lists for students to learn before reading a chapter and a list of comprehension questions for students to answer at the end of the chapter. We want to discourage you from this type of teaching. Think back to your middle school years. Many of you probably had teachers who taught

Middle level readers like reading paperback books.

Collier, J. L. (1984). *My brother Sam is dead.* New York: Simon & Schuster.

Earley, T. (2001). *Jim the boy: A novel.* New York: Little, Brown & Company.

Hesse, K. (1997). *Out of the dust.* New York: Scholastic Inc.

Lasky, K. (2001). *Elizabeth I, red rose of the house of Tudor.* New York: Scholastic.

Rinaldi, A. (2001). *My heart is on the ground: The diary of Nannie Little Rose, a Sioux girl.* New York: Scholastic.

Rose, R. (1983). *Twelve angry men: A play in three acts.* New York: Dramatic Publishing Company.

Speare, E. G. (1958). *The Witch of Blackbird Pond.* New York: Houghton Mifflin.

Taylor, M. (1976). *Roll of thunder, hear my cry.* New York: Bantam.

Zindel, P. (1983). *The pigman.* New York: Bantam Starfire.

FIGURE 12.1   Sample Middle Level Book List

novels using these techniques. Did they help you learn how to read better? Did they help you think deeply about the selection? Did they engage you and your classmates in learning? Probably not to a great extent. In fact, by having to do so much paperwork, you may have lost all enjoyment in the novel. Instead, you should use strategies that engage readers in text, strategies that you have learned about already in this book and those still to come.

Banned books. We encourage you to use YA literature as a basis for teaching Critical Readers, but you will have some additional steps to follow before you select books to teach. When you use a basal reading series or a literature anthology, a panel of authorities has approved the selections. The contents of some selections may have been modified for young teens. Even classic stories include words and phrases that would not be appropriate to say in school. Many of the books of interest to middle level students include words or passages that could be objectionable to some parents. Since that is the case, before you teach any piece of YA literature, you will need to find out whether your school has a policy on book challenges. Some schools will even offer lists of approved classroom novels from which you must choose. Other schools will have lists of banned books—books that you cannot use for instructional purposes or even have in your classroom. Once you have discovered which books you can and cannot use to teach, you can make decisions about a list of books for your classroom instruction.

If your school does not have a list of approved books, create your own list with care and show that list to your department head or your school administrator. Make sure they have seen the list and have authorized you to teach those books. Then ask your administrator whether or not you need parents to sign a consent letter stating that they agree that their children can read the books on the list.

Book challenges. Most of you who teach middle school will not have your book selections challenged, but some of you will. Some parents will not want their children to read literature that seems acceptable to you.

If parents challenge a book you have selected to teach, obtain a copy of your school's censorship policy to keep with your letters of consent. If your school does not have a policy for challenged material, we recommend that you develop your own. Judy Blume (1997), a well-known author who has written about censorship, believes that one of the reasons her books were censored was that schools did not have a policy for parents who challenged a book. Therefore, we suggest that you prepare your own policy for book challenges and ask your building administrator to approve it. In your policy, you might include the National Council of Teachers of English/International Reading Association (NCTE/IRA) statement on intellectual freedom:

> All students in public school classrooms have the right to materials and educational experiences that promote open inquiry, critical thinking, diversity in thought and expression, and respect for others. Denial or restriction of this right is an infringement of intellectual freedom. (NCTE/IRA, 1988)

In addition to a policy on challenged books, Simmons and Dresang (2001) suggest that you prepare a rationale for teaching all books that you use for instruction. You can find rationales for some books that have been challenged on a CD-ROM that was developed by the NCTE/IRA (1988). If a parent still requests that a child refrain from reading a specific book after reading your rationale for teaching the book, have a list of alternate books the student can read. That way you'll have alternate assignments ready, and you won't have to jettison your entire teaching plans for one student.

Making the Decision

You might seem overwhelmed with choices right now. Should you use a basal reading series, a literature anthology, YA literature, or a combination of materials? You should have an opinion about the instructional materials you want to use as you prepare to become a teacher. However, you may not be able to make that decision yourself once you obtain a teaching position. Many schools have textbook adoption committees that make the decision for you. Some states even have textbook adoption committees at the state level. In these situations, you might have some latitude about supplemental texts, but you will not have free rein.

If you do have complete autonomy over your instructional materials or if you serve on a textbook adoption committee, you should consider two principles before deciding which type of materials to use.

Principle 1: What do students need and want to read?   Your first consideration should be your students. As you think about your students, ask yourself the following questions:

- Do my students need to have a more structured text such as a basal reading series?
- Do students need to be introduced to the elements of fiction or do they come with some understanding about text structures?
- Do students prefer paperback books?
- Are students motivated to learn?
- How many students can read English?
- How many students need more challenging materials?
- How many students need less challenging materials?

Principle 2: What do you need to be an effective teacher?   Just as you should consider the needs of your students, you should also think about your own strengths and weaknesses as a beginning teacher. If you don't feel confident teaching novels without the many teaching ideas that can be found in a basal reading series, you should choose a basal. If you believe you can teach reading skills and strategies but don't feel confident teaching the elements of fiction, you might want a literature anthology. If you feel confident that you can prepare teaching lessons that teach reading processes and the structure of texts but you need content that is deeper and of greater interest to students, you should choose YA literature. Or, you might decide to use a combination of all three approaches.

There is no one correct answer about selecting teaching materials. You should use whatever material will provide the best instruction for the students that you teach. And remember, your own strengths and weaknesses will change during your teaching career. If you need more structure during your first few years, that's fine. You might move to less prescribed materials as you gain experience teaching.

SEE FOR YOURSELF

Interviewing Middle School Teachers

Visit the message board for Chapter 12 on our Companion Website at *www.prenhall.com/lenski* to discuss your findings.

Interview two or three middle school teachers about their experiences selecting classroom materials. First, ask about their state, district, or school policies. Find out whether the teachers made their own decisions about classroom materials, whether they have an approved book list, and whether they have a policy for book challenges. Then ask the teachers what type of text they prefer and why they prefer it. Finally, ask them for recommendations for books to teach at each of the middle school grade levels. Post your findings on the Companion Website *(http://www.prenhall.com/lenski).*

PREPARING FOR READING

Once you have selected a common text for students to read, you need to consider your instructional goals. Say you have decided to teach the classic *Farewell to Manzanar* by Jeane Wakatsuki Houston and James D. Houston (1973), a true account of a Japanese American family that was sent to an internment camp during World War II. In addition to selecting a text, you need to think about how you will engage students in the text, how you will address individual differences, and what reading processes and strategies you want students to learn.

Teaching middle level students to read is different from teaching them the content of the novel. Here's an example of what we mean. Think back to your literature classes in high school and college. What activities did the teacher prepare? What did you learn? If you are like many college students, you learned some of the historical background of the novel; you probably learned about the author; and you may have read examples of a literary analysis of the novel. These activities were designed to help you learn about the literature selection——a worthy goal, but they may not have helped you become a more strategic reader or to enjoy reading.

Teaching reading is not teaching literature, although you may certainly use YA literature as text. Humphrey (2002) notes that many middle level teachers were trained to be secondary English teachers. As English teachers, they were trained to teach creative expression, grammar, spelling, drama, writing, and literature. However, they were not trained in ways to teach reading. If your instructional goal is to teach middle level students to become critical, strategic readers, you need to focus on instructional aspects of the reading process. If you design activities that promote strategic learning, rather than the reading of literature, your students can continue to become better readers who *choose* to read throughout middle level grades and beyond.

Generating Interest in the Text

The first step you should take as you design instructional activities that promote reading is to generate student interest in the text you have selected. Middle level students will not be automatically interested in a book even though you may think it's really good. Remember how changeable middle level students are? It's very difficult to choose a novel that all students will find interesting. You can, however, engage students in text by developing activities that draw them into the topic.

Opinionnaire/Questionnaire.   Students often become interested in text if you personalize the subject matter by asking for their opinions about a central concept in their reading (Lenski, Wham, & Johns, 2003). Identifying opinions before reading is a strategy that many readers use. For example, let's say that you are reading an essay on capital punishment for a political science class. Before you read about the author's stance, it's helpful to identify your own opinion on the matter: whether you're in favor of it, against it, ambivalent, or uncertain. Identifying your own opinion increases your interest in whether the author agrees with you or can persuade you to change your mind. Good readers subconsciously identify their own thoughts, beliefs, and opinions before they read.

A strategy that elicits student opinion is the Opinionnaire/Questionnaire (Reasoner, 1976). This strategy examines students' attitudes and has them express their opinion about a topic. To develop an Opinionnaire/Questionnaire, read through the text and find important concepts and ideas and find items appropriate for a survey. Then devise a series of questions and true–false statements about the topic. Type the questions and true–false statements, duplicate the paper, and distribute copies to each student. Have students take the Opinionnaire/ Questionnaire independently, and then have them discuss their answers in small groups and then with the entire class. An example of an Opinionnaire/Questionnaire can be found in Figure 12.2.

Character Quotes.   Another way to generate student interest is to have them engage in predictive activities. A strategy that encourages predictions and generates interest is Character Quotes (Buehl, 2001). The Character Quotes strategy helps students think about characters in a novel before they read. To design this activity, identify a character in the selection and list several quotations from that character on a sheet. Divide the class into small groups and have students generate a list of qualities the character might possess. Have students share their lists of qualities and from that list have students develop a personality profile for the character.

By working in small groups, students can share ideas and generate interest and enthusiasm for reading. They will want to read the text to find out if their predictions were "correct." Another advantage to the Character Quotes strategy is that students work in groups to develop their list of characteristics and their personality

---

1. Why do you think Japanese Americans were sent to internment camps during WWII?

    _____ The Japanese wanted to live together in a gated community.

    _____ The Japanese were being trained to fight in the war.

    _____ Many American people were afraid of the Japanese.

    _____ Many Americans of all nationalities were sent to internment camps.

2. What words would you use to describe internment camps?

    _____ hard labor camps

    _____ jails

    _____ relocation facilities

    _____ historical fiction

    _____ punishment

    _____ other _____

3. Which of the following statements do you believe to be true?

    _____ Japanese volunteered to be relocated in internment camps.

    _____ Internment camps were dreary places.

    _____ No Japanese Americans were allowed to fight in WWII.

    _____ The American government was concerned about the loyalty of Japanese Americans after the attack on Pearl Harbor.

FIGURE 12.2 Opinionnaire/Questionnaire

profiles. Middle level students are social beings and working in groups is another way to help them become engaged in learning. Finally, the Character Quotes strategy is also a reflection of the reading process of sophisticated readers. As you read, you continually process information and develop an ongoing character analysis. You may notice that you are doing this when you think, "This character would *never* say or do this!" Using the Character Quotes strategy provides Critical Readers with an example of the thinking process of good readers and can help them become more interested in the text they will read. An example of Character Quotes can be found in Figure 12.3.

Name **Brandon**   Date **4/12/02**
Novel **Out of the Dust**   Author **Hesse**
Character **Billie Jo**

Character Quotes:
"Daddy named me Billie Jo. Instead, got a long-legged girl with a wide mouth and cheekbones like bicycle handles. He got a redheaded, freckle-faced, narrow-hipped girl with a fondness for apples and a hunger for playing the piano."

"I handed Livie the memory book we'd all filled out with our different slants. I couldn't get the muscles in my throat relaxed enough to tell her how much I'd miss her."

"How does that singing plowboy know something I don't? And how much more is out there most everyone else has heard of except me?"

"We don't talk much. My father was never a talker. Ma's dying has changed that. I guess he lets the sound out of him with the songs he sings."

"I am so filled with bitterness, it comes from the dust, it comes from the silence of my father, it comes from the absence of Ma."

From *Out of the Dust* by Karen Hesse. Copyright © 1997 by Karen Hesse. Reprinted by permission of Scholastic Inc.

Character Qualities
1. **Insecure**
2. **Courageous**
3. **Determined**
4. **Uptight**

Personality Profile
Billie Jo seems insecure and uptight. She's afraid she isn't good enough for her father and at school, but she can't express her feelings. She also wants more in life, so I think she must be courageous. She faced real problems. Billie Jo must also be determined. She keeps trying in spite of hardships.

FIGURE 12.3 Character Quotes

Activating Prior Knowledge

Reading comprehension is based on what readers bring to the text, what they learn from the text, and the connections they make. Teaching middle level students to activate prior knowledge is important because middle level readers come to reading events with a wide range of experiences. Because students have been reading for several years by the time they reach the middle level, they each have deep pockets of information that they bring with them to reading situations. For example, let's say you are teaching the novel *Farewell to Manzanar*. Some of the students in your classroom may be totally unaware of how Japanese Americans were treated in America during World War II. However, some students of Japanese descent may have had family members who experienced internment. And students who have an interest in World War II may also have a great deal of knowledge about the topic.

Not only is the range of differences great in the amount students know, some topical knowledge may be buried deep within students' knowledge structures. Getting students to remember what they know about a topic may take a bit of time. It's like when you sit in class and think, "I've never heard that before," but as the professor continues teaching, the topic begins to sound familiar. The same holds true with middle level students, which is why they need to activate their prior knowledge before reading.

You've read about the importance of activating prior knowledge in other chapters in this book. What other strategies can you use to help students activate their prior knowledge?

Guided writing procedure.   The guided writing procedure (GWP) (Smith & Bean, 1997) is an effective strategy for helping students activate and share prior knowledge in small groups. To implement GWP, select a topic of importance from the novel that you are teaching. If you are teaching *Farewell to Manzanar,* you might choose the topic of the American government's treatment of Japanese during World War II. Then have students individually list the facts they know about the topic. After students have completed their lists, divide the class into groups of three or four students and have students organize their ideas into a semantic web and write a short essay about the topic, either in groups or individually.

Although the GWP can be used at any level, it is especially good for middle level readers. Students in the middle grades are often fluent writers and are able to use writing as a tool for thinking and learning. Furthermore, most middle level students are very social and are responsive to learning from each other. After participating in a GWP, students have not only activated their prior knowledge about the topic under discussion, they have shared knowledge so that more students have a basis of information to use during reading. In addition, you can evaluate how much students know about the topic as they are working in small groups. If few students know about the topic, you should take the opportunity to preteach some information.

Find Someone Who. . . .   Another interactive strategy that activates background knowledge is Find Someone Who. . . , which is described by Stephens and Brown (2000). The Find Someone Who. . . strategy is similar to an icebreaker that you might play at a party, but it serves several academic purposes. First, it helps students activate their own background knowledge about a topic. It also provides a venue for students to share their knowledge while they move around the classroom. (Remember, young teens need to talk and move, not stay in their desks all of the time.) As students participate in Find Someone Who. . . , you can observe and evaluate the amount of background knowledge students have about a topic.

Find Someone Who...	
Has accessed a website on the Japanese involvement in WWII. Comment *It was cool. I'll give you the URL later.* Signature Nick	**Knows someone who fought in WWII.** Comment My great uncle Signature Sharon
Has read a book about WWII. Comment **Facts About WWII** Signature Taylor	**Knows the name or location of WWII internment sites of Japanese.** Comment IOWA Signature JEFF
Has witnessed discrimination of American-born Asians. Comment *My grandfather is Korean, and he was ignored at a restaurant.* Signature Lee	**Has seen a movie or television program about Japanese in WWII.** Comment *Special on last week* Signature *Kim*

FIGURE 12.4   Find Someone Who. . .

To prepare a Find Someone Who. . . activity, divide a sheet of paper into six or eight boxes. In each box, list a fact or activity around a central topic of a novel. Under each item, draw a line for a comment and another line for the student's signature. Duplicate the sheets for each member of the class. Distribute the Find Someone Who. . . sheets and have students circulate around the room asking for other students to sign their sheets. After a set amount of time, have students discuss the general topic. As students discuss, they share their individual background knowledge and, as a result, all students increase their knowledge in preparation for reading. Figure 12.4 provides an example of a Find Someone Who. . . activity based on *Farewell to Manzanar.*

Identify Story Elements

If you're teaching a novel to your entire class, you should review the elements of fiction so students can read with the book's story elements in mind. Story elements, also called story grammar, define the structure of fictional text. You've learned that

Book _____

Author _____

Problem _____

_____

Events

  • _____

  • _____

  • _____

  • _____

  • _____

  • _____

  • _____

  • _____

  • _____

Resolution _____

_____

FIGURE 12.5   Plot Outline

to comprehend text, readers need to identify the structure of the text whether the text is fictional or informational. In this chapter, we discuss only fictional text.

Fictional texts have story elements such as characters, plot, setting, theme, and mood. Before you teach a novel, you should decide which of the fictional elements should be emphasized. For example, the setting of some books is critical for comprehension; for other books you might emphasize characterization, the plot, or the theme. To set the stage for reading, you might choose to design a prereading activity that highlights fictional elements such as a plot outline.

Plot outline.   By the middle level students should be quite familiar with plot, but they may have learned that a plot is a series of events. In middle school you can take students further in their understanding of plot by drawing a plot outline on the chalkboard (Figure 12.5) and describing the stages of the plot.

The plot generally begins with an *introduction*. In the introduction of many books, the setting and characters are described. Each plot has a *conflict,* which is the

Informational texts will be discussed in detail in Chapter 13. Why is text structure important to teach?

problem that is introduced for the characters to solve. Four types of conflicts can occur in fiction:

- Character against nature,
- Character against society,
- Characters against other characters, and
- Characters against themselves.

The conflict of the story is usually presented early in the book at the point of the *rising action*. As the conflict is played out, the action rises until it reaches a *climax*, where the conflict is at its peak and is resolved. After the conflict is resolved, the plot enters the stage of *falling action*. The complications that have occurred as a result of the conflict are solved. The story ends with a *conclusion* or *resolution*.

Strategic readers are aware of plot structure and use what they know about plot as they read (Stein & Glenn, 1979). Therefore, reviewing a plot outline before reading can help students prepare for reading.

YOU TRY IT

Strategy Teaching

The best way to learn about teaching is to teach. When you teach, you learn how to prepare a lesson, how to pace a lesson, and how to engage students in the text. Several prereading strategies were presented in this section: Opinionnaire/Questionnaire, Character Quotes, Guided Writing Procedure, Find Someone Who. . . , and plot outlines. Develop a lesson using one of these strategies for one of your favorite trade books. If you have the opportunity, teach the lesson to middle level students, or teach it to members of your class. As you teach, explicitly tell students how the strategy mirrors the active process of strategic readers. After teaching, reflect on the success or failure of the lesson by answering several of the following questions:

- How did the lesson prepare students for the upcoming reading?
- Did students exhibit interest, curiosity, or motivation to read the text?
- Were students engaged in the activity?
- Did students activate their prior knowledge?
- Do I need to preteach necessary information?
- Are students aware of the structures of fictional materials?
- Will students be able to successfully read this book?

WORD KNOWLEDGE

When you teach a common text to a group of middle level students, you should address the issue of word knowledge. *Word knowledge* consists of vocabulary instruction and word study. Vocabulary instruction is different from using cueing systems to problem solve unknown words, and it's different from decoding words. Vocabulary instruction is the teaching of the meanings of words. Word study, on the other hand, consists of teaching word parts. Middle level students should have learned the basic phonetic rules that govern the English language. But just because students know sound–symbol relationships doesn't mean that they don't need to learn more about words. Middle level students should continue to learn about words through the study of word parts.

As you think about how you will teach middle level students to learn new words, take a moment and reflect on the activities that have helped you become a successful reader. Also, remember the activities that were a waste of time. For example, many of you probably were taught about new words through vocabulary workbooks or by locating words in the dictionary. Although vocabulary workbooks are useful for some students, they generally do not encourage engaged learning or thoughtful reading.

Teaching through workbooks does not match the social constructivist belief system. Why?

Vocabulary Instruction

A critical aspect of reading is understanding the words on the page. If there are too many words that a reader doesn't know, comprehension suffers. You've probably had this experience. If you've ever tried to read a book about a totally new subject, you might have had difficulty understanding the text because you didn't know the meanings of the words. Just in case you haven't had this experience, read the paragraph in Figure 12.6 and without looking up any new words think about how well you understand the passage.

Were you able to understand the passage? It's about a mountain climber named Odd (a Norwegian name) who was climbing one of the highest peaks in the world. As you read, you were probably able to decode the words by using what you know about the context of words and the word parts. For example, you could probably pronounce the word *serpentine,* but that doesn't mean you know the meaning of the word in the passage. To be able to read with comprehension, you need to know the meanings of most of the words that you read.

Designing Effective Vocabulary Instruction

How do readers learn the meanings of words? Educators have different opinions about how readers learn words. Many researchers believe that extensive wide reading accounts for most of the words students learn. In fact, most middle level students learn between 3,000 and 4,000 words each year (Graves, 2000). Obviously, you wouldn't have the time to teach that many new words in a year. It's clear, therefore, that students learn new words without instruction—by reading, listening to others speak, watching television, and so on. But that doesn't mean you shouldn't teach students the meanings of words that they will encounter in the text that you teach.

As a middle level teacher, you should have an organized plan for teaching vocabulary. Blachowicz and Fisher (2000) recommend that students should be active participants in developing their understanding of words and ways to learn them, and that you should design activities that personalize word learning for students. Therefore, you will have two instructional goals as you develop vocabulary instruction. You will need to design activities that encourage students to independently learn new words, and you should also develop activities that help students apply new words to their own lives. The strategies that follow accomplish one or both of these goals.

Odd moved to a wide shelf sheltered by a serac wall along the spur. We passed the cwm on the way to the col. A serpentine track formed. The col was more extensive than I had imagined.

FIGURE 12.6   Vocabulary Lesson

A concept/definition map is an extension of the type of word map called Four Square that you learned about in Chapter 8. How are these two strategies alike and how are they different?

Concept/definition map.　Learning the definition of a word doesn't always help students improve their comprehension. For example, say you were teaching the novel *Holes* by Louis Sachar (1998) and you were discussing the theme of the novel: redemption. Now picture a student asking you the meaning of the word *redemption,* and your giving him a dictionary definition: "the act of redeeming." The student asks what the word *redeem* means and you give another dictionary definition, "to restore or make amends." Although these definitions fit the context of the novel's theme, they don't really explain the complex concept of redemption. Instead of using a dictionary definition, Schwartz and Raphael (1985) suggest using a concept/definition map.

A concept/definition map encourages students to provide information about the word by asking for the category of the word, properties, and illustrations. An example of a concept/definition map is given in Figure 12.7.

Possible Sentences.　Students can personalize vocabulary words when they use them in writing. Possible Sentences (Moore & Moore, 1986) is a strategy that encourages students to use new words by predicting how the words will be used in the text they read. First, identify several words that you want students to learn—some words should be unfamiliar and some should be vaguely familiar. Here is an example of a list of words from the book *Holes* (Sachar, 1998):

forbidden	curse	jumpsuit
wasteland	canteen	convince

Do not explain the meanings of the words just yet. Divide the class into small groups and have students discuss the words. Encourage students to share what they know about the words even if their understanding is incomplete. Then have students write a sentence that they think could be in the novel using two of the words on the list. For example: "The thirsty boy walked through the barren *wasteland,* his empty *canteen* dangling from his belt."

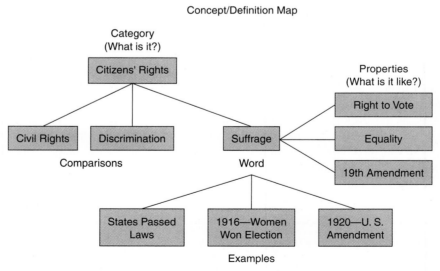

Concept/Definition Map

Adapted from Schwartz, R., & Raphael, T. (1985). Concept of definitions: A key to improving students' vocabulary. The Reading Teacher, 39, *296–304. Copyright by the International Reading Association. All rights reserved.*

FIGURE 12.7　Concept/Definition Map

Encourage the groups of students to share their sentences. After you have shared all of the sentences, have students discuss their ideas about the meanings of the new words. Add your own ideas to those of the students at this time.

Creating a glossary.   Vocabulary activities directed by you engage students in reading and encourage students to learn new words. However, students also need to learn how to identify words they want to learn and to become self-directed learners. To encourage independent learning, Carroll (1998) suggests that you have students create their own glossary of new words from a book they are reading. A glossary is list of words with short definitions that apply directly to the context of that book. Show students glossaries that are at the back of textbooks, such as social studies or science books. Tell them that they will be developing their own glossary for the book they are reading. Provide students with paper stapled to form a small book that is sized to fit into the back of the book they are reading. Have students write the title "Glossary" on the top of the first page. Encourage students to write one or more glossary entries each time they read a chapter from the book. Tell students that glossary entries are typically written in alphabetical order if they are found at the end of a book, but that they could also be organized by chapter. Explain to students that this glossary will be organized by chapters.

◼ YOU TRY IT

Creating A Glossary

Create a glossary for some of the new words and terms that you learned in this chapter. Discuss how creating a glossary helped you understand some of the more difficult concepts you encountered. You may consider developing glossaries for other chapters in this book.

Word Study

You know that you need to teach phonics to younger students, and you might have thought that you won't need to teach middle level students how to figure out unknown words. Middle level students, however, also need to learn about words; it's just that what you teach older students is different. By the time students reach middle level grades, most of them are able to understand the rudiments of phonics, but they may not know how to decode polysyllabic words. Remember, your goal is for students to be able to read with comprehension, and to do this, they will need to understand the words in the text. In an article on teaching word study to adolescents, Hennings (2000) reminds us: "Knowledge of words, ability to access that knowledge efficiently, and ability to integrate new concepts into existing conceptual schemata are key factors in reading and listening comprehension" (p. 269). Research indicates that some students will be able to figure out word meanings independently if they are able to identify word parts (Baumann, Bradley, Edwards, Font, & Hruby, 2000).

Affixes.   Word parts that are attached to the beginning or the end of a root word are called affixes. You probably remember them as prefixes and suffixes. Prefixes are word parts that can be added to the beginning of a word such as *rerun*. *Re-* is the prefix, and *run* is the root word. When you add *re-* to *run* you change the meaning of the word. A suffix is a word part that is added to the end of a word that changes the meaning or is used to make the word grammatically correct. For example, when the suffix *-ing* is

Prefix	Meaning(s)	Suffixes	Example
ab-	away, from, off	-ed	drafted
ad-	at, to, toward	-ing	jogging
be-	make, against, to a great degree	-s/es	books, washes
com-	with, together, in association	-al	national
de-	separation, away, opposite of, from	-er/or	bigger, janitor
en-	cause to be, put in or on	-ible/able	possible, affordable
ex-	from, out of, former, apart, away	-ion/tion	region, generation
in-	into, in, within	-ity	popularity
in-	not, opposite of, reversal	-ly	mainly
pre-	before in place, time, rank, order	-ment	government
pro-	before, forward, for, in favor of	-ness	kindness
re-	again, back	-y	tardy
sub-	under, beneath, subordinate		

FIGURE 12.8   Frequently Occurring Prefixes and Suffixes

reacquaint	rebuild	reheat	replay
readjust	recharge	rehire	resell
readmit	recheck	reload	restring
realign	recopy	reinvest	restyle
reappear	redecorate	relive	retell
reappoint	rededicate	relocate	rethink
rearm	redirect	rematch	reunite
reassemble	redraw	renumber	reuse
reassign	reenter	reorder	revisit
reawaken	refasten	repack	
reborn	refuel	repaint	

FIGURE 12.9   Word Tower

added to *run,* the word becomes *running.* Middle school students can learn the common prefixes and suffixes and how they are used in English. Figure 12.8 includes a list of prefixes and suffixes that you should consider teaching middle level students.

Word tower.   Once students have learned several prefixes and suffixes, you might teach them how to create a word tower (Hennings, 2000). A word tower lists words that can be generated from a common base (not necessarily a root word), or words that can be generated from a single prefix or suffix. An example of a word tower using the prefix *re-* can be found in Figure 12.9.

DESIGNING COMPREHENSION INSTRUCTION

The purpose of reading is comprehension, or the understanding of text. As you've learned in previous chapters of this book, there is not just one "meaning" for any text; meaning is individually constructed by each reader. Readers bring their background, knowledge, and abilities to reading situations, and they develop their own personal meaning from text. How readers construct meaning and how teachers should design instruction to facilitate comprehension has been the topic of reading research for several decades.

When educators based their teaching practices on behaviorism, they believed that "comprehension abilities improved through instruction in the numerous skills identified in basal reading programs" (Dole, 2000, p. 52). Since the movement toward a belief in social constructivism, however, reading educators have redefined comprehension instruction. Researchers such as Michael Pressley (1999) have detailed what it means to teach students how to comprehend text through teacher explanation and modeling of reading processes. Despite the research on methods of teaching comprehension, the majority of teachers in schools today do not really teach comprehension (National Reading Panel, 2000); instead, they assign and test.

Think about your own experiences reading in middle level grades. What did your teachers do to help you construct meaning from text? If your teachers were typical, they may have conducted a prereading activity, assigned vocabulary words to memorize, assigned you to read a section or a chapter, conducted a class discussion, and then gave you a quiz. These practices *did not* teach comprehension. At best, they encouraged you to read books, but they did not provide ways for you to develop meaning from your reading.

What Is Reading Comprehension?

You might be wondering right now what reading comprehension really is and how to teach it. Blachowicz and Ogle (2001) describe reading comprehension as skillful, strategic reading. They list the strategies good readers use when reading:

- Previewing the text,
- Predicting from the preview,
- Setting purposes for reading by asking questions,
- Choosing an appropriate reading speed,
- Checking understanding while reading,
- Integrating new information with known information,
- Monitoring understanding,
- Making ongoing predictions,
- Summarizing and synthesizing what has been read,
- Responding to the text,
- Cross-checking with other information,
- Checking for fulfillment of the purpose of reading, and
- Using what is read.

 You've learned many ways to promote comprehension in other chapters of this book. What strategies have you learned that apply to middle level students?

You might be surprised at the number of strategies good readers use and at the complexity of the thinking processes that occur during reading. You might also be wondering how you will teach students to use all of these strategies. One way to model comprehension processes is through the use of instructional strategies. As you model comprehension, you should explain to students how to internalize the strategies so they become part of the students' thinking processes during reading.

Preview-Predict-Confirm charts.   Good readers preview texts before reading—even if it's just to read the back cover, read the author's biography, check the length of the book, and scan through it to see if the book has any interesting textual features such as photographs. Along with previewing, readers should also make preliminary predictions about the content of the book. A strategy that can be used to facilitate previewing and prediction is a Preview–Predict–Confirm chart (Yopp & Yopp, 2001).

To use a Preview–Predict–Confirm chart, have students scan through a book to anticipate words, ideas, and concepts that they think might occur in the story. Have students independently generate a list of words that they predict will be found in their reading. After students have developed their own lists, have them meet in groups and share ideas to develop a combined list. Have students use this list as they read to confirm their predictions. A Preview–Predict–Confirm chart based on *Walk Two Moons* by Sharon Creech (1994) is shown in Figure 12.10.

Elaborative interrogations.   During reading, good readers ask themselves questions to keep actively engaged in reading and to construct meaning from text. To understand this better, think about your own reading habits. You may not be aware of the many questions you ask during reading. As you read this section, make your thinking processes visible by jotting down the questions that you ask while reading. An example of the thinking process of one reader of this text follows:

> I read the subtitle, elaborative interrogations, with interest. I immediately connected interrogations with police work, and I wondered how it applied to teaching reading. I like the term *elaborative,* so I predicted that the strategy encourages students to ask lots of questions. Then I started reading the paragraph, and I found myself agreeing with the authors: I believe good readers do ask questions while reading, but I wondered whether many middle school students actually do. I don't remember thinking about my reading very much when I was that young.

A questioning strategy that promotes deep questioning is elaborative interrogations (Pressley, Symons, McDaniel, Snyder, & Turnure, 1988). When using elaborative interrogations, students don't just ask questions during reading, they ask questions that actively promote the connection of their background knowledge to the information they are reading. The elaborative interrogations strategy consists of four questions that readers ask during reading:

1. Why?
2. What I am learning now?
3. What do I already know about this?
4. What relationships can I find?

Title: *Walk Two Moons*

Author: Sharon Creech

Predictions	Appeared in Text?	
	Yes	No
Yellow boa	X	
Car trip	X	
Camp		X
Hospital	X	

FIGURE 12.10   Preview–Predict–Confirm Chart

Model how to ask these questions during the reading of the text you are using. Encourage students to use elaborative interrogations by providing them with sticky notes or a notebook to record their questions and answers. Remind students that good readers ask these questions while they read.

■▰▰▰ **YOU TRY IT** ▰▰▰▰▰▰▰▰▰▰▰▰

Elaborative Interrogations

Read a passage of a young adult book that would be appropriate to teach middle level readers. From that passage ask yourself the four questions used in elaborative interrogations:

1. Why?
2. What I am learning now?
3. What do I already know about this?
4. What relationships can I find?

Write the answers to these questions to use as an example of the thinking processes of good reading. Share your examples with your classmates. You can use these examples to demonstrate elaborative interrogations when you have the chance to teach this strategy to students in schools.

ReQuest.   Questioning during reading is one of the most important strategies students can use. If students ask questions during reading, they become more actively involved in the text. The elaborative interrogations strategy is designed for self-questioning, but the ReQuest strategy (Manzo, 1969) is better suited for students to ask questions in pairs or small groups. When students participate in ReQuest, they have the benefit of listening to questions developed by their classmates.

To use the ReQuest strategy, have students read a chapter of their novel or a passage of the text independently or in pairs. After students have read the passage, ask them to generate questions and to write them on index cards. Collect the index cards and distribute them randomly to students in the class. Make sure you take a card too. Each student who holds a card can ask that question of another student (or of you). Monitor the answers to make sure that students are getting accurate information and encourage students to keep asking questions as they read.

Rereading.   Have you ever read a passage of a text over several times just because you liked the rhythm of the language or the actions of the characters? Or maybe you've reread portions of textbooks to remember information for your classes in school. Middle level students can also benefit from rereading passages according to Faust and Glenzer (2000). Readers might reread simply for pleasure, or they may reread to clarify confusions during reading. Faust and Glenzer found another purpose for rereading that might surprise some teachers. They had eighth-grade students reread a book, *Roll of Thunder, Hear My Cry* (Taylor, 1976), that the students had read in fifth grade. The researchers reported that the eighth-grade students benefited from rereading the book. One student said that when she read the book in fifth grade, she only read for the main plot, but on rereading, she was able to identify themes in the book that related to her life. Other students agreed, stating that they enjoyed rereading the book and recommended that teachers use this strategy more often.

You can have students reread passages from their texts for a variety of different purposes without having them reread an entire book. Rereading lessons should fit the context of the story, but a few general purposes for rereading are:

- To understand the characters' motivation,
- To get a sense of the mood of the story,
- To listen to the characters' dialogue, and
- To find additional reasons for the conflict.

Classroom Discussions

Comprehension is socially constructed in several ways, one of which is through classroom discussions. When students enter into discussions, they offer their current constructions of meaning, which are subsequently influenced by the ideas of their classmates (Almasi, 1996) and the discussion itself (Lenski, 2001a). As the discussion progresses, students revise their original understandings and create new meanings about their reading. In this way, students' comprehension deepens.

If you think about times you have discussed books or movies with friends, you'll see how discussion promotes comprehension and also how it is influenced by social interactions. Think about one of the books you read for literature class in college. Were there times when you talked about the book with a friend and found you had richer, deeper understandings? That's what it can be like for students when they engage in classroom discussions; their comprehension deepens.

Not all classroom discussions promote comprehension. Have you ever been in a class where the discussion did nothing to help you learn more? Courtney Cazden (2001) found that teachers dominate many discussions to the extent that students have little meaningful input. She found that typical classroom discussions follow the

Book discussions can be invigorating.

same structure: The teacher initiates a question, the students respond, and the teacher evaluates the students' answers. Cazden labeled those types of discussions I-R-E (intiate, respond, and evaluate). Almasi (1996) suggests that students learn more from discussions that are not dominated by teachers but are led by students.

Student-led discussions.   There are a number of ways to let students have more control over classroom discussions. One way is to rearrange the seating arrangements during class discussions and to sit with students. If you teach in a typical classroom, you won't have room to move the desks into a circle, but you can organize the desks into a type of double oval (Figure 12.11). When students are facing each other, rather than all facing you, they are more likely to discuss more freely (Almasi, 1996). Once you have arranged the desks so that they are not in rows facing you, sit with students and participate with them rather than asking questions. Try to think of your class as a large group of friends freely talking about a book.

Another way to share the lead with students is to allow one or more students to co-teach with you. Invite several students to lead classroom discussions with you, give them time to prepare for the discussion, and provide them with support as they ask questions. Encourage students to ask open-ended questions that require thinking and conversation. You might have students develop questions before the discussion so that they are successful discussion leaders.

Socratic questioning.   The questions that you or your student leaders prepare make the difference between a stagnant talk and a lively discussion. Tanner and Casados (1998) suggest using Socratic questioning to promote rich discussions. Socratic questioning leads students to develop their own conclusions. To engage in Socratic questioning, the leader simply prepares one open-ended question. After

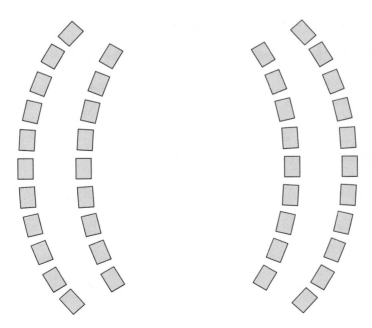

FIGURE 12.11   Double Oval Seating for Discussions

posing that question, the leader guides the discussion participants to form their own opinions using prompts like the following:

- What are your ideas on the subject?
- How are your ideas like those other students have offered?
- How is your point of view different from those discussed?
- How did you reach your point of view?
- Where do you think your ideas take us?
- What are the reasons for your thinking?
- What evidence do you have to support your ideas?

It may take a few sessions for students to become comfortable participating in this type of discussion, but, with practice, most students can learn to engage in rich Socratic questioning.

EXTENDING MEANING

As students read, they generate a provisional interpretation of text; they construct meaning, but that meaning may be superficial. Often students read just to finish the text, or do what Mackey (1997) calls "good-enough" reading. "Good-enough" reading is reading that gets finished but isn't necessarily thoughtful. You experience this type of reading when you read a Stephen King novel over a vacation, and you read for the plot, not to discover a universal truth. Contrast that type of reading with the reading you've done for college classes. You probably read college textbooks with much more thought.

Mackey (1997) found that students often read classroom texts superficially, or just to get them done. When students were questioned about the intensity of their reading, they replied that a quick reading was "good enough" for school. When students read quickly, just to finish, they don't move beyond their initial interpretation of text to a deeper understanding.

Comprehension can be extended through a variety of thinking activities. As a teacher, you'll have to decide which type of activity you want students to participate in based on your instructional goals. If you want students to think more deeply about the text, you may develop activities that have students look back in the text for further learning. Another instructional goal is to have students think critically about the text. Each of these types of activities has merit, and you should do both of them throughout a unit of study.

Getting the Facts/Making Inferences

At times you'll want to make sure students are getting the facts of the story. Middle level students will be reading more complex texts than they have in the past, and they sometimes have difficulty following the plot of some books. Some of the books that you teach will have a straightforward plot, but students will also encounter books that have plots with flashbacks and other sophisticated literary devices. When this occurs, students may take notes as they read, underline key passages, or develop a timeline. Each of these strategies can help readers follow complex texts. Just as you need strategies to help you understand the plots of literature you've read in college, middle level readers need to learn strategies to help them follow their texts.

Follow the character.   Some of the books you teach will have rich, multidimensional characters. Students will need to pay close attention to the facets of the characters so that they can understand the character's actions and motivations. One strategy that is useful in keeping track of a character is Follow the Character (Buehl, 2001). Follow the Character is an organizational grid that students can use to keep track of a character's thoughts, actions, speech, changes, and what other characters think or say about him. To use the Follow the Character strategy, design a grid similar to the example shown in Figure 12.12. Write the title of the book at the top of the page, and identify the conflict in the center circle. At the top of the page write what the character does, on the right side write what the character says or thinks, on the bottom write how others feel about the character, and on the left side write how the character changes.

Students may find the Follow the Character strategy to be challenging until they have had several opportunities to use it with the entire class or in small groups. Make sure you model the strategy several times, then have students Follow the Character independently. As students become confident using the strategy, encourage them to change or adapt it to fit their needs.

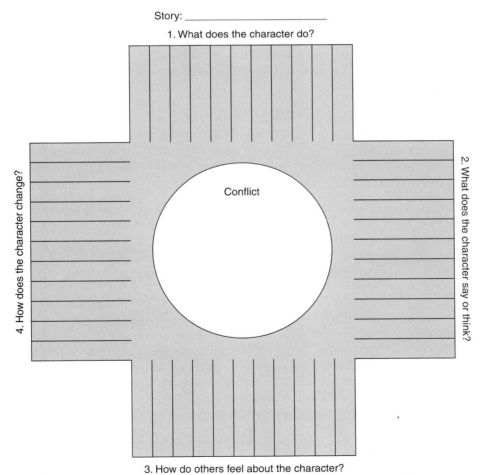

From Buehl, D. (2001). Classroom strategies for interactive learning (2nd ed.). Newark, DE: International Reading Association.

FIGURE 12.12 Follow the Character

Technology topic: Character home page.   By middle level grades, many students will be competent using new technologies. In fact, many students may have computer skills that surpass yours. Even the students who have few technical skills will be familiar with home pages on the Internet, and many students will have had experiences designing websites. A good way to incorporate computer skills and reading is to have students create a home page for a character from a book you are reading (Stephens & Brown, 2000). When students have to design a character home page, they will need to recall many facts about the character, and, if they can't remember, they'll have to go back into their books to find more information.

To have students design character home pages, divide the class into small groups and have students identify a character that is of interest to them. Then have students pretend they are the character. Have them design a home page that includes personal information such as age, family, school, friends, characteristics, interests, hobbies, problems, and home. Students can be creative and incorporate pictures and music on the home page.

Reading Critically

 Critical literacy was introduced in Chapter 1 and discussed in Chapter 10. What is your understanding of critical literacy?

One of the differences between middle level students and younger readers is their ability to read critically. Reading from a critical perspective is the positioning of text in social and political arenas (Green, 2001). Most middle level students will have the potential for reading critically, but they will need guidance, practice, and demonstrations.

Perspective guide.   One aspect of reading critically is in identifying the perspective the author is taking. Texts are not neutral; authors subtly, and not so subtly, express opinions through print. Therefore, readers need to take note of the perspective the author takes. A strategy that guides students to look at the author's perspective is a perspective guide (Lenski et al., 2003).

To develop a perspective guide, choose two or more texts that have been written around a central theme. You can choose two short stories, or you can choose a fictional text and another text genre. Identify four to eight quotations from each of the texts that relate to the central theme. Write the quotations on paper, duplicate the sheet, and distribute it to your students. Divide the class into small groups and have them try to identify the source of the quotations. Encourage students to discuss their rationale for their choices.

Discussion web.   A key aspect of critical reading is the ability to view an issue from alternate views. A strategy that promotes discussion about two views on a subject is a discussion web (Alvermann, 1991). To implement a discussion using a discussion web, pose a central question for students to answer. Then have them divide into groups and answer the question from both points of view giving reasons for each point of view. Encourage students to discuss both sides as objectively as possible. After the discussion, have students independently reach their own conclusions. Some students may have difficulty viewing an issue from an alternative perspective, but with practice, they can learn. An example of a discussion web can be found in Figure 12.13.

Opinion Proof.   Students will be exposed to many different opinions during their middle level years. Differing opinions will come through reading, through classes, through other students, and through the media. A strategy that helps students learn how to evaluate the logic of an opinion is the Opinion Proof strategy (Santa, Dailey,

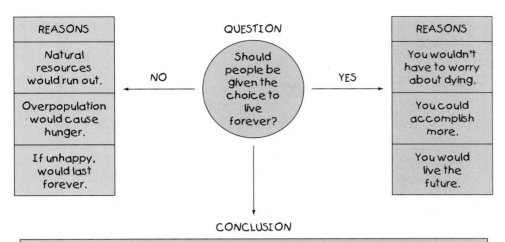

FIGURE 12.13   Discussion Web for *Tuck Everlasting* (Babbit, 1975)

Appealing to authority: Invoking authority as the last word.

Appealing to emotion: Using emotion as proof.

Appealing to force: Using threats to establish the validity of a claim.

Appealing to the people: Justifying a claim based on its popularity.

Arguing from ignorance: Arguing that a claim is justified because its opposite cannot
  be proved.

Begging the question: Making a claim and producing arguments that do not support
  the claim.

Contradiction: Presenting information that contradicts a claim.

Evading the issue: Talking around the issue rather than addressing it.

False analogy: Comparing unmatched elements.

False cause: Crediting an effect to a cause without evidence.

Hasty generalization: Drawing a conclusion from too few examples.

Poisoning the well: Overly committed to one position and explaining everything in
  light of that position.

FIGURE 12.14   Reasoning Fallacies

& Nelson, 1985). The Opinion Proof strategy helps students form an opinion, look
for reasoning fallacies, and revise their thinking through writing.

   To implement the Opinion Proof strategy, write an example of an opinion that
relates to the text you are using. Tell students that you need evidence to support the
opinion. Divide the class into small groups and have students generate evidence that
they think will support your opinion. Have the groups share their evidence and list it
on the chalkboard. Explain to students that not all evidence supports any statement.
Then discuss the reasoning fallacies listed in Figure 12.14. Have students discuss each

bit of evidence and determine whether it actually supports the opinion or is faulty reasoning. Use this strategy frequently so students can become familiar with all of the reasoning fallacies.

Social action.   The epitome of critical reading is taking social action. Print is a social and cultural reality that influences how people think and act. Many middle level students have a deep concern about social issues and are interested in promoting social justice. When middle level students use critical literacy in practice, they reach a better understanding of the power of print.

Many middle school students are currently experiencing how to use literacy to promote equality. An example is that of students who read about the potential strip mining of a nearby mountain (Powell, Cantrell, & Adams, 2001). These middle level students used their literacy skills to research the issue, write letters, and speak at public forums about the pros and cons of the strip-mining venture. The students also interviewed the potential employees of the mine, and after careful deliberation, the students reached a reasoned opinion. They made their opinion known to local politicians and eventually changed the scope of the strip-mining project. The use of critical literacy made an actual difference to the students in this school and to the entire community.

ASSESSING STUDENT LEARNING

Many teachers give traditional tests at the end of novels to assess comprehension and vocabulary knowledge. These tests often consist of multiple-choice, true–false, or essay questions and are called *criterion-referenced tests* or *book tests*. With these types of tests, you are trying to determine how much students know about a specific content; in this case the content is a piece of literature. Teachers who give book tests typically grade students in comparison to the class rather than individually (Marzano, 2000). You're familiar with this type of grading; it's probably the way you were graded in school. However, giving book tests and grading students in comparison with their class does not actually assess how well a student can comprehend in general; it measures how well a student understood the piece of literature and how well the student was able to read and understand and respond to the test.

Classroom Assessment

Written Retellings

An alternative way to assess students' knowledge is for them to give written retellings of the book or story. A retelling is a summary of the story that includes all of the story elements such as characters, setting, plot, and theme. Written retellings are appropriate for middle level students because most of them will be fairly fluent writers who are able to express themselves in print. To assess students' written retellings, determine when you want to assess your students—after reading a few chapters, half of the book, or all of the book. Ask them to summarize the story in a page or two. Remind students to thoroughly explain the plot, setting, characters, and theme.

You can evaluate written retellings using scoring guidelines similar to those shown in Figure 12.15. When you evaluate papers using scoring guidelines, you need to determine which score most accurately reflects the paper. This type of assessment is subjective in that you are making judgments based on a standard that can change. Therefore, you should be as consistent as you can as you score written retellings.

Students who are unable to write coherent English paragraphs may need a different type of assessment. In what other ways can you assess comprehension?

Score	Description
3	The response is complete. It indicates a solid understanding of the story. It provides accurate, relevant details in a logical order.
2	The response is not complete, but indicates some understanding of the story. The paper provides some details, but not necessarily in a logical manner.
1	The response has accurately reported parts of the story, but with enough gaps that comprehension is questionable.
0	The response is inaccurate and indicates little or no understanding of the story.

FIGURE 12.15 Written Retelling Scoring Guideline

CONNECTIONS: WHAT'S NEXT?

In this chapter we discussed how to teach middle level students fictional text in whole groups (Figure 12.16). If you teach middle level English or language arts, one of your biggest decisions will be the type of text to use: basal readers, literature anthologies, or trade books. No matter which type of text you select, you should teach students how to approach unfamiliar words through word analysis and vocabulary knowledge. You should also teach comprehension strategies through explanation, modeling, and encouraging students to internalize the thinking processes that should occur during reading. As you work with students to promote strategic reading, you should also help them think critically. Middle level students have the abstract thinking ability and the interest in the world to analyze text and to determine how the text fits into cultural and social norms.

Another aspect of middle level reading that we didn't address in this chapter is reading and writing informational text, or content-area material. In middle level grades, students take content-area classes: science, social studies, math, and so on, where they read textbooks to learn. Many of the strategies that you've learned in this chapter and in previous chapters of the book can be applied to reading in the content areas. Informational text has a different organizational pattern, however, so additional strategies for reading and writing in content areas will be presented in the next chapter.

FIGURE 12.16 A Developmental Approach to the Teaching of Reading

	Early Readers	Interpretive Readers	Critical Readers
Theories underscored as readers develop:	Social Constructivism Psycholinguistic Critical Transactional	Social Constructivism Psycholinguistic Critical Transactional	Social Constructivism Psycholinguistic Critical Transactional

continued

FIGURE 12.16 *Continued*

	Early Readers	Interpretive Readers	Critical Readers
Whole-group instruction through:	• Read-alouds • Shared texts • Comprehension strategies • Working with words	• Read-alouds • Using basals • Literature-based models • Word-building strategies • Comprehension strategies	• Read-alouds • Common texts (e.g., basals, anthologies, trade books) • Comprehension strategies • Vocabulary instruction and word analysis • Researching • Critical reading • Reading content area texts • Studying and note-taking
Assessment ideas for whole group:	• Observations • Kidwatching • Anecdotal notation	• Portfolios • Open-ended questions • Rubrics	• Written retellings • Research projects • Interest inventories • Content-area histories • Cloze procedure
Small-group instruction through:	• Guided reading • Teaching for strategies • Working with words	• Basal readers • Literature anthologies • Fluency practice • Guided silent reading • Literature circles • Inquiry groups	• Book clubs • Trade books
Assessment ideas for small groups:	• Running Records • Retellings • Discussions with children	• Names test • Fluency checklist • Peer assessment • Inquiry rubric	• Student information card • Bio poem • "I Used to… But Now I…" poem • Observational checklist • Student self-assessment • Norm-referenced tests
Independent learning through:	• Independent reading • Reading/writing workshop • Making books • Reading the room	• Independent reading • Reading/writing workshop • Responding through writing • Reading logs	• Sustained silent reading and writing
Sociocultural contexts:	• Literacy partnerships with parents • Parents in the classroom • Home–school communication	• Reading/writing connection for life • Oral histories • Home literacy activities • Parent programs	• Parents as coaches • Funds of knowledge • Parent–student book clubs

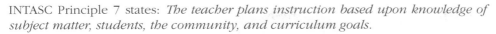

FOR YOUR PORTFOLIO

ENTRY 12.1   *Using State Standards*

INTASC Principle 7 states: *The teacher plans instruction based upon knowledge of subject matter, students, the community, and curriculum goals.*

Locate your state standards for teaching reading to middle level students. Identify the standards that apply to teaching reading skills and strategies with fictional text. You might have to sift through language arts standards to find those that apply to reading. Then explain how you will incorporate state standards into your overall reading program.

ENTRY 12.2   *Understanding Word Knowledge*

IRA/NCTE Standard 6 states: *Students apply knowledge of language structure, language conventions (e.g., spelling and punctuation), media techniques, figurative language, and genre to create, critique, and discuss print and nonprint texts.*

To teach word knowledge at the middle level grades, you need to have an understanding of the types of word analysis skills that are appropriate for Critical Readers. Locate a reading or language arts teacher's manual that includes a scope and sequence of word analysis skills. Identify the skills that you think would be most appropriate for middle level learners, and then prepare a list of terms that you will teach students. (For example, you'll want to teach students about prefixes and suffixes.) If any of the terms are unknown to you, look them up in a literacy dictionary.

TO LEARN MORE

Helpful Websites

Visit our Companion Website at *http://www.prenhall.com/lenski* to link to the following sites:

Censorship

> This is the official website of the National Coalition Against Censorship.
> *http://www.ncac.org*

Office for Intellectual Freedom

> Visit the website of the subgroup on intellectual freedom from the American Library Association professional organization.
> *http://www.ala.org/oif.html*

Vocabulary

> Provides lesson plans and vocabulary games.
> *http://www.education-world.com/a_lesson/lesson241.shtml*

Teaching K–8

> Contains teaching ideas with many helpful links.
> *http://www.teachingk-8.com/*

Critical Literacy

> This interactive site helps you learn, understand, and apply the concept of critical literacy.
> *http://students.washington.edu/jmcarney/critlit.html*

chapter **13**

Reading in the Content Areas

Essential Learning Questions

- How does instruction using informational texts differ from teaching young adult novels?
- Why is it important to teach students strategies to learn from text?
- How does researching apply to social constructivist theory?
- What assessment tools does a middle level teacher need to make decisions about student learning?
- How can content-area teachers meet the needs of students with special needs?

As a teacher of middle level students, you might teach one of the content areas: mathematics, social studies, science, fine arts, or physical education as well as language arts, reading, or English. When you teach a content subject, your main focus will be to teach the material from that subject, but you'll also need to teach students how to read informational texts and how to learn from texts.

In your university content classes you probably learned how to teach science, history, or math using hands-on approaches. Someone might have even told you that you don't need textbooks to teach content knowledge. It's true that reading textbooks isn't the only way to access information; however, reading is definitely one of the ways to learn. Authors of content-area literacy textbooks (e.g., Alvermann & Phelps, 2002; Vacca & Vacca, 2002) take the stance that reading is one of the primary ways for students to learn content-area information. Granted, students learn from experiences, but the knowledge they gain from texts should not be ignored.

The way you teach content-area reading will be different from teaching students how to read fictional text. You might remember that readers can take different stances toward text: an aesthetic or an efferent stance. Readers can identify with the text, they can take information away from the text, or both. When you teach reading in content-area classrooms, you'll be focusing on teaching your students to take an efferent stance as they read to learn, or to read so that they learn from text.

TEACHING INFORMATIONAL TEXT

Many students, even good students, have difficulty reading textbooks. NAEP data indicate that the majority of middle level readers are able to read at a basic level, but few are able to read and interpret informational texts (Donahue, Voelkl, Campbell, & Mazzeo, 1999). Students have difficulty reading textbooks in science, history, or math for a number of reasons. First, most students have had few experiences reading informational texts. Also, research reported by the National Reading Panel (2000) suggests that teachers generally don't teach the strategies that students need to use when reading textbooks. That may be because many secondary teachers don't know which strategies help students comprehend informational text (Spor & Schneider, 1999).

Another more subtle reason why students have difficulty reading textbooks is that they don't view reading textbooks as "reading" (Feathers, 1998). School reading is different from the reading students choose to do on their own. In schools, teachers tend

Visit the online journal in Chapter 13 on our Companion Website at *www.prenhall.com/lenski* to answer these questions. Save your answers to your hard drive or to a disk to compile an online journal.

You can adapt most of the teaching strategies you already know to content-area subjects. Which strategies do you think would work best?

to focus on facts rather than the larger issues presented in the text (Feathers, 1998). The focus on facts prevents students from understanding what they have read, which, in turn, causes students to become frustrated with the type of reading done in content-area classrooms. And, too often, students avoid reading textbooks as a tool for learning.

Students who use strategies as they read, however, are much more likely to be successful readers (Rand Study Group, 2002). Some students automatically use reading strategies as they read, but many do not. Those who do not, have difficulty constructing meaning from text. There are teaching strategies, however, that you can demonstrate to help students learn how to use reading strategies independently and to help them gain information from the texts they read.

Reading strategically is one component of the reading act. Another component of reading, however, is the text itself. Remember, reading is an interaction between the reader, the text, and the context. As you think about teaching students to read informational text, therefore, you should help them access the text.

Friendly and Unfriendly Texts

You've probably noticed that some textbooks are more difficult to read than others. Think about the textbooks you've read in college that were especially difficult to read. Those texts may have been difficult for you because you didn't have much background knowledge about the topic or the readability level was higher than you were comfortable reading. Another aspect of difficulty is that some texts are "friendly" and some are "unfriendly" (Armbruster, 1984).

An "unfriendly" text has certain attributes that cause readers to work especially hard to comprehend the ideas presented in the text. These attributes include an organization that is hard to decipher, a writing style that is too difficult, passages that are too long, and/or graphics that are difficult to read (Olson & Gee, 1991; Smith, 1997). When students are expected to read a text that is "unfriendly," too many of them decide that the effort they must expend to read is not worth it.

Text coherence.   If a text is to be readable for middle level readers, it must be written in a style that they can access, and it must also exhibit textual coherence (Armbruster, 1984). *Coherence* refers to how clearly the material is presented. Two types of coherence must be evident if a text is to be readable: global coherence and local coherence.

Texts that exhibit global coherence are organized so that readers can identify the major concepts being presented. Some textbooks are organized in small chunks that in the minds of the authors are related but that in the minds of young adolescents are difficult to connect. Friendly textbooks have an organizational pattern that "connects the dots" for its readers.

A second type of coherence is local coherence, which refers to the transitions between ideas within clauses or sentences. Sometimes textbook authors omit transitional words and phrases in order to keep their sentences short. They may want to shorten sentences in order to adhere to a readability formula. If some sentences contain long passages with many multisyllabic words, the readability may be calculated as a higher readability. In those cases, the authors often rewrite the material so that the sentences are shorter, thus fitting the readability formula. Short sentences, however, are not always easiest to understand, especially if the sentences have to omit important transitional wording. When that occurs, the writing tends to lack local coherence and is difficult for middle level students to read.

Readability formulas were described earlier in this text. In what ways does the readability of a text impact its friendliness?

Since the concept of "friendly" texts was introduced in the 1980s, textbook publishers have made significant progress in producing textbooks that are easier to read for middle level students. You may be surprised when you look at the current content-area textbooks. In most cases, contemporary textbooks are much more friendly than the textbooks you might remember from your schooling.

■■■■ YOU TRY IT ■■■ ▌ ▌ ▌ ▌ ▌ ■ ▄▄

Identifying Friendly Content-Area Textbooks

Find three different textbooks in a content area that you may teach, or use three textbooks from different subjects. For this activity, try to use textbooks that are actually used in the schools in your geographic area. Rate each of the textbooks using the teacher survey that follows. After you have rated each of the textbooks, post your findings on the Companion Website (http://www.prenhall.com/lenski) so that others can read your opinions about the friendliness of different books.

How Friendly Is This Textbook?
Teacher Assessment

Name _____   Date _____

Title of text _____

Publisher _____

Date of publication _____   Grade level _____

1. Pacing of new concepts

3	2	1
Too many new concepts	Appropriate number	Not enough new concepts

2. Concepts clarified with examples

3	2	1
Not enough examples	Appropriate number of examples	Too many examples

3. Degree of prior knowledge required

3	2	1
Too much prior knowledge	Adequate prior knowledge	Not enough prior knowledge

4. Vocabulary load

3	2	1
Too many new words	Appropriate number of new words	Not enough new words

5. Number of abstract terms

3	2	1
Too many abstract terms	Appropriate number of abstract terms	Not enough abstract terms

continued

6. Important information

3	2	1
Not easily identified	Easily identified	Too simple

7. Organizational patterns

3	2	1
Too difficult	Appropriate	Too easy

8. Sentence length

3	2	1
Too complex	Appropriate	Too simple

9. Text features: subheadings, pictures, graphs, etc.

3	2	1
Not enough	Appropriate	Too many

10. Concept load

3	2	1
Too difficult	Appropriate	Too easy

Rating Scale:
Textbooks receiving a score of 20 are the friendliest texts for your students. If a book received between 21 and 30, the text may be too difficult for your students, and if it received between 10 and 19, it may be too easy.

Overall impression:
As you rate a textbook, you will also be making subjective judgments about the book that will not appear on the rating scale. Write your overall impressions of the appropriateness of the book for the course that you will teach.

Organizational Patterns

All texts can be classified as one of three patterns: narrative, expository, or mixed. Narrative text is organized in a pattern, sometimes called story grammar, that includes a plot, setting, theme, and characters. Expository text can be organized into several patterns: simple listing, sequence, compare–contrast, cause–effect, problem–solution. Mixed patterns are used in books such as biographies that have aspects of both narrative and expository texts.

Differences between informational text and narrative text.   Feathers (1998) describes the three major differences between narrative and expository text as the point of view, the orientation, and the linkages. Students are used to reading narrative texts with a first- or third-person point of view. First-person point of view is being used when the author tells the story using first-person pronouns (such as I). Edgar Allan Poe's, "The Tell-Tale Heart," is a good example of a story told in the first person. In the case of third-person narratives, the story is told from the point of view of a character, using the pronouns *he, she,* and *it*. Most popular fiction is written in third person. In the famous Sherlock Holmes stories, for example, Watson is the narrator and he tells the readers what occurs in the story, what Holmes does, and the outcome of

Advice for New Teachers

Text Patterns

Dear Linda,

I know I need to teach my middle level students how to identify the organizational patterns of my content-area textbook, but I have trouble figuring them out myself. What should I do?

Dear New Teacher,

I have the same problem. The textbook I use in my social studies class is not as "friendly" as I would wish. I know how the ideas should be related, but the connections aren't that clear to a reader unfamiliar with the content. This year I decided to teach text patterns using *News for You,* a newspaper written for middle school readers, during the first semester. *News for You* is written in easily identifiable text patterns that are ideal for teaching organizational patterns. By the second semester, I'll transition into teaching the text patterns that I can identify in my textbook.

the plot. Readers are able to identify the narrators and can make predictions based on the telling of the story. Expository text is not written with an identifiable narrator. Readers, therefore, have to form their own judgments without a narrator's assistance.

A second difference between the texts involves orientation. Narratives are agent oriented; they describe characters involved with real-life situations and have characters that act within a plot. Narratives are easy for readers to understand because they are based on life. Readers are able to identify with the characters or the situation, so they are able to access background knowledge, which promotes their comprehension. Expository texts are not agent oriented, they are subject oriented. They focus on topics or subject matter about which students may or may not have background knowledge.

The third difference is the way in which texts are linked. Narrative texts are typically connected by chronological order and progress sequentially through time. Even when stories have flashbacks or foreshadowing, they move in ways that are familiar to most readers. Informational texts, however, are organized differently. They are organized mainly by simple listing, steps in a series, comparison–contrast, cause–effect, and problem–solution. Their organization is identified by transitional words, examples, topic sentences, and lists. Some students may have difficulty understanding how texts are linked because they are less familiar with the mental processes that connect informational text than they are with the links in narrative texts. For this reason, researchers suggest that teachers in the early grades should spend much more time exploring expository texts with their students (Richgels, 2002).

You learned ways to teach fictional text patterns in Chapter 12. Which ideas can you apply to informational text patterns?

Teaching Informational Text Patterns

Just as you teach middle level learners how to read fictional texts, you can teach them how to read informational texts. Teaching text patterns can influence how well students understand what they are reading (Goldman & Rakestraw, 2000), and it's not as difficult as you might think. You teach informational text patterns in the same way that you teach fiction; the patterns are just different.

Think-Alongs.   Since the majority of students in middle level grades have had few experiences reading informational texts independently, you may have to begin with a teacher modeling activity called a Think-Along (Ehlinger & Pritchard, 1994). A Think-Along imitates the thinking processes that occur as a reader makes sense of a passage or text. Let's say you want your students to read and understand this passage from *Science Voyages* (2000):

> The Global Positioning System, or GPS, is a satellite-based, radio-navigation system that allows users to determine their exact position anywhere on Earth. Twenty-four satellites orbit 200km above the planet. Each satellite sends an accurate position and time signal. The satellites are arranged in their orbits so that signals from at least six can be picked up at any given moment by someone using a GPS receiver. By processing the signals coming from multiple satellites, the receiver calculates the user's exact location. GPS technology is a valuable navigational tool. It is also used to create detailed maps and to track wildlife. (p. 226)

You notice that the passage is organized by the main idea–detail organizational structure. To help students understand the passage, you might say, "In reading this paragraph, I notice that the first thing the author does is to define a Global Positioning System. I know what a GPS is, but I don't know the formal definition, so I'd better write it down. Then the author explains other features of the GPS through the rest of the paragraph." By making the text organization explicit through a Think-Along, you can help students develop the thinking processes needed to understand informational text.

Identifying signal words.   Another way to help students understand text structure is through the use of signal words. Certain words in the English language signal types of text organization (Figure 13.1). As a middle level teacher, you will need to help stu-

Sequence/Time Order	Cause–Effect/Problem–Solution	Compare–Contrast
After	Accordingly	Also
Before	As a result	But
Finally	Because	Conversely
First, second, third, etc.	Consequently	Differently
In the past	Due to	Either . . . or
Initially	Eventually	However
Later	Hence	In comparison
Next	If . . . then	In contrast
Now	Since	Likewise
Previously	Subsequently	More than
The following	The outcome	Not only... but also
When	Therefore	While
	Thus	Yet

FIGURE 13.1   Words That Signal Text Structure

dents connect different signal words to the ways informational texts are organized. Signal words can also help middle level students write expository prose since they can be used as transitional words that increase the local coherence of their own writing.

Diversity Issue: Familiarity With Text Patterns

When you teach a content subject to your entire class, you should be aware of the different reading backgrounds of your students. The majority of the students in your class may not know the types of text patterns that you teach, although students from the mainstream culture have had many more experiences with expository textual patterns than students from backgrounds outside the mainstream. For example, when students listen to the news on television, or even when they listen to adults talking, they hear information through a series of factual statements that are linked in some way. Conversely, students from some cultures have heard very few of these types of discussion patterns (Au, 1993). The conversational patterns of some cultural groups revolve around storytelling, rather than information giving. Some of the students in your classes, therefore, may be unfamiliar with the

Teaching text patterns is important for all students.

organizational patterns of content-area texts and may need more explicit instruction and more experiences with informational text before they are able to read content texts independently.

LEARNING FROM TEXT

When you teach a content-area subject, you should use the same types of comprehension strategies that you learned about in earlier chapters in this book. Your instructional goals will be a bit different, though. As a teacher of a content area, your main objective will be for students to personalize, learn, and remember the content you are teaching. This objective differs from your goals as a teacher of reading, in which your main goal is for students to improve their ability to read. In other words, students in content-area classes learn with text rather than learn the reading process.

Taking Notes

Taking notes is a way for readers to identify important points to remember. The process students use to take notes, the very selection of information, helps students learn (Anderson & Armbruster, 1991). As students select words or phrases from their reading, reduce these ideas into their own words, and write notes into an organized form, they are mentally processing information. Mentally processing information is necessary for learning to occur. If ideas from a text are not mentally processed, most students will forget at least half of what they've read (Vacca & Vacca, 2002).

Think back to your experiences in middle school and high school. Did your teachers expect you to know how to take notes, or did they teach you different note-taking strategies? Teachers of middle level learners often expect their students to be able to take notes independently. Taking notes from difficult material, however, is a sophisticated mental strategy that many young teens find difficult. Many early adolescents think concretely and need support when they're asked to think abstractly. As a middle level teacher, therefore, you should teach most of your students how to take notes by modeling different types of note-taking strategies. After students have learned how to take notes, you should encourage them to adapt these strategies to fit their learning preferences and the type of notes they need to take. An example of a middle level student's notes is given in Figure 13.2.

Power notes.   At times, students will need to take notes from textbooks and organize these notes into a hierarchy of ideas. In the past, students have been taught how to develop outlines, but middle level students can easily get bogged down in the process of outlining. They forget when to write a capital letter, when to use a number, or when to indent. A version of outlining that arranges information in a main idea–detail pattern that is easy for middle school students is called Power Notes (Santa, Havens, & Macumber, 1996).

Power Notes use the same type of a format as outlining but with a different numbering system. The main points are assigned a power of 1; details are assigned a power of 2; examples are a power of 3 as in the following example:

1. Football positions
   2. Offense
      3. Quarterback
      3. Halfback
      3. Fullback

8/15

Chapter 6 (1781—88)– |Section 1|

①Unicameral:—one-house legislature (Pennsylvania)
②Sovereign:supreme power (could not be shared)
③Confederation:alliance
1781– Articles of Confederation go into effect after finally being
        approved by Maryland
1787– Northwest Ordinance:provided a guide for establishing
        territories
1785– Land Ordinance:reserved one lot in every township for schools
        The Articles of Confederation gave these powers to
        the federal government:
                        — power to declare war
                        — power to make peace
                        — Power to sign treaties
                        — borrow money
                        — set standards for coins and
for weights and measures
                        — establish a postal service
                        — "deal with the indians"
        *States feared a strong national government
        The Northwest Ordinance provided these:
                        — the establishment of not less than 3
nor more than 5 territories p. 141 P4.
                        — religion, morality and knowledge being
necessary to good government, means of education forever
encouraged
                        — one lot in every township reserved for the
maintainence ~~reserved for the m~~ of public schools
                        —no slavery nor involuntary servitude
other than for crimes
                        — the utmost of good faith to be observed
toward the indians

FIGURE 13.2   Middle Level Student's Notes

    2. Defense
        3. Linebacker
        3. Cornerback
        3. Lineman

Some students may find Power Notes easy to understand, but others will have
difficulty with the concept of classifying information, and many students will have

difficulty applying Power Notes to material from their textbooks. Tell students that they can use headings and subheadings as ideas for their outline, but remind students that some textbooks aren't very "friendly," and the headings may not be arranged in a hierarchical organization. You can also support students' learning by providing them with some of the main headings and having students fill in the rest of the outline.

After students become proficient taking Power Notes, tell them that this form of outlining is an intermediate step and that when they reach high school, they may be asked to outline information using the traditional outline form.

◢◣◢◣ YOU TRY IT ◢◣◤◢◥◣◢

Taking Power Notes

The best way to understand a reading strategy is to experience it yourself. That holds true for note-taking strategies as well. To learn how to use Power Notes, choose a chapter from this textbook and take notes using the Power Notes format. Then reflect on how much this strategy helped you learn and remember information from the text.

Record–Edit–Synthesize–Think (REST). Students in schools usually have to take notes from both textbook reading and from the class lecture or discussion. Oftentimes students have difficulty synthesizing what they have learned in class and what they have learned from textbook reading. A note-taking strategy that combines the two sources of knowledge is called REST (Morgan, Meeks, Schollaert, & Paul, 1986). When students use REST, they record what they have heard in class on one side of a double-column sheet; they record what they learned from reading the text on the other side; they edit their notes by omitting irrelevant material; they synthesize the two versions of the content; and they think about the topic. (See Figure 13.3 for an example based on a music textbook.)

Flexible Reading Rate

Strategic readers read flexibly. They know how to approach a text—whether they need to read from an aesthetic or an efferent stance, whether they need to remember big concepts or small details, and whether they can read quickly or slowly and carefully. Many middle level readers, however, do not realize that they can vary their reading rate to fit a reading selection. Middle level readers tend to read everything at the same rate rather than adjusting their rate to fit the text and their purposes. As a content-area teacher, therefore, you should teach your students how to read flexibly.

There are four main types of reading speeds: skimming, scanning, pleasure reading, and precise reading. Skimming is the type of reading you do to get a general impression or a main thought. When you read newspaper or magazine articles, you probably skim them rather than reading every word carefully. When you skim, you're probably reading 800 to 1,000 words per minute (Fry, 1978). With the vast amounts of print information you have to read, skimming should be one of your frequently used skills.

When you scan, you read even faster—up to 1,500 words per minute. You scan material when you read to locate information such as looking up a telephone number or looking for a word in a dictionary. You might not even consider scanning

Topic: Music from the 1960s	
Notes From Class Discussion	Notes From Text
Examples/Artists	
"Blowing in the Wind" by Bob Dylan	Folk music—addressed social and political issues
Beach Boys	Surf music
Chubby Checker	The Twist
Many groups	Rock concerts—Woodstock
Beatles, Rolling Stones	Rock and roll; British rock groups popular
Summary	
During the 1960s, a variety of music was popular such as folk music as sung by Bob Dylan, surf music popularized by the Beach Boys, and rock and roll sung by the Beatles. One of the new dances was the Twist. Music was performed in small and large venues, including big open-air concerts such as Woodstock.	

FIGURE 13.3   REST Example

reading because you are not really comprehending text, but scanning is a reading strategy that all of us use.

The third type of reading is pleasure reading. Pleasure reading is the type of reading you do when you read novels or texts for enjoyment. You're reading quickly, but you're also reading every word and comprehending the text. Pleasure reading is the type of reading you do at the beach, and the type of reading your students do when they read during independent reading.

The final type of reading speed is precise reading. Precise reading requires careful, thoughtful reading during which you analyze an author's words, and you think about the meaning. Precise reading is the type of reading you're doing as you read this textbook (although we hope it's also pleasurable). Your students should read much of their content-area textbooks using precise reading.

When students read textbooks, they should use each of these types of reading speeds. As they preview a section of text, students should skim the pages they are to read. They might use scanning to look for specific information, and they certainly will read much of the text precisely. Many textbooks also include narrative accounts, primary sources, and anecdotes that students can read for pleasure. However, many middle level students aren't aware of the types of reading speeds that they should use as they read textbooks.

 Reading speed has an impact on a reader's comprehension. What other factors influence comprehension?

Selective reading guides.   You can teach middle level students how to read flexibly by using a selective reading guide (Cunningham & Shabloak, 1975). A selective reading guide imitates the types of decisions strategic readers use as they approach text flexibly. To create a selective reading guide, select a portion of text so that students can apply several of the types of reading speeds. Then develop specific directions that help students know which type of speed to use when reading. Figure 13.4 contains an example of a selective reading guide from a history book.

1. Skim pages 342–343 to identify the topic of the section.
2. Scan the new terms in the margin of page 342. Decide if any of the terms are new to you. Watch for new terms during reading.
3. Read the introduction, "The Big Picture," precisely and carefully. Connect the information to your existing knowledge of the topic.
4. Read the first section of this chapter, "The First Central Government," precisely, taking notes as you read.
5. Scan the illustration of Shays's Rebellion for information that connects with the passage reading.

FIGURE 13.4   Selective Reading Guide

Technology topic: Internet reading.   Students who read websites on the Internet automatically use a variety of reading speeds. As they access a website, readers scroll down the site—sometimes skimming and sometimes scanning as they look for information. Once they find what they're looking for, readers slow down and begin precise reading. Because most of your students will be experienced web readers, you might compare the reading of websites to the reading of textbooks. Tell students that reading textbooks is similar to Internet reading in that reading speed should vary in both cases. However, remind students that the proportion of skimming, scanning, pleasure, and precise reading will be different for textbook reading than for Internet reading.

Many middle level students are proficient at reading Internet pages.

Summarizing

As students read content texts, they should continually summarize as they are reading. Summarization is a thinking process that strategic readers use to learn information. To learn, readers need to encode the ideas from the text into their own words (Friend, 2000/2001). This cognitive process helps readers connect the information they're reading to their prior knowledge.

By middle level grades, students should be familiar with summarization processes, even if they haven't written summaries before. When students participate in strategies such as the Directed Reading–Thinking Activity, for example, they review what they have read before making a prediction. This reviewing process is very similar to summarizing. As readers summarize, they also review what they have read, but they take the process one step further. Summarization also rephrases and synthesizes the text.

 Some strategies cause readers to stop, think, and summarize. Which strategies promote these processes?

Summary microtheme.   An easy way to teach students how to summarize during reading is by teaching them to write a summary microtheme (Brozo & Simpson, 1995). A summary microtheme is a one-sentence summary of a portion of text. To model this strategy, read a short portion of text and write a one-sentence summary as in Figure 13.5. Then have students read another passage. Give each of your students a small index card and ask them to write one sentence that sums up the passage. Have students share their microthemes with each other. Students are likely to interpret the passages in slightly different ways. Encourage differences in interpretations as long as they represent a reasonable construction of meaning.

What Are Friends For?

Christopher and Suzanne are friends who hang around with the same group of friends. One day they were talking together after school when Suzanne started talking about a problem she was having with Ouida, a girl Christopher likes and has just asked out Friday night.

Christopher said, "You know, she's really nice."

"I'm not saying she's not nice," protested Suzanne. "I'm saying I have a problem with her. She has an attitude sometimes."

"Well it makes me mad when you talk that way about someone I like. You're disrespecting her and me."

"So when I have a problem with someone I can't talk to you about it, even though we've been friends for years. Is that what you're saying? It makes me mad when someone who is supposed to be my friend won't listen to me."

Christopher felt very frustrated. "I just don't want you talking that way about Ouida!"

"You can't tell me what to talk about!" Suzanne snapped.

Microtheme

Suzanne wants to tell Christopher about problems she's having with a mutual friend, Ouida, but Christopher considers the conversation disloyal.

From Kreidler, W. J. (1997). Conflict resolution in the middle school. *Cambridge, MA: Educators for Social Responsibility.*

FIGURE 13.5 Summary Microtheme

Studying

When you study, you're performing a different type of thinking process than any other type of reading. Studying is not just reading; it's reading and remembering for a specific task (Anderson & Armbruster, 1984). You might think that precise reading is the same as studying, but it's not. You can understand the distinction between reading for information and studying by the following example: Let's say you are planning a trip to Mexico, and you begin reading several travel books. You carefully read the section about health hazards because you want to know if your immunizations are current. In that case, you're reading slowly and carefully for a purpose, and you might even remember the information, but that's still not studying.

Studying is when you're reading to perform a task. Typically, someone else determines the task and evaluates your performance. You've had lots of experiences with studying for tests in college. Other tests that you may have studied for are teacher certification tests, driver's license tests, and citizenship tests.

Studying is a unique skill, and it's also idiosyncratic: Everyone studies in different ways. If you asked your classmates, roommates, or children how they study, you would probably get different answers from each group. If studying is individual, you're probably wondering whether you should teach middle level students how to study. You should. Middle level students are novices at studying because they haven't had much experience studying for tests before the middle grades. But by the middle level, many students know that they need to learn how to study, and they want to learn study strategies (Hornberger & Whitford, 1983). Therefore, you should teach your students a variety of study strategies and encourage them to develop their own systems of study.

Classroom Assessment

Study habits survey.   Because middle-grade students are new at study skills, you might consider surveying them to determine what they already know and what they need to learn. Davis (1990) developed a survey for middle-grade students that she used as a pre- and posttest in conjunction with instruction on study strategies (Figure 13.6). In addition to providing information about the students' study habits, the survey also had the result of alerting students to the types of behaviors they should engage in as they develop effective study habits.

Study techniques.   One of the most popular study techniques is SQ3R (Robinson, 1961). SQ3R stands for Survey, Question, Read, Recite, and Review. When studying, students should first survey the information they need to learn. As they survey the chapters, they should ask questions about the topic. For example, if students were surveying Chapter 2 from *People in Time and Place* (1991) about Ancient Greece, they would encounter four sections: Myths and History, The Cities of Greece, Alexander the Great, and Greek Achievements. Students might ask themselves questions such as "Who were the Greek gods and goddesses?" "How did Pericles rule Sparta?" and "How does the Greek vision of democracy compare to current ones?"

After students survey and question the chapter, they should read it, or reread it. During this reading, students should pay close attention to graphic representations and new vocabulary terms. You should encourage students to carefully read graphs, charts, and pictures because, if left on their own, most middle level students skip these graphic aids entirely (Gillespie, 1993). After students are ready, they should recite and review the important information from the text.

SQ3R is one of the study strategies that students use. What other study strategies have you found to be successful?

Study plans.   Good readers don't just say they're going to study; they develop a study plan. Developing a study plan is especially important for middle level stu-

Name _____   Date _____

1. I read material more than once if I don't understand it the first time.

Always		Sometimes		Never
5	4	3	2	1

2. I try to identify the most important points as I read.

Always		Sometimes		Never
5	4	3	2	1

3. I preview reading assignments before reading.

Always		Sometimes		Never
5	4	3	2	1

4. I concentrate when I study.

Always		Sometimes		Never
5	4	3	2	1

5. I study with a friend when I think it will help.

Always		Sometimes		Never
5	4	3	2	1

6. I try to "overlearn" material as I study.

Always		Sometimes		Never
5	4	3	2	1

7. I take notes that help me when I study.

Always		Sometimes		Never
5	4	3	2	1

8. I study in an environment that is conducive to learning.

Always		Sometimes		Never
5	4	3	2	1

9. I set goals for each study time.

Always		Sometimes		Never
5	4	3	2	1

10. I enjoy learning what I study.

Always		Sometimes		Never
5	4	3	2	1

Adapted from Davis, S. J. (1990). Applying content study skills in co-listed reading classrooms. Journal of Reading, *33, 277–281. Copyright by the International Reading Association. All rights reserved.*

FIGURE 13.6   Study Skills Self-Assessment

dents. Middle level students tend to employ "magical thinking" when they study. They say, "I'm going to study for this test and get an A," but in reality, they spend their time in a distracting environment with a book open but with very little real studying occurring. A strategy that encourages students to plan their study sessions is called PLAE (Nist & Simpson, 1989), which stands for preplan, list, activate, and evaluate.

When using PLAE, students preplan each study session and list the strategies they need to use. For example, if students are studying for a test on Ancient Greece, they might develop a study plan that looks something like this:

Monday: Reread notes from class and write a list of ideas that I don't understand
Strategies: Careful reading, questioning
Tuesday: Find information from text to supplement class notes
Strategy: Skimming to find information
Wednesday: Memorize terms and dates
Strategy: Memory devices
Thursday: Review important concepts
Strategy: Summarization
Friday: Test

The third step of PLAE is to activate the plan, and finally, students should evaluate their study plan. In this example, students should determine whether they received the grade they expected. If not, students should evaluate their plan and decide what they need to change so that they are successful.

Test-Taking Strategies

Sometimes middle level students use appropriate study strategies, yet do poorly on tests. One reason for low test scores despite adequate studying is because students don't know how to take a test. This is especially true for middle school students who have not had many experiences with test taking.

Think about your reactions to testing situations. Do you find tests challenging? Do you get anxious? Are you nervous when you take a test? Many people don't like tests and suffer from test anxiety. Test anxiety is an unreasonable fear of taking tests, but research indicates that teaching test-taking strategies can reduce test anxiety and improve test scores (Flippo & Caverly, 1991).

Preparing for tests.   When you know you will be given a test, what is one of the first questions you ask the teacher? You should ask what type of test will be given. As a student, you know that the type of studying you do will depends on the type of test you will take.

Most middle school students don't know to ask this question. As a middle school teacher, therefore, you should help the students ask the appropriate questions that will guide their studying. Lenski, Wham, and Johns (2003) suggest teaching middle level students to ask the following questions:

- What is the exact day of the test?
- How much time will we have for the test?
- Can we use any resources during the test?
- What kind of test is it?
- Will a choice of questions be offered?
- What specific chapters are covered on the test?
- What study strategies might be useful?

Objective tests.   As a content-area teacher, you probably will give students objective tests, with true–false, multiple-choice, matching, and fill-in-the-blank questions. For objective tests students can study effectively by applying the acronym SCORER

(Ritter & Idol-Maestas, 1986). SCORER stand for *schedule* your time, use *clue* words, *omit* difficult questions at first, *read* questions carefully, *estimate* your time, and *review* your responses. If students follow these suggestions, they will become better test-takers.

True-false questions.   You can offer students additional tips to learn how to answer true–false questions. Although true–false questions seem easy to answer, some students have difficulty determining the correct answer. The tips that follow help students learn how to approach these types of tests.

- Interpret statements at face value. Don't read too much into them.
- Assume that a statement is true unless you're sure it is false.
- Watch for absolutes such as *always, never,* and *all.* These statements are usually false.
- If a statement is partially false, it is false.
- Never leave a true–false statement blank. Guess if you don't know.

Multiple-choice questions.   Multiple-choice questions are probably the most challenging type of objective test item. Students have to read the test stem and decide which of four or five answers is the one best answer. To make matters more difficult, many multiple-choice questions have at least one additional answer that *could be* considered correct. Figure 13.7 offers tips for answering multiple-choice questions that you can teach your middle level students.

Essay tests.   Studying for an essay test is entirely different from studying for a test with objective questions. To answer an essay test, students need to remember details, and they also need to be able to apply their knowledge in various ways. Some

Middle level students benefit from learning how to study.

1. Read the stem *before* reading the choices and try to predict the answer.
2. Read all the choices carefully before making a final choice.
3. A response that is only partly correct is *probably* not the best choice.
4. Note any negatives and be sure your choice fits the stem.
5. If a choice is much longer and more detailed than the others, it *may* be the correct answer.
6. If a word in a choice also appears in the statement, it *may* be the correct answer.
7. Improve your chances by eliminating one or more unreasonable choices.
8. When two of the choices are similar, they are both *probably* incorrect.
9. When two of the choices are opposites, one of them is always wrong, and the other choice is *usually* correct.
10. If answer choices do not fit grammatically with the question stem, they are probably incorrect.
11. A choice that includes one or more of the other choices is *likely* to be correct.
12. If *none* or *all* is used in a choice, it is usually incorrect.
13. If *some* or *often* is used in a choice, it is *likely* to be correct.
14. If *all of the above* is a choice, determine whether at least two of the other choices seem appropriate before selecting *all of the above*.
15. If one choice is more precise or technical, it is more likely to be correct than a more general choice.
16. If you are unsure about a response and the correct choice for many items on the test tends to be longer, select the longer choice.
17. For a difficult question, put a mark beside it and go to the next question. Come back to the question at the end of the test.
18. Be alert to clues in the stem of other questions that may be helpful with a difficult question.
19. Mark your answer sheet carefully.
20. Make a calculated guess if you are not sure of the right answer, unless there is a penalty for guessing.

From Reading & Learning Strategies for Middle & High School Students *by Susan Davis Lenski, Mary Ann Wham and Jerry L. Johns. Copyright © 1999 by Kendall/Hunt Publishing Company. Used with permission.*

FIGURE 13.7 Twenty Tips for Taking Multiple-Choice Tests

students will find essay tests much easier than objective tests, whereas others will have a great deal of difficulty answering essay questions.

The first thing you can do to help your students learn how to answer essay questions is to teach them the meanings of verbs that are commonly used to frame the essay question (Figure 13.8). By providing students with examples and these essay question verbs in your content area you can help students learn how to answer essay questions. You can also encourage students to write practice answers.

TEACHING RESEARCHING

Research papers can be the best learning experience for middle level students that you can provide. They can also be the worst. If you think back to your school experiences, including college, you may have been assigned a research topic that you

Verb	Meaning
Analyze	To identify basic parts
Compare	To point out similarities
Contrast	To discuss differences
Explain	To make plain
Illustrate	To explain with examples
Summarize	To describe important points

FIGURE 13.8   Essay Question Verbs

really didn't care about. Because the topic wasn't personally meaningful, you may have waited until the last moment to conduct your research and write the paper—maybe even the night before it was due. As a result, your paper may have been uninspiring, and it may even have bordered on plagiarism.

You may also have had powerfully positive experiences with research—in school or out of school. For example, some of you may have researched what college to attend. You developed a research question, such as "Which college has the best teacher education program in my price range?" Many of you looked through college catalogs, accessed websites, talked with school counselors, questioned friends, and conferred with parents or spouses. You collected and synthesized data, and then you generated conclusions. You didn't write a formal report, but you were researching nonetheless.

Now let's think about why researching is a perfect learning activity for middle level learners. First, think back to the characteristics of middle level learners. You learned that middle level learners don't like to sit at desks and listen to adults lecture. Instead, they like to actively work with their peers to accomplish specific goals. Middle level learners are curious and inquisitive, wondering how the world works and what their relationship is to the world at large. They also are concerned with promoting social justice and are beginning to think abstractly, critically, and creatively.

If you are a teacher who applies social constructivist philosophy, you'll want your students to conduct research, but you may want to approach the activity in different ways than those you experienced in school.

Rooted Relevance

Alexander and Jetton (2000) suggest that teaching in middle and high schools should have "rooted relevance." We've already discussed the importance of making learning relevant to middle level learners, but teachers complain that they also need to teach a written curriculum or satisfy a set of standards. To meet both needs, Alexander and Jetton suggest linking academic learning to students' lives. We would add that you should also teach students how to form those connections between their lives and the curriculum. And, what better way to accomplish rooted relevance than through researching?

Although you may not have thought about this before, researching is part of our lives, and it is part of the lives of middle level students. Students research whenever they search for answers to an inquiry. It makes sense, therefore, that researching should be a vital part of the middle level curriculum—in all subjects.

Researching Strategies

Researching consists of the following strategies: generating a topic for inquiry; locating, selecting, organizing, and synthesizing information; and conveying the findings (Spivey, 1997). Researchers, however, do not always follow the steps of research in this order. Lenski and Johns (1997) conducted a study of middle level students doing research and found that some students followed the steps of research in a linear progression, but others spiraled back through the process several times, and still others moved through the stages in random order. This means that you should approach research in the same way you approach the teaching of writing: as a process. You can teach the steps of researching, but you should not expect every student to follow the steps in a particular order.

Developing research questions.   You may be wondering how you should go about teaching middle level students to conduct research in your content-area class without having students resort to the bad habit of plagiarism, or the copying of phrases, sentences, or paragraphs from printed sources without citations. Many students are confused about plagiarism and think that if they give credit to another source, they can copy as much as they want. Copying sections of another's work is only acceptable if the writer has placed quotation marks around the words.

One of the best ways to combat plagiarism is to have students develop their own questions for researching (Davis, 1994). When students have authentic questions to answer and real reasons for researching, they rarely resort to plagiarism because they are writing about topics of real personal interest. Your challenge in helping students generate their own questions will be to develop interesting activities that promote learning in your content area that include the posing of authentic questions.

One way for students to develop authentic questions is through problem-based learning (PBL). Problem-based learning deals with problems that are close to real-life situations and, therefore, it promotes the asking of questions that students want to research and answer (Delisle, 1997). An example of a PBL question is having students research a school or community problem, as is done in Figure 13.9.

Technology topic: Locating sources.   There is no lack of sources for any topic. Just think about your latest research on the Internet. After entering a search request you may have had thousands of hits. As your students research, the first thing they'll have to do is decide whether to use print sources or electronic sources. Many middle school students will automatically begin researching on the Internet, but the Internet is not necessarily the best place to begin researching. Instead, you should ask students to decide which type of source to use by asking these questions:

- Do I need to read a general synthesis of the topic such as can be found in an encyclopedia?
- How important is it that the source material has been reviewed by a panel of experts?
- Do I want to read primary sources such as original documents?
- Do I want to read personal opinions such as those found on the Internet?
- Is the library or the Internet more convenient for my researching needs?

Technology topic: Evaluating Internet sources.   If students choose to use the Internet as a researching tool, they need to understand the differences between Internet text and print text and the impact the differences can have on researching. First, the Internet is not linear like print texts; it is multilinear (Bolter, 1998). When read-

Scenario: A group of eighth-grade social studies students want to take a trip to Washington, D.C., in conjunction with their study on American history. The social studies teachers suggest that the students research the project and present their findings to the administrative council and the school board.

Research Question: How could eighth-grade students organize and raise funds for a trip to Washington, D.C.?

Possible topics of study:

Faculty sponsors	Parental permission
Insurance	Connection to school curriculum
Funding	Student interest
Destinations	Travel arrangements
Safety	Accommodations

Procedures:
Students research topics of study and present their findings in a multimedia report to the administrative council and the school board.

FIGURE 13.9 Problem-Based Learning

ing a print text, students know that there is a beginning and an ending to the text. Internet texts, on the other hand, are linked to other sources and sites. Readers of the Internet don't merely read texts from start to finish; they explore them in various ways. One reader may read part of a website while another reader may read the entire site and four of the links. Still another reader may read the first half of the site and six of the links.

Furthermore, the processes students use to conduct research on the Internet might be very different from the process that students use when reading print text. In a study of technologically experienced preservice teachers, Lenski (2001b) found that undergraduate students used a sophisticated array of conflicting strategies as they researched on the Internet: defining search requests flexibly yet accurately, filtering and evaluating the content of websites, becoming distracted and refocusing on the topic, working alone and working with others, and feeling in and out of control. Although the strategies the preservice teachers used in this situation may not be the only strategies needed to research on the Internet, they indicate the complexity of Internet research.

One of the strategies that experienced researchers use is to evaluate their sources. Evaluating print sources is much different from evaluating Internet sources. When reading Internet sources, students can't be certain that the information is accurate. Therefore, students need to evaluate Internet sites as they read. One way to teach students the skills they need to evaluate Internet sites is to teach them to use a website evaluation guide as presented in Figure 13.10.

 Evaluating the validity of a website is an important critical reading strategy. In what ways does it illustrate critical literacy theory?

Recording information. Middle level students will have the same types of difficulties taking notes for research that they have when taking notes for class. When reading research, however, students come across more difficult, unfriendly texts than they do from textbooks. To read this difficult text, Poorman and Wright (2000) suggest that students use dialectical journals to record information. A dialectical journal (Figure 13.11) is a type of two-column journal in which information from texts is written on the left side of the page and responses on the right.

| 1. Who is the author of the site? |
| 2. What are the author's qualifications? |
| 3. What are the purposes of the site? |
| 4. What other sources can verify the information on this site? |
| 5. What author bias is present? |
| 6. On what date was the site produced? Updated? |
| 7. How valid do you think this site is? |

FIGURE 13.10 Website Evaluation Guide

Text on Left	Response on Right
Summaries	Your comments
Quotations	Your thoughts
Interesting words or phrases	Connections
Key information	Reflections
Questions	Answers to questions

FIGURE 13.11 Dialectical Journals

Synthesizing and writing research.   As all writers know, synthesizing information from a variety of sources is the most difficult part of conducting research. One strategy that Zorfass (1998) suggests for use with middle level students is using the I-Search paper (Macrorie, 1984). An I-Search paper is different from a traditional research paper: It tells the story of the research process. In an I-Search paper, students wouldn't just write the *results* of research, they would tell the story of their research and what they found. For example, let's think back to the problem-based learning question discussed earlier in Figure 13.9. If a student were researching "Destinations" for part of the paper, she might begin writing something like this:

> I started my research by deciding whether to look in the library or on the web. I know that I could find travel books about Washington DC in the library, but I doubt if they're current. Therefore, I began my search on the Internet.
>
> When I started searching, I used my favorite search engine, Lycos, to begin. I typed in Washington DC, and I got over 5,000 hits, many of them having nothing to do with our project. The first site I clicked on was a home page describing a family vacation. That one wasn't very helpful, so I continued with my search. I then found a site that described the landmarks I could see in the area. It also had links to the home pages of those landmarks. I gathered much of my information from that site and the related links.

Evaluating research projects.   When you evaluate research projects, you should remember that researching is a process that should be assessed as a process. Just as you don't "grade" process writing papers by merely assigning a letter grade, you should assess research papers using a rating scale or a rubric. To develop a scale for evaluating researching, think of the components of the paper you want to evaluate and the criteria for assessment. Then assign a point continuum. An example of a rating scale for researching can be found in Figure 13.12.

Classroom Assessment

Topic	No		Yes
The topic is interesting.	1	2	3
The topic is important.	1	2	3
The topic is limited in scope.	1	2	3
Question			
The question is clear.	1	2	3
The question is meaningful.	1	2	3
Sources			
The sources are varied.	1	2	3
The sources are appropriate.	1	2	3
Final Paper			
The paper answers the research question.	1	2	3
The paper is organized.	1	2	3
The paper is interesting.	1	2	3

FIGURE 13.12   Research Paper Evaluation

You've already learned a variety of assessment strategies throughout this book. Which strategies would you use as a content-area teacher to help students comprehend text?

ASSESSING STUDENT PROGRESS

When you think about assessing students in content areas you probably think about giving classroom tests. Classroom or unit tests are one way to assess content knowledge, and you probably learned about this type of assessment in your other educational course work. There is another way to think about assessing student progress in content areas: how well students can read content textbooks.

Assessing Student Interest

Many content-area teachers don't think about whether students are interested in the topic they're teaching; they just teach. You know from your own experiences and material earlier in this textbook that motivation plays a key role in the reading and learning of all students, but particularly middle level students. If students are interested in a topic, they'll read extremely difficult texts. If they're not interested, it's worse than pulling teeth.

You can use a variety of prereading strategies such as those that you learned about in other chapters of this book. But another tack is to survey students about their interests on a particular topic and to provide more reading for those topics of interest.

Classroom Assessment

Interest inventories.   To survey students on their interests, preview a chapter of a text you are using and list the topics represented in the text. Create a survey such as the one found in Figure 13.13. Compare your students' interest with the treatment of the topic in the text, then assign reading according to student interest.

Assessing Background Knowledge

You know that each student brings different knowledge and skills to any learning situation and nowhere is that more evident than in content-area classes. Some students will have an interest in your topic and a great deal of background knowledge. Many middle level learners are proficient readers, and some students will have read a number of books about your subject. Others will have very little knowledge. You can assess the background knowledge of your students by having them create a content-area history (McLaughlin, 2000).

Below is a list of topics pertaining to an Immigration Unit we will be beginning next week. Please check those items that you would like to read about.

_____   Fears and hopes

_____   Voyages

_____   Ellis Island

_____   Countries of origin

_____   Adjustment difficulties

_____   Treatment by local citizens

_____   How immigrants influenced existing culture

FIGURE 13.13   Interest Survey

Content-area histories.   A content-area history (Figure 13.14) details a student's development in a content subject from earliest memories. Tell students that you want to know about their experiences with your subject. Encourage them to create a time line that chronicles their experiences from early years to the present. Then have students develop a scrapbook, a Power Point presentation, a poem, or a mosaic to illustrate their development. When you review these content-area histories, you'll have a better understanding of the background knowledge, interests, and attitudes of your students. You can then adjust your teaching to comply with your students' knowledge.

Classroom Assessment

Assessing Reading Ability

You can assess your students' ability to read your content-area textbook the same way you assess younger students: by having them read a portion of text aloud, recording miscues, and assessing comprehension through retelling. Because middle level teachers usually teach from 60 to 150 students, individual assessments such as recording miscues should be reserved for students who are experiencing unusual difficulty reading the textbook or when you don't know whether a student is *able* to read the textbook.

Cloze procedure.   If you want to determine whether your students can read your textbook, you can give a group assessment to the class called a *cloze test*. A cloze test is a type of fill-in-the-blank test using a section from the textbook. To make up a cloze test, type several 250-word passages from your textbook, skipping every fifth word. (See Figure 13.15 for an example.) Duplicate and distribute the passages to the students and have them write in the missing words. Tell students that they need to read the passage carefully because you will only consider words correct if they are actually used in the original text.

Classroom Assessment

Because cloze tests are very difficult, your scoring of them will be unlike anything you have done before. Remember, when you score the tests, only the exact word from the book counts as correct. Therefore, if students score at the 50 percent

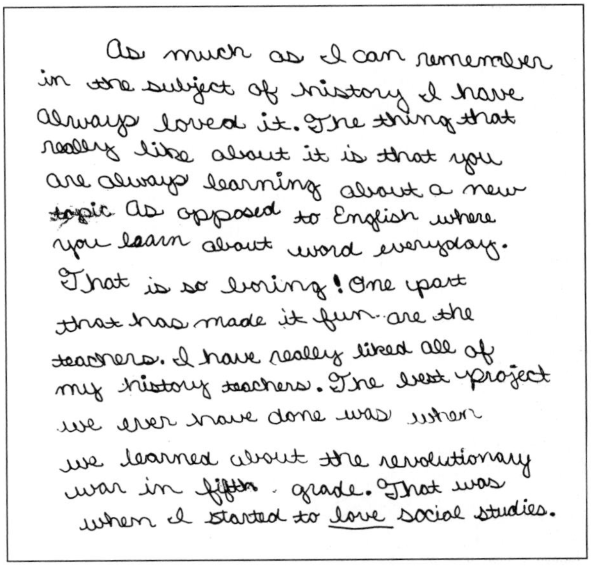

As much as I can remember in the subject of history I have always loved it. The thing that really like about it is that you are always learning about a new topic as opposed to English where you learn about word everyday. That is so boring! One part that has made it fun are the teachers. I have really liked all of my history teachers. The best project we ever have done was when we learned about the revolutionary war in fifth grade. That was when I started to love social studies.

FIGURE 13.14   Content-Area History

Paris itself is home _____ about 8.7 million people. _____ literacy rate of 99 _____ shows that France prizes _____. Paris, a world center _____ art and learning, is _____ to many universities, museums, _____ other cultural sites. It _____ also France's leading center _____ industry, transport, and communications. _____ of tourists from all _____ the world visit Paris _____.

(Answers: to, France's, percent, education, of, home, and, is, of, Millions, over, annually)

From Geography: The world and its people. *(1998). Peoria, IL: Glencoe McGraw-Hill.*

FIGURE 13.15   Cloze Example

level, you can consider the textbook appropriate for reading in class. If students score below 40 percent, the book is too difficult for them (Bormuth, 1975).

MEETING STUDENTS' NEEDS

In most content-area classes, students will evidence a wide range of abilities to read and to learn. You'll have students who are mainstreamed from special education classes, students who have difficulty reading, students who don't speak English, students who love your subject, students who can read and learn but who won't, and students who know more than you do about your subject. It is your job to teach all of your students, no matter who they are and which abilities they bring to your classroom. To teach all students, you will have to address individual needs—not just teach from your textbook.

Students With Reading Difficulties

What happens when students can't read the textbook from your content-area class? Should you simply refrain from requiring those students to complete reading assignments? Or, should you assign the material anyway, hoping that students have someone to help them read at home? Unfortunately, there are no really good answers. There are, however, some principles that you should consider as you make decisions about students who can't read your textbook.

Vogt (2000) suggests that content-area teachers use the following strategies to make content and text accessible to students who have difficulty reading:

- Use several modalities as you teach: writing on overheads, speaking, videos, etc.
- Begin lessons with the main concept you are presenting.
- Introduce new vocabulary words in class.
- Use demonstrations, modeling, and hands-on activities to teach new concepts.

Using picture books.   Another strategy used to teach struggling readers and still use texts is to use picture books to teach content-area subjects (Albright, 2002; Carr, Buchanan, Wentz, Weiss, & Brant, 2001). Many students, not just those who have difficulty reading, will enjoy your use of picture books to supplement your classroom teaching. For students who struggle with reading, the picture books may be the only reading they can accomplish independently. Figure 13.16 lists picture books appropriate for middle level content-area classes.

Flexible grouping.   At times you will want every student to read about a topic even though you know that the textbook won't be appropriate for many of your students.

Bailie, A. (1994). *Rebel.* New York: Ticknor.

Bridges, R. (1999). *Through my eyes.* New York: Scholastic.

Bunting, E. (1990). *The wall.* New York: Clarion.

Bunting, E. (1996). *Going home.* New York: HarperColllins.

Cech, J. (1991). *My grandmother's journey.* New York: Bradbury.

Cherry, L. (1993). *The great Kapok tree.* San Diego: Harcourt Brace.

Cordova, A. (1997). *Abuelita's heart.* New York: Simon & Schuster.

Goble, P. (1992). *Love flute.* New York: Bradbury.

Grimes, N. (1999). *My man Blue.* New York: Scholastic.

Hart, T. (1994). *Antarctic diary.* New York: Macmillan/McGraw-Hill.

Hoffman, M. (1991). *Amazing Grace.* New York: Dial.

Isadora, R. (1991). *At the crossroads.* New York: Scholastic.

Keller, L. (2000). *Open wide, tooth school inside.* New York: Henry Holt.

Martin, J. (1998). *Snowflake Bentley.* Boston: Houghton Mifflin.

Polacco, P. (1990). *Just plain Fancy.* New York: Dell.

Scieszka, J. (1995). *Math curse.* New York: Viking.

Tarbescu, E. (1998). *Annushka's voyage.* New York: Clarion.

Williams, S.A. (1992). *Working cotton.* San Diego: Harcourt Brace.

FIGURE 13.16 Content-Area Picture Books

For those times, you should consider grouping students by reading ability and giving the struggling readers adapted or easy-to-read textbooks. Once you have assessed students' general ability to read the content-area textbook, you can occasionally require different reading from different students. Struggling readers can read a textbook that is written at a lower reading level; some students can read the regular textbook; and others can read trade books. After students have completed their reading, they can share their knowledge in small groups. This way the struggling readers have read a text and have contributed to classroom learning through group sharing.

At times you will want students to read the same textbook, not different texts. For those times, you might consider having students read in pairs or in small groups. At no time should you have the entire class read portions of the textbook aloud—what we call round-robin reading. As stated earlier in this book, round-robin reading does not benefit anyone; it makes struggling readers nervous and competent readers frustrated. And, students don't listen to each other read. Instead of round-robin reading, try having students read to each other in some configuration of small groups.

 You've learned a variety of ways to teach small groups. Which ones apply best to content-area classrooms?

Gifted Readers in Content-Area Classes

Gifted readers are often just as neglected as struggling readers. They can be bored in content-area classrooms because the instruction moves too slowly for them. How should you cope with students who are gifted, either in reading or in your content area?

Again, there are no easy answers to challenging gifted students. One thing you should not do is consistently use the gifted student as a tutor for struggling students. Gifted students deserve challenging assignments, just as struggling readers deserve texts they can read.

Some of your content-area classes will be tracked, so the gifted students will not be as obvious in your class. In heterogeneous classes, however, gifted students will need differentiated instruction. You don't need to differentiate every day, but you do need to address the needs of the gifted. One way to address the needs of the gifted is to provide challenging reading in flexible groups several times during the year. Another idea is to occasionally provide tiered activities (Tomlinson, 1999). Examples of tiered activities follow:

- Students are given packets of readings that vary in reading levels, from early elementary to high school.
- All students are required to take notes, but some students are given Power Note outlines and others are not.
- All students are asked to use the Internet for research and are given different sites to read.
- All students are required to write a research paper, but some are required to cite more sources than others.

Tiered assignments can meet your needs to differentiate classroom instruction. However, note this word of caution about any type of differentiation: You need to reassure students that assigning different activities at times is fair. You might make an analogy to sports to help students understand. Explain that coaches don't always give every player the same drills to prepare for a game. Some players need practice at simple skills, whereas others need practice at more complex skills. Let students know that the same principle holds true in a classroom. At times, all students will be assigned the same activities, but at other times, students will be given different assignments.

Another danger in differentiation is that you, as the teacher, might make incorrect assessments of student ability and progress. Often teachers do not expect students from minority cultures to perform as well as students from the mainstream culture. To counteract that possibility, allow students to move to a more difficult assignment at any time.

CONNECTIONS: WHAT'S NEXT?

In this chapter you learned instructional strategies to teach students to learn with text. These strategies are especially appropriate if you're teaching content-area classes, such as history, science, and mathematics. The strategies you learned in this chapter can also be applied to the teaching of any informational text. Even if you never teach a content subject, you still will need to teach your students, whether they are at the middle level or not, how to comprehend informational text.

As with all of the information from this textbook, the strategies presented in this chapter can be applied to other grade levels. Although some strategies work better with older students, many of them can be adapted for Early and Interpretive Readers. As a teacher, you should select strategies to teach that you think will work best for your students. As you know by now, teachers need to creatively adapt ideas to their teaching situations.

In the part on Critical Readers so far we've provided background and information about students, and we've presented ideas and strategies to teach fictional and informational text to the entire group (Figure 13.17). We stressed whole-group teaching for middle level learners because much of your teaching for this age group is directed to the entire class. At times, however, you'll want to teach small groups of students and have students work independently. Chapter 14 will discuss those ideas. In addition, we would like you to think about how to assess middle level students. Although we've presented a few assessment strategies in Chapters 12 and 13, we will discuss assessment in detail in Chapter 14. We will also discuss the role parents play in their middle level child's literacy learning. Taken together, these chapters should give you a foundation for teaching Critical Readers.

FIGURE 13.17 A Developmental Approach to the Teaching of Reading

	Early Readers	Interpretive Readers	Critical Readers
Theories underscored as readers develop:	Social Constructivism Psycholinguistic Critical Transactional	Social Constructivism Psycholinguistic Critical Transactional	Social Constructivism Psycholinguistic Critical Transactional
Whole-group instruction through:	• Read-alouds • Shared texts • Comprehension strategies • Working with words	• Read-alouds • Using basals • Literature-based models • Word-building strategies • Comprehension strategies	• Read-alouds • Common texts (e.g., basals, anthologies, trade books) • Comprehension strategies • Vocabulary instruction and word analysis • Researching • Critical reading • Reading content area texts • Studying and note-taking
Assessment ideas for whole group:	• Observations • Kidwatching • Anecdotal notation	• Portfolios • Open-ended questions • Rubrics	• Written retellings • Research projects • Interest inventories • Content-area histories • Cloze procedure
Small-group instruction through:	• Guided reading • Teaching for strategies • Working with words	• Basal readers • Literature anthologies • Fluency practice • Guided silent reading • Literature circles • Inquiry groups	• Book clubs • Trade books
Assessment ideas for small groups:	• Running Records • Retellings • Discussions with children	• Names test • Fluency checklist • Peer assessment • Inquiry rubric	• Student information card • Bio poem • "I Used to… But Now I…" poem • Observational checklist • Student self-assessment • Norm-referenced tests

continued

FIGURE 13.17   *Continued*

	Early Readers	**Interpretive Readers**	**Critical Readers**
Independent learning through:	• Independent reading • Reading/writing workshop • Making books • Reading the room	• Independent reading • Reading/writing workshop • Responding through writing • Reading logs	• Sustained silent reading and writing
Sociocultural contexts:	• Literacy partnerships with parents • Parents in the classroom • Home–school communication	• Reading/writing connection for life • Oral histories • Home literacy activities • Parent programs	• Parents as coaches • Funds of knowledge • Parent–student book clubs

FOR YOUR PORTFOLIO

Companion Website

ENTRY 13.1   *Use of the Internet*

INTASC Principle 6 states: *The teacher uses knowledge of effective verbal, nonverbal, and media communication techniques to foster active inquiry, collaboration, and supportive interaction in the classroom.*

The Internet is an important tool for learning for yourself as a new teacher and also for your students. Develop a content-area lesson plan that uses the Internet and other media to teach a specific topic. Incorporate links in your lesson plan to websites with audio and video footage.

ENTRY 13.2   *Professional Organizations*

INTASC Principle 9 states: *The teacher is a reflective practitioner who continually evaluates the effects of his/her choices and actions on others (students, parents, and other professionals in the learning community) and who actively seeks out opportunities to grow professionally.*

Most content areas have professional organizations to further a teacher's knowledge in that subject. Professional organizations typically offer publications, conferences, and websites that provide information, teaching ideas, research studies, and opportunities for networking. Access information about a professional organization that interests you. If you hope to teach mathematics, for example, you should learn about the National Council of Teachers of Mathematics. After learning about the organization, join either at the national level or one of the local, regional, or state groups. Be prepared to discuss how professional organizations can provide opportunities for your continued learning.

ENTRY 13.3   *Knowledge of Reading Strategies*

IRA/NCTE Standard 3 states: *Students apply a wide range of strategies to comprehend, interpret, evaluate, and appreciate texts. They draw on their prior experience, their interactions with other readers and writers, their knowledge of word meaning and of other texts, their word identification strategies, and their under-*

standing of textual features (e.g., sound–letter correspondence, sentence structure, context, graphics).

As middle level students learn to read with texts, they need to employ a variety of reading strategies. An example of a strategy that readers use is to vary reading rate to match the purposes and difficulties of the text. Each of these reading strategies has one or more instructional strategies that you should demonstrate in your teaching lessons. List the reading strategies that middle level students will need to use to learn with text. Create a chart that includes the name of the reading strategy, a definition of the strategy, and the instructional strategy that you would use for demonstration. Use strategies that you've read about throughout this book. An example follows:

Strategy Name	Definition	Instruction
Reading flexibly	Determining how fast you read by your purpose and how difficult the text is.	**Selective reading guide** **Teach skimming and scanning** **Teach Internet reading**

TO LEARN MORE

Helpful Websites

Companion Website

Visit our Companion Website at *http://www.prenhall.com/lenski* to link to the following sites:

Evaluating Websites

Kathy Schrock's Guide for Educators is a list of sites on the Internet that are useful for enhancing curriculum and teachers' professional growth. Includes website evaluation guides.
http://discoveryschool.com/schrockguide/index.html

Literacy Assistance Center

Provides information on resources and links to literacy on the Net. Its website links and e-mail contacts can connect teachers and students around the world.
http://www.lacnyc.org

Cloze Tests

Helps you create cloze activities.
http://www.auburn.edu/~mitrege/knowledge/cloze.html

Assessment

This site is a clearinghouse for articles and books about assessment and assessment tools.
http://www.ericae.net

Reading Content-Area Textbooks

Offers a set of strategies for teaching students to read content-area texts.
http://www.Idonline.org/Id_indepth/teaching_techniques/understanding_textbooks.html

Instructing Critical Readers in Small Groups Independently and With Families

Essential Learning Questions

- What are some ways to assess Critical Readers?
- How can middle level teachers motivate students to read?
- How could the Book Club Program fit into a middle level reading program?
- In what ways should parents be involved in their middle level child's literacy learning?

As a middle level teacher, most of your instruction will be directed to the entire class, but not all. You've learned that you can't address individual differences if you only teach to the whole group—either as a reading teacher or as a content-area teacher. So you know that you need to have other options as a teacher, and those options include instructing Critical Readers in small groups and independently and by encouraging parental involvement.

As you think about the entire menu of instructional practices that you've already learned, you know that you need to develop engaging lessons targeted to the whole group that encourage students to become strategic readers. You'll want to use good teaching techniques and reading strategies to help students learn from text. These strategies and practices will be the foundation of your teaching, but students should also have the opportunity to learn in other ways.

It's a bit more difficult to teach small groups in the middle grades because typically you have less scheduling flexibility. If middle level teachers are to group their students, they have to assess students so they can make informed decisions about that grouping. Too often middle level teachers only "grade" their students; they don't assess reading progress. But if you want to address the needs of all students, you will have to assess their reading so you can tailor instruction and teach students in a variety of grouping patterns.

ASSESSING CRITICAL READERS

You've already learned many ways to assess reading progress, and you may be wondering how you can apply your knowledge of assessment to large groups of students. Remember, if you teach at the middle level, you will probably teach from 60 to 180 students every day in time blocks of 45 to 90 minutes. You will have far less time to administer individual assessments like Running Records or miscue analysis, but you will need to develop some sort of assessment plan. That assessment plan should include ways to assess both reading processes and content knowledge. In addition, you will need to understand the role of norm-referenced testing (e.g., achievement tests) in your decision making, and you will need to think about how to assign grades.

Getting to Know Your Students

The only way for you to assess the reading processes of your students is to get to know each student individually. This may seem obvious to you, but it's difficult to get to know more than 100 middle-grade students in a short period of time. No matter how many students you have, you'll need to spend some time at the beginning of the year developing a classroom community and learning about your students' backgrounds and interests. Learning about students' backgrounds and interests is crucial for success as a middle level teacher. Personal interest, motivation, and learning are closely connected, so part of the bedrock of assessing Critical Readers will be to get to know them individually as people.

Classroom Assessment

Student information cards.   Picture this: You have a position as a seventh-grade language arts teacher. You are teaching four classes of students, each with 35 students. You are responsible for teaching 140 students the entire language arts curriculum, including reading. The students file into class on the first day calling out to each other, greeting old friends. You assign the students seats according to your seating plan, you distribute books, and you're ready to begin. You have 90 minutes to make an attempt to get to know 35 students.

One way to get to know your students is to have students write about themselves on an index card. Ask students to write down pertinent information about themselves such as their address, phone number, and e-mail address. (You might consider having each of the students e-mail you. Then, you'll have a "class list" of e-mail addresses.) Also ask students to list their favorite hobbies, after-school activities, movies, television programs, friends, preferred reading materials, and books. You might also consider attaching a picture of the student to the front of the card. If you have access to a Polaroid camera, take pictures of the students as they are completing the cards, or you can ask students to bring a school photograph from home.

As you are getting to know your students, also remember that students want to get to know you. Before you ask students to complete a student information card, show them a copy of a card you have written about yourself. (Leave the address and phone number blank on your card.) Also, show students a sample card from someone their age as is shown in Figure 14.1.

Visit the online journal in Chapter 14 on our Companion Website at *www.prenhall.com/lenski* to answer these questions. Save your answers to your hard drive or to a disk to compile an online journal.

You learned how to build a classroom community in earlier chapters. Which ideas could you apply to middle level learners?

Classroom Assessment

Bio poems.   Another beginning activity that helps you get to know your students is having students write bio poems. A *bio poem* is a patterned poem that reveals information about the author. In this case, bio poems can encourage classroom community and can also help you quickly learn about the students in your classrooms.

Read the sample bio poems from Figure 14.2 to students. Explain to them that not all poetry needs to rhyme, but that poetry is a way to combine imagery through language to portray emotions or ideas. After reading the bio poems, show students how they are constructed. Encourage students to be thoughtful and creative as they write their own bio poems.

Classroom Assessment

"I used to..., But now I..." poems.   Students in middle level grades are entering puberty and are growing and changing in many ways. At this age, many students are interested in writing about some of the changes that they are experiencing. The poem form "I used to..., But now I..." is especially relevant for middle level students.

To teach the poem form, "I used to..., But now I..." have students reflect on the ways they have changed from their elementary school years. Give students time to think about these changes and then encourage them to discuss their ideas with their classmates in small groups. After students have spent time discussing, read several "I used to..., But now I..." poems that you have written or use those found in

Name:	*Samantha Monckton*
Address:	*812 Oahwood Rd, Homeland, JL 61611*
Email:	*angel22531@home.com*
After school activities:	*Talking on the phone* *Watching T.V.* *Shopping*
Hobbies:	*Dancing* *Volleyball* *Softball*
T.V. programs:	*Friends* *7th Heaven*
Movies:	*John Q* *A Walk to Remember*
Friends:	*Morgan* *Jody* *Nikki*
Preferred reading materials:	*magazines* *Science fiction* *mystery*
Favorite books:	*Haunted Sister* *The Giver Cages* *A Break with Charity*

FIGURE 14.1   Student Information Card

Figure 14.3. Then have students write one or more poems about themselves. After students have finished their poems, encourage them to share with their classmates, and then collect the poems to learn more about your students.

YOU TRY IT

Poems About Yourself

As a teacher, your students will want to learn about you as a person, not just as their teacher. You can reveal some of your experiences, thoughts, and emotions by writing the same sorts of poems you assign to your students. Write several poems about yourself, using the two poetry forms suggested in this text, bio poems and "I used to. . . , But now I. . . ." You may want to write other types of poems about yourself as well. Post the poems on the Companion Website *(http://www.prenhall.com/lenski).*

Line 1	Name
Line 2	Four traits
Line 3	Related to. . .
Line 4	Cares deeply about. . .
Line 5	Who feels. . .
Line 6	Who needs. . .
Line 7	Who gives. . .
Line 8	Who fears. . .
Line 9	Who would like to see. . .
Line 10	Resident of. . .

Desirea
Funny, smart, shy, silly
Related to Danielle, Laura, and Danny
Cares deeply about her dog, D.J.
Who feels nervous in front of people she doesn't know
Who needs to set better study times
Who gives good effort to school work
Who fears getting bad grades
Who would like to see Hawaii and Montecello (Jefferson's home)
Resident of Smithville.

Dylan
Talkative, nice, serious, outgoing
Related to Tami and Clint
Cares deeply about my mom
Who feels scared when I get in trouble
Who needs more sleep at night
Who gives respect to others
Who fears the assistant principal
Who would like to see New York
Resident of Oak Lake

FIGURE 14.2   Bio Poems Format and Samples

Monitoring Reading Progress

A second aspect of assessing Critical Readers is to conduct ongoing progress monitoring. Reading is a difficult process to assess because it's an internal, cognitive process. Some younger children talk out loud during the reading process, while older readers remain silent when they're struggling with print so you don't know what strategies they are or are not using. You have already learned several assessment strategies that can become windows into the reading processes of students. You can adapt these strategies for large groups of students so that you have enough information to inform your instructional decisions.

I used to watch T.U. 24/7,
But now I read as much as I can.

I used to get a couple C's on
my report card and not care,
But now I get A's and am happy.

I used to spend time alone,

But now I go shopping with

my friends.

FIGURE 14.3   "I Used to…, But Now I…" Sample Poems

Observational checklist.   Middle level teachers should assess students in many of the same ways elementary teachers do: They should conduct ongoing assessment of authentic literacy tasks (Brenner & Pearson, 1998). As a middle level teacher, therefore, you will need to develop a streamlined version of the assessment strategies you've already learned in this text. Some teachers like using an observational checklist to help them structure their informal assessments.

As a teacher, you'll continually be making judgments about your students. For example, as you conduct a classroom discussion, you might think, "I'm not sure Tonya understands the theme of this novel," or "Jonathan really is making good inferences about the character's motivations." You've learned in previous chapters that you can formalize these thoughts by writing them down as anecdotal notes. Anecdotal notes should also play a key role in informal assessment in the middle grades. These notes should be made and analyzed on a regular basis.

Another way to collect informal data is to listen to students read during paired reading. As students read quietly in pairs, you can listen in to determine whether students are reading fluently and whether they are having difficulty with the vocabulary of the selection. After you listen to the students, record your observations on the checklist.

A third way to collect data for the observational checklist is to use students' reading logs and journal entries to make evaluations of students' reading progress. Let's say that you collect the reading logs of your third-period class after school has been in session for 4 weeks. You notice that all of the students have read four or five books

Classroom Assessment

Monitoring reading progress is an important instructional task. What are some ways you can monitor the progress of readers?

with the exception of Venetta and Thomas, who have each read only one book. Those reading logs provide data about the reading interests of your students, and, more importantly, they give you direction for your instruction. You know that you need to work with Venetta and Thomas to help them select books that interest them.

Journal entries and think sheets such as prediction charts also provide input into the reading progress of your students. As you read your students' prediction charts you can note whether the students are making informed predictions. These data, again, can be part of your overall evaluation of a student's reading progress.

The observational checklist in Figure 14.4 shows the notes Linda wrote about Angel's progress during the first semester. Notice that the entries are spaced over several months and that they were taken in a variety of situations.

Classroom Assessment

Student self-assessment.   Students in middle level grades are becoming self-reflective and should be given the opportunity to assess their own reading progress. A student self-assessment of reading progress is different from asking students to assign themselves a grade. A self-assessment encourages students to think beyond classes and grades and guides them to consider their strengths and weaknesses as readers. Students who reflect honestly on their reading progress are more likely to become aware of the learning they need to do (Mueller, 2001).

Introduce the self-assessment (Figure 14.5) to students early in the first semester and tell them that you will be asking them to think about their reading progress throughout the year. Show students the items on the self-assessment periodically so that students continue to think about their reading progress. Then at the end of a unit of study or at a time when you intend to make changes in your classroom instruction, have students complete the reading self-assessment. Use the assessment to modify how you teach your class.

Linda makes observations while she teaches.

Student's Name: **Angel García** Date: **Sem 1**

Class: **Language Arts** Period: **4**

Strategy	Date and Comments
Exhibits interest in reading	9/12 Classroom observation Good use of time during SSRW 10/30 Classroom observation "Lost in book"
Reads a variety of material	9/30 Reading log—reads mainly fiction (Discussed other options with her.) 11/15 Reading log—some nonfiction (Praised her efforts. Also discussed poetry and plays.) 12/20 Reading log—good balance (Praised her balance of reading.)
Reads fluently	9/15 Listened to paired reading—Good fluency
Applies reading strategies • Predicting • Sequencing • Identifying key ideas • Summarizing • Drawing conclusions	10/1 Classroom discussion Good use of predicting 11/5 Classroom discussion Summarized chapter of novel—excellent 12/12 Classroom discussion Identified key ideas in informational text
Uses text structure to comprehend • Story grammar • Nonfiction text structures	10/1 Written retelling (novel) Understands fictional structures 11/13 Science essay Confused when reading graphic aids
Monitors comprehension • Rereading • Visualization • Questioning	10/3 Think aloud Needs work on questioning (Small-group instruction needed.)
Interprets text fairly	11/7 Discussion Web Could not provide both pro and con

FIGURE 14.4 Observational Checklist

Name _Nick Jones_   Date _11-7-01_

Class _7 gold / Reading_   Period _I_

1. Do I consider myself a reader? _Yes, I read a lot and enjoy it._

2. What do I like to read? _I like reading fantasy/action books with medi-evil style settings, plots, etc_

3. What are my reading strengths? _I comprehend well, read at a good speed, large vocabulary_

4. What areas need improvement? _I want to Improve my speed without losing comprehension._

5. What are my reading goals? _read as much as possible_

6. What are my favorite reading activities in this class? _just reading._

FIGURE 14.5   Student Self-Assessment

Norm-referenced tests.   Your students may be given standardized tests that are norm-referenced tests as part of school or district policy. Some teachers use the information on these tests to assess student learning. You should know that norm-referenced tests, such as the *Iowa Test of Basic Skills* and the *Stanford Achievement Tests,* do not provide the kind of information that you can use to assess individual students. Instead, norm-referenced tests are given to determine how well students do in comparison to a large group of students of the same age or grade level. The data you get from norm-referenced tests should not be used to make instructional decisions (Popham, 2001).

Assessing Content Knowledge

Many of the novels or content-area textbooks that you teach will have tests associated with them that have been developed by the books' publishers. These tests do not assess reading processes, but they do assess students' knowledge of the novel or the content. It is often from these types of assessments, coupled with the assignments you give, that you will assign grades.

Assigning grades for schoolwork is common in most schools today, especially in middle level grades. The vast majority of schools have policies that require teachers to give traditional grades: A, B, C, D, and F. Different schools have different requirements for grades, but, in general, you will be assigning grades based on students' content knowledge rather than reading progress.

Many teachers assign grades based not only on academic achievement, but also on effort, attendance, and behavior (Marzano, 2000). Your school may have a policy on whether you can include nonacademic factors when you assign a grade. As you assess content knowledge, you might decide to record grades from student work in the following areas: vocabulary knowledge, class discussion, chapter tests, daily work, and homework. These factors do not indicate how well a student can read, but they do point to students' successes in learning the content of your class.

SEE FOR YOURSELF

Assigning Grades

Visit the message board for Chapter 14 on our Companion Website at *www.prenhall.com/lenski* to discuss your findings.

Interview two or three middle level teachers and ask them questions such as these about grading:

- How do you determine reading (or language arts) grades for your students?
- Do you grade homework? If so, what kinds of assignments do you give?
- How do you grade class participation?
- What percentage of a grade is made up of tests on stories and novels?
- Do you grade effort?
- Do you take into account a students' ability when you assign a grade?
- What's the most difficult part of grading reading (or language arts)?

Synthesize the information you gather from your interviews and develop your own grading plan. Post the plan on the Companion Website *(http://www.prenhall.com/ lenski).*

FOSTERING INDEPENDENT READING AND WRITING

Early adolescence is a time when students are beginning to develop their own personal identities, when the academic differences between students become even more apparent, and when students are chafing against institutional constraints. Schooling for young teens, however, rarely matches their developmental needs. Too many middle level teachers still operate under the assumption that "teaching" means to stand in front of the classroom and "tell" students what they need to learn. By now you recognize this type of teaching as matching the behaviorist theory of learning, and you know that we're recommending that you instead teach from the social constructivist position. If you're operating from a social constructivist theory base, you'll see teaching differently—from the standpoint of student engagement and student learning.

Researchers Ivey and Broaddus (2000, 2001) have been concerned with what they see as a mismatch between middle level instruction and the needs of young teens, so they conducted a series of studies to find out what middle level readers were thinking. In their studies, Ivey and Broaddus (2001) surveyed and interviewed middle school readers to determine how to make instruction more appropriate. Among their findings, these researchers concluded that the "typical reading demands in middle

The type of teaching that matches social constructivist perspectives emphasizes student engagement and active learning. What motivational strategies could you apply to middle level learners?

schools rarely take into consideration the developmental and personal differences be-tween students" (p. 353). Instead, most students reported their schooling as a "one-size-fits-all" model; teachers did not attempt to consider differences among students. Ivey and Broaddus concluded that this mismatch between students' needs and school routines could foster both negative attitudes toward reading and school failure.

The type of teaching in many middle schools prevents students from learning to their potential. When hearing about this disparity, some teachers might say, "But what else can I do? How should I teach?" Fortunately, researchers have some answers. One answer is to devote time for students to pursue independent reading and writing.

Providing students with independent reading and writing is the one instructional decision that a teacher can make that fits well with what young teens find worth-while (Worthy, Turner, & Moorman, 1998). When students have control over their own reading choices, they are more interested in reading, and they tend to use more sophisticated reading strategies during self-selected reading than they do for as-signed reading (Bintz, 1993). So, encouraging independent reading and writing in middle level classes is both successful for student learning and provides opportuni-ties for students to become more strategic readers—a major goal for middle level reading instruction. "But what do I as the teacher do?" you're probably wondering right now. Well, you don't simply say, "OK, everybody, you can just read now." For successful independent reading and writing time you need to address student moti-vation to read, and you need to carefully organize sustained silent reading and writ-ing time.

Motivating Students to Read

Middle level students may be more difficult to motivate to read than very young chil-dren, but teachers still can influence them to be readers. The interactions that occur between teachers and students can boost motivation because teachers' messages have an impact on students' beliefs about themselves (Schlosser, 1992). You may have memories of teachers who motivated you to read during middle school. Per-haps you had a teacher who introduced you to some of the popular young adoles-cent authors such as Gary Paulsen. Perhaps you really enjoyed reading the stories in your literature anthology and that motivated you to read other books. Or, perhaps you never had a teacher who truly motivated you to read. As a teacher yourself, how-ever, you need to remember that what you do as a middle level teacher and how you treat your students makes a difference in how they perceive themselves as read-ers and how motivated they are to read. In addition to treating students as readers, you can also motivate students by providing reading choices, reading aloud to them, acting like a reading role model, and encouraging internal engagement.

Reading choices.   Students of all ages need to have choices of reading materials, but middle-grade students need choice even more than their younger counterparts. In their interviews of middle level students, Ivey and Broaddus (2001) found that "personal choice was closely aligned with positive experiences reading" (p. 363). The range of reading levels in middle grade will be greater than in other elementary grades; you might have students in the same class reading at a third-grade level and students reading high school books. The only way to accommodate all of the read-ing abilities and interests in a class is to allow students to choose their own books to read—at least some of the time.

Middle-grade readers can be influenced by the books you read aloud and by your recommendations, but their peers influence them to a greater extent. Students' peers become more important to young teens than they are for younger students, and you can use this knowledge to your advantage. Middle-grade students help each other decide what books to read (Guice, 1991), so providing students with a venue for recommending books can promote reading motivation. For example, you might have an interactive bulletin board with student recommendations where students can post a recommendation whenever they find a book they enjoy, or you might encourage brief, informal book talks in which students present a title and do an advertisement for their peers, advocating the book.

Reading aloud. Middle-grade students are not too old to hear books read aloud. In fact, reading aloud to young teens can encourage them to become lifelong readers (Sanacore, 2000). Reading aloud kindles students' imaginations, lengthens their attention spans, and helps them identify reading as a pleasurable experience (Lesesne, 1998). Reading aloud to middle level students won't be a "cure-all" for students who struggle with reading, but it will improve many students' attitudes toward reading and their motivation to read (Trelease, 2001).

You might be wondering how you can fit reading aloud into your classes in a departmentalized setting. Some teachers spend the first few minutes of each class period reading a passage of a chapter to their students. Other teachers prefer to read to students for 20 or 30 minutes once a week. Having a regular schedule for reading aloud is as important as when you read. A regular reading time signals to students that reading aloud is a vital part of reading instruction.

After you have scheduled the time you want to spend reading aloud, you have the opportunity to select books to read to your classes. As a middle level teacher you'll probably teach several different groups of students in a day, and you might decide to read different books to different classes. The benefit of reading different books is that your students will discuss the books among themselves and even compare their reactions to the books. That way you'll expose students to more titles even though you're not directly reading all of these books to the students.

The books you choose will, in part, determine the success of your read-aloud sessions. Variety in your book selection is crucial. At times you should choose the books to read, but you might also read books that students recommend. You can read picture books, single chapters from longer books, entire short books, and you might even decide to play audio books. As you read, though, you should pay close attention to your students' reactions. If the majority of your students dislike one of your reading selections, stop reading and choose a book that many students will enjoy. A list of suggested read-aloud titles can be found in Figure 14.6.

Bauer, J. (2000). *Hope was here.* New York: Putman.

Fleischman, P. (1997). *Seedfolks.* New York: HarperCollins.

Giff, P. R. (1997). *Lily's crossing.* New York: Yearing.

Lisle, J. T. (2000). *The art of keeping cool.* New York: Atheneum.

Peck, R. (1998). *A long way from Chicago.* New York: Scholastic.

Peck, R. (2000). *A year down yonder.* New York: Dial.

Rawls, W. (1999). *Summmer of the monkeys.* New York: Laureleaf.

Sachar, L. (1998). *Holes.* New York: Dell Yearling.

Spinelli, J. (1997). *Wringer.* New York: Scholastic.

Zindel, P. (1989). *A begonia for Miss Applebaum.* New York: Harper & Row.

FIGURE 14.6 Recommendations for Read-Alouds for Middle Level Readers

Reading role model.   No matter how you view yourself as a reader, if you want to be a teacher, you have to be a reading role model to motivate middle level students. Reif (1992) writes, "All teachers must be readers and writers, but teachers of language arts *must* be writers and readers. How many schools hire home economics teachers who do not cook or sew, industrial arts teachers who will not use power tools, coaches who nave never played the game, art teachers who do not draw, Spanish teachers who cannot speak Spanish?" (p. 10). That doesn't mean you have to read only novels—showing your students that you're a reader is more important than what you read. Bring your own reading into the classroom frequently. For example, let's say you were reading an article in a sports magazine about a popular basketball player. Mention it to your students. Or suppose you were experimenting with a new pasta maker and that you had difficulty reading the directions. Tell your students about it. Or perhaps you were reading a spellbinding novel. Relate your experience of staying up late to finish your book. As often as you can, bring your own reading experiences into the classroom so that your students know that you're a reader. In that way, you can be a reading role model.

Becoming a reading role model is critical for students of all ages. What are some reading experiences you could share with your students?

Internal engagement.   You've learned about the importance of engagement on motivation and you know how to create a classroom environment for maximum student engagement. When students reach the middle grades, they also need to be engaged in learning—engagement increases motivation. Because middle-grade students have a greater capacity for introspection than do younger students, you can discuss ways in which students can learn how to motivate themselves. In his research with high-achieving students, Csikszentmihalyi (1991) found that students who did well in school were able to motivate themselves to begin tasks. Once they began a task, these students entered a state of "flow." A flow state is a time when you become thoroughly engaged in an activity, so immersed that time passes without realizing it. You have experienced a flow state at various times in your lives: when you were hiking in the woods and the day passed like a blink of an eye or when you were shopping at the mall and hours went by like minutes. You have most likely also experienced flow when you engaged in literacy activities. Think about a time when you were so involved in a literacy activity that you didn't even think about time passing. You might have been reading an engrossing novel, writing a paper for a class, conducting library research, reading Internet sites, or even listening to a professor. As a middle-level teacher, you can discuss internal engagement with your students and encourage them to work toward entering a flow state when reading.

Sustained Silent Reading and Writing

As a reader yourself you know how important it is to have time to read, especially books of your own choosing. In college, you have a great deal of assigned reading, and although we hope you enjoy most of those assignments, many college students would rather read books that they have selected. The same principle holds true with middle level students. Middle level students want time to read independently in school, and they appreciate it when a teacher sets aside a specific time for them for sustained silent reading and writing (SSRW) (Stewart, Paradis, Ross, & Lewis, 1996). In discussing independent reading time, students found SSRW "as a way to make more sense of the text at hand, since time set aside freed them to concentrate, comprehend, and reflect without being disturbed or distracted by some other tasks" (Ivey & Broaddus, p. 367, 2001).

To organize SSRW, you need to decide how much time to set aside for students to read books of their own choosing and to write for their own purposes. SSRW is different from reading and writing workshops because you're not instructing using focus lessons, you're not assigning the reading, and you're not requiring students to complete specific work associated with their reading or writing. Instead, you provide time and guidelines, and the students read and write.

How much time you devote to SSRW depends on the length of your class periods, the goals you have set for your teaching, and what you are expected to accomplish during that time. Some of you might teach all of the language arts during a short amount of time, whereas others will have two classes devoted to the language arts. However, you should remember that middle level students need time to read for their own purposes, and you should allocate at least 15 to 30 minutes once or twice a week for SSRW.

While you won't be instructing students during SSRW, you need to monitor students' reading and writing. Many teachers ask students to keep a reading/writing log or a journal in which students record the page numbers of the book they are reading or the type of writing they are working on. Furthermore, you can occasionally use the time when students are participating in SSRW to make informal observations about students' engagement with literacy tasks. During much of the SSRW time, however, you also need to be reading or writing—another way to model the joy of literacy for your students.

Materials. A successful independent reading program hinges on having materials available to students during the time they are expected to read or write. Most students will get their reading material from bookstores and libraries, but some will come to class without anything to read—even if you remind them repeatedly to be prepared. In general, middle school classrooms are rarely stocked with materials that students like to read (Worthy, Moorman, Turner, 1999). You may be wondering what middle level students like to read. Of course, you won't know what individual students like reading until you ask them, but, in general, the reading preferences of middle level students are well known and are listed in Figure 14.7.

Classical literature versus series books. As you read the list of students' reading choices given in Figure 14.7, you might be concerned that if students read whatever they want that they won't be exposed to classical literature. You need to remember that SSRW is only a part of your reading program, and that you'll be teaching other types of literature during your reading class. During independent reading, students

---

1. Magazines
2. Adventure books
3. Mysteries
4. Scary stories
5. Joke books
6. Informational books about animals
7. Comic books
8. Series books
9. Informational books about sports
10. Books about peer groups
11. Fantasy
12. Science fiction
13. Newspapers
14. Poetry books
15. Biographies
16. Picture books
17. Historical fiction
18. Science books
19. Informational books about history

From Ivey, G., & Broaddus, K. (2001). "Just plain reading": A survey of what makes students want to read in middle school classrooms. Reading Research Quarterly, 36, *350–377. Copyright by the International Reading Association. All rights reserved.*

FIGURE 14.7 Preferred Reading Materials of Middle Level Students

should be able to choose whatever they want to read, within reasonable boundaries. Some students may want to bring questionable reading materials to independent reading, and you have every right to refuse to allow those types of materials in the classroom. But you should allow students to read magazines and books that you wouldn't ordinarily teach, such as *Popular Mechanics* or Stephen King novels.

One type of book that is very popular with middle level students is series books, such as the Hardy Boys, Nancy Drew, and Harry Potter. Students frequently read series books because they are easy to find in bookstores and libraries, and students already know the characters in the books after they've read one of the books. Reading a book series gives students a "head start" and is easier than reading a brand new book (Greenlee, Monson, & Taylor, 1996).

Not all series books are the same, however. Jim Trelease (2001) differentiates between commercial series like Nancy Drew, Goosebumps, and the Baby-Sitters Club, and more sophisticated series books like the *Chronicles of Narnia* and Harry Potter stories. The commercial series books are written by teams of authors and are often written using a plot pattern. Series such as the Harry Potter books, however, are written by a single author and contain more complex characterization and plot structures.

 A list of series books can be found in Chapter 10. What additional series books would middle level students enjoy?

Book selection.   Some students who have the chance to read during SSRW won't read because they don't know how to choose books of interest to them. These students may find reading "boring." In *Lifers,* a book about struggling adolescent readers, Mueller (2001) described her experiences interviewing young teens about reading. She found that students who found reading to be boring usually were not interested in the topic they were reading about. As a teacher, you won't be able to manufacture interest for students, but you can help students find ways that books and reading can be relevant to their own lives.

You can use student information cards and other data you collect about students to find materials that are of interest. You can also help students develop their own book selection strategies. Williams (2001b) states that one of the most useful book selection strategies for students is to have them ask their peers for book recommendations. Young teens are much more likely to read a book suggested by a friend than by a teacher or a librarian. She also suggests that you remind students to look for books by favorite authors. Other selection strategies include looking at the front cover and title, reading the summary on the back cover, and noting the book's length. While these strategies may seem like common sense to you, they may be new to some of your students and can help them make wise choices for independent reading.

Technology Topic: Internet Workshops

A way to foster independent reading and writing connected with technology is through an Internet workshop (Leu, 2002). An Internet workshop consists of an "independent reading of information on the Internet around a topic and a location initially designated by the teacher; it concludes with a short workshop session where students can share and exchange the ideas and strategies they discovered during their work on the Internet" (p. 466).

Internet workshops work best when you connect them with something you're teaching. For example, if you're teaching students about Mark Twain, you could connect to sites dealing with him and his books. Then give groups of students different sites to access. You might ask students to take notes or to print some of the information they have learned. Because some students will be still novice Internet users, it's important that you have the students discuss their searching strategies after they've read the websites. During the discussion, you can also discuss what students learned about the topic.

GROUPING PRACTICES FOR CRITICAL READERS

A recurring theme throughout this text is that an effective reading teacher will develop a variety of instructional practices to meet the varied needs of students. Nowhere is this more important than in the middle grades. The differences among students are far greater in middle grades than at any of the other elementary grades. Despite the wide range of student achievement in reading and the many individual and cultural differences among students, middle school teachers admit that they rarely differentiate their teaching to accommodate the differences between the students in their classes (Tomlinson, Moon, & Callahan, 1998).

One of the reasons why middle level teachers have been so resistant to differentiate instruction is that middle schools (or junior high schools) were patterned after high schools. High school teachers generally teach four to six classes of 30 or more students for short periods of time (45 minutes or so), and in that time, they would teach primarily to the whole group. Much of this teaching is typically lecture and discussion. Because many middle school teachers were trained to teach high school, these instructional patterns are routine for them.

With the advent of the middle school and the changes in learning theory from behaviorism to constructivism, teachers began experimenting with different types of teaching for students at the middle level. Further, middle school policy statements such as *Turning Points* (Jackson & Davis, 2000) encouraged teachers to develop creative ways to address individual differences and to consider the range of abilities of students in classrooms.

Some middle schools have taken the challenge and have begun to adopt practices that consider students as individual learners. For example, one school faculty studied the research on grouping practices and took an in-depth look at the way they grouped students. Many middle schools schedule students in heterogeneous, or mixed-ability, classes for language arts or reading. Other schools group students in homogeneous, or ability, groups. There are reasons why both heterogeneous and homogeneous groupings are troublesome in the middle grades, so this school decided that they would offer one class period of language in mixed-ability groups and another period of language arts for ability-based groups (Lisandrelli & Lisandrelli, 2000). They found that having different types of grouping practices built into their scheduling solved an educational problem.

As a new teacher, you probably won't have input into scheduling of classes; you'll probably have to just take what you get. However, you have already learned several ways to group students in your own classroom that are applicable to middle level teaching. You've already learned about guided reading, reading and writing workshops, and literature circles. Each of these grouping options could be appropriate for different middle level teaching situations. In addition, we'd like to introduce you to another type of grouping practice that works well for middle level students—the Book Club Program.

The Book Club Program

The Book Club Program was developed as an instructional practice and was based on social constructivist learning theory. It's somewhat like book clubs that adults join at public libraries or that Oprah promoted, but the Book Club Program has several distinguishing features that are unlike the more informal book clubs that you might know.

The Book Club Program is based on the Vygotskian principles that (1) language plays a key role in the development of thought processes, (2) learning is best accomplished at the zone of proximal development with the guidance of a "more knowledgeable other," and (3) that new learning needs to be internalized through extending activities (Raphael, Pardo, & Highfield, 2002). A fourth principle underpinning the Book Club Program based on Bruner's (1989) work is that learners will not learn unless they are actively engaged in learning activities.

"But what does a Book Club look like?" you're probably wondering. A Book Club includes some of the features of grouping practices that you already know. In a Book Club, you might begin the class with a community share, which is similar in some respects to beginning the class with a focus lesson for reading and writing workshops. Then students gather in heterogeneous groups to read a common text. After students have read a part of a text, they write responses to their reading, and finally students engage in either small-group or whole-class discussions. When students participate in small-group discussions, the *students* lead the discussions.

Community Share.   The Community Share is the name for the Book Club equivalent of short focus lessons on reading or writing for whole-class discussions and for community building. A vital part of Book Clubs is developing a classroom community where literacy discussions and events are enacted. The placement of the Community Share depends on its purpose; it can be held at the beginning of the class period, in the middle, or at the end.

The reading strategies you've learned in earlier chapters are ideal for focus lessons. Which strategies do you think would be most appropriate for middle level students?

Raphael and Goatley (1997) write about the Community Share as providing time for "instructing, modeling, building intertextual connections among different book clubs within a unit or across units over time, initiating 'repair activities' when interpretations of story events conflict with conventional knowledge, and in general, helping students participate as active members of their educational community" (p. 27). This is the time for teacher-led activities such as setting the stage for the day's events, introducing new strategies, summarizing story events, and modeling strategies.

Reading the text.   The text you select for your Book Club Program should be one that has wide appeal for the majority of your students such as Lois Lowry's novel, *The Giver* (1993). Once you have selected a book, you need to purchase enough copies for every student in the class. (In some schools, students purchase their own paperback novels for Book Clubs.) After each student has a copy of the book, and *you've* read the book carefully, you can begin Book Club.

You'll probably want to begin a Book Club unit with a Community Share where you introduce the book and the author and possibly explore students' perspectives about the themes of the book. Then students begin reading.

You can structure the reading time in different ways depending on your class and your teaching goals. You might read parts of the story aloud, you can have students read in pairs or in groups, or you can give students time to read independently. Most middle level teachers find a combination approach works best. You can read aloud those parts that hold dramatic interest, and you can divide students into pairs or groups for the difficult, complex chapters. Much of the reading, though, should be done independently because middle level readers typically prefer reading silently.

The days you assign paired or group reading are especially useful to you for making informal assessments of students' reading. As students read, walk around the room and stop to listen in to the reading of students that you've identified before the session begins. If you have questions about a particular student's reading, you can have that student read with you individually in a conference setting. (Be sure you make notes about your observations.)

One of the most interesting features of the Book Club Program is its use of heterogeneous groupings for reading texts. The reasons for mixed-ability grouping are (1) middle level students have a variety of factors that influence their learning other than reading ability, (2) discussions can be richer if students from different perspectives participate, and (3) students demonstrate different strengths and abilities when they take part in student-led discussions (McMahon, 1997).

Responding to reading. As students read, they should be actively constructing meaning from the text. During reading, students should be visualizing the story, trying to understand the characters' feelings, making connections to other books or events, thinking about their own lives, interpreting the author's message, and critiquing the story (Raphael, Kehus, & Damphousse, 2001). All of these mental processes are fertile grounds for responding to reading. Students should have a journal or notebook with them as they read, and you should encourage them to write responses to their reading immediately after they have finished a section. These responses might be words, phrases, or even page numbers to remember with a short note. They do not need to be long narratives that students sometimes dread writing. Figure 14.8 illustrates an example of a student's written response to reading the novel *Roll of Thunder, Hear My Cry* (Taylor, 1976).

Class discussions. You have experienced hundreds of school discussions in your life, and you may have noticed that classroom discussions generally follow the same pattern. Typically, the teacher initiates a question, the students respond, and the teacher evaluates the answer (Cazden, 2001). During these types of classroom discussions, students often try to "guess" what the teacher is thinking, and they are discouraged from volunteering their own constructions of meanings. Although there are times when whole-class discussions are appropriate, one of the distinguishing features of Book Clubs is that students discuss their reading in student-led discussion groups.

Student-led discussions will probably not be successful unless you prepare students in advance of the discussion time. During Community Share, you can model good discussion group etiquette and present ideas for discussion. Your goal for these discussion groups is for students to talk about their readings naturally, like dinner

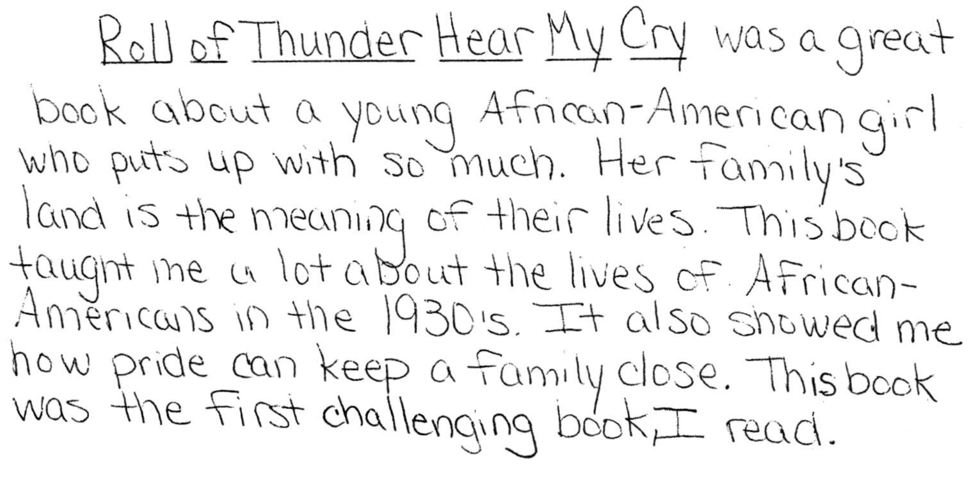

> *Roll of Thunder Hear My Cry* was a great book about a young African-American girl who puts up with so much. Her family's land is the meaning of their lives. This book taught me a lot about the lives of African-Americans in the 1930's. It also showed me how pride can keep a family close. This book was the first challenging book I read.

FIGURE 14.8 Responding to Reading

table conversations. To achieve natural discussions, however, you'll need to help students learn how to discuss without a teacher directing them. In addition, you might consider assigning students to Book Club groups during your first few discussions.

To better understand how a Book Club discussion operates, think about discussing a book with friends over lunch. One of you might mention a book you are reading—you might talk about the characters, parts of the plot that you especially like, author's techniques such as humor, or other related books. As you discuss the book, others join in with their own opinions. You share ideas, maybe agreeing or disagreeing with each other; at the end of the discussion, you leave with a deeper understanding of the book. It's this type of discussion that you want students to replicate during Book Club discussions.

If you implement Book Club, you should be aware of the hazards of student-led discussions. Unlike friendly book discussions over lunch, some students can feel silenced by overly aggressive student leaders (Hinchman & Young, 2001). As students discuss, you should be aware of students who are not able to participate in discussions and of students who try to control the group. If a situation arises, you can give more suggestions on ways to take turns during discussions, or you can change group membership.

Scheduling Book Clubs.   The Book Club Program was developed for middle level readers so it is particularly appropriate if you teach grades 6 through 8. As with other grouping practices, such as literature circles, reading and writing workshops, and guided reading, you need to remember that one instructional practice should not take up all of your teaching time. Instead, you need to allow time for reading aloud, independent reading, book talks, and teaching with a common text. As you develop your reading schedule, you can reserve Book Clubs (or other grouping practices) for part of a class period, part of a week, or part of a semester. You will not have time to use each of these instructional practices every day. The schedule in Figure 14.9 gives an idea of ways to implement Book Club with other teaching practices.

Grouping Options

Book Clubs are one of the many grouping options you should consider as a middle level teacher. You might be wondering which one of these options will work best for you and your students. As you make your decision, you should consider the

Monday	Tuesday	Wednesday	Thursday	Friday
Community Share (15 minutes)	Read aloud (15 minutes)	Community Share (20 minutes)	Student-led discussion (30 minutes)	SSRW 25 minutes
Reading in pairs or groups (35 minutes)	Responding to reading (20 minutes)	Silent sustained reading and writing (30 minutes)	Read aloud (20 minutes)	Community Share (15 minutes)
	Community Share (15 minutes)			Book talks (10 minutes)

FIGURE 14.9   Reading Schedule Using Book Clubs With a 50-Minute Class Period

Advice for New Teachers

Grouping Options

Dear Linda,

I want to group my middle level students and I've learned about guided reading, reading and writing workshops, literature circles, and Book Clubs. I feel as if I have too much information. How do I decide which one to use in my classroom?

Dear New Teacher,

All of the grouping options that you've listed are wonderful ways to have students read materials with support. Making the decision between the options is pretty much a personal choice, and it's not a choice that is irrevocable. Last year I began with Book Clubs and I transitioned students to reading and writing workshops. One of my colleagues uses guided reading in a class of struggling readers. So, you're on your own with this one. Use the information you have to make the best decision you can. Stay flexible and you'll be surprised at how successful you'll be.

needs of your students and your curriculum requirements. The grouping options that have been described in this book and a rationale for their use follows.

Use guided reading when a majority of students still need support using the cueing system and reading fluently.

Use literature circles when you have compatible texts at different levels, if students need the structure of assigned roles in their discussions, and if you want to group students by reading ability.

Use reading and writing workshops when students are at many different reading levels and are motivated to read and write independently.

Use the Book Club Program when you want students in heterogeneous groups, if students are able to lead discussions, and if you want to integrate reading and writing.

ENCOURAGING PARENTAL INVOLVEMENT

Another context for learning is the home, but it may be easier to teach middle school students than it is to parent them. Middle school students are challenging; they're beginning to break free of adult control, and they often test the limits of adult restrictions. You may remember this behavior from your adolescent years or perhaps you are the parent of an adolescent yourself. As middle school students are breaking away from parents and finding their own identity, parents are also learning how to relate to young adolescents who will soon be independent adults. Both parents and their children are transitioning to a new stage in life, and often parents don't know whether they should continue to be closely involved in their child's schooling.

Because of the changes that are taking place in the relationship between parents and their middle school children, the number of parents who are highly involved in their children's schooling decreases from that of younger students. The U.S. Department of Health and Human Services (1998) estimates that only 24% of parents of students in grades 6 through 8 are highly involved in their child's schooling. The decrease of parental involvement comes at a high cost. Young adolescents whose parents are not involved in their lives tend to have lower self-esteem, less self-reliance, and are less successful in school (Steinberg, Brown, & Dornbusch, 1996). It's important, therefore, that middle school teachers continue to encourage parents to stay involved in their child's schooling, especially their literacy learning.

Understanding Changing Parental Roles

By the time a student has reached middle school, many changes are occurring, not only in the student, but in the family structure. The roles of parents begin to change, providing the student with more freedom, more decision-making ability, and less guidance. The relationship parents have with teachers in schools also begins to weaken (Epstein, 1996). Some parents would like to be closely involved in their middle school child's work, but they find the academic work challenging and simply can't help their child with homework any longer. Furthermore, middle schools tend to be located further away from parents' homes than elementary schools, and many more parents work longer hours than when children were younger (Jackson & Davis, 2000).

When their children reach middle school, many parents believe that their relationship with schools should change. In a survey about parental roles of middle schools students, the findings indicated that parents believe that their role should be one of mentor and coach. The parents surveyed thought their role in school should be to encourage their children to study and to respect the teachers. Teachers, however, disagreed. They thought parents should attend conferences and volunteer to help with school events (Jackson & Davis, 2000).

Some students become ambivalent about their parents at this age. Although many parents and children maintain good relationships, during the middle school years many children begin to become "embarrassed" by their parents. Middle school students may not want to be seen with parents in public, eat with the family at restaurants, and, especially, have their parents come to school. However, many middle school students expect their parents to attend their sporting events, concerts, and other school events. It's hard to predict exactly what middle school students want from their parents, and most likely the students don't know either. This shifting family dynamic has an impact on the role parents take in school.

◼◼◼ YOU TRY IT ◼◼◼

Reflections on Middle School Years

Think back to your middle school years, or talk with a middle-school-aged student about her experiences. Remember how you felt when your parents attended schools events. How did you feel when your parents watched you participate in school activities such as sporting events, plays, or concerts? Did your parents participate in school in other ways? Did they volunteer at the school, attend conferences, attend open house or curriculum night, or visit the classes you were in? Did your parents know your teachers socially outside of school? How did you feel when your parents saw your teachers at community events?

Talk with your parents about the role they played in school during your middle school years. What do they remember about their involvement? How did they perceive your reaction to their involvement? Write about your experiences. Based on your experiences as a middle school student and your interviews with your parents, develop a plan for yourself as a middle school teacher. What role do you think parents should play in the schooling of middle school students? How can you encourage this involvement?

Parents as coaches.   Parents and teachers agree that parents should monitor their child's homework. When you're a teacher, you'll find that some middle school students need close monitoring at home while others don't need much guidance at all. For the students who need their parents to check their homework, you can institute a homework assignment sheet (see Figure 14.10). This assignment sheet should be filled in by the student at school and signed by you or another teacher. The student takes the assignment sheet home so that the parent can review all homework assignments. Using an assignment sheet helps middle school students stay organized to complete their multiple assignments, keeps parents informed, and provides parents with an active role in making this happen.

Diversity Issue: Respecting Cultural Differences

Middle school is difficult for many students and for many parents. The physical and emotional changes that occur during young adolescence tend to make middle school students unpredictable. The normal changes of adolescence are compounded when the students come from a home culture that is different from that of the school. Some students come to school with what Bourdieu and Passeron (1977) have termed

SUBJECT	ASSIGNMENT	DUE DATE
Reading	Read last part of *Monster*	1/13
English	Work on biography	1/16
Math	P.P. 126–127 1–45 odd	1/13
Science	Write lab results	1/14
History	Work on research project	1/20
Exploratory	None	

Date: *January 12*

Teacher's Signature *Ms. Terrell*

Parent's Signature *Patricia Evans*

FIGURE 14.10   Sample Assignment Sheet

cultural capital; that is, they possess culturally valued advantages as a result of family background or life experiences. Cultural capital is respected and reproduced in schooling. For example, Standard English is valued and expected in American schools. Those students whose home cultures are steeped in Standard English have language as an aspect of cultural capital. Students who speak another language or dialect at home may not have as firm a grasp on some of the subtleties of the English language. Cultural capital is not equally available to all students.

What happens to the relationship of middle school children and their parents when students come from home cultures that are different from the valued culture of school? The clash between school culture and home culture can distress parents. In a sensitive article describing this clash, Cline (1998) articulates the pain some parents feel when their culture is not valued in schools and their children are caught in the middle of the two cultures.

Identifying funds of knowledge.   What can you do when you find that your middle school students come from cultures unlike the culture of schooling? Gonzalez, Rueda, and Moll (in press) suggest that teachers value parents' "funds of knowledge." Funds of knowledge are the things people know and can do that are valued in life but are not evident in schooling. Funds of knowledge are easy to understand if you think about your friends and the talents they have that are not connected with schoolwork. For example, perhaps you have said something like this about a friend: "She may not get top grades, but she's an expert at hair styles, a really talented musician, and a great friend." These are funds of knowledge. They are talents or gifts unrelated to schooling.

Funds of knowledge can be found in all areas of life. What are some of your own funds of knowledge?

You can respect the parents of your students for their funds of knowledge and make your respect obvious to your students, especially to a parent's child. For example, suppose you request a conference with a student who you know emigrated from El Salvador. The parents don't attend, and you find out that both parents work two jobs and are unable to take off work. Your response can make a difference. Even though you believe that a conference with parents is important to the student's progress, you can respect the parents for working so hard and you can convey that message to the student.

Sharing life experiences.   Your response to parents is one way to respect their funds of knowledge. Another way is to encourage parents to volunteer in the classroom by sharing their life experiences or skills with the students. You can respect and admire the lives of the many parents who are fluent in English and a second language. You can show your respect for their linguistic ability by asking dual-language parents to act as translators for non-English-speaking students or parents. Asking parents to serve on PTO boards or to supervise students on field trips is another way to respect their talents. Many parents welcome invitations to share leadership in the school. All parents have funds of knowledge, and you can promote parental involvement by acknowledging the many gifts and talents of parents of your students.

Encourage Parental Participation

When children reach early adolescence, they may have an ambivalent attitude toward their parents, but they still rely on their parents for encouragement and support, and parents influence their child's actions and attitudes (Baker, 2000). After all, students who stay in school from kindergarten through 12th grade will have spent only 9% of their time in school, which leaves 91% of their time outside school and under their parents' guidance (Kearns, 1993). The time middle school students spend at home can encourage or discourage their literacy learning.

Jim discusses a book he's reading with his son Eric.

Parental role models. One important way parents can encourage their child's literacy learning is to be reading role models for their children. Middle level students are influenced by actions far more than words, so knowing that their parents value reading is important for students. Students may not recognize all of the reading that their parents do, so it's up to you to make parental reading more visible. You can make reading visible by sending home a flyer requesting that parents visit your class to speak about the reading they accomplish on their jobs. Many jobs require much more reading and writing than middle level students realize. Inviting parents to share job-related reading helps middle school students understand the enduring need for reading.

Another way parents can be reading role models is to talk about reading at home. Ask if you can make a "public service announcement" at a school event. During the announcement ask parents to talk to their children about the reading that they do in the course of their everyday lives. Give several examples, such as "I was reading a sports magazine last night, and I found out the background of my favorite baseball player," or "Last week I read a movie review that convinced me to see the movie. I was amazed at how different my reaction was to the movie compared to the movie critic's." Frequently remind parents that they should encourage their child's reading and writing by talking about their own literacy.

Parent-student book clubs. Book clubs are springing up in unlikely places, including those promoted by talk show hosts. You can take advantage of the popularity of book clubs by beginning a parent–student book club. Select a list of books that could be of high interest to middle school students and their parents. These books would need to have themes that transcend adolescents but to which young teens can relate. Encourage parents and students to purchase copies of these books and hold monthly meetings after school to discuss them. You might choose to be the

Both parents and teachers can be reading role models. How can you make the ways parents use reading outside school visible for students?

discussion leader for the first meeting, but ask a parent or student to co-lead the group during subsequent meetings. At the book club meetings, spend time discussing the book and, just like classroom book clubs, set some ground rules before the book discussions, such as allowing everyone to tell their understanding of the story without negative comments. Parent–student book clubs can be a wonderful way to promote parental involvement on a new sphere where parents and students are equal partners in literacy.

CONNECTIONS: WHAT'S NEXT?

In this chapter you've learned some instructional options for teaching Critical Readers. You don't have to teach students to read through whole-group instruction alone. Instead you can organize a reading program that is based on the knowledge you gather about your students' reading progress through informal assessment. Using that information, you can make decisions about instructional groupings. You may at times want to divide students for small-group instruction so you can address individual differences. Book clubs are one type of grouping option that works well for middle level learners, but other options presented in this book can also be used. Middle level learners also like to make choices about the books they read, so SSRW should also have a prominent place in your reading program. Finally, you need to remember that the parents of middle level students also have a role in their children's learning. Although it can be more difficult to make space for parent participation with Critical Readers, it's important for you to respect and value the contributions parents make in the lives of their children. Look through Figure 14.11 to see how independent and small-group learning of Critical Readers fits into the larger context of reading instruction.

In the final chapter of this book, you'll see how all of the previous chapters fit together as you become a teacher of reading. In the first chapter we focused on you as an individual—who you are, what you know, and what you believe—because teaching always begins with the individual. In Chapters 2 through 14 we focused on the students you will teach and discussed how to organize a classroom for instruction, how to assess students' reading progress, and how to provide culturally relevant instruction. In Chapter 15, we return the spotlight to you by asking you to apply what you've learned in the previous chapters of this book. You'll find as you read the final chapter that you are indeed becoming a teacher of reading.

FIGURE 14.11   A Developmental Approach to the Teaching of Reading

	Early Readers	**Interpretive Readers**	**Critical Readers**
Theories underscored as readers develop:	Social Constructivism	Social Constructivism	Social Constructivism

FIGURE 14.11 *Continued*

	Early Readers	**Interpretive Readers**	**Critical Readers**
Whole-group instruction through:	• Read-alouds • Shared texts • Comprehension strategies • Working with words	• Read-alouds • Using basals • Literature-based models • Word-building strategies • Comprehension strategies	• Read-alouds • Common texts (e.g., basals, anthologies, trade books) • Comprehension strategies • Vocabulary instruction and word analysis • Researching • Critical reading • Reading content area texts • Studying and note-taking
Assessment ideas for whole group:	• Observations • Kidwatching • Anecdotal notation	• Portfolios • Open-ended questions • Rubrics	• Written retellings • Research projects • Interest inventories • Content-area histories • Cloze procedure
Small-group instruction through:	• Guided reading • Teaching for strategies • Working with words	• Basal readers • Literature anthologies • Fluency practice • Guided silent reading • Literature circles • Inquiry groups	• Book clubs • Trade books
Assessment ideas for small groups:	• Running Records • Retellings • Discussions with children	• Names test • Fluency checklist • Peer assessment • Inquiry rubric	• Student information card • Bio poem • "I Used to… But Now I…" poem • Observational checklist • Student self-assessment • Norm-referenced tests
Independent learning through:	• Independent reading • Reading/writing workshop • Making books • Reading the room	• Independent reading • Reading/writing workshop • Responding through writing • Reading logs	• Sustained silent reading and writing
Sociocultural contexts:	• Literacy partnerships with parents • Parents in the classroom • Home–school communication	• Reading/writing connection for life • Oral histories • Home literacy activities • Parent programs	• Parents as coaches • Funds of knowledge • Parent–student book clubs

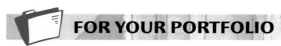

FOR YOUR PORTFOLIO

ENTRY 14.1   *Learning about Students' Backgrounds*

INTASC Principle 10 states: *The teacher fosters relationships with school colleagues, parents, and agencies in the larger community to support students' learning and well-being.*

Background knowledge is a key factor in learning to read in the middle grades, especially in content-area subjects. You'll find that students from cultures different from your own have funds of knowledge that are unfamiliar to you. Develop a plan for learning about the different backgrounds of your students and their families and try it out on a hypothetical student. For example, suppose you had a group of students who came to the United States from Guatemala. Find out about the culture, politics, and climate of Guatemala by looking at Internet sites, reading books, and interviewing people familiar with the country.

Then develop a list of topics that you might use as you develop lesson plans. Using the Guatemalan example, you might have the following list:

- Volcanoes,
- Oceans,
- Tropical climate,
- Civil war,
- Guerrillas,
- Fincas (plantations),
- Indigenous people,
- Weaving and embroidery,
- Catholicism,
- Spanish influence, and
- Maize (corn).

Using your knowledge about the country or culture, prepare several lesson plans that you would use with students who may have background knowledge in those topics. As you prepare your lesson plans, however, remember that not all children from a country will be familiar with every topic you list.

ENTRY 14.2   *Learning about Students' Languages*

IRA/NCTE Standard 9 states: *Students develop an understanding of and respect for diversity in language use, patterns, and dialects across culture, ethnic groups, geographic regions, and social roles.*

As a middle level teacher, one of your goals will be for your students to respect the different languages and dialects that make up your school community and other geographic regions. An ideal place to start in learning about different languages or dialects is with the parents of the students you teach. Develop a plan that enumerates ways you can use parents to foster your students' language learning. Include necessary artifacts that you could use right away when you get your first teaching position. For example, in your plan you might include a letter to parents written in English and Spanish (and other languages represented in your area) that invites them to come to school to teach the class a few words in their language.

ENTRY 14.3   *Strategic Writers*

IRA/NCTE Standard 5 states: *Students employ a wide range of strategies as they write and use different writing process elements appropriately to communicate with different audiences for a variety of purposes.*

Your goal as a teacher will be to teach your students to become strategic readers and writers. Throughout this book, we've provided you with ideas to facilitate student writing, especially as it relates to reading. Describe the elements of the writing process, list some of the strategies writers use as they compose text, and prepare a list of audiences for student writing.

TO LEARN MORE

Helpful Websites

Visit our Companion Website at *http://www.prenhall.com/lenski* to link to the following sites:

National Association for Bilingual Education

This is the home page of the professional organization on bilingual education.
http://www.ncbe.gwu.edu/

ERIC Clearinghouse on Assessment and Evaluation

Provides information on assessment and ideas for practicing teachers.
http://ericae.net/

Index to Internet Sites: Children's and Young Adults' Authors & Illustrators

Lists helpful links to information on authors and illustrators.
http://falcon.jme.edu/~ramseyil/biochildhome.htm

Helping Your Child With Homework

Explains ideas parents can use to help their children with homework.
http://www.ed.gov/pubs/parents/Homework/index/html

PTA National

Lists a variety of links to articles that deal with communicating and interacting with parents.
http://www.pta.org/programs/invstand.htm

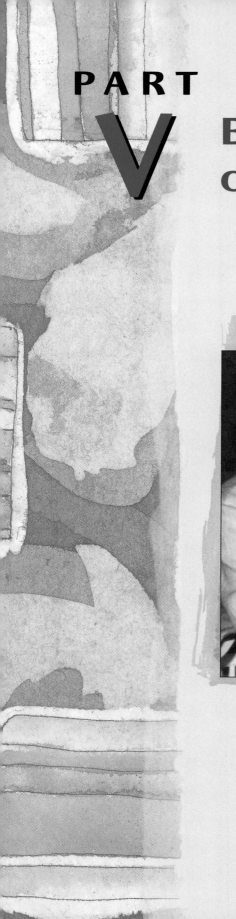

BECOMING A TEACHER OF READING

You have worked hard to understand important information about the teaching of reading. In the process of doing so, you have remembered your own experiences as a literacy learner, questioned your own beliefs about teaching and learning, and explored many new concepts about literacy. This is just a beginning for you. We hope that you are excited about becoming a teacher, but you may still be wondering if you'll know *what to do* when you are responsible for a classroom of students.

No good teacher ever ceases learning how to teach, and our students never quit teaching us how to be better teachers. However, our hope is that you have a clear sense of how to begin literacy instruction in your first classroom and that you have constructed new and valuable knowledge that has started you on your path toward becoming an outstanding teacher of reading.

At the beginning of this text, we used a lens metaphor to describe your experiences in learning to become a teacher of reading. We noted that we would end the book with a telescopic stance, allowing you to see the whole picture. The telescope that we will use to look at the whole picture is positioned on a "social constructivism setting" as it focuses on the teaching of reading. That means that as you think about all you have learned about reading, your understandings should be embedded in a foundational belief about teaching/learning events: The construction of meaning occurs through social interactions and *active* participation.

Calkins (1994) writes that we each need a vision of what's essential in order to teach well. In this final part, we reaffirm the vision we have as literacy educators concerning what we believe is essential to teach well: the enthusiasm to become a responsive teacher, the knowledge to address the needs of the complexity of teaching, and an acknowledgment that it all comes back to you.

chapter **15**

Becoming a Responsive Teacher

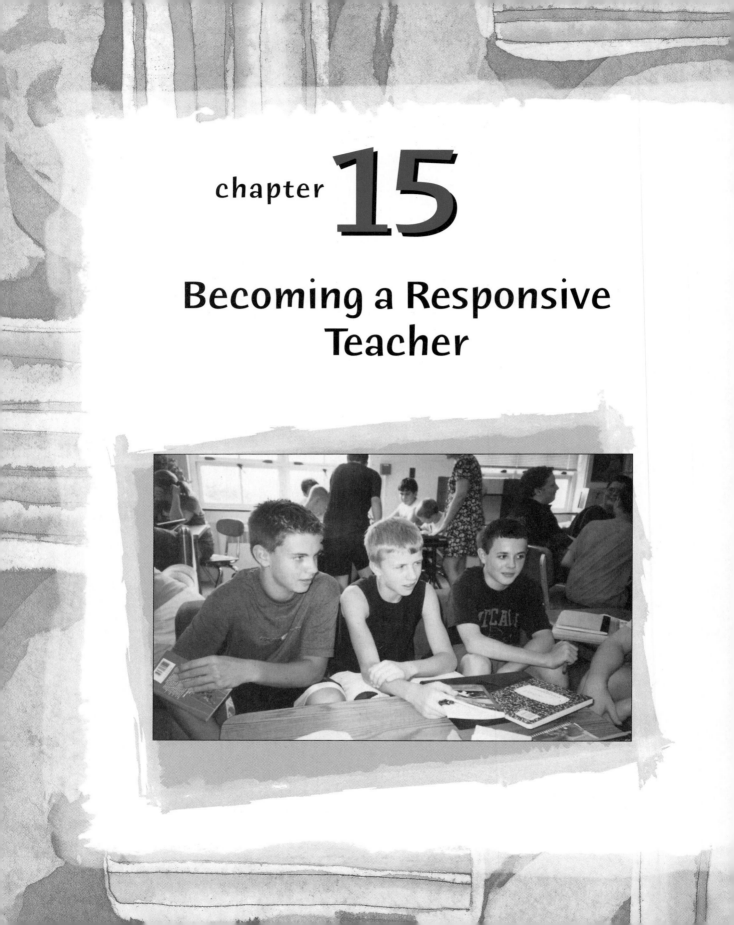

Essential Learning Questions

- What does it mean to be a responsive teacher?
- How can the Responsive Teaching Model help you think about decision making in response to students' needs?
- How does culturally relevant teaching benefit your students?
- How can you facilitate literacy learning for students whose first language is not English?
- What are some of the factors that contribute to the complexity of teaching?
- What is meant by this statement: Your theory of literacy learning will always be evolving.

Visit the online journal in Chapter 15 on our Companion Website at *www.prenhall.com/lenski* to answer these questions. Save your answers to your hard drive or to a disk to compile an online journal.

The centrality of assessment has been stressed throughout this text. Why is knowing about your students essential to responsive teaching?

What does it mean to be a responsive teacher? We believe it means that you are reactive and sensitive to your students' strengths and needs as learners. In terms of responsive teaching, the *centrality of assessment* is a core understanding that we hope you have internalized.

Responsive teachers make decisions based on what they know about their students. You know now that assessment is so much more than giving tests and assigning grades. Each child in an elementary classroom who is learning to read has different strengths and needs as well as different ways of approaching literacy tasks. As an effective, responsive literacy teacher, you will assess each child and make instructional decisions for that child based on the findings from the assessments. Each of the assessment measures you use, such as Running Records, retellings, and anecdotal notation, is designed to give you a view of the in-the-head strategies that a reader is or is not using. One of most important ways you will become more effective at teaching reading is through responding to your students' needs. Becoming a responsive teacher is your primary goal. You will continue to develop your ability to "see" children through careful observation and by using informal and formal assessments.

THE RESPONSIVE TEACHING MODEL

The Responsive Teaching Model will help as you reflect on all you have learned about being a responsive teacher. *Responsive* is used in the context of this model to define a teacher who is learner centered, understands that assessment informs instruction, and makes teaching decisions in *response* to students' strengths and needs. Remember that at the heart of your teaching is your evolving theory of how children learn best. Your philosophy will affect every instructional decision that you make.

Know that while this model provides a representation of responsive teaching, it is not a rigid game plan. Due to the unique characteristics and changeability of students, teaching decisions will often be made without following the model in a strictly sequential manner. Instead, as a responsive teacher, you should always keep the needs of your students foremost in your mind and let their needs guide your teaching actions in flexible ways.

FIGURE 15.1   The Responsive Teaching Model

 You noticed that the Responsive Teaching Model in Figure 15.1 has your theory of how children learn placed in the center. Why is it located in the center of the diagram and what does that indicate?

In Figure 15.1 the inner circle characterizes students' activities in this student-centered model, and the teachers' actions are shown in the outer circle, even though all participants in the classroom are continuously interacting, as the arrows indicate. Notice that the teacher engages in the following pattern: assessment, which leads to evaluation and planning, then to teaching or modified teaching as students' needs change, and back to assessment. In this hypothetical example, we use guided reading as the instructional approach. Start at the top of the diagram with assessment, where all good teaching begins. The activities are described below using guided reading as an example.

Assessment: Knowledge of students and what students need.
- Students need to become more strategic, independent readers.

Teaching: Using guided reading, the teacher flexibly and temporarily groups children according to their strengths and needs; selects and introduces appropriate texts; and monitors children's reading.
- Students participate in the prediction process and begin independent, silent reading of the text.

Ongoing assessment: The teacher makes sure that the book selected is suitable, that children in the group have similar strengths and needs, and notices problems children are encountering in their reading.

- Students meet with too much difficulty in the text the teacher has presented. They need to develop and use more effective strategies for solving unknown words.

Evaluation and planning: Based on ongoing assessment, the teacher acts *responsively* and decides that students need extra support from a different text, such as an easier nonfiction book. The teacher also decides that students need to learn and use the word-solving strategy of "skip it and come back."

Modified teaching: The teacher brings in an easier, nonfiction text and demonstrates the "skip it" strategy for students.

- The students read the nonfiction text with more self-confidence and understanding. They also relate the information in the text to their own lives.

Assessment: The teacher listens to the children read the new book, then asks children to do a retelling and conducts a discussion to assess comprehension. During listening to students read, students apply the new strategy that was introduced.

Evaluation and planning: The teacher discovers that this group of students responds more readily to a nonfiction text but they still need to work on fluent reading. Therefore, she provides them with more nonfiction texts and demonstrates fluent reading strategies. She plans to allow the students more time for talking about books and making connection to their lives.

Teaching: The teacher brings in another nonfiction text. This time she invites a rich and lively discussion about the book. The teacher then introduces choral reading as an approach to foster more fluent reading.

- The students participate in an animated book discussion. They also practice fluent reading by dividing into pairs and alternately read the book aloud.
- The teacher makes notes about the teaching decisions and observations she has made. Then the Responsive Teaching Model begins all over again.

We used the guided reading method as an example of responsive teaching. However, every classroom activity is an opportunity to form judgments about student learning and to assess your teaching. As you become more comfortable in your role as a responsive teacher, you will begin to make quick judgments about what you need to change in order to make literacy teaching and learning interactions more effective. Ongoing assessment will guide your instructional planning and influence what you do as a teacher.

Knowing your students well will provide you with information to ensure that you are reaching all children by being a responsive teacher. Knowing your students well affects more than just the instructional decisions that you make, however; it also affects the relationships you establish with your students and the learning environment you create in the classroom. In these arenas, being a responsive teacher means that you understand and react to children's needs as diverse and cherished *people*.

DIVERSITY IN THE CLASSROOM

As you have learned, today's classrooms are increasingly diverse in terms of linguistic, cultural, racial, ethnic, and socioeconomic composition. When you are a teacher you should capitalize on the rich cultural and language backgrounds that children bring to school from their homes and communities. We are living in a multicultural, multilingual society, and teachers need to be prepared to facilitate learning in all settings. But

We have used the term *culture* throughout this text. What attributes comprise one's culture?

this ability cannot be encapsulated into a formula for success. It takes an attitude of openness on your part as well as a willingness to learn more and stretch yourself beyond your comfort zone. Embracing diversity is another aspect of responsive teaching.

Diversity Issue: Culturally Relevant Teaching

Students' out-of-the-classroom, real-life experiences should be legitimized and valued as well as their abilities to express themselves orally as indicators of their developing literacy skills (Delpit, 1994; Ladson-Billings, 1994). Diller (1999) writes that she extended her connection to her students by becoming a responsive teacher and dialoguing with both students and their parents to discover cultural knowledge that was unfamiliar to her; she invited her students and their families to teach *her*.

 "Parents and students can teach *us.*" What is meant by this statement?

As responsive teachers in cultures that are unfamiliar to us, whether African American, Asian, Hispanic, or European cultures, "we must find help through children's literature, colleagues who know about that culture, and the children and parents themselves" (Diller, 1999, p. 826).

 YOU TRY IT

Develop a Literacy Lesson With Cultural Relevance

Culturally relevant lessons have significance to students because they can relate the lesson's content to their prior knowledge and cultural experiences. Therefore, develop a literacy lesson that addresses the cultural needs of students in your community. Remember to consider diversity in all its aspects including religious, ethnic, and linguistic traditions. Post your lesson on the Companion Website (http://www.prenhall.com/lenski) so that you and your classmates can learn from one another's contributions.

Diversity Issue: Children in Need

Unfortunately, more children in the United States are living in poverty and are suffering at the hands of adults who inadequately care for them. In his book *Uncertain Lives: Children of Promise, Teachers of Hope,* Bullough (2001) wrote case studies of 34 children who attended a school in an urban area. (He notes, however, that poverty rates among children are not limited to urban settings; they are rising in rural and suburban areas as well.) The children studied faced the challenges of "poverty, missing fathers, parental drug use, abuse, injury and death, and family instability" (p. 9).

Bullough (2001) discovered remarkable findings, including the resilience of these children of promise and their willingness to keep on trying. While Bullough's portraits are heartbreaking, he offers suggestions as to how we can be "teachers of hope." He draws on the work of Haberman (1991) to define when good teaching is occurring versus a "pedagogy of poverty" that does not meet students' needs. A pedagogy of poverty is described as telling information, asking factual, low-level questions, assigning worksheets, reviewing worksheets, giving tests, reviewing tests, giving homework, reviewing homework, punishing noncompliant students, and giving grades. In contrast, Haberman believes that good teaching is going on when these things occur:

- Students are involved with issues that they regard as important.
- Students are involved in planning what they will be doing.
- Students are involved with applying fairness or justice to their classroom worlds.

- Students are actively involved in real-life experiences.
- Students are often grouped heterogeneously.
- Students are engaged in redoing and polishing their work.
- Students are encouraged to reflect on their own lives and how they have come to believe what they do.

 How can you be a "teacher of hope" rather than engage in a "pedagogy of poverty?"

You may notice that the preceding list reflects elements of both social constructivism and critical theory that you learned about earlier. Literacy practices grounded in these theories empower students to exert more control over their lives and also motivate students to become engaged in literacy learning. Bullough (2001) calls for more tutoring programs, including those that enlist volunteers, to help prevent "early reading failure, which is crucial to school success and to building legitimate and productive self-esteem" (p. 108).

When we consider children whose lives are in desperate conditions, Cazden (1999) reminds us that we should not create or reinforce stereotypes and lower expectations for students. Further, Delpit (1995) writes, "there is a tendency to assume deficits in students rather than to locate and teach to strengths. To counter this tendency, educators must have knowledge of children's lives outside of school so as to recognize their strengths" (p. 172).

 Many children in our country today live in poverty. How can you modify your teaching to address these children's needs?

Diversity Issue: English Language Learners

Children whose first language is not English will be in your future classrooms. One in five Americans speaks a language other than English at home (Kottler & Kottler, 2002). Further, in some regions of our country, other spoken languages outnumber English. Let's review some general principles that involve facilitating English Language Learners (ELLs).

Learning about English Language Learners' lives. As a responsive teacher, it is up to you to learn as much about a particular culture as possible for you to understand the way to approach your interactions with students from that culture. Kottler and Kottler (2002) offer these social and cultural dimensions that you should be aware of as you get to know the ELL students in your classroom:

Classroom Assessment

- If the child has been in school, is he used to active or passive involvement?
- How is time viewed? Is punctuality valued?
- Does the student's culture encourage/allow meeting adults' eyes?
- Does the student nod when he understands, or just to be polite?
- Do parents regard teachers as experts and, therefore, refrain from contacting teachers if problems occur?
- Does the student avoid asking questions out of fear of bothering the adult?
- Is education or work valued more by the family?
- Is speaking or listening the preferred method of communication?

Each of the answers to these questions has implications for teaching as you've already guessed. As you know, too, because of the variety of cultures that may be represented in your classroom, there are no strict guidelines for you to follow except to find out about the child, his family, and his cultural background. This will guide you in how you teach English.

Valuing the students' first language. While English is the "power code" (Delpit, 1995) in this nation, meaning that speaking English is almost always a prerequisite to achieving financial and social status, the tendency is to give the message to students that English is "better" than their native tongues (Jiménez, 2000). This, of course, diminishes students' self-esteem and social standing in your classroom. You will have to work diligently to keep this from happening. In addition, forming respectful relationships with your ELL students is fundamental. They must be able to trust you and know that risk taking is encouraged as is asking for help.

Teaching strategies for ELLs.   Peregoy and Boyle (1997) offer teaching approaches for facilitating oral language development in a second language. These include using songs/music, drama, tape recording students' re-creations of wordless picture books, choral reading, riddles and jokes, and even taping then dubbing a television show.

When you enter into the literacy arenas of reading and writing, you use approaches that closely imitate those you would use with emergent readers and writers in the early grades such as read-alouds and shared reading, while simultaneously tailoring your topics and interests to the ages of your students. For example, ELLs can be helped to make alphabet books, along with books that contain "noun pictures" of words that would be most useful to them. An example of a noun picture book would be one made up of foods found at the grocery store, with their various labels and packaging, so that students could begin to learn and associate foods with their English names.

Inquiry approaches.   Beach and Myers (2001) suggest an inquiry approach to the teaching of English, especially when you are teaching middle level students. Through inquiry-based instruction, students use their own social worlds as the basis for learning more proficient speaking, reading, and writing of English. This approach is effective for all learners and could be the motivation for ELLs to become engaged in learning a new language.

As a teacher, you should capitalize on what middle level students are interested in: their social worlds. This includes peers, school and sports, family and romance, community and workplace, and virtual worlds (Beach & Myers, 2001). For instance, let's say you are working with eighth-grade boys from Mexico who are learning to speak English and at the same time are extremely interested in sports, especially soccer. An inquiry-based project that could motivate your students might be to help them make a film/video that highlights their favorite team and players. Students could use multiple print media such as newspapers and magazines, as well as television clips, for their project. Their task of putting the film together as well as narrating it would develop their English speaking and reading and also provide authentic purposes for their learning.

Striving to meet the needs of all learners in your future classrooms is an awe-inspiring task and illustrates the challenge and complexity of teaching.

Inquiry approaches involve letting students choose topics of interest to explore. How could inquiry be an effective approach for ELL middle level students?

EMBRACING THE COMPLEXITY OF TEACHING

Throughout this text, you have reflected about yourself and the attributes that responsive teachers possess. Along the way you may have remembered a favorite teacher or teachers who made a difference in your life. Did you notice that those teachers made everything they did look easy? In fact, that is a problem that we teachers face when the public looks at what good teachers do; it looks like anyone could do it (Larabee, 2000). You have taught lessons to your peers and perhaps taught a lesson to a group of children. You know that it isn't as easy as it looks. For example, perhaps you have taught Sunday School, or been a scout leader, or were in charge of children at camp. If so, you have already encountered chances to plan activities; manage children, materials, and time; deal with emergencies; keep a smile on your face; and show up the next day. You know how difficult teaching can be.

Relationships

Many societal factors make teaching a very difficult profession. Larabee (2000) observes that to be an effective teacher, you have to achieve a reciprocal teacher–student relationship. Reciprocity is seen in many forms in a successful classroom. You have to respect your students, and they have to respect you. You must expect much from your students, and they must expect much from you. You must care that your students learn, and your students must care about learning. Dewey (1933) concurs, believing that an exact equation exists between teaching and learning just like the equation between selling and buying. As a teacher you will be responsible for creating the classroom conditions that will motivate students to "buy what you are selling" and draw them into learning (Cambourne, 1995; Turner & Paris, 1995).

You may have had opportunities to create conditions for learning if you have served in leadership positions such as an officer in your sorority, fraternity, or residence hall. Perhaps you were in charge of facilitating an informational meeting where you had to establish a comfortable environment, invite your peers to participate and give their input, and help your fellow members in achieving consensus. You may have discovered that unless, as the leader, you set the conditions for positive interactions, your meeting may not have proceeded as you intended.

Teachers who build emotional relationships with students positively affect learning in the classroom. In what ways did teachers whom you remember as special establish those relationships with you?

Creating optimal learning conditions also necessitates your establishing and maintaining emotional relationships with students. Unlike other professionals such as doctors and lawyers, who strive to maintain emotional *distance,* teachers must build emotional relationships with students in order to understand their unique learning strengths and needs (Fenstermacher, 1990). There are no guide books that tell you how to do this; it is a skill that good teachers develop over time.

Handling Isolation

Another challenge that makes teaching difficult is the isolation in which you conduct your work. While you may be fortunate to cultivate collaborative relationships with your colleagues, in most school settings you will be established in your own classroom where you will be charged with creating a community of learners in your own little world with its own rules and customs. This can be especially problematic for new teachers as classroom management challenges and teaching dilemmas arise, with no one to support them in their problem solving. This tends to reinforce the notion that teaching is often private and lonely (Lortie, 1975).

The IRA's website is *http:// www. reading.org.* Besides joining professional organizations, how else do you plan to reach out to other professionals in the field of literacy to prevent feelings of isolation?

To resist the isolation that can occur, you need to seek out colleagues in your school as mentors and friends. You do not have to face your challenges alone. Consider joining a local chapter of the International Reading Association (IRA) or creating a study group of new teachers who support one another through commiseration as well as through reading professional books together, searching out teaching ideas on the Internet, and attending literacy conferences.

Intensity

A further challenge that we will consider that makes teaching such a difficult profession is the intensity of the work. Palmer (1998) writes, "the students we teach are larger than life and even more complex. To see them clearly and whole, and respond to them wisely in the moment, requires a fusion of Freud and Solomon that few achieve" (p. 2). Ayers (1993) agrees when he says:

> I know that becoming an outstanding teacher is an heroic quest: One must navigate
> turbulent waters, overcome a seemingly endless sea of obstacles, and face danger

and challenge (often alone), on the way to an uncertain reward. Teaching is not for the weak or the faint-hearted; courage and imagination are needed to move from myth to reality. (p. 10)

As you can see, good teaching is extremely difficult. The difficulty of your chosen profession eludes many people who believe that because they have been to school, they can teach. That just isn't true. You may have had an appendectomy, but could you perform a surgical appendectomy on a patient? Expert teaching is just as difficult as expert surgery; it is extremely complex because of myriad variables and unpredictable outcomes. You will experience complexity daily in your teaching career and nowhere more intensely than in your work with developing readers.

Handling Pressure

It's no secret that teachers today face tremendous pressure from many sources including school administrators, parents, media, politicians, and our society at large, especially in the arena of literacy. As a teacher of reading, not only will various stakeholders hold you responsible for teaching children to read, some of the many pressures on you will be to ensure that your students score well on standardized tests and also meet literacy standards set by your state and district.

Standardized tests.   We are sure you are familiar with standardized tests since you were probably a participant in many throughout your educational experiences, including perhaps the ACT or SAT required for entrance to your university. Standardized tests are "tests for which norms on a reference group, ordinarily drawn from many schools, are provided" (Harris & Hodges, 1995, p. 242). Standardized test are often norm referenced by comparing scores with pupils of the same age or grade across the country. Scores are typically represented in *percentile rank,* which indicates the percentage of students who got the same score or lower as the student whose results are being reported/analyzed.

Standardized tests can be useful when a school or district is trying to paint a broad picture by comparing their students to others in the nation. However, extreme caution must be taken when interpreting the scores that individual students make on such tests. First, remember that scores reflect just one measure of competence on a single day in time (and no test is perfectly constructed). Second, there is great danger that such tests have high stakes attached to them. *High-stakes testing* has emerged as a real threat to the true purpose of assessment: to provide information to improve instruction. Instead, in some areas of the country teachers and schools are being punished for the scores their students are making on high-stakes tests. Teachers and schools are being placed on probation with threats of financial consequences if scores don't improve.

The IRA issued a policy statement concerning such tests in 1999. The IRA lists the following concerns and recommendations for various stakeholders:

- Teachers have the responsibility to create rich assessment environments in their classrooms. In addition, teachers should be systematic and rigorous in their assessment of literacy learners and use that knowledge to inform their instruction.
- Researchers should continue to examine better ways to assess students in order to further educational goals. Researchers should also challenge the value of high-stakes testing by offering viable, more effective options.

- Parents must "consider cost, time, alternative methods, and emotional impact on students as a result of these tests" (IRA, 1999, p. 262). Furthermore, parents should lobby for classroom-based assessments that offer more complete pictures of their children's literacy development and that help their children become better readers.

 Standardized exams are often referred to as *high-stakes tests.* What does that mean and how do standardized tests compare to authentic assessment?

Literacy learning standards.   In this textbook we referenced the literacy learning standards created by the IRA and the National Council of Teachers of English (NCTE). Generally, there are two main kinds of standards: content and performance (Noddings, 1997). Content standards are curriculum related and are created to determine the topics/concepts and the order of their presentation in various subjects and grade levels.

Performance standards, on the other hand, specify what students should be able to *do.* Performance standards could become a source of pressure for you if your effectiveness as a teacher is judged solely on your students' ability to meet your state's performance standards. If standards are used as benchmarks to help you set goals, however, and the various stakeholders have a say in their creation and use, then standards can be helpful.

When you teach, you will be responsible for planning instruction based on the literacy learning standards established by the state in which you teach. It will behoove you to research and understand your state's learning standards (both content and performance) as you prepare for your first classroom. Some schools, for example, require that each lesson plan reference the performance standard being addressed.

SEE FOR YOURSELF

State-by-State Standards

Visit the message board for Chapter 15 on our Companion Website at *www.prenhall.com/lenski* to discuss your findings.

On the Companion Website *(http://www.prenhall.com/lenski)* you will find links to standards in literacy education from the 50 states. Connect to the state where you are living to explore the literacy/language arts standards as defined by your state. State-by-state references to content standards as well as national standards are available at this website: *http://www.education-world.com/standards/.*

Accepting Complexity

The discussion here is not to discourage you, but to help you recognize how very skillful and complex the teaching profession is; and to assure you that through self-reflection of the *teacher in you,* you have a propensity for handling this complexity. Many of you have already discovered that you thrive on complexity; you juggle university classes and a job, you play different roles in your daily life such as student, worker, friend, parent, and confidant. Your personal relationships cause you to communicate effectively and appropriately, you enjoy being a leader and making decisions, and you are likely looking forward to the challenge of teaching in your own classroom. Embracing the intricacies and the ambiguity of your chosen profession will be essential for you to be successful. Learning to become a teacher of reading is a career-long process, requiring relentless commitment, hard work, reading to keep up with the field, and further study.

Articulating what you understand about literacy learning and teaching helps you clarify your knowledge. How does expressing your understandings help you become a better teacher?

PUTTING IT ALL TOGETHER

Putting it all together involves taking a telescopic stance again. During the progression of this textbook, you have been articulating your beliefs in an effort to make sense of what you were learning. Now, it will be helpful for you to express in writing what you have learned throughout this experience in order to see the big picture.

Twice you articulated your evolving theory of literacy learning. Each time you kept in mind that your theory of literacy learning will *always be evolving*. Your continuing knowledge acquisition coupled with your experiences in teaching and learning with students will result in changes to your theory. At this point, however, it is important to look back over the course and integrate your new understandings into your evolving philosophy of literacy learning.

A Mock Interview: Questions Concerning Literacy Learning and Teaching

To stimulate your thinking even further, see if you can answer the following questions as part of your evolving philosophy of literacy learning. The questions that we pose here could very well be those asked of you in a job interview setting as you seek your first teaching position.

- What are some of your beliefs about literacy teaching and learning?
- What do you consider to be important components of your literacy block of time in _____ grade? Describe a typical day.
- How will you work with students in whole-group, small-group, and independent settings?
- How can you help young children who are struggling with learning to read? How can you help older students who are struggling?
- Describe the reading process. What are the cueing systems and how do readers use the cueing systems to construct meaning from text?
- Discuss the role of phonics instruction in your classroom.
- What is *phonemic awareness* and what are some teaching strategies you might use to develop phonemic awareness?
- Talk about the role of assessment in your literacy classroom. Describe the kinds of assessment measures you will use.
- You used the term *guided reading*. What does that mean? How does guided reading differ from traditional reading groups?
- What will you do about grouping for instruction?
- When you're working with a small group of children, what will the other children be doing?
- What kinds of materials will you select for the readers in your classroom?
- What are literature circles? Where do literature circles fit in the framework for teaching children to read?
- How will you motivate older children to *choose* to read?
- How do you incorporate reading in content areas?
- What role can literacy play in promoting social justice?

SEE FOR YOURSELF

Questions About Literacy Learning

Visit the message board for Chapter 15 on our Companion Website at *www.prenhall.com/lenski* to discuss your findings.

Perhaps you found our list of questions about literacy learning difficult to answer. On the Companion Website *(http://www.prenhall.com/lenski)* you will find that we posed some of the same questions to teachers whose practices we consider exemplary. Remember, though, these teachers are still learning more about teaching and their philosophies of literacy learning are still evolving. Additionally, their responses will not necessarily match yours; your understandings are uniquely yours.

Creating a Job Search Portfolio

Throughout your experiences in this course, you were given directives about creating a portfolio based on the INTASC principles and the IRA/NCTE standards for the English language arts. Although this is your first professional preparation on your path to becoming a teacher of reading, you now have the basis of a portfolio that can grow and change with you.

One effective way for you to capitalize on all that you've learned from this book is to use the portfolio entries from this text as a foundation. Then you can add other pieces such as selections from the You Try It, See for Yourself, and To Learn More features, as well as other assignments from your instructor to expand your portfolio. You could even include the "mock interview" questions we posed. In this way, you will have created a portfolio that effectively pulls all of the pieces of the text together into a coherent and usable document that can be further developed in other literacy courses. Eventually, this portfolio can be refined into a job search portfolio—one that you will take to job interviews to showcase your abilities as a literacy teacher.

An elementary school principal notes that prospective teachers' portfolios should highlight actual teaching experiences that show what teachers know and can do (McCormick, 2002). This principal comments that "the language arts dominate the elementary program....Therefore, [teacher] candidates should capitalize on artifacts anchored in the language arts...that demonstrate basic competencies such as planning for instruction or diagnosing student needs, while at the same time demonstrating an understanding of the basic precepts of reading and writing instruction" (p. 37).

When you reach the stage in your teacher preparation that you are taking a job search portfolio to interviews, school principals, who often have a key role in the hiring process, have advice for you. Principals who participated in a study concerning their viewpoints about teaching portfolios believed that they should be concise, easy to read, about 15 pages long, spaced well and tabbed, and contain instructions for reading (Pardieck, 2002). Pardieck's model in Figure 15.2 reflects principals' suggested contents for a job search portfolio which could also be housed on a CD-Rom.

IT ALL COMES BACK TO YOU!

Many of you may be finishing up a literacy course with the word *Methods* in the title. *Methods* implies a recipe-like approach to the teaching of reading: If you do this, students will do that. You already know that almost never happens. In fact, in your

Resume	Student Work Samples	Assessment Strategies
Letters of recommendation	Checklist/rubric	Unit overview/rationale
State certification	Reflection	Photographs with captions
Educational philosophy	Transcript	Books/resources/materials
Lesson plan	Technology use	Sample newsletter for parents
Professional development plan	Achievements	Classroom floor plan
Activity web	Placements/school experiences	

From Pardieck, S. C. (2002). Development of job search teaching portfolio. Journal of Reading Education, *27(2), 24–30.*

FIGURE 15.2 Principals' List of Job Search Portfolio Elements

teaching career you will see literacy teaching methods come and go, as those who would reduce literacy teaching to an easy process, with quick fixes for those who find learning to read difficult, introduce "the perfect method" for teaching reading. Although new approaches deserve your attention, always keep in mind that the teaching process always comes back to you.

Duffy and Hoffman (1999) write: "The answer is not in the method; it is in the teacher. It has been repeatedly established that the best instruction results when *combinations* of methods are orchestrated by a teacher who decides what to do in light of children's needs" (p. 11). Further, they have found that the most effective teachers are eclectic and thoughtfully adaptive, what we've defined as being a responsive teacher. In summary, Duffy and Hoffman note that we need to replace the perfect method mentality with "a commitment to developing independent, problem-solving, and spirited teachers who understand that their job is to use many good methods and materials in various ways according to students' needs" (p. 15).

How Will You Teach Reading?

> "I'm so afraid I'll fall back on the way I was taught, not the way I want to teach!"
> —Kara, February 2002

The above statement was made by one of our undergraduate students during a literacy class. She was expressing her apprehension that rather than challenge herself to take her new understandings and build on them in her future classrooms, she would rely on patterns of literacy instruction that were familiar to her and comfortable. Because this student is aware of the "pitfall of comfort," we believe that she will continue to stretch herself to employ research-based, best practices in her literacy teaching, thoughtfully adapting her teaching to her students' needs. We are confident that she will grow into a competent and responsive teacher of reading.

How about you? We are convinced that it is the *teacher* who makes the difference in the classroom, who sets the conditions for learning, who creates a community of learners, who uses assessment to inform instruction, who knows and is responsive to *every* child in the classroom, and who persists in learning better ways to teach and reach students.

We believe that you are now equipped with strategies, approaches, and philosophical stances that help you feel ready to become a teacher of reading. You have developed an evolving philosophy of literacy learning that will continue to evolve as long as you teach; new experiences and new knowledge will continually change your vision of how children learn and how you should teach. All the while, you will always be looking back in the mirror to reflect on yourself as a teacher; it all begins with and comes back to you!

FOR YOUR PORTFOLIO

ENTRY 15.1 *Create Your Own Responsive Teaching Model*

Figure 15.1 illustrates responsive teaching. We then used guided reading as an example of a teaching strategy. For this portfolio entry, select another teaching approach presented in this text and create your own diagram that exemplifies the various components: the teacher's roles, the students' roles, ongoing assessment, modifying teaching, evaluation, and knowledge of students.

ENTRY 15.2 *My Evolving Philosophy of Literacy Learning*

For this portfolio entry we ask that you revisit your evolving philosophy of literacy learning for the last time. You will expand your reflection by answering additional questions stemming from your growing knowledge base. Look back at what you wrote at the beginning of the book and midway through, and determine changes you would make in articulating your philosophy of literacy learning.

- How do children learn to read?
- What should I teach when helping children learn to read?
- How should I teach children to read?

Finish these statements, relating them to literacy learning:

- All children can. . .
- All children need. . .
- Children learn. . .
- Everyone in the classroom. . .
- Learning should be. . .
- Children need opportunities to. . .
- Teachers need to. . .
- Teachers can. . .
- Teachers have a responsibility to. . .

TO LEARN MORE

Helpful Websites

Visit our Companion Website at *http://www.prenhall.com/lenski* to link to the following sites:

Websites with lesson plans and ideas for beginning teachers:

http://www.toread.com
http://www.teachers.net
http://www.4teachers.org/
http://www.atozteacherstuff.com/
http://www.ericsp.org/
http://www.sitesforteachers.com/
http://teams.lacoe.edu/documentation/places/newteachers.html (site for beginning teachers)
http://www.ash.udel.edu/ash/index.html

Appendix A

INTASC Principles

Principle 1: The teacher understands the central concepts, tools of inquiry, and structures of the discipline(s) he or she teaches and can create learning experiences that make these aspects of subject matter meaningful for students.

Principle 2: The teacher understands how children learn and develop, and can provide learning opportunities that support their intellectual, social and personal development.

Principle 3: The teacher understands how students differ in their approaches to learning and creates instructional opportunities that are adapted to diverse learners.

Principle 4: The teacher understands and uses a variety of instructional strategies to encourage students' development of critical thinking, problem solving, and performance skills.

Principle 5: The teacher uses an understanding of individual and group motivation and behavior to create a learning environment that encourages positive social interaction, active engagement in learning, and self-motivation.

Principle 6: The teacher uses knowledge of effective verbal, nonverbal, and media communication techniques to foster active inquiry, collaboration, and supportive interaction in the classroom.

Principle 7: The teacher plans instruction based upon knowledge of subject matter, students, the community, and curriculum goals.

Principle 8: The teacher understands and uses formal and informal assessment strategies to evaluate and ensure the continuous intellectual, social and physical development of the learner.

Principle 9: The teacher is a reflective practitioner who continually evaluates the effects of his/her choices and actions on others (students, parents, and other professionals in the learning community) and who actively seeks out opportunities to grow professionally.

Principle 10: The teacher fosters relationships with school colleagues, parents, and agencies in the larger community to support students' learning and well-being.

Appendix B

International Reading Association and National Council of Teachers of English Standards for the English Language Arts

1. Students read a wide range of print and nonprint texts to build an understanding of texts, of themselves, and of the cultures of the United States and the world; to acquire new information; to respond to the needs and demands of society and the workplace; and for personal fulfillment. Among these texts are fiction and nonfiction, classic and contemporary works.

2. Students read a wide range of literature from many periods in many genres to build an understanding of the main dimensions (e.g., philosophical, ethical, aesthetic) of human experience.

3. Students apply a wide range of strategies to comprehend, interpret, evaluate, and appreciate texts. They draw on their prior experience, their interactions with other readers and writers, their knowledge of word meaning and of other texts, their word identification strategies, and the understanding of textual features (e.g., sound–letter correspondence, sentence structure, context, graphics).

4. Students adjust their use of spoken, written, and visual language (e.g., conventions, style, vocabulary) to communicate effectively with a variety of audiences and for different purposes.

5. Students employ a wide range of strategies as they write and use different writing process elements appropriately to communicate with different audiences for a variety of purposes.

6. Students apply knowledge of language structure, language conventions (e.g., spelling and punctuation), media techniques, figurative language, and genre to create, critique, and discuss print and nonprint texts.

7. Students conduct research on issues and interests by generating ideas and questions, and by posing problems. They gather, evaluate, and synthesize data from a variety of sources (e.g., print and nonprint texts, artifacts, people) to communicate their discoveries in ways that suit their purpose and audience.

8. Students use a variety of technological and informational resources (e.g., libraries, databases, computer networks, video) to gather and synthesize information and to create and communicate knowledge.

9. Students develop an understanding of and respect for diversity in language use, patterns, and dialects across cultures, ethnic groups, geographic regions, and social roles.

10. Students whose first language is not English make use of their first language to develop competency in the English language arts and to develop understanding of content across the curriculum.

11. Students participate as knowledgeable, reflective, creative, and critical members of a variety of literacy communities.

12. Students use spoken, written, and visual language to accomplish their own purposes (e.g., for learning, enjoyment, persuasion, and the exchange of information).

References

Ada, A. F., & Zubizarreta, R. (2001). Parent narratives: The cultural bridge between Latino parents and their children. In M. de la Luz Reyes & J. J. Halcón (Eds.), *The best for our children: Critical perspectives on literacy for Latino students.* (pp. 229–244). New York: Teachers College Press.

Albright, L. K. (2002). Bringing the Ice Maiden to life: Engaging adolescents in learning through picture book read-alouds in content areas. *Journal of Adolescent & Adult Literacy, 45,* 418–428.

Alexander, P. A., & Jetton, T. L. (2000). Learning from text: A multidimensional and developmental perspective. In M. L. Kamil, P. B. Mosenthal, P. D. Pearson, & R. Barr (Eds.), *Handbook of reading research* (Vol. III, pp. 285–310). Mahwah, NJ: Erlbaum.

Allen, C. A. (2001). *The multigenre research paper: Voice, passion, and discovery in grades 4–6.* Portsmouth, NH: Heinemann.

Allington, R. L. (1983a). The reading instruction provided readers of differing abilities. *Elementary School Journal, 83,* 548–559.

Allington, R. L. (1983b). Fluency: The neglected reading goal. *The Reading Teacher, 36,* 556–561.

Allington, R. L. (1998). The schools we have. The schools we need. In C. Weaver (Ed.), *Reconsidering a balanced approach to reading* (pp. 495–519). Urbana: IL: National Council of Teachers of English.

Allington, R. L. (2001a, August 1). Educators become students at Purdue workshop. *The Journal and Courier,* pp. C1–C2.

Allington, R. L. (2001b). *What really matters for struggling readers: Designing research-based programs.* New York: Longman.

Allington, R. L., & McGill-Franzen, A. (1989). Different programs, indifferent instruction. In D. K. Lipsky & A. Gartner (Eds.), *Beyond separate education: Quality education for all* (pp. 75–94). Baltimore, MD: Paul Brookes.

Almasi, J. F. (1996). A new view of discussion. In L. B. Gambrell & J. F. Almasi (Eds.), *Lively discussions! Fostering engaged reading* (pp. 2–24). Newark, DE: International Reading Association.

Alvermann, D. (1991). The discussion web: A graphic aid for learning across the curriculum. *The Reading Teacher, 45,* 92–99.

Alvermann, D. E., Moon, J. S., & Hagood, M. C. (1999). *Popular culture in the classroom: Teaching and researching critical media literacy.* Newark, DE: International Reading Association.

Alvermann, D. E., & Phelps, S. F. (2002). *Content reading and literacy: Succeeding in today's diverse classrooms* (3rd ed.). Boston: Allyn & Bacon.

Ames, C. (1992). Classrooms: Goal, structures, and student motivation. *Journal of Educational Psychology, 84,* 261–271.

Anderman, E. M., & Maehr, M. L. (1994). Motivation and schooling in the middle grades. *Review of Educational Research, 64,* 287–309.

Anderson, R. C., Hiebert, E. H., Scott, J. A., & Wilkinson, I. A. G. (1985). *Becoming a nation of readers: The report of the Commission of Reading.* Washington, DC: National Institute of Education.

Anderson, R. C., & Pearson, P. D. (1984). A schema-theoretic view of basic processes in reading comprehension. In P. D. Pearson, R. Barr, M. L. Kamil, P. Mosenthal (Eds.), *Handbook of reading research* (pp. 255–291). New York: Longman.

Anderson, R. T., & Armbruster, B. B. (1984). Studying. In P. D. Pearson, R. Barr, M. Kamil, & P. Mosenthal (Eds.), *Handbook of reading research* (pp. 657–679). New York: Longman.

Anderson, T. H., & Armbruster, B. B. (1991). The value of taking notes during lectures. In R. F. Flippo & D. C. Caverly (Eds.), *Teaching reading & study strategies at the college level* (pp. 166–194). Newark, DE: International Reading Association.

Armbruster, B. (1984). The problem of inconsiderate text. In G. Duffy, L. Roehler, J. Mason (Eds.), *Comprehension instruction* (pp. 128–143). New York: Longman.

Aronson, E., Stephens, C., Siles, J., Blaney, N., & Snapp, M. (1978). *The jigsaw classroom.* Beverly Hills: Sage.

Askew, B. J., & Fountas, I. C. (1998). Building an early reading process: Active from the start! *The Reading Teacher, 52,* 126–134.

Atwell, N. (1987). *In the middle: Reading, writing, and learning with adolescents.* Portsmouth, NH: Heinemann.

Au, K. H. (1993). *Literacy instruction in multicultural settings.* Fort Worth, TX: Harcourt Brace Jovanovich.

Au, K. H. (2001). What we know about multicultural education and students of diverse backgrounds. In R. F. Flippo (Ed.), *Reading researchers in search of common ground* (pp. 101–117). Newark, DE: International Reading Association.

Ayers, W. (1993). *To teach: The journey of a teacher.* New York: Teachers College Press.

Baker, A. J. (2000). Parent involvement for the middle level years: Recommendations for schools. *Schools in the Middle, 6,* 27–30.

Baker, C. (1993). *Foundations of bilingual education and bilingualism.* Philadelphia: Multilingual Matters.

Banks, J. A., & Banks, C. A. M. (2001). *Multicultural education: Issues and perspectives* (4th ed.). New York: John Wiley & Sons.

Barillas, M. (2000). Literacy at home: Honoring parent voices through writing. *The Reading Teacher, 54,* 302–308.

Barrett, M., & Boggiano, A. K. (1988). Fostering extrinsic orientations: Use of reward strategies to motivate children. *Journal of Social and Clinical Psychology, 6,* 293–309.

Baskin, B. (1998). Call me Ishmael: A look at gifted middle school readers. In K. Beers & B. G. Samuels (Eds.), *Into focus: Understanding and creating middle school readers* (pp. 65–79). Norwood, MA: Christopher-Gordon.

Baumann, J. F. (1991). Teaching comprehension strategies. In B. L. Hayes (Ed.), *Effective strategies for teaching reading* (pp. 61–83). Needham Heights, MA: Allyn & Bacon.

Baumann, J. F., Bradley, B., Edwards, E. C., Font, G., & Hruby, G. G. (2000, December). *Teaching generalizable vocabulary-learning strategies: A critical review of the literature.* Paper presented at the National Reading Conference, Scottsdale, AZ.

Baumann, J. F., & Heubach, K. M. (1996). Do basal readers deskill teachers? A national survey of educators' use and opinions of basals. *The Elementary School Journal, 96,* 511–526.

Baumann, J. F., & Schmitt, M. C. (1986). The what, why, how, and when of comprehension instruction. *The Reading Teacher, 39,* 640–646.

Beach, R., & Myers, J. (2001). *Inquiry-based English instruction: Engaging students in life and literature.* New York: Teachers College Press.

Bean, T. W. (2000). Reading in the content areas: Social constructivist dimensions. In M. L. Kamil, P. B. Mosenthal, P. D. Pearson, & R. Barr (Eds.), *Handbook of reading research* (Vol. III, pp. 629–644). Mahwah, NJ: Erlbaum.

Bear, D. R., Invernizzi, M., Templeton, S., & Johnston, F. (2000). *Words their way: Word study for phonics, vocabulary and spelling instruction.* Upper Saddle River, NJ: Merrill/Prentice Hall.

Beaver, J. (1997). *Analyzing children's writing for signs of growth.* Seminar for Reading Recovery Teacher Leaders at Purdue University, West Lafayette, IN.

Beck, I., & McKeown, M. G. (1981). Developing questions that promote comprehension: The story map. *Language Arts, 58,* 913–918.

Beck, I. L., McKeown, M. G., Hamilton, R. L., & Kucan, L. (1997). *Questioning the author: An approach for enhancing student engagement with text.* Newark, DE: International Reading Association.

Beers, K. (1998). Choosing not to read: Understanding why some middle schoolers just say no. In K. Beers & B. G. Samuels (Eds.), *Into focus: Understanding and creating middle school readers* (pp. 37–63) Norwood, MA: Christopher-Gordon.

Bell-Gredler, M. E. (1986). *Learning and instruction: Theory into practice.* New York: Macmillan.

Berger, K. S., & Thompson, R. A. (1991). *The developing person through childhood and adolescence* (3rd ed.). New York: Worth.

Berger, L. R. (1996). Reader response journals: You make the meaning . . . and how. *Journal of Adolescent & Adult Literacy, 39,* 380–385.

Berk, L. E. (1996). *Infants, children, and adolescents* (2nd ed.). Boston: Allyn & Bacon.

Bernal, E. M. (1974). Gifted Mexican-American children: An ethno-scientific perspective. *California Journal of Educational Research, 25,* 261–273.

Berzins, M. E., & Lopez, A. E. (2001). Planting the seeds for biliteracy. In M. de la Luz Reyes & J. J. Halcon (Eds.), *The best for our children: Critical perspectives on literacy for Latino students* (pp. 81–95). New York: Teachers College Press.

Bintz, W. P. (1993). Resistant readers in secondary education: Some insights and implications. *Journal of Reading, 36,* 604–615.

Blachowicz, C. Z. (1986). Making connections: Alternatives to the vocabulary notebook. *Journal of Reading, 29,* 543–549.

Blachowicz, C. Z., & Fisher, P. (2000). Vocabulary instruction. In M. L. Kamil, P. B. Mosenthal, P. D. Pearson, & R. Barr (Eds.), *Handbook of reading research* (Vol. III, pp. 503–523). Mahwah, NJ: Erlbaum.

Blachowicz, C. Z., & Fisher, P. J. (2002). *Teaching vocabulary in all classrooms.* Upper Saddle River, NJ: Merrill/Prentice Hall.

Blachowicz, C., & Ogle, D. (2001). *Reading comprehension: Strategies for independent learners.* New York: Guilford.

Bloom, B. (1956). *Taxonomy of educational objectives: Handbook I, Cognitive domain.* New York: David McKay.

Blume, J. (1997). Censorship: A personal view. In J. Blume (Ed.), *Places I never meant to be* (pp. 1–13). New York: Simon & Schuster.

Bodrova, E., & Leong, D. J. (1996). *Tools of the mind: The Vygotskian approach to early childhood education.* Columbus, OH: Merrill/Prentice Hall.

Bolter, J. D. (1998). Hypertext and the question of visual literacy. In D. Reinking, M. C. McKenna, L. D. Labbo, & R. D. Keiffer (Eds.), *Handbook of literacy and technology: Transformations in a post-typographic world* (pp. 3–13). Mahwah, NJ: Erlbaum.

Booth, D. (2001). *Reading & writing in the middle years.* York, ME: Stenhouse.

Bormuth, J. R. (1975). Literacy in the classroom. In W. D. Page (Ed.), *Help for the reading teacher: New directions in research* (pp. 60–90). Urbana, IL: ERIC Clearinghouse on Reading and Communication Skills.

Bourdieu, P., & Passeron, J. C. (1977). *Reproduction in education, society and culture.* Los Angeles: Sage.

Brenner, D., & Pearson, P. D. (1998). Authentic reading assessment in the middle school. In K. Beers & B. G. Samuels (Eds.), *Into focus: Understanding and creating middle school readers* (pp. 281–310). Norwood, MA: Christopher-Gordon.

Brisk, M. E., & Harrington, M. M. (2000). *Literacy and bilingualism: A handbook for ALL teachers.* Mahwah, NJ: Erlbaum.

Bromley, K., & Modlo, M. (1997). Using cooperative learning to improve reading and writing in language arts. *Reading and Writing Quarterly, 13*(1), 21–35.

Bromley, K. D. (1996). *Webbing with literature: Creating story maps with children's books.* Boston: Allyn & Bacon.

Brown, B. B., & Theobald, W. (1998). Learning contexts beyond the classroom: Extracurricular activities, community organizations, and peer groups. In K. Borman & B. Schnieder (Eds.), *The adolescent years: Social influences & educational challenges* (pp. 109–141). Chicago: University of Chicago Press.

Brown, K. J. (2000). What kind of text—For whom and when? Textual scaffolding for beginning readers. *The Reading Teacher, 53,* 292–307.

Brozo, W. G. (2002). *To be a boy, to be a reader: Engaging teen and preteen boys in active literacy.* Newark, DE: International Reading Association.

Brozo, W. G., & Simpson, M. L. (1995). *Readers, teachers, learners: Expanding literacy in secondary schools* (2nd ed.). Columbus, OH: Merrill/Prentice Hall.

Bruner, J. (1989). Vygotsky: A historical and conceptual perspective. In J. V. Wertsch (Ed.), *Culture, communication, and cognition* (pp. 21–34). New York: Teachers College Press.

Buehl, D. (2001). *Classroom strategies for interactive learning* (2nd ed.). Newark, DE: International Reading Association.

Bullough, R. V. (2001). *Uncertain lives: Children of promise, teachers of hope.* New York: Teachers College Press.

Burke, C. (1980). The reading interview. In B. P. Farr & D. J. Strickler (Eds.), *Reading comprehension: Resource guide.* Bloomington, IN: Language Education, Indiana University.

Buss, K., & Karnowski, L. (2000). *Reading and writing literary genre.* Newark, DE: International Reading Association.

Butler-Por, N. (1987). *Underachievers in school: Issues and intervention.* Chichester, England: Wiley.

Cadiero-Kaplan, K. (2002). Literacy ideologies: Critically engaging the language arts curriculum. *Language Arts, 79,* 372–381.

Calkins, L. M. (1986). *The art of teaching writing.* Portsmouth, NH: Heinemann.

Calkins, L. M. (1994). *The art of teaching writing* (2nd ed.). Portsmouth, NH: Heinemann.

Cambourne, B. (1995). Toward an educationally relevant theory of literacy learning: Twenty years of inquiry. *The Reading Teacher, 49,* 182–192.

Cambourne, B. (1999). Explicit and systematic teaching of reading—A new slogan? *The Reading Teacher, 53,* 126–127.

Cambourne, B. (2000). Observing literacy learning in elementary classrooms: Nine years of classroom anthropology. *The Reading Teacher, 53,* 512–515.

Cambourne, B. (2001). Why do some students fail to learn to read? Ockham's razor and the conditions of learning. *The Reading Teacher, 54,* 784–786.

Carr, K. S., Buchanan, D. L., Wentz, J. B., Weiss, M. L., & Brant, K. J. (2001). Not just for the primary grades: A bibliography of picture books for secondary content teachers. *Journal of Adolescent & Adult Literacy, 45,* 146–153.

Carroll, P. S. (1998). A w(hole) in the middle: Language study for transformed middle schools. In J. S. Simmons & L. Baines (Eds.), *Language study in middle school, high school, and beyond* (pp. 20–40). Newark, DE: International Reading Association.

Cazden, C. (2001). *Classroom discourse: The language of teaching and learning* (2nd ed.). Portsmouth, NH: Heinemann.

Cazden, C. B. (1999). Foreword. In C. Ballenger, *Teaching other people's children: Literacy and learning in a bilingual classroom* (pp. vii–viii). New York: Teachers College Press.

Chapman, A. (1993). *Making sense: Teaching critical reading across the curriculum*. New York: College Board.

Chomsky, C. (1971, March). Write first, read later. *Childhood Education*, pp. 296–299.

Chomsky, N. (1994). *Language and thought*. Wakefield, RI: Moyer Bell Publishers.

Clay, M. M. (1966). *Emergent reading behavior*. Unpublished doctoral dissertation, University of Auckland, New Zealand.

Clay, M. M. (1979). *The early detection of reading difficulties: A diagnostic survey with reading procedures*. Aukland, NZ: Heinemann.

Clay, M. M. (1985). *The early detection of reading difficulties* (3rd ed.). Auckland, NZ: Heinemann.

Clay, M. M. (1991). *Becoming literate: The construction of inner control*. Portsmouth, NH: Heinemann.

Clay, M. M. (1993). *An observation survey of early literacy achievement*. Portsmouth, NH: Heinemann.

Clay, M. M. (1998). *By different paths to common outcomes*. York, ME: Stenhouse.

Clay, M. M. (2000). *Running records for classroom teachers*. Portsmouth, NH: Heinemann.

Cline, Z. (1998). Buscando su voz en dos culturas—Finding your voice in two cultures. *Phi Delta Kappan, 79*, 699–702.

Comber, B. (2001). Classroom explorations in critical literacy. In H. Fehring & P. Green (Eds.), *Critical literacy* (pp. 90–102). Newark, DE, and Norwood, South Australia: International Reading Association and Australian Literacy Educators' Association.

Consortium on Reading Excellence (1999). *Assessing reading: Multiple measures for kindergarten through eighth grade*. Novato, CA: Arena.

Cordova, D. I., & Lepper, M. R. (1996). Intrinsic motivation and the process of learning: Beneficial effects of contextualization, personalization, and choice. *Journal of Educational Psychology, 88*, 715–730.

Council of Chief State School Officers. (1992). *Interstate New Teacher Assessment and Support Consortium*. Retrieved August 15, 2002, from *http://www.ccsso.org/intascst.html*

Csikszentmihalyi, M. (1991). Literacy and intrinsic motivation. In S. R. Graubard (Ed.), *Literacy* (pp. 115–140). New York: Noonday.

Csikszentmihalyi, M., & Schmidt, J. (1998). Stress and resilience in adolescence: An evolutionary perspective. In K. Borman & B. Schnieder (Eds.), *The adolescent years: Social influences and educational challenges* (pp. 1–17). Chicago: University of Chicago Press.

Cunningham, P. M. (1995). *Phonics they use: Words for reading and writing* (2nd ed.). New York: HarperCollins.

Cunningham, P. M. (1990). The Names Test: A quick assessment of decoding ability. *The Reading Teacher, 44*, 124–129.

Cunningham, P. M. (2000). *Phonics they use: Words for reading and writing* (3rd ed.). New York: Longman.

Cunningham, P. M., & Allington, R. L. (1994). *Classrooms that work: They can all read and write*. New York: HarperCollins.

Cunningham, P. M., & Hall, D. P. (1994a). *Making big words: Multilevel, hands-on spelling and phonics activities*. Torrance, CA: Good Apple.

Cunningham, P. M., & Hall, D. P. (1994b). *Making words: Multilevel, hands-on, developmentally appropriate spelling and phonics activities*. Torrance, CA: Good Apple.

Cunningham, R., & Shabloak, S. (1975). Selective reading guide-o-rama: The content teacher's best friend. *Journal of Reading, 18*, 380–382.

Cushnew, K., McClelland, A., & Safford, P. (1992). *Human diversity in education: An integrative approach* (3rd ed.). New York: McGraw-Hill.

Dahl, K. L., & Scharer, P. L. (2000). Phonics teaching in whole language classrooms: New evidence from research. *The Reading Teacher, 53*, 584–594.

Daniels, H. (2002). *Literature circles: Voice and choice in books clubs & reading groups* (2nd ed.). Portland, ME: Stenhouse.

Daniels, H., & Bizar, M. (1998). *Methods that matter: Six structures for best practice classrooms*. Portland, ME: Stenhouse.

Darling-Hammond, L. (2000). How teacher education matters. *Journal of Teacher Education, 51*, 166–173.

Davey, B. (1983). Think-aloud: Modeling the cognitive processes of reading comprehension. *Journal of Reading, 27*, 44–47.

Davis, S. J. (1990). Applying content study skills in co-listed reading classrooms. *Journal of Reading, 33*, 277–281.

Davis, S. J. (1994). Teaching practices that encourage or eliminate plagiarism. *Middle School Journal, 25*, 55–58.

Davis, S. J., & Jepson, D. C. (1991). Beyond response to literature: Literary criticism in the middle school. *Illinois Reading Council Journal, 19*, 25–32.

Deci, E. L., Koestner, R., & Ryan, R. M. (1999). A meta-analysis review of experiments examining the effects of extrinsic rewards on intrinsic motivation. *Psychological Bulletin, 125*, 627–668.

Delisle, R. (1997). *How to use problem-based learning in the classroom*. Alexandria, VA: Association for Supervision and Curriculum Development.

Delpit, L. (1992). Education in a multicultural society: Our future's greatest challenge. *Journal of Negro Education, 61*, 237–249.

Delpit, L. (1995). *Other people's children: Cultural conflict in the classroom*. New York: New Press.

Denton, P., & Kriete, R. (2000). *The first six weeks of school*. Greenfield, MA: Northeast Foundation for Children.

Dewey, J. (1913). *Interest and effort*. Cambridge, MA: Riverside.

Dewey, J. (1933). *How we think*. Lexington, MA: D.C. Heath.

Dewey, J. (1938). *Experience and education*. New York: Macmillan.

Díaz, E., & Flores, B. (2001). Teacher as sociocultural, sociohistorical mediator. In M. de la Luz Reyes & J. J. Halcon (Eds.), *The best for our children: Critical perspectives on literacy for Latino students* (pp. 29–47). New York: Teachers College Press.

Diller, D. (1999). Opening the dialogue: Using culture as a tool in teaching young African-American children. *The Reading Teacher, 52,* 820–828.

Dole, J. A. (2000). Explicit and implicit instruction in comprehension. In B. M. Taylor, M. R. Graves, & P. van den Broek (Eds.), *Reading for meaning: Fostering comprehension in the middle grades* (pp. 52–69). Newark, DE, and New York: International Reading Association and Teachers College Press.

Donahue, P. L., Voelkl, K. E., Campbell, J. R., & Mazzeo, J. (1999). *NAEP 1998 reading report card for the nation and states*. Washington DC: National Center for Educational Statistics, U.S. Department of Education.

Duffelmeyer, F. A. (2002). Alphabet activities on the Internet. *The Reading Teacher, 55,* 631–635.

Duffy, G. G., & Hoffman, J. V. (1999). In pursuit of an illusion: The flawed search for a perfect method. *The Reading Teacher, 53,* 10–16.

Dugger, C. W. (1998, March 21). Among young of immigrants, outlook rises. *New York Times,* pp. A1, A11.

Eccles, J. S., & Midgley, C. (1989). Stage-environment fit: Developmentally appropriate classrooms for young adolescents. In C. Ames & R. Ames (Eds.), *Research on motivation in education* (pp. 139–186). New York: Academic Press.

Edwards, P. A., & Danridge, J. C. (2001). Developing collaboration with culturally diverse parents. In V. J. Risko & K. Bromley (Eds.), *Collaboration for diverse learners: Viewpoints and practices* (pp. 251–272). Newark, DE: International Reading Association.

Ehlinger, J., & Pritchard, R. (1994). Using Think Alongs in secondary content areas. *Reading Research & Instruction, 33,* 187–206.

Elkonin, D. B. (1973). U.S.S.R. In J. Downing (Ed.), *Comparative reading*. New York: Macmillan.

Epstein, J. L. (1996). Perspectives and previews on research and policy for school, family and community partnerships. In A. Booth & J. F. Dunn (Eds.), *Family–school links: How do they affect educational outcomes?* (pp. 209–246). Mahwah, NJ: Erlbaum.

Epstein, J. L. (1997). A comprehensive framework for school, family, and community partnerships. In J. L. Epstein, L. Coates, K. C. Salinas, M. G. Sanders, & B. S. Simon (Eds.), *School, family, and community partnerships: Your handbook for action* (pp. 1–25). Thousand Oaks, CA: Corwin.

Ernst-Slavit, G., Han, J. W., & Wenger, K. J. (2001). Reading at home, reading at school: Conflict, communication, and collaboration when school and home cultures are different. In V. J. Risko & K. Bromley (Eds.), *Collaboration for diverse learners: Viewpoints and practices* (pp. 289–309). Newark, DE: International Reading Association.

Evans, K. S. (2001). *Literature discussion groups in the intermediate grades: Dilemma and possibilities*. Newark, DE: International Reading Association.

Fader, D. N. (1976). *The new hooked on books*. New York: Berkely Publishing Company.

Faltis, C. J. (2001). *Joinfostering: Teaching and learning in multilingual classrooms* (3rd. ed.). Upper Saddle River, NJ: Prentice Hall.

Farr, R., & Tone, B. (1994). *Portfolio and performance assessment: Helping students evaluate their progress as readers and writers*. Orlando: Harcourt Brace.

Faust, M. A., & Glenzer, N. (2000). "I could read those parts over and over": Eighth graders rereading to enhance enjoyment and learning with literature. *Journal of Adolescent & Adult Literacy, 44,* 234–239.

Fawson, P. C., & Reutzel, D. R. (2000). But I only have a basal: Implementing guided reading in the early grades. *The Reading Teacher, 54,* 84–97.

Feathers, K. M. (1998). Fostering independent, critical content reading in the middle grades. In K. Beers & B. G. Samuels (Eds.), *Into focus: Understanding and creating middle school readers* (pp. 261–280). Norwood, MA: Christopher-Gordon.

Fehring, H., & Green, P. (Eds.). (2001). *Critical literacy*. Newark, DE, and Norwood, South Australia: International Reading Association and Australian Literacy Educators' Association.

Fennimore, B. S. (2000). *Talk matters: Refocusing the language of public schooling*. New York: Teachers College Press.

Fenstermacher, G. D. (1990). Some moral considerations on teaching as a profession. In J. I. Goodlad, R. Soder, & K. A. Sirotnik (Eds.), *The moral dimensions of teaching* (pp. 130–151). San Francisco: Jossey-Bass.

Fields, M. V., & Spangler, K. L. (2000). *Let's begin reading right: A developmental approach to emergent literacy* (4th ed.). Upper Saddle River, NJ: Prentice Hall.

Fletcher, R., & Portalupi, J. (1998). *Craft lessons: Teaching writing K–8*. York, ME: Stenhouse.

Fletcher, R., & Portalupi, J. (2001). *Writing workshop: the essential guide*. Portsmouth, NH: Heinemann.

Flippo, R. F., & Caverly, D. C. (Eds.). (1991). *Teaching reading & study strategies at the college level.* Newark, DE: International Reading Association.

Ford, D. Y., & Harris III, J. J. (1999). *Multicultural gifted education*. New York: Teachers College Press.

Ford, M. P., & Opitz, M. F. (2002). Using centers to engage children during guided reading time: Intensifying learning experiences away from the teacher. *The Reading Teacher, 55,* 710–717.

Fosnot, C. T. (1996). Constructivism: A psychological theory of learning. In C. T. Fosnot (Ed.), *Constructivism: Theory, perspectives, and practice* (pp. 8–33). New York: Teachers College Press.

Fountas, I. C., & Pinnell, G. S. (1996). *Guided reading: Good first teaching for all children.* Portsmouth, NH: Heinemann.

Fountas, I. C., & Pinnell, G. S. (1999). *Matching books to readers: Using leveled texts in guided reading, K–3.* Portsmouth, NH: Heinemann.

Frank, C. R., Dixon, C. N., & Brandts, L. R. (2001). Bears, trolls, and pagemasters: Learning about learners in book clubs. *The Reading Teacher, 54,* 448–462.

Freebody, P., & Luke, A. (1990). "Literacies" programs: Debates and demands in cultural context. *Prospect, 5,* 7–16.

Freire, P. (1985). *The politics of education.* South Hadley, MA: Bergin & Garvey.

Fresch, M. J. (1999). Alice in computerland: Using the Internet as a resource for teaching reading. *The Reading Teacher, 52,* 652–653.

Friend, R. (2000/2001). Teaching summarization as a content area reading strategy. *Journal of Adolescent & Adult Literacy, 44,* 320–329.

Fry, E. (1978). *Skimming and scanning.* Providence, RI: Jamestown.

Fry, E., Fountoukidis, D. L., & Polk, J. K. (1985). *The new reading teacher's book of lists.* Englewood Cliffs, NJ: Prentice Hall.

Galda, L., & Guice, S. (1997). Response-based reading instruction in the elementary grades. In S. A. Stahl & D. A. Hayes (Eds.), *Instructional models in reading* (pp. 311–330). Mahwah, NJ: Erlbaum.

Galda, L., & West, J. (1995). Exploring literature through drama. In N. L. Roser & M. G. Martinez (Eds.), *Book talk and beyond: Children and teachers respond to literature* (pp. 183–190). Newark, DE: International Reading Association.

Gambrell, L. B. (1996). Creating classroom cultures that foster reading motivation. *The Reading Teacher, 50,* 14–25.

Gambrell, L. B., Palmer, B. M., Codling, R. M., & Mazzoni, S. A. (1996). Assessing motivation to read. *The Reading Teacher, 49,* 518–533.

García, G. E. (2000). Bilingual children's reading. In M. L. Kamil, P. B. Mosenthal, P. D. Pearson, & R. Barr (Eds.), *Handbook of reading research* (Vol. III, pp. 813–834). Mahwah, NJ: Erlbaum.

García, G. E., & Pearson, P. D. (1991). Modifying reading instruction to maximize its effectiveness for *all* students. In M. S. Knapp & P. M. Shields (Eds.), *Better schooling for the children of poverty: Alternatives to conventional wisdom* (pp. 31–60). Berkeley, CA: McCutchan.

Garner, H. (1985). *The mind's new science: A history of the cognitive revolution.* New York: Basic Books.

Gates, A. I., & Bond, G. L. (1936). Reading readiness. A study of factors determining success and failure in beginning reading. *Teachers College Board, 37*(5), 679–685.

Gay, G. (2000). *Culturally responsive teaching: Theory, research & practice.* New York: Teachers College Press.

George, P., & Lawrence, G. (1982). *Handbook for middle school teaching.* Glenview, IL: Scott, Foresman and Company.

Gersten, R., & Jiménez, R. (1994). A delicate balance: Enhancing literature instruction for students of English as a second language. *The Reading Teacher, 47,* 438–449.

Gilbert, P. (2001). (Sub)versions: Using sexist language practices to explore critical literacy. In H. Fehring & P. Green (Eds.), *Critical literacy* (pp. 75–83). Newark, DE, and Norwood, South Australia: International Reading Association and Australian Literacy Educators' Association.

Gill, S. G. (2000). Reading with Amy: Teaching and learning through reading conferences. *The Reading Teacher, 53,* 500–509.

Gillespie, C. (1993). Reading graphic displays: What teachers should know. *Journal of Reading, 36,* 350–354.

Giorgis, C., Johnson, N. J., Colbert, C., Conner, A., Franklin, A., & King, J. (2000). What makes a good book? *The Reading Teacher, 53,* 344–352.

Goldman, S., & Rakestraw, J. (2000). Structural aspects of constructing meaning from text. In M. Kamil, P. Mosenthal, P. D. Pearson, & R. Barr (Eds.), *Handbook of reading research* (Vol. III, pp. 311–335). Mahwah, NJ: Erlbaum.

Gonzalez, N., Rueda, R., & Moll, L. C. (in press). *Theorizing practices: Funds of knowledge in households and classrooms.* Cresskill, NJ: Hampton.

Goodman, K. S. (1965). A linguistic study of cues and miscues in reading. *Elementary English, 42,* 639–643.

Goodman, K. S. (1967). Reading: A psycholinguistic guessing game. *Journal of the Reading Specialist, 6,* 126–135.

Goodman, K. S., & Buck, C. (1997). Dialect barriers to reading comprehension revisited. *The Reading Teacher, 50,* 454–468.

Goodman, Y. (1978). Kidwatching: An alternative to testing. *National Elementary Principals Journal, 57,* 41–45.

Goodman, Y. M. (1985). Observing children in the classroom. In A. Jaggar & M. T. Smith-Burke (Eds.), *Observing the language learner* (pp. 9–18). Newark, DE, and Urbana, IL: International Reading Association and the National Council of Teachers of English.

Goodman, Y. M., Watson, D. J., & Burke, C. L. (1996). *Reading strategies: Focus on comprehension.* Katonah, NY: Richard C. Owen.

Goswami, U., & Bryant, P. (1990). *Phonological skills and learning to read.* Hillsdale, NJ: Lawrence Erlbaum.

Graves, D. (1983). *Writing: Teachers and children at work.* Portsmouth, NH: Heinemann.

Graves, D. (1994). *A fresh look at writing.* Portsmouth, NH: Heinemann.

Graves, M. (2000). A vocabulary program to complement and bolster a middle-grade comprehension program. In B. M. Taylor, M. R. Graves, & P. Van Den Broek (Eds.), *Reading for meaning: Fostering comprehension in the middle grades* (pp. 116–135). Newark, DE, and New York: International Reading Association and Teachers College Press.

Gray, W. S., & Rogers, B. (1956). *Maturity in reading: Its nature and appraisal.* Chicago: University of Chicago Press.

Gredler, M. E. (1999). *Classroom assessment and learning.* New York: Longman.

Green, P. (2001). Critical literacy revisited. In H. Fehring & P. Green (Eds.), *Critical literacy: A collection of articles from the Australian Literacy Educators' Association.* Newark, DE, and Norwood, South Australia: International Reading Association and Australian Literacy Educators' Association.

Greenlee, A. A., Monson, D. L., & Taylor, B. M. (1996). The lure of series books: Does it affect appreciation for recommended literature? *The Reading Teacher, 50,* 216–225.

Guice, S. (1991). *Sixth graders as a community of readers: An interpretive case study from the emic perspective.* Unpublished doctoral dissertation, The University of Georgia.

Gunderson, S. (2002). *The reading/writing connection.* Unpublished manuscript, Purdue University, West Lafayette, IN.

Gunning, T. G. (2000). *Phonological awareness and primary phonics.* Boston, MA: Allyn & Bacon.

Gupta, A. (2000). Ditto reading strategy. *The Reading Teacher, 53,* 370–371.

Guthrie, J. T., & Wigfield, A. (1997). *Reading engagement: Motivating readers through integrated instruction.* Newark, DE: International Reading Association.

Guthrie, J. T., & Wigfield, A. (2000). Engagement and motivation in reading. In M. L. Kamil, P. B. Mosenthal, P. D. Pearson, & R. Barr (Eds.), *Handbook of reading research* (Vol. III, pp. 403–422). Mahwah, NJ: Erlbaum.

Guthrie, J. T., Wigfield, A., Metsala, J. L., & Cox, K. E. (1999). Motivational and cognitive predictors of text comprehension and reading amount. *Scientific Studies of Reading, 3,* 231–256.

Haberman, M. (1991). The pedagogy of poverty versus good teaching. *Phi Delta Kappan, 12,* 290–294.

Haggard, M. E. (1986). The vocabulary self-collection strategy: Using student interest and word knowledge to enhance vocabulary growth. *Journal of Reading, 29,* 634–642.

Hall, M. (1981). *Teaching reading as a language experience.* Columbus, OH: Merrill/Prentice Hall.

Hansen, J. (1998). *When learners evaluate.* Portsmouth, NH: Heinemann.

Hansen, J. (2001). *When writers read* (2nd ed.). Portsmouth, NH: Heinemann.

Harris, T. L., & Hodges, R. E. (Eds.). (1995). *The literacy dictionary: The vocabulary of reading and writing.* Newark, DE: International Reading Association.

Harste, J. C., Woodward, V. A., & Burke, C. L. (1984). *Language stories & literacy lessons.* Portsmouth, NH: Heinemann.

Havighurst, R. (1952). *Developmental tasks and education.* New York: Longmans, Green.

Hefflin, B. R., & Barksdale-Ladd, M. A. (2001). African American children's literature that helps students find themselves: Selection guidelines for grades K–3. *The Reading Teacher, 54,* 810–819.

Heilman, A. W. (2002). *Phonics in perspective* (9th ed.). Upper Saddle River, NJ: Merrill/Prentice Hall.

Hennings, D. G. (2000). Contextually relevant word study: Adolescent vocabulary development across the curriculum. *Journal of Adolescent & Adult Literacy, 44,* 268–279.

Herber, H. L. (1978). *Teaching reading in content areas* (2nd ed.). Englewood Cliffs, NJ: Prentice Hall.

Hiebert, A. H., & Raphael, T. E. (1998). *Early literacy instruction.* San Diego: Harcourt Brace.

Hill, B. C., Noe, K. L. S., & Johnson, N. J. (2002). *Literature circle resource guide.* Norwood, MA: Christopher-Gordon.

Hill, B. C., Ruptic, C., & Norwick, L. (1998). *Classroom based assessment.* Norwood, MA: Christopher-Gordon.

Hinchman, K. A., & Young, J. P. (2001). Speaking but not being heard: Two adolescents negotiate classroom talk about text. *Journal of Literacy Research, 33,* 243–268.

Hodgkinson, H. (2000/2001). Education demographics: What teachers should know. *Educational Leadership, 57,* 6–11.

Hoffman, J., Cunningham, P. M., Cunningham, J. W., & Yopp, H. (1998). *Phonemic awareness and the teaching of reading.* Newark, DE: International Reading Association.

Hoffman, J. V., McCarthey, S. J., Abbot, J., Christian, C., Corman, L., Curry, C., et al. (1994). So what's new in the new basals? A focus on first grade basal reading program. *Journal of Reading Behavior, 26,* 47–73.

Hoffman, J. V., McCarthy, S. J., Elliot, B., Bayles, D. L., Price, D. P., Feree, A., et al. (1998). The literature-based basals in first-grade classrooms: Savior, Satan, or same-old, same-old? *Reading Research Quarterly, 33,* 168–197.

Holdaway, D. (1979). *The foundations of literacy.* Sydney, Australia: Aston Scholastic.

Hootstein, E. W. (1996). Motivating at-risk students to learn. *The Clearing House, 70,* 97–100.

Hornberger, N. H. (1990). Creative successful learning contexts for bilingual literacy. *Teachers College Record, 92,* 212–229.

Hornberger, T. R., & Whitford, E. V. (1983). Students' suggestions: Teach us study skills! *Journal of Reading, 27,* 71.

Humphrey, J. W. (2002). There is no simple way to build a middle school reading program. *Phi Delta Kappan, 83,* 754–757.

Hurley, S. R., & Tinajero, J. V. (Eds.). (2001). *Literacy assessment of second language learners.* Boston: Allyn & Bacon.

Igoa, C. (1995). *The inner world of the immigrant child.* New York: St. Martin's Press.

International Reading Association. (1997, January). *The role of phonics in reading instruction: A position statement of the IRA.* Newark, DE: Author.

International Reading Association. (1999). High-stakes assessments in reading. *The Reading Teacher, 53,* 257–263.

International Reading Association. (2000). *Making a difference means making it different: Honoring children's rights to excellent reading instruction.* Newark, DE: Author.

International Reading Association and National Association for the Education of Young Children. (1998, May). Learning to read and write: Developmentally appropriate practices for young children, Part 4: Continuum of children's development in early reading and writing, a joint position of IRA and NAEYC). Newark, DE: Authors.

International Reading Association and National Council of Teachers of English. (1996). *Standards for the English language arts.* Newark, DE, and Urbana, IL: Authors.

Invernizzi, M., Abouzeid, M., & Gill, J. T. (1994). Using students' invented spellings as a guide for spelling instruction that emphasizes word study. *Elementary School Journal, 95,* 155–167.

Irvin, J. L. (1991). *Teaching reading comprehension processes* (2nd ed.). Boston: Allyn & Bacon.

Irvin, J. L. (1998). *Reading and the middle school student: Strategies to enhance literacy* (2nd ed.). Boston: Allyn & Bacon.

Ivey, G., & Broaddus, K. (2000). Tailoring the fit: Reading instruction and middle school readers. *The Reading Teacher, 54,* 68–78.

Ivey, G., & Broaddus, K. (2001). "Just plain reading": A survey of what makes students want to read in middle school classrooms. *Reading Research Quarterly, 36,* 350–377.

Jackson, A. W., & Davis, G. A. (2000). *Turning points 2000: Educating adolescents in the 21st century.* New York: Teachers College Press.

Jacobson, J., Thorpe, L., Fisher, D., Lapp, D. Frey, N., & Flood, J. (2001). Cross-age tutoring: A literacy improvement approach for struggling adolescent readers. *Journal of Adolescent & Adult Literacy, 44,* 528–536.

Janes, H., & Kermani, H. (2001). Caregivers' story reading to young children in family literacy programs: Pleasure or punishment? *The Reading Teacher, 44,* 458–466.

Jiménez, R. T. (2000). Literacy and the identity development of Latina/o students. *American Educational Research Journal, 37,* 971–1000.

Jiménez, R. T. (2001). "It's a difference that changes us": An alternative view of the language and literacy needs of Latina/o students. *The Reading Teacher, 54,* 736–742.

Johns, J. L., & Bergland, R. L. (2002). *Fluency: Questions, answers, evidence-based strategies.* Dubuque, IA: Kendall/Hunt.

Johns, J. L., & Lenski, S. D. (2001). *Improving reading: Strategies and resources* (3rd ed.). Dubuque, IA: Kendall/Hunt.

Johnson, D., & Pearson, P. D. (1975). Skills management systems: A critique. *The Reading Teacher, 28,* 757–764.

Johnson, D. W., & Johnson, R. T. (1990). Cooperative learning and achievement. In Shlomo Sharan (Ed.), *Cooperative learning: Theory and research* (pp. 22–37). New York: Praeger.

Johnson, P. (2000). *Making books: Over 30 practical book-making projects for children.* Portland, ME: Stenhouse.

Johnston, F. R. (1999). The timing and teaching of word families. *The Reading Teacher, 53,* 64–75.

Johnston, P. H., & Winograd, P. N. (1985). Passive failure in reading. *Journal of Reading Behavior, 27,* 279–301.

Jongsma, K. (2001a). Literacy links between home and school. *The Reading Teacher, 55,* 58–61.

Jongsma, K. (2001b). Using CD-ROMs to support the development of literacy processes. *The Reading Teacher, 54,* 592–595.

Jordan, G. E., Snow, C. E., & Porche, M. V. (2000). Project EASE: The effect of a family literacy project on kindergarten students' early literacy skills. *Reading Research Quarterly, 35,* 524–536.

Juel, C. (1988). *Learning to read and write: A longitudinal study of fifty-four children from first through fourth grade.* Paper presented at the annual meting of the American Educational Research Association, New Orleans, LA.

Kagan, J., & Moss, H. A. (1962). *Birth to maturity: A study in psychological development.* New York: Wiley.

Kearns, D. T. (1993). Toward a new generation of American schools. *Phi Delta Kappan, 74,* 773–776.

Kempe, A. (2001). No single meaning: Empowering students to construct socially critical readings of the text. In H. Fehring & P. Green (Eds.), *Critical literacy* (pp. 40–57). Newark, DE, and Norwood, South Australia: International Reading Association and Australian Literacy Educators' Association.

Klare, G. R. (1984). Readability. In P. D. Pearson (Ed.), *Handbook of reading research* (pp. 681–744). White Plains, NY: Longman.

Koskinen, P. A., & Blum, I. H. (1984). Paired repeated reading: A classroom strategy for developing fluent reading. *The Reading Teacher, 40,* 70–75.

Kottler, E., & Kottler, J. A. (2002). *Children with limited English* (2nd ed.). Thousand Oaks, CA: Corwin Press.

Krashen, S. (2001, April/May). Do teenagers like to read? Yes! *Reading Today,* p. 16.

Labbo, L. D., & Teale, W. H. (1997). Emergent literacy as a model of reading instruction. In S. A. Stahl & D. A. Hayes (Eds.), *Instructional models in reading* (pp. 249–281). Mahwah, NJ: Erlbaum.

LaBerge, D., & Samuels, S. J. (1974). Toward a theory of automatic information processing in reading. *Cognitive Psychology, 6,* 293–323.

Ladson-Billings, G. (1994). *The dreamkeepers: Successful teachers of African American children.* San Francisco: Jossey-Bass.

Lapp, D., Fisher, D., Flood, J., & Cabello, A. (2001). An integrated approach to the teaching and assessment of language arts. In Hurley, S. R., & Tinajero, J. V. (Eds.), *Literacy assessment of second language learners* (pp. 1–26). Boston: Allyn & Bacon.

Lapp, D., Flood, J., & Goss, K. (2000). Desks don't move—students do: In effective classroom environments. *The Reading Teacher, 54,* 31–36.

Larabee, D. F. (2000). On the nature of teaching and teacher education: Difficult practices that look easy. *Journal of Teacher Education, 51,* 228–233.

Lee-Daniels, S. L. (2000). DEAR me: What does it take to get children reading? *The Reading Teacher, 54,* 154–155.

Lenski, S. D. (2001a). Intertextual connections during discussions about literature. *Reading Psychology, 22,* 313–335.

Lenski, S. D. (2001b). Netscape strategies of experienced teachers. In W. Linek, E. G. Sturtevant, J. R. Dugan, & P. E. Linder (Eds.), *Celebrating the voices of literacy* (pp. 179–192) Commerce, TX: College Reading Association.

Lenski, S. D., & Johns, J. L. (1997). Patterns of reading-to-write. *Reading Research and Instruction, 37,* 15–38.

Lenski, S. D., Wham, M. A., & Johns, J. L. (1999). *Reading & learning strategies for middle & high school students.* Dubuque, IA: Kendall/Hunt.

Lenski, S. D., Wham, M. A., & Johns, J. L. (2003). *Reading and learning strategies: Middle grades through high school.* (2nd ed.). Dubuque, IA: Kendall/Hunt.

Lepper, M. R. (1988). Motivational considerations in the study of instruction. *Cognition and Instruction, 5,* 289–309.

Lerner, J. W. (1993). *Learning disabilities: Theories, diagnosis, and teaching strategies.* Boston: Houghton Mifflin.

Lesesne, T. S. (1998). Reading aloud to build success in reading. In K. Beers & B. G. Samuels (Eds.), *Into focus: Understanding and creating middle school readers* (pp. 245–260). Norwood, MA: Christopher-Gordon.

Leu, D. J. (2001). Internet project: Preparing students for new literacies in a global village. *The Reading Teacher, 54,* 568–572.

Leu, D. J. (2002). Internet workshop: Making time for literacy. *The Reading Teacher, 55,* 466–472.

Lisandrelli, C. A., & Lisandrelli, E. S. (2000). Creating lifelong learners: Strategies for success. In M. McLaughlin & M. Vogt (Eds.), *Creativity and innovation in content area teaching* (pp. 231–257). Norwood, MA: Christopher-Gordon.

Lortie, D. C. (1975). *Schoolteacher: A sociological study.* Chicago: University of Chicago.

Lowery-Moore, H. (1998). Voices of middle school readers. In K. Borman & B. Schnieder (Eds.), *The adolescent years: Social influences and educational challenges* (pp. 23–35). Chicago: University of Chicago Press.

Luke, A., O'Brien, J., & Comber, B. (2001). Making community texts objects of study. In H. Fehring & P. Green (Eds.), *Critical literacy* (pp. 112–123). Newark, DE, and Norwood, South Australia: International Reading Association and Australian Literacy Educators' Association.

Lukens, R. J. (1999). *Critical handbook of children's literature.* Reading, MA: Addison-Wesley.

Lyons, C. A., Pinnell, G. S., & DeFord, D. E. (1993). *Partners in learning: Teachers and children in Reading Recovery.* New York: Teachers College Press.

Mackey, M. (1997). Good-enough reading: Momentum and accuracy in the reading of complex fiction. *Research in the Teaching of English, 31,* 428–458.

Macrorie, K. (1984). *Searching writing.* Upper Montclair, NJ: Boynton/Cook.

Manzo, A. V. (1969). The ReQuest procedure. *Journal of Reading, 13,* 123–126.

Maria, K. (1989). Developing disadvantaged children's background knowledge interactively. *The Reading Teacher, 42,* 296–300.

Martin, P., & Midgley, E. (1999). Immigration to the United States. *Population Bulletin, 54,* 1–44. Washington DC: Population Reference Bureau.

Martinez, M., Roser, N. L., & Strecker, S. (1998/1999). "I never thought I could be a star": A readers theatre ticket to fluency. *The Reading Teacher, 52,* 326–334.

Marzano, R. J. (2000). *Transforming classroom grading.* Alexandria, VA: Association for Supervision and Curriculum Development.

McCarrier, A., Pinnell, G. S., & Fountas, I. (1999). *Interactive writing: How language and literacy come together, K–2.* Portsmouth, NH: Heinemann.

McCormick, J. (2002). Would you like to see my portfolio? Portfolio assessment and the education of reading teachers. *Journal of Reading Education, 27*(3), 36–38.

McCormick, S. (1999). *Instructing students who have literacy problems* (3rd ed.). Columbus, OH: Merrill/Prentice Hall.

McGill-Franzen, A. (1992). Early literacy: What does "developmentally appropriate" mean? *The Reading Teacher, 46,* 56–58.

McGinley, W. J., & Denner, P. R. (1987). Story impressions: A prereading/writing activity. *Journal of Reading, 31,* 248–253.

McKenna, M. C., & Kear, D. J. (1990). Measuring attitude toward reading: A new tool for teachers. *The Reading Teacher, 43,* 626–639.

McKenna, M. C., Kear, D. J., & Ellsworth, R. A. (1995). Children's attitudes toward reading: A national survey. *Reading Research Quarterly, 30,* 934–956.

McLaughlin, M. (2000). Assessment for the 21st century: Performance, portfolios, and profiles. In M. McLaughlin & M. Vogt (Eds.), *Creativity and innovation in content area teaching* (pp. 301–327). Norwood, MA: Christopher-Gordon.

McLaughlin, M., & Allen, M. B. (2002). *Guided comprehension: A teaching model for grades 3–8.* Newark, DE: International Reading Association.

McLoyd, V. (1979). The effects of extrinsic rewards of differential value on high and low intrinsic interest. *Child Development, 50,* 1010–1019.

McMahon, S. I. (1997). Book clubs: Contexts for students to lead their own class discussions. In S. I. McMahon & T. E. Raffael (Eds.), *The book club connection: Literacy learning and classroom talk* (pp. 89–106). Newark, DE, and New York: International Reading Association and Teachers College Press.

McPhail, J. C., Pierson, J. M., Freeman, J. G., Goodman, J., & Ayappa, A. (2000). The role of interest in fostering sixth grade students' identities as competent learners. *Curriculum Inquiry, 30,* 43–69.

Meece, J. L., and Miller, S. D. (1999). Changes in elementary school children's achievement goals for reading and writing: Results of a longitudinal and an intervention study. *Scientific Studies of Reading, 3,* 207–230.

Meier, D. R. (2000). *Scribble scrabble: Learning to read and write; success with diverse teachers, children, and families.* New York: Teachers College Press.

Miller, H. M. (2001). Including "the included." *The Reading Teacher, 54,* 820–821.

Moles, O. C. (1993). Collaboration between schools and disadvantaged parents: Obstacles and openings. In N. Feyl Chavkin (Ed.), *Families and schools in a pluralistic society* (pp. 21–49). Albany: State University of New York Press.

Moll, L. C. (2001). The diversity of schooling: A cultural–historical approach. In M. de la Luz Reyes & J. J. Halcon (Eds.), *The best for our children: Critical perspectives on literacy for Latino students* (pp. 13–28). New York: Teachers College Press.

Mooney, M. E. (1990). *Reading TO, WITH, and BY children.* Katonah, NY: Richard C. Owens.

Moore, D., & Moore, S. (1986). Possible sentences. In E. Dishner, T. Bean, J. Readence, & D. Moore (Eds.), *Reading in the content areas: Improving classroom instruction* (2nd ed.). Dubuque, IA: Kendall/Hunt.

Morgan, R. F., Meeks, J. W., Schollaert, A., & Paul, J. (1986). *Critical reading/thinking skills for the college student*. Dubuque, IA: Kendall/Hunt.

Morningstar, J. W. (1999). Home response journals: Parents as informed contributors in the understanding of the child's literacy development. *The Reading Teacher, 52,* 690–697.

Morrow, L. M. (1997). *The literacy center: Contexts for reading and writing*. York, ME: Stenhouse.

Moss, B., Leone, S., & Dipillo, M. (1997). Exploring the literature of fact: Linking reading and writing through information trade books. *Language Arts, 74,* 418–429.

Moutray, C. L., Pollard, J. A., & McGinley, J. (2001). Students explore text, themselves, and life through reader response. *Middle School Journal, 32,* 30–34.

Mueller, P. N. (2001). *Lifers: Learning from at-risk adolescent readers*. Portsmouth, NH: Heinemann.

Nagel, G. K. (2001). *Effective grouping for literacy instruction*. Needham Heights, MA: Allyn & Bacon.

National Center for Educational Statistics, U.S. Department of Health, Education, and Welfare. (1993). *Digest of educational statistics*. Washington, DC: U.S. Government Printing Office.

National Council of Teachers of English and International Reading Association. (1988). *Rationales for challenged books (CD ROM)*. Urbana, IL, and Newark, DE: Authors.

National Reading Panel. (2000). *Report of the National Reading Panel*. Washington, DC: National Institute of Child Health and Development.

Nespor, J. (1987). The role of beliefs in the practice of teaching. *Journal of Curriculum Studies, 19,* 317–328.

Nessel, D., & Jones, M. (1981). *The language experience approach to reading*. New York: Teachers College Press.

Neuman, S. B. (2001). Access to print in low-income and middle-income communities: An ecological study of four neighborhoods. *Reading Research Quarterly, 36,* 8–27.

Neuman, S. B., & Bredekamp, S. (2000). Becoming a reader: A developmentally appropriate approach. In D. S. Strickland & L. M. Morrow (Eds.), *Beginning reading and writing* (pp. 22–34). New York: Teachers College Press.

Neuman, S. B., & Celano, D. (2001). Books aloud: A campaign to "put books in children's hands." *The Reading Teacher, 54,* 550–557.

Newman, D., Griffin, P., & Cole, M. (1989). *The construction zone: Working for cognitive change in schools*. Cambridge, England: Cambridge University.

Nierstheimer, S. L. (2000). "To the parents of . . . ": A parent's perspective on the schooling of a struggling learner. *Journal of Adolescent & Adult Literacy, 44,* 34–36.

Nist, S. L., & Simpson, M. L. (1989). PLAE, a validated study strategy. *Journal of Reading, 33,* 182–186.

Nistler, R., & Maiers, A. (2000). Stopping the silence: Hearing parents' voices in an urban first-grade family literacy program. *The Reading Teacher, 53,* 670–680.

Noddings, N. (1995). Teaching themes of care. *Phi Delta Kappan, 76,* 675–79.

Noddings, N. (1997). Thinking about standards. *Phi Delta Kappan, 79*(3), 184–189.

Norton, D. E. (1997). *The effective teaching of language arts* (5th ed.). Columbus, OH: Merrill/Prentice Hall.

Norton, D. E. (2001). *Multicultural children's literature: Through the eyes of many children*. Columbus, OH: Merrill/Prentice Hall.

Ogle, D. M. (1986). K–W–L: A teaching model that develops action reading of expository text. *The Reading Teacher, 40,* 564–570.

Oldfather, P. (1993). Students' perspectives on motivating experiences in literacy learning. *Perspectives in Reading Research, 2,* 1–16.

Oldfather, P., & Wigfield, A. (1996). Children's motivation for literacy learning. In L. Baker, P. Afflerbach, & D. Reinking (Eds.), *Developing engaged readers in school and home communities* (pp. 89–113). Mahwah, NJ: Erlbaum.

Ollmann, H. E. (1992). Two-column response to literature. *Journal of Reading, 36,* 58–59.

Olson, M. W., & Gee, T. (1991). Content reading instruction in the primary grades: Perceptions and strategies. *The Reading Teacher, 45,* 298–307.

Opitz, M. F., & Rasinski, T. V. (1998). *Good-by round robin: 25 effective oral reading strategies*. Portsmouth, NH: Heinemann.

Padrón, Y. (1998). Latino students and reading: Understanding these English language learners' needs. In K. Beers & B. G. Samuels (Eds.), *Into focus: Understanding and creating middle school readers* (pp. 105–122). Norwood, MA: Christopher-Gordon.

Pajares, M. F. (1992). Teachers' beliefs and educational research: Cleaning up a messy construct. *Review of Educational Research, 62,* 307–332.

Palmer, P. J. (1998). *The courage to teach: Exploring the inner landscape of a teacher's life*. San Francisco: Jossey-Bass.

Pappas, C. C., & Brown, E. (1987). Learning to read by reading: Learning how to extend the functional potential of language. *Research in the Teaching of English, 21,* 160–184.

Pardieck, S. C. (2002). Development of job search portfolios for preservice teachers. *Journal of Reading Education, 27*(2), 24–30.

Paris, S. G. (2001). Developing readers. In R. F. Flippo (Ed.), *Reading researchers in search of common ground* (pp. 69–77). Newark, DE: International Reading Association.

Paris, S. G., Lipson, M. Y., & Wixson, K. K. (1983). Becoming a strategic reader. *Contemporary Educational Psychology, 8,* 293–316.

Paris, S. G., Lipson, M. Y., & Wixson, K. K. (1994). Becoming a strategic reader. In R. B. Ruddell, M. R. Ruddell, and H. Singer (Eds.), *Theoretical models and processes of reading* (4th ed., pp. 788–810). Newark, DE: International Reading Association.

Parsons, L. (2001). *Response journals revisited: Maximizing learning through reading, writing, viewing, discussing, and thinking.* Portland, ME: Stenhouse.

Paul, D. G. (2000). Rap and orality: Critical media literacy, pedagogy, and cultural synchronization. *Journal of Adolescent & Adult Literacy, 44,* 246–251.

Paul, R. W. (1993). *Critical thinking: How to prepare students for a rapidly changing world.* Santa Rosa, CA: Foundation for Critical Thinking.

Pearson, P. D., & Gallagher, M. C. (1983). The instruction of reading comprehension. *Contemporary Educational Psychology, 8,* 317–344.

Pearson, P. D., & Spiro, R. (1982). The new buzz word in reading is schema. *Instructor, 5,* 46–48.

Peregoy, S. F., & Boyle, O. F. (1997). *Reading, writing, & learning in ESL: A resource book for K–12 teachers* (2nd ed.). New York: Longman.

Phillips, D. C. (1995). The good, the bad, and the ugly: The many faces of constructivism. *Educational Researcher, 24,* 5–12.

Phillips, W. (1997). The smartest thing you can do for your baby. *Parenting, 8,* 107–108.

Piaget, J. (1952). *The origins of intelligence in children.* New York: International Universities Press.

Piaget, J. (1954). *The construction of reality in the child.* New York: Basic Books.

Piaget, J. (1972). Intellectual evolution from adolescence to adulthood. *Human Development, 15,* 1–12.

Piaget, J. (1977). *Equilibration of cognitive structures.* New York: Viking.

Piirto, J. (1999). *Talented children and adults: Their development and education.* Columbus, OH: Merrill/Prentice Hall.

Pinnell, G. S., & Fountas, I. C. (1998). *Word matters: Teaching phonics and spelling in the reading/writing classroom.* Portsmouth, NH: Heinemann.

Pinnell, G. S., & Fountas, I. C. (2002). *Leveled books for readers grades 3–6.* Portsmouth, NH: Heinemann.

Pipher, M. (1994). *Reviving Ophelia: Saving the selves of adolescent girls.* New York: Ballantine.

Plato. (1983). *Parmeides.* R. E. Allen (trans.). Minneapolis: University of Minnesota.

Poorman, L., & Wright, M. (2000). Middle schools students learning to research: An inquiry-based approach. In M. McLaughlin & M. Vogt (Eds.), *Creativity and innovation in content area teaching* (pp. 259–280). Norwood, MA: Christopher-Gordon.

Popham, J. W. (2001). *The truth about testing: An educator's call to action.* Alexandria, VA: Association for Supervision and Curriculum Development.

Powell, R., Cantrell, S. C., & Adams, A. (2001). Saving Black Mountain: The promise of critical literacy in a multicultural democracy. *The Reading Teacher, 54,* 772–781.

Powers, S., & Wagner, M. J. (1984). Attributions for school achievement of middle school students. *Journal of Early Adolescence, 4,* 215–222.

Pressley, M. (1999). Self-regulated comprehension processing and its development through instruction. In L. B. Gambrell, L. M. Morrow, S. B. Neuman, & M. Pressley (Eds.), *Best practices in literacy instruction* (90–97). New York: Guildford.

Pressley, M. (2000). What should comprehension instruction be the instruction of? In M. L. Kamil, P. B. Mosenthal, P. D. Pearson, & R. Barr (Eds.), *Handbook of reading research* (Vol. III, pp. 545–561). Mahwah, NJ: Erlbaum.

Pressley, M. (2002). Comprehension strategies instruction. In C. C. Block & M. Pressley (Eds.), *Comprehension instruction: Research-based best practices* (pp. 11–27). New York: Guilford.

Pressley, M., Allington, R. L., Wharton-McDonald, R., Block, C. C., & Morrow, L. M. (2001). *Learning to read: Lessons from exemplary first-grade classrooms.* New York: Guilford.

Pressley, M., Symons, S., McDaniel, M., Snyder, B., & Turnure, J. (1988). Elaborative interrogation facilitates acquisition of confusing facts. *Journal of Educational Psychology, 80,* 268–278.

Primeaux, J. (2000). Shifting perspectives on struggling readers. *Language Arts, 77,* 537–542.

Purcell-Gates, V. (2000). Family literacy. In M. L. Kamil, P. B. Mosenthal, P. D. Pearson, & R. Barr (Eds.), *Handbook of reading research* (Vol. III, pp. 853–870). Mahwah, NJ: Erlbaum.

Purves, A. C., & Beach, R. (1972). *Literature and the reader: Research in response to literature, reading interest, and the teaching of literature.* Urbana, IL: National Council of Teachers of English.

Radencich, M. C., & McKay, L. J. (1995). *Flexible grouping for literacy in the elementary grades.* Boston: Allyn & Bacon.

Rand Study Group. (2002). *Reading for understanding: Toward and R&D program in reading comprehension.* Santa Monica, CA: Author.

Raphael, T. E. (1982). Question-answering strategies for children. *The Reading Teacher, 36,* 186–190.

Raphael, T. E., & Goatley, V. J. (1997). Classrooms as communities: Features of community share. In S. I. McMahon & T. E. Raffael (Eds.), *The book club connection: Literacy learning and classroom talk* (pp. 26–46). Newark, DE, and New York: International Reading Association and Teachers College Press.

Raphael, T. E., Kehus, M., & Damphousse, K. (2001). *Book club for middle school.* Lawrence, MA: Small Planet Communications.

Raphael, T. E., Pardo, L. S., & Highfield, K. (2002). *Book club: A literature-based curriculum.* Lawrence, MA: Small Planet Communications.

Rasinski, T. V. (2000). Speed does matter. *The Reading Teacher, 54,* 146–151.

Rasinski, T. V., & Zutell, J. B. (1990). Making a place for fluency instruction in the regular reading curriculum. *Reading Research & Instruction, 29,* 85–91.

Readence, J. E., Moore, D. W., & Rickelman, R. J. (2000). *Prereading activities for content area reading and learning* (3rd ed.). Newark, DE: International Reading Association.

Reasoner, C. (1976). *Releasing children to literature* (rev. ed.) New York: Dell.

Reif, L. (1992). *Seeking diversity: Language arts with adolescents.* Portsmouth, NH: Heinemann.

Reis, S. M. (1998). *Work left undone: Choices and compromises of talented females.* Mansfield Center, CT: Creative Learning.

Reutzel, D. R. (1999). Organizing literacy instruction: Effective grouping strategies and organizational plans. In L. B. Gambrell, L. M. Morrow, S. B. Neuman, & M. Pressley (Eds.), *Best Practices in literacy instruction* (pp. 271–291). New York: Guilford.

Rhodes, L. K., & Nathenson-Mejia, S. (1992). Anecdotal records: A powerful tool for ongoing literacy assessment. *The Reading Teacher, 45,* 502–509.

Rhodes, L. K., & Shanklin, N. L. (1993). *Windows into literacy: Assessing learners K–8.* Portsmouth, NH: Heinemann.

Richards, M. (2000). Be a good detective: Solve the case of oral reading fluency. *The Reading Teacher, 53,* 534–539.

Richek, M. A., Caldwell, J. S., Jennings, J. H., & Lerner, J. W. (2002). *Reading problems: Assessment and teaching strategies.* Boston: Allyn & Bacon.

Richgels, D. J. (2002). Informational texts in kindergarten. *The Reading Teacher, 55,* 586–595.

Rief, L. (1999). *Vision and voice: Extending the literacy spectrum.* Portsmouth, NH: Heinemann.

Rinne, C. H. (1998). Motivating students is a percentage Game. *Phi Delta Kappan, 79,* 620–627.

Ritter, S., & Idol-Maestas, L. (1986). Teaching middle school students to use a test-taking strategy. *Journal of Educational Research Quarterly, 79,* 350–357.

Robinson, F. P. (1961). *Effective study I* (rev. ed.). New York: Harper & Row.

Robinson, L. (1998). Understanding middle school students. In K. Beers & B. G. Samuels (Eds.), *Into focus: Understanding and creating middle school readers* (pp. 3–22). Norwood, MA: Christopher-Gordon.

Rodriguez, T. A. (2001). From the known to the unknown: Using cognates to teaching English to Spanish-speaking literates. *The Reading Teacher, 54,* 744–746.

Rodríguez-Brown, F. V. (2001). Home-school connections in a community where English is the second language: Project FLAME. In V. J. Risko & K. Bromley (Eds.), *Collaboration for diverse learners: Viewpoints and practices* (pp. 251–272). Newark, DE: International Reading Association.

Roe, B. D. (2000). Using technology for content area literacy. In S. B. Wepner, W. J. Valmont, & R. Thurlow (Eds.), *Linking literacy and technology: A guide for K–8 classrooms.* Newark, DE: International Reading Association.

Roehler, L., & Duffy, G. (1991). Teachers' instructional actions. In R. Barr, M. L. Kamil, P. B. Mosenthal, & P. D. Pearson (Eds.), *Handbook of reading research* (Vol. II, pp. 861–884). White Plains, NY: Longman.

Rogavin, P. (2001). *The research workshop: Bringing the world into your classroom.* Portsmouth, NH: Heinemann.

Rogoff, B. (1990). *Apprenticeship in thinking: Cognitive development in social context.* New York: Oxford University Press.

Romano, T. (1995). *Writing with passion.* Portsmouth, NH: Boynton/Cook.

Rosenblatt, L. (1978). *The reader, the text, the poem: The transactional theory of the literacy work.* Carbondale, IL: Southern Illinois University Press.

Rosenblatt, L. (1994). The transactional theory of reading and writing. In R. B. Ruddell, M. R. Ruddell, & H. Singer (Eds.), *Theoretical models and processes of reading* (4th ed., pp. 1057–1092). Newark, DE: International Reading Association.

Rosenshine, B., Meister, C., & Chapman, S. (1996). Reciprocal teaching: A review of the research. *Review of educational research, 64,* 479–530.

Routman, R. (1991). *Invitations.* Portsmouth: NH: Heinemann.

Routman, R. (2000). *Conversations.* Portsmouth, NH: Heinemann.

Rumelhart, D. E. (1977). Toward an interactive model of reading. In S. Dornic (Ed.), *Attention and performance VI* (pp. 573–603). Hillsdale, NJ: Erlbaum.

Rumelhart, D. E. (1980). Schemata: The building blocks of cognition. In R. J. Spiro, B. C. Bruce, & W. F. Brewer (Eds.), *Theoretical issues in reading comprehension* (pp. 33–58). Hillsdale, NJ: Erlbaum.

Ryan, R. M., & Deci, E. L. (2000). Self-determination theory and the facilitation of intrinsic motivation, social development, and well-being. *American Psychologist, 55,* 68–78.

Ryan, R. M., Stiller, J., & Lynch, J. H. (1994). Representations of relationships to teachers, parents, and friends as predictors of academic motivation and self-esteem. *Journal of Early Adolescence, 14,* 226–249.

Salomon, G., & Perkins, D. N. (1998). Individual and social aspects of learning. In P. D. Pearson & A. Iran-Nejad (Eds.), *Review of research in education* (pp. 1–24). Washington DC: American Educational Research Association.

Sanacore, J. (2000). Promoting the lifetime reading habit in middle school students. *The Clearing House, 73,* 157–161.

Santa, C., Havens, L., & Macumber, E. (1996). *Creating independence through student-owned strategies.* Dubuque, IA: Kendall/Hunt.

Santa, C. M., Dailey, S. C., & Nelson, M. (1985). Free-response and opinion proof: A reading and writing strategy for middle grade and secondary teachers. *Journal of Reading, 28,* 346–352.

Santrock, J. W. (1998). *Child Development* (8th ed.). Boston: McGraw-Hill.

Scala, M. (2001). *Working together: Reading and writing in inclusive classrooms.* Newark, DE: International Reading Association.

Schlosser, L. K. (1992). Teacher distance and students' disengagement: School lives on the margin. *Journal of Teacher Education, 43,* 128–140.

Schwartz, R., & Raphael, T. (1985). Concept of definition: A key to improving students' vocabulary. *The Reading Teacher, 39,* 198–205.

Schwartz, R. M. (1997). Self-monitoring in beginning reading. *The Reading Teacher, 51,* 40–48.

Science Voyages: Exploring life, earth, and physical science (2000). Columbus, OH: Glencoe/McGraw-Hill.

Serafini, F. (2000/2001). Three paradigms of assessment: Measurement, procedure, and inquiry. *The Reading Teacher, 54,* 384–393.

Shanker, J. L., & Ekwall, E. E. (1998). *Locating and correcting reading difficulties* (7th ed.). Upper Saddle River, NJ: Merrill/Prentice Hall.

Shepard, L. A. (2000). The role of assessment in a learning culture. *Educational Researcher, 29,* 4–14.

Short, K. G., Harste, J. C., & Burke, C. (1996). *Creating classrooms for authors and inquirers* (2nd ed.). Portsmouth, NH: Heinemann.

Short, K. G., Schroeder, J., Laird, J., Kauffman, G., Ferguson, M. J., & Crawford, K. (1996). *Learning together through inquiry: From Columbus to integrated curriculum.* York, ME: Stenhouse.

Siegel, M., & Fernandez, S. L. (2000). Critical approaches. In M. L. Kamil, P. B. Mosenthal, P. D. Pearson, & R. Barr (Eds.), *Handbook of reading research* (Vol. III, pp. 141–151). Mahwah, NJ: Erlbaum.

Siegel, M. G. (1984). *Reading as signification.* Dissertation. Bloomington, IL: Indiana University.

SilverBurdett & Ginn. (1991). *People in time and place.* Morristown, NJ: Author.

Simmons, J. S., & Dresang, E. T. (2001). *School censorship in the 21st century: A guide for teachers and library media specialists.* Newark, DE: International Reading Association.

Sipe, L. R. (2001). Invention, convention, and intervention: Invented spelling and the teacher's role. *The Reading Teacher, 55,* 264–273.

Skinner, B. F. (1953). *Science and human behavior.* New York: Free Press.

Slavin, R. E. (1988). Cooperative learning and student achievement. *Educational Leadership, 46*(2), 31–33.

Smith, C. C., & Bean, T. W. (1980). The guided writing procedure: Integrating content reading and writing improvement. *Reading World, 19,* 290–302.

Smith, D. (1992). Common ground: The connection between reader-response and textbook reading. *Journal of Reading, 35,* 630–635.

Smith, F. (1997). *Reading without nonsense.* New York: Teachers College Press.

Soter, A. O. (1999). *Young adult literature & the new literary theories: Developing critical readers in middle school.* New York: Teachers College Press.

Spielman, J. (2001). The Family Photography Project: We will just read what the pictures tell us. *The Reading Teacher, 54,* 762–770.

Spivey, N. N. (1997). *The constructivist metaphor: Reading, writing, and the making of meaning.* San Diego: Academic Press.

Spor, M. W., & Schneider, B. K. (1999). Content reading strategies: What teachers know, use, and want to learn. *Reading Research & Instruction, 38,* 221–231.

Stanovich, K. (1986). Matthew effects in reading: Some consequences of individual differences in the acquisition of literacy. *Reading Research Quarterly, 21,* 360–406.

Stauffer, R. G. (1969). *Teaching reading as a thinking process.* New York: Harper and Row.

Stein, N. L., & Glenn, C. G. (1979). An analysis of story comprehension in elementary school children. In R. O. Freedle (Ed.) *New directions in discourse processing* (pp. 53–120). Norwood, NJ: Ablex.

Steinberg, L., Brown, B. B., & Dornbusch, S. M. (1996). *Beyond the classroom: What school reform has failed and what parents need to do.* New York: Simon & Schuster.

Steineke, N. (2002). *Reading and writing together: Collaborative literacy in action.* Portsmouth, NH: Heinemann.

Stephens, E. C., & Brown, J. E. (2000). *A handbook of content literacy strategies: 75 practical reading and writing ideas.* Norwood, MA: Christopher-Gordon.

Stevens, L. P. (2001). South Park and society: Instructional and curricular implications of popular culture in the classroom. *Journal of Adolescent & Adult Literacy, 44,* 548–555.

Stewart, R. A., Paradis, E. E., Ross, B., & Lewis, M. J. (1996). Student voices: What works in literature-based developmental reading. *Journal of Adolescent & Adult Literacy, 39,* 468–478.

Strickland, D. S., Ganske, K., & Monroe, J. K. (2002). *Supporting struggling readers and writers: Strategies for classroom intervention 3–6.* Portland, ME, and Newark, DE: Stenhouse and International Reading Association.

Sutherland-Smith, W. (2002). Weaving the literacy web: Changes in reading from page to screen. *The Reading Teacher, 55,* 662–669.

Swanson, D. P., Spencer, M. B., & Petersen, A. (1998). Identity formation in adolescence. In K. Borman & B. Schnieder (Eds.), *The adolescent years: Social influences and educational challenges* (pp. 18–41). Chicago: University of Chicago Press.

Szymusiak, K., & Sibberson, F. (2001). *Beyond leveled books: Supporting transitional readers in grades 2–5.* Portland, ME: Stenhouse.

Taberski, S. (2000). *On solid ground: Strategies for teaching early reading K–8.* Portsmouth, NH: Heinemann.

Tannenbaum, A. J. (1983). *Gifted children.* New York: Macmillan.

Tanner, M. L., & Casados, L. (1998). Promoting and studying discussions in math classes. *Journal of Adolescent & Adult Literacy, 41,* 342–351.

Taylor, A. R. (1996). Conditions for American children, youth and families: Are we "world class"? *Educational Researcher, 25,* 10–12.

Teale, W. H. (1986). Home background and young children's emergent literacy development. In W. H. Teale & E. Sulzby (Eds.), *Emergent literacy: Writing and reading* (pp. 173–206). Norwood, NJ: Ablex.

Teale, W. H. (1995). Emergent literacy. In T. L. Harris & R. E. Hodges (Eds.), *The literacy dictionary: The vocabulary of reading and writing* (p. 71). Newark, DE: International Reading Association.

Teale, W. H., & Sulzby, E. (1986). Emergent literacy as a perspective for examining how young children become writers and readers. In W. H. Teale & E. Sulzby (Eds.), *Emergent literacy: Writing and reading* (pp. vii–xxv). Norwood, NJ: Ablex.

Teale, W. H., & Sulzby, E. (Eds.). (1986). *Emergent literacy: Writing and reading.* Norwood, NJ: Ablex.

Tharp, R. G., & Gallimore, R. (1988). *Rousing minds to life: Teaching, learning, and schooling in social context.* Cambridge, England: Cambridge University.

Thomas, M. D., & Bainbridge, W. L. (2001). All children can learn: Facts and fallacies. *Phi Delta Kappan, 82,* 660–662.

Thomas, S., & Oldfather, P. (1995). Enhancing student and teacher engagement in literacy learning: A shared inquiry approach. *The Reading Teacher, 49,* 192–205.

Thorndike, E. L. (1913). *Educational psychology: The psychology of learning.* New York: Teachers College Press.

Tierney, R. J., & Readence, J. E. (2000). *Reading strategies and practices: A compendium* (5th ed.). Boston: Allyn & Bacon.

Tinajero, J. V., & Ada, A. F. (Eds.). (1993). *The power of two languages: Literacy and biliteracy for Spanish-speaking students.* New York: Macmillan/McGraw-Hill.

Tomlinson, C. A. (1992). Deciding to differentiate instruction in the middle school. *Gifted Child Quarterly, 39,* 77–89.

Tomlinson, C. A. (1999). *The differentiated classroom: Responding to the needs of all learners.* Alexandria, VA: Association for Supervision and Curriculum Development.

Tomlinson, C., Moon, T. R., & Callahan, C. (1998). How well are we addressing academic diversity in middle school? *Middle School Journal, 19,* 3–11.

Trelease, J. (1995). *The read-aloud handbook.* New York: Penguin Books.

Trelease, J. (2001). *The read-aloud handbook* (5th ed.). New York: Penguin.

Turner, J., & Paris, S. G. (1995). How literacy tasks influence children's motivation for literacy. *The Reading Teacher, 48,* 662–673.

Unrau, N. J. (1997). *Thoughtful teachers, thoughtful learners: A guide to helping adolescents think critically.* Scarborough, Ontario: Pippin.

U.S. Census Bureau. (1998). *Statistical abstract of the United States* (118th ed.). Washington, DC: U.S. Government Printing Office.

U.S. Department of Education. (1993). *National excellence: A case for developing America's talent.* Washington, DC: U.S. Government Printing Office.

U.S. Department of Education. (1998). *To assure the free appropriate pubic education of all children with disabilities.* Twentieth annual report to Congress on the implementation of Individuals with Disabilities Education Act. Washington, DC: U.S. Government Printing Office.

U.S. Department of Health and Human Services, Office of the Assistant Secretary for Planning and Evaluation. (1998). *Trends in the well-being of American's children & youth.* Washington, DC: Author.

Vacca, R. T., & Vacca, J. L. (2002). *Content area reading: Literacy and learning across the curriculum* (7th ed.). Boston: Allyn & Bacon.

Valdés, G. (1996). *Con respeto: Bridging the distances between culturally diverse families and schools: An ethnographic portrait.* New York: Teachers College Press.

Valmont, W. J. (2000). What do teachers do in technology-rich classrooms? In S. B. Wepner, W. J. Valmont, & R. Thurlow (Eds.), *Linking literacy and technology: A guide for K–8 classrooms* (pp. 160–202). Newark: DE: International Reading Association.

Van Hoose, J., & Strahan, D. (1988). *Young adolescent development and school practices: Promoting harmony.* Columbus, OH: National Middle School Association.

VanTassel-Baska, J. (1998). *Excellence in educating gifted & talented learners* (3rd ed.). Denver: Love Publishing.

Veskauf, J. A. (1999). Open doors: Parents volunteering as tutors in the classroom. *Illinois Reading Council Journal, 27,* 18–23.

Vogt, M. (2000). Content learning for students needing modifications: An issue of access. In M. McLaughlin & M. Vogt (Eds.), *Creativity and innovation in content area teaching* (pp. 329–351). Norwood, MA: Christopher-Gordon. Vygotsky, L. S. (1962). *Thought and language.* Cambridge, MA: The MIT Press.

Vygotsky, L. S. (1978). *Mind in society: The development of higher psychological processes.* Cambridge, MA: Harvard University Press.

Vygotsky, L. S., & Luria, A. R. (1930/1993). *Studies in the history of behavior: Ape, primitive, and child.* Hillsdale, NJ: Lawrence Erlbaum.

Watson, B. (1999). Creating independent learners. In J. S. Gafney & B. J. Askew (Eds.), *Stirring the waters: The influence of Marie Clay* (pp. 47–74). Portsmouth, NH: Heinemann.

Watson, D. J. (1994). Whole language: Why bother? *The Reading Teacher, 47,* 600–607.

Watson, M. W. (1984). Development of social role understanding. *Developmental Review, 4,* 192–213.

Weaver, C. (1994). *Reading process and practice: From socio-psycholinguistics to whole language* (2nd ed.) Portsmouth, NH: Heinemann.

Weaver, C. (1998). Toward a balanced approach to reading. In C. Weaver (Ed.), *Reconsidering a balanced approach to reading* (pp. 11–74). Urbana, IL: National Council of Teachers of English.

Weinstein, R. S. (1976). Reading group membership in first grade: Teacher behaviors and pupil experience over time. *Journal of Educational Psychology, 68,* 103–116.

Wells, G. (1986). *The meaning makers: Children learning language and using language to learn.* Portsmouth, NH: Heinemann.

Westberg, K. L., Archambault, Jr., F. X., Dobyns, S. M., & Salvin, T. J. (1993). The classroom practices observation study. *Journal for Education of the Gifted, 16,* 120–146.

Whitehead, D. (1994). Teaching literacy and learning strategies through a modified guided silent reading procedure. *Journal of Reading, 38,* 24–30.

Whitmore, J. (1980). *Giftedness, conflict, and underachievement.* Boston: Allyn & Bacon.

Wilkinson, L. (1999). An introduction to the explicit teaching of reading. In J. Hancock (Ed.), *The explicit teaching of reading* (pp. 1–12). Newark, DE: International Reading Association.

Williams, M. (2001a). Making connections: A workshop for adolescents who struggle with reading. *Journal of Adolescent & Adult Literacy, 44,* 588–601.

Williams, M. (2001b). Trying books on for size: A book selection strategy for middle school students who struggle with reading. *Illinois Reading Council Journal, 28,* 46–50.

Wilson, L. (2001). Critical literacy and pop music magazines. In H. Fehring & P. Green (Eds.), *Critical literacy* (pp. 137–141). Newark, DE, and Norwood, South Australia: International Reading Association and Australian Literacy Educators' Association.

Wilson, R. M., Hall, M., Leu, D. J., & Kinzer, C. K. (2001). *Phonics, phonemic awareness, and word analysis for teachers: An interactive tutorial* (7th ed.). Upper Saddle River, NJ: Merrill/Prentice Hall.

Wimsatt, W., & Brooks, C. (1964). *Literacy criticism.* New York: Alfred A. Knopf.

Wink, J. (1997). *Critical pedagogy: Notes from the real world.* New York: Longman.

Winner, E. (1996). *Gifted children: Myths and realities*. New York: BasicBooks.

Winograd, P. N. (1989). Introduction: Understanding reading instruction. In P. N. Winograd, K. K. Wixson, & M. Y Lipson, (Eds.) *Improving basal reading instruction* (pp. 1–20). New York: Teachers College Press.

Winograd, P. N., Wixson, K. K., & Lipson, M. Y. (Eds.). (1989). *Improving basal reading instruction* (pp. 1–20). New York: Teachers College Press.

Wise, A. E., & Leibbrand, J. A. (2000). Standards and teacher quality: Entering the new millennium. *Phi Delta Kappan, 4,* 612–621.

Wittlesea, B. W. (1987). Preservation of specific experiences in the representation of general knowledge. *Journal of Experimental Psychology: Learning, Memory, & Cognition, 13*(1), 3–17.

Wixson, K. K., & Peters, C. W. (1984). Reading redefined: A Michigan reading association position paper. *The Michigan Reading Journal, 17,* 4–7.

Wolfram, W., Adger, C. T., & Christian, D. (1999). *Dialects in schools and communities*. Mahwah, NJ: Erlbaum.

Wong, M. G. (1980). Model students? Teachers' perceptions and expectations of their Asian and White students. *Sociology of Education, 53,* 236–247.

Wood, C. (1997). *Yardsticks: Children in the classroom ages 4–14*. Greenfield, MA: Northeast Foundation for Children.

Wood, D., Bruner, J. S., & Ross, G. (1976). The role of tutoring in problem solving. *Journal of Child Psychology and Psychiatry and Applied Disciplines, 17,* 89–100.

Worthy, J., Broaddus, K., & Ivey, G. (2001). *Pathways to independence: Reading, writing, and learning in grades 3–8*. New York: Guilford.

Worthy, J., Moorman, M., & Turner, M. (1999). What Johnny likes to read is hard to find in school. *Reading Research Quarterly, 34,* 12–27.

Worthy, J., Turner, M., & Moorman, M. (1998). The precarious place of self-selected reading. *Language Arts, 75,* 296–304.

Wylie, R. E., & Durrell, D. D. (1970). Teaching vowels through phonograms. *Elementary English, 47,* 787–791.

Yopp, H. K., & Yopp, R. H. (2000). Supporting phonemic awareness development in the classroom. *The Reading Teacher, 54,* 130–143.

Yopp, R. H., & Yopp, H. K. (2000). Sharing informational texts with young children. *The Reading Teacher, 53,* 410–423.

Yopp, R. H., & Yopp, H. K. (2001). *Literature-based reading activities* (3rd ed.). Boston: Allyn & Bacon.

Zimelman, S., Daniels, H., & Hyde, A. (1998). *Best practice: New standards for teaching and learning in America's schools* (2nd ed.). Portsmouth, NH: Heinemann.

Zorfass, J. M. (1998). *Teaching middle school students to be active researchers*. Alexandria, VA: Association for Supervision and Curriculum Development.

Zutell, J. B., & Rasinski, T. V. (1991). Training teachers to attend to the students' oral reading fluency. *Theory into Practice, 30,* 211–217.

Children's Literature Cited

American Girl. (2002). *Molly's Route 66 adventure*. Middleton, WI: Pleasant Company.

Babbit, N. (1975). *Tuck everlasting*. New York: Farrar, Straus & Giroux.

Barrett, J. (1978). *Cloudy with a chance of meatballs*. New York: Scholastic.

Bedard, M. (1992). *Emily*. New York: Scholastic.

Blaxland, W. (1996). *Lunch at the zoo*. New York: Scholastic.

Blume, J. (1978). *Freckle juice*. New York: Yearling Books.

Bridges, R. (1999). *Through my eyes*. New York: Scholastic.

Canizares, S., & Chanko, P. (1998). *Water*. New York: Scholastic.

Canizares, S., & Moreton, D. (1998). *This bird can't fly*. New York: Scholastic.

Carle, E. (1969). *The very hungry caterpillar*. New York: Philomel.

Chimo, S. (1989). *The Egyptian Cinderella*. New York: HarperTrophy.

Collier, J. L., & Collier, C. (1974). *My brother Sam is dead*. New York: Scholastic.

Creech, S. (1994). *Walk two moons*. New York: HarperTrophy.

Creech, S. (2001). *Love that dog*. New York: HarperCollins.

Crowley, J. (1986). *Uncle Buncle's house*. Bothell, WA: The Wright Group.

Dahl, R. (1964). *Charlie and the chocolate factory*. New York: Puffin.

Freeman, D. (1976). *Corduroy*. New York: Penguin.

Giblin, J. (2000). *The amazing life of Benjamin Franklin*. New York: Scholastic.

Guarino, D. (1991). *Is your mama a llama?* New York: Scholastic.

Hall, D. (1994). *I am the dog, I am the cat*. New York: The Trumpet Club.

Havill, J. (1989). *Jamaica tag-along*. New York: Scholastic.

Hess, K. (1997). *Out of the dust*. New York: Scholastic.

Hess, K. (2001). *Witness*. New York: Scholastic.

Hoban, R. (1992). *A bargain for Frances*. New York: HarperCollins.

Hobbs, W. (2001). *Down the Yukon*. New York: HarperCollins.

Hobbs, W. (2002). *Wild Man Island*. New York: HarperCollins.

Houston, J. W., & Houston, J. D. (1973). *Farewell to Manzanar*. New York: Bantam.

Keller, L. (1998). *The scrambled states of America*. New York: Scholastic.

Kraus, R. (1971). *Leo the late bloomer*. New York: Windmill Books.

Lee, F. (1999). *Can you see me?* Littleton, MA: Sundance.

Lobel, A. (1970). *Frog and Toad are friends*. New York: HarperCollins.

London, J. (1964). *White Fang*. New York: Airmont.

Louie, A. (1982). *Yeh-Shen: A Cinderella story from China*. New York: Philomel.

Lowell, A. (1992). *The three little javelinas*. Flagstaff, AZ: Northland.

Lowry, L. (1989). *Number the stars*. New York: Bantam Doubleday Dell.

Lowry, L. (1993). *The giver*. Boston: Houghton Mifflin.

Martin, R., & Shannon, D. (1992). *The rough-faced girl*. New York: Putnam.

Munsch, R. N. (1988). *Thomas' snowsuit*. New York: Firefly.

Noble, T. H. (1980). *The day Jimmy's boa ate the wash*. New York: Dial.

Numeroff, L. J. (1985). *If you give a mouse a cookie*. New York: Harper.

Osborne, M. P. (1998). *Lions at lunchtime*. New York: Random House.

Park, B. (1996). *Mick Harte was here*. New York: Scholastic.

Paterson, K. (1977). *Bridge to Terabithia*. New York: HarperCollins.

Pfetzer, M., & Galvin, J. (1998). *Within reach: My Everest story*. New York: Scholastic.

Rylant, C. (2001). *Henry and Mudge and the tall treehouse*. New York: Simon and Schuster.

Sachar, L. (1978). *Sideways stories from wayside school*. New York: Avon.

Sachar, L. (1998). *Holes*. New York: Dell Yearling.

Seldon, G. (1960). *The cricket in Times Square*. New York: Dell.

Smothers, E. F. (1992). *Down in the piney woods*. New York: Random House.

Speare, E. G. (1958). *The Witch of Blackbird Pond*. Boston: Houghton Mifflin.

Spinelli, J. (2000). *Stargirl*. New York: Alfred A. Knopf.

St. George, J., & Small, D. (2000). *So you want to be president*. New York: Philomel.

Stone, J. (1971). *The monster at the end of this book*. Racine, WI: Western Publishing.

Taylor, B. (1999). *Pole to pole*. Hauppauge, NY: Barron's Educational Series, Inc.

Taylor, M. (1976). *Roll of thunder, hear my cry*. New York: Bantam.

Wells, R., & Jeffers, S. (1999). *Hitty: Her first hundred years*. New York: Simon & Schuster.

Williams, S. (1989). *I went walking*. New York: Voyager.

Index

Page numbers followed by f indicate figures.